M000248910

PRAISE FOR
LUTHERAN PRAYER COMPANION

Lutheran Prayer Companion is yet another treasure from our church's past that Concordia Publishing House has resurrected for our edification in our own day. Filled with over 450 prayers on every imaginable topic (and a few one might never have thought of), it provides a marvelous compendium to guide the Christian through life. Though some of the topics covered seem at first not to be applicable to one's own situation, it quickly becomes evident that even those prayers are a rich blessing as they remind us to pray for the needs of others.

—REV. PAUL J. GRIME, PhD, DEAN OF SPIRITUAL FORMATION AND DEAN OF THE CHAPEL
CONCORDIA THEOLOGICAL SEMINARY, FORT WAYNE, IN

Do we really need another prayerbook? After using this gem, the answer is a decided yes! Through this fresh translation into modern English, Matthew Carver has done the church a tremendous service. Scripturally saturated prayers for the days of the week, the seasons of the year, and the seasons of life. Some are short "sighs," others thankful for blessings, still others pour out the heart in deep cries of anguish. What other prayerbook has a "Prayer of a woman who has a gloomy and unfriendly husband"? The prayers in this volume do not mince words; they confront directly the real situations people face. I had searched in vain all my life for a prayerbook like this; it will be my close companion for the rest of it.

—REV. CHRISTOPHER S. ESGET, SENIOR PASTOR, IMMANUEL LUTHERAN CHURCH, ALEXANDRIA, VA
LCMS SIXTH VICE-PRESIDENT

Lutheran Prayer Companion helps to restore a rich heritage in Lutheran piety, and in The Lutheran Church—Missouri Synod in particular. Prayers for each day of the week are tied to the seven petitions of the Our Father and give a catechetical flavor to each day's devotion. It is refreshing to have prayers for each Sunday of the Church Year, and not merely for the feast days. Indeed, all the seasons of life, including various vocations, are included in this marvelous gem.

In our watered-down, superficial age, this resource will help us not only learn how to pray but also give solid meat throughout a person's life. I have long enjoyed *The Abridged Treasury of Prayers*. Now, no longer restricted to the Epitome, we can enjoy the fullness of the larger *Gebetsschatz* in our native prayer language.

—REV. DR. WALTER R. STEELE, PASTOR, RESURRECTION LUTHERAN CHURCH, QUARTZ HILL, CA

Lex orandi, lex credendi. That's an old-fashioned way of saying that how we pray discloses what we believe, and what we believe shapes how we pray. In *Lutheran Prayer Companion*, Matthew Carver's translation of *The Evangelical Lutheran Prayer Treasury*, you get to pray along with Luther, Gerhard, Arndt, and scads of other great Lutheran teachers of old. When you do, you step into their world of faith: a world that is formed in the Scriptures and filled with the church's song. From the first time I encountered the German original, I've known how very blessed Lutherans of today would be to have this whole treasure chest of prayer opened for them in English. And Carver has pulled this off, putting them into English and yet maintaining the "feel" of the original. Dig in, folks! Through this volume, the rich spirituality that shaped our church in years gone by is let loose in our own language.

—REV. WILLIAM WEEDON, DIRECTOR OF WORSHIP FOR THE LUTHERAN CHURCH—MISSOURI SYNOD, CHAPLAIN OF THE INTERNATIONAL CENTER OF THE LCMS

LUTHERAN
PRAYER
COMPANION

LUTHERAN
PRAYER
COMPANION

ORIGINALLY PUBLISHED IN GERMAN AS

The Evangelical-Lutheran Prayer Treasury:
A compendious collection of the prayers
of Dr. Martin Luther
and other orthodox Lutherans
reproduced without alteration;
along with 106 orthodox hymns
for home devotional use.

TRANSLATED FROM THE GERMAN
By Matthew Carver

CONCORDIA PUBLISHING HOUSE • SAINT LOUIS, MISSOURI

Published by Concordia Publishing House
3558 S. Jefferson Avenue, St. Louis, MO 63118-3968
1-800-325-3040 • cph.org

Translated from *Evangelisch-Lutherischer Gebets-Schatz: Vollständige Sammlung von Gebeten Dr. Martin Luthers und anderer rechtgläubiger, gesalbter Beter der ev.-luth. Kirche in unverändertem Abdruck. Nebst einem Hausgesangbüchlein, 106 alte rechtgläubige Lieder für den Hausbedarf enthaltend* (St. Louis: Concordia Publishing House, 1881).

Manufactured in the United States of America

3 4 5 6 7 8 9 10   27 26 25 24 23 22 21

CONTENTS

TRANSLATOR'S NOTE

As it says in the "Preliminary Remarks" below, the German original of the present book was to be considered a sequel or second part for the older St. Louis hymnal, which has already been translated into English under the title *Walther's Hymnal*. That book contains 443 hymns and an appendix of a couple dozen prayers. This one is the reverse; it is predominantly prayers—482 of them, if you count the hymn stanzas, verses of comfort, and litanies—and an appendix of 106 hymns. Thus it is above all a prayerbook, and indeed, was designed as the prayerbook to end all prayerbooks. It was to be larger, more exhaustive, and more orthodox than any others which Lutherans then might have availed themselves of, and to do so by including the best of the many prayerbooks which so proliferated from the earliest days of the Lutheran confession. At the same time, the *Gebetsschatz* (or "prayer treasury") as it was called, is somewhat different in application and tone. It is meant primarily for use in the Christian home, to be prayed and sung by individuals and families. That is not to say, of course, that these prayers and hymns were supposed to stay at home! Indeed, several of these hymns eventually entered later English-language hymnals of the Missouri Synod and other church bodies intended for singing in church and have proved profitable in that context. As the hymns, so the prayers. Some prayers eventually found their way into an abridged *Gebetsschatz*, first in German, then in English. Designed for greater portability, this constituted perhaps as little as one fifth of the present material, often preferring shorter prayers and collects.

The exhaustive *Gebetsschatz*, which is translated here in its entirety, includes many longer, more meditative and reflective hymns appropriate to the use of the individual and family. Such lengthier scripted prayers may be unfamiliar to many nowadays, but that by no means diminishes their benefit. On the contrary, they are terrific windows into the godly minds and piety of previous generations and teach us godliness in a manner similar to the recorded words and actions of the prophets, apostles, and martyrs. First, they ground themselves solidly by constant reference to God's Word—indeed, the language of the Bible is so interwoven in these prayers, it is often difficult to distinguish quotation and the writer's voice (where possible, we have attempted to use the familiar wording of the English Standard Version to make this more noticeable). In addition, these prayers also teach us in the midst of prayer and help us meditate and reflect more deeply on our need and on God, who answers that need. They poke and pry the conscience and the heart in ways deeper than our own extemporaneous powers can reach.

Yet many of the prayers are short, what Lutherans have traditionally called *Seufzer*, "sighs." Such above all are those characteristic compositions by the blessed Dr. Luther himself. Many are appropriate for, or all but assume, a church context (which might well be prayed silently while sitting or kneeling in the pew). Others, as hinted above, are not prayers at all, but rather hymn stanzas and verses to be read or spoken aloud for the comfort of the sick or those otherwise afflicted or in distress. There are even a few litanies to be prayed, ideally in the company of others with one leading and the rest responding. Clearly, this prayerbook was designed to be useful in the entirety of a Christian's life.

Regarding the translation, it must be recognized that, in the adoption of a common, modern English (slightly elevated, as usual for religious purposes), a somewhat unconventional method has been used to address problems relating to the modern idiom. This is particularly the case with the grammar of the relative clause ("who . . .") following the address (e.g., "O God . . .") of almost every prayer. In the mid-twentieth century, knowledge of the historic language was still strong enough that in the switch to modern use of "You" for "Thou" in the second person, a close agreement between the grammatical person of the address and that of the relative clause was maintained, so that the second person "You" or "God" (where "You" was implied) was always followed in the relative clause by the analogous form of the verb to be used with "you" ("are, have, do," etc.).

Sometime in the last two or three decades, an uneasiness seems to have grown around this usage. This phenomenon seems largely to have spared the earlier materials of some other confessions, such as the Anglican and Roman Catholic, but to be more widespread in the Lutheran tradition in America and to have grown more notable in the last twenty years. In fact, recognition of this error in some quarters seems to have led to the adoption of a new solution: the elimination of the relative pronoun altogether and the transformation of the relative clause ("who is, who has") into a pure declarative ("You are, You have"). This succeeds in its quest to improve the grammatical deficiency, but it may be doubted whether it adequately conveys in every way the sense originally intended. Thus the old method has been used here, in which the relative pronoun, the second-person verb of the relative clause, and the whole unity of the grammatical structure, is maintained. It might be objected that this sounds incorrect or unfamiliar to our ears, but this is because of an unfortunate period of incorrect usage preceding and may soon be remedied by constant attention to the coordination and agreement between the addressee (with or without the explicit "You") and the verb in the relative clause ("who do, who are, who have"). I am satisfied by substantial use of materials in this form that the correct idiom quickly begins to feel normal, and the sense originally intended is in this way best conveyed.

As in *Walther's Hymnal*, the hymns in the appended *Hymns for Home Use* have been maintained in their original "traditional" language form (where already existing) or else translated in an equivalent idiom (where a new one was required) for the sake of relative continuity and simplicity. Likewise, the absence of hymn notation is continued from the original German *Gebetsschatz*, with melodies indicated by name. In addition to this, the *Gebetsschatz* includes several less-familiar melodies in notation after the hymn texts, which feature has been replicated here. For additional melodies which do not appear in our most recent hymnals (*Lutheran Service Book, Lutheran Worship*, and *The Lutheran Hymnal*) reference is made to Karl Brauer's ("Br") *Mehrstimmiges Choralbuch zu dem Kirchengesangbuch für Evangelisch-Lutherische Gemeinden Ungeänderter Augsburgischer Confession* (St. Louis: Concordia Publishing House, 1906). This reference is readily available online.

Finally, for their helpful advice, criticism, and advancement of this work, the translator thanks especially Dr. Joseph Herl, Dr. Benjamin Mayes, Mr. Nathaniel Jensen, Mr. Scott Gercken, Mr. Philip Fillion, and Rev. Karl Hess; and for the design of this volume, my dear Amanda.

Matthew Carver
Nativity of John the Baptist, 2018

LIST OF PRAYERS
WITH DESCRIPTIONS

B. The clerical estate

VIII. Repentance, Confession & Communion

IX. Catechism

X. Weather

XI. Cross & tribulation

XII. Praise & thanksgiving

XIII. Sickness & dying

PRELIMINARY REMARKS (1865)

Although there is already such a large number of prayerbooks that to add to them by way of the present volume might seem to some superfluous, yet not a few of those now available are of rather poor quality, while others contain bad material mingled with the good, and still others are not comprehensive. For this reason, faithful pastors have up to now been quite at a loss as to which book they might in good conscience recommend when those entrusted to their charge ask them for a good prayerbook covering all kinds of situations. The collectors of the present *Lutheran Prayer Companion* hope that they have thus met a need which has become increasingly urgent. The collection before you, designed not for church use but home use, is not only as exhaustive as possible, but also includes only those prayers which both confess the doctrines of God's Word purely and possess a language of genuine devotion devoid of anything naturalistic, diseased, or enthusiastic. In this regard, our *Lutheran Prayer Companion* might well surpass not only the more recent collections but also most of the older, exhaustive ones.

As for the appended *Hymns for Home Use*, we have only to note that only such hymns have been included as are not already found in the *Kirchen-Gesangbuch der deutschen evangelisch-lutherischen Synode von Missouri, Ohio und anderen Staaten*[1]. Therefore our *Hymns for Home Use* may be viewed as the second part of said hymnal.

It is hoped that the included indexes, which is to say, the alphabetical indexes located at the end of this book, will be welcome to readers and of service for quickly locating a fitting prayer for every occasion.

It is further hoped that this *Lutheran Prayer Companion* may become for a great many seekers of salvation an effective treasury for their souls, and that those who use it for their prayer may do so in such a way that they not only recite the prayers contained in it with their lips and heart, and come before God in true faith and in the name of Jesus Christ, but also that they may learn from it and be encouraged to pour out their heart before the throne of grace with prayer, invocation, praise, and thanksgiving, even in their own words. To this

---

1 Published in English as *Walther's Hymnal*. St. Louis: Concordia Publishing House. © 2012.

end we have included below from Luther, that anointed man of prayer, some instructions for praying so as to be truly answered (this is taken from his Church Postil). We strongly recommend that all who intend to use this *Lutheran Prayer Companion* make careful study of these instructions and take them to heart.

St. Louis, Missouri. May, 1864.
The German Evangelical-Lutheran
Pastoral Conference of St. Louis, Missouri.

LUTHER'S INSTRUCTIONS
FOR PROPER PRAYER

In order for a prayer to be truly good and receive an answer, it is well to note first that five things are needed. First, one has to have a promise or pledge from God and know beforehand that God will take note of it, and by this be moved to pray with more confidence. Had God not asked us to pray and promised to answer, the whole creation would not be able to get one grain, no matter how much it asked. It follows from this that no one gets something from God because of the worthiness of himself or his prayer, but only from God's goodness, which precedes all asking and requesting. By His gracious pledge and promise, He moves us to ask and request, so that we learn how much more He provides for us and is more ready to give than we to receive and look for, and so that we are emboldened to pray with confidence, since He offers everything and more than we can ask.

Second, it is necessary not to doubt the promise of the true and faithful God. That is precisely why He promised to answer—indeed, why He commanded us to pray. You can therefore rest assured and believe firmly that it will be answered, as He says (Matthew 21, Mark 11): "All that you ask in prayer, only believe, and you will receive it." And in Luke 11 He says, "I say to you also, 'Ask, and you will receive; seek, and you will find; knock, and it will be opened to you. For whoever asks, receives, and whoever seeks, finds, and whoever knocks, it will be opened to him. What son among you asks his father for bread and he would give him a stone instead? And if he asks for a fish, he would give him a scorpion instead? Therefore, if you who are wicked are able to give good gifts to your children, much more will the Father in heaven give the Holy Spirit to those who ask Him." You must console yourself by pondering this and similar promises and commands and pray with true confidence.

Third, if anyone prays in such a way that he doubts whether God will answer him, and only ventures to pray on the chance that it might or might not be answered, he makes two mistakes. First, he negates his own prayer and labors in vain. For James (chapter 1) says, "Whoever would ask of God, let him ask in faith, and not doubt; for whoever doubts is like a wave of the sea which is driven and tossed by the wind; let such a man not think that he will receive something from the Lord." He means by this that that man's heart is not still, so God can give him nothing. Faith, however, keeps the heart still and makes it capable of receiving divine gifts.

The second wrong is that he regards his most faithful and truest God as a liar and a worthless, unreliable man, as someone who cannot or will not keep his promises. Thus by his doubting he robs God of His glory and His name of faithfulness and truth and in the process sins so greatly that by this very sin a Christian is made a pagan and denies and loses his own God. And if he persists in this, he cannot but be condemned eternally without any hope. And if he should be given something that he asks for, it is given him not for his happiness but for his temporal and eternal harm. Neither is he then given something because of his prayer, but because of God's wrath, that He might reward those good words which are spoken in sin, unbelief, and disrespect of God.

Fourth, some say, "Well, I would be sure that my prayer is answered if I were worthy and behaved well." I reply: if you decided not to pray until you knew or felt that you were worthy and well-prepared, you would never pray again. As I said before, our prayer must not be based or depend on the worthiness of ourselves or our prayer, but on the unchangeable truth of God's promise. If it is based on itself or something else, it is false and deceptive, even if your heart is torn asunder by great devotion and weeps utter drops of blood. The reason why we pray is that we are not worthy to pray, and the way that we become worthy to pray and to be answered is by believing that we are unworthy and confidently leaving it to the faithfulness of God. No matter how unworthy you are, look at this and consider with all seriousness that it is a thousand times more important that you honor God's truthfulness and do not turn His promise into a lie by doubting. Your worthiness does not help you; your unworthiness does not hinder you. But mistrust condemns you, and reliance makes you worthy and sustains you.

Therefore, as long as you live, make sure that you never regard yourself as worthy or well-prepared to ask or to receive until you find that you are one who can freely rely on the true and certain promises of your gracious God, who will so reveal to you His mercy and goodness that, just as He has promised you an unsolicited answer out of pure grace, even though you are unworthy and undeserving, He will actually answer you, too, out of pure grace, even though you are unworthy to pray. This He will do to the glory of His truthfulness and promise, so that you give thanks not for your own worthiness but for His truthfulness by which He fulfilled the promise, and for His mercy by which He made the promise, verifying the words of Psalm 25, "The ways of the Lord are good-ness and faithfulness to those who keep His covenant and testimony." Good-ness or mercy in the promise, faithfulness or truth in the fulfillment or hearing of the promises. And in Psalm 85, he says, "Goodness and faithfulness meet, righteousness and peace kiss each other." That is, they come together in every work and gift which we get from God by asking.

Fifth, having this confidence, you should behave in such a way that you do not assign God a goal, prescribe Him the day or place, or specify the manner or measure of His answer to your prayer, but commit it all to His will, wisdom, and almighty power, and simply wait with confidence and joy for His answer, not wishing to know how and where, how soon, how long, and by what means. For His divine wisdom will find the immeasurably better manner and means, time and place, than we can imagine, even if it should take a miracle of the sort found in the Old Testament. When the children of Israel trusted that God would redeem them, even though there was no possible way in sight or in any of their powers of thought: then the Red Sea opened and let them pass through and drowned all their enemies in a single stroke.

The holy woman, Judith, did the same thing. When she heard that the cit-izens of Bethuliah would hand over the city in five days unless God delivered them during that time, she rebuked them and said, "Who are you, that you put God to the test? These are not the means to obtain grace but to stir up more disfavor. Would you prescribe for God a time to have mercy on you, and spec-ify a day according to your whim?" [Judith 8:11ff.] And God helped her in a miraculous way, so that she struck off the head of the great Holofernes and the enemies were driven away.

Likewise, St. Paul says in Ephesians 3 [:20] that it is God's way to do immea-surably higher and better than we ask or comprehend. Therefore we should acknowledge that we are too little to be able to identify, designate, or portray time, place, manner, measure, and other circumstances for what we ask of God, but leave everything entirely to Him and steadfastly believe without shifting that He will answer us.

SOURCES
*from which the prayers contained in
this Lutheran Prayer Companion have been drawn.*

Alard, Wilhelm (1572–1645), superintendent in Crempe.[1]

Albinus, Johannes (1624–79), pastor in Naumburg.[2]

Albrecht, Bernhardus (1569–1636), senior in Augsburg.[3]

Arndt, Johann (1555–1621), general-superintendent in Celle: *Paradiesgärtlein.*[4]

Bugenhagen, Johann (1485–1558), chief pastor in Wittenberg, contemporary and friend of Luther.

Crüger, Johann (1598–1662), cantor and composer in Berlin: *Übung der Gottseligkeit.*[5]

Dedekenn, Georg (1564–1628), pastor in Hamburg.[6]

Dilherr, Johann Michael (1604–69), chief pastor in Nuremberg: *Weg zur Seligkeit.*[7]

Drechsler, Johann Gabriel (d. 1677), teacher in Halle.[8]

Eichorn, Johann (ca. 1518–64),[9] *Rüst- und Schatz-kammer* (1715).[10]

---

1 Works include the devotional prayerbook, *Girrendes Turteltäublein,* revised (Rinteln/Weser: P. Lucius, 1633).

2 I.e., Johann Georg Albinus the Elder, notably author of the hymn, *Straf mich nicht in deinem Zorn;* also translated and wrote devotional works.

3 Works include *Haus- und Kirchen-Schatz,* revised and enlarged (Ulm: B. Kühne, 1666).

4 In numerous editions, e.g., *Paradis-Gärtlein voll Christlicher Tugenden . . .* (Sondershausen: L. H. Schönermarck, 1708).

5 This entry is amended because of confusion with a similarly named pastor of Stettin (d. 1616). Our Crüger's hymnal had several eds., e.g., *Praxis Pietatis Melica, Das ist: Ubung der Gottseligkeit in Christlichen und trostreichen Gesängen . . .* (Berlin: C. Runge, 1653).

6 Works include *Thesaurus conciliorum et decisionum* (1623, 1671).

7 *Weg zu der Seeligkeit . . .* (Nuremberg: W. Endter d. Ä, 1655).

8 Name originally given as "Johann Georg Drechsler." Works include a student prayerbook, *Anchora Sacra Studiosorum e Verbo Dei fabricata, oder Andächtige Gebet und Gesänge vor Studirende . . .* eighth edition (Leipzig: J. C. Cörner, 1696).

9 The birthdate has been supplied by the translator. No further biographical details can be satisfactorily connected to the author of the *Rüst- und Schatz-Kammer.*

10 In several editions, e.g., *Geistliche Rüst- und Schatz-Kammer in vier Theil . . .* (Frankfurt / Oder: Rösner, 1660). *Die Geistliche Rüst- und Schatz-Kammer, voll auserlesener Geistreicher Gebete . . .* (Nürnberg: Miltenberger, 1696, 1702).

Emdenius, Joachim (1595–1650), pastor in Nordhausen.[11]

Facilides, Christoph Siegmund (1625–84), pastor in Frankenberg, *Güldene Rauchwerk-Schaale.*[12]

Feinler, Johann (1609–90), pastor in Gleina: *Trostührlein.*[13]

Gerhard, Johann (1582–1637), professor at Jena: *Übung der Gottseligkeit.*[14]

Haas, Nicolaus (1665–1715), *Das in Gott andächtige Frauenzimmer.*[15]

Habermann, Johann (1516–90), superintendent in Zeitz: *Christliches Gebet-buch.*[16]

Hartmann, Johann Ludwig (1640–84), superintendent in Rotenburg: *Hand-buch.*[17]

Heermann, Johann (1585–1647), pastor in Köben: *Buß-Leiter.*[18]

Liscovius, Salomo (1640–89), pastor in Otterwisch: *Der zu seinem Jesu sich na-hende Sünder.*[19]

Löscher, Valentin Ernst (1673–1749), superintendent in Dresden: *Unschuldige Nachrichten.*[20]

---

11 Native of Magdeburg, pastor of the old St. Nicolai Church in Nordhausen. A transcription of his epitaph shows the date of his death to be October 10, 1650. Works include a collection of funeral sermons.

12 C. S. Facilides's works include *Güldener Rauch-Altar, ein Hand- und Bet-Büchlein* (Nuremberg: Hoffmann, 1676). The specified prayerbook, *Güldene Rauchwerck-Schaale* (Stößel, 1735) is rather the work of his son, Johann Gottfried Facilides, pastor in Ottendorf.

13 Works include *Krancker Christen Lehr- und Trost-Ührlein* (St. Annaberg, 1674); *Wahrer Christen Creutz-Schul* (Naumburg, 1676); *Geistlich Bet-Ührlein in 12 Stunden*; *Kinder-Gebet-büchlein.*

14 That is, *Schola Pietatis oder Übung der Gottseligkeit* (Jena: Steinmann, 1622–23), also trans. from the Latin as *Johann Gerhard's tägliche Uebung der Gottseligkeit* (Sulzbach: Seidel, 1842).

15 *Das in Gott andächtige Frauenzimmer, Wie es so wohl alltäglich . . . erscheinen, und in brüns-tiger Andacht . . . ausschütten könne . . .* (Leipzig: Gledisch, 1722).

16 In numerous eds., e.g., *Christliche Gebet, auff alle Tag in der Wochen zu sprechen . . .* (Hartmann, 1593), *Christliche Gebet für alle Noth und Ständte . . .* (Nuremberg: Fuhrmann, 1605), *D. Johann Habermanns Christliches Gebet-Buch . . .* (Reiss, 1672), *D. Johann Habermanns Christliche Morgen-Abend-Beicht-Communion- und andere Gebete . . .* (Roth: Meyer, 1765).

17 *Hand-Buch für Seelsorger in Sechs Theilen vorstellend . . .* (Rotenburg: von Millenau, 1680).

18 *Johann Heermanns, Pfarrers zu Cöben, Buß-Leyter: Beicht-Büchlein: und Communicanten-Büchlein* (Frankfurt: Götzen, 1653).

19 Originally published in 1670; editions include *Der mit rechtschaffenem Hertzen und bittern Thränen zu seinem Jesu sich nahende Sünder, Bestehet in auserlesenen Buß- Beicht- und Com-munion-Andachten . . . Wie auch Morgen- und Abend-Andachten* (Leipzig: Schönermarck, 1749), not to be confused with Benjamin Schmolck's (1672–1737) *Der mit rechtschaffenem Hertzen zu seinem Jesu sich nahende Sünder* (Chemnitz: Stößel, 1743).

20 *Unschuldige Nachrichten von Alten und Neuen Theologischen Sachen . . .* (Leipzig: Braun, 1710).

Luther, Martin (1483–1546): *Gebetklöcklein* (through Peter Trewer).[21]

Mathesius, Johann (1504–68), pastor in Joachimsthal: *Andächtige und christliche gemeine Gebetlein.*[22]

Olearius, Johann (1611–84), professor in Leipzig.[23]

Pancratius, Andreas (1529–76), superintendent in Hof: *Haus- und Kirchenbuch.*[24]

Quirsfeld, Johann (1642–86), archdeacon in Pirna: *Geistlicher Myrrhen-Garten.*[25]

Scherertz, Sigismund (1584–1639), *Seelen-Arznei und Spiegel der geistlichen Anfechtungen.*[26]

Schimmer, Georg (1652–95), *Biblisches Seelen-Kleinod.*[27]

Schrader, Johann (fl. 1592–1624).[28]

Scriver, Christian (1629–93), *Gebetskleinod.*[29]

Zeämann, Georg (1580–1638), *Geistliches Vade Mecum.*[30]

---

21 *Beteglöcklin Doctoris Martini Lutheri Von allen wolklingenden Geystreichen, hertzlichen, starcken und feurigen Gebetten . . . Treulich und auffs neu zugericht durch M. Petrum Trewer Coburgensem* (Strassburg: Jobin, 1579).

22 *Andächtige und christliche gemeine Gebetlein für alle Noth der Christenheit*, new edition (Nuremberg: Raw, 1836).

23 Works include *Geistliches Hand-Buch der Kinder Gottes* (Halle, 1668), *Geistliche Singe-Kunst* (Leipzig, 1671), *Exemplarische Bet-Kunst der Kinder Gottes* (Leipzig, 1672), *Biblische Erklärung* (Leipzig, 1679).

24 Pancratius's summaries and prayers in their earlier form were known as *Uber der Sonntäge Epistel und Evangelia kurtze Summarien und Gebetlein . . .* (Nuremberg: Geißler, 1565).

25 *M. Johann Quirsfelds geistlicher Myrrhen-Garten . . . Nebenst einem kurtzen Gebet-Buche in allerhand Creutz und Elend* (Leipzig: Wittigau, 1692).

26 Pastor in some West-Bohemian parishes, later superintendent in Lunenburg. The full title of this work is *Fuga Melancholiae cum Speculo Tentationum Spiritualium, et Poculo Consolationis, Oder: Drey Geistreiche Bücher, Das Erste: Seelen-Atzney Wider die Melancholey, Traurigkeit und Schwermuht des Geistes, etc. Das Ander: Spiegel der Geistlichen Anfechtungen, Warüm sie Gott über uns kommen lasse. Das Dritte: Trost-Becher, Für alle traurige, wehemühtige, auch mit seltzamen und wunderlichen Gedancken geplagte Christen* (Lunenburg: Stern, 1682).

27 *Biblisches Seelen-Kleinod oder Neu-vollständiges Gebetbuch* (Leipzig: Fritsch, 1706).

28 Pastor in Alvensleben. Most notable work is *Formular-Buch, Allerhand Christlicher Wort, und Ceremonien . . .* (Magdeburg, 1621), revised, in three volumes (Frankfurt & Leipzig, 1660).

29 Pastor in Magdeburg, later Quedlinburg. Editions of the work include *M. Christian Scrivers Güldenes und in seinem Seelen-Schatze beygelegtes Gebet-Kleinod, Oder: Auszug Aller Gebete und Seuffzer, so in dessen herrlichen und erbaulichen Schrifften hin und wieder enthalten . . .* (Nuremberg: Hoffmann, 1713).

30 *Geistlich Vade Mecum* (Nuremberg: Endter, 1675).

An old prayerbook (title page lacking).
Die Himmlische Braut-Kammer.[31]
Großes und vollkommnes Gebetbuch of Michael Cubach (1655).[32]
Himmlisches Freudenmahl.[33]
Israels Trost und Freude (1660).
Krone der Alten.[34]
The Nuremberg Children's Catechism.[35]
The Prayerbook of Elector Christian I (1589).[36]
The *Riga Prayerbook* (1719).[37]
The Torgau Catechism and Handbook (1676).[38]

31 Christian Zeis, *Die Himmels-schöne Königliche Braut-Kammer, Welche der überirrdische Salomo, und hochverliebte Menschen-Freund, Christus Jesus seiner liebsten Sulamithin . . . zubereitet . . . Bestehend aus einem . . . Gebet- und Gesang-Buch . . .* (Oetingen, 1674; Leipzig: Eyssel, 1722).

32 In several editions, e.g., *Einer gläubigen und andächtigen Seelen tägliches Bet- Buß- Lob- Und Danck-Opffer, Das ist: Ein groß-vollkommnes Gebet-Buch . . .* (Leipzig: Gleditsch/Weidmann, 1713).

33 M. Johann Rittmeyer (1636–98), several editions, e.g., *Himmlisches Freuden-Mahl der Kinder Gottes auf Erden. Oder geistreiche Gebehte . . .* (Hamm, 1703), *Himlisches Freuden-Mahl der Kinder Gottes auf Erden. Oder: Geistreiche Gebete . . . mit einem Anhang von Morgen- und Abend-Gebetern . . .* (Lüneburg: Stern, 1769); Traugott Siegmund [=Philipp Räthjen], ed., *Himmlisches Freudenmahl: Ein Communionbuch . . .* (Leipzig: Sinhuber, 1860), *Himmlisches Freudenmahl der Kinder Gottes. Ein Communionbuch . . .* (Neu-Ruppin: Buchbinder, 1860). Not to be confused with J. M. Dilherr, *Himmlisches Freudenmahl auff Erden . . .* (Nuremberg: Dümler, 1647).

34 Johann G. Olearius et al., *Krone der Alten, Das ist: Neu-vollständiges Gebet Buch: Vermittelst dessen, und der darinn enthaltenen so wohl . . . Geistreichen Gebete und Seuffzer . . .* (Klinger, 1693; Eyffel, 1732).

35 *Nürnbergisches Kinderlehrbüchlein, darinnen jede Frage wieder durch neue unter dem Text gesetzte Fragen zergliedert wird* (1711); or, *Nürnbergisches Kinder-Lehr-Büchlein . . .* (Nuremberg: Felßecker, 1719).

36 See Dr. Johann Konrad Irmischer, ed., *Betbuch Christian des Ersten, Herzogs und Churfürsten zu Sachsen, vom Jahre 1589. Mit Gebeten des Churfürsten August von Sachsen* (Erlangen: Deichert, 1853).

37 Editions from 1664, e.g., *Rigisches Viel-vermehrtes Haus- und Kirchen-Gebet-Buch . . .* (Leipzig: Gleditsch, 1699); *Neu Rigisches Gebetbuch, Bestehend aus Andacht- und Trostvollen Hertzens-Seuffzern . . .* (Riga: Nöller, 1700). Later editions are attached to a hymnal, e.g., *Neu-Vielvermehrtes Rigisches Gesang-Buch . . . nebst einem Andacht- und Trost-vollen Gebetbuche . . .* (Riga: Frölich: 1750, 1784, etc.).

38 By Dr. Paul Hofmann, superintendent. First printed in 1594, later revised, expanded, and illustrated: *Torgauischer Catechismus, oder Fürstlicher und andrer Gottfürchtiger Kinder Hand-Buch* (Fritzsch, 1676; Torgau: Hempe, 1675).

Breslau Hymnal (1751).[39]

Eisenach Hymnal (1760).[40]

Freiberg Hymnal.[41]

Leipzig Hymnal (1730).[42]

Marburg Hymnal.[43]

Schwarzburg Agenda (1650).[44]

Seckendorf's Hymnal.[45]

39 I. e., "Burg's Hymnal." Johann Friedrich Burg (1689–1766), inspector of Breslau: *Allgemeines und vollständiges Evangelisches Gesang-Buch für die Königliche Preußische Schlesische Lande . . . Nebst angefügtem Gebet-Buch . . .* (Breslau: Korn, 1751).

40 *Neu eingerichtetes Sachsen-Weimar-Eisenach- und Jenaisches Gesang-Buch . . .* (Weimar: Hoffmann, 1755). *Neu eingerichtetes Eisenachisches Gesangbuch . . .* (Eisenach: Hof-Buch-druckerei, 1776).

41 *Neueingerichtetes Freybergisches Gesangbuch nebst einigen Gebeten zur Kirchen- und Husandacht* (Freyberg: Barthel, 1780/1782); or possibly, *Gesangbuch für die Stadt und Diöces Freyburg* (Freyberg/Unstrut, 1798).

42 *Das Vollständige und vermehrte Leipziger Gesang-Buch Worinnen Die auserlesensten Lieder . . . nebst einem Wohleingerichteten Gebet-Buche . . .* (Leipzig: Barnbeck, 1729).

43 *Vollständiges und Neu-eingerichtetes Marburger Gesangbuch . . . Sampt einem Gebet- Beicht-Buß- und Communion-Büchlein . . .* (Marburg: Stock, 1681); or else, *Vollständiges Marburger Gesangbuch . . . nebst schönen . . . Gebätern . . .* (Marburg/Franckfurt: Brönner, 1799).

44 *Agenda Schwartzburgica, Das ist: Verzeichniß der Ceremonien . . .* (Arnstadt, 1650; rev. Arnstadt: Meurer, 1675; Rudolstadt: Freyschmid/Fleischer, 1675).

45 *Seckendorffisches Familien-Gesangbuch . . . mit etlichen schönen Gebetern . . .* (Nürnberg: Felßecker, 1708, 1723).

PRAYERS

I. PREPARATION

1. For true devotion

Lord, because You desire and direct me to pray and come to You, therefore I come, bringing many reasons for prayer, particularly that which most hinders me and keeps me from You, which is my sin which weighs on me and oppresses me, that You might take it away from me and forgive me; through Jesus Christ. Amen.

2. For true worthiness to pray

Lord, it is for Your glory and Your worship, by which You are extolled, that I come as a beggar before You. Therefore, dear Lord, do not regard how unworthy I am, but see how I am in need of Your help, and You are for all sinners the true and only help in time of need. Therefore it is to Your glory that I call on You; nor can I do without Your help, but You can and will give to those who ask. Amen, amen.

3. Thanksgiving that God makes us worthy for prayer

I am well aware, O gracious God, that I am an unworthy person and deserve to be the devil's brother and not Christ's. Yet Christ has said that I, as one for whom He died and rose again, no less than St. Peter, am His brother; and it is His earnest desire that I should believe Him without any doubting or wavering and not regard or consider the fact that I am unworthy and full of sins, since He Himself will not consider or contemplate taking revenge or punishing me (as He is well within His rights and has good reason to do), but all is forgotten and blotted out from His heart—in fact, it is dead and buried. Why then should I not let it be so and heartily thank, praise, and love my dear Lord for being so gracious and merciful? Amen.

4. Comfort against any sins or unworthiness

Who I am is of no concern to me. Even if I am a sinner, I know that my Lord Christ is not a sinner but is always righteous and gracious. Therefore I will confidently cry out and call on Him and turn nowhere else. I do not have time now to deliberate whether I am elect or not, but I sense that I am in need of help and, therefore, come looking for it in all humility. Dear God, the Canaanite woman was a Gentile, and as such was able, indeed, was required, to conclude that she was not chosen. But as she approached the Lord Jesus and did not let such thoughts keep her from praying, I will do the same and say, Lord, I come now, requiring this and that. Where else will I receive or seek except with You in heaven, through Your Son, my Savior, Jesus Christ? Amen.

5. Prayer based on God's command and promise

Dear Lord, You know that I do not come to You of my own accord, in my own presumption, or on my own worthiness. If I considered that, I would not be able to lift my eyes up before You, nor would I know how to begin to pray. Rather, I come because You Yourself have commanded us, and earnestly direct us, to call on You. You also swore an oath, and even sent Your own Son, who taught us what to pray and gave us the words. Therefore I know that such prayer pleases You. And however great my presumption may seem when I call myself a child of God before You, I must obey You, who desire it to be that way, lest I call You a liar and sin against You even more severely than my other sins, both by despising Your commandment and disbelieving Your promise.

6. Assurance of being heard because of Christ

O God, Creator of heaven and earth, You sent Your Son, Jesus Christ, into the world, that for my sake He might be crucified, die, on the third day rise again, and ascend into heaven, that, being seated at Your right hand, He might hold all things in His own hand and send us His Spirit, that we might wait for His coming to judge both the living and the dead and so receive with Him the eternal kingdom, our inheritance, which You desire to give us through Him. To this end, O Lord God, You have given and instituted for us Baptism and the Sacrament of the body and blood of Your Son, for in His sacraments He has joined Himself with us Christians and revealed Himself to us. If we take hold of Him there, we have certainly found Him. But as for other things which we have not been commanded, let us abandon them, or else we will miss Him by a great distance.

7. *For a gracious hearing*

Father in heaven, I know that You love me, for I love Your Son, my Redeemer, Jesus Christ. In this trust and confidence, I will now pray, assured that You will hear me and give me what I ask, not because I am holy and pious but because I know that You eagerly desire to grant and give us all things for the sake of Your Son, Jesus Christ. In His name I come before You to pray, having no doubt that this prayer, regardless of who I am, is certainly heard. Amen.

8. *Before the Lord's Prayer*

O heavenly Father, dear God: I am a poor, unworthy sinner, unfit to lift my eyes and hands toward You in prayer. But because You have commanded us all to pray and promised to hear and, through Your dear Son, our Lord Jesus Christ, personally taught us both the words and way to pray, therefore, I come on the basis of Your commandment, in obedience to You, relying on Your gracious promise, and in the name of my Lord Jesus Christ, I pray with all Your holy Christians on earth, even as He taught me:

Our Father who art in heaven, hallowed be Thy name, Thy kingdom come, Thy will be done on earth as it is in heaven. Give us this day our daily bread; and forgive us our trespasses as we forgive those who trespass against us; and lead us not into temptation, but deliver us from evil. For Thine is the kingdom and the power and the glory forever and ever. Amen.

II. DR. LUTHER'S MORNING & EVENING BENEDICTION

9. Morning benediction

In the name of the Father and of the Son and of the Holy Spirit. Amen.

I believe in God, the Father Almighty, Maker of heaven and earth;

And in Jesus Christ, His only Son, our Lord, who was conceived by the Holy Spirit, born of the Virgin Mary, suffered under Pontius Pilate, was crucified, died and was buried. He descended into hell. The third day He rose again from the dead. He ascended into heaven and sits at the right hand of God, the Father Almighty. From thence He will come to judge the living and the dead.

I believe in the Holy Spirit, the holy Christian church, the communion of saints, the forgiveness of sins, the resurrection of the body, and the life everlasting. Amen.

Our Father who art in heaven, hallowed be Thy name, Thy kingdom come, Thy will be done on earth as it is in heaven. Give us this day our daily bread; and forgive us our trespasses as we forgive those who trespass against us; and lead us not into temptation, but deliver us from evil. For Thine is the kingdom and the power and the glory forever and ever. Amen.

I thank You, my heavenly Father, through Jesus Christ, Your dear Son, that You have kept me this night from all harm and danger; and I pray that You would keep me this day also from sin and every evil, that all my doings and life may please You. For into Your hands I commend myself, my body and soul, and all things. Let Your holy angel be with me, that the evil foe may have no power over me. Amen.

10. Evening benediction

In the name the Father and of the Son and of the Holy Spirit. Amen.

I believe in God, the Father Almighty, Maker of heaven and earth;

And in Jesus Christ, His only Son, our Lord, who was conceived by the Holy Spirit, born of the Virgin Mary, suffered under Pontius Pilate, was crucified, died and was buried. He descended into hell. The third day He rose again from the dead. He ascended into heaven and sits at the right hand of God the Father Almighty. From thence He will come to judge the living and the dead.

I believe in the Holy Spirit, the holy Christian church, the communion of saints, the forgiveness of sins, the resurrection of the body, and the life everlasting. Amen.

Our Father who art in heaven, hallowed be Thy name, Thy kingdom come, Thy will be done on earth as it is in heaven. Give us this day our daily bread; and forgive us our trespasses as we forgive those who trespass against us; and lead us not into temptation, but deliver us from evil. For Thine is the kingdom and the power and the glory forever and ever. Amen.

I thank You, my heavenly Father, through Jesus Christ, Your dear Son, that You have graciously kept me this day; and I pray that You would forgive me all my sins where I have done wrong, and graciously keep me this night. For into Your hands I commend myself, my body and soul and all things. Let Your holy angel be with me, that the evil foe may have no power over me. Amen.

III. TABLE PRAYERS

11. *Before the meal*

The eyes of all look to You, O Lord, and You give them their food at the proper time. You open Your hand and satisfy the desires of every living thing.

Then the Lord's Prayer and the following prayer:

Lord God, heavenly Father, bless us and these Your gifts which we receive from Your bountiful goodness, through Jesus Christ, our Lord. Amen.

12. *Another*

Come, Lord Jesus, be our Guest
And let Thy gifts to us be blest. Amen.

13. *Another*

Feed Thy children, God most holy,
  Comfort sinners poor and lowly;
O Thou Bread of Life from heaven,
  Bless the food Thou here hast given!
As these gifts the body nourish,
May our souls in graces flourish
  Till with saints in heavenly splendor
  At Thy feast due thanks we render. (*TLH* 659)

14. *Another*

Watch yourselves lest your hearts be weighed down with dissipation and drunkenness and cares of this life. (Luke 21:34)

Lord, bless to us these gifts of Thine
  That they may nourish those who dine,
And thereby strengthen and refresh
  Upon this earth our feeble flesh.

(cont.)

For not by bread alone are we
  Sustained for all eternity:
Thy Holy Word alone can feed
  Our soul, and give us life indeed. (*WH* 306)

15. *After the meal*

Give thanks to the Lord, for He is good. His love endures forever. He gives food to every creature. He provides food for the cattle and for the young ravens when they call. His pleasure is not in the strength of the horse, nor His delight in the legs of a man; the Lord delights in those who fear Him, who put their hope in His unfailing love.

Then the Lord's Prayer and the following prayer:

We thank You, Lord God, heavenly Father, for all Your benefits, through Jesus Christ, our Lord, who lives and reigns with You and the Holy Spirit forever and ever. Amen.

16. *Another*

Godliness is a means of great gain when accompanied by contentment. For we have brought nothing into the world, so we cannot take anything out of it either. If we have food and covering, with these we shall be content. (1 Tim. 6:6–8)

We thank and praise our Lord in heaven
  For all the gifts which He has given,
And ask Him also evermore
  To feed us all as heretofore.
Thy Word our nourishment let be
  Now and in all eternity
And let at length us occupy
  Our heavenly mansions when we die. (*WH* 310)

Glory to God the Father, who made us:
Glory to God the Son, who redeemed us:
Glory to God the Holy Spirit, who sanctified us:
Glory to the Holy and Most Blessed Trinity
From this time forth and for eternity!

IV. PRAYERS FOR EVERY
DAY OF THE WEEK

17. Morning benediction on Sunday

O Lord, heavenly Father, everlasting God, blessed be Your divine power and omnipotence! Praised be Your boundless goodness and mercy! Glorified be Your eternal wisdom and truth! During this dangerous night You covered me with Your hand, and caused me to abide and sleep safely under the shadow of Your wing, and preserved me and tenderly sheltered me from the evil foe and all his secret wiles and cunning. Therefore I praise You for Your goodness and wondrous works to the children of man, and I desire to extol You in the congregation. Your praise shall continually be in my mouth. My soul shall make its boast in You, my Lord, at all times. All that is within me will bless Your holy name and will not forget all Your benefits. Be pleased, therefore, with the sacrifice of praise out of my mouth, which I offer to You this morning in the simplicity of my heart.

With my whole heart I cry to You, that You would keep me this day also from every danger of body and soul and command Your angels concerning me, to guard me in all my ways. Make a hedge around me with Your shield, and lead me in the path of Your Commandments, that I may walk purely in service to You, like the children of the day, to Your good pleasure. Restrain the evil foe and all the offensive things of this world, and curb my own flesh and blood, lest, being overpowered by them, I offend You and anger You with my sins. Govern me with Your Holy Spirit, that I may not endeavor, do, say, or think anything but what is pleasing to You and attains to the honor of Your divine majesty. Behold, my God, I present and offer myself wholly to Your will this day, with body and soul and all my powers and faculties, inside and out. Make me a living sacrifice for Yourself, holy and pleasing to You, that I may give You reasonable and acceptable worship.

Therefore, holy Father, almighty God, let me be Your own possession. Direct my heart, mind, and soul, that I may know and understand nothing but You. O Lord, in the morning may You hear my voice; in the morning I will direct my prayer to You and watch; in the morning I will praise You, and in the evening I will not cease; through Jesus Christ. Amen.

18. Another

Almighty, everlasting God and Father, I give You thanks and praise from my heart that You have mercifully kept me this night from every evil and danger of body and soul; and I pray from my inmost heart that You would forgive me all my sins with which I have ever angered You, and that You would kindle my heart with Your Holy Spirit, that I may daily grow and increase in the knowledge of You. Grant me grace that throughout the coming day I may keep myself from sin and shame and be found in Your divine will, that I may so walk that, being defended from every evil, I may keep You in my heart and mind continually without ceasing. When my last hour draws near and I must depart this world, let me fall asleep blessedly in the true knowledge of Your dear Son, Jesus Christ, and come to life everlasting. Amen.

19. Prayer from the first petition of the Lord's Prayer

Abba, Holy Father, to the honor of whose holy and glorious name the cherubim and seraphim in heaven above with uplifted voice unceasingly sing, "Holy, Holy, Holy Lord God of Sabaoth. Heaven and earth are full of Your glory!" Grant grace that Your name may be duly sanctified and honored today and at all times by Your whole beloved Church on earth. Help me and all men rightly to know Your power, to tremble with fear at Your righteousness, safely to hope in Your truth, heartily to love Your mercy, piously to wonder at Your wisdom, always to rejoice in Your goodness, and in all things zealously to seek Your glory.

O God, on this Sunday make my dear pastor, as well as other faithful teachers and preachers, vessels of Your mercy and instruments of Your grace, and let their ministry attain to the praise of Your glory and to the welfare and blessedness of every soul entrusted to their care. Grant that their lips may continually preserve the truth of Your doctrine in its purity and give no room to any devilish heresy or any error which corrupts the soul. Clothe them with power from on high, that they may preach purely and without mingling the Word of life to Your congregation, which Christ purchased so dearly by His blood, instruct the unlearned with holy doctrine, rebuke the ungodly by opening their mouths boldly, and uplift the afflicted with mighty comfort. Give Your divine growth to their holy labor, that Your Word may never return to You empty, but succeed in the thing for which You sent it, and in my heart and the hearts of all hearers, bring forth fruit a hundredfold unto life everlasting. Teach them in their life and conduct to do Your will, and let Your good Spirit lead them on level ground, that they may put no obstacle in anyone's way, so that no fault may be found with their ministry.

O merciful Jesus, let me and all godly Christians learn well the whole counsel of God concerning our salvation, which You reveal to us by these Your ministers and messengers, and blessedly observe it. Enlighten the eyes of our understanding, that we may have strength to comprehend with all the saints what is the breadth and length and height and depth of Your love with which You loved us; and kindle in us a true, heartfelt, and sure trust, that in life and death we may steadfastly confide in You and Your merit, and a holy and sincere love, that we may cease from all sin and unrighteousness. For we are called by Your name, and neither angels nor rulers nor powers, nor height nor depth, nor things present nor things to come, will be able to separate us from You.

O God the Holy Spirit, sanctify us, one and all, in Your truth, and grant that we may with right devotion and holy reverence attend to Your precious Word, which is able to save our souls, write it and seal it on our hearts by true faith, conform our lives to it most diligently for the glory of Your great name, and one day come to Your eternal glory, and in the choir of all the holy angels and elect forever worship and glorify You. Amen.

20. *Evening benediction on Sunday*

Eternal God, merciful Father, I lift up my hands to You as the evening sacrifice and give You praise, honor, and thanks from my heart that You have graciously kept me this day, and the whole time of my life, from every evil and misfortune by Your dear angels' protection against the evil foe. I pray that You would forgive me all my sins where I have done wrong and continue to surround me with Your holy angels this night, that they may encamp around me, and set up a barricade around me, that I may escape the snares and wicked cunning of the evil foe. Receive me, Your poor creature, into Your goodness and mercy. Protect me with Your outstretched arm, for I sincerely long for You this night, and my spirit within me keeps watch for You continually. I wait for Your goodness, and my soul hopes in You, O living God, for You are my refuge and my faithful Savior. Behold, O Lord, whether we sleep or wake, we are Yours. Whether we live or die, You are our God, and You made us. Therefore I cry to You. Let Your grace not be far from me. Cover me with Your shield. Uphold me that I may lie down in peace and sleep pleasantly and arise in good health. Hide me in Your shelter in the day of trouble; conceal me under the cover of Your tent; lift me high upon a rock, and I will not be afraid. Even though I walk through the valley of the shadow of death, I will fear no evil, for You are with me; Your rod and staff, they comfort me. Only grant me Your grace that my body may sleep while my soul is always awake to You, and that I may always have You in my heart and never let You out of my mind, lest the night of sin overtake me. Preserve me from evil and shameful dreams, from restless waking and useless worry, from wicked, heavy thoughts and from every torment. Behold, my God, to Your gracious keeping I commend myself, my body and soul, my dear brothers and sisters, and all who are related to me by blood or otherwise. Be pleased, O Lord, to deliver us! Do not restrain Your mercy from us. Let Your steadfast love and Your faithfulness ever preserve us. Cover us during this night with Your loving kindness; encompass us with Your grace on every side; and support us with Your mercy, that we may be defended in body and soul. Amen.

21. Another

O Lord, almighty God, heavenly Father, I thank You from my inmost heart for all Your mercies and benefits which You have kindly shown me this day, and that You have kept me in good health and safe from every evil. And I pray, as Your dear child, that You would graciously continue to keep me in Your only saving Word until my final breath, and enlighten my heart with Your Holy Spirit, that I may know what is good and evil. In Your mercy blot out all my sins which I have knowingly done this day, along with all hidden faults, and grant me this night a Christian rest, that I may arise in good health, ready to praise You. Help me also, dear Father, by Your grace, to begin a new life, pleasing to You and salutary to my soul; through Jesus Christ, Your beloved Son, our only Savior. Amen.

22. Morning benediction on Monday

Immortal and merciful God, forasmuch as in Your law You commanded Your people to make a burnt offering to You every morning, to praise You and thank You for Your gracious protection, therefore I now offer up to You a sacrifice of praise, that is, the fruit of my lips, and worship Your holy name, because You have so graciously and mercifully protected me this night from all evil and harm of body and soul, and with fatherly kindness defended me from my adversary, the evil foe. If You had not been my shield and stay, countless evils would have laid waste to me, and I would not have risen in good health. From my inmost heart I cry to You, in the morning my prayer comes before You. I seek You early and pray that this day You would continue to protect me and all who are in my charge from the craft and power of the devil and from sin, disgrace, and every evil. Go before me with Your grace this morning hour, for without You I can do nothing. Help me this day also, in Your name, to begin all my labors in Christian fashion and to bring them to blessed completion to the honor of Your divine majesty and to the benefit of my neighbor. Guard my soul, mind and reason, thoughts and senses, and all that I do or do not, that the wretched devil may have no power to hurt me. Protect me from the destruction that wastes at noonday; defend me from all my enemies, visible and invisible, so that they cannot hurt or harm me with their wiles and cunning, enchantments, poisonings, and all their violence and mischief—secret and open. O Lord God, Father and Lord of my life, keep me from the sight of uncleanness, and dispel from me every wicked passion. Let me not fall into gluttony or unchastity, and guard my heart from shamelessness. Help me by Your grace to tear out any eye that causes me to sin and to throw it away by shunning the wicked and impure desires of my heart. Take from me anything that is hateful to You and hurtful to myself; give to me whatever is pleasing to You and profitable to myself, that I may serve You in true faith. O Savior of the whole world, look upon me with the eyes of Your mercy, and enlighten my heart and my eyes, that, walking in the radiance of Your grace which has risen upon me, I may never lose You, the Light everlasting. Amen.

23. Another

O good and faithful God, heavenly Father, I praise, honor, and worship You from the bottom of my heart for causing me to rest and sleep safely this past night, and for waking me up to good health by Your fatherly love. I heartily pray that You would also mercifully keep me, along with my dear parents, brothers and sisters, and all faithful Christians, today and at all times, from evil and danger of body and soul, that I may be found daily in Your will. For into Your divine protection and keeping I commend myself, my body and soul, heart and mind, thoughts and senses, all my hopes and endeavors, my movement and rest, my sitting up and lying down, my going in and going out, my life and death, and all that I am or may be. Let Your holy angel be with me, that no misfortune may come to my soul or body. This grant me for the sake of Your dear Son, Jesus Christ. Amen.

24. Prayer from the second petition of the Lord's Prayer

Abba, almighty Father, Lord of heaven and earth, I praise You with my whole heart for delivering me and my faithful fellow Christians (while we were by nature children of sin and slaves of the devil) from the domain of darkness and transferred us to the kingdom of Your beloved Son, Jesus Christ. In Him we have redemption through His blood, the forgiveness of our trespasses, the righteousness of faith, peace of conscience, and the certain hope of eternal life. O all-powerful God, sustain and confirm with Your mighty hand and omnipotent arm this kingdom which You have among us, that the gates of hell may never prevail against it. Dwell continually in and among us until the end of the world with Your saving Word, which is the joy and comfort of our hearts, and let us never be deprived of the Holy Sacraments, the dearest treasures of our souls. Protect and defend Your Christian congregation from every false doctrine and offensive sinfulness as from the true abomination of desolation. Crush wretched Satan under our feet. Restrain the powerful enemies of our faith. Curb the raging persecutors of Your Church, and do not permit Your people, whom You have chosen for Your own possession and who are called by Your name, to be suppressed by them.

Rather, by Your superabundant grace enlarge and increase this Your kingdom of grace and bring to it the poor, blind heathens, Jews, Turks, and other sons of unbelief, who still remain under the dominion of the devil. Look, O loving Savior, with pitying heart and compassionate eyes upon their sorrow and distress, put away the veil that hangs before their blinded hearts, and turn them, if they may be turned, from those ways which they walk to destruction and damnation. They were not created for eternal death, but when they fell into it by the devil's envy, O my Jesus, You by Your bloody merit redeemed them even as You did us. Oh, then do not let Your labor and toil, Your agony and pain, Your cross and death be wasted and in vain for them, but help them, that they may be able to come to the knowledge of the truth and obtain eternal salvation.

O Lord God, Holy Spirit, direct me and other Christians, whom You have adopted in Holy Baptism as fellow citizens of Your kingdom, that we may renounce all ungodliness and worldly passions and shun all works of the flesh, such as adultery, sexual immorality, impurity, sensuality, idolatry, sorcery, enmity, strife, jealousy, fits of anger, rivalries, dissensions, divisions, envy, murder, drunkenness, orgies, and things like these, about which You warned us before by Your chosen instrument, Paul, that those who do such things will not inherit the kingdom of God. Strengthen us in the true faith and in true godliness, that in the kingdom of Christ we may lead a Christian life, and serve Him without fear, in holiness and righteousness before Him. Finally, take us to heaven, the eternal kingdom of joy and glory, and when our soul must leave the body, let it hear the gracious voice of our Jesus: "Come, you blessed of My Father; inherit the kingdom prepared for you from the beginning of the world." Amen.

25. *Evening benediction on Monday*

O mighty and living God, the Father of our Lord Jesus Christ, I thank You that You have graciously kept me this day from every harm and danger by Your divine protection, and preserved me from calamity by fire, and from drowning by flood, and from mauling by wild animals, from cutting by the edge of the sword, from murder by the enemy, from wounding by the wicked, from harm and injury by thieves and robbers; and that I did not cause my own death by lack of caution, nor injure myself in any way, and in short, experienced no danger of life or limb. For all this I have only Your mercy to thank, for You have kept me in all my ways, wherever I have gone. I further pray that You would forgive me all my sins which I have committed against You, and that You would graciously preserve me, together with all my family and those under my care, both this night and the whole time of our lives, from all anguish and difficulty, and from the devil's craft and cunning, with which he seeks day and night to ensnare us. Defend us also from the deadly pestilence that stalks in darkness; save us from the snare of the enemy; deliver us, that we may not fall into the net of the fowler who seeks after our souls. Protect us also from the grievous trials and terrors of Satan and from every evil of body and soul. For You are our mighty fortress, our shield, and weapon. All our hope and confidence rest in You. Therefore, O faithful God, let Your eyes be open upon us and preserve us during this night from all violence and assaults of the evil foe. Be our keeper and watchman. Surround us with Your protection, that the devil may have no power to hurt us; for our salvation is only in You. To You alone I lift up my eyes. From where does my help come? My help comes from the Lord, who made heaven and earth. Behold, as the eyes of servants look to the hand of their master, as the eyes of a maidservant to the hand of her mistress, so our eyes look to the Lord our God, till he has mercy upon us. Have mercy upon us, O Lord, have mercy upon us; for we are poor and miserable. Lift up the light of Your countenance upon me, and light up my eyes, lest I sleep the sleep of death; for You live and reign forever. Amen.

26. Another

Gracious God, merciful Father, I thank You with my whole heart that You have graciously kept me this day until the present hour, and I pray that for the sake of Jesus Christ, Your beloved Son, You would graciously forgive all my sins, which I have again committed against You this day in thought, word, and deed, and forget them forever. And now, as I lie down to rest, I pray that You would kindly keep me this night from every evil of body and soul, that I, being defended from the crafts and assaults of the devil and from evil, unprofitable, and harmful dreams, may rest and sleep soundly, and arise from sleep refreshed and in good health. Now therefore, I commend myself entirely into Your divine hand; You have redeemed me, O Lord, God of truth. Amen.

27. Morning benediction on Tuesday

Blessed be God, the maker of heaven and earth! Blessed be the Lord, who alone does wondrous things, and blessed be His holy name forever, who by His divine wisdom created the day and the night and separated them, so that while the earth remains they shall not cease, that at night man may find rest and in the day return to his labor! O Lord, how manifold are Your works! In wisdom You have made them all; the earth is full of Your riches. For these Your benefits, it behooves us to rise before the sun to give You thanks and to worship You at the dawning of the light. Therefore I worship You now, because You have caused me to sleep and rest safely this night, and to arise in joy and good health, and have kindly protected me from all the assaults and wickedness of the enemy. I pray that You would enclose my soul in Your hands, sustain the health of my body according to Your will, and preserve me from all evil and injury. Be my mighty shield and strong support, my shelter from the scorching heat and my shade from the noonday sun, my guard against stumbling and my help against falling, that no evil may befall me. O gracious God, the hour has come for us to wake from the sleep of sin and all unrighteousness; for our salvation is now very near. The night is far gone; the day is at hand. Help us therefore to cast off the works of darkness and to put on the armor of light, that we may walk properly as in the daytime, not in orgies and drunkenness, not in sexual immorality and sensuality, not in quarreling and jealousy, but that we may put on Jesus Christ in true faith and with a Christian way of life. Therefore awaken me each morning: awaken my ear, that I may hear Your Holy Word with a heart of faith and keep it firm in my memory; that I may incline my ears to the cries and supplications of the poor and not forsake them in their need. And when I cry to You in my anguish, hear the voice of my supplication also, and do not despise the groaning of my final distress. Early in the morning let my prayer come before You; incline Your ear to my cry! Satisfy us in the morning with Your steadfast love, that we may rejoice and be glad all our days; through the same Jesus Christ, Your beloved Son, our Lord. Amen.

28. Another

O Lord Jesus Christ, only Savior of the world, I lift up my heart and mind to You and thank You once more for keeping me safe and sound from the crafts and assaults of the evil foe by Your unfathomable mercy. O Lord Jesus Christ, my possession and my inheritance, in Your hands my salvation resides; neither do I know of any helper in heaven or earth besides You. Therefore I pray that, for the sake of Your unspeakable agony, anguish, and utterly contemptible and bitter death, which You, dear Lord Jesus Christ, in Your great love suffered for me, a poor sinner, You would be gracious and merciful to me, and bless, guard, and keep me this day and as long as I live, and preserve me from sin and every evil of this wearying and wretched age, until at last You mercifully summon me to eternal joy and blessedness, for the sake of Your most holy name. Amen.

29. Prayer from the third petition of the Lord's Prayer

Abba, dear Father! I acknowledge in childlike humility that all that I am is obliged to submit obediently to Your divine pleasure and to help to accomplish Your holy will in my station and every part of my life with a willing heart, according to the example of the elect citizens of heaven. But, alas, You know that nothing good dwells in my flesh. For I have the desire to do what is right, but not the ability to carry it out. For I do not do the good I want, and the evil I do not want to do is what I keep on doing. O Lord, Your all-seeing eyes perceive how the ancient serpent, which is known as the devil and Satan, deceives the whole world by his cunning assaults; how the world, which lies in the power of the evil one, along with the desires of the flesh and the desires of the eyes and pride of life, always incite me to live according to their wicked will and to strive against Your own will, which is ever good. Therefore, O my God, do not reckon my disobedience unto damnation, but be gracious to me according to Your great goodness, and blot out the sins of my stubbornness according to Your boundless mercy.

O Jesus, my Jesus, who were obedient to Your heavenly Father even unto death on the cross, supply what I lack from the riches of Your perfect obedience, and by virtue of Your merit mightily support me against the devil and the world, that they may no longer hinder me from carrying out the will of the Most High. O Holy Spirit, give me a new heart and a new spirit, and make me a new man from henceforth, walking in the Commandments of God, keeping His statutes, and acting according to them.

O Lord, faithful God, it is Your fatherly will that I should also prove myself to be Your servant in trials, afflictions, and needs. Jesus has said to me that if I would be His faithful follower, I must deny myself and take up my cross daily and follow Him. Behold, my spirit is willing, to Your glory, to suffer all that Your wisdom has appointed for me; but the flesh is weak. Nevertheless, I ask nothing contrary to Your will, and hereby offer myself wholly and completely up to You, and submit to You in love and loss, in honor and dishonor, in life and death. At Your feet I lay my body and soul, my heart and mind, my reason and senses, my powers and abilities, my wealth and possessions, and all that I have. You are the Lord; do to me as pleases You. You will not impose on me more than I can bear, but in the end will turn all things to my good and blessing. But according to the riches of Your glory, give me and all Your children power to grow daily stronger in the inner man, and as far as possible, to live here on earth according to Your will until You take us and transfer us to Your heavenly Jerusalem, where true righteousness dwells and Your will is perfectly observed. Amen.

30. *Evening benediction on Tuesday*

O Lord, gracious God, Holy Father, in the daytime I cry aloud to You; I call to You when my heart is faint, and in the evening I remember Your steadfast love and faithfulness which You have shown me. And now especially I praise You, because You have, out of pure grace and mercy and without any merit or worthiness in me, so tenderly protected me this past day from countless harms and dangers which could have befallen me, so that Satan could not kill me by a sudden and evil death; and I was not injured by tempest, hail, or lightning; and no severe winds caused me harm; and the evil foe did not destroy me with poison while I ate and drank, nor with his countless other devices; and my arms and legs were not broken. For all these things I give You thanks and praise now and forever. And I pray, for the sake of the bitter sufferings of Jesus Christ, that

You would pardon all my wrongdoings which I have committed against You this day and would mercifully preserve me in the coming night from my wicked adversary, the devil, from the fears and terrors of the night, that no monster or phantasm may deceive or injure me. Defend me and all that I own from calamity by fire and water, from every evil of body and soul. Let me fall to sleep peacefully, free from cares and worries, that even in the darkness the eyes of my heart may see the light of Your divine radiance shining upon me. For You are the bright and true light that lightens all the dim shadows which surround us. You, Lord God, are with me. You are my rock and my fortress and my deliverer, my rock in whom I take refuge, my shield, the horn of my salvation, and my stronghold. O Lord my God, I lift up my hands to You in the night; come to me like the evening shower that waters the earth. Stay with us, Lord, for the day is now far spent, and in this darkness there is none other who can defend us, save You only, O our God. Make haste to help me, and protect me in this night, that my spirit may not sleep in sin and my body encounter no evil. Awaken me at the proper and acceptable time, and let me hear joy and gladness; for I have a desire for Your Word and testimonies, which are the comfort of my heart. Grant that no message of sorrow may come into my ears, and turn away the anguish of my soul; for You alone can save my life and fill me with all blessings in Jesus Christ, our Lord. Amen.

31. Another

O eternal, merciful, and bountiful God of heaven, who of great grace and fatherly providence have granted me to complete another day in health and safety, for which it behooves me to thank You with my whole heart; and inasmuch as I have, alas, not passed this day to Your glory and honor and to the benefit of my neighbor, seeing my corrupt nature is always inclined more to evil than to good, therefore, O faithful God, grant that I, who was conceived of sinful seed, may acknowledge my failings and be made a partaker of Your divine grace. Teach me to consider my end often, that I may prepare for it in true repentance, and when it draws near, that I may blessedly and confidently depart this miserable estate, and with all believing Christians be transferred into the heavenly paradise. Until which time, as long as I have life in me, take me into Your almighty protection, and mercifully defend me in soul and body from every harm and danger; through Jesus Christ, Thy beloved Son. Amen.

32. *Morning benediction on Wednesday*

Almighty, merciful God, as all Your creatures endlessly praise and glorify You, among them the birds in the sky, which with their tongues and voices most sweetly extol You toward the dawning of the day, so I thank You now with my heart that You have kept me this night, and all the time of my life previous, under Your protection and shelter until the present hour, and have awakened me from the sleep and darkness of this night and caused me to rise in joy and good health. And I pray, by the salutary resurrection of Jesus Christ from the dead, that You would also keep me and all my family and other relatives safe from every calamity and evil. O Lord, save Your people and bless Your heritage! Be their shepherd and carry them forever.

May You also in this morning hour fill me with Your mercy, that I may joyfully pass the entirety of this day in Your Commandments. Show me Your grace as a mist of the morning dew; and as a fruitful dew that spreads in the early morning and waters the earth, so cause Your goodness to extend over me; refresh my weary spirit, that I may soberly and joyfully do Your will. Direct me with Your Holy Spirit, that I may serve You with a pure heart, in perfect righteousness and holiness before You. Keep me this day, that I may not sin against You, nor stain my conscience with the passions of the flesh, which wage war against my soul. Also keep my tongue from evil and my lips from speaking deceit. Far be from me all filthiness and foolish talk and crude jesting, which are out of place for Christians! Help me not to offend, speak evil, judge or condemn, slander or scorn anyone with my lips. O that I might set a guard over my mouth and a seal upon my lips so that I may not fall because of them, and my tongue may not destroy me! Grant grace that, when I fail, I may be aware of it and reproach myself, that I may not fall under Your stern judgment and decree. This grant to me, O eternal God, through Christ, Your beloved Son. Amen.

33. *Another*

O Almighty, merciful God, gracious Father in heaven, since You have again kept me this night by the protection of Your heavenly spirits, the holy angels, and granted me to rise in happiness and health, I give You praise, honor, and eternal thanks with my heart, and also ask, dear heavenly Father, that, even as I place all my action and inaction, beginning and ending in Your will, You would also continue to have mercy on me and rule all my thoughts and desires, heart, mind, reason, and senses, and all my words and works with Your Holy Spirit, that I may know what is good and evil, and that I may so walk and live in this wicked and perverse world today that I, above all being released from all my sins, may heartily desire the eternal country which Christ, my Savior has purchased and won for me, and not lose it by a wicked and sinful life. Mercifully grant this to me with Thy divine love and the power of the Holy Spirit through Jesus Christ, Thy beloved Son. Amen.

34. Prayer from the fourth petition of the Lord's Prayer

Abba, most gracious Father, You know all things, and You see that I sorely need Your fatherly goodness for my support in this temporal life each day, indeed, each hour and moment, so let it also rise upon me anew every morning with the sun. You know best how much I need in this valley of sorrow. Therefore, as the eyes of servants look to the hand of their master, as the eyes of a maidservant to the hand of her mistress, so my eyes look to You, my God, that You might shower from Your generous hands of blessing whatever pertains to the nourishment and necessity of my needy body. You said that You would not forsake or neglect those who trust in You and wait for Your goodness. You will also graciously fulfill this toward me and not let me suffer any distress or want in my service to You.

Two things I ask of You; deny them not to me before I die: give me neither poverty nor riches; feed me with the food that is needful for me, lest I be full and deny You and say, "Who is the Lord?" or lest I be poor and steal and profane the name of my God. I brought nothing into this world, and I cannot take anything out of it. Therefore help me always to be content with Your gifts and blessings and to use them for the furthering of Your honor, for my own nourishment and clothing, and for the assistance and service of my poor neighbors, that when I must give an account of this, I may stand unmoved before Your court.

O Lover of life! Grant life to me and all those dear to me in this world for as long as pleases You, and uphold us in good health, that we may be able to serve You in our station always and without hindrance, and with united heart and mouth praise and honor You at all times. O God of peace! Bestow continually the blessing of peace in our times, that every man may sit safely under his vine and under his fig tree as long as he lives. Make a wall of fire all around our land with Your holy angels, that no enemy may draw near its borders. O Lord of glory, crown our princes and all Christian rulers here and abroad with

Your blessing from on high, and bring to fulfillment all their good and pleasing endeavors. Give them long and contented life, happy government, faithful ministers and counselors, pious and obedient subjects, powerful victory against their enemies, and indeed, whatever good their heart desires, that under their protection and defense, we may lead a peaceful and quiet life, godly and dignified in every way.

O Father of all mercies, grant all fathers and mothers to prosper in earning their living. Bless the fruit of the womb, that they may see their children increase in wisdom and in stature and in favor with God and man. Bless the fruit of the field, and open the windows of heaven, that the early and the latter rain may fall in due season. Preserve for us the fullness of the yearly harvest. Bless the fruit of their cattle, and let them tend well their fields, enjoy the fruits of their difficult toil, and eat their bread with satisfaction. Bless the works of their hands, that they may not labor in vain, for they are the offspring of the blessed of the Lord. Let me and all Your Christians be blessed with all spiritual and physical blessings in earthly and heavenly riches; through Jesus Christ our Lord. Amen.

35. *Evening benediction on Wednesday*

O Holy Trinity in one divine Unity, You are my life, salvation, and eternal comfort! I thank and praise You with my heart and mouth, that You have graciously kept me this day. I pray that of Your divine goodness You would cover all my iniquities, especially the sins which I have committed this day against You and against Your holy Commandments with my tongue, with vain and careless words, with foolish talk, and otherwise. And I pray that You would also keep me this coming night from all harm and danger. For all my trust is in You alone. As Your name, O God, so Your praise reaches to the ends of the earth. Your right hand is filled with righteousness. Into Your hands I therefore commend my body and soul. The divine Majesty bless me, the Holy Trinity conceal me, and the eternal Unity uphold me. The unfathomable mercy of God protect me, the unspeakable clemency of God defend me, the infinite sweetness of God gladden me, the highest truth of God cover me, the deepest knowledge of Christ strengthen me, the boundless goodness of the Lord preserve me. The grace of the Father direct me, the wisdom of the Son refresh me, the power of the Holy Spirit enlighten me. My Maker assist me, my Redeemer save me, my Comforter be with me. The Lord bless me and keep me, the Lord make His face shine upon me, and be gracious unto me; the Lord lift up His countenance upon me and give me peace. This protection and blessing of the only Godhead be this day and ever between me and all my enemies visible and invisible, that they may not be able to touch me or do me harm. As the pillar of cloud in the wilderness came between the host of the Egyptians and the host of Israel, that one might not come near the other, lest the children of Israel suffer any hurt, so may You be a wall of fire and a division between me and all my enemies. Sustain me also in the hour of my death. When my eyes can no longer see, my ears no longer hear, my tongue no longer speak, my hands no longer hold, and my feet no longer walk, O most blessed Trinity, assist me, that the evil foe may have no power over me. Amen.

36. Another

I thank You, mighty God, most gracious Father, that You have again graciously kept my body and soul from all harm and danger this day. I pray You of Your divine goodness that You would cover all the sins which I have committed against You this day with heart and mouth and otherwise, and not forsake me, Your own creature, which You have dearly purchased with the blood of Your beloved Son, Jesus Christ; and that You would protect me this night under Your almighty wings of grace against the evil foe, who prowls around like a roaring lion, seeking to devour me. Let me rest and sleep safely under the shadow of Your goodness and mercy, that the evil foe may not have the power to come near me nor to do me any harm. Amen.

37. Morning benediction on Thursday

O Lord Jesus Christ, You are the eternal, true light which drives away the darkness of the night and shadow of death. I will bless Your name. I will sing to You and praise You, because You have mercifully kept me this night and brought me from darkness to light. You preserved me from the terror by night, from the dread of the devil and unclean spirits, from the deadly pestilence that stalks in darkness, from various illnesses and diseases which might easily have befallen me. You also surrounded and guarded my soul with Your shield, as a shepherd guards his flock. And all that I have has been kept safe by Your great mercy. To You be praise and honor for this gracious protection and for all Your benefits. I will sing of Your strength; I will sing aloud of Your steadfast love in the morning. For You have been to me a fortress and a refuge in the day of my distress.

O my Strength, I will sing praises to You, for You, O God, are my fortress, my strong deliverer, my faithful God in whom I take refuge. You make my heart rejoice and make my face glad. I beseech You by Your holy birth and incarnation that You would let Your mercy rise on me this day, and break forth like the radiant dawn, and fall on me like the early rain. Lighten my blind nature and darkened heart with Your radiance, that the morning star may arise in my heart, even the true light which lightens men to eternal life. Defend me also from every evil. O Lord, be gracious to me; I wait for You. My soul waits for You from one morning watch to the next. Be my arm every morning, my salvation in the time of trouble. Hide my body and soul, that no evil may be allowed to befall me, and no plague come near me. Drive far away from me all evil spirits. Rise up for me against the wicked; stand up for me against evildoers. Protect me, that the hand of my adversaries may not touch me. O Lord, our God, establish the work of our hands upon us; yes, establish the work of our hands, and strengthen our arms, and teach our fingers to keep Your Commandments, that we may not sin against them today. Grant us these things for the sake of Your mercy, which endures forever throughout all generations. Amen.

38. Another

O God the Father, God the Son, and God the Holy Spirit, most blessed Trinity, I commend myself to You, body and soul, from henceforth and forevermore, and give You hearty praise and thanks that You did not grant the evil foe power to hurt me this night, but by the protection of Your angels I have been kept safe and sound. What shall I render to You? How shall I praise You for this? I will in repentance and sorrow give You a broken and contrite heart, full of blood-red sins. Graciously accept it, wash it white as snow with the precious blood of Your beloved Son, my Redeemer, and conceal it in His holy, innocent wounds. In this way graciously let me find forgiveness for all my sins. And since I cannot know when You will come, help me to live in Christian readiness today and every day, so that, however and whenever You bid me leave this life, I may be blessedly conveyed to eternal joy. Grant me this, O gracious God and Father, for the sake of Your dear Son, Jesus Christ. Amen.

39. Prayer from the fifth petition of the Lord's Prayer

Abba, merciful Father, I confess with a repentant heart that I am not worthy of Your benefits. I deserve not grace but wrath and punishment, because I have, alas, done evil in Your sight, and throughout the time of my life have broken Your holy Commandments with countless, weighty sins. My iniquities, with which I have offended You, are more than the hairs on my head, more than the sand in the sea. My debts which I owe You are great, reaching up to the heavens, and will drag me down into hell like an unbearable burden. If You dealt with me according to Your strict justice, You would have to cast me away from Your face to the abominable devil to the place of eternal torment. But, O Lord, have patience with me, and temper the strictness of Your Law with grace. O God, my God, be gracious to the poor sinner who falls at Your feet and takes refuge in Your fatherly love! Remember Your solemn oath which You swore: "As surely as I live, I have no pleasure in the death of the wicked, but that he turn and live." Your dear Son's bitter Passion see, His holy wounds and agony. These, these are the redemption price that paid for all men's sin and vice. These are my comfort evermore. With hope Your mercy I implore.*

O Jesus, my Redeemer and Bridegroom! Heartily receive my poor, sinful soul to Your care, and do not let it die and perish in sin. With Your crimson blood cross out the black tally of my sins and the stern writing of the Law against me, even with the blood by which You made atonement for me, that the debt of my sins may no more be remembered in the sight of God and before His seat of judgment. For the sake of Your perfect satisfaction with which You appeased the righteous God in my place, graciously turn away from me all the temporal and eternal punishments for my transgressions, and give me Your precious, purchased righteousness and eternal salvation.

O God the Holy Spirit, renew my heart from henceforth, that I may not let the heavy debt of my sins increase anew, nor the righteous wrath of God heap upon my soul by unrepentance, but that, as long as I live, I may have the words of the Lord before my eyes, and consent to no sin against His Commandments. Yet should I sin out of human frailty by the seduction of Satan and my own flesh and blood, stir me up at once to genuine repentance, and help me with all humility both to seek the forgiveness of my transgressions and to receive it. Strip my heart of all callousness and bitter feeling, and kindle in it true and fervent love for my neighbor, that I may forgive the faults of my brothers and sisters from my heart, bless those who curse me, do good to those who hate me, pray for those who injure and persecute me, and so demonstrate that I am a true, obedient child of my Father in heaven.

* From the hymn "Nimm von uns, Herr, du treuer Gott," st. 5. Cf. *WH* 225.

Enlighten and convert all other sinful men and women, all unholy, hardened, and impenitent souls, that they may truly acknowledge their great sins, fear the fiery wrath of God, recoil from the ceaseless torments of hell, repent of their iniquities, in true faith take hold of the bloody merit of Jesus, amend their ungodly lives, and be sustained to eternal salvation; through the blood and wounds of Christ. Amen.

40. *Evening benediction on Thursday*

Blessed be God the Father through Jesus Christ in the Holy Spirit, forever one God, who by His manifold mercies this day has graciously preserved me, a poor sinner and wretched person, from all the fiery darts of Satan that fly by day and from the destruction that wastes at noonday, and has tenderly preserved me from a sudden and evil death and from every harm. Your steadfast love, O Lord, extends to the heavens, Your faithfulness to the clouds. You are gracious and merciful; full of splendor are Your works! O bountiful God, I pray that You would graciously pardon all that I have done against You this day in thought, word, and deed. Direct Your mercy also to me, and let me sleep and rest the coming night, that I may not now or ever forsake You, who are the eternal rest, but may abide in You by faith, and dwell safely under Your shelter, that the evil foe may not draw near to me or have the power to do me any harm. O Lord, You are my light and my salvation; whom shall I fear? You are the stronghold of my life; of whom shall I be afraid? In You my heart trusts, and I am saved. You are my comfort and strong shield. Your right hand supports me; Your right hand comforts me; and in the shelter of Your arms, I take refuge. O my God, I cry by day, and You answer, and by night I am not silent, and You hear me. I remember You upon my bed and meditate on You in the watches of the night. For You have been my help, and in the shadow of Your wings I will sing for joy. My soul clings to You; Your right hand upholds me. When I sit in darkness, the Lord will be my light and my salvation. O gracious God, grant me grace that, when the hour of my death draws near and I lie down on my deathbed to everlasting rest, I may by Your help fall asleep with confidence and courage in true and steadfast faith and receive the blessing of eternal life. Meanwhile keep me in Yourself, that I may always be awake, leading a sober and moderate life, and be found in Christian readiness, since I cannot know at what hour You will come, O God, and bid me leave this life, that I may be found worthy to stand before the Son of Man and not be put to shame in His judgment; for You live and reign for all eternity. Amen.

41. *Another*

Merciful, tender God, eternal Father, what sincere love and fatherly care You have for me, a poor sinner! You have graciously protected me from all the wiles of the devil and from the dangers and perils of the corrupt and wicked world every day and every hour from my childhood to the present day. I humbly pray that, according to Your fatherly love which You have for me, You would remember no more all the things which I have done against You today, but graciously grant me pardon, and be merciful to me for the sake of Your beloved Son, Jesus Christ. And I pray that You would keep me and all my family this night from a sudden and evil death, from calamity by fire and water, from pestilence and from all misfortune. To this end I commend myself, my body and soul and all that I have into Your fatherly keeping. Let Your holy angel be with me, that I may fear no evil. Amen.

42. *Morning benediction on Friday*

Blessed be God, my Maker; blessed be God my Savior; blessed be God, my highest Comfort, who gives me health, life, and blessing, who is my Rock and my Salvation. Great and greatly to be praised is His mercy, according to which He has kept me this past night in body and soul from the various devices of Satan and granted me to reach this day in good health. O heavenly Father, I pray that You would take me this day into Your divine protection. Shelter me and attend to me within and without, that no wicked thing may befall me. Today and for all time, I commend into Your hands my poor soul, my miserable body, my needy life, my senses, reason, understanding, and intentions, all my thoughts, words, and works, what I do or do not, my going out and coming in, my movement and rest, my sitting and lying, my decisions and counsels, my hopes and desires, my faith and confession, and all my inward being and ability, the end of my life, the day and the hour of my death, my dying and rising again. O Lord God, do with me as You will and as You know will best redound to Your glory and to my salvation. Uphold me in the fear and true knowledge of You. Keep me from the works of unrighteousness, and if I sin against You out of weakness, I pray that You would not remove Your mercy from me, nor turn Your grace from me, nor withdraw Your help from me. For there is no other God or helper. None like You has been before You, and none like You shall arise after You. You, even You, are the First and the Last, and beside You there is no god! Therefore I cry out to You alone. Let Your goodness abound upon me.

Let me hear Your grace early, for I hope in You. Lead my foot in the even way, that I may not walk in the counsel of the ungodly, nor stand in the path of sinners, nor sit in the seat of the scornful, but have all the desire and love of my heart in Your Word and Commandments, and train myself in them day and night; through Jesus Christ, our Lord, who lives and reigns with You and the Holy Spirit forever. Amen.

43. Another

In Your name I now arise, O crucified Lord Jesus Christ, who on the tree of the holy cross, as the true patient Lamb for the slaughter, suffered the most shameful death for me and with Your crimson blood redeemed me from all my sins! Govern my heart by Your Holy Spirit, refresh it with the heavenly dew of Your grace, preserve me this day with Your divine love, and hide me, body and soul, in Your holy wounds. Wash me thoroughly from all my iniquities, uphold me in all good works, and lead me out of this valley of tears to eternal joy and glory, O most faithful Savior, Jesus Christ, my only comfort, hope, and life. Amen.

44. Prayer from the sixth petition of the Lord's Prayer

Abba, faithful Father, behold, our adversary, the devil, as a roaring lion, walks around Your Christians in these latter days, seeking whom he may devour! Together with the wicked world he seeks only to mislead Your elect into damnable error and unbelief and horrible sins and vices, and finally to cast them down into ultimate despair and eternal perdition. Stretch forth Your mighty hand to protect the people of Your right hand, and preserve me, Your child, and all godly hearts, that we may not fall into the tribulation and temptation of the evil one of hell. But if, according to Your just judgment, You permit Satan to have any power over us, let us not be tempted above our ability, but cause the temptation to have an end, that we may be able to bear it.

O Jesus, my Jesus, You appeared in order to destroy the works of the devil, and for our sake overcame Satan and cast him down at Your feet; therefore be our helper, and shelter us in the shadow of Your wings. Pray for us above in heaven, that our faith may not fail or cease, but by Your blood obtain the victory.

O Holy Spirit, when the evil last hour comes, put on us the whole armor of God, that we may be able to stand against the schemes of the devil. Equip us with the shield of faith, that we may be able to extinguish all the flaming darts of the evil one. Teach us to wield the sword of the Spirit, which is the Word of God, that we may do well in all things and hold the field.

But until that day, O triune God, graciously attend all troubled souls who endure with anguish Satan's sieve of tribulation. Incline Your ears to their cries and supplications, and do not be silent at their fervent tears. In Your power be their strength in weakness, and let not the smoldering wick of their faith be quenched. Comfort them then at the proper time with Your gracious help, and uphold them with Your willing Spirit. Amen.

45. *Evening benediction on Friday*

Blessed be the Lord, who alone does wondrous things. Blessed be His glorious name forever! May the whole earth be filled with His glory! In God I will boast continually, and in the evening my mouth will give thanks to His name forever. For when I cry, He hears me, and when I pray, He inclines His ears to me; when I make my plea, He is attentive to my voice. The Lord is my refuge and strength, my very present help in the troubles which beset me. Therefore, O eternal God, I give You thanks and praise, that You have kindly kept me this day from all calamity and harm which might have befallen me. My heart exults and my soul magnifies You for all Your goodness and mercy. My tongue will sing of Your Word and say continually, "blessed be God above all, and blessed be His holy name." I beseech You graciously to release all the sins which I have committed against You this day and to protect me this coming night, together with all who are in my charge. Be my keeper and my shade at my right hand. Defend me, O Lord, from every evil; defend my soul. Be merciful to me, for in You alone I take refuge. I trust in the Lord, and I cry to God Most High, to God who puts an end to my calamity. Behold, He who keeps me will not slumber. Behold, He who keeps Israel will neither slumber nor sleep. He will hold my steps fast on the path of uprightness, that I may not stumble and my feet may not slip; He will not let my foot be moved, for His Word is a light to my path. Therefore when I lie down, I will not be afraid, but my sleep will be sweet. I will not be afraid of sudden terror or of the storm of the wicked when it comes. For You will keep my foot from being caught and deliver me from the snares of death. O Lord God, lift up the light of Your countenance upon me, that I may rest and sleep in perfect peace, and dwell safely in Your shelter, for You alone help me. In Your name I will lie down to my rest and give slumber to my eyelids. You, Lord God, will awaken me with joy, to the praise and honor of Your divine majesty; through Jesus Christ, Your beloved Son, our Lord, who lives and reigns with You in the unity of the Holy Spirit. Amen.

46. Another

O Lord Jesus Christ, the patient sacrificial Lamb and holy Propitiation for all my sins, and not for mine only but also for those of the whole world: I thank You once again from the depths of my heart that You have so kindly kept me this day in body and soul by Your protection. And I pray that You would graciously pardon and forgive me all my sins which I have done this day out of the weakness of my corrupt nature and by the instigation of the evil one, which weigh heavily and oppress my heart and conscience. And as I now intend to lie down to rest and sleep, spread Your wings of grace over me and help me, that with my body I may sleep in rest and peace this night, but with my soul I may always be awake to You, and await Your glorious coming for judgment, and with heartfelt groaning wait for You, until I go forth to meet You. Grant me this, O faithful God, who with Your beloved Son and the Holy Spirit are most blessed forever. Amen.

47. Morning benediction on Saturday

O true, immortal God and Father of our Lord Jesus Christ, I lift up my mind to You in due gratitude. I will not hide Your deliverance within my heart; I will speak of Your faithfulness and Your salvation. I will not conceal Your steadfast love and Your faithfulness from the great congregation, and of all the good that You have done to me I will not keep silent. For it is good to give thanks to the Lord and to sing praise to Your name, O Most High, to declare Your steadfast love in the morning and Your faithfulness by night. Therefore my soul magnifies You, for You have protected me this night by Your abundant mercy. Blessed are You, O Lord of Sabaoth, who are gracious to all who seek You, to those who love Your salvation! Blessed is Your name in all the earth, which is our protection and help. I pray that You would also keep me this day, that the evil foe may have no power to hurt me nor the hand of the wicked to touch me. O Lord God, my Savior, I rise to You early; early I call to You! Help me diligently and faithfully to accomplish the works of my vocation and the things committed to my charge, to the praise of You and the good of my neighbor, that I may not misuse them for sin or vanity, nor offend You with my actions or omissions, nor transgress the covenant of my Holy Baptism. And grant me grace to avoid the six things which You hate, and the seven which are an abomination to You: haughty eyes, a lying tongue, hands that shed innocent blood, a heart that devises wicked plans, feet that make haste to run to evil, a false witness who breathes out lies, and one who sows discord among brothers. From these things and similar vices, preserve me, O my God, that I may never fall into them or agree with them. But teach me to do Your will, for You are my God and Lord. Let Your good Spirit lead me on level ground, that I may serve You in blameless conduct and that all my deeds and life may please You; through Jesus Christ, Your beloved Son, our Lord, who lives and reigns with You in the unity of the Holy Spirit from everlasting to everlasting. Amen.

48. Another

O faithful Father in heaven, if only I might sufficiently praise and thank You for all Your benefits which You have so kindly shown me throughout my life until this hour, but it is not in my power to do so, for I am flesh and blood and can do only evil. Nevertheless, You cause great good beyond measure to befall me each day. In particular, during this night, You were my shield and stay. The devil's power could have hurt me in many ways and prevented me from rising in good health, but by Your gracious protection I have been kept unharmed. I sincerely ask that You would shower me with Your grace today, and as I am Your property purchased by the blood of Christ, mercifully keep me from now on, even to eternal life. Amen, amen. O Lord Jesus, take my soul in Your hands and look after it. Amen.

49. Prayer from the seventh petition and conclusion of the Lord's Prayer

Abba, faithful Father, You are the Redeemer and Helper of those who take refuge in You. You said, "Call on Me in the time of trouble, and I will deliver you." My heart reminds You of Your words when You gave the command, "Return to Me, for I have redeemed you." Oh, then hear the voice of my supplication, and do not despise my prayer, which I now send to You, for gracious deliverance out of all troubles. Mercifully turn away from me and my family every evil thing which is able to harm the salvation of our souls. And from all sin and unrighteousness, from the craft and power of the devil, from hardness of heart and unrepentance, from unbelief and despair, from a sudden and evil death, and the eternal fire of hell, defend us, dear Lord God! Protect our life and limb from the pestilence which stalks in darkness and other contagious diseases, from war and bloodshed, from famine and starvation, and every plague which would be a hindrance to our temporal welfare. Preserve our goods and possessions from calamity by fire and water, hail and tempest, theft and plunder, and other ruinous evils which would deprive us of them. Finally, defend our honor and reputation from lies and slander, from public shame and mockery, from defamation, and from any disgrace that would injure them.

But if it pleases You to visit cross and misery upon me and my family and to discipline us, grant that I may not murmur against Your discipline but kiss the rod of Your fatherly care with all humility, not faint under trials but bear them boldly, not lose heart when Your help is withdrawn but wait for it in quiet patience. By Your power from on high, strengthen my anxious soul; remove the appointed burden from my shoulders at the proper time, and after the gloomy storms of adversity, cause at last the sun of Your grace to shine brightly upon me.

O my God, this last day of the week reminds me that my life has an end, and I will have to leave it. Therefore, when the day and hour of my death shall come, grant that I may be done with all the sorrows of this life; fall peacefully asleep, trusting in the bloody merit of Jesus; and, leaving this valley of tears, enter into Your eternal joy and heavenly rest. O Jesus, bloody Lamb of God, in my final distress appear to me as You appeared on the cross when You generously poured out Your blood and died. Uphold me with Your willing Spirit. Heal me with Your wounds. Wash me with the sweat of Your death in my final hour, and when it pleases You, take me in true faith from this world to Your elect. O most worthy Savior, on the Last Day be my advocate in God's strict judgment, and save me in that day because of Your wounds, that I may be found written in the Book of Salvation. Neither will I doubt that You will do so, since You have already judged the enemy and made propitiation for my trespasses. O God, the Holy Spirit, do not forsake me, but abide with me constantly until the final moment of my life, and keep Your powerful comfort close at hand to oppose all the tribulations of the evil one. Be my strength in greatest weakness, that my last meal in this world may be the Holy Supper, my last thought to imagine Jesus crucified and dying, my last word may be to call out with my mouth, "Father, into Your hands I commend my spirit."

O Most High God, mighty to save, I also pray for all my brothers and sisters suffering distress, whoever and wherever they may be, and commend them to Your steadfast love and mercy. Oh, establish and confirm by Your grace all the weak in faith. Enlighten, convert, and restore all the wandering and misguided. Give joy, peace, and comfort to every afflicted heart and troubled conscience. Be the physician, attendant, and helper of the sick. Nourish, care for, and uphold the poor, the comfortless, and the forsaken. Be the Father, Judge, and Counselor of widows and orphans. Release and set free those in barbaric service or otherwise innocently imprisoned. Be the Savior, Protection, and Refuge of those afflicted and persecuted for the sake of Your doctrine and glory. Preserve and bring to safe delivery those who travail. Sustain in true repentance and faith, love and hope, those struggling in the final throes of death. Relieve their pains, and by Your angel bring their souls into the blessed bosom of Abraham for eternal quickening. O Lord, give ear and hear me and all men whenever we call to You in our troubles and afflictions, and save us how, when, and where we need and desire Your help.

Indeed You will do this, O Lord, for You are our Father, and You not only created, redeemed, and sanctified us, Your children, but also have promised to love, protect, and help us. You can do it because You can do all things in heaven and earth, and according to Your almighty power, You are able to do far more abundantly than all that we ask or think. And You will surely do it, because You are to be heartily loved and gloriously praised and honored, here in time and there in eternity. Amen. O my Lord and my God, may You also answer, amen, amen.

50. *Evening benediction on Saturday*

Praise to You, O Most High and Immortal God, praise to Your generous goodness and mercy, praise to Your eternal wisdom and truth, for You have kept me this day from all harm and evil. I pray that You would mercifully bring to completion the good work which You have begun in me, and let me dwell in Your shelter, O Most High, and cover me with Your pinions, and under Your wings let me find refuge, that I may fear no misfortune. O God, keep me as the apple of Your eye; hide me in the shadow of Your wings. O Lord, You are my portion and my inheritance; my salvation is in Your hands. Save me by Your steadfast love, that fear and trembling may not come upon me, and the terror by night may not overtake me. Be merciful to me, for in You my soul takes refuge; in the shadow of Your wings, I will take refuge. In the day of my trouble, I seek the Lord; in the night my hand is stretched out without wearying; my soul has no other comfort, nor do I know of any helper in heaven and earth but You alone. At midnight when I rise, I remember Your name, for it is pleasant, and Your steadfast love and faithfulness which You have shown me; and I give thanks to You, because of Your righteous judgments. When I am troubled, I remember God; when my heart is afflicted, I speak of my Savior. For He drew my soul up from the pit of destruction and delivered me from the bonds of death. O Lord, God of my salvation, I cry out day and night before You, that You might forgive me all my iniquities by which I have offended You this week and this day. O Lord, deliver my life for the sake of Your steadfast love. Gracious are You and righteous; our God is merciful. The Lord preserves the simple. When I am brought low, He saves me. Therefore I will rejoice and glorify You, and remember You on my bed. For my life will be like the morning, and I will feel secure, because You, O God, are my hope and rest in life and death. I shall lie down, and none shall make me afraid. Therefore into Your hands I now commend my body and soul; You have redeemed me, O faithful God; through Jesus Christ, our Lord. Amen.

51. Another

O merciful and gracious God and Father, I give You thanks and praise from my heart once more that You have so tenderly cared for me throughout my life and have graciously kept me this day, and throughout this week until the present hour, from every evil of body and soul. And I pray that, through the grace which all repentant sinners have in You, You would cover and remember no more all my sins which I have knowingly or unknowingly committed this day and throughout this week against You and against my neighbors. Graciously help me to step from the old week into a new Christian life pleasing to You and to all the elect in heaven. Keep me in Your gracious arms this coming night, that I may rest and sleep in safety and arise refreshed and in good health to the furthering of Your praise. When my last hour is at hand, O Lord Jesus Christ, take me to Yourself; for I am Yours and You are mine. How heartily I long to be with You now! Amen.

V. TIMES & OCCASIONS

A. DAILY PRAYERS

52. *General confession*

My dear Father, I always confess and You see that, for my own part, in all my comings and goings, inside and out, hide and hair, body and soul, I deserve nothing but the everlasting fire of hell. Taking it all in all, You, my Father, indeed know that there is nothing good in me, not even a hair on my head. It all deserves nothing but to go to the wretched devil in the pit of hell. Why should I use many words? Nevertheless, O my dear Father, I implore You, in spite of all that I am, not to fix Your eyes on me and behold me, or I must perish and be destroyed, even if there were a hundred thousand worlds between us. Rather, I pray that You would fix Your eyes upon and behold the face of Your dear Son, Jesus Christ, Your Anointed, and my Mediator, High Priest, Advocate, Savior, and Redeemer. For His sake, and not for my own, O my Father, I pray that You would be gracious and merciful to me. For the sake of Your dear Son, Jesus Christ, grant me a blessed end and a joyful resurrection, and help my body here and my poor soul in the world to come. By the crimson blood which Your Son, Jesus Christ, so generously shed on the cross for the forgiveness and remission of my sins, I pray now, O my Father, that in Your righteousness You would not change or alter the blood of the same Jesus Christ, Your dear Son, nor withhold it from me, a poor creature, because of my manifold sins which cannot be named. But according to Your boundless mercy, allow the benefit and fruit of that blood to avail for me, to which purpose You ordained it from eternity and Your dear Son, Jesus Christ, shed it on the cross, that You might let it suffice and avail for the pardon and forgiveness of my sins. Thus I pray continually, O my Father, that at whatever hour or moment, by day or night, You will come and knock and summon my spirit which You first breathed into me, and that You would let my spirit, which is my soul, be commended into Your hands; through the blood, Passion, and death of Your beloved Son, Jesus Christ. Amen.

53. *Prayer for a blessed death*

Dear God and Lord, I live, yet know not how long. I die, yet know not when. Only You, my heavenly Father, know. Very well! If this day (night) shall be the last day (night) of my life, O Lord, Your will be done! Your will is best, and by it I am ready to live or die, truly believing in Christ, my Redeemer. Only vouchsafe to me this petition, O God, that I may not die suddenly in my sins and so perish. Give me true knowledge, remorse, and sorrow over the sins which I have committed, and set them before my sight in this life, that they may not at the Last Day be set before me and I be put to shame before angels and men. Grant me sufficient time and opportunity for repentance, that I may heartily acknowledge and confess my transgressions and from Your saving Word obtain forgiveness and comfort. O merciful Father, do not forsake me, and do not take Your Holy Spirit from me. O Searcher of hearts, my heart and its confidence, founded on Jesus, are well known to You. Sustain me in that confidence to life eternal. Let me die whenever You will; only, if it is possible, grant me a lucid, peaceful, and blessed death. Amen.

Lord Jesus Christ, of all things Best,
I pray Thee, through Thy blood out-pressed,
To let my final end be blest.

O God, be gracious and merciful to me, a poor sinner! Amen.

B. GENERAL SUNDAY PRAYERS

54. *Before the sermon*

Dear God, through Your beloved Son You call those blessed who hear Your Word. How much more fitting it would be, O eternal, merciful Father, for us unceasingly, with joyful hearts, blessedly to honor You, give thanks to You and praise You, that You have treated us poor worms with such kindness, indeed, with such fatherly care, and that You speak with us concerning the greatest and highest matters: eternal life and salvation. Nevertheless You do not forget, by Your Son, to draw us tenderly to hear Your Word when He says, "Blessed are those who hear the Word of God and keep it." It is as if You could not do without our hearing, as if we, who are dust and ashes, are not many thousand times more in need of Your blessed Word. O how unspeakably gracious and wonderful Your steadfast love and patience are! Yet alas and woe to the ingratitude and blindness of those who are not only unwilling to hear Your Word, but even maliciously despise, persecute, and slander it.

55. Thanks upon hearing the Word of God

O God, the Father of all mercy, we thank You exceedingly and continually that, according to the abundant riches of Your grace, You have led us to the treasury of Your Word, in which we have knowledge of Your beloved Son, that is, a certain pledge of our life and salvation to come in heaven, prepared for all who in pure faith and fervent love remain steadfast to the end, to which we hope and pray You will sustain us, and make us perfect with all the elect, in the same mind, conformed to the image of Your beloved Son, Jesus Christ, our Lord. Amen.

C. PRAYERS FOR THE SUNDAYS AND FEASTS OF THE CHURCH YEAR

56. Prayer for a fruitful hearing of the sermon

Gracious God, since it pleased You by the preaching of the Holy Gospel to save those who believe therein, I pray that You would enlighten my mind and open my heart that I may not only understand Your Word with the ears of my body, but also take hold of it, keep it with my heart, and act according to it. Let me not be a forgetful hearer, but a doer of the Word. O Lord, I love the habitation of Your house and the place where Your glory dwells. Let Your teaching drop from the preacher's mouth as the rain and Your speech distill as the dew, that I may meekly receive it, preserve it in my heart, and bring forth the good fruit of faith. Curb the evil one, that he may not pluck the precious seed from my heart, nor make me fall away in cross and persecution, nor mortally wound my heart by the thorns of the cares, riches, and pleasures of this world. Grant that I may be born again through Your living Word, the imperishable seed, and sustained unto eternal life. Amen.

57. Another

O merciful God and Father, You see how because of my corrupt nature, I have no desire for Your Word and how the devil, my own flesh and blood, the children of the world, and false teachers and preachers, indeed, other paltry causes, so easily hold me back and make me lazy, slow, and reluctant to hear and keep

Your Word. Therefore I pray, O eternal God, that You would pardon me for this laziness and sloth within me and give me a heart willing and eager to hear and listen to Your Word. Awaken in me such hearty desire that, like a newborn infant, I may long for the pure, spiritual milk of God's Word. Help me to find my greatest delight and happiness in Your Word. Let nothing in this world be dearer to me than Your Word, that I may love Your Word above gold, above fine gold, and always regard it as my greatest treasure. And since, alas, I have lived to see the day about which Your beloved Son prophesies, that false christs will arise and perform great wonders so as to lead astray, if possible, even the elect, therefore I pray that You would graciously keep and preserve me from error and false doctrine. Uphold me in Your truth, for Your Word is truth, that I may cling to it as to heavenly truth and remain steadfast in it until my end. All these things grant for the glory of Your most holy and worthy name. Amen.

58. *Prayer after the sermon*

We praise and worship You, Lord God, Father of heaven and earth, that in Your steadfast love and mercy, You have richly provided for our bodies with daily bread and our souls with the heavenly food of Your Holy Word. Grant, O faithful God, that it may remain in our hearts and profit much to Your glory and to our salvation. We also beseech You of Your fatherly grace not to remove Your pure Word and ministry from us, nor to reward us for any trespasses and sins which we may have profaned this day, but to pardon us according to Your abundant goodness and by the bitter sufferings and death of Your beloved Son, Jesus Christ. Finally, receive us into Your divine protection and fatherly blessing this day and throughout our poor life in this valley of tears, and let Your holy angels encamp around us, that the evil foe may have no power over us.

But now that it is toward evening in this world, and the day is far spent, grant to us the grace of Your Spirit, that we may keep constant vigil and in living faith, fervent love, firm hope, and holy conduct, wait for the blessed appearing of the glory of our great God and Savior, Jesus Christ, when He shall come to judge the living and the dead, that we may then worthily receive Him with joy, enter with Him into eternal life, and with all the elect attain to and keep the eternal day of rest and gladness. Have mercy, O Lord, on all Christendom, and unburden Your poor, persecuted Church of all oppression, mockery, and tyranny; comfort all afflicted, troubled consciences by the true Counselor, the Holy Spirit, and send us all Your peace; through Jesus Christ, our advocate and only mediator. Amen.

59. Another

I thank You, my heavenly Father, that in Your great mercy You have caused Your Holy Word to be so freely proclaimed and presented to us for our comfort, poor sinners though we be. O God, press and seal it upon our hearts, that we may follow it in living and dying. Grant that we may always grow and increase in the knowledge of You. Let it be known and published not only to ourselves but also to all nations, that it may stir and water the hearts of all men, as the rain and the snow water the earth and make it fruitful. Let us so know, call upon, honor, and thank You, eternal God, that, ruling all our deeds according to Your Holy Commandments, we may ever be found obedient children, and finally be made partakers of eternal life and the inheritance purchased for us by Jesus Christ. Amen.

60. Prayer on the First Sunday in Advent

Lord God, heavenly Father, it behooves us ever to thank, praise, and glorify You that for us poor men, who for our sins had else remained under the tyranny of death and Satan, You appointed Your Son as King, that He might be a just King and Savior, that is, that by His death He might deliver and save us from our sins. And we pray that You would enlighten, direct, and lead us by Your Holy Spirit, that we may cling only to that true King and Savior, and not, like the world, be offended at His lowly form and despised Word, but by firm trust in Him receive eternal salvation. Amen.

61. Prayer on the Second Sunday in Advent

Lord God, heavenly Father, who by Your Son have revealed to us that heaven and earth shall pass away, our bodies shall rise again, and we all shall be brought before the judgment seat: we beseech You that by Your Holy Spirit, You would keep us in Your Word and the true faith, graciously defend us from sin, and preserve us in all temptations, that we may not burden our hearts with gluttony and drunkenness and cares of this life, but watch and pray continually, and in the certain confidence of Your grace, await with joy the coming of Your Son and through Him receive eternal salvation. Amen.

62. Prayer on the Third Sunday in Advent

O Lord God, heavenly Father, who caused Your Son, our Lord Jesus Christ, to become man and to come into this world to break Satan's tyranny; to deliver us poor men from sin and death; and to give us eternal salvation: we beseech You that You would so lead and rule our hearts with Your Holy Spirit that we may look only to Your Word and so, avoiding every offense to which our reason inclines us, be found in Your flock, even the flock which is not offended at Your Son, Jesus Christ, but by Him has eternal salvation. Amen.

63. *Prayer on the Fourth Sunday in Advent*

O Lord God, heavenly Father, it behooves us to thank You that You first instituted by St. John the Baptist the blessed and grace-giving Sacrament of Baptism and have caused us also to receive that Sacrament, in which You have promised us forgiveness of sins, the Holy Spirit, and eternal life for the sake of Your beloved Son, Christ Jesus. We beseech You to sustain us in such confidence in Your grace and mercy, that we may never doubt, but in various tribulations take comfort in it. Grant us also by Your Holy Spirit that we may avoid sin and remain in the innocence which we receive by Baptism, and whenever we may fall and in our human weakness cannot rise again, that we may not remain lying in sin, but may by true repentance turn away from it and take comfort again in Your promise, and so by Your grace obtain eternal salvation.

64. *Prayer of preparation on Christmas Day*

O Lord of Sabaoth, Holy God, how heartily we rejoice at the return of this sacred time, that we may go into Your house to gaze upon the beauty of Your worship and to inquire in Your temple, that in the assembly we may hear of the mystery which is great indeed: that God, Your Son, was manifested in the flesh and, according to the flesh, born of the seed of David! Grant us, we beseech You, life and blessing, that throughout this day and at all times we may go around Your altar, where thanksgiving is proclaimed aloud and all Your wondrous deeds are told, and that we may go with the throng and lead them in the procession to the house of God with glad shouts and songs of praise, a multitude keeping festival. Give our preachers and ministers a mouth and wisdom, that they may preach to us what You command them, and that, in opening their mouth boldly, they may so instruct us that their doctrine may flow like a life-giving spring. In so doing, may they save both themselves and us. O Lord, open our hearts, that we may with joy and heartfelt devotion hear and hold fast the comforting and graceful sermons on the saving birth and incarnation of Your beloved Son, our Savior, Jesus Christ. Grant, O faithful Father, that we may greatly rejoice in the Lord, and our soul may exult in our God and Savior and sing glad songs of salvation in the tents of the righteous. Create in us clean hearts, O God, that by true repentance we may duly and worthily prepare and ready ourselves for the sacred occasion now approaching. Preserve us in these solemn days and at all times from fire, sedition, murder, and manslaughter. Curb all the works of the flesh, as adultery, sexual immorality, impurity, sensuality, idolatry, sorcery, enmity, strife, murder, drunkenness, and gluttony. Restrain the devil, who, being a liar and murderer, eagerly seeks to hinder our good devotion and drive us to such sins. And help us to conclude these solemn days with good health, rest, and peace, for our own comfort and blessed edification, that we may partake of all the benefits of our dear newborn Christ unto our eternal salvation. Amen.

65. Prayer on Christmas Day
Lord God, heavenly Father, we thank You that of Your abundant mercy You sent Your only-begotten Son to be made man, thereby graciously causing us to be saved from sin and eternal death. And we pray that You would enlighten our hearts by Your Holy Spirit, that we may give thanks to You for this Your grace and take comfort in it in every distress and tribulation, and so by Your Son, our Lord Christ, obtain eternal salvation. Amen.

66. Prayer on the Sunday after Christmas
Lord God, heavenly Father, who by St. Simeon prophesied that Christ, Your Son, was appointed for the fall and rising of many in Israel: enlighten our hearts, we beseech You, by Your Holy Spirit, that rightly knowing Your Son, Christ Jesus, we may cling to Him in every distress and danger, rise in Him, and not be offended at Him with the blind and complacent world, but be bold and confident in whatever suffering and tribulation we meet for the sake of Your Word and confession. For it is certain that those who persecute Your Word have no part in Your kingdom, but those who believe and abide in it have eternal salvation. Amen.

67. Prayer on New Year's Eve
O Lord God, You have been our dwelling place in all generations. Before the mountains were brought forth, or ever You had formed the earth and the world, from everlasting to everlasting You are God. When You created all things, You made the lights in the expanse of the heavens to separate the day from the

night and let them be for signs and for seasons and for days and years. We acknowledge Your steadfast love especially at this time when the old year departs and the new year enters in. We must not only extol Your wisdom, which by these lights gave us this year with its signs and seasons, days and nights, but also honor Your great attention in so wonderfully providing food and drink, clothing and nourishment, care and protection, and Your grace and blessing on all our good endeavors. We humbly beseech You to let all Your grace and truth abound to us, that with the old year our sins may be sealed shut, and with the new year the door of grace may be open to us anew; that with it we may also find new power of body and soul, and so be enabled to walk in newness of life; that it may be well with us and our children forever. O trustworthy God, as You once brought faithful Noah out of the ark and set a limit to his sadness with the old year, so lead us out of the ark of sadness and grant grace, that with the old year the old tempest may pass over us, and with the new year a new and joyful sunshine may arise. And as of old You gave Your plentiful blessings in Egypt not one year only, but seven, year after year, so let Your blessing always be upon us, so that we are obliged to extol and magnify it every year, both in the old and in the new. May we not only remember this as befits a Christian people, but also give You thanks for it at all times; through Jesus Christ, the Alpha and the Omega, the beginning and the end. Amen.

68. Prayer on New Year's Day

Lord God, heavenly Father, we thank You for Your great, unspeakable grace in receiving the needy into Your care and subjecting Your Son to the Law for our sake, that He, by His perfect obedience, might satisfy Your wrath and repair our disobedience. We beseech You so to enlighten our hearts by Your Holy Spirit that we may take comfort in this obedience over against our sins and wicked conscience, and by the help of Your Holy Spirit begin our life as obedient children and finally obtain eternal salvation; through Jesus Christ. Amen.

69. Prayer on Sunday after New Year

Lord God, heavenly Father, who together with Your Holy Spirit revealed Yourself in a most gracious manner at the Baptism of Your beloved Son, who bore all our sins, and by Your voice directed us to Him, that through Him we might have forgiveness of sins and all grace: we beseech You, sustain us in such confidence, and inasmuch as, in accordance with the command and example of

Your Son, we also are baptized, strengthen our faith by Your Holy Spirit, and bring us to eternal life. Amen.

70. Prayer on the Feast of the Epiphany

Lord God, heavenly Father, who have caused Your dear Word, the true star that shows us the infant Jesus, to shine on us: we beseech You to put Your Holy Spirit into our hearts, that we may receive that light and make salutary use of it, so that like the Wise Men we may follow that star and let no toil or danger frighten us, but with our whole heart cling to Your Son, Christ Jesus, the only Savior, and dispose of all our temporal possessions for the building up of Your poor Church and for the glory of Jesus Christ, Your Son. Amen.

71. Prayer on the First Sunday after the Epiphany

Lord God, heavenly Father, I thank You for Your grace in causing me to come to Holy Baptism and to the knowledge of Your divine Word and will. I beseech You to put Your Holy Spirit into my heart, that I may study Your Word and not neglect or despise it, but mark it well, that true godly fear would grow and increase in me, and that in Your Word I may finally die a blessed death and obtain eternal salvation. Amen.

72. Prayer on the Second Sunday after the Epiphany

Lord God, heavenly Father, I thank You that You have given me Your grace and brought me to the holy estate of marriage and thereby kept me from sin. And I beseech You to give me Your Holy Spirit, that He may so lead and guide me in that estate that I may be one with my spouse, give no cause for anger or strife, but lead a loving and godly life, that although tribulation may not be avoided, we may nevertheless always be sensible of Your gracious help and blessing, raise our children according to Your will, live with one another in all godliness, and finally obtain eternal salvation through Your Son, Jesus Christ. Amen.

73. Prayer on the Third Sunday after the Epiphany

Lord God, heavenly Father, who of great love and mercy gave us Your Son to be made man and die on the cross for us: put Your Holy Spirit into our hearts, that we may confide wholly in Your Son alone, and by Him believe as firmly in the forgiveness of our sins and eternal life as the centurion believed that He would save his sick servant with a word. We have His word that whoever believes in Him will never perish. Grant therefore, dear Father in heaven, that we may believe it with a resolute heart and remain steadfast in it until our final end. Amen.

74. Prayer on the Fourth Sunday after the Epiphany

Lord God, heavenly Father, who in Your good and fatherly wisdom subject Your children here on earth to the cross, sending various tempests upon us to curb our sin and train us in faith, hope, and prayer: we beseech You to have mercy on us, hear our prayer in every trial and need, and provide Your gracious help, that we may acknowledge Your grace and fatherly assistance, and with all the saints forever praise and bless You, who with the Son and the Holy Spirit are the only everlasting and almighty God. Amen.

75. Prayer on the Fifth Sunday after the Epiphany

O Lord God, heavenly Father, we thank You that You have sown the good seed of Your Holy Word in our hearts, and we beseech You by Your Holy Spirit to quicken that seed in us, bring forth fruit, defend us from the evil foe that he may sow no tares in us, keep us from complacency, uphold us in Your fear, and help us in every tribulation, until at last we obtain salvation. Amen.

76. Prayer on Septuagesima *[Latin: 70 days before Easter]* **Sunday**

Lord God, heavenly Father, who by Your precious Word have called us into Your vineyard: we beseech You to send Your Holy Spirit into our hearts, that we may labor faithfully in that vineyard, keep ourselves from sin and every offense, study Your Word and will, and put all our hope only in Your grace, which You have plentifully demonstrated to us through Your Son, Jesus Christ, and so obtain eternal salvation. Amen.

77. Prayer on Sexagesima *[Latin: 60 days before Easter]* **Sunday**

Lord God, heavenly Father, we thank You that You have sown Your precious Word among us by Your Son, Jesus Christ, and we beseech You by Your Holy Spirit to prepare our hearts so that we may hear that Word diligently, keep it in a good heart, and in patience bring forth fruit, that we may not pursue sin but subdue it by Your help, and in every persecution find certain comfort in Your grace and perpetual help. Amen.

78. *Prayer on Quinquagesima [Latin: 50 days before Easter]* **Sunday**

Lord God, heavenly Father, who by Your Son, Jesus Christ, mercifully opened the eyes of the blind man and granted Him to see the light: we poor sinners beseech You to enlighten our hearts by Your Holy Word, that through Christ, Your Son, who died on the cross for us and made atonement for our sins, we may rightly learn to know Your gracious help and mercy and in all troubles and trials look only to that, seeking it by faithful prayer, and so find comfort and deliverance from the devil, sin, and death, and obtain salvation. Amen.

79. *Prayer on the First Sunday in Lent*

Lord God, heavenly Father, we beseech You that, whereas the wicked enemy constantly stalks us, and as a roaring lion walks around, seeking whom he may devour, You would for the sake of Christ, Your Son, come to our aid and by Your Word strengthen our hearts, that the foe may not overpower us, but that we may abide in Your grace eternally and at last obtain salvation. Amen.

80. *Prayer on the Second Sunday in Lent*

Lord God, heavenly Father, we beseech You by Your Holy Spirit to fix and confirm in our hearts true faith and hope in Your grace and mercy, that although, because of our conscience, sin, and unworthiness, we have cause to fear, yet in Your grace we may, like the Canaanite woman, persevere steadfastly and through Christ find in You help and deliverance in every trial and need. Amen.

81. *Prayer on the Third Sunday in Lent*

Lord God, heavenly Father, who sent Your Son, our Lord Jesus Christ, to be made man, that He might crush the devil's tyranny and protect us men from our wicked adversary: we thank You for this gracious help, and we beseech You in all tribulations graciously to come to our aid, to keep us from complacency, and by Your Holy Spirit mercifully to sustain us in Your Word and holy fear, that we may abide in peace from the evil foe until our end, and through Your Son obtain eternal salvation. Amen.

82. *Prayer on the Fourth Sunday in Lent*

Lord God, heavenly Father, who by Your Son in the wilderness bountifully fed five thousand men, besides women and children, with only five loaves and two fish: we beseech You graciously to visit us also with Your blessing and to protect us from covetousness and cares for this life, that we may seek first Your kingdom and righteousness, and mercifully be made to know Your generous, fatherly goodness in all our needs of body and soul; through Jesus Christ, our Lord. Amen.

83. Prayer on the Fifth Sunday in Lent

O Lord God, heavenly Father, Your beloved Son, our Savior, Jesus Christ, says, "Whoever keeps My Word will never see death." We beseech You to send Your Holy Spirit into our hearts, inasmuch as You came to us for Your Son's Word and caused us to hear the same, that we might also keep it, depend on it with our whole heart, and in the midst of death take comfort in it and never see eternal death; for the sake of Your dear Son, our Savior. Amen.

84. Prayer on Palmarum [Latin: Palm Sunday]

O Lord God, heavenly Father, who in Your fatherly grace did not spare Your only Son, but gave Him into death, even to the death of the cross: we beseech You to send Your Holy Spirit into our hearts, that we may take heartfelt comfort in this grace, continue to avoid sin, and patiently bear whatever You appoint for our suffering, that through Him we may have eternal salvation. Amen.

85. Prayer of preparation for Easter

Lord God, we praise You; Lord God, we thank You that You have granted us this year to see the holy day of Easter in peace and good health. Most especially we glorify You for giving us the victory against all our enemies by the resurrection of Jesus Christ, Your beloved Son. O Lord Jesus, we thank You for Your triumphant resurrection from death by which You have opened heaven to us, destroyed death, and obtained for us the comfort that You are the resurrection and the life. O God the Holy Spirit, we thank You for Your paschal message, and we pray that You would plant the paschal joy in our hearts and increase and sustain it in us. And as by Your power the troubled hearts of the disciples were made glad on Easter, so comfort us with Christ's resurrection and that we have a gracious God, we shall live forever, hell and Satan have no power over us, and the world cannot hurt us. O Holy Trinity, God the Father, Son, and Holy Spirit, sustain Your Church against all her enemies, spiritual and physical. Grant that after this life we may all keep the joyful feast of Easter in Your life of gladness, and with all the angels praise, extol, and glorify You, most blessed forever. Amen.

86. Prayer on Easter

Lord God, heavenly Father, who delivered up Your Son for our trespasses and raised Him for our justification: we beseech You to give us Your Holy Spirit, and by Him to rule and guide us, sustain us in the true faith, and keep us from all sins in newness and purity of life; and through Your Son, Jesus Christ, awaken us after this life to life everlasting. Amen.

87. Prayer on Easter Monday

Lord God, heavenly Father, who revealed Your Son, Jesus Christ, to the two disciples in Emmaus: we beseech You that You would enlighten our hearts by Your Word and Holy Spirit, that we may be strengthened and confirmed in the faith, cling steadfastly to Your Word, proclaim it eagerly, and use it diligently, so that even though we must suffer here on earth after the example of Christ, yet by Your Word we may have and retain the true consolation that after this life we shall be awakened to eternal life by Your beloved Son. Amen.

88. Prayer on Quasimodogeniti *[Latin: as newborn babes]* Sunday

Lord God, heavenly Father, we thank You for Your great, unspeakable grace in appointing through Your Son, our Lord Christ, the Holy Gospel and Holy Sacraments for our comfort, that in them we might find forgiveness of sins. And we beseech You to put Your Holy Spirit into our hearts, that we may heartily believe Your Word, and that by the Holy Sacraments our faith may be daily strengthened until at last we obtain salvation; through Jesus Christ, Your Son, our Lord. Amen.

89. Prayer on Misericordias Domini *[Latin: mercy of the Lord]* Sunday

Lord God, heavenly Father, who have tenderly remembered us miserable men and have set Your Son over us as our keeper, not only to feed us with Your Word but also by His protection to deliver and preserve us from sin, death, and the devil: we beseech You to grant by Your Holy Spirit that, just as this Shepherd knows us and has assumed our troubles as His own, so in all our pressing concerns, we may also cling to Him, seek and expect help and comfort from Him, heartily follow His voice, and so through Him obtain eternal salvation. Amen.

90. *Prayer on Jubilate* [Latin: shout for joy] **Sunday**

Lord God, heavenly Father, who in Your fatherly goodness are pleased to chasten Your children on earth with the rod of discipline, that we may be conformed to the likeness of Your only-begotten Son in both present suffering and future glory: we beseech You to comfort us with Your Holy Spirit in tribulation and cross, that we may not despair but cling firmly to this comfort, according to the promise of Your Son that our suffering will be but little, and then shall follow eternal joy, that by such hope we may patiently overcome all misfortune and through Jesus Christ obtain salvation. Amen.

91. *Prayer on Cantate* [Latin: sing (to the Lord)]**Sunday**

O Lord God, heavenly Father, who by Your Son promised to us the Holy Spirit, to convict the world concerning sin and righteousness and judgment: we beseech You to enlighten our hearts, that we may acknowledge our sin, and by faith in Christ attain eternal righteousness, and in every trial and need hold fast the certain comfort that Christ is the Lord over the devil, death, and all things and will graciously save us from all evil and give us eternal salvation. Amen.

92. *Prayer on Rogate* [Latin: to ask] **Sunday**

O Lord God, heavenly Father, who by Your Son promised to us that whatever we ask in His name You will give to us: preserve us, we beseech You, in Your Word, and grant Your Holy Spirit to rule and guide us according to Your will. Keep us from the tyranny of the devil, from false teaching, and from improper worship, and preserve our body and being from every evil. Grant Your blessing and peace, that we may always know Your gracious help, and through Christ honor and praise You as our gracious Father both now and forever. Amen.

93. *Prayer on Ascension Day*

O Jesus Christ, Son of the Most High God, who having left Your earthly humility, are seated at the right hand of Your Father as Lord over all things: we beseech You to send us Your Holy Spirit, give us faithful ministers, preserve Your Word, curb Satan and every tyrant, and mightily uphold Your kingdom on earth until Your enemies are all laid at Your feet and we through You are victorious over sin, death, and all things. Amen.

94. *Prayer of preparation for Whitsunday*

Lord God, Holy Spirit, who on the sacred day of Pentecost filled the hearts of the apostles with new gifts: enlighten our hearts also and grant that we may keep the feast devoutly. Come, precious Guest of our hearts; come, only Treasure of our souls. Dwell in us as in Your temple; purify our hearts from sin. Make us all the anointed of the Lord, and help us by Your power to resist all our spiritual enemies and to obtain the victory. In our prayers and thanksgivings, intercede for us with groanings too deep for words. Comfort all troubled hearts, that the bones that You have broken may rejoice. Support us by Your power against the accusations of our heart and conscience, that there may be no condemnation for us. May Your peace, which surpasses all human understanding, guard our hearts and our minds unto joy everlasting. Give and grant us, O God, Holy Spirit, sincere joy in this holy feast, and when this life is done, let us ever proclaim Your wondrous works; who with the Father and Son are most blessed forever. Amen.

95. *Prayer on Whitsunday* [Old English title for Pentecost Sunday

Lord Jesus Christ, Son of the Most High God, we beseech You to put Your Holy Spirit into our hearts by Your precious Word, that He may rule and guide us according to Your will, comfort us in all trials and misfortunes, and, refuting all error, lead us into Your truth, that we may continue steadfast in the faith, increase in charity and all good works, and by the certain hope of Your grace, which You have purchased with Your death, obtain eternal salvation; for You reign with the Father and the Holy Spirit. Amen.

96. *Prayer on Whit Monday* [Monday after Pentecost Sunday]

Lord God, heavenly Father, who of Your fatherly love for us poor sinners have given us Your Son, that we should believe in Him and by faith obtain salvation: we beseech You to put Your Holy Spirit into our hearts, that we may persevere in such faith unto the end and obtain salvation; through Christ, our Lord. Amen.

97. *Prayer on Trinity Sunday, or the Feast of the Holy Trinity*

O almighty, everlasting God, Father, Son, and Holy Spirit, who showed Your grace to us men and made Your mercy bountifully evident, first, O eternal Father, in making us as men; and eternal Son of God, in being made man for us and making atonement for our sins on the cross; and eternal Spirit, who proceed eternally from the Father and the Son, in giving us faith and sanctifying us by the Holy Gospel: we beseech You, the only, eternal, and almighty God, Father, Son, and Holy Spirit, to sustain us in Your grace until the end and to give us eternal salvation. Amen.

98. Another

Lord God, heavenly Father, we poor sinners confess that nothing good dwells in us, and if left to ourselves, we must perish in sin and eternal death, since that which is born of the flesh is flesh and cannot see Your kingdom. But we beseech You to be gracious and merciful, and send Your Holy Spirit into our hearts for the sake of Your Son, Jesus Christ, and make of us new men, that we may confidently believe in the forgiveness of sins through Christ, as promised to us at our Baptism, and daily increase in charity toward our neighbor and all other Christian virtues, until we at last obtain salvation. Amen.

99. Prayer on the First Sunday after Trinity

Lord God, heavenly Father, we beseech You so to rule and govern our hearts by Your Holy Spirit that we may not, like the rich man, hear Your precious Word unfruitfully, nor so handle things temporal that we thereby forget the eternal, but readily and freely assist the poor according to our means and not sin with arrogance and excess. When we are oppressed with cross and calamity, let us not despair, but place our hope wholly in Your eternal help and grace, and in patience overcome all things. Amen.

100. Prayer on the Second Sunday after Trinity

Lord God, heavenly Father, we thank You that You have by Your precious Word invited us to Your banquet of eternal life, and we beseech You to awaken our hearts by Your Holy Spirit, that we may not hear Your Word in vain nor permit this temporal life to keep us from it. Amen.

101. Prayer on the Third Sunday after Trinity

Lord God, heavenly Father, we all, alas, like sheep have gone astray, having allowed Satan and our sinful flesh to lead us away from the right path. But we beseech You to be gracious and to forgive us all our sins for the sake of Your Son, Jesus Christ. Awaken our hearts by Your Holy Spirit, that we may hold fast

Your Word, and in true repentance and genuine faith continue in the fold of Your Christian Church till our end, and obtain eternal salvation. Amen.

102. Prayer on the Fourth Sunday after Trinity

Lord God, heavenly Father, who are merciful, and by Your Son, Jesus Christ, promised to forgive all our sins: we heartily beseech You not to judge us according to our wicked life, unrighteous conduct, and many sins committed out of human weakness, but as our heavenly Father, to whom our weakness is well known, to pardon and forgive these all according to Your divine, fatherly heart and to bestow on us the crown of eternal salvation; and further, to soften our hearts of stone, that we may gladly forgive our neighbors, show them mercy, judge and condemn no one falsely with a premature, unreasonable, and precipitous judgment, as often happens, but with all our hearts gladly pardon and forgive all men, and first being true, honest, and good judges only of our own selves, consciences, hearts, and souls, lead a Christian life in Your fear and die a blessed death. Amen.

103. Prayer on the Fifth Sunday after Trinity

O Jesus Christ, Son of the living God, who have given us Your precious Word and blessed us with every physical blessing: we acknowledge that we are unworthy of all these things and have certainly deserved much worse, and we beseech You to forgive us our sins, as You did Peter's, and bestow success and health to our calling, that we, being supported and defended by You both now and forever, may praise and glorify You for eternity. Amen.

104. Prayer on the Sixth Sunday after Trinity

O Lord God, heavenly Father, we confess that we are, alas, miserable sinners, in whom there is nothing good at all! Our heart, flesh, and blood are so poisoned that we can never be without wicked desires. Therefore, dear Father, forgive us those sins, and purify our hearts by Your Holy Spirit, that we may have a desire and love for Your Word and follow it, and through Christ abide in Your grace eternally. Amen.

105. Prayer on the Seventh Sunday after Trinity

Lord God, heavenly Father, who by Your Son in the wilderness bountifully fed four thousand men, besides women and children, with only seven loaves and a few fish: we beseech You graciously to visit us also with Your blessing and to protect us from covetousness and cares for this life, that we may seek first Your kingdom and righteousness and mercifully be made to know Your generous, fatherly goodness in all our needs of body and soul; through Jesus Christ our Lord. Amen.

106. Prayer on the Eighth Sunday after Trinity

Lord God, heavenly Father, we thank You with our whole heart that You have caused us to come to the knowledge of Your precious Word, and we beseech You graciously to preserve us in that Word and to grant us a blessed death in the same. Mercifully defend from every evil all godly preachers who faithfully proclaim Your Word, and sustain their life. But if any handle Your Word unfaithfully and, having the appearance of godly sheep, are ravenous wolves, punish them according as they deserve, and graciously restrain them and keep Your poor Christendom from them; through Jesus Christ, Your Son, our Lord. Amen.

107. Prayer on the Ninth Sunday after Trinity

O Lord God, heavenly Father, who have abundantly given to us rich blessings and daily bread: we beseech You to keep us from coveting and to awaken our hearts, that we may gladly give to the poor and share with them, that we may be found as faithful stewards over Your goods and not be left to starve for eternity when we are summoned from the stewardship and come before Your judgment seat. Amen.

108. Prayer on the Tenth Sunday after Trinity

Almighty, everlasting God, who by Your Holy Spirit have revealed and made known to us Your Word concerning Your Son, Jesus Christ: we beseech You to awaken our hearts, that we may receive it earnestly and not cast it to the wind nor listen carelessly, as did Your people, the unbelieving Jews, that we may daily live and increase in Your fear and in true confidence in Your mercy, and at last obtain salvation; through Your Son, Jesus Christ. Amen.

109. Prayer on the Eleventh Sunday after Trinity

O Lord God, heavenly Father, I beseech You so to rule and govern me by Your Holy Spirit that I may not forget my sins nor grow complacent, but live in continual repentance and take comfort only in this, that for the sake of Your

Son, Jesus Christ, You will be gracious to me, forgive all sins, and give me salvation. Amen.

110. Prayer on the Twelfth Sunday after Trinity

Almighty, everlasting God, gracious maker of all things, I thank You that You have given me a sound body and graciously protected my tongue, ears, and other members from the evil foe; and I beseech You to grant me Your grace, that I may use my ears and tongue rightly, with my ears diligently hearing and marking Your Word, with my tongue praising and extolling Your grace, that no one may be caused to stumble by my tongue, but that everyone may be edified thereby. Amen.

111. Prayer on the Thirteenth Sunday after Trinity

Lord God, heavenly Father, we thank You from our inmost heart that You have granted us to see this blessed time in which we hear the blessed doctrine of Your Gospel, and by it are able to know Your will and fatherly heart and behold Your Son, Jesus Christ. We beseech You of Your boundless mercy graciously to sustain the blessed light of Your Word, and so to rule and direct us by Your Holy Spirit that we may never turn aside from it, but rather forsaking all things, cling firmly to it, and at last obtain salvation. Amen.

112. Prayer on the Fourteenth Sunday after Trinity

Lord God, heavenly Father, who by Your Son, Jesus Christ, through Your Word and Holy Baptism, have graciously saved us believers from the detestable leprosy of sin and still demonstrate Your gracious help each day in all that we need: we beseech You to awaken our hearts by Your Holy Spirit, that we may never forget these benefits, but live continually in Your fear and hearty confidence in Your mercy, and with a joyful heart give thanks and praise to You forevermore. Amen.

113. Prayer on the Fifteenth Sunday after Trinity

Lord God, heavenly Father, we thank You for all Your benefits in giving us life and limb and graciously sustaining them until now, and we beseech You not to take Your blessing away from us, but keep us from covetousness, that we may serve You alone, love You, and cling to You, and not sin by idolatry and the harmful worship of mammon, but put all our hope, comfort, and confidence only in Your mercy and grace; through Jesus Christ, our Lord. Amen.

114. *Prayer on the Sixteenth Sunday after Trinity*

Lord God, heavenly Father, who sent Your Son to be made man, that by His death He might pay for our sins and save us from eternal death: we beseech You to preserve us in such hope, that we may not doubt that, even as our dear Lord Christ, by His word, raised up the widow's son, He will also raise us up at the Last Day and give us eternal salvation. Amen.

115. *Prayer on the Seventeenth Sunday after Trinity*

Lord God, heavenly Father, we beseech You to so rule and direct us by Your Holy Spirit that we may keep ourselves in Your fear and not grow proud, but with our whole heart hear and receive Your Word and truly keep the Sabbath holy, that we being sanctified by Your Word may, first, put all our trust and hope in Your Son, Jesus Christ as our only righteousness and redemption, and secondly, amend our lives according to Your Word and avoid all offense, until by Your grace in Christ we obtain eternal salvation. Amen.

116. *Prayer on the Eighteenth Sunday after Trinity*

O Lord God, heavenly Father, we are poor, miserable sinners. We know Your will, but we are too weak to fulfill it. Flesh and blood are too strong in us, and the wicked adversary, the devil, leaves us no peace. Wherefore we beseech You, pour out Your Holy Spirit into our hearts, that we may cling to Your Son, Jesus Christ, with a firm faith, take comfort in His death and Passion, and believe that by Him we have complete forgiveness of all our sins, and so lead a holy life in Your will and obedience here on earth, and die a blessed death in Your grace; through Jesus Christ. Amen.

117. *Prayer on the Nineteenth Sunday after Trinity*

Almighty, everlasting God, who by Your Son, Jesus Christ, graciously caused the paralytic to be healed in body and soul: I beseech You of Your boundless mercy to be gracious to me also, and forgive me all my sins, strengthen my faith by Your Word and Holy Spirit, and so direct me that I may not by sin and weakness cause hardship for others, but may continue in Your fear, and so be released from wrath and punishment temporal and eternal. Amen.

118. *Prayer on the Twentieth Sunday after Trinity*

Lord God, heavenly Father, I thank You for Your abundant mercy and steadfast love in inviting me through Your dear Word to come to the glad wedding feast, and by Your Son forgiving me all my sins. But because daily tribulations, offenses, and dangers are so numerous, and we for our own part are very weak and inclined to sin, I beseech You by Your Holy Spirit graciously to keep me from all calamity. But should I fall and defile my garment which Your beloved Son, Jesus Christ, put on me, graciously restore me, lead me to genuine repentance and true faith in Your mercy, and never let me fall. Amen.

119. Prayer on the Twenty-First Sunday after Trinity

Almighty, everlasting God, who by Your Son have promised us forgiveness of our sins, justification, and eternal life: we beseech You so to govern and quicken our hearts by Your Holy Spirit that we may by daily prayer, especially in all trials, seek such help from Him, and by steadfast faith in His Word and promise, be sure to find and receive it, and through Him at last obtain eternal salvation. Amen.

120. Prayer on the Twenty-Second Sunday after Trinity

Almighty, everlasting God, we acknowledge that we are sinners and the list of our debts is great. But we thank You heartily that You have removed those debts from us and laid them on Your beloved Son, Jesus Christ, and appointed Him to pay for us. And we beseech You also graciously to sustain us in such faith, and by the Holy Spirit so to lead and direct us here on earth that we may live after Your will and gladly show all love, service, and help to our neighbors. Conversely, let all wrath, impatience, and vengefulness subside, that we may not stir up wrath against ourselves, but ever have a gracious Father toward us; through Jesus Christ, who with You and the Holy Spirit lives and reigns from everlasting to everlasting. Amen.

121. Prayer on the Twenty-Third Sunday after Trinity

Lord God, heavenly Father, we thank You that You have until now granted us a gracious season of peace and with fatherly care defended us from war and foreign rule. We beseech You to grant Your continued grace, that we may live in Your fear and according to Your will, and not by sin give rise to war and other similar punishments. So govern and guide our authorities that they may not hinder obedience to You, but nurture it, and that we under their governance enjoy more blessing and prosperity. Amen.

122. Prayer on the Twenty-Fourth Sunday after Trinity

O almighty God, who by Your Son have promised to us the forgiveness of sins and deliverance from eternal death: we beseech You to strengthen us by Your Holy Spirit, that we may daily increase in such confidence in Your grace through Christ and hold fast the hope that we will not die but sleep in peace, and by Your Son, Jesus Christ, be raised up again on the Last Day unto eternal life. Amen.

123. Prayer on the Twenty-Fifth Sunday after Trinity

Lord God, heavenly Father, we thank You heartily that by Your Word You have brought us out of the pernicious error of the papacy and restored us to the true light of Your grace. And we beseech You that You would graciously sustain us in that light, preserve us from all error and heresy, and keep us from following the Jews in ingratitude, despising and persecuting Your Word, but let us receive it with our whole heart, amend our lives in accordance thereto, and place all our confidence only in the grace and merit of Your beloved Son, Jesus Christ; who lives and reigns with You and the Holy Spirit from everlasting to everlasting. Amen.

124. Prayer on the Twenty-Sixth Sunday after Trinity

O Lord God, heavenly Father, Your beloved Son, our Lord Jesus Christ, bids us feed the hungry, give drink to the thirsty, clothe the naked, and visit the sick, and in this way show our neighbors charity and loyalty. Yet, dear Father, You know how cold, reluctant, and lazy, alas, our hearts naturally are toward all such things, and how fiercely the wicked devil hinders charity in us. Accordingly, we heartily beseech You that You would pardon and forgive us all that we have done contrary to this good and salutary command, and govern us by Your Holy Spirit, that we may increase daily in brotherly love, and continue steadfast in it until the end, and at last with all the saints enter into the kingdom of eternal joy and salvation. Amen.

125. Prayer on a birthday

My Lord and my God, in You I live and move and have my being, both in life and death. I praise You, for I am fearfully and wonderfully made. Wonderful are Your works; my soul knows it very well. You knitted me together in my mother's womb. My frame was not hidden from You when I was being made in secret, intricately woven in the depths of the earth. Your eyes saw my unformed substance; in Your book were written, every one of them, the days that were formed for me when as yet there was none of them.

Today I recall the day of my birth, the beginning not only of my temporal life but also of my spiritual life; for then I was soon brought to Holy Baptism, reconciled with God, cleansed by the washing in the Word, and washed of my sins, and I received the Holy Spirit. For this I give You sincere thanks and praise. I glorify You, O God, my maker, that You delivered me, a human being, from my mother's womb today, though it was with sorrow and weeping, that You brought me to a place where Your name is truly acknowledged and Your Holy Word is taught in its purity, and that in this way I have come to the true faith by Your help.

I also thank You, Lord Jesus Christ, for all Your benefits which You have frequently showered upon my body and soul from my mother's womb until this present hour, nourishing and sustaining my body and protecting my temporal life in various ways by the holy angels, who always behold the face of God in heaven, and daily and richly providing me with food, drink, and clothes. But most especially, by Your Word You have shared with me spiritual and imperishable gifts and given me new birth in Holy Baptism, the washing of rebirth, that I might be a new creation and firstfruits of Jesus Christ, and granted me the forgiveness of sins, the Holy Spirit, and the inheritance of eternal life. And when in weakness or willful disobedience I turned aside from God, neglected His Commandments, and with many terrible sins transgressed against God in heaven and my neighbor on earth, more than seventy times seven times, You did not enter into judgment with me, nor fall upon me with the sudden punishment that I deserved.

O God, Holy Spirit, how shamefully I have spent my life, for how many years and in how many places I have terribly slipped and committed sins which cry to heaven! Yet, O God, Holy Spirit, how often You came after me, a lost sheep, and brought me back to the right way! How often You sanctified, comforted, and governed me, sustained me in my duty, curbed the devil, and repelled countless physical and spiritual dangers, in which I would have perished long ago if You had not been with me!

O Holy Trinity, there is a time to be born. Help all unborn children and give them a joyful day of birth, forgiveness of sins, and eternal life. Let me pass my birthday, and every day of my life remaining, free from damnable sin, and let me be mindful of my humble origin and lowly estate. Sustain me in health and life until the appointed goal, grant me patience in all cross and suffering, and comfort me in all misfortunes and troubles. Forgive me my sins each day, and grant me to remain steadfast unto the salvation of my soul, that I may serve You in true, saving faith and a good conscience until my end; through Jesus Christ. Amen.

VI. VOCATION

A. THE DOMESTIC ESTATE

126. Prayer of the parents for their children

O faithful God and Father, maker and upholder of all creatures: I thank You from my heart for the offspring which You have given me by Your blessing. And whereas You said that You will give the Holy Spirit to all who ask You for Him, I heartily beseech You to grace my poor children with Your Holy Spirit, that He may kindle in them the true fear of the Lord, which is the beginning of wisdom, and a good understanding, which if anyone practices it, his praise endures forever. Bless them with true knowledge of You; keep them from all idolatry and false teaching; let them increase in the true, saving faith and in all godliness; and continue therein until their end. Give them a believing, obedient, humble heart with true wisdom and understanding, that they may grow and increase in stature and in favor with God and man. Oh, plant in their hearts a love for God's Word, that they may be devout in prayer and worship, respectful to the servant of the Word, upright in their dealings with all men, modest in behavior, self-controlled in manner, true in words, faithful in works, diligent in labors, successful in carrying out their duty and office, judicious in their affairs, right in all things, and meek and kind to all men. Keep them from all the offenses of the wicked world, that they may not be led astray by bad company, fall into the mire of immodesty, unduly shorten their own lives, nor do harm to any other. Be their protection in all danger, that they may not die a sudden death. Let me not live to see dishonor and shame in them, but joy and honor, that by them also Your kingdom may be increased and the number of believers enlarged, and that they may sit in heaven around Your table like heavenly olive shoots, and with all the elect give honor, praise, and glory to You; through Jesus Christ, our Lord. Amen.

Here Psalm 127 and 128 may be prayed.

127. Prayer when parents send their children to school

Faithful God, heavenly Father, who in Your Word have earnestly commanded us parents to bring up our children in the way that pleases You: I beseech You from my inmost heart that I, and all others, may duly acknowledge the great importance of bringing up young children. Grant that I may preside fittingly over my family, and, as I have decided in support of that purpose, to send my child to school in Your name, O Most High. I pray that You would fill my child with the gifts of Your Holy Spirit, direct him (her) to the knowledge and fear of You and to diligent learning and obedience, that by Your grace he (she) may daily increase to Your glory and to his (her) and his (her) neighbor's good; for the sake of Your own child, Jesus Christ, my Lord. Amen.

128. *Prayer of parents for their adult children, that God would give them a godly spouse*

Almighty, gracious, merciful God, who instituted, ordained, and blessed the holy and chaste estate of marriage, and desiring that man should not remain alone throughout his life, therefore made and appointed for every man a helper with whom he might provide for the necessities of this life in tender love and faithfulness, and increase himself in chastity and honor: because You have given and graciously bestowed on us parents in the holy estate of marriage sons and daughters, who by daily increase have now reached the age of maturity, and today or tomorrow, according to Your divine will, may well enter the estate of marriage, and because, in Your divine Word, it is charged and committed to parents to provide for them particularly in this respect, and to take wives for their sons and husbands for their daughters; therefore, we beseech You, good and gracious God, to enlighten and govern our hearts and minds with Your Holy Spirit, that we may provide our dear children with godly and faithful spouses. Grant us, moreover, good occasion, and show us those persons at the proper time which You have chosen in Your wisdom. And since a godly spouse can only come from You, we commend our children into Your divine care, O good and faithful God, beseeching You to send each his portion in due season. Meanwhile, dear God, protect them from all evil, from offense, and from wicked company, that they may not be led astray, but behave modestly and decently in Your fear, honorably awaiting the time of their marriage; for the sake of Your beloved Son, Jesus Christ, our Lord. Amen.

129. *Prayer of a mother for wayward children*

Almighty God, merciful Father, turn to the prayer and supplication of Your poor maidservant, and forgive me all my sins for the sake of Your most beloved Son, Jesus Christ! Do not be angry that I have taken it upon myself to pour out my heart to You and to speak to You in my great concern and sorrow. There is no other God besides You who can save me. I know of none other in whom I might take refuge. On You was I cast from my birth, and from my mother's womb You have been my God. Lord, You already know the cause of my pain. All my longing is before You; my sighing is not hidden from You. You see and behold the grief which my motherly heart feels over the disobedience and detestable wickedness of my son (daughter). I received him (her) from Your hand as a precious gift and in turn devoted him (her) to You in Holy Baptism. I have commended him (her) to You by daily and heartfelt prayer, and, as far as in me lay, never ceased to admonish him (her) to keep his (her) way pure and to guard it according to Your Word. Yet how shamefully he (she) has corrupted his (her) way and been led astray by the devil and delinquent company! Having been a vessel of honor consecrated to You, he (she) has become a vessel of wrath and must perish eternally unless You have mercy on him (her), wash him (her) in the waters of Your grace, cleanse him (her) with the blood of Your dearest Son, Jesus Christ, and deliver his (her) poor soul. O Lord, look mercifully upon him (her) for the sake of Your dearly beloved and perfectly obedient child, Jesus Christ! Do not remember the sins of his (her) youth and all his (her) transgressions. Receive his (her) poor soul into Your care, that it may not perish, but be snatched like kindling from the flames and preserved from eternal damnation.

O Jesus, dearest Savior! You take no pleasure in the death of the ungodly but desire that he should turn from his evil ways and live. For this reason also You became obedient to Your Father in heaven unto death, even the death of the cross, and made atonement for the disobedience of all the sons of men, and on the cross reconciled all things, in heaven or on earth, by Your blood. O let Your blood and death not be lost on this wicked man (woman), but govern him (her) by Your Spirit, that he (she) may acknowledge his (her) transgressions, consider well the temporal and eternal punishment for the disobedient children and unrepentant sinners, and be genuinely converted to You.

O Lord, Your heart was once moved with pity when You wept for Your friend, Lazarus, while he was dead and lay in the tomb. How willing You were then to restore him to life! Let the tears and sighs of Your poor maidservant also move Your heart to pity as I weep like Rachel for my son (daughter), because he (she) is dead in his (her) sins, although living. O Jesus, You can dry my tears and turn my sadness and grief into joy. You have the keys of Death and Hades. If You are willing, You can give life again to this sinner who is dead in his (her) sins and trespasses. Cry aloud in his (her) heart, "Awake, O sleeper, and arise from the dead, and Jesus Christ will shine on you!" Help him (her) to hear this, to forsake the tomb of iniquity and sin, to begin a new life, and by Your merits to obtain eternal life in heaven.

Lord God, Holy Spirit, who hold the hearts of all men in Your hands and govern them as You will: You moved the prodigal son to acknowledge his prolonged wickedness, repent sincerely, return to his father, and become another man. I call on You from the depths of my heart to incline the heart and mind of my wayward son (daughter) to good, change his (her) reasoning, direct his (her) feet back to the way of true godliness, and make of him (her) a man (woman) that walks in Your Commandments, keeps Your laws, and acts accordingly. Grant that he (she) may abandon the evil society of perverse men and rather join the prodigal son in returning and saying, "Father, I have sinned against heaven and before you. I am no longer worthy to be called your son," that I may be moved with all in my household to rejoice and say, "Let us celebrate; for this my son (daughter) was dead, and is alive again; he (she) was lost, and is found." Then there will be joy before the angels of God in heaven over this sinner. Then I will praise and extol You for this grace with all my powers, both now and forever.

O Lord, triune God! Have mercy upon me, hear my prayer, comfort and strengthen me in my great cross. Restore to me the joy of Your salvation for the glory of Your name. Amen.

130. *Prayer for comfort in trials relating to one's calling [Luther on Matthew 7]*
Dear Lord, I have Your Word and occupy an estate pleasing to You; this much I know. As You see, there is such deficiency on all sides that I know of no help apart from You. Help, therefore; for You have directed us to ask, seek, and knock and told us that we will certainly receive, find, and have what we desire. Amen.

131. *Another*
Dear God, what I do now I will do in the name of Jesus and in the obedience in which I have been placed by God and will do so with joy. If something happens to me in the process and the devil afflicts me, what harm does it do me? I am still in an estate where God's Word teaches and comforts me. Whatever I do or endure, it is well, and God will take pleasure in it and accompany me with His grace. Amen.

132. *Travel prayer of a father moving his family to a new residence*

Faithful, heavenly Father, who long ago commanded Abraham to go from his country and kindred to another country unknown to him and there made him into a great people; and who brought Jacob out of the Promised Land to Mesopotamia and to Egypt, and with a mighty hand and outstretched arm brought his descendants, the children of Israel, back again by the Red Sea and by the harsh wilderness, going before them in a pillar of fire by night and a pillar of cloud by day throughout their journey; and who by means of a miraculous star safely guided the Wise Men from the East even to Bethlehem: according to Your wonderful will and counsel, You have laid upon me a long, difficult, and dangerous journey, directing me to go to a land which I do not know. But because it is Your divine call and ordinance, I will obey You by faith, according to the example of Abraham, and with my dear wife and children begin the pilgrimage in Your name.

O Lord, keep our going out and our coming in; be our shade on our right hand, that the sun may not strike us by day, nor the moon by night. Let Your holy angels encamp around us and set up a barricade around us, that no evil may befall us by land or sea and no plague come near us. Command Your strong champions to keep us in all our ways. On their hands let them bear us up, lest we strike our feet against a stone or fall into the hands of the wicked. Let us find good Christians who faithfully come to our aid.

O dear Father, we are too weak and faint and do not know what to do or how to manage this difficult journey. But our eyes are toward You only, O Lord. You are our strength and refuge, our rock and our fortress and our deliverer, our God, our rock in whom we take refuge, our shield, and the horn of our salvation, our stronghold. You have kept count of all our wanderings; indeed, the hairs of our head are all numbered, and not one will fall to the ground apart from Your will. Therefore, though we walk through the valley of death, and many thousands of people set themselves against us all around, we will fear no evil, for You, O Lord, are with us; You are a shield about us, our glory, and the lifter of our heads. Ah, Lord! You have the hearts of all men in Your hand and in Your power. Incline to us the hearts of those to whom we come, that they may show us works of mercy. Make us glad for as many days as You have afflicted us, and for as many years as we have seen evil. Dearest Father, be and abide with us, Your children, for the whole length of our journey, and uphold us with Your righteous right hand. Be our faithful leader and guide, that we may come in peace and good health to the place which You have appointed for us; and there, if so be Your holy will, conclude our life in a good old age; through Jesus Christ. Amen.

133. Prayer of a legal guardian

Almighty, everlasting God, who are the Father of orphans, defender of widows, and a swift witness against those who abuse the widow and the fatherless and treat them unjustly, and are therefore pleased when there are those who bring justice to the fatherless and assist the widow's cause and in all ways address the needs of such people; even as You regard whatever is done to the least of these as done to Yourself: behold, I have been persuaded to take up such concern and to care for children who have been forsaken by father and mother. Therefore, since You require no more of such stewards than that they be found faithful, fill my heart with love and faithfulness for the children in my care.

Above all, let me see to it that they are brought up in the discipline and instruction of the Lord, that they may increase in the fear of God and grow up in every way into Him who is the head, into Christ Jesus, especially since godliness is of value in every way, as it holds promise for the present life and also for the life to come. And nothing better can be instilled in children than the knowledge of God, in which eternal life is found.

Incline my heart to Your testimonies and not to selfish gain, that I may do no violence to their inheritance, nor seize their fields, nor take their houses for my own, but so manage their property and means as to answer faithfully to You, omniscient God, and to men. Let me rather protect their inheritance from all violence, as far as possible, and deliver them from the hands of all who hate them, that they may not be treated unjustly or fall prey to any man. And since You do not despise the supplication of the fatherless, hear them from Your holy height and bless them with blessings from heaven. Above all, sustain them in Your fear, that they may have You before their eyes and in their hearts throughout their lives and consent to no sin, nor knowingly break Your Commandments, that I may one day bring these my charges with me into heaven and say, "Behold, here am I, and the children whom You, the Lord, have given me," and that they enter with me into the eternal kingdom of Your glory. Amen.

134. Prayer of children

Almighty God, heavenly Father, since You have earnestly commanded me in

the Fourth Commandment to honor my father and my mother and have graciously promised to reward this service with long life and prosperity, I pray
from the depths of my heart that You would give me an obedient heart that in
all things will obey, with due submissiveness, my dear parents and all who are
set in the place of my parents, to honor them in word and deed with patience,
and not to aggravate, ignore, or despise them as long as I live, that the blessing
may come upon me. Grant that I may keep their words, commandments, and
precepts; store them up in my heart and, indeed, bind them on my heart always
and tie them around my neck; and accept their reproof; and not forget their
teaching, that I may live the longer. Govern me also by Your good Spirit, that
I may obey my father's command and not forsake my mother's teaching, that
I may be a joy and comfort to them. Grant that I may carefully consider, in all
that I do or do not, the pattern of my Lord and Savior, who as an example to
all godly children, was subject to his dear mother, the Virgin Mary, and to his
guardian, Joseph. Give me a thankful and humble heart, that I may repay my
dear parents and serve them in turn, and especially that I may care for them
in their old age and excuse them when they become childlike and strange, not
forgetting that I came from them. Graciously forgive whatever I have done
against them out of the weakness or ignorance of youth. Keep me from bad
company and careless men, so that when sinners entice me, I may not consent,
nor walk in the way with them, but may hold back my foot from their path and
not fall into disgrace and iniquity. O Lord, You have led me till now as a man
leads his son! Grant that I may incline my ear and hear the words of the wise,
and so learn in my youth that I may gain knowledge and discretion. Help me
to increase in wisdom and in stature and in favor with You and men; through
Jesus Christ. Amen.

135. *Prayer of a servant*

Merciful God, who by the sufferings and death of Your beloved Son, Jesus Christ,
have redeemed and released me from eternal servitude, the power of sin, the
dominion of darkness, and the cruel tyranny of the devil: grant me grace, I beseech You, that in my estate of physical service into which You have, according
to Your will and pleasure, placed me here on earth, I may not grow weary and
not impatiently murmur, as it may be, against Your ordinance, nor envy others
for their higher estate, but that I may do Your pleasure with my whole heart and
a good will, regarding it as if I were serving You, God in heaven, and not man

on earth. So, dear God, help me to serve You, the Most High Lord in heaven and earth, in true knowledge and proper fear, to love You above all things, to place all my hope and blessedness in You, and to walk blameless in Your Commandments; and further, that I may in all things which are not contrary to You, patiently be subject to my physical master and mistress, not only to the good and gentle, but also to the unreasonable and unjust, with all fear, and in the simplicity of my heart, as to Christ, my Lord, not with eye-service, as a pleaser of men, but from my heart for the sake of Your direction and command. Grant grace that I may be found faithful in all that is committed to me and placed in my charge, not neglect or confound anything, nor let anything be damaged or ruined through carelessness. Let me not covet or embezzle another's property which is entrusted to me and put into my hands. Preserve my health, strengthen my limbs and all my bodily powers, and endow me with reason and wisdom, that I may provide for my master and mistress and improve their livelihood by Your divine assistance, that they may be blessed by my diligence and increased abundantly, and that all that I carry out or accomplish may serve for Your divine glory and for the blessed training of my faith; through Jesus Christ, Your beloved Son, who lives and reigns with You in the unity of the Holy Spirit, from everlasting to everlasting. Amen.

136. *Prayer of young people seeking to enter the estate of holy matrimony*
Behold, dear God, I hear that the estate of matrimony is Your created work and pleases You well. Upon Your Word I therefore purpose to enter it. However You wish it may be for me, that will please and suit me. Ah, dear God and Father of our Lord Jesus Christ! Grant me, Your poor child, a godly (husband/wife) with whom I may, by the grace of the Holy Spirit, live a godly life in the estate of marriage. Amen.

137. *Another*
Lord God, You have created me to be a husband. You see that I cannot live chastely. I call upon You and ask You to guide my plans and give them success. Provide good counsel and help me. Choose for me one with whom I can live honorably and serve You and by faith and prayer overcome the misfortune and difficulties which occur in the estate of marriage. Amen.

138. *Prayer of young people for a faithful spouse*
O almighty, everlasting God, maker, upholder, and multiplier of all mankind,

who in the Garden of Eden instituted the holy estate of marriage, and at Cana in Galilee honored it with the first sign of Your beloved Son, our Savior, Jesus Christ, and who made me for that estate and have brought me to the proper age: I heartily beseech You that You would grant me a prudent, Christian, and God-fearing spouse, whom I may heartily love and with whom I may, in true godly fear and Christian conduct, live on earth in peace and concord and make an honest living to Your praise, as a good example to others, and for the good and welfare of body and soul of ourselves and all men. You are the searcher of hearts, knowing the characters and dispositions of all men. A prudent spouse is from You, for it is a present and gift of the Most High. Therefore I call to You, that I may find such a one and heartily beseech You, dear Lord God, by Your Holy Spirit to enlighten my heart and the hearts of my parents, to choose rightly, and to receive the matter into Your own fatherly care; through Jesus Christ. Amen.

139. Prayer of a young man who will propose marriage

Gracious, merciful God, heavenly Father, I have now, after long prayer, looked for a spouse with whom I may (according to my thinking) make a good living and dwell together in Christian marriage. If, therefore, the person whom You have appointed for me is ____name____, and if this marriage will attain to Your divine glory, to the edification of others, and to the bodily and spiritual welfare of her and myself, grant Your grace that it may be transacted by regular, Christian means. But if it should attain rather to Your dishonor, O God, to the offense of others, and to the hindrance of my own soul's salvation, then, O Lord God, change my heart and mind, that I may not desire or undertake anything contrary to Your will. Your will be done, Lord God. Give special attention to this matter, and grant Your Holy Spirit to that end. Amen.

140. Prayer of a young woman who is asked to be married

Everlasting, almighty, and gracious God, my heavenly Father, since You have created me for the estate of marriage, and I am now given the opportunity to enter that estate by the honorable proposal made to me by ___name___, therefore if marriage with this person is in Your divine will, and if he is the one whom You have supplied and chosen as my husband, and if it will attain to Your glory and my welfare, I heartily pray that You would grant grace and blessing that this honorable prospect may happily proceed. And as I perceive that this honest person's heart and mind have love and respect for me, incline my heart and mind likewise toward him, that I may love him in turn with propriety and decency, and willingly submit myself to my dear parents' counsel and opinion. But if it is not to be, and I may not be well provided for by this person, O Lord, then hinder this affair, and turn his thoughts from me, and grant him and myself our separate portions according to Your gracious will and pleasure. For I leave everything to Your will, heavenly Father, and commend this matter entirely to You and to my dear parents. Order it as You know will be best for both parties. Whatever You counsel and advise me in this matter by my dear parents I will gladly obey, not doubting that You will certainly provide well for me at my humble petition; for the sake of Your beloved Son, Jesus Christ. Amen.

141. Prayer of the betrothed

O gracious, loving, and merciful God, the Father of our Lord Jesus Christ, maker of heaven and earth, who in the special counsel of Your divine wisdom instituted and foreordained that man and wife should dwell together in marital union, particularly for the propagation of mankind and the filling of the kingdom of heaven: we give You thanks and praise from our hearts that we, being now betrothed as bride and groom, need await nothing more for the completion of our marital estate than our regular and public joining or union at the hand of the pastor. We therefore humbly beseech You meanwhile to sustain us both in good health, that we may joyfully live to see that honored day and the public service in the church, and to observe it in a Christian manner. For the time being, as we anticipate our marriage, grant us the grace and blessing to consider and take to heart how we may begin our wedded estate in a Christian manner, live blessedly therein, and honor and glorify You always; through Jesus Christ, our Lord, who lives and reigns with You, one God, most blessed forever. Amen.

142. Prayer of the betrothed on the wedding day

Almighty God, heavenly Father, who instituted, ordained, and blessed the holy estate of marriage: we give You praise and thanks that You have called us to that estate and graciously kept us from disgrace until this present time. But because we know that the devil is very hostile to this Your ordinance, we beseech You this day that You would send us Your holy angel to protect and preserve us from murder and lies of the devil and demons in this our estate. Direct and govern us by Your Holy Spirit that we may above all love Your divine Commandments and serve You with faithful hearts, and that we, as spouses, may show each other all marital fidelity, love, honor, and good, that we may live long together in good health, peace, quiet, unity, and trust, have children according to Your divine will, and direct all our actions to Your divine praise, honor, and worship, that we may both, by Your grace, possess eternal life. Amen.

143. A husband's prayer

Almighty, gracious God, who instituted the holy estate of marriage and by the first sign of Your dear Son, Jesus Christ, honored and adorned it as an estate pleasing to You, and in which many holy patriarchs and prophets lived godly lives and were pleasing to You: because You have brought me to holy matrimony, ordained me to the management of a household, and take especial pleasure in three things, namely, when brothers agree, and neighbors love each other, and man and wife live well together, therefore, I beseech You from the depths of my heart to grant that I may dwell together with my wife in Christian love and unity with discernment, knowing that she is the weaker vessel, give her due honor as a fellow heir of the grace of life, and lead her, our children, and our household to the knowledge of You and godly honor in all propriety and decency. To that end grant grace that she may follow and submit to me in every good thing and to all godliness. Preserve our marriage from the demons, that no division or conflict may come between us, and if we should be overtaken in our weakness and fall into dispute, grant that we may be quickly reconciled. Grant me grace that I may not covet the wife of any other, nor look lustfully upon her, to desire her. Preserve me, my wife, children, and household from sickness according to Your will. Grant that as Your servant, I may attend diligently to my calling, eat my bread by the sweat of my brow, and not be aggravated by the heaviness of the toil, since You have made it so. Bestow success and health on my living, that it may be increased by Your blessing without harm or disadvantage to others. Grant me godly servants and faithful workers. Preserve my house and home and all that You have given me. Help us patiently to bear the cross in our estate, and after this life gather us together with all godly spouses in Your kingdom. Amen.

144. A wife's prayer

Gracious God, faithful Father, forasmuch as You have graciously called me to the holy estate of marriage for the management of a household, in which it is possible for me to serve and please You, my God, grant grace that I, Your servant, may always have Your divine fear before my eyes and love You, my Maker and Redeemer, above all things and trust in You; and after You, that I may fear, honor, and love my husband and covet no other. Help me according to Your commandment to subject my desires to my husband and to obey him in all willingness. Let my adorning be the hidden person of the heart with the imperishable beauty of a gentle, quiet spirit and all manner of virtues, as were the holy women long ago, who trusted in their God and obeyed their husbands. Give me, Your maidservant, chaste, self-controlled conduct in fear and humility, that with soft and seasonable words, I may turn away and appease the wrath and displeasure of my husband and counter him with kindness; that I may bring up my children and servants with gentleness to the praise and glory of Your holy name; that I may be a true helper for my husband and diligently keep the provisions which You graciously grant us; that I may lose nothing, but labor and help to produce what is available to me in my vocation, so that I may have something to give to the needy and reach out my hand to the poor. Defend us from unfaithful laborers and wicked servants who diminish and squander our possessions. Grant me grace also, that I may patiently bear the cross in the estate of marriage, and not at once grow shy or timid when suffering appears, knowing that by tribulation and adversity our faith is tested. O Lord God, into Your almighty power I commend myself, my dear husband, all my children, and servants. Defend us from sin, disgrace, and all suffering; through Jesus Christ, our Lord. Amen.

145. Prayer for the blessing of children in marriage

Lord, You are God Almighty, and the earth is full of Your steadfast love. All Your works are truth, and Your ways are just. You Yourself said, "Be fruitful and multiply, and fill the earth," and it shall not cease so long as the earth remains. For this reason it is sometimes Your punishment that we have barren wombs and dry breasts. And holy women long ago, before God was manifest in the flesh, regarded it as a miserable and contemptible thing to die without children. Therefore, when at times their hearts were troubled, they prayed to You, the Lord, and poured out their hearts to You, and You granted their request. For You can do as You please, O Lord, and with You nothing is impossible. You are He who gives the barren woman a home, making her the joyous mother of children. Indeed, You can make laughter for her who is old and full of days. For children, O Lord, are a heritage from You, and the fruit of the womb is Your reward. Therefore I will turn my face toward You, my Lord, who are able to do far more abundantly than all that we ask or think. I, who am called, as it were, barren, acknowledge You to be the God who can give me the fruit of the womb, and I beseech You, according to Your will, O my God, to hear me. O Lord of Sabaoth, remember me and do not forget Your maidservant. Wonderful are Your works; my soul knows it very well. Your eyes see the unformed substance. So in this matter also I commit my ways to You and trust in You, knowing that You will manage it well. You are the Lord; do what is pleasing to You. If You will look upon Your maidservant, I will sing praises to You, O my God. But if I am to have no child until the day I die, O Lord, Your will be done. You know all that is hidden and concealed. To die childless is better than to have ungodly children, especially in these last days when abominable times have come in which many are disobedient to their parents and when wickedness perverts the mind and false teaching deceives the soul. So it is even among innocent hearts, as mothers are everywhere bereaved by the sword, so that they often start to say, "Blessed are the barren and the wombs that never bore and the breasts that never nursed!" But above all, grant that Jesus Christ may be formed in me and that I may be fruitful in all good works until the resurrection, when we will be like the angels of God in heaven. Give ear, O God, to the prayer of Your maidservant and her supplication for the Lord's sake. To Your name be eternal glory and praise. Amen.

146. Prayer when the blessing of children is detected

Lord God Almighty, maker of heaven and earth, You spoke Your divine blessing upon the holy estate of marriage, willing that out of the blood of one, all the families of men should come to dwell on the face of the whole earth. Indeed, You alone are He who gives the barren woman a home, making her the joyous mother of children. For children are a heritage from the Lord, and the fruit of the womb is a reward. By Your grace I, too, have become a partaker of this Your blessing, which is still hidden under my heart. But because You imposed on womankind, as a consequence of sin, that she should bear children in pain, and a woman with child is subject to dangers, I beseech You of Your generous mercy, in the name of Your only and dearest Son, Jesus Christ, who by the overshadowing of the Holy Spirit, was conceived and born of the pure and chaste

Virgin Mary for me and for my offspring, and thereby sanctified our sinful conception and birth, that You would let me know Your will, help me to bear my pain in patience, strengthen the fruit of my womb, bless this child, and grace this child with Your Holy Spirit. Give me Your angels to be my guardians on the way. Preserve me on highways and byways from all misfortune. Let me not fall or carelessly slip. Keep my eyes from seeing anything unsightly. Let me not have a miscarriage or bear my offspring prematurely. Graciously deliver me at the proper time. Give me and my husband joy to see a happy delivery, and let the poor infant come to Holy Baptism. For I devote myself wholly to You in body and soul, with my child and all my members. You created and redeemed me. I am Yours. In You I put my trust. My salvation is in Your hands. I will live and die to You. O Lord, hear me, and let me not be put to shame in my hope. Amen.

147. Prayer when a wife is fearful before the birth

Lord Jesus Christ, who are alive from everlasting to everlasting, and hold the keys of life and death: behold, my hour has come; sorrow is at hand. Oh, how anxious I am! My heart pains me within my body. I justly feel the pain that was proclaimed for all womankind before one woman had ever been born, since by womankind transgression entered the world. Let my plea come before You, O faithful Savior, who by Your holy birth and incarnation have sanctified the sinful birth of man, indeed, who by the example of a woman giving birth have confirmed all Your dear Christendom, that they may not waver, but look forward to the joy that will quickly follow. Oh, strengthen me, Lord, in this hour! Do not turn Your face from me. Let me see You again, and let my heart rejoice because You are so eager to help. It is Your work only. You only are the strong Lord able to draw us from our mothers' wombs. Therefore I flee to You and beseech You for the sake of Your blood and death to assist me in these needs, where the help of man is of no avail. Send me the power of the Holy Spirit, that He may awaken in me a heartfelt confidence in Your grace, strengthen my faith, and grant me Christian patience. Almighty and gracious God, who commanded us to call upon You in the time of need, behold my sorrow and misery; do not leave me comfortless and helpless. I know that You see, for You behold the misery and sorrow. They are in Your hands. Therefore demonstrate Your wonderful steadfast love and almighty power in me. You who have blessed me with the fruit of the womb and have given me joy with hope, let me not be put to shame in that hope. Grant me to see a joyful sight, and after the weeping and mourning, overshadow me with joy. But if it be Your holy will that this should be my final hour, and I must give up my spirit because of this birth, then give me constancy, spare the poor creature whom You have redeemed, and let it enter this world alive and be written in the Book of Life by Holy Baptism. Comfort and refresh those who are troubled by my departure. Lord, be their Father; provide for them and care for them like a true guardian, and receive my soul into Your hands of grace. For You said, "A woman will be saved through the begetting of children, if she remains in the faith and in charity." I believe, dear Lord! Strengthen my faith, seal in me Your grace and Your promise to take me up like a child into eternal joy and glory. O Lord, listen! O Lord, be merciful! O Lord, pay attention, and do it. Behold, I am the handmaid of the Lord; let it be for me according to Your will. Amen.

148. Prayer when the hour of birth draws near

Dear God, I have no more time to wait. At any moment, I may expect You to call me to the labor of childbirth. To Your almighty keeping and shelter I commend myself entirely, body and soul. Do with me according to Your fatherly will and pleasure, as You know will be best and most beneficial for me in body and soul. O Lord Jesus Christ, after You instituted the Holy Supper, in Your comforting farewell sermon which You preached to Your disciples, You mentioned the pains and sorrows of a woman in childbirth and thereby wished to comfort the Church after her sorrows. I beseech You by Your mortal agony and bloody sweat, by Your cross and death, assist me by the help, assistance, comfort, and strength of the Holy Spirit, that when I have endured the pain and sorrow, I may be gladdened by the joyful sight of my child and the gracious delivery from my pains. But if the hour for me to depart this world is at hand, and I must give up my spirit during this birth, I beseech You from my heart that You would not let Your bitter sufferings and death be in vain for me. Take my husband (and young infants) into Your care, even as You call Yourself the Father of the fatherless, seeing that I, while I live, am only appointed as a caretaker. Therefore I deliver and commend all things into Your fatherly provision. Whatever You do, it is all very good. If I live, I will serve You as long as I am here; if I die, take me in the midst of my duties to eternal life. To You, eternal Father, Son, and Holy Spirit, be unceasing praise, honor, and worship both now and forever. Amen.

149. Prayer when there is a risk of dying in childbirth

Almighty, merciful God and Father in heaven, I beseech You by the mortal agony and anguished sweat and affliction of my only Savior and Redeemer, Your beloved Son, Jesus Christ, that You would bestow on me, a weak and weary woman, strength, power, patience, and comfort in this exceedingly great distress, and grant me the joyful sight of my child. For You alone work salvation and help in the midst of the earth. But if I and my baby may not survive, oh, then baptize this the fruit of my womb with the precious blood of Your beloved Son and grant me a blessed end! Let me live in joy and die in blessing. Receive my soul into Your divine hands, for Christ is my life. And according to Your holy will, I have a desire to be released and to be with Christ Jesus, my Brother and Immanuel, from whose hands no one shall pluck me. O Lord Jesus Christ, Son of the living God, help me and comfort me in this great trial, and give strength and power to me and the fruit of my womb, which is Your own handiwork and blessing, that we may not perish! O God, Holy Spirit, supreme Comforter in every need, comfort me with Your divine comfort; let me not waver, but be my support, O mighty God, for the sake of Your truth and the honor of Your name. Amen, O Holy Trinity! Amen.

150. Another

O Lord, how long will You forget me? How long will You hide Your face from me? Dearest Father, have You forgotten to be gracious to me and turned cruel to me, that You might persecute me with the might of Your hand? Oh, that God would have mercy! Shall I not moan like Zion, "The Lord has forsaken me; my Lord has forgotten me"? Look, O faithful God, and see if there is any sorrow like my sorrow, which was brought upon me. I am in anguish and out of breath because the child is about to be born, and yet there is no strength in me to give birth. O Jesus, Son of the living God! Have mercy on me and help me, whether it be for my life or for my death. And because I know that a woman will be saved through childbearing if she continues in faith, and the hour of my departure seems to be at hand, O Lord, Thy will be done on earth as it is in heaven! Only have mercy on my poor soul, which You have redeemed not with perishable gold or silver but with Your precious blood, and receive my spirit. If it is not possible for my child of sorrow to be born into the world and must die in my womb or be stillborn, I hereby commend his (her) soul and mine into Your hands. I live to You, I die to You, I am Yours, whether I live or die. Amen.

151. Thanksgiving after a successful birth

O gracious and merciful God, who have especially and graciously shown us that You alone are God, who give life to the dead and call into existence the things that do not exist: You have graciously given us living, true offspring after Your own image, without any merit of our own, so that we are obliged to show our gratitude no less than were Elkanah and Hannah, Zechariah and Elizabeth, Joachim and Anna, and others like them, whom You wonderfully and graciously provided with a blessed and joyful birth. Therefore we humbly give You thanks and praise for this unspeakable grace and benefit and earnestly pray that You would grant grace, that our infant, together with any others which You might grant us hereafter, according to Your will, may grow and increase in Your divine honor, fear, virtue, godliness, and service, in good health until life's end, that You may take pleasure and that we may find blessed joy in our child, without any shame or vice, and that we may praise, honor, and worship You, our Lord and maker, both here and hereafter forever and ever. Amen.

152. Prayer of a husband after his wife delivers a stillborn child

Dear, faithful God, because it has pleased Your wisdom, in the birth of our child, to call him (her) out of this life and to take him (her) to Yourself, it must please us also. Neither will we doubt that You have received and taken him (her) into all grace for the sake of Your beloved Son, as we have earnestly prayed, and that now he (she) is assuredly a beloved child of eternal salvation, where he (she) is best provided for and preserved from all evil, of which he (she) would otherwise have had to endure much in this wicked world. I also thank You from my heart that You, in this difficult time of childbirth, have nevertheless preserved the life of my dear wife and plucked her from the midst of death and brought her back, for the good of myself (and my young children). Help her to recover her faculties, which have been strained and nearly lost in this great trial and difficult labor, and I will praise and worship You and extol Your mercy here in time and hereafter in eternity; through Christ our Lord. Amen.

153. Prayer of a mother who has given birth to a disabled child

O gracious, merciful God, I give You thanks from my heart that You have by Your almighty hand saved me from peril of life and limb and graciously delivered me of my maternal burden. Yet since You have given me a [child with disabilities], thereby making clear to me my own spiritual disability as the misshapenness of my corrupt nature and unsightliness of my grave sins, help me also, O faithful God, to acknowledge my faults and to keep myself from sins henceforth. Heal my disabled child and make him (her) whole by the holy washing of Baptism, and make up for his (her) bodily deficiencies with godly fear and other excellent gifts and virtues, and enable and equip him (her) for the kingdom of heaven. And grant me grace that I may not hate this child because of his (her) disability, but may love Your creation, nourish him (her), and bring him (her) up unto every good thing, as befits a Christian mother; for the sake of Your dear Son, Jesus Christ. Amen.

154. Prayer of a mother when her newborn dies before being baptized

Almighty God, merciful Father, You see the great sorrow of Your maidservant and know that I am concerned in this troubled state not so much with the death of my child as with his (her) salvation. I acknowledge and revere the power that You have over the fruit of my womb, Your own creation, that, as You have given him (her) life and breath according to Your pleasure, You are also free to take these back. Yet it troubles me deeply, and like a sword pierces through my own soul, that this poor child has departed before he (she) could be incorporated by Holy Baptism into the covenant of Your grace. O gracious God, take this sorrow from my heart and let the comfort of Your Word refresh me. You graciously heard my prayers and supplications which I made for my unborn child, that this my child, by virtue of the promise that You gave to Abraham and to every believing Christian, might nevertheless be included in Your covenant of grace, since You said, "I am your God, and the God of your seed after you." Indeed, You could save men without Baptism in cases of necessity.

O Jesus, dearest Savior, who are a sincere friend of children and say, "Let the children come to Me, and do not prevent them, for of such is the kingdom of God": how eagerly I would let my dear child come to You in Holy Baptism and lay him (her) in Your bosom of grace, if only he (she) had not been prevented by a too sudden death. But I know by Your own divine mouth that it is not the will of the Father in heaven that any of these little ones should perish; and I believe steadfastly that God did not create this my child for eternal destruction, and that You, O only-begotten Son of God, have washed away his (her) sins with Your precious blood, and with Your death on the cross redeemed him (her) from the eternal power of death, and so will receive his (her) soul into Your keeping, that it may not perish. Since You promised paradise to the converted robber on the cross, who never received the Sacrament of Holy Baptism, why would You not also transfer this child of my womb into Your eternal kingdom without Baptism? Yet, O my Savior, strengthen in me my weak faith, and grant that I may take comfort and confirm myself in this.

O Lord God, Holy Spirit, God of patience and comfort! Send forth the light of Your grace and consolation to scatter the dark clouds of sorrow from my soul. Let me ponder the glorious benefits which God by this death has given to my child, promptly delivering him (her) from the burdens of sin and toils of this life, bringing him (her) from death to life, from misery to happiness, and from anguish to repose, receiving his (her) soul into the fellowship of the holy angels, and instantly crowning him (her) at the beginning of his (her) course. Help me in the contemplation of these things soon to forget my grief and not to weep as the pagans do, which have no hope, but with godly David to rest assured in my heart that although my child will not return to me in this world, nevertheless I will come to him (her) some day and see him (her) again in the glory and joy of heaven. And for this I will extol and worship You with God the Father and my Savior Christ for all eternity. Amen.

155. *Prayer of a mother observing her churching*

God the Father, Son, and Holy Spirit, only and eternal God, thanks and praise be to You that You have visited me with Your power and might in the pains of my childbirth and granted me a healthy child, and especially that You have brought him (her) to Holy Baptism and incorporated him (her) as a true member of Your Christian Church, and that You have tenderly sustained, refreshed, strengthened, and cared for me and my dear child during my lying-in. I now go to appear in Your divine presence and offer to You my dear child, which You have given me, even as dear Hannah did, earnestly praying that You would always be his (her) dear God and Father. And as You received and adopted him (her) in Holy Baptism as Your own child, let him (her) forever be an heir of Your heavenly riches and eternal salvation in Jesus Christ, Your only Son. Preserve him (her) in the time of his (her) life from all evil of body and soul, and grant me Your divine help and blessing that I may, as a faithful mother, bring up my dear child in all Christian virtues to Your glory, to my and my husband's joy, to my neighbor's benefit, and to my child's own welfare, temporal and eternal. Deign to do so for the sake of Your beloved Son, Jesus Christ, in whom the infants of all baptized Christians are heartily pleasing and acceptable; to whom be blessing, honor, and glory with You and the Holy Spirit from this time forth and forevermore! Amen.

156. *Prayer of a husband who has a bad wife*

Lord God, heavenly Father, I know and am assured that this estate in which You have placed me is pleasing to You and that all that I do and suffer for You in this estate and vocation is an acceptable offering to You because of Jesus Christ, Your beloved Son, my Redeemer and Savior, whom I honor, love, and confess. You see what sorrow and misery I am in and that my peril is so great that no human help can deliver me. I, a poor and afflicted husband, regret to say that I have an unhappy marriage with my wife because of her stubbornness, disobedience, wickedness, and lack of diligence in the management of the household, and it is difficult beyond measure for me in such an existence to live and dwell together with my spouse at length, because I do not have a happy, restful, or peaceful hour with her and am concerned that my entire household will collapse and be destroyed by this. Therefore in my distress I call to You with a troubled heart and cry to You with a voice of supplication, that You would take necessary, fatherly, and gracious regard for this matter, bring timely resolution, and grant my wife grace and spirit to live together with me in a Christian manner, with true sense and understanding, to be always kind, patient, and gentle with me, to have genuine appreciation and fondness for me, and not to be so contrary, stern, and serious with me, that the evil foe may be given no cause or impulse to work any more disunity and discord between us, by which we are hindered in our prayers, and therefore in the blessing and prosperous welfare of body and soul. O Lord, teach us to act according to Your will, and let Your good Spirit lead us on the even way, that we may walk in true, unfeigned marital love, and especially pursue the laudable virtue of domestic harmony, overlook each other's faults and yield to one another, that we may finish our lives in good peace and worthy happiness until we relinquish our marital estate in this world and live forever with You in the heavenly kingdom hereafter and be able to extol and magnify Your wondrous works of majesty. Amen.

157. *Prayer of a wife who has a bad husband*

O merciful God and Father, omniscient Lord, You know my misery better than I can relay and describe it to You. My spouse, whom You have joined to me, is, I regret to say, not as he ought to be, and I suffer from a heavy and almost daily domestic cross with him, so that I do not know what I will do in this miserable and troubled condition, where vile Satan makes my marriage very difficult by way of my ill-natured husband. We cannot leave each other since we have already been joined together, so that nothing but death can separate us. Now I turn to You, O Lord my God, without whose counsel and will and without whose permission nothing can be done. I must accept that You wish to chasten me with the evil behavior of my husband, as with a special cross which I have certainly deserved from You otherwise. Yet give me the patience for it, and with Your loving, fatherly hands help me to bear this burden. Neither let us live together always in such conflict, but govern the heart of my husband so that he may change and act as befits and becomes a devout Christian husband. Restrain the vile demon which attacks marriage and other wicked mouths by which my husband is often deceived, and in his heart plant true fear of God and an honest, upright love for me, that we may dwell with one another in peace and unity from now on, and our domestic life and livelihood may continue together so as to afford pleasure to both God and man. Bless us also from above with Your heavenly blessing, that we may as obedient children walk according to Your Commandments and always be the blessed of the Lord, both here in time and hereafter in eternity. Amen.

158. Prayer of a woman who has a gloomy and unfriendly husband

Lord God, heavenly Father, I know and am certain that this estate in which You have placed me is pleasing to You and that all that I do and endure in my estate and vocation is a sacrifice acceptable to You because of Your dear Son, my Redeemer and Savior, Jesus Christ, whom I honor, love, and confess. But You see in what misery and sorrow I am and that I am in such danger that no human help can deliver me out of it. I, a poor, troubled wife, am unfortunately in an unhappy marriage with my husband because of his stubborn, undutiful, wicked, and remiss behavior in the support of the family due to his drinking, gambling, violent anger, and slothfulness in his vocation, and it strikes me as unbearably difficult in this way of life to live and share a house for much longer with my spouse. I cannot find a moment of happiness, peace, or quiet with him and am concerned that my family will be entirely destroyed by it. Therefore I cry to You with a troubled heart in this time of need and implore You to intervene in a fatherly and gracious way and do what is necessary to amend this situation in due time and to grant my husband the grace and spirit to live with me in a reasonable, understanding, and Christian manner, to be kind, patient, and gentle with me at all times, to love me honestly, hold me dear, and not to be so contrary and stern with me, that the wicked, evil foe may not be given the opportunity to incite any more discord and strife between us, lest he hinder us in our prayers, and so in all happiness and welfare of body and soul. O Lord, teach us to do Your will, and let Your good Spirit lead us on level ground, that we may walk in true, unadulterated, and honest love, and especially that we may pursue the worthy goal of domestic peace, forgive one another, and defer to one another, that in goodly peace and worthy prosperity, as befits Christian spouses, we may live our lives to the full, until we lay aside our estate of marriage here and live with You forever in Your heavenly kingdom hereafter and extol and praise Your glorious wonders. Amen.

159. Prayer when one spouse has abandoned the other

Almighty God, I lay before You my great sorrow, for which I am unable to shed sufficient tears. My spouse has proven unfaithful to me and shamefully deserted me without any substantial cause. No one knows how to help or advise me but You, my faithful God. Therefore give me Your grace that I may recognize this heavy domestic cross as Your fatherly chastisement and in childlike humility submit to Your fatherly will. O Searcher and Governor of hearts! You see his (her) heart. If it can still be guided to correction, please govern and guide it and bind it again to my heart with true marital love and fidelity, that we may, as befits true wedded spouses, live together to Your honor. But if his (her) heart cannot be won back, come to my aid and provide for me, as You promised to poor widows (widowers) in Your Word, for the glory of Your most worthy name. Amen.

160. Prayer of a widower

Lord, almighty God, the Father of mercies and God of all comfort, whose hand both wounds and heals: with a troubled heart I lay before You my unspeakable grief and sorrow. You have taken away from me by temporal death the delight of my eyes, my faithful helper, the jewel of my house, whom my heart could trust in all things touching my temporal welfare. O Lord, behold my weeping, hear my groaning and lamentation, consider my affliction and my trouble, and forgive all my sins. Turn to me and be gracious to me, for I am lonely and afflicted. The troubles of my heart are enlarged; bring me out of my distresses. Heal me, O Lord; restore my soul. Let me not waste away in my grief. Cast me not off; forsake me not, O God of my salvation. I humbly beseech You, let Your Holy Word be my comfort, that I may not faint in my misery. Sustain what You have given to me and my family till now (have mercy on the poor and uninstructed orphans), defend my house and home, goods and reputation. Give me faithful servants. Turn away all dangerous diseases, thieves, robbers, calamity by fire and water, and every evil of body and soul. In You, O Lord, I put my trust; let me never be confounded. Be my comfort, my shelter, my strength, my help, my joy, that I may praise and bless You eternally for Your faithfulness.

161. *Prayer of a widow*

O faithful, helping, kind, and gracious God, who have called Yourself a Father of the fatherless and judge of widows—a Father of the fatherless, because they have no father on earth who so tenderly loves them as His own dear children, who so carefully and solicitously provides for them, as a physical father, who gives them what they need, as their father who raises them, comforts them, pities them in sickness and distress even as a father pities his children: You have offered to take up this kind and gracious fatherly office as Your own; therefore You will also exercise it toward me, my family, and all poor orphans with all fatherly care and faithfulness, and You will tenderly love, support, nourish, and bring up all poor orphans, comfort them, and pity them even as a sincere father does. And You have called Yourself a judge of widows because they must endure much suffering from the wicked world; have no protection or comfort; and, like needy, comfortless, and forsaken souls, must allow every tempest to pass over them. Therefore I humbly beseech You that, as You have said, "The Lord your maker is your husband, the God of the whole earth He is called," take me also as a comfortless and forsaken soul into Your almighty protection, and do not permit me to suffer violence and sorrow at the hand of the wicked world, but preserve and encompass me and my troubled heart with Your holy promise that You will not permit widows to be mistreated: "They will cry out to Me, and I will hear their cry, and your wives shall become widows and your children fatherless." Let Your Word be a strong wall around me and my poor fatherless children. Stir up godly hearts to remember that pure and unblemished religion is to visit widows and orphans in their affliction, that is to visit them with counsel, help, and comfort. Defend me, dear Father, from lying lips and false tongues. Give me Your grace that in my solitude I may put my hope only in You, find all my comfort in You, and cling to You with genuine faith and mighty assurance. Bless my jar of flour, and let it not be spent, even as You did for the widow of Zarephath who received the prophet Elijah. And let my jug of oil not run dry, as You did for that widow who, after the blessing of the prophet Elisha, filled all her vessels from her jug of oil and nourished her children by

God's Word and blessing alone. Grant me thus to see that You are my Father, Sustainer, Comfort, and Protection; through Jesus Christ, Your beloved Son, our Lord. Amen.

162. Prayer of a distraught widow

Merciful God, according to Your holy will You have severely afflicted me by making me a widow. I am now forsaken by the world, and a double-edged sword has, as it were, pierced my own soul. Alas, my sun has set at noon, and my glory and the joy of my heart has ceased! Surely, the crown has fallen from my head; my dancing has been turned to mourning and weeping. But because You, dear Lord, are called a judge of widows and do not despise the widow when she laments, and because even the tears that run down her cheeks cry out to You, I take refuge, O Lord, in You alone and beseech You heartily to lend me Your aid and let my trouble move Your heart. Turn to me and be gracious to me, for I am lonely and afflicted. The troubles of my heart are enlarged; bring me out of my distresses. Be to me a true helper and to my poor fatherless children a true Father. For there is no confiding in the help of men. Widows and orphans especially are made, as it were, a rug to be trod upon by others. Therefore I devote myself to You entirely. Receive me into Your fatherly keeping and let my light not be utterly quenched. Behold, here am I, dear heavenly Father, and the children which You have given me. Help, O Lord, protect, provide, bless me. I can give myself neither counsel nor aid. But I know in truth that if anyone serves God, he will be comforted after his tribulation and delivered from affliction, and after his chastisement he will find grace. For after the storm, You let the sun shine again, and after wailing and weeping, You shower us with joy. Grant me a morsel of bread, and show me faithful people to take up my cause with advice and action, just as You provided for the widow of Zarephath in time of great scarcity and sent to her the prophet Elijah. But above all, govern me by Your Holy Spirit, that in time of need I may place all my hope on You, the living God, and continue in prayer both day and night and, likewise, that I may cultivate a godly, chaste, self-controlled, moderate life and conversation, that I may not cause anyone offense by actions, words, or works, nor heaping sin upon myself, be found dead, although alive, but that I may act in such a way that no one will have cause to speak ill of me. Protect me from lying lips and false tongues. Be gracious to me, O Lord, be gracious to me, for I am lonely and afflicted. The troubles of my heart are enlarged. Have mercy upon me for the sake of Jesus Christ, Your beloved Son. Amen.

163. *Prayer of a midwife*

Lord, almighty God, wonderful Maker of man: I thank You for appointing me to be an instrument of Your divine power and strength and giving me the vocation of supporting mothers in the delivery of their infant children and of being of help and service to them in their birth. But I also pray that You would grant Your grace that the work of my vocation may always be performed with success and completed with joy. Dear God, let me not fail to do anything that is necessary for me in such cases, lest anyone be neglected and the life of mother and child be endangered. I pray that, as You form children in the mother's womb, and preserve them therein until the time of their birth, You would also apply Your own hand when those infants are born and brought into the light of day, that our work may be the more efficacious. Let me do all things with due deliberation and wisdom, that I may not cause difficulty with my words or actions. Let me not bring the mother to labor before the time comes, lest she be wearied unnecessarily and have no more strength at the proper time. Let my words to others not be harsh, but gentle, lenient, and kind, that no one may have difficulty because of me. Keep me from strong drink, lest by excess thereof I commit irresponsible mistakes. Let all secret witchcraft, superstition, and abuse of Your divine name be far from me. If there is too much difficulty, let me not grow impatient because of it, nor even abandon anyone, as the case may be, in order to visit others from whom more profit may be expected. Rather, let me serve rich and poor alike with equal attention, since it is the preservation of mother and child, and not my own profit, which is most important. And when the child is delivered, let me not omit anything that pertains to his (her) spiritual regeneration, nor willfully undertake emergency Baptism, so that Your ordinance is not disturbed. Dearest Lord and God! Let me be found Christlike, God-fearing, disciplined, full of holy faith, in prayer and true devotion in all that I do, that the work given to me may be the more prosperous and blessed. Amen, amen.

164. *Prayer of young people*

O Father of all grace and mercy, who are a holy God and desire that we also should lead holy lives without ungodly passion and desire of our sinful flesh: I lay before You my weakness and inborn sinful deficiency. I have the desire, but I do not find the fulfillment. Three great and powerful enemies rage against me—the lust of the flesh, the lust of the eyes, and the pride of life—desiring to seduce me from Your grace. Therefore I pray, O my Father, that You would create and preserve in me a clean heart. Grant that I may avoid every place and situation in which occasion for impurity is given, and that I may fear to make of the members of my body, as the members of my Savior, Christ Jesus, members of fornication. Rather let me always be burning with ardent devotion and heartfelt longing for heaven, that I may live as a temple of God the Holy Spirit and not cease loving Jesus Christ, my love, who was crucified and gave Himself into death for my sake. Let me love heavenly wisdom, that I may never end up on the byways of deception. O righteous and holy God! You search out the heart and reins. Grant that I may so cling to You in this world that I may not be parted from You in eternity either. Amen.

165. *Prayer of a young man*

O holy and chaste God, who take great pleasure in holy conduct and godliness, and therefore in chaste and self-controlled hearts, and desire that young men and women should be holy and chaste in body and spirit, for which reason also Your servant Paul writes, "Flee youthful passions and pursue righteousness, faith, love, and peace, along with those who call on the Lord from a pure heart," and "encourage younger men as brothers, and younger women as sisters, in all purity": that I may attain to this, I pray You from my inmost being that You would create in me a clean heart, that I may lead a chaste and self-controlled life in thoughts, words, and works, and serve You with a pure soul and unpolluted body, as long ago Joseph, being a chaste young man, served You in Egypt with a pure soul and unpolluted body when he refused to lie with the wife of his master.

Preserve me from indecent sights, and turn away from me all wicked desires. Let me not fall into debauchery and unchastity, but keep me from a shameless heart. Guard me against all recklessness in words and actions, from lazy speech, shameful words, folly, and jesting, which does not befit us as Christians; from idleness and laziness, as the cords and snares of the devil; from excess of eating and drinking, which lead to a disordered life; from adultery and all impure society, which commonly arises from idleness, as the devil's pillow, and from drunkenness, as the mother of all evils. Extinguish in me the flames of carnal desires, and put to death in my members adultery, impurity, shameful burning, and wicked passion, that I may not devote myself to the lust of the flesh, to carry on shame and vice with immoral people, nor make of the members of Christ members of fornication. Preserve me also from evil company and from those situations which give occasion and incitement to sin and shame. Whenever scoundrels tempt me, grant that I may not follow them.

Moreover, since a godly and reasonable spouse comes from You, O faithful God, it behooves us to seek one from You. If, then, it is Your holy will that I should someday enter the estate of marriage, grant me a godly, pious, and reasonable spouse with whom I may pass the time of my life in godliness and honor, peace, love, and unity, and grant that I may undertake the same estate in Your name and in Your fear, and with the counsel and consent of my parents and friends, not out of impudence and for lack of self-control, but because of Your ordinance and out of the desire for children, by which Your holy name may be forever worshiped and praised. But if it pleases You that I should remain unmarried, as Your servant Paul and others were unmarried, help me to follow the words of Paul, where he writes, "The unmarried man is anxious about the things of the Lord, how to please the Lord." In all these things, do what is pleasing to You and profitable to me, heavenly Father, who hold the hearts of all men in Your hand and direct them where You will, most blessed forever. Amen.

166. Prayer for a Christian household

O almighty, everlasting, and merciful God, because You have sufficiently shown with words and works that You provide for us as a faithful Father and have graciously adopted us as children and given to each his own vocation, in which he is to serve You and his neighbor, we beseech You heartily, dear Father, grant grace, that we may diligently attend to our vocation and always be found in obedience as Your faithful children. Further the works of our livelihood so that our hearts are not set on the goods of this world and we give no cause for offense to anyone. But let us use and enjoy with daily thanksgiving, in quietness, all the temporal goods and gifts that we have received by Your blessing. Turn away from us all idleness, excessive worry about nourishment, and all that displeases You, and further in us all that pleases You, that in all our doings we may pursue Your command, and in true faith cast all our cares and burdens on You. For You know all that we need and lack. May You graciously grant us the same. Amen.

167. Prayer of a housefather who is a farmer

Lord, almighty God, who give to each man whatever You deem fit: before the fall, You created Adam, the first man, as heir, master, and father of the world, and set him in the garden of Paradise, to tend and keep it, and after the fall compelled him to eat his bread by the sweat of his brow and the toil of his hands. By Your blessing I, too, have a house and livelihood, field and farm, and make my living by the toil of my hands. Dear Father, You have blessed us with all spiritual blessings and heavenly goods in Christ. If it is for Your glory and the salvation of my soul, bless my temporal goods also, that my living may increase and expand. Command a blessing to be on all that I do. Give me of the dew of heaven and of the fat of the earth, and let me see the streams and rivers of water flowing with honey and butter. The gods of the heathen can offer no goods, but You fill the earth with Your bounties and bless us in every place, that we may enjoy the good of the land. Your blessing makes rich without effort, and You give it to Your own while they sleep. Open Your storehouses to us, and give us true goods which abide and prosper forever. Let us order our house well, deal circumspectly and prudently, and so manage our affairs that we harm none and burden none. Let us not love wine and oil, live in feasting and idleness, esteem lightly our own livelihood, squander Your goods, and wickedly waste them, lest trouble and poverty take us unawares.

Dear Father, who are the true housefather in heaven and on earth, let me take Your Word and command to heart and manage my affairs accordingly, that I may impress Your Commandments upon my children and servants and all who belong to me and speak to them about them at home and in the field, when I lie down and rise up, that they, O Lord, may keep Your ways and do what is right and good, that all the good that You have spoken may come to them, that I may honor the Lord and do good to the poor and needy from my own income, that the blessing may remain in my house and last continually. Let me use the present good for life and not for sin, that by Your blessing and in Your fear, I may eat and drink and enjoy the fruits of my own labors, and another man not consume them. O rich God on Your throne! Give me neither poverty nor riches; feed me with the food that is needful for me, lest I be full and deny You and say, "Who is the Lord?" or lest I be poor and steal and profane the name of my God and my ruler. Dear Lord and Master, who govern all things with leniency and great clemency: let me preside well over my house, govern my children and servants in a Christian manner, and not mistreat my workers and day-laborers, lest the unpaid wages of laborers and farmhands, and of those who have harvested our land, cry to heaven against me and be counted as sin against me, but that I may give them their wages on the day, before the sun sets. Let me not take usury and interest from my neighbor and injure him, lest my blessing be turned into a curse and everything dissolve under my hands, that I may be content and pleased with what there is, whether I have little or much. And give me grace that I may act as a Christian father in all my doings and life and be faithful with Your goods, that I may stand on the day of accounting and as a good and faithful servant, be set over much, enter into the joy of my master, and obtain salvation for the sake of Christ. Then I will give You thanks here in time because You have satisfied me with Your goods and worship You forever hereafter with Your servants Abraham, Isaac, and Jacob in heaven. Amen.

168. Prayer of a merchant

O Lord, who are pleased with honest commerce and industry and have called me to the estate of a merchant: grant me, I beseech You, that I may keep myself diligently in Your fear and not grasp too far at the expense of my brother, but deal rightly with temporal goods in buying and selling. Keep me from doing intentional wrong or injury to my neighbor and from enlarging my goods with usury or interest and persisting in such, but let me do unto others as I would have them do unto me. Preserve me from vicious greed, that I may not love temporal things more than You, who are my highest Good, nor seek to enrich myself by inordinate means, lest I fall into temptations and snares and many foolish and harmful lusts, which bring men down to destruction and damnation. Grant that I may be content and rather make use of present goods than ponder others. Direct me, that I may lay up for myself treasures in heaven, and seek first Your kingdom and its righteousness, that I may be lacking no good thing; in Christ Jesus. Amen.

169. Prayer of an elderly person who has been abandoned

O Lord Jesus Christ, my only Savior, who do not scorn the sighing of the afflicted and do not despise the longing of the contrite heart: with great sorrow in my heart I lay before You my complaint that I have been abandoned by everyone in my old age, in this time when I am unable to do many things. I am so alone and miserable that I have even become estranged from my relatives and acquaintances. My friends have forgotten me and my neighbors have withdrawn from me. I humbly beseech You to look in grace upon my misery and not to forsake me in this loneliness as other friends have done, but to hold me firmly according to Your trustworthy promise. O Lord, if I have You only, I ask for nothing in heaven and earth. And though all the world forsake me, yet You are the only comfort of my heart, and my sure and faithful friend in life and death. *I trust, O Lord, Your holy name, leave me not evermore in shame. Amen.*

170. Prayer of an elderly person

Lord God, our dwelling place in all generations, our life and length of days, in whose hand our times are found: behold, I have reached such an age that I find little pleasure in it. Since my powers at this age are markedly decreased and difficulties and frailties have multiplied on every side, I humbly beseech You, according as You have so graciously and tenderly delivered me from the womb of my mother and have been my hope and trust from my youth, that You would not forsake me in my maturity either, when I have become gray and weak, but continue to uphold, carry, and deliver me until my life's blessed cessation. But especially I pray, O gracious Father, that You would govern and guide me by Your Holy and goodly Spirit, that with Christian conduct, prayer, and supplication, I may devote the rest of my life wholly to You and be enabled increasingly to prepare myself as a Christian for a blessed death so that, when the end of my life shall come, whether it be today or tomorrow, I may take my peaceful leave with old Simeon and depart this world for eternal life. Amen.

171. Prayer when choosing a vocation

O wise and faithful God, who have created all created things and appointed for them their number, measure, and weight, and above all have appointed particular estates, desiring that man should live in a certain vocation and walk in its ways and have promised to give him success and blessing, now that I have reached maturity and am considering what vocation I should undertake, that I may do honorable work therein, honestly support my own, and secure Your blessing with a good conscience, neither is it in anyone's power how he shall walk, but You must counsel him, therefore I beseech You with childlike trust to grant that I may first direct the thoughts of my heart toward You, before I undertake anything herein. Let me search Your will by prayer and take counsel with You, that I may accordingly choose what is right and what pleases You. Let me also hear the counsel of other good and judicious men and not despise it, indeed, not undertake anything beyond my own means. But especially, govern my mind, that in this endeavor I may look more to Your divine honor and my neighbor's advantage than to my own honor, imagined riches, and other idolatries, and acknowledge what is good or evil, worthy of praise or shameful.

Therefore, when I have made a decision about my future and have chosen a certain path in life with regard to vocation, grant it Your divine success, and govern me by Your Spirit, that all that I do may have a Christian beginning, a successful continuance, and a blessed ending; through Jesus Christ. Amen.

172. Prayer when a person begins a business

I give thanks to the Lord with my whole heart and recount all Your wondrous works. I rejoice and am glad in You and praise Your name, O Most High, that You not only have been with me since my youth and kept me in my ways, but have always given me bread to eat and clothes to wear, and in addition to this, have brought me to the point of carrying on my own business and attending to my temporal nourishment. O dear God! I am too small for all the faithfulness and all the mercies which You have shown to me, especially when I consider the sins of my youth and how I rejected Your Commandments and did not have them continually before my eyes as I ought. Oh, how great has Your steadfast love been toward me, that You have helped me thus far and not driven me from the land, nor caused me to wander the earth because of my sins, but rather have appointed me a place and position, where I may remain in the land and support myself honestly. Now, dear God, I begin this vocation and livelihood in Your name, and at Your word I will let down my net. Only bless me from heaven with Your blessing, and receive from henceforth the works of my hands. Send me help from Your sanctuary and strengthen me out of Zion. Support the work of my hands from henceforth; indeed, help me to do honest work with my own hands, that I may have something to share with anyone in need. And whereas the race is not to the swift, nor bread to the wise, nor riches to the intelligent, nor favor to those with knowledge, but time and chance happen to them all, show me Yourself the acceptable time and occasion, and grant me success and progress, that I may conduct my affairs properly, and all that I do may prosper. Let Your fear always be in my heart and before my eyes, that I may do no violence or injustice to anyone, and that no iniquity may be found in all my toil. O Father of lights, from whom every good and perfect gift comes down from above, grant me health, happiness, and life also in my vocation, that I may the more easily attain my goal and be able to accomplish what You have committed to me. And if there should ever be any displeasure in earning my living, let me not weary of it, but remember that it is Your will that I and all men should eat our bread in the sweat of our faces. Help me not to be earthly minded, nor to burden my heart with the cares of this life, but to seek first Your kingdom and Your righteousness, and what is above, where Christ is seated at the right hand of God, and I know that, as regards temporal things, they will be added to me according to Your generous mercy, and I will not lack any good thing. Save me, I pray, O Lord! O Lord, I pray, give me success! Amen.

173. Prayer when a person has something important to do

O Lord, who do great things beyond searching out and marvelous things beyond number, whose power is made perfect even in weakness: I call on You, O Most High! Let my doings prosper, and graciously help me accomplish the work that I have undertaken with complete trust in You. O Lord God, strengthen me in this hour, and do not forsake Your servant, who puts all his hope in You and without You can do nothing. Clothe me with power from on high, and give me the wisdom that sits by Your throne, that it may be with me and labor with me. All depends on Your divine blessing. Therefore remember me for my good, O my God, and bless all that I do, that I may begin all things wisely and finish them successfully. Say yes to each endeavor, / All to my good work ever; / Beginning, middle, ending, / Lord, to the good be bending (*WH* 304:9). For to You I commend my going out and my going in; to You I will also gratefully ascribe all the glory and progress of the task which I perform. Amen. In Jesus' name, Amen, Amen!

174. Prayer for the proper performance of one's duties

Merciful, faithful God! You have directed that each person should occupy an estate and faithfully attend thereto. You see and know, omniscient Lord, what I ought to do and how, without Your grace, power, and blessing, I can do nothing, and in how many ways I can go astray. Therefore I pray You from my heart that You would grant me understanding and strength and give me a bold and fearless courage, that I may act reasonably, confidently overcome all adversity that may arise, and by Your fatherly governance obtain a blessed end. O my God, in You I trust; let me not be put to shame; let not my enemies exult over me. Indeed, none who wait for You shall be put to shame. Make me to know Your ways, O Lord; teach me Your paths, for You are the God of my salvation. For You I wait all the day long. Oh, guard my soul and deliver me, and save me from all my troubles. Let me not be put to shame, for I take refuge in You. O Lord my God, be not far from me. O my God, make haste to help me, O Lord, my salvation. Amen, Amen, Amen.

175. *Prayer before going to work*

Eternal and merciful God! I will now return refreshed to my labors and the tasks of my regular calling in which You have placed me, Your servant. I will take them up with confidence and perform them according to Your provision, for the service of my neighbor and the earning of my bread. I heartily beseech You, therefore, to grant me, according to Your gracious promise, the sense, intelligence, understanding, success, health, and blessing for the labor and work to be performed, that in Your name and by Your fatherly assistance I may both begin it well and bring it to good conclusion, and in Your fear and a clean conscience, attend faithfully to my duty at all times. To You I commend my work. Promote my endeavors and prosper the things which I undertake in Your name, that light may ever shine on my ways to the glory and praise of You and to the welfare and good of my family, my neighbors, and myself; through Jesus Christ, Your beloved Son, our Lord. Amen. O Lord Jesus, in Your name and at Your word I will let down my net. Save me, I pray, O Lord! O Lord, I pray, give me success! Amen.

176. *Prayer for blessing in the work of one's vocation*

O Lord, who assign to each person a labor according to the measure given him and desire that we should eat our bread in the sweat of our faces, live from the toil of our own hands, and so prosper until we return at last to the dust: behold, at Your word I will let down the net of my vocation. Let my effort and labor not be in vain, but help me to do honest work with my own hands, that I may have something to share with anyone in need. Let there always be success and blessing, on which all depends, that I may accomplish my task and do wrong to no man, that I may honor the Lord out of my property and provide for those who belong to me, especially the members of my own household. Bless us ever increasingly, bless our basket and our surplus, for Your blessing makes the diligent hand rich without effort. O Lord, make my heart rejoice, make my face glad, give me health, life, and blessing. All this I ask, O Lord, according to Your will. Hear my prayer. I commit my way to You; I trust in You, knowing You will act. Blessed be the Lord daily. Amen.

177. *Prayer for the household*

Faithful God, heavenly Father, lover of order and God of peace, who have placed the sons of men on earth into certain estates, and so bound them one to another that they must always lend their hand to their neighbor and be of help to all men in troubles of body and soul: I thank You from my heart that You have caused Your Holy Word to be preached daily for the food of my soul and my eternal welfare and so preserved me by the protection of temporal authorities that I am able to lead a quiet and peaceable life in all godliness and honesty. And I beseech You, let Your grace continue to abound upon my house, that it may be built up more and more by Your blessing. It is in vain that I build the house if You, O Lord, do not build it. It is in vain that I labor, plant the seed, and water, if You, O Lord, do not give the increase. Indeed, it is in vain that I rise up early and go late to rest, eating the bread of anxious toil if You do not give to me while I sleep, as You give to Your beloved.

O Lord Jesus Christ! By Your saving knowledge salvation has indeed already come to my house. Therefore let it continue not to lack Your blessing or any other thing. All that I do I will do in Your name and thank God the Father through You. Your name is to me a strong tower; I run with the righteous into it and am safe. O precious Comforter, Holy Spirit! Let my house, as hitherto, continue to be Your workplace, that I and the members of my household, being led by You on the even way, may learn to do according to God's pleasure. In ourselves we are not capable of good, and of ourselves have neither the desire nor the fulfillment. Our sufficiency comes from God by Your grace. In this we confide and humbly pray that You would comfort us in all our labor and toil upon the earth, which the Lord has cursed because of our sin. Unite our hearts in Christian love, that we may not make this life more difficult by disunity, but may dwell together in peace and abundantly enjoy the blessing of God.

Especially, O God, govern those who serve in this house, that they may fear You and remember that they serve God and not men, and that each one, whatever good he shall do, is to receive it from You. Give them understanding and skill, that they may be enabled to prevent with wisdom whatever may harm the house and may wholesomely promote whatever is beneficial thereto. Govern their hearts, that they may fulfill their duty faithfully with us and do what You have committed to them, and our hearts will be continually directed to You. And as the eyes of servants look to the hand of their master, as the eyes of a maidservant to the hand of her mistress, so our eyes look to the Lord our God, till He has mercy upon us. Be merciful to us, O Lord! Be merciful to us and bless our household, all who dwell in our house, and all that belongs thereto, as You know that our temporal and eternal welfare require it, according to Your

fatherly goodness; through Jesus Christ, in the grace and power of the Holy
Spirit. Amen.

178. Luther's prayer on the verse, "Cast all your anxieties upon God, because He cares for you."

Heavenly Father, You are my Lord and God, who created me when I was nothing and redeemed me by Your Son. You have committed and assigned to me
this office and work, in which it is not as I will, and there is so much that would
oppress and afflict me that I find in myself no help or solution. Therefore take it
into Your own hands. Provide the help and solution, and be all things in these
matters. Amen.

179. Prayer of one whom God has blessed with earthly goods

O my most gracious and merciful God, Your holy name be praised because You
have abundantly furnished and provided me, an unworthy man and sinner,
with all excess of temporal goods. What have I deserved above others beside
me, who must pass their miserable lives anxiously in want and neediness? But
I find in Your Holy Word, not without movement of my heart, and read that
in my riches I am in great danger of losing my soul when Your dearest Son
Himself says that it is difficult for a rich man to enter the kingdom of heaven,
and that it is easier for a camel to pass through the eye of a needle than that
a rich man should enter the kingdom of God; therefore my heart is fearful at
this and wishes that I might be the poorest man on earth. However, it comforts
me that my Jesus also quickly adds that it is impossible for men, but with God
all things are possible. Therefore I beseech You, my God, with all my heart, in
deepest humility, for the sake of the most precious merit and blood of Jesus
Christ, to be gracious and merciful to me, and let it not be that You have given
me my wealth for my damnation, nor that I may perish eternally. I place it in
Your holy will, O my God, whether to permit to continue, and sustain, what I
by Your divine blessing have received and possess through inheritance, marriage, business, and the like; or, if it hinders and harms my salvation, to take it
all away and make me utterly poor, and in so doing to save me. For what would
it avail me if I won the whole world and forfeited my soul? Or what could I give
to redeem my soul? It is nothing at all if the whole world calls me blessed and
I am utterly content with my own condition! If Your almighty hand and great
goodness do not deliver me from Satan's net and preserve me from hell, I am

the most pitiable of men, and it were better that I never had a penny in the world, indeed, that I were never born. Therefore I beseech You of Your mercy, for the sake of my Lord Jesus Christ, who purchased me at so high a price, to assure my heart by Your Holy Spirit that my soul is eternally saved.

Let me appreciate Your salutary cross, that a spiritually poor, contrite, and humble heart may be found in me. Be my highest and only good, that I may heartily love You above all things, and out of love for You be charitable also to my poor neighbor, supply the needs of the saints, and be eager toward works of mercy. But if wealth is given to me, let my heart not cling to it, but to You, my God, and let me seek and find more joy and comfort in Your fear, worship, praise, and glory than in all temporal goods. Hear and vouchsafe this to me, O Father of mercies and God who are rich toward all for the sake of Jesus Christ, my Savior. Amen.

180. Prayer when beginning a journey

My God! If I live, I live to You, and if I die, I die to You. So then, whether I live or whether I die, I am Yours, and in Your name I have begun my journey. I rely on Your fatherly care, I trust in Your almighty power, and I leave to Your keeping all my going and staying, my journey home, and my return. Preserve my going out and my coming in, and let all things be done for Your glory and for my good. Be with me and go before me on the road that I travel. Command Your angels to accompany me on the way and to encamp around me everywhere I stay. Grant me knowledgeable guides to direct me, good drivers to transport me, faithful companions to journey with me, and friendly people in the inn to receive me and thus bring me in due time to my destination. Preserve my health also in the foreign air; bless me at all times with food and drink to the extent that I can find it. Guard the provisions which I take with me. Let me deal wisely at all times with those whom I meet and exercise caution with those whom I do not know. Yet help me always to find favor with men. Grant me needful lodging even outside my own country. Let all my transactions prosper. Grant that in every place I may learn from all that I see and hear in others, and finally, when it is time, help me to return home joyfully to my family. Amen.

181. Prayer during a journey

O Lord Jesus Christ, most merciful Lord and Savior, who for our sakes became a guest and stranger on the earth! I come to You with a humble heart, imploring You to accept my whole life and conversation in this world. Mercifully defend me by Your angel guard during every part of this journey, that I may be defended from all evil and misfortune, from all calamity and danger to soul and body, that I may prosper in all my endeavors and, alert and healthy, finally return home to my dear family. To You, O Lord, alone I commend my body and my soul, my property and possessions during my whole journey. Direct my path and conversation as is good and salutary for me. And while I am gone, faithfully watch over my dear family at home, that in good health we may happily meet again. And when I have completed the pilgrimage of my life here in this world, receive and accept me through a gentle and blessed death into Your glory, my heavenly fatherland. Amen.

182. Prayer when going to sea

Behold, eternal God, I now embark and commit myself to the wild and reckless sea, where, between heaven and earth, I shall move upon the waters in this small and frail vessel and ship which cannot protect or save itself, much less me. In what, then, shall I, a poor man, confide? Ah, in You alone and in Your fatherly strength and provision, O God and Lord! For neither man nor any created thing can deliver me. The wind blows where it will; the sea lifts up her waves. Below me I see no solid ground, above me only naked sky, beside me men in similar danger and apprehension. Therefore, O God, I lift up my eyes only to You, from whence comes my help. My help comes from the Lord, who made heaven and earth! I commend myself to You as Your own possession in body and soul, life and belongings! I look to You alone, I trust in You, my hope is in You; the help of men is nothing! Carry this vessel on Your wings, preserve me in it, and be with me, O Lord, or else we pass away; yet if I have You only, I ask for nothing in heaven and earth! Yea, as I now depart this soil and leave dry land behind me, help me to forsake and renounce all confidence in earthly and human help and to rely on You alone. Behold, O Lord, I leave myself wholly to Your will; do with me as You please and as You know will most benefit the salvation of my soul. I entrust myself to Your hands, for You have engraved me on the palms of Your hands, and no man will pluck me out of Your hands, since I am the sheep of Christ and of His pasture, in which, by the help of the Holy Spirit, I will gladly live and die. Amen.

183. Prayer of a passenger at sea during a storm

Almighty God, the God of the just! You made the sea and dry land and have all things in Your hand. You raise the stormy wind, which lifts up the waves of the sea. In our ship we mount up to heaven; we go down to the depths. We reel and stagger like drunken men and are at our wits' end, as the Holy Spirit says. We, too, are in such great trouble and distress as we journey in this ship. Therefore, since You have said, "Call upon Me in the time of trouble, and I will deliver you," we come to You in our great trouble, from which no created thing can deliver us, but only You, and with a heart believing in Your words, we humbly beseech You to show Your power according to Your great mercy. Rebuke the wind and sea that they may be calm, graciously preserve us from shipwreck and injury, support and protect us with Your hand of grace, and graciously deliver us from this danger. So shall we praise Your name as long as we live, be ever mindful of Your benefits, and amend our lives in conformity to Your Holy Word from henceforth. O Lord, be merciful to us, and forgive us our sins for the sake of Jesus Christ. Oh, save us, or we will perish! O Lord, deliver us for Your mercy's sake! But if it should be Your will to end our lives here, grant us Christian patience, keep us in the true faith, and give us the end of faith, which is the soul's salvation. O Lord, be with us! Do not forsake us! You can deliver from death; You can also deliver from this danger! Hear us, hear us, hear us, Lord God the Father, for the sake of Jesus Christ! Lord Jesus, for Your five holy wounds! Lord God, the Holy Spirit, for Your grace and mercy! Help us, Lord God the Father! Help us, Lord God the Son! Help us, Lord God the Holy Spirit, for Your sake, for the honor of Your name, and because of Your boundless mercy. Amen.

184. *Prayer in great peril by water*

O Lord, You promised me, "When you pass through the waters, I will be with you; and the rivers will not overwhelm you." And since You are the almighty Lord, You can certainly keep Your promise; help me in this extreme danger, and bring me to shore alive, for You are the Lord my God, the Holy One of Israel, my Savior. And even if it is Your will that I drown here, yet I know that You could pull me out as You pulled Your servant Moses from the reeds. And even if You do not do so here in time, yet You will bring me with You to heavenly life in eternity. Save us, O Lord, save us, for we are perishing! I have come into deep waters, and the flood sweeps over me. But if You save me, I shall be saved. Therefore I commend myself, body, soul, life, blood, and belongings into Your hands. I live to You, I die to You; whether I live or whether I die, I am Yours;

for You are mine and I am Yours, and where You are, there will I also be; where I abide, You will not forsake me. For You are Immanuel, God with us. Amen.

B. THE CLERICAL ESTATE

185. *Prayer of a preacher*

O faithful God, merciful Father, who have called me, a poor, unworthy servant, to the holy preaching office and appointed me a fisher of men, to catch many souls for the kingdom of heaven, and by regular means set me apart to declare the Gospel to my parishioners: I beseech You by Your grace to make me, an incapable man, capable to bear the office of the New Testament, that I may preside well over my office as a faithful servant and steward of Your divine mysteries, not under compulsion but willingly, not for filthy lucre but of a ready mind, for the love of Your holy name, and that I may faithfully feed the sheep entrusted to my care with wholesome doctrines, attend to the weak, heal the sick, bind up the wounded, restore those who have gone astray, seek out the lost, and with a meek spirit bring again into the way those who have fallen into error. Send me Your Holy Spirit, that He may give me the mouth and wisdom to speak and to divide Your Word rightly. Let me not be a worthless instrument of Your grace, but work through me powerfully and prosper me abundantly. Dear God, You set me as a watchman over Your people! Help me to warn the ungodly and to teach transgressors Your ways, that I may turn sinners unto You, and that many of them may be drawn to Your kingdom. Grant also that I may live conformably to Your Word and be an example to the flock, lest after preaching to others I myself should be disqualified; also, that I may not by unchristian conduct give the enemy reason to blaspheme Your name, nor cause any other offense. Give Your Holy Spirit to me and all my listeners, that we may know You, the only true God, and Jesus Christ, whom You have sent; increase in true and genuine faith, fear, and love; and in firm hope with a repentant heart continue steadfast until our end, and so receive together the imperishable crown of glory at the appearing of the Arch-Shepherd, Jesus Christ, our Savior; who lives and reigns with You and the Holy Spirit, one God, forever and ever. Amen.

186. Another

Dear God, gracious Father, You have called me to be a preacher of Your saving Word, and You know that I have no power to handle Your mysteries worthily except by Your divine help and assistance. Therefore I heartily beseech You to give me Your Holy Spirit, that He may lead, guide, and direct me, that in this my vocation I may not think, speak, act, or undertake anything other than what attains to the honor and glory of You, O Lord, and to the benefit and comfort of those Christians committed to my care.

Defend me, gracious God, from the father of lies, who is the sworn enemy of the holy preaching office, that I may teach nothing other than Your Word, which alone is truth, and which brings with it life. Let me so live that Christians are not offended by my life, but edified by it, and that it gives no reason for Your holy and gracious Word to be blasphemed by unbelievers.

But especially I beseech You, my Lord and my God, to remember this day Your gracious, fatherly, and comforting promise which You made through Your servant Isaiah, that Your holy Word which goes out from Your mouth shall not return empty, but accomplish what You please, and succeed in the thing for which You send it; and mercifully to fulfill and realize that promise to me, Your servant, as well as to those who shall hear it, that my preaching may attain to the praise and thanksgiving of You, O Lord God, and to the improvement of my and all my listeners' lives, the comfort of our weak consciences, the strengthening of our faith, and finally, the salvation and blessedness of all our souls; through Jesus Christ, Your beloved Son, our Lord. Amen.

187. Yet another

Lord God, You have appointed me as a bishop and parson in the church. You see how unequipped I am to fulfill rightly so great and heavy an office, and if it were not for Your counsel, I would long since have ruined it all. Therefore I call upon You. I eagerly desire to lend and apply my mouth and heart to the purpose; I want to teach the people; I want to be always learning Your Word myself and studying it and meditating on it diligently. Use me as Your instrument; only do not forsake me, dear Lord. For if I am left to myself, I will easily ruin it all. Amen.

188. Yet another

Lord God, I have begun to preach and to instruct the people, but there is no progress; impediments arise on every side. Yet no matter. Since You have commanded me to preach Your Word, I will not stop. If it fails, it fails for You; if it succeeds, it succeeds for me and for You. Here is Your command; on this basis I will go forth and cast my net and let You worry about the results. Amen.

189. Prayer of a preacher for fruitful study of Holy Scripture

O dear God, if it pleases You to accomplish something through me for Your glory and not for my or any man's boast, grant me out of pure grace and mercy a right understanding of Your Word. Amen.

190. Another

Grant Your grace, dear Lord God, that I may rightly understand Your Word and, far more, that I may do it. Yet, beloved Lord Jesus Christ, if my studying does not attain to the glory of You alone, let me rather fail to understand the least word. Give me only so much as will benefit me, a poor sinner, for Your glory. Amen.

191. Assurance and comfort of a diligent preacher in his studies

Dear Lord and God, I go to sleep in Your name, knowing that even my slumber is well-pleasing to You, but when I wake and do my customary work in my vocation—writing, reading, meditating or contemplating, and praying—I do not doubt that this work also is acceptable to You. Yet if I knew that it displeased You, I would far rather refrain from it. But of this I am certain, that I am well-pleasing to You in all my doings, not because of myself who do these things, but because of You who have mercy on me, forgive me my sin, love me, lead me, and govern me by the Holy Spirit. Amen.

192. Prayer of a preacher before the sermon

Eternal God, heavenly Father, I, a poor, miserable servant of Your Gospel, confess that of myself, I am too little and ill-equipped for this high and holy ministry of preaching, and that without the help and assistance of Your Son's Spirit, I could bring forth no lasting fruit. Wherefore I heartily call on You, in the name and at the word of Your eternal Son and Spokesman, our only High Priest and Bishop, that You would let Your Spirit of grace speak through me this day and open my lips and fill my mouth, that my tongue may seek Your glory and the good of this church; and that I may discern, distinguish, and present Your precious Word to my parishioners with wise and judicious teaching; and that my sheep may be enabled to learn and keep its teachings, comforts, and admonitions; that Your praise may be sung in all the world, Satan's murder and lying destroyed by the mouths of nursing infants and simple men; faith, love, comfort, life, patience, self-control, deference, and obedience be planted in the hearts of my designated flock by Your Spirit, and I, after preaching to others, not be myself disqualified; for You alone through Your Son give good gifts and power to Your Gospel, most blessed forever.

Our Father who art in heaven, hallowed be Thy name, Thy kingdom come, Thy will be done on earth as it is in heaven. Give us this day our daily bread; and forgive us our trespasses as we forgive those who trespass against us; and lead us not into temptation, but deliver us from evil. For Thine is the kingdom and the power and the glory forever and ever. Amen.

193. Another

O eternal God, heavenly Father, I, a poor servant of Your Holy Gospel, confess that, on my own, I am too little and ill-equipped for this high ministry, and without the help and assistance of Your Holy Spirit, I cannot begin or complete any good. Therefore I heartily call upon You, beseeching that You would let the Spirit of grace speak now through me, a poor, feeble instrument, and open my lips and fill my mouth, that my tongue may seek Your glory and the good of this church; through Jesus Christ, Thy Son, our Lord. Amen.

194. Yet another

O my Lord Jesus Christ, God, our Brother, God and Man, Immanuel, our Savior, who said, "Without Me you can do nothing": in Your name and at Your command, I now ascend the pulpit, beseeching You for the sake of my sermon to give me Your Holy Spirit, whom You received without measure from Your Father. Open my lips, that my mouth may declare Your praise. Strengthen my memory, understanding, speech, and feeble bodily powers, that Your Holy Word may be set forth in a pure, plain, and profitable manner; Satan's murders and lying destroyed; the saving faith implanted in the hearts of my hearers; and eternal salvation nurtured in us all. Amen.

195. Yet another

Veni Sancte Spiritus! Veni dator munerum! Dona mihi os et sapientiam, ad annunciandum laudem tuam; effice, ne quod verbum mihi imprudenter excidat, quo possit aut nominis tui gloria, aut conscientia mea laedi; sed, ut cum fructu doceam. Da successum, accende corda auditorum, ut attente et magna cum reverentia verbum tuum audiant, atque inde emendentur. Amen.

Cor, mentem, linguam, Tu rege, Christe! meam.*

196. Prayer of a preacher after the sermon

O very Son of God and eternal Spokesman: at Your command, I, a poor servant, have sown Your Word and dealt to my dear parishioners what You apportioned and gave to me. Now, therefore, I beseech You, my dear Lord Jesus, to give strength to Your thunder and Your Word and confirm in my flock what You have worked in them through me, and through Your Spirit speak prosperity on what I have planted and watered, that we may together bring forth many enduring fruits, and Your Word may increase and abound in them. Seal, O Lord, Your Word in their hearts, that Your name may be hallowed, and I with my little talent may win many souls for You, whom I may bring with me before Your face when You distribute imperishable crowns to faithful teachers and diligent hearers. For we confess that without Your Spirit and blessing, all our toil and efforts are in vain. Open their hearts, therefore, and preserve Your Word in them, that no anguish, distress, or devil may pluck it from them. For You are mighty and active in Your ministry of preaching, and by the proclaimed Word You gather to Yourself an eternal Church from all nations, who praise and glorify You with Your Father and the Holy Spirit, here and in all eternity. Amen, dear Lord Jesus! Amen.

197. Another

Eternal God, gracious Father, I heartily thank You that You have filled my mouth and graciously given me the ability to proclaim Your Word, and I pray You for the sake of Your dear Son that You would cause Your Word to take root, increase, and multiply by Your Spirit in the hearts of my dear parishioners and speak Your prosperity upon them, that it may bring forth much fruit in them.

* Although this prayer, of the genre of ministers' Latin pulpit prayers and titled in at least one German prayerbook "Prayer of a preacher when he ascends the pulpit," was left in Latin in the *Gebetsschatz*, as were several "Veni Sancte Spiritus . . ." prayers in earlier Lutheran prayerbooks, which were otherwise in the vernacular—nevertheless, for the sake of those not versed in Latin, I include the following English rendering: "Come, Holy Spirit! Come, Giver of gifts! Grant me the mouth and wisdom to speak Your praise. Let not my word go forth unwisely, lest it thereby do injury either to the glory of Your name or to my own conscience, but that I may teach fruitfully. Prosper Your Word, and kindle the hearts of my hearers that they may hear it attentively and with great reverence, and be amended thereby. Amen. — My heart and mind and tongue, Christ, to Your rule belong." —MC

Build a hedge around their hearts, that the wicked foe may not suffocate that Word with the cares of this world, nor pluck it clean out of their hearts, that teachers and hearers may keep the faith and a good conscience and continue in Your truth until the end. So may we appear as one before Your face and receive the imperishable crown which You have graciously prepared for all Your faithful servants and disciples for the sake of Your Son's blood. For You by Your Gospel are gathering for Yourself an eternal Church out of the human race and this congregation, and with Your Son's Spirit are mighty in the preached and believed-on Word, most blessed by all godly preachers forever and ever! Amen.

198. Prayer of a preacher before the rite of Confession & Absolution

O almighty, everlasting God, I must now perform that great and lofty work which seems marvelous to reason and without doubt even to angels: namely, forgiving sins in Your stead. You know how entirely unworthy and ill-equipped for that purpose I confess myself to be, since I myself am a poor sinner, and it is so greatly abused. But You have faithfully commanded us not to give what is holy to the dogs nor to cast such precious pearls before the swine. And although You have bestowed on me Your Holy Spirit for the performance of my office, I regret to say that I have often grieved Him with my manifold sins. Yet since You will require from my hands the blood of any who have been led astray through me, I am all the more sincerely and deeply sorry that I have ever offended You. Furthermore, since You do not want us to forsake our office, I beseech You from the depths of my heart, for the sake of Jesus Christ, Your dearest Son, that You would pardon, forget, and forgive all my iniquities, errors, and trespasses, and not take Your Holy Spirit from me, but would rather grace, enlighten, sanctify, direct, and guide me by Him, that I, who cannot see into people's hearts, may comfort and strengthen terrified hearts but terrify the unrepentant, that by the power and operation of Your Holy Spirit, they may heartily rejoice in both Your grace and Your mercy, abuse it all the less, and with heart, mouth, and deed, turn increasingly to You with ever greater desire, giving thanks to You for the praise and honor of Your most holy name, for their own welfare and the salvation of their souls, and for the preservation of my conscience, and as a correction and good example for others; through Your beloved Son, Jesus Christ, our Lord. Amen.

199. *Prayer of a preacher when he has something difficult to do*

Merciful God, You see what a difficult task lies before me, and You know that I am far too weak and insufficient to accomplish it without disgrace and harm. Wherefore I humbly beseech You to grant me Your gracious assistance in it. O Lord, do not forsake me, for I put all my hope and trust in You, but strengthen me with heavenly power, and equip me with holy wisdom, that I may not grow timid nor act unreasonably, but may fruitfully complete the work given to me. For to You I commend my going out and my coming in, and to You will I gratefully ascribe all the glory and advancement of my endeavors. Amen, in Jesus' name, Amen, Amen.

200. *Prayer of a preacher before visiting a sick person*

Almighty, everlasting God, the Father of our Lord Jesus Christ and source of all true comfort: behold, I, a poor servant, now go, as called by my vocation, to comfort a sick, afflicted, and perhaps even dying person. Since this does not depend on human but on divine help, grant me Your Holy Spirit, that He may put Your words in my mouth and so govern my tongue and lips that my speech may flow and be sweet like honey, and quicken and strengthen the invalid in faith, hope, and patience, or else gently help him (her) to have a swift and happy death; for the sake of Your only-begotten Son, our Lord and Savior Jesus Christ. Amen.

201. *Prayer of a minister during an epidemic*

Lord, almighty God, it is an evil and dangerous time, and the epidemic increases daily because of our sins. But because he is cursed who does his work with slackness (Jer. 48:10), and it behooves me, by virtue of my office as a shepherd, to stand with my sheep, I beseech You to be merciful to me, a poor sinner. Keep me as the apple of Your eye; hide me under the shadow of Your wings. O Lord, my breath is in Your hand, and all my ways are Yours; and You send out the angels as ministering spirits for the service of those who shall inherit salvation, as You preserved Daniel in the midst of the lions; Jonah in the belly of the fish; Aaron, David, and Isaiah in terrible pestilence between the dead and the living. O Lord, be with me also in my distress; give Your angels charge over me to keep me in all my ways, that no evil may befall me nor any plague come nigh my dwelling. Give me courage and the Spirit of wisdom and strength, so that I shall not be afraid for the terror by night, nor for the pestilence that stalks in the darkness, nor for the sickness that wastes at noonday. And help me, as a faithful servant, to make ready use of prayer, the weapon of my office, and so to fight for my flock, and to do without fear all else that is committed to me for my office, and to have my life as a prize of war. O Lord, You are my strength and my fortress, my refuge in the day of trouble. You are with me to help me and deliver me; though a thousand fall at my side and ten thousand at my right hand, it shall not come nigh me. In this safe conduct which You have promised me I trust wholeheartedly; for Your truth is a shield and buckler. But if You have other plans for me, and it is now my turn to put off my tabernacle—for in any case, my end is known, and there is a measure to my days and I must depart; for to You my days are a handbreadth, and my life is as nothing before You—then, O Lord, Your will be done. Only help me to abide in the faith sincerely and without offense, to receive the end of faith, the salvation of my soul. Finally, O defender of widows and Father to the fatherless, receive my flock into Your care, for the sake of Jesus Christ. Amen.

202. *Thanksgiving of a preacher after completing the work of his office*
Dear Lord Jesus Christ, who have justified and saved us and given me the strength and power to explain Holy Scripture, and my hearers to hear it: Sustain and strengthen me and my hearers in this doctrine, and grant grace that we may continually grow and increase in the knowledge of Your grace and unalloyed faith, and defend us from sects and false teaching, that we may be found blameless and without reproach in the blessed day of our redemption. To You, with the Father and the Holy Spirit, be praise and thanksgiving forever. Amen.

203. *Another*
Merciful, gracious God, who are the beginning and ending, through whom all things were created and are still preserved: I thank You that You have let me finish this work which I began in Your name. Grant me also the grace that this work may be profitable and fruitful. If there is any deficiency in it, it is mine; for what is good in it comes only from You. Mercifully forgive me my failings, and rectify them with Your full perfection, until You shall cause me also to attain to perfection in heaven. Amen, for the sake of Christ Jesus, Amen, Amen.

204. *Prayer of a teacher*
Merciful, gracious God and Father, I heartily thank You that according to Your gracious will and pleasure, You have placed me in this office, in which I am to

feed Your lambs, the children purchased with Your dear Son's precious blood, and to lead them to every good thing. I humbly beseech You to govern my heart with Your Holy Spirit, that at all times I may so conduct all my endeavors, desires, knowledge, and abilities with due diligence that all those under my care may daily increase in wisdom and stature and in favor with God and man and may grow in true godliness, piety, and ability, like beautiful trees planted by the rivers of Your Holy Word, to the glory and honor of Your name and to their eternal salvation. O my God and Father, grant all these children Your Holy Spirit. Give them an obedient heart and with it continual health, wisdom, understanding, and good power of memory, that God and man may be heartily pleased by them, and that they may study well, advance worthily, behave rightly as befits a Christian, and in time be well employed in useful tasks and positions. Oh, let none of them perish, and let me live to see no shame or dishonor in any of them, but further honor and joy in each and every one according to Your fatherly will and pleasure, to Your glory and to their eternal salvation, that I may joyfully present them to You on the Last Day, and say, "Here am I, and the children which You gave me!" God the Father grant it to me through Jesus Christ in the power of the Holy Spirit. Amen.

205. Another

O invisible and only wise God! I have been charged with the office of imparting sure teaching and clearly instructing the inexperienced, who apply to me and come to school to learn what they do not know. Indeed, You Yourself have set me apart and appointed me to build and plant, and to instruct the young in Your fear. Now I am myself weak and insufficient in knowledge, but Yours is both wisdom and strength. You give to the wise their wisdom and to the knowledgeable their knowledge. Therefore I come before You, pleading with my whole heart: O Lord, help me to do my work with wisdom, reason, and skill; to feed Your flock and to watch it well, yet not for shameful gain, but with sincerity of heart; and above all to show young people how they should conduct themselves from their youth up according to Your Word, fearing You and fleeing from sin, seeing that the fear of the Lord is the beginning of wisdom, that You chiefly, O Lord our ruler, may be glorified through Jesus Christ. And help me as a good steward of Your manifold gifts to serve others with the gift which I have received. At the same time, grant me that as I prescribe, advise, and teach young people many things, they may submit their neck to the yoke of wisdom and be willingly led forward. Grant to them, O Father of glory, the Spirit of wisdom and revelation for the knowledge of Yourself. Give them skill and understanding in all manner of writing and wisdom, that they may learn and study to the astonishment of many. Enlighten their souls by wisdom, that they may remember that the thoughts and imaginations of their hearts are wicked from their youth up, lest they think themselves wise, but that they fear You and shun evil; that they willingly submit to correction, and by it attain knowledge; that they give thanks to You continually and pray You to govern them. In all that they do, let them follow Your Word, that here and hereafter they may be our hope and the crown of our glory, indeed, our honor and joy, the adornment of their parents and delight of their friends, and that by wisdom they themselves may finally obtain salvation. But if in the meantime, if even as I increase knowledge in them I must suffer much sorrow, and find only ingratitude for my good works, grant that I may nevertheless work with quietness and not weary of well-doing, that I may carry out my office honestly, and that I may be patient toward all people, looking not at the things which are seen but at the things which are not seen, remembering that my reward shall be great in heaven. Amen. Blessing and glory and wisdom and thanksgiving and honor and power and might be to our God forever and ever! Amen.

206. *Prayer of a student*

Lord God, heavenly Father, assist me with Your Holy Spirit, and bless my labor, studies, and undertakings, that I may daily increase in godliness, piety, and ability, indeed, in wisdom and stature and in favor with God and man. Not unto us, O Lord, not unto us, but to Your name give glory, through Jesus Christ. Amen.

207. *Prayer of a college student*

Lord, gracious God, merciful Father, it pleases Your divine, most wise, and holy will to prepare for Yourself praise and a power of Your glory from the mouths of young men and children, and by godly rulers and people in churches and schools to sustain and nourish them, among whom I also find myself by Your favor, dearest God, and so I cry to You from a believing heart: O Lord, give me Your Holy Spirit, and fill my heart with the brightness of Your grace, that I may serve You with an eager and devout heart and mouth, and use all the benefits which I receive to the glory of Your holy name, the building up of Your Christian Church, and the temporal and eternal salvation of my soul. Enlighten my understanding, merciful Father, and by Your light and power invigorate all my faculties of body and mind for the glorious advancement of Your praise and the edification of Your Christian Church, that I may diligently and eagerly cultivate godliness and the proper habit of attending church and school, and other Christian virtues; and that I may by constant diligence and daily practice, with all my ability, search out and seek to know wisdom, Yourself, and Your works, and to sing praises to Your holy name, and grow each day and hour in the wholesome knowledge and profitable use of Your Holy Word and musical arts, and with zeal and careful attention overcome the frailty of my youth. O loving Father, graciously receive into Your care my youth, my studies, and all that I do, and come to my aid in all things with Your grace and Holy Spirit, that I may offer up to You the time of my youth through genuine righteousness and holiness and continue in wisdom and knowledge of all holy things until the desired end; and by the generous hands of Christian and benevolent men, obtain further alleviation of my poverty. Oh, keep my soul, dearest God, from all manner of sin and vice, by which the glory of Your holy name is infringed upon and my welfare is injured, and sustain me in the fear and true knowledge of You, indeed, in godly and worthy exercise of all duties and obligations, that until my end I may have You as a gracious God and loving Father, and afterward be exalted by my most beloved Redeemer, Jesus Christ, to eternal and unspeakable joy. Grant this all to me by grace, dearest God, for Your glory and my good! Amen.

208. *Prayer of a student who is tempted to quit school because of poverty*

Lord Jesus Christ, into whose hand the heavenly Father has given all things, without whom we can think or do nothing: You know, my Savior, that I have begun my studies in Your name not for worldly pleasure, honor, riches, or other worthless things, but only for Your glory, that Your name may be hallowed among us and the good of our neighbor advanced. But since You know well our human frailty, especially how my severe poverty threatens to hinder and deter me from my good intentions, therefore I beseech You to visit me with Your perfect and plentiful grace and to continue to direct my understanding, strength, and abilities which You have given me in the work which I have undertaken, that I may complete it happily and with success. Give me perseverance, means, and good counsel, that the needy may see it and rejoice that You have dealt well with Your servant, that they also may be strengthened in their endeavors. Indeed, be my strength and consolation, the beginning and the end, that having received Your gracious help, I may praise and glorify You for all eternity. Amen.

209. *Prayer of a student of theology*

My God, up till now I have studied wisdom, knowledge, arts, and languages. Give me grace further to pursue my intentions earnestly and zealously and to make good use of my time. Let me consider well what an account I will have to give for wasting the flower of my youth in idleness, drunkenness, gluttony, indecent dancing, gambling, and other sinful foolishness, and squandering my parents' sweat and blood and dashing the hopes of my fatherland. At the same time, let me also remember that it is not enough to use my natural gifts well, practice and master all fields of study, and know all that the world can teach me, if in doing so I still lack the chief thing, which is heavenly wisdom, the saving knowledge of Jesus Christ, the art of faith, the law of love, the practice of godliness, and the knowledge of dying a blessed death. With worldly studies I may endear myself to the world, but without these spiritual arts, I cannot please You, my God. And what would I gain if in pleasing the world I were yet detestable in Your sight?

Therefore I humbly beseech You in the name of Jesus Christ to enlighten my heart with Your heavenly light of grace, to hallow and sanctify my diligence and labor, and, according to Your pleasure, to prepare me for Your holy ministry. Grant that I may cultivate a good conscience in all respects, both toward You, O God, and toward other men, that I may walk in Your godly fear; call frequently to mind my baptismal covenant; live in humility, meekness, chastity, and moderation; and keep myself unstained from the present ungodliness of the world. I am one of the Nazarites of Your Church, a dedicated servant of God separated for Your holy service. I am a young tree from which many simple souls hope someday to have many fruits of doctrine, comfort, and edification. Therefore, my God, give me a renewed, enlightened, godly heart, that I may cultivate a holy way of life. O God, my Father and Lord of all loving kindness, give me that wisdom which constantly surrounds Your throne, for I am a feeble man, and of a short time, and fall short of the understanding of judgment and laws; for if one be perfect among the children of men, yet if Your wisdom be not with him, he shall be nothing regarded. Send her out of Your holy heavens and from the throne of Your glory; send her, that she may be with me and may labor with me, that I may know what is pleasing to You. And if it be Your divine will, my Father, some day to place me in a certain post, or if You will even grant that I may serve You in Your Church (my mind and thoughts being so directed by the inward urging of Your Holy Spirit), then make me perfectly equipped for that purpose. I know, O almighty God, that in Your most wise counsel You have already set the time, place, and occasion. Far be it from me, then, that I should dictate and prescribe these for You, let alone acquire them by the means which this present world adores and which are used by those whom You Yourself have called "runners" (Jer. 23:21), but which are not in accord with Your Holy Word, but contrary thereto, and for that reason not compare myself to the world nor imitate their thinking. Send me where You wish, only grant that it may serve for the glory of Your most holy name and the salvation of all who hear me. Let me then be full of power and spirit, full of right and might, full of living knowledge, full of faith, full of love, full of godly zeal, full of heavenly wisdom, full of piety, humility, meekness, chastity, moderation, and other virtues, that I may become and be a new creature in Christ, a truly enlightened, converted, and holy man, an example for the faithful in word and conduct, charity and patience, that I may hold the mystery of the faith in a pure conscience, and so in all things adorn the doctrine of God our Savior. Amen.

210. Prayer of a student of theology before beginning his studies

Assist me, my God, Father of light, from whom every good and perfect gift comes down to us, and govern me with Your Holy Spirit, that I may read, ponder, and perform whatever is true, whatever is right, whatever accords with Your divine Word, whatever edifies the Christian Church and is profitable and salutary to myself, to the praise and glory of Your most holy name; through Jesus Christ. Amen.

211. Prayer of a student of theology after completing his studies

Glory be to God on high for the grace and assistance of the Holy Spirit, which even at this time He has so richly bestowed on me! Continue to do so, O God, dear Father, since without the light of the Holy Spirit, nothing good is done in men; and confirm the good which You have begun in me. Enlighten my understanding, strengthen my memory, govern my will and actions, that I may obey You and glorify You, and rightly understand all that I read, and carefully keep all that I understand, and use for benefit all that I keep. Make me a wholesome vessel of Your grace to the praise and glory of Your name and the increase of Your Church; through Jesus Christ. Amen.

C. THE POLITICAL ESTATE

212. *Prayer of a person in governmental authority*

O God, my Father and Lord of all things, who have made all things with Your Word and have ordained the wise man, that he should have dominion over the creature that was made by You, that he should order the world with holiness and righteousness and execute judgment with an upright heart: You have chosen me, among others, to be a ruler of Your people and a judge of Your sons and daughters; but I am a feeble man, and of a short time, and fall short of the understanding of judgment and laws, and know neither my going in nor my going out. Indeed, if one be perfect among the children of men, yet if Your wisdom be not with him, he shall be nothing regarded. Therefore I come before Your face, heartily beseeching You and calling on You with my prayer, for You alone give wisdom, and from Your mouth come knowledge and understanding. You are great in counsel and mighty in deed. Now therefore, let the Spirit of the Lord rest upon me, the Spirit of wisdom and understanding, the Spirit of counsel and might, the Spirit of knowledge and the fear of the Lord. Give Your servant an obedient heart to govern Your people, that I may discern between good and evil.

Give me wisdom and knowledge, that I may go in and out before this people and preside over them as fitting. Send wisdom out of Your holy heavens and from the throne of Your glory; send her, that she may be with me and may labor with me, that I may know what is pleasing to You. So let me understand righteousness and judgment and equity, yea, every good path, and fear You in earnest. Defend me from pride, that I may not let it have dominion over me either in my words or in my heart, since pride goes before destruction. For You desire that a king's heart not be lifted up above his brethren. Incline my heart to Your testimonies and not to covetousness, that I may not accept bribes nor pervert justice and so hinder the way of the needy, but that I may hear the poor gladly, and give him a kind and gentle answer; that I may give justice to the poor and the fatherless and maintain the right of the afflicted and destitute; that in judgment I may not respect any person, but may hear the lowly as well as the great, and fear no man's person, since the office of judgment is Yours, and we are not to conform ourselves to men but to You, who are in judgment with us. Help me not to be deceived by liars who resist the truth and devise wicked schemes to destroy the poor with lying words and thereby justify the cause of the ungodly, so that their judgment is sustained. In this way let me act in the fear of the Lord faithfully and from a true heart, and my work shall be acceptable to You, and I will judge Your people rightly. Lord God, grant that we and all authorities, which are ordained by You, may govern their land and people with counsel and understanding of Scripture and in peace, and constantly remember the name of the Lord. In addition, help Your people to be subject to every ordinance of man for Your sake, and to walk uprightly with true hearts, and to pray for us, that they may lead a peaceful and quiet life in all godliness and honesty. Bless us, O our God, and enlarge our border; let Your hand be with us and keep us from harm. Lord, let come what I ask. I trust in You, O Most High; therefore through Your mercy I shall not be moved. To You, the King of kings and Lord of lords, who alone have immortality, be honor and eternal dominion! Amen.

213. Prayer of a person in judicial authority

Lord, almighty God, who are judge among the gods and who give us good and faithful judges and take them away: by Your divine providence I have been chosen and called by Your instruments to pronounce judgment and to decide and judge every disagreement and dispute which occurs between brother and brother, friend and friend, and so between each person and his neighbor. Lord, I acknowledge my inability and my lack of understanding. Make me, O God of justice, capable of this office; grant me understanding and give me a heart to hear and give justice to the less as the great and the poor as the rich, that I may search out unfamiliar matters well and learn them rightly, and see whether it is as I am told, or whether it is not; that I may be sure not to honor, regard, respect, or prefer any person in judgment, nor to hesitate to give any man due punishment, nor to turn a blind eye to any man. O righteous Judge, who tests heart and reins, who see into every heart: every way of a man is right in his own eyes, but You, O Lord, weigh the heart. Lead me in Your fear, which causes wise performance in all things. Let me love righteousness and truth, hating covetousness, that bribes may not blind me to pervert justice nor to make the just cause unjust, nor to condemn any man unjustly, that I may not, like the judges of Beersheba and Babylon, deal in lies or pronounce perverted judgments. Do not permit me to burden anyone with undue fines and excessive costs or to defer the matter to the unrighteous judge, but to deliver the abused from the abuser, to bear witness to the innocence of the guiltless, and to guard myself against injustice, and so to conduct and perform my office in the fear of

God, nor to punish in anger. O Judge of the world, let wrath and envy not be judges, that I may not take vengeance on an old hatred, nor take out my anger on anyone, but may judge with righteous judgment, follow justice and uphold it, assist no one in an unjust cause, nor withhold justice from the righteous, that I may punish not according to appearance but according to the measure and degree of the trespass, and so judge and administer all things according to the Word of God. Let me remember that, when I give unjust judgment, acquit the guilty, and condemn the innocent, my sins will finally come upon me, and in due time You will ask what I have done and search out what I have ordained. Let me also remember that those who abuse their power will be punished severely. You have said, Keep far from a false matter. Let Your commandment be before my eyes and my heart far from false matters, that I may not devour iniquity and pervert all that is right. O Judge of the living and the dead, let me be counted among the godly judges in Holy Scripture, and with them receive a glorious reward in this world and the one to come; for Your own sake. Amen.

214. *Prayer of a juror who is to decide a criminal case*

O Lord, zealous and powerful God, who desire that we should put away from among us the wicked and according to their transgression, punish them in body and life, and who nevertheless regard the blood of man highly and as a precious thing and do not desire that it should be shed innocently: since the order of my vocation has called me to sit in judgment of body and life, and I must bind myself upon my oath and salvation that said judgment is right and just, I beseech You to give me the Spirit of wisdom, that I may with good understanding sufficiently discern the matter or transgression of those who have sinned and may consider well whether the judgment assessed is too severe for the transgression in question. O Lord my God, let me not participate in an unjust case nor help to deprive the innocent of his life! But if I find it just in my conscience, give me, O Lord, a fearless spirit to speak as my conscience instructs me and to consent valiantly and confidently with the drafted verdict; for it is better to cut off from the body a rotten limb and to remove a wicked man from the community by lawful means than to spare the wicked through leniency and to cause Your wrath to be kindled upon the whole community for vengeance and chastisement. O Lord, grant wisdom and understanding, character and courage in all parts of my vocation. Amen, Amen.

215. *Prayer of an officer, jurist, or councilman*

Almighty, everlasting God, heavenly Father, You ordained and directed that I should study law and learn and speak what is just. Therefore grant Your grace and blessing to the end that I may seek only truth and find and do only what is pleasing to You, to Your glory, and to the good of the country and its people, for the sake of Christ, Your beloved Son, my Lord and Savior. Amen.

216. *General prayer of a soldier*

Heavenly Father, according to Your divine will I am here in this external work and service to my superior, as is my duty firstly to You and then to the same superior for Your sake, and I give thanks to You that of Your grace and mercy You have placed me in this work, which I am certain is not sin, but just, and a pleasing act of obedience to Your will. But because I know, and have learned through Your gracious Word, that none of our good works can help us, and no one can be saved simply because he is a soldier, but only because he is a Christian, I will not rely on this act of obedience and work, but I do it freely as an act of service to Your will, believing in my heart that I am saved only by the innocent blood of Your beloved Son, Jesus Christ, my Savior, which blood He shed for me in obedience to Your gracious will. On this faith I stand; on this faith I live and die; on this faith I fight and do all things. Sustain this faith, dear Lord God and Father, and strengthen it in me by Your Holy Spirit. Amen.

(*If you wish, follow this by saying the Creed and the Lord's Prayer, or else let this suffice, and hereby commending body and soul into God's hands, draw your sword and strike your blow in His name.*)

217. *Another*

Lord Jesus Christ, heavenly victor, conqueror over sin, death, and the devil! I beseech You to grant Your gracious blessing to my performance in battle and not to deny me on account of all my countless sins, for which You have made abundant satisfaction. Give me a godly heart, that I may keep myself from cursing, swearing, boasting, unseemly taking of spoil and plunder, and other sins; that I may remain faithful and obedient to my superiors and not shrink from my enemy, but in Your name attack vigorously and without fear; that in every danger I may trust firmly in You and let neither wounds nor death make me waver from You. If it pleases You that I should be captured, wounded, or left lying half-dead on the battlefield, grant me patience in my affliction, and let me acknowledge and accept it all as Your fatherly will. And if You wish to take me utterly away by fire and sword or any other means, grant me, for the sake of Your sorrowful and contemptible death, a blessed end, and let me never be parted from You. Amen.

218. *A soldier's morning prayer*

Lord, almighty God, dear, merciful Father, we thank You from the depths of our hearts that You have so graciously preserved and protected the time of our lives, including this past night, and we beseech You in the name of Jesus Christ, Your Son, that for the sake of His precious suffering and death, You would pardon all our sins, and by Your Holy Spirit You would ever enlighten and govern us more and more, that we may sincerely repent, walk in Your fear, trust in You alone, love You, and keep ourselves from all shame and vice. Defend us this day also from every evil, and bless our going out and our going in, our action and inaction, that it may attain to the glory of Your holy name, the deliverance of Your Church and our fatherland, and all our temporal and eternal welfare. Above all, govern our general with Your Spirit, and protect him as the apple of Your eye. Be his shelter and defense, O Lord, and bring his plans to completion. Turn to nothing all the wicked plans and great power of the enemy. Prevent and destroy all treachery. Govern, preserve, and bless all our other senior and junior officers and the whole military force; O Lord of Sabaoth, mighty prince of war, assist us. Give us all a fearless and confident heart, take the field with our host, grant us the desired victory, and let Your fatherly grace abound upon us; for the sake of Your most beloved Son, Jesus Christ, our only Savior. Amen.

219. *Another*

Almighty, merciful God and Father, I give You praise, honor, and thanks for sheltering and preserving me with such fatherly care, even though I have sinned in so many ways against Your divine will, grace, and loving kindness. And I beseech You, Lord my God, that You would be gracious and merciful to me and pardon and forgive me all my iniquities. Take away my heart of stone, remove from me the old man, renew my heart and spirit, that I may know and perfectly love You, my highest treasure, and diligently contemplate Your holy Commandments, and with highest diligence and holy obedience walk blamelessly therein. Lord, almighty, faithful God, I beseech You by the bitter sufferings and death of Your beloved Son, Jesus Christ, to defend me this day and always from dishonoring Your holy name and transgressing against Your divine will. Take from me my evil, poisoned nature, and give me to You, that in true serenity I may be wholly free from myself and devote myself to You by true and living faith, strong hope, and fervent love. O Lord Jesus Christ, my duke and captain, I beseech You by the love of Your heavenly Father, go before me with Your grace, lead me through this errant and mischievous world in the right way of Your salutary Word, that I may not be deceived by anyone, fall away from Your Word, forget You, or live an unchristian life. But protect me, my dear Lord Jesus, and all men from sin and unbelief; from wicked thoughts, words, and deeds; and from an offensive way of life, that in and through us You may be praised, honored, and worshiped with Your heavenly Father and the Holy Spirit. May He move us with heartfelt and fervent devotion to pray in Spirit and in truth and say: Our Father who art in heaven, hallowed be Thy name, Thy kingdom come, Thy will be done on earth as it is in heaven. Give us this day our daily bread; and forgive us our trespasses, as we forgive those who trespass against us; and lead us not into temptation, but deliver us from evil. For Thine is the kingdom and the power and the glory forever and ever. Amen.

220. A soldier's evening prayer

Almighty, gracious God and Father, we give You praise and thanks with all our hearts that You have sustained, directed, and protected us this day with such fatherly care. And we beseech You further in the name of Your most beloved Son, Jesus Christ, and for His sake to have mercy on our iniquities, which are very great, and to keep us this night also from all the cunning and might of Satan, from sin and shame, from hostile attack and from all harm. Turn us also by the power of Your Holy Spirit, and grant that in true faith and a godly life, as befits a Christian, we may serve You and keep an uninjured, good conscience. Lord, our God, who neither slumber nor sleep, mercifully receive our general into Your almighty protection, govern him always by Your Spirit, protect him from all evil through Your holy angels, and bless all his good designs. Preserve also our other senior and junior officers and the whole military force. Destroy all the cunning and might of our enemies, and protect us also from all treachery and wicked devices. Be a wall of fire round about us. For if You do not preserve us, O Lord, the watchman watches in vain. If You do not help, the strength of man is powerless. Into Your hands, therefore, O heavenly Father, we commend our bodies, souls, and all that You have given us, in the name of Your Son, our only Savior, Jesus Christ, who taught us to pray: Our Father who art in heaven, hallowed be Thy name, Thy kingdom come, Thy will be done on earth as it is in heaven. Give us this day our daily bread; and forgive us our trespasses as we forgive those who trespass against us; and lead us not into temptation, but deliver us from evil. For Thine is the kingdom and the power and the glory forever and ever. Amen.

221. Another

Almighty, merciful God and Father, I give You heartfelt thanks that You have kept me, a poor sinner, with such fatherly care this day and preserved my body and soul, life and health. You covered me with Your wings so that no evil befell me and gave Your angels charge over me to defend me against Satan's violence. I thank and praise You, O God, that You are my defender and helper, and I beseech You of Your boundless mercy to forgive me my sins in word or deed, thought or action, by which I have angered You. Leave my sins in the setting of the sun, but Your grace in the rising of the sun on account of the overabundant payment of Your beloved Son, my only Redeemer, Jesus Christ, in whom You are pleased to forgive us all our sins. And I pray further that You would love me till the end and prepare mercy and truth, which may preserve me. Defend me this night from all harm and danger, and let me sleep and rest peacefully in safety. Or if, because of my estate, I must rise quickly, give me wakeful eyes, a confident heart, and ready hands and feet, that I may be untiring and successful in the performance of my duty. And if I should be taken by surprise this night and go the way of all the world and die unawares, nevertheless lift up my soul with Your consolation, and let no danger befall me apart from Your will, but make a way to escape, so that I may be able to bear it. But if it is pleasing to Your will and profitable to my soul, deliver my life from destruction, and awaken me at the right and acceptable time, that alive, healthy, and happy, I may behold the blessed sun and return joyfully to my calling and faithfully serve You and my neighbor. For this I will give You praise and thanks in time and eternity and conclude my evening benediction, saying: Lord, bless and preserve me; Lord, make Your face to shine upon me and be gracious unto me; Lord, lift up the light of Your countenance upon me and give me peace. God the Father, Son, and Holy Spirit bless me from this time forth, even forever. Amen.

222. Prayer for courage

Strong and mighty God, who according to Your good pleasure give courage to those who trust in You: I beseech You, since I am now in a very dangerous position in which I certainly have need of strength, power, and courage, that You would remove from me all natural timidity and fearfulness to which I, a sinful man, am by nature inclined. Do not punish me with a terrified heart and wavering spirit, lest I be very troubled. Yet if it pleases You according to Your divine wisdom to make my heart fearful, that I may learn to rely not on my own strength but on Your help, then let me not sink utterly; in the midst of my apprehension give me a glimpse of Your strength, that I may take comfort in the fact that You are with me and will powerfully protect me in every danger and turn all heartaches away from me. Neither let me fall into madness and impudence, from which harm and ruin follow, but let my heart fear You, having You always before my eyes and believing certainly that You lead me with Your right hand, lest I fall and perish. I know that the works of man are nothing, and on his own he cannot be self-assured without Your assistance. Therefore I call on You for this lofty gift, of which I have need daily in my office and estate, that I may do without hesitation what is proper, to the honor of Your name. Lord, You are my rock, my fortress in whom I heartily trust both now and till my end. Amen.

223. Prayer while on guard duty

Dear Lord Jesus Christ, I stand here on the edge of the camp to keep watch against our enemy. But if You, O Lord, do not keep us, the watchman watches in vain. I beseech You, forgive me all my sins and cover us with Your favor as with a shield. Let Your holy angels stand around us to protect and preserve us that we may not be taken by our enemies unawares. Let me not be afraid of the terror by night. Preserve me from the specters and illusions of the devil. Open my eyes and ears, that I may see the coming of the enemy and be careful for myself and the whole host. Keep me from sleep and laziness in my service. Let my heart constantly call upon You as I stand forlorn in this quiet place, and incline Yourself to me with Your powerful presence. Be with me when I am alone, and strengthen me in body and soul, that I may keep my strength in cold and heat and in all tempests, and return in good health to the glad company of my brothers; so shall I praise Your name and glory in Your protection while I live. Amen.

224. Prayer before battle

[If a soldier's army is weak, he should not doubt, but pray to the Lord God for victory and say:] Lord, all strength and victory is in Your power! Lord, help me! *[etc. Likewise, if you are stronger and have a greater host than your enemy, do not rely on that or be certain of victory, but pray to God and say:]* Lord, the triumph and victory are in Your power. If You decide to give them to me, I will give You thanks. But if You wish to punish our sins with harm and misery, Lord, I am here and will endure it patiently. Amen.

225. Exclamation during battle

My spirit, Lord, now be Thy lot,
My God, my God, forsake me not!—
Into Thy hands receive me!
God, let me go
From every woe,
And at my end relieve me!

—*A. Reusner*

I live to You, Jesus!
I die to You, Jesus!
I belong to You, Jesus,
Whether I live or die!
Save me and take me on high! Amen.

226. Prayer after winning a battle

Make a joyful noise to the Lord, all the world! Come into His presence with singing. Behold the works of the Lord, how He has brought desolations on the earth: He has made wars cease to the end of the earth; He has shattered the enemy's spears, broken their bows, and burned their chariots with fire. O merciful Father, how can we repay You for the great benefits which You have mercifully bestowed on us, who are not worthy to lift our eyes up to You in heaven. Neither have You dealt with us according to our sins, nor repaid us according to our iniquities, but You have graciously heard our prayer and done what we asked and besought of You. O Lord of Sabaoth, continue to be with us; O God of Jacob, be our refuge. Sustain and protect evermore Your Christian Church on earth. Keep her as the apple of Your eye, hide her under the shadow of Your wings, and give us peace in our time, for there is none other who can fight for us but You alone, O our God. To You belong glory and majesty, dominion and power both now and ever. Amen.

227. *Prayer of one who is wounded*

O faithful God! I lie surrounded by weakness, yet none can save me but You alone. With my detestable sins I have surely deserved worse than this fatherly rod; but You, O Lord, graciously correct me, as a father corrects his son. Therefore, if it is Your fatherly will, pleasing to You, and profitable to my salvation, then cure and heal me, for You are my greatest physician. You have the power to save. Death and life, weakness and health are in Your hands. You alone know what is best for me. Do as You please. If You wish me to live longer so that I may be of further use and service to You and my neighbor in this estate, You can heal me instantly with a single word. But if, by this wound, You wish to call me away, O Lord, I am ready and willing even to die a blessed death in You. Amen.

228. *Prayer in great pain*

O dear Father in heaven, what great pain, anguish, and distress I suffer in my body, all of which, and more, I have surely deserved with my sins! Dear Father, see how my infirmity continues to sting, rage, rave, torment, and burn, and have pity on me; for I am Your dear child and the brother of Your beloved Son, Jesus Christ. An earthly father is pained and stung to the heart when he sees his child suffering distress and sorrow. May You be all the more so toward me, and in such compassion come and help me in this great physical distress. Diminish my pain, and if it pleases You, take it all away. How long, O Lord? Will You forget me forever? Hasten to my aid, or I will despair in this anguish. You commanded me to call on You for help in the time of trouble, and promised to deliver me from it, and said that when I ask You, You will help me out of it. O gracious God, come to my aid, therefore, and if I must conclude my life with such sorrow and great distress, yet do not hide Your fatherly, tender, and gracious face from me, but in my distress help me by the Holy Spirit to have before my eyes the unspeakably great sufferings and torment of my Lord Christ and to bear my own suffering patiently after Him, that I may not sin because of this physical distress, but like the blessed martyrs may abide steadfast in faith and prayer until my end; through Jesus Christ, Your dear Son. Amen.

229. Prayer before undergoing surgery

My Lord and my God, to whom shall I flee in this great distress which has come upon me according to Your holy will, but to You, who commanded: "Call on Me in the time of trouble, and I will deliver you, and you shall glorify Me"? Where shall I seek for help in my misery but in You, who alone work salvation in the midst of the earth? You have torn me; You can also heal me. Your hand has struck me down; it will also bind me up. You have laid me on the bed of sorrow and let me fall into the peril of death; You can raise me up again that I may live before You.

I confess before Your holy presence that I, with my countless, grievous sins, have earned not only Your fatherly rod, by which You have chastised me before now, but also the punishment of eternal damnation, the agony and torment of hell. But I am heartily sorry that I have angered and offended Your high, divine majesty; my soul is in anguish over the multitude and enormity of my errors; my eyes flow with tears because I have (alas!) not kept Your Commandments. Yet I know that You, O merciful Father, take no pleasure in the death of the wicked, but will that the sinner should turn from his evil ways and live. Therefore I also turn to You with a broken spirit, and You firstly to forgive all my sins by grace. Ah, turn Yourself to me, O Lord, and have mercy upon me, for I am desolate and afflicted. The troubles of my heart are enlarged; bring me out of my distresses. To You do I flee; reject me not as I deserve. O God, do not be angry; enter not into judgment! Your Son has made atonement for me.

I firmly believe that if anyone has sinned, we have an advocate before Your throne, even Jesus Christ, who is righteous, who is the propitiation for our sins. On this my Jesus, on His bloody sufferings and agonizing wounds, on His most perfect satisfaction and most powerful intercession, I rely completely this hour, doubting not that I shall find favor with You and obtain mercy. Likewise, I am certain in faith that I am and remain Your child, because You sent the Spirit of Your Son into my heart, who cries without ceasing, "Abba, dear Father!" and represents me to You with unspeakable sighs. Therefore, "since Thou my God and Father art, I know Thy true paternal heart will not forsake Thy child; I am but dust and clay by birth, I have no comfort on this earth."* Have mercy on me, a poor and miserable being, as a Father has mercy on his children, and let Your heart be moved by my distress.

O Lord, You are the helper of all who trust in You, and You have pledged

* From the hymn "Warum betrübst du dich, mein Herz" (H. Sachs, 1552), st. 3.

Your help to all who seek and cry to You, so be my helper now also. O Lord, be not far from me, for trouble is near! Hasten to help me, O Lord, my salvation! Be pleased to deliver me. My God, do not delay! You give strength to the weary, and power enough to the powerless. Those who wait on You receive new strength. Oh, behold, Lord, how weary I am from sighing and sorrow, how infirmity has sapped my strength! My hope and trust are in You only, wherefore let Your strength be powerful in my weakness. Comfortingly assure my soul, "Fear not, for I am with you; be not afraid, for I am your God. I will strengthen you, yea, I will help you by the right hand of My righteousness."

O faithful physician of Israel, give grace and blessing from heaven to the ordinary means which I will use in Your name for the recovery of my health. Grant the physician wisdom and understanding for the difficult and painful work, and lead and govern his hand with Your hand of grace, that all may go well and achieve success. Grace me also, O God of patience and comfort, with true courage and Christian patience, that I may confidently overcome and endure such severe pains.

O Lord, help; O Lord, grant success for the sake of the great sorrows and bitter anguish and death of my Redeemer, Jesus Christ! Let me find comfort, rest, and refreshment in Your fatherly love, in Your Son's bloody wounds, and under the Holy Spirit's wings of grace, until the anguish and pain are past. But if in the intensity of the pain I should fall into some error from human weakness and sin against You, great God, with my lips, ah! then do not reckon it to my damnation, nor turn Your gracious countenance and helping hand from me, but accept the blood of my Jesus as a propitiation for this sin also. And if according to Your counsel I am to end my life in the great distress which lies before me and give up the ghost, bind my soul in the bundle of the living and elect, that it may not perish and be lost. Preserve me in the true faith, believing in my Redeemer and Savior, Jesus Christ, that in my final distress I may think of nothing but His cross and painful death, and by His open wounds enter into Your heavenly paradise. Let Your Holy Spirit bear witness to my spirit that I am a child of God and that heaven is my inheritance. Let my final word be that with which Your dearest Son sealed His lips on the cross: "Father, into Your hands I commit My spirit!" And when I can no longer speak, then, O Lord, receive my final sigh; through Jesus Christ. Amen.

230. Prayer in sickness

O merciful, gracious God and Father, I lament and confess to You that I have passed my life, which You have given me, wickedly up till now, and not for Your glory but for the fulfilling of the pleasures of my flesh. I have lived more to myself and to the world than to You. O Lord, how heartily sorry I am that I have so wickedly used the brief time of my life! Therefore I discern now that You are visiting my sins upon me and sending me this sickness in order to call me to repentance. You are right, O Lord, to judge and correct me, that I may not be damned with the ungodly world. By this sickness You remind me of my mortality and wish to teach me that my life is measured and I must leave it. Oh, how empty are all men who live complacently! They go about as a shadow! Surely for nothing they are in turmoil; man heaps up wealth and does not know who will gather. Now therefore, O Lord, in what shall I take comfort? Deliver me from my sins. O Lord, I know that my life is in Your hand. You wrote in Your book all my days which are yet to come when none had yet been. My bones were not concealed from You when I was formed in my mother's womb. Therefore because it is Your will that I should be sick, let me do this will of Yours gladly. O Lord, Your arrows pierce me, and Your hand presses me; there is nothing sound in my body because of Your threatening, and there is no peace in my bones because of my sins! For my sins pass over my head, and as a heavy burden they have become too heavy for me. O my God, preserve my soul from all tribulations! Let my physical infirmity be a remedy to my soul, that by it my soul may be healed. Preserve my heart and mind, and by the peace of my Lord Jesus Christ cover me with Your shield and buckler from all the fiery darts of the devil. You know, Lord, that I am the work of Your hands, that You have made me out of clay. We are clay, You are our potter. Oh, how broken I am! Therefore spare me, O dear Lord; You will not cast away and break in wrath the work of Your hands. You took me from my mother's womb and were my confidence when I was still at my mother's breast. You are the source and Lord of my life, and You have the power to take it again if You wish. Therefore, if it is Your will, have mercy on me as You did on King Hezekiah, to whose life You added fifteen years. Behold, I am very anxious for consolation! Come heartily to the aid of my soul, that it may not be destroyed, and cast all sins behind You. If this sickness is not unto death, restore me again and heal me, Lord, for I am very weak. O heavenly physician, Lord Jesus Christ, receive me into Your care, diminish my pains, and heal me by Your wounds. Let Your bitter sufferings and death be my remedy. Lord, let me touch the hem of Your garment, Your Word and Sacrament in which You have clothed Yourself, and heal me, that I may be healed by Your power which goes out from You. But if it is Your will that I, through this sickness, should go the way of all the world, no matter! I am no better than my fathers. I only ask, Lord, that You let Your servant go in peace according to Your word; for my eyes have seen You, my Savior, who were prepared before the face of all people: a light to lighten the Gentiles, and the glory of Your people Israel. Amen.

231. *Prayer of thanksgiving and repentance after one has been delivered from various dangers*

O Father of mercy and God of all comfort, who have been my God from my mother's womb and have wonderfully sheltered and protected me under the shadow of Your wings during the time of my life: I will praise You now in quietness and glorify Your name forever. I can never repay You for all Your benefits which You have shown me, delivering me from many dangers and daily demonstrating much good in body and soul. For in the war to which You sent me, the sword devoured man after man, shots were fired from rampart and field, and many brave soldiers died, not a few falling before me and beside me, and death often a step away. Yet Your hand covered me so that I was kept alive and brought my life away as a prize of war. It is You only who have equipped me with strength, taught my hands to fight, and given me sufficient powers. With You I was frequently able to surmount the walls of danger and to evade many misfortunes. Thus I am still alive this hour and can sing of the wonderful victory in the tents of the righteous, so that the humble shall hear of it and be glad. And therefore, O God, I justly thank You for delivering me from so many dire distresses and worship the glory of Your name because You have been the strength of my life and my salvation up till now. But because I have not walked in a manner worthy of my calling, nor always had You before my eyes and in my heart, but have committed many sins, from which I now have a stain in my conscience, therefore, I implore You like a child to be gracious to me according to Your loving kindness and blot out my transgressions according to Your great mercy. By the blood of Jesus Christ, which cleanses us from all our sins, wash me of all my iniquities and cleanse me from my sins, for I acknowledge my iniquities, and my sin is ever before me. And where I have been unmerciful, for the sake of Christ let me not have judgment without mercy, but deliver me from my bloodguiltiness, O God, my God and Savior, that my tongue may sing aloud of Your mercy, here in time and hereafter in eternity. Amen.

232. Prayer of Christian soldiers to speak in assembly

Lord of heaven and earth, great and mighty God, we thank You heartily through Jesus Christ that You have so graciously protected and preserved us up till now. We beseech You, faithful, heavenly Father, mercifully to pardon us poor sinners of our grievous and manifold sins for Jesus Christ's sake. Convert and govern our hearts by Your Spirit, that we may not imitate the wicked example of the multitudes, nor lead a heathen and ungodly life, but a Christian and godly life, love and fear You, and cultivate and keep a good conscience in all places. And bestow on us all wisdom, strength, health, constancy, and valiant courage, to fight bravely for the fatherland against the enemy. And since human forces, aid, arms, and strategies are utterly powerless without Your support, fight for us, Lord, mighty God, and bless our going out and coming from this time forth and forevermore. Go before us and drive back our enemies; give them hopeless hearts and heavy hands, that our poor fatherland may be saved, Your Church preserved, the sorrowful comforted, and the downtrodden and oppressed restored again. Surely, O Lord, we are of ourselves unworthy of Your help, for we have all sinned grievously. Yet, Lord, we beseech You to regard the holy, precious merits of Jesus Christ, Your Son; look upon the sorrow and misery of Your Church; and hear the sighs of all the poor, afflicted, devastated, suffering, godly hearts which in childlike trust never cease crying to You with fervent tears for help and deliverance. For their sake, O Lord, assist us and grant us success and victory, that Your glory may be known in all the earth, and all men may see that You are Lord, the true and only helper in time of need, who makes wars cease, shatters the spear and the bow, repels all attacks as He wills, and finally comes to the aid of those who are His, even when it is least expected. Into Your keeping, O Lord, let all Christian rulers be commended, along with all our military officers and the whole force. Escort and defend us all by Your holy angels, and to those in our military force whom You have appointed to die, mercifully grant steadfast faith and true repentance, comfort them at their final moment by Your Holy Spirit, and take their souls to Yourself in eternal joy and blessedness for the sake of Jesus Christ, Your beloved Son, who commanded us to pray in His name: Our Father who art in heaven, hallowed be Thy name, Thy kingdom come, Thy will be done on earth as it is in heaven. Give us this day our daily bread; and forgive us our trespasses as we forgive those who trespass against us; and lead us not into temptation, but deliver us from evil. For Thine is the kingdom and the power and the glory forever and ever. Amen.

233. *Prayer of a soldier for his family at home*

Lord of all grace and sole defender of the faithful! I thank You with all my heart that You have graciously protected and preserved me till now in all the dangers of my calling, and I beseech You to take me into Your fatherly protection also henceforth. And I beseech You of Your boundless loving kindness and mercy to surround with Your protection my house and all that pertains to me, that no evil may come near my dwelling nor what little I have to live on, nor anything that I have left behind be damaged or taken from me. But above all, I commend into Your hands what is most dear to me, my dear wife and children, who melt my heart and are my greatest treasure. Be their help and their protection that they may not fall, and turn away from them all dangers of body and soul. Preserve them today and always, that they may fear Your majesty and not consent to intentional sins, nor act against Your Commandments. Give Your angel charge over them, to keep them in all their ways and comfort them even in all their toil and labor. Grant that they may continue in prayer, and practice all works of godly fear. And if, after a successfully completed campaign, You will bring me back home in good health and grant that I and my family may be found healthy, we will with one heart and mouth worship and glorify You for all the good which You have shown us in soul and body. Amen.

234. *Prayer of those at home for the soldiers in the field*

O most beloved God and Father, we are indebted to pray not only for ourselves but also for our family, yea, for all men; wherefore I pray from the depths of my heart on behalf of my dear husband (father, son, brother, relative), who has gone to war in Your name according to his calling. But because I cannot be with him this day at this time as much as I would wish, O Lord in heaven and on earth, be and remain with him today and always! Protect and shelter him in body and soul, preserve him in good health, defend him from all evil, provide for him as a father, lead him as faithful guide, protect him in all danger, and bless him in all his deeds and endeavors. And because Satan walks about all lands, laying snares especially in the paths of Your godly children to bring them into calamity, O Lord, mighty God, then preserve my dear husband (father, son, brother, relative) from all the cunning works, ways, and deeds of vile Satan and his accursed horde! O Lord of hosts, give Your holy angels charge over him, to encamp round about him and to keep him in all his ways. Govern and lead him by Your Holy Spirit this day and always, and bring him happily again to us, that we may see him unharmed and unscathed once more. So will we together gladly praise You, faithful God, all our life long and worship You eternally hereafter. Amen.

235. *Prayer in the fear of death*

Dear Lord Jesus Christ, although I have not fulfilled the Law, and though sin is still at hand and I fear death and hell, yet I know from the Gospel that You have given and imputed to me all Your works. I am certain of this; You do not lie. You will keep Your promise faithfully. And I have received Baptism as a pledge of this, in which I confide. Therefore, dear God, since You are mine I will happily die, for it pleases You, dear Father, and death cannot harm me. It has been swallowed up in victory. And thanks be to You, dear Lord, that You have given us that victory; through Jesus Christ, our Lord. Amen.

236. *Three prayers in the throes of death*

1. *To God the Father*

Almighty God, the Father of mercy and God of all comfort: Have mercy on me as a father has mercy on his children. Remember that Your dear Son, Jesus Christ, was made man for my sake. Remember that You so loved the world that You gave Your only-begotten Son, that whoever believes in Him should not perish but have eternal life. In this faith my soul comes to You, bringing with it Your dear Son, Jesus Christ, whom You have given me. For His sake be mindful of me and receive me into Your favor. To You I commend my soul. Let me, Your dear child, abide forever in Your grace, and be merciful to me while I live and when I die; through Jesus Christ, Your dear Son.

2. *To God the Son*

Lord Jesus Christ, my only comfort and my only help, who bore my sickness and were wounded for my transgressions, the Lamb of God, who take away the sin of the world: Be my righteousness, my sanctification, and my redemption. Heal my afflictions by Your wounds. Let Your innocent blood not be wasted on me; take not Your Holy Spirit from me. Forsake me not in my final distress, but help me pass quickly through to eternal life. Remember that I was Your poor sheep, and You my faithful shepherd. Take me up in Your arms and carry me into joyful paradise. Let me also see Your kind face and Your glory. Amen.

3. To God the Holy Spirit

O God the Holy Spirit, only comfort of all the afflicted! Strengthen and comfort my fearful and sorrowful heart. Uphold my faith which You work in me, and let the smoldering wick not be quenched. Guard me from the tribulations of the wicked foe. Let my heart not shrink or despair at death. Repel all impatience; make me to be willingly obedient to the Lord my God. Help me to conclude my life in a blessed and joyful manner. Keep my heart and my senses in the peace of my Lord Jesus Christ. And when I can no longer speak, preserve and seal in my heart the remembrance of the holy name of Jesus Christ, and therewith let me fall blessedly asleep. Amen.

237. Prayer for peace

Grant peace, we pray, in mercy Lord,
Peace in our time, oh, send us!
For there is none on earth but You,
None other to defend us;
You only, Lord, can fight for us.

Give to our land and all authority peace and good government, that under their guidance we may lead an honest, peaceful, Christian existence in all truth and God-pleasing devotion. Amen.

238. The Lesser Litany

Lord God the Father in heaven, Maker of all things, have mercy upon me and hear me!

Lord God the Son, Savior of the world, have mercy upon me and intercede for me!

Lord God, the Holy Spirit, the Comforter in all trouble, have mercy upon me and make supplication within me!

Holy, Holy, Holy, most blessed Trinity, have mercy upon me and be gracious to me, a poor sinner. Forgive me all my sins, preserve unto me Your pure and saving Word, and give me Your temporal, spiritual, and eternal peace. Amen.

VII. INTERCESSION

239. Prayer of Christian women for a mother in travail

O almighty and powerful God, we beseech You through Jesus Christ, Your dear Son, to help this mother in this time of such great distress as she lies here in her maternal calling, according to Your divine will, and have mercy on Your creature, and so attend mother and child as will be beneficial and serviceable to them in body and soul. For You have never forsaken any man who cried out to You and have at last helped all mothers who in their travail took refuge and put their confidence in You. Lord, gracious helper in every need! Now is the time of distress and anguish, the time to deliver and help. If You, Lord, do not help, the help of all the world is in vain. For the child has reached the time to be born, and there is no one who can help but You, Lord, our God, You only. You know best the proper hour and moment. Hour by hour we wait on Your help and hope in Your Word. Yea, though it tarry till the night, and till the morning waken, our heart shall never doubt Your might nor count itself forsaken. Your helping hand no limit knows, it sounds our deepest sorrow. Sure faith from hence we borrow.* We have no doubt about this. Your Word cannot deceive us; for You know well what hour is best; no devious thought is in Your breast; here let our trust be founded. Though it may seem You hear us not, we fear us not forsaken; though You may not reveal our lot, Your plan is not mistaken. Your Word is sure, here is our stay, and though our heart say only Nay, our faith shall not be shaken.† O God, strengthen our faith and help us for the glory of Your name. Amen. Let us pray together: Our Father who art in heaven, hallowed be Thy name, Thy kingdom come, Thy will be done on earth as it is in heaven. Give us this day our daily bread; and forgive us our trespasses as we forgive those who trespass against us; and lead us not into temptation, but deliver us from evil. For Thine is the kingdom and the power and the glory forever and ever. Amen.

* Cf. *TLH* 329:4–5.
† Cf. *WH* 237:12.

240. Prayer of mother for her newborn

O my Lord Jesus, I thank You that You have deemed me worthy to be the mother of a child and that You give me the grace to quiet my child with my own breast! I fill him (her) with mother's milk; fill him (her), my Redeemer, with Your love and holy fear. Let him (her) always remain a living member of Your body! By Your Holy Spirit blot out inherited sin and all wickedness in him (her). Give him (her) Your Holy Spirit, govern his (her) heart and mind, preserve him (her) from the offense and seduction of the sinful, wicked world, sanctify and bless him (her) in body and soul, let him (her) daily increase in physical stature, wisdom, maturity, and in favor with You, O God in heaven, and with men on earth. Amen.

241. Prayer of one who will stand as godparent

O triune God, I herewith commend to You my godchild, beseeching You not to reckon to his (her) condemnation his (her) sinful impurity, in which he (she) was conceived and born, but to cover them with the holiness and righteousness of Christ, Your Son, to lift him (her) up and receive him (her) into the number of Christians, to keep him (her) steadfast in Your grace, and after this life to give and bestow on him (her) true salvation. Amen.

242. Prayer of parents for their child who is traveling

O almighty, merciful, and gracious God and Father, who wonderfully accompanied young Tobias on a long and distant road by the angel Raphael, preserved him from all danger, and granted him grace to return home again to his parents (who awaited his return with great longing) with all fortune, blessing, and benediction, by the name of Jesus Christ, Your dear Son, our Lord, who is the Way, the Truth, and the Life: I beseech You, almighty, faithful Father, that You would grant my dear child grace, fortune, salvation, blessing, and benediction on his (her) journey, to preserve the same from all danger, injury, and adversity, both in soul and body, in all his (her) paths and ways by water and land, and to send him (her) Your holy angel as a prosperous escort, to protect him (her) here and there, and shelter him (her) from all that is harmful to him (her) in soul and body, reputation and goods, so that he (she) might, with healthy body, successfully come home again. May that be granted him (her) by the divine blessing of the Holy Trinity, God the Father, the Son, and Holy Spirit. Amen.

243. *Prayer for a son who is abroad*

Merciful God and Father over all that are called children in heaven and earth! Mercifully hear the prayer and supplication which Your poor maidservant now offers before You. O Lord, You know how I have shed and poured abroad many tears over my son and with what grief my heart has frequently been filled. I want nothing more than that he may fear You and learn what is proper and profitable and keep in a sound body a soul unscathed and a pure conscience. And therefore I call on You (from whom every good and perfect gift comes down) in deepest humility and from the bottom of my heart: Dear Father, govern him with Your Holy Spirit, that in all places and at all times he may have You before his eyes and Your Word in his heart, that he may not become wicked and consent to sin contrary to Your Commandments. Let him be with You in grace and mercy, keep Your eyes open toward him, lead and protect him by Your angels, which are mighty champions, on all his ways, that no evil may befall him and no destroying adversity come nigh to him.

Lord Jesus, the Savior of those who trust in You, who were sent to earth from Your heavenly Father, for the good of the children of men: receive my Son into Your provision, attention, love, and affection. Grant that he may follow Your footsteps in all things as You have given him an example and increase day by day not only in age but also in godliness and virtue, in wisdom and skill (in business and conduct, etc.), in favor with God and man. Bless his doings and endeavors, and cause what he begins in Your name to succeed well. And finally bring him home again in health and joy, that he may, according to Your will, be the staff and comfort of my old age, but especially that he may remain the heir of heaven and of eternal salvation through Your merits.

God, the Holy Spirit, governor and guide of youth! Teach this young man to walk his course blamelessly, and lead him in the right way, to live according to Your holy Commandments. Grant that he may walk before You with an upright heart, believe certainly that godliness is profitable unto all things, and seek to have always a conscience void of offense toward both God and man. Incline to him the hearts of influential, honest, and pious men, that they may receive him when he has need of them and show him every good. Yet preserve him also from the deceit and craft of Satan, and the offensive example of the world, from false teaching and tempting company, from sin and shame, robbers and murderers, harm and danger, and a sudden and evil death. Make him a man who is of service to Your glory, useful to his neighbor, and who for this and all Your gracious benefits worships You with heart and mouth forever and ever. Amen.

244. *Prayer for a sick child*

Almighty God, dear Father, You not only promised Abraham, "I am your God, and your seed's after you," but also assured us through Your apostles that this promise was for us and our children. Therefore do not be angry that I take it upon myself to speak with You and pour into Your lap my prayer and sighs on behalf of my sick child. Lord, he (she) is Your creature and the work of Your hands! You fashioned him (her) in his (her) mother's womb, gifted him (her) with body and soul, and added life and goodness to him (her). You brought him (her) to the light of this world, received him (her) as Your child in Holy Baptism, and have kept him (her) in Your grace until now. Receive him (her) therefore into Your care at this time also when he (she) is in weakness. Oh, do not count against him (her) his (her) sin, in which he (she) was conceived and born, and with which he (she) has transgressed Your most holy Commandments in his (her) life. Have mercy on him (her) according to Your great goodness. Relieve his (her) pains and sickness, and if You will, restore him (her) soon to health. Lord, it is in Your hand and power to restore him (her) to complete health, and You will do so, too, if You find that it is profitable to Your glory, my welfare, and his (her) own salvation. But if, according to Your holy counsel, You do otherwise with him (her), and he (she) must lie in recovery longer, or else must die prematurely, then not my will but Yours be done, for it is always the best. Lord Jesus, precious Lamb of God who takes away the sin of the world, behold this poor lamb which You have purchased with the most valuable redemption price for Your own possession. Wash him (her) and cleanse him (her) from all his (her) sins with Your innocent blood, strengthen him (her) by Your Holy Spirit in true faith in You and Your merit, in Christian patience under the cross which You have laid upon him (her), and in the good hope of Your gracious help. If it pleases You that this child should be brought up in Your fear, and to see that he (she) keep increasing in all Christian virtues from year to year by Your blessing, I will praise Your name forever and ever. Lord, only speak a word and he (she) shall be healed and live! But if You have decided to take him (her) to Yourself by a blessed death (for You have a greater right to him [her] than I), I will be at peace, knowing that You will bring his (her) soul by Your holy angels to the spirits of the perfectly righteous in heaven, and on the Last Day, in the resurrection of the righteous, You will clothe his (her) body with blessed immortality and make him (her) like Your glorified body.

God the Holy Spirit, the Spirit of adoption and God of all comfort: fill my grieving soul and my sick child's heart with Your powerful comfort. Assist his (her) weakness by Your heavenly power, and represent him (her) before God with sighs too deep for words. Grant me grace also that I may submit obediently to the will of God, humble myself under Your mighty hand, await the departure of this sickness with a quiet spirit, and say nothing more than this: You are the Lord, do as You please. Up till now I have seen in the godliness and good nature of this child that he (she) belongs to You; let him (her) also be devoted and dedicated to You in his (her) living and dying. If he (she) is taken from my bosom and embraced by death, then transport him (her) to the bosom of Your grace, and You will satisfy him (her) in heaven with the breast of Your consolation, that at God's right hand he (she) may partake of the fullness of joy and pleasures forevermore.

Amen, Lord, triune God! Say to my prayer and supplication: Amen. Yes, yes, it shall be so. Amen!

245. Intercession of children for their father delayed on his travels

Eternal Son of God, faithful Savior of all who call on You in faith: we, Your children, who are baptized in Your blood and consecrated with Your Spirit as royal priests and chosen by grace as Your brothers and fellow heirs, cry out to You with our innocent tongues, praying heartily that, since our dear father is traveling for his work and calling, You would graciously protect him on his way, let him do his business well, and bring him back to us in health and joy, just as You protected Your servant Jacob on his journey and accompanied him with Your angels, O eternal and faithful escort and companion of all who fear You and hope in Your steadfast love. Amen.

246. Prayer of godly children for their parents

O gracious, merciful God, dear Father, the true Father of all that are called children in heaven and earth! I thank You sincerely that You have given me my dear parents—Father and Mother—and kept them in good health and prosperity until now. Honor, thanks, and praise be Yours for this great benefit! I pray that You would graciously forgive me my disobedience with which I have often sinned against my dear parents, and turn away from me the punishment which You have threatened in the Fourth Commandment. Give me an obedient and thankful heart toward them, that I may honor, fear, love, and gladden them with my obedience and Your godly fear, that I may recognize them as God's ordinance and accept with patience their fatherly and well-intended punishments. Teach me also to remember how difficult I have been to my mother and with what great toil and effort she has raised me; let me honor her in turn with obedience, love, humility, and fear in word and deed, that I may inherit the blessing and not the curse, but long life. Let me always have before my eyes the example of my Lord Jesus Christ's obedience, who obeyed His Father even to death on the cross. Give me the obedience of Isaac, the fear of Jacob, the discipline of Joseph, and the godly fear of Tobias, and give my dear parents the faith of Abraham, the blessing of Isaac, the protection of Jacob, the fortune of Joseph, and the mercy of Tobit. Let them grow old in a good and quiet life, in peace and concord; lighten their cross and help them bear it; hear their prayers and bless their livelihood; protect them from all evil of body and soul, and when their time comes, let them go to sleep gently and quietly, and take them to Yourself in the eternal fatherland; through Jesus Christ. Amen.

247. Prayer of children for their father who is traveling

Almighty, merciful, and gracious God and Father, who have not only created and made us, but also keep us daily and give us all that we need in body and soul: I heartily beseech You on behalf of my father, who has set out to do his work abroad, that You would mercifully keep, sustain, and preserve him from all danger and harm, accompany him by Your holy angels, and, after he has finished his business, bring him happily home again. O Lord, hear me! Hear my prayer and supplication, O Lord, and be his guide and escort and give success and blessing to his undertaking. Sustain him in good health and good humor, that we may see him again soon and celebrate together in You through Your Son. Amen.

248. Prayer of pious children for their sick father (mother)

Almighty, everlasting God, the Father of our Lord Jesus Christ! You say in Your holy and divine Word, "Call on Me in the time of trouble and I will deliver you, and you shall glorify Me." Now that great trouble has stricken us poor children, and You have visited our dear father (mother) with physical weakness because of our sins, we come with humble hearts before Your divine majesty, calling on You in the name of Your dear Son, Jesus Christ, our dear Lord, Savior, and Redeemer, not to punish us in Your wrath, nor to chasten us in Your displeasure. Be merciful to us, O Lord, be merciful to us and lighten the heavy cross which

You have sent to our dear father (mother). Comfort him (her) by Your Holy Spirit; grant him (her) health of body, strength, and power, and do not remove him (her) from us immature children so quickly; but, according to Your divine and gracious will, let him (her) live with us longer on this earth, that he (she) may be a comfort and help to our dear mother (father) and raise us in the fear and true knowledge of You, and that we may in time serve Your Christian Church and worship, honor, praise, and glorify You, our God. Graciously restore our dear father (mother) to health, and grant that our dear father and our dear mother may find comfort and joy in us, and that we in turn may care for and attend to them in their old age and show them all love and goodness, as they have shown us when they were younger. O Lord, be gracious to us, do not count against us the sins and iniquities of our youth, with which we angered You and deserved these punishments; but look on us with the eyes of Your mercy, in Your dear Son, Jesus Christ, and measure it according to the weakness of our dear father (mother), that it may be for the honor, praise, and glory of Your name and for the salvation and welfare of our dear father's (mother's) body and soul. Graciously hear us, Your dear children, for the sake of Jesus Christ, Your dear Son, our dear Lord and Savior. Amen.

249. *Prayer of baptismal sponsors*

Lord Jesus Christ, only Savior and Redeemer of all mankind! You said, "Whoever believes and is baptized shall be saved." And again, "Unless someone is born of water and the Spirit, he cannot enter the kingdom of the God." Therefore I thank You heartily that You have so tenderly and graciously blessed the dear parents of my godchildren with the fruit of the womb, and bestowed on me the grace that in this most holy week they should incline to me in Christian affection and be pleased to choose me as their godparents over any others, that in the stead of my unspeaking godchild, I, though unworthy, should and will renounce the wicked foe and all his horde and confess You, the true God, with heart, mouth, and true faith, and commend and devote to Your most gracious keeping and protection my dear godchild in body and soul, now and forever. As You commanded: "Let the children come to Me . . . for of such is the kingdom of God"; therefore I devote and commend to You, O God of Abraham, Isaac, and Jacob, God of our fathers, this unspeaking infant, my dear godchild, that You would enlighten him (her) with the light of Your fatherly mercy, bless him (her), protect him (her), and not turn away Your face from him (her), but receive him (her) into the number of all Your believers in Christ and sustain him (her) in Your divine grace here in time and hereafter in eternity, and after this life to give him (her) everlasting joy and salvation. Amen.

250. Intercession for confirmands

O almighty, true, living God, eternal and merciful Father of our Savior Jesus Christ, who in loving kindness revealed Yourself to us: You say of Your dear Son, Jesus Christ, "This is My beloved Son, to whom you shall listen"; and this Your beloved Son Himself said, "Let the children come to Me, and do not forbid them, for of such is the kingdom of God." Therefore since these children present have been brought to Your dear Son, Jesus Christ, in Holy Baptism and are baptized into His death, washed with His blood, and buried with Christ by Holy Baptism, we beseech You, merciful God and Father, of Your lavish goodness, to renew in these Your children once more the Holy Spirit, whom You poured out on them richly in Holy Baptism, that their hearts may be lightened with the radiance of the Holy Gospel. Increase in them, O gracious God, both the pure knowledge of Your beloved Son, Jesus Christ, and the true faith, that they may believe firmly in You, the true God, and in Jesus Christ, Your Son, whom You have sent, and with firm confidence abide steadfast in You. Deliver them from the power of darkness and set them in the kingdom of Your beloved Son, in which we have redemption and forgiveness of sins. Put in their minds the peace of Christ and the joy of the Holy Spirit, and the love of God and neighbor. Fill them with the gifts of the Holy Spirit, that He may instruct and guide them into all truth, and make them fit to serve in Your holy congregation, to put to death the deeds of the flesh, to overcome the devil in all his guile and temptation, and to serve You in holiness and the righteousness pleasing to You, that together with all the faithful they may look for and await the coming of Your beloved Son with a cheerful heart and active prayer in soberness, righteousness, and godliness, to Your glory and the edification of Your poor Church; for You live and reign with Jesus Christ, Your only-begotten Son, in the power and unity of the Holy Spirit forever and ever. Amen.

251. Prayer of a master for his servants or staff

O faithful God, heavenly master! In Your Holy Word You have explicitly portrayed for all manservants and maidservants and all domestic staff their fitting office, how they are to act as Christians toward their regular authorities. But in these last days we find largely the opposite; wherefore we beseech You, dear Master and Father, to give Your Holy Spirit, that the domestic staff may discharge their calling as befits them, first committing themselves to all Christian obedience, yielding to their masters in all honest things, then performing with due diligence their assigned tasks and laboring in the sweat of their brows, not in fear and compulsion but in Christian love, with a good will, for the benefit of their masters and for their own temporal and eternal welfare; and finally, earnestly guarding themselves from all frivolity, treachery, and falsehood, that they may keep a good conscience here in time, so that, on their deathbed and especially on the Last Day, when Christ Himself shall call for an accounting of their stewardship, they may stand and may hear the glad voice, "Come, blessed servant, you have been faithful in a little; I will set you over much. Enter into the joy of your master"; through the same Your dear Son, our only Lord and Savior. Amen.

252. Prayer for the sick in general

O great and mighty God, the strength which is made perfect in weakness, the power of those who wait upon You, the true help in every need at the inopportune hour! I beseech You on behalf of all the sick, those burdened with physical weakness, or those in the throes of death, that You would grant them to know Your holy will and to accept, suffer, and bear it patiently. By Your Holy Spirit also strengthen and comfort them, refresh them on their sickbeds, and save them from all their diseases. Have mercy on them according to Your great goodness, and for the sake of the bitter sufferings of Jesus Christ, Your beloved Son, pardon them all their sins and iniquities with which they have ever angered You and given cause for any of their infirmities; and if it is not contrary to Your holy and divine will and the salvation of their souls, help them to recover and heal and strengthen them in body and soul. For if You will, You can cleanse them. You are our dear physician, our best hope, and when all human help ends, You are most happy to help. Therefore look down from heaven and see the misery and sorrow of all the sick. Let it move Your heart, and give aid and regular means through Your divine wisdom. Bring succor with Your outstretched arm, that they may be saved and healed. But as for those for whom it is more profitable to leave this present misery, according to Your divine will, rather than to linger in this valley of sorrows any longer—let them be gathered in true, firm faith and strong hope with a blessed end to Yourself in eternal joy. Assist them with Your Holy Spirit at their final hour. Give them grace that they may prepare themselves willingly and well to die, not least of all by receiving Christ's most Holy Supper, insofar as it may be provided, and be with Him in the flock of all the elect. Shorten their physical pain and agony, which they now suffer; help them to overcome all pangs of death, that they may press through to eternal life. Turn their sorrow into joy, which shall not be taken from them. Take in Your hands their souls, which You created and redeemed; through Jesus Christ, our Lord. Amen.

253. *Prayer for a sick man*

Lord, look upon him whom You love, and who loves You, who is sick. Oh, have mercy upon him! Help him, and he shall be helped in body and soul. Amen.

254. *Three intercessions for one who is possessed*

The First

Lord Jesus Christ, who descended into hell and bound Satan fast: we beseech You to descend into this pit of hell which Satan has established in the heart of the possessed. Destroy it; bind the wicked foe, that he may accomplish nothing; drive him out of him; destroy his kingdom and work in him; and speak in his soul Your blessing, Your consolation, and Your peace, Your delight and joy. Amen.

The Second

Lord Jesus Christ, who with Your almighty Word mercifully assisted a poor, dumb, and deaf man and heartily groaned at all our misery: we lament to You that Satan has also injured this young person bodily and terribly corrupted him toward every good, and no one can help him but You, Lord Jesus Christ, alone. We beseech You, have mercy upon his misery, touch his heart with the finger of the Holy Spirit, speak Your powerful word in his soul. Say to him, "Ephatha," that the iron bonds of sin with which he is bound may be instantly burst asunder. Open his ears to hear Your Holy Word blessedly. Open his mouth to speak what is pleasing to You and salutary for him, that he may always worship and glorify Your holy name with a thankful heart, a holy mouth, and a joyful voice, and be able to say the beautiful saying, "He has done all things well in heaven and on earth." Grant this to him, Lord Jesus Christ, blessed forever. Amen.

The Third

O almighty, eternal Holy Trinity, Father, Son, and Holy Spirit, single, eternal divine Essence, we thank You from our hearts for all the benefits and for the riches of Your grace shown to us and beseech You of Your eternal Godhead, holiness, and glory, have mercy on us and keep us in Your Word and truth, in the true knowledge of Your being and will, in firm confidence, in holy love of Your name and obedience to Your will, that we may praise, honor, and fear You. O Lord, let Your great love and mercy blot out the sin of the possessed; let Your unspeakable goodness come to his aid in all his misery; let Your almighty authority be his strength against Satan and all adversity; let Your truth help him out of all trouble; let Your love, favor, and goodness assist and comfort him!

O eternal power of God, the Father, Son, and Holy Spirit, strengthen him. O eternal Godhead of God, have mercy on him and be gracious to him. O most holy Majesty of God, help him in all his troubles, preserve him to the glory of Your name and the salvation of his soul; through Jesus Christ. Amen.

Lord God, the Father, who sent Your Son to destroy the works of Satan and bring us into Your kingdom: we beseech You, make a blessed beginning of Your divine kingdom in the possessed, and destroy in him the work of Satan. Amen.

Eternal, true Son of God, Jesus Christ, our Lord and King, Victor over Satan: we cry to You, humbly beseeching You to drive out from him the evil foe with the power of Your finger; grant us the strength, protection, and arms to resist Satan. Help us ourselves to fight, struggle, conquer, and overcome. Amen.

O Holy Spirit, fill us with power from heaven to resist Satan and claim the victory over him. Amen.

255. *Prayer for a person possessed by Satan*
Lord God, heavenly Father, who by Your beloved Son have commanded us to pray and ordained and instituted the preaching office in the holy Christian Church, that we might with a gentle spirit instruct any brother who has fallen into error and restore him; and this Your beloved Son, Christ, Himself says that He came only because of our sins: we therefore beseech You on behalf of this Your servant that You would forgive him his sins, enclose him again in the article of the forgiveness of sins, and receive him back into the bosom of the holy Church; for the sake of Your dear Son, Christ our Lord. Amen.

256. *Prayer for a sick woman who is in tribulation*

Lord God, heavenly Father, who have called us to pray for the sick: we beseech You through Jesus Christ, Your dear Son, that You would redeem this Your maidservant from her sickness and from the devil's bonds. Spare, dear Lord, her soul, which You by the shedding of Your dear Son Jesus Christ's blood, purchased and saved from sin, death, and the power of the devil. Amen.

257. *Prayer at a committal service*

Almighty God, dear Father, how are all the men who live in the world nothing. You have set a measure to our life which we cannot exceed or surmount. Yet we have now accompanied a brother (sister) to the grave. O Lord, teach us to number our days! Govern us by Your Holy Spirit, that we may always be ready when You shall come and summon us. Let us not be afraid of death, but with a fearless heart await our release, and after this wretched life live forever with You. Then turn our sufferings into joy, and wipe away all our tears. Fetch home, Lord, Your servants when it pleases You; only grant a blessed death. To the deceased, therefore, grant a gentle rest in the bosom of the earth and a joyous resurrection with all the elect on the day of Your beloved Son's appearing. Comfort the survivors mightily with Your Holy Spirit. Be their God, their Father and Protector, to the praise and honor of Your holy name because of Your great mercy. Amen.

258. *Prayer of a hearer on behalf of his minister*

Almighty, gracious God, heavenly Father, I beseech You on behalf of my dear minister that You would gift him with all manner of boldness to speak Your Word against false doctrine and error and to make known the mystery of Your Gospel. Keep him in pure doctrine and a salutary life. Give him a sound body, powers, and strength, that he may preside over us fruitfully and beneficially a long time. Let him rebuke all sin and vice, as is fitting, that I and many others may be won over to Your kingdom. Open my heart and ears, that I may hear my minister with delight and love, devotion of mind and attention of heart, and with true faith walk in a godly manner according to his teaching and preaching, and bring forth fruit, that Your Word, going forth from You, may not return to You void, but accomplish that which You please, and prosper in the thing for which You sent it. Help me to receive with a good will all fatherly reproof and admonition from my preacher and to be corrected thereby, to cease from my sins, and to live in Your obedience. Keep us always in true faith and a Christian life, that in them we may daily increase and persevere until the end, and then be eternally saved; through Jesus Christ, Your beloved Son. Amen.

259. *Prayer of a parishioner*

Eternal, gracious God, heavenly Father, I beseech You on behalf of my minister that You would give him Your Word, along with a boldness in opening his mouth, to speak without fear against all error, false doctrine, and abuse, that he may reveal and make known to us the mystery of Your Gospel and pluck all false delusions from our hearts. Keep him in pure, saving doctrine and in Christian conduct, that he may go before us to eternal life. Preserve his body and health, that he may preside over us fruitfully and beneficially a long time and preach Your divine Word without any hesitation, fear, or apprehension, without hypocrisy, not from favoritism, hatred, envy, or personal gain, but speak the pure truth without adulteration and rebuke vice, as is fitting, that I and many others may be won over to Your kingdom. Open my heart and ears, that I may hear Your salutary Word with delight and love, devotion of mind and attention of heart, and with true faith walk in a godly manner according to it, and bring forth fruit to Your divine glory, that Your Word, going forth from You, may not return to You void, but accomplish that which You please, and prosper in the thing for which You sent it. Therefore take from me all sloth and idleness of heart, and plant in my mind a true hunger and earnest longing for the abundant riches of Your grace, which are presented to us in pure preaching. Give me grace that I may know my minister and regard him as Your servant and the steward of Your divine mysteries, that I may receive Your Word from his mouth as though it were from You Yourself and not despise the holy ministry which You have committed to men, and that I may not hold Your Word in less esteem because of any deficiencies in the man who preaches and proclaims it. Help me to receive peaceably and willingly all fatherly reproofs and admonitions from my preacher, to understand them as well-intended, and to be corrected thereby, to cease from my sins, and not to hate or reject discipline, or oppose or slander those who rebuke me. Keep us always in true faith and a Christian life, that in them we may grow, increase daily, persevere steadfast until our end, and be eternally saved; through Jesus Christ, Your beloved Son. Amen.

260. Prayer for true preachers, to be prayed especially in a vacancy

O almighty God, who by Your beloved Son, Jesus Christ, commanded us to pray for laborers in Your harvest and graciously promised to hear us: I beseech You for the sake of the same, Your dear Son, to give Your Church true ministers and preachers of Your Holy Word in great number and multitude. Send us wise men well-versed in Scripture, and grace with Your Holy Spirit those whom You send us. Fill them with true understanding of Your Word, that they may rightly point us the way to life everlasting, expound the Scriptures without distortion, and warn us of improper faith and human inventions together with all things poisonous to the soul, that we may be found in the pure doctrine and faith without adulteration. For how shall we believe in Him of whom we have not heard? And how shall we hear without preachers? And how shall they preach except they be sent? Therefore, O most beloved Father, place in Your Church learned bishops, Christian parsons, pure preachers, faithful shepherds, and godly teachers and curates, who by Your Holy Spirit faithfully feed the congregation which Your dear Son purchased with His own blood, who declare and spread abroad fruitfully and to great profit the Holy Gospel, Your precious and worthy Word, to the glory of Your divine name; who turn sinners to repentance, strengthen the weak in faith, comfort faint consciences against all the temptations of Satan and the wicked world; who are mighty to admonish by holy doctrine and to rebuke those who contradict it, that they may with great force resist their adversaries, beat them back and prevail over them, and destroy and lay waste the devil's kingdom; and who precede the flock and congregation of God with a good example and godly conduct, that all offense may be prevented and no one kept from the faith by an ungodly life. O merciful God, send not into our land a hunger and famine of Your Word, nor let us be deprived of pure preachers. Let us not be repaid for our ingratitude. But from wicked laborers, unfaithful hirelings, and all who run forward of their own accord and are not sent by You, preserve us, dear Father; through Jesus Christ, Your dear Son, our Lord. Amen.

261. Prayer at a Bible festival

O faithful, gracious, and merciful God, we thank You for the great grace, love, and faithfulness which You have shown to us poor, needy men by the revelation of Your holy, divine Word and the institution of Your most worthy Sacraments. The Spirit of the Lord spoke by the prophets, and His words came through their mouths. By these means You gave us to know in what knowledge of You eternal life consists; by these means You called us to the community of Your holy Church. Your Holy Gospel is also a power of God to save all who believe in it: by it You awake faith within us, You give us the Holy Spirit, You cause us to proclaim the forgiveness of sins, by which we receive the true, living comfort in all cross and in the distress of death; by it You still our sad minds; by it You gladden our sad hearts; by it You feed our souls as with the true bread of heaven; by it You make us new creatures; by it You come to us and make Your home among us; by it You relieve the distress of our death so that we will not taste death forever; by it You enlighten our souls; by it You govern and lead us in our calling and in the course of our whole life as with a light to our path and a lamp unto our feet, that our feet may not stumble. O Lord! If Your Word had not been our delight, we would have perished in our afflictions. For Your Word is the joy and comfort of our hearts. By the Word of God we are sanctified and blessed in body and soul; therefore, O Lord, he who rejects Your Word has rejected You Yourself and all his temporal and eternal blessing and can by no means have the blessing, but will have the eternal curse; and the heaven will stay from her dew, and the earth will stay from her fruit; the heaven will be as iron and earth as brass, and all their strength shall be spent in vain. O Lord, we thank You for this noble, precious treasure! For the Law of the Lord is perfect, refreshing the soul; the testimony of the Lord is sure, making wise the simple. The statutes of the Lord are right, rejoicing the heart; the Commandments of the Lord are pure, enlightening the eyes. The fear of the Lord is clean, enduring forever; the precepts of the Lord are true and righteous altogether. They are more desired than gold, yea, than much fine gold. They are sweeter than honey and the honeycomb. By them Your servant also is made glad, and he who keeps them has a great reward. Your Word, O Most High, is the foundation of wisdom, and her source is the everlasting commandment. He who honors her does true worship, and him who loves it God loves in turn.

The King of Israel says of God, "I am like the cedars of Lebanon, and as the cypresses on the mountains of Hermon. I am exalted like a palm tree by the water, and as a rose plant in Jericho, as a fair olive tree. I give a sweet smell like cinnamon and myrrh and frankincense. Come, all you who desire me, and fill yourselves with my fruits. My memorial is sweeter than honey, and my gift than the honeycomb. He who eats of me will always hunger for me, and he who drinks of me will always thirst for me. This is the book of the covenant made with the Most High God, even the Law of Moses, from which Wisdom has flowed as the Euphrates when it is enlarged, as the Jordan in the time of the harvest, like the Nile in the autumn. There has never been one who learned her perfectly, nor will he ever be who can fathom her. For her thoughts are richer than any sea, and her word is deeper than any abyss. There flow into the gardens many brooks from her; and there the brooks become rivers, and the rivers great waters. For her instruction shines as far as the bright day and sends forth her light in the morning. And they pour out doctrine and prophecy which abide to all generations" (Ecclesiasticus 14:13–33).For this high and precious treasure we give You thanks, O God, the Father, Son, and Holy Spirit, most blessed forever. Amen.

262. Prayer for mission services

I beseech You, my heavenly Father, through Jesus Christ, Your dear Son, our Lord, graciously to have mercy on all unbelievers, whoever and wherever they may be, who are still walking in darkness, who do not have the light of Your Gospel, whom the devil has stricken with blindness and darkened their ignorant hearts, who through the ignorance that is in them are estranged from the life which is from God, who seek guidance from dumb idols, and in their blindness curse and blaspheme Your dear Son, Jesus Christ, the propitiation for our sins. Therefore, O faithful God, remove the veil that still hangs before the hearts of the Jews, who fall on the stone of stumbling and on the rock of offense. Enlighten their eyes, that they may acknowledge the true Messiah, the Savior of the world. Bring the heathen and all unbelievers who regard Your Word as foolishness into the true fold and assembly of Christians, the fellowship of the saints, that with us and all believers, they may honor, praise, and worship the Father in the Son and the Son with the Father and Holy Spirit, one true God and Lord. Open the understanding of all men who do not put their salvation and trust solely upon the foundation and cornerstone, Christ Jesus, that they may know Him whom You have sent, and with genuine faith and true and hearty confidence receive as their Savior and Redeemer Him who by His obedience and fulfilling of the Law through His bitter death has obtained eternal redemption. May You also bring all who have departed from the Christian faith, or else have gone astray in certain points and are burdened with false doctrine, and restore them to the eternal truth of Your Word. God of all grace, have mercy on those who are not of the true faith, who sit in the shadow of death and walk in an uneven way according to the darkness of their minds. Seek the lost, bring back the erring, enlighten the blind, open the ears of the deaf, open the mouths of the dumb, who do not confess You, raise up the fallen, bring back those who have gone away, gather together the scattered, restore the erring and misled, for Your mercy. Amen.

263. *Prayer for the Church*

Lord, merciful and gracious God, inasmuch as these are only Your citizens and fellow residents which are built upon the foundation of the prophets and apostles, in which Jesus Christ is the chief cornerstone, and You bless with grace only those who walk in Your light, therefore I beseech You to let Your Word so shine in the world that in many places there may be a house where the voice of Christ is heard and Your Word learned, that everywhere men may keep the Commandments of God and faith in our Lord Jesus Christ. So may the congregation of believers grow ever greater, and there be many thousands upon thousands of the chariots of God to enter into the gates of righteousness, to dwell in Your house, and so to leave all unrighteousness, and to serve You alone in holiness and righteousness before You. O Lord Jesus Christ, who are the founder and perfecter of the faith, and greatly to be feared in the assembly of the saints: govern the hearts of men by Your inward grace, that they may turn to You. Give Your thunder, that is, the preaching of the power of Your Word. Let it prosper in the thing for which You send it. Enlighten and strengthen the hearts of men that they may not be separated from Your Church, but walk eagerly with the flock in the house where Your Word and Holy Sacraments are expressed and administered purely and without distortion. Although it is a little flock, a poor, unimpressive people, beaten by every storm and having almost no solace anywhere in the world, yet that little flock is to have no fear, for it is Your good pleasure to give them the kingdom of Your glory, where You will take away the disgrace of Your people and draw to Yourself all those who persevered with You in Your tribulations, that they may eat and drink at Your table in Your kingdom, and sit on thrones, judging the twelve tribes of Israel. Do not grant the devil his desire, who is opposed to You and Your Word, hindering it where he can so that it is not heard or believed. Glorify Your name, that many souls may be added to the number of the elect, even those who dwell in Your house, ever singing Your praise. Amen.

264. *Prayer for the Christian Church and against her enemies*

Almighty, everlasting, merciful God and Father of our dear Lord and Savior, Jesus Christ: we see and sense the condition of Your Church in this life, what sort of fortune she has, and the various ways she is afflicted by the devil and the world. We therefore beseech You for the sake of the same, Your only-begotten Son, firstly, to comfort and strengthen our hearts with Your Holy Spirit, that we may not be defeated or cast down by many great dangers; and secondly, that You would not only hinder the counsels and endeavors of the enemy, but with Your faithful and wonderful help also show, declare, and demonstrate to the world that You nurture, govern, protect, preserve, and deliver Your Church; for You live and reign with the Son and the Holy Spirit, one eternal God, forever and ever. Amen.

265. *Prayer against the antichrist, or Roman pope, and all his party*

Dear God and Father of our Lord Jesus Christ, we beseech You to visit us once more according to all Your wondrous works and to show us the day of the coming of Your Son's glory, that that villain, the Antichrist, the very man of lawlessness and son of perdition, may be destroyed and brought to nothing, and an end be made of the monstrous errors of the devil, by which (alas!) at every moment many thousand souls are ruined and snatched to hell, solely to preserve intact the tyranny of the abominable and apostate chair of Rome; to which may all the world say Amen, Amen.

266. *Prayer of faithful teachers and preachers at pastors' conferences*

Gracious and merciful God, in exceptional grace You called us to the preaching office and laid on us the spiritual works of teaching, preaching, baptizing, absolving, and giving Communion. Now we are willing and ready, and we have a hearty desire to do it. But You see how weak and incapable we are for these spiritual works of our own powers. You also see how fiercely they are attacked by the devil and his horde. Therefore, dear God, further these works, give strength and power to the end that we may faithfully discharge them! Hinder and restrain the devil and all his followers that they may not defile these works: that the Law and Gospel may not be confounded by false teaching and hypocrisy, nor Baptism and Communion despised by Anabaptists and Sacramentarians, nor the Absolution twisted by false indulgences and popish lies, but that every person may continue in his strength and dignity, and that Your Holy

Spirit, who dwells in us, may not be grieved by our sins, but mighty and active in all these things, that we may always be found Your faithful servants. Amen.

267. Prayer for constancy and preservation in the saving Word, to conclude pastors' conferences

Lord God, Father of all bounties and strength! Mercifully confirm and strengthen us by Your Holy Spirit in the work which You have begun, that Satan may not weaken us by any might or cunning, nor make us weary so that we forsake Your Word and kingdom. For this is a dangerous time, when many are being led away or even falling away through sectarian spirits, and many are becoming apathetic and cold, so that, deceived by Satan's guile, they come to believe that they are content, can do all things, and are in no danger, and so grow lazy and ungrateful, and are soon worse than before. Therefore let us remain fervent in the faith, that we may daily increase therein, through Jesus Christ, our true and only helper. Amen.

268. Prayer in congregational assemblies

Merciful, gracious God, who have taught and commanded us to seek first Your kingdom and its righteousness before all else: I beseech You to grant grace that Your Holy Word may be preached in its purity to all the world, and we may bring our reason into captivity to the obedience of the faith, and as children of God also lead holy lives in accordance thereto, as is pleasing to You, that Your kingdom may come in and to us and be increased, and many of those who do not believe in the Word may be won over by a Christian conduct. Help us, dear God, that by grace we may be delivered from the power of darkness and transferred to the kingdom of Your dear Son, Jesus Christ, in whom we have redemption through His blood, the forgiveness of sins, that we may dwell in His kingdom, continue steadfast in sound doctrine, and walk worthily in all godliness and honesty as children of the light. But since the kingdom of God does not come by outward actions, nor consists of words, but of power and Spirit, grant grace that by Your saving Word and Holy Spirit, we may be born anew and regenerated from on high, as fellow heirs of life, that we may dwell with our minds in heaven, and continually strive for the imperishable, unblemished, and incorruptible inheritance. Help us to be spiritually poor and humble, to be sorry for our sins; give us a hunger and thirst, that is, a heartfelt longing, for righteousness, and that at the same time we may be meek, merciful, pure in heart, and peaceable, and for the sake of righteousness and truth, patiently endure and overcome all manner of persecution and hostility, evil backbiting, and undeserving slander. Keep us from all offenses by which Your holy name is blasphemed and confounded and Your kingdom hindered and weakened. Grant grace that we may put our faith into practice by all manner of works of charity and mercy involving food and drink, clothing, lodging, and comforting and visiting the poor and needy in this world, that we may hear on that Day the joyful and gracious voice of Your dear Son: "Come, you blessed of My Father, inherit the kingdom prepared for you from the foundation of the world." Amen.

269. Prayer for the church in congregational assemblies

Lord and God, because Your godly have ceased and Your faithful are few on earth, and it is to be feared that, with so few godly men, all places will be filled with the ungodly, O arise, therefore, and help Your poor and needy, that those who are now sighing may not be destroyed! Let Your divine truth be taught with confidence and confessed without hypocrisy before all. Spread abroad Your Word, which as silver refined in the fire is pure and unadulterated, and defend us from the wicked generation of those who set forth vain things instead of Your Word, or else do not take the religion seriously. Increase the little flock, that it may stand firm against the great multitude of the ungodly, and all the gates of hell may not prevail against it; through Jesus Christ. Amen.

270. Prayer for peace in the congregation

O almighty, everlasting God, dear, heavenly Father, God of unity and peace, who not only are one with Your only-begotten Son, Jesus Christ, and the Holy Spirit, but also have promised in Your Holy Word to give us a unified heart, mind, and disposition if we call upon You for that purpose: we beseech You devoutly and with one accord to curb and restrain all discord; to beat down Satan, the founder of discord, under our feet, that we may give no room to his suggestions; and to give to us generally and individually a meek, humble, and peaceable heart, that we may live together in unity as brothers, establish and preserve peace with kind actions and gracious words, and be diligent to hold the unity in the Spirit through the bond of peace, so that all of us who believe in Your name and are members of one body may be one in soul and mind, and may thereby show ourselves to be Your dear children in deed. O loving God of peace, who have so wondrously mingled the human body that the needy member is given the most honor, that there may not be a division in the body, but all members may care for and be united with each other: grant us that we may faithfully guard ourselves against all discord and conflict, threatening, quarreling, and strife, and rather cultivate sincere brotherly love, peace, and concord, that we being bound together here in this time with the bond of charity, may lead a peaceable and godly life, have a quiet conscience, and after this time, O God of peace, may rejoice with You and all holy angels, believers, and the elect in the awaited eternity of the heavenly land of peace, indissoluble unity, and unspeakable glory, when our blessed peace of heaven shall never cease. O dear Lord and God, let us depart in peace from the unrest of this world to the eternal peace of heaven which You purchased for us with Your sharp and bitter death. Amen.

271. *Prayer for the conversion of the deceived*

Gracious God and Father, who desire all men to be saved and to come to the knowledge of the truth! I beseech You to have mercy on all unbelievers who still dwell in darkness and the shadow of death, whose minds are darkened and blinded by the devil from seeing the bright light of Your Gospel, that they may be turned from the error of their way and their souls be saved from death. Open the eyes of the blind and lead them in the way that they do not know. Take away the veil that hangs before their eyes and heart, that they may know You and Him whom You sent, even Jesus Christ. O Lord, who long ago beheld the misery of Your people Israel in Egypt and heard and answered their sighs and lamentations, will You not also hear the sighs of the needy who are oppressed, constrained, afflicted, and tormented by the Antichrist with an unbearable burden? You regard and look upon what is miserable and afflicted. Therefore arise and grant help, that we may teach with confidence. Convert the poor who have been enchanted by false teachers and blind leaders so that they do not obey the truth, but go to dumb idols as they are led, and put on a yoke of true bondage, toil like slaves, act defiantly, and submit to be stricken in the face. Oh, if only they knew, they would surely consider what things make for their peace! But this is the hour and power of darkness, for their hearts are hardened and dull, and their ears are hard of hearing, and their eyes are shut with slumber. O Lord, enlighten them, that they may no longer harden their hearts to the Holy Gospel, but may acknowledge the powerful error in which they lay and come out of Babylon and give glory to God. Turn those who have fallen away, who may yet be turned again, and take certain ones among the fat, take them from the depths of the sea and bring them to Your fold. Grant that they may always let the earnest voice of Your Son ring in their ears: "Saul, Saul, why do you persecute Me? It is hard for you to kick against the goads." Enlighten also, O Lord, all who believe their own reason rather than Your Word, that they may see the light and know what is not light. O God, founder and preserver of the truth, sanctify me in the truth which I have come to know, that I may fearlessly stand up for Your divine glory, the majesty of Your Word, and the purity of the faith, and remain steadfast until the end; through Jesus Christ, Your only-begotten Son, in the power of the Holy Spirit. Amen.

272. *Prayer against atheism and Epicurean complacency*

Help, Lord! The godly have ceased, and the faithful fail from among the children of men! There is no truth, no love, no Word of God anymore in the land, but only sin and Epicurean complacency, and it is the very time of which Your dearest Son spoke, saying that when He would come, He would hardly find faith on the earth. For the faces of the multitude witness against them, and they declare their sins like Sodom, and they are sorry that they can do no worse; indeed, many fools and brutish persons say in their hearts, "There is no God, but we were born by chance, and by chance we will return," and it seems that, on Your Last Day, which will come like a snare upon all who dwell on the earth, You will come and take away many thousands of such ungodly atheists and Epicures and command them, as the eternally accursed, to depart from Your presence into the hellfire which is prepared for the devil and his angels. O dear God, I know in whom I believe and am assured that You, God the Father, Son, and Holy Spirit, are alone the true God, and not a God who takes pleasure in wickedness, and he who is evil does not stand before You; oh, then never let such wicked thoughts enter my heart, as that there is no God, nor let me live so securely that I think in my sins, "The Lord does not see it, and the God of Jacob does not regard it." For where shall I go from Your Spirit, and where shall I flee from Your presence if Your hand does not lead me there, and Your right hand does not uphold me? Therefore let me remember well that in You we live, move, and have our being, and that there is no word on my tongue, but You, Lord, know it altogether. And let me therefore conduct myself well and serve You in holiness and righteousness pleasing to You. Help me to renounce ungodliness and worldly lusts, and to live a chaste, upright, and godly life in this present world. Yet also by Your infinite power curb all Epicureanism and atheism, that all men may know that You are the great Lord who made the sun and the whole earth and preserve and uphold all things by Your mighty Word, that You are round about us, whether we walk or lie down, and see all our ways. And because he who turns a sinner from the error of his way saves a soul from death and covers over a multitude of sins, give me the heart and spirit not to run with thieves, nor to have fellowship with adulterers, but to warn these and all other sinners of their complacency, that they may be instructed and consider that He who made the eye sees all things, and He who made the ear hears all things, and eventually all that was concealed in darkness shall be brought to light, and the counsel of every heart be revealed. Assist me also, that I may have You before my eyes and heart as long as I live, that I may not transgress Your commandment, but at Your last coming may be accounted worthy to escape all these things which will come to pass and to stand before the Son of Man. Amen.

273. Prayer for the marital estate

Holy God, merciful Father, who Yourself instituted the marital estate and are pleased that man and wife should dwell together in marital love to fill the world, enlarging Your Church by the begetting of children, that thereby Your holy name may be forever praised and worshiped: therefore because Satan, as an enemy of all Your divine ordinances, fiercely attacks this estate with all cunning and opposes it forcefully, I beseech You to grant all Christian spouses grace to acknowledge You, the founder of their ordinance, and to be comforted in their conscience with the knowledge that they are in an estate which is good and pleasing to You, in which they can also serve You and have salvation, that they may be the more willing to do with a good will all that their vocation requires. Help them to fear You, to dwell together as Christians in true charity and unity, to eat their bread in the sweat of their faces, to raise their children in all godliness, and also to bear patiently their mutual cross, which is not absent from this estate. Restrain the devil who causes discord in marriage, that he may not disturb or spoil Your creation and ordinance and not cause spouses, it may be, to tire of their estate or come to hate it, nor to catch them in his net by unbelief, nor to sow and intersperse between them his seed of all kinds of strife and discord by embittering their hearts, lest they be incited to break Your commandment by adultery or unchastity or by forsaking each other, and be led astray into other great sin, shame, and vice, or into quarreling, strife, and discord, or to live ungodly lives at the expense of their consciences, whereby their prayer and all practice of Christianity is hindered, the Church and the Holy Spirit offended. Help, merciful God, that all disagreeing spouses may be reconciled again in Your name, forgive each other from the depths of their hearts, remember their marital covenant and pledge, dwell together in true love and fidelity, learn Your Holy Word with all diligence and keep it in all honor, hope and build upon You in the midst of all adversity, and sanctify and praise You with their prayer and Christian conduct, that they may be found in Your service and good pleasure, and after this fleeting life be gathered to all godly spouses in Your kingdom. Amen.

274. Prayer when new authorities are to be elected

O almighty, merciful God and Father, You desire that Your people should be provided with just judges and officers, that Your law may be enforced according to Your entire pleasure: I beseech You heartily to give us leaders and rulers who inquire after Your will and are inclined with their whole heart so to govern Your people that Your praise and glory may be advanced and the common peace preserved; through Jesus Christ. Amen.

275. Prayer for temporal authorities

Almighty, everlasting God, King of kings, from whom all rank and power proceed, who instituted temporal authority and committed to it the sword for the punishment of the wicked and the protection of the good: lead all temporal lords and rulers in Your way, that they may keep the common peace, turn away from us war and sedition, and nurture whatever makes for peace, honor, and justice. To that end, O Lord of hosts, give them Your divine blessing, the righteousness of Moses, the meekness of David, the zeal of Phinehas, the strength of Samson, and the wisdom of Solomon. Make and keep them steadfast in good, courageous in adversity, confident in affliction, joyful in sorrow, reliable in distress, victorious in temptation, unmoved in prosperity, and wise, strong, and prosperous in all their endeavors. Let their government serve for the suppression of all tyrants, peace in this present time, and the protection of Christians, to the praise and eternal worship of Your holy name; through Jesus Christ, our Lord and Savior. Amen.

276. Prayer for the prosperity of the fruits of the earth

Lord God Almighty, King of heaven and earth, who of Your abundant goodness adorn and fill the whole earth with all manner of fruits, by which man
and beast are nourished: I beseech You of Your mercy to bless our land, that it
may yield its fruits and increase, since of ourselves we cannot bring one grain
from the soil, nor can we help it if You do not grant success. Therefore grant
these fruits fair weather, that they may increase and mature well. Harbor them
from hail and tempest, destruction, and especially from vermin and any cause
of harm. Do not cause the land to lie fallow in Your wrath, lest it be desolate
and remain unfruitful. Do not shut up the heavens in Your anger because of
our sins, lest they be made like iron and the earth like bronze; but give us the
early and the latter rain and fruitful seasons. Visit the earth and water it, and
greatly enrich it, for the river of God has fullness of water. O Lord, let our grain
prosper, for so You prepare the land. Water its furrows, and moisten its ridges
with rain; make it soft, and bless its growing. Crown the year with Your goodness, that Your tracks may drop fatness, and the pastures in the wilderness will
be fattened also, so that they drip, and the hills rejoice on every side, and the
meadows are filled with sheep, and the valleys are thick with grain, that we may
shout for joy and sing.

Therefore, dear God, graciously watch over the seed and all the fruits of
the whole earth. Preserve them in frost, cold, ice, and snow, in wind, heat, and
drought, in rain and every kind of weather, that they may not be harmed. Defend us from unfruitfulness, famine, hunger, and care. Behold, we confess our
sins with penitent hearts and cry to You, our God, that You would hear in heav-
en, Your dwelling place, and forgive the sins of Your people and not forsake us
with bodily nourishment, but provide for us, that in all things we may gratefully
acknowledge Your divine power and bountiful hand and glorify You, who so
richly feed us in body and soul, here in time and hereafter in eternity. Amen.

277. Intercession for those who do good

O good and faithful God! Inasmuch as I hear and discern from Your divine
Word that You are displeased by all ingratitude, and the punishment shall not
be absent from the house of the thankless, seeing the hope of an ungrateful
person will suddenly pass away like thin frost before brightness of the sun and
melt away like useless water: therefore I beseech You, grant me grace, that at every moment I may give You thanks from my inmost heart for all Your benefits,

nor may be found ungrateful toward those who have ever done me any good. Therefore I thank You, Lord God, almighty Father, for You are good, and Your mercy endures forever. You are faithful and keep Your covenant to the thousandth generation. To You, O God, the eternal King, the immortal, invisible, and only-wise, be glory and honor forever. I pray You on behalf of all men who have shown me good, who have raised and sustained me from my youth up, who have instructed, disciplined, and directed me for good, who have helped me along with words and works, and for those for whom I am otherwise obliged to pray, whose names and necessities are familiar to You, dear God, that You would take them into Your care, do good to them in body and soul, here in time and hereafter in eternity. Grant me grace and Your blessing, that I may be able to repay their well-doing in due time and requite it to their children. And as I have received good, let me also, according to my means, be helpful and beneficial to others from henceforth, that my leaves may not wither, nor I be uprooted as a dry, unfruitful tree. Let me not become reluctant, weary, and careless because of the ingratitude of others, nor cease from doing good to all men, especially to my fellows in the faith, since You, the heavenly Father, are also gracious and cause Your sun to shine on the wicked and on the good, and let rain fall on the just and unjust. Let us follow Your example in this, that we may prove that we are Your true children and let our light so shine before men that they may see our good works and glorify You, the true God in heaven, that with our well-doing we may silence the ignorance of foolish men, that Your divine name may not be profaned and blasphemed among us, nor Your glory disgraced; for You live and reign, one true, almighty God, forever and ever. Amen.

278. Intercession for one's enemies

Almighty, everlasting God, who by Your dear Son have earnestly commanded us to love our enemies, to do good to those who hurt us, and to pray for those who persecute us: we cry to You earnestly that You would visit all our enemies, mercifully grant them true repentance for their sins, and give them a tender, God-fearing, peaceable, and unanimous mind and heart with us and with all Christians; through Jesus Christ our Lord. Amen.

279. Heartfelt prayer and sigh for Christ's coming again

O Lord Jesus Christ, faithful watcher of men, I heartily thank You that You have not left us uninformed of Your coming again, but have willed faithfully to warn us in advance. Waken me, dear Lord, from the sleep of complacency, that I may diligently guard myself from sins against conscience, and as a wise servant be always ready and await Your return from heaven with the greatest joy and longing, as that on which our only and final hope depends in this lamentable age. Come, Lord Jesus, make haste, Lord, conclude the wicked days, that the poor flock may not despair utterly. O heavenly cornerstone and foundation, strike the image in its feet, which are of clay and iron, and crush them, and bring us into the new heaven and the new earth, in which righteousness dwells. Let Your saints one day take the kingdom and possess it forever. Be moved to this by Your divine promise and fervent love toward us, Your dearly purchased bride, as well as by the heartfelt longing of all nature and the unceasing sighs of Your faithful Christians, and also by the blood of so many thousand martyrs which was shed for Your name. Therefore come, dear Lord Jesus, and hasten Your judgment. Yet let Your praiseworthy and majestic voice be heard so that heaven and earth quake. Not a day goes by that we do not await You and wish that we were soon with You. Amen, Lord Jesus! Amen.

VIII. REPENTANCE, CONFESSION & COMMUNION

280. Self-examination from the Ten Commandments

First Commandment

O holy and righteous God, who see and hear all things: I come before You now to examine carefully the condition of my soul and to learn how I am, and whether I am on the way of destruction. I am far too corrupt, my heart far too false and deceiving, for me to do it myself. Search me Yourself, O God! Try me and know my thoughts, and make me aware of them by Your Word and Spirit. Have I remembered You often, great Maker and Sustainer, Redeemer and Sanctifier? — Have I used Your will and Your Commandments as my guidepost in what I do and do not, and have I always asked myself, "Is this in line with God's commandment?" — Have I entertained any detestable thoughts, such as, "There is no God"? — Have I not honored many idols and thought of myself highly, followed only my own will, and sought only my own glory and satisfaction? — Have I not feared other men more than God, revered their presence more than God's presence, and made a greater effort to gain their favor than God's grace, and done more in love toward them than I would do love in to God? — Have I not put my trust in great benefactors and in the favor of men? — Has my heart found its rest, etc., in temporal things such as money, goods, honor, and an easy life instead of seeking its only delight and joy in the eternal good from which all others come? — Have I perhaps sought the help of Satan and his sorcerers rather than the help of God and feared their power more than the strength of God? — Have I had a proper conception of God's power, omnipresence, righteousness, and grace in order to move myself to childlike fear? — Has my fear of God also borne true fruit, such as obedience, hatred of evil, remorse for sin, humility, patience, vigilance, and the like? — Have I sought to know God as the highest good and to love Him above all things? — Have I to that end diligently sought God's perfection, majesty, goodness, mercy, power, wealth, and benefits? — Has my love arisen merely for the sake of those benefits and temporal happiness? — Have I also detected in myself the fruits of true and genuine love of God, such as hatred of sin, contempt for the world, long-suffering, desire for greater union with God, praise, thanksgiving, and joy? — What form has my trust toward God taken? Is it a well-founded and childlike trust? — Have I founded it on God's goodness, truth, omnipotence, and promise? — Has this trust worked true fruit in me, such as hope, serenity, courage, and constancy? — Likewise, what form has my knowledge of God taken? Is it a living or dead knowledge? And do I seek to increase in that knowledge? Do I earnestly guard myself against all errors? — Are all, or even most of, my desires centered on God and His grace?

Second Commandment

How have I treated God's name, or everything in which God is revealed in His glory? — Have I not frequently spoken the names of God and Jesus irreverently? — How often have I prayed without true devotion and conception of God's majesty? — What form has my reading and meditation of God's Word taken? — Have I not sometimes quoted verses of Holy Scripture in an unfitting manner to bring attention to myself or to make a joke? — Have I, in the contemplation and use of created things, reverently regarded the Creator's wisdom, goodness, and almighty power? — Have I misused my mouth for cursing, swearing, and slander after the manner of brazen sinners? — Have I clung to superstition or magical things? — Have I been a liar and deceiver in spiritual things and knowingly twisted God's Word, or even deceived others through hypocrisy? — What form have my praise and thanks taken?

Third Commandment

Have I regarded the Sabbath with due reverence and tried to sanctify it in a way pleasing to God? — Have I on Sundays allowed my mind to rest from temporal concerns and my body from the regular work of my vocation, that God might do His work in me and I might rest in God? Have I, to that end, prepared myself in the morning with sincere prayer? — Have I come to God's house at the proper time? — Have I behaved as a child of God in thoughts, words, and actions, and heard the Word devoutly as the Word of God and prayed and sung with sincerity? Have I acted like a child of the world at church and used my clothing to show off, chatted about worldly things, looked down on other people, judged the preacher's recitation only by human favor, sought prestige before others through a special position, or passed much of the time sleeping? — Have I recalled the sermon at home, or thought over those points which especially pertain to my situation? — Have I passed the rest of my Sunday with holy activities, such as reading, praying, singing, examining myself, contemplating God's works and benefits, renewing my good resolution, and so on? — Have I tried to instruct, stir up, and edify others, used good speech, and assisted and comforted the poor and afflicted? — Or have I joined the world in seeking all manner of carnal amusements and passed the time with sinful jokes, foolishness, even gambling, and looked to my own contentment on the Lord's day in indolence, excessive eating and drinking, or frivolous parties? — Have I been serious about serving God and being properly edified and amended?

Fourth Commandment

How have I treated my parents, my teachers, and my authorities? — Have I humbly acknowledged and honored the image of God affixed to them? — Have I made an effort to show them all love, fidelity, obedience, and gratitude, and called on God for their physical and spiritual welfare?

Fifth Commandment

Have I not frequently held a grudge against my neighbor, hated him in my heart, envied him, rejoiced at his misfortune, and planned revenge on him? — How often has my anger exceeded bounds of moderation? — Have I not wrongly addressed my actions in wrath and expressed angry, mocking, insulting words and evil wishes? — Have I not perhaps concealed my enmity and mischief and sought to injure my neighbor treacherously through false kindness and courtesy? — Has my rage gone so far at times that I have actually hurt my neighbor with respect to his body and health? Have I fed my enemy, given him something to drink, and prayed for him? — Have I let my neighbor fall in danger of life or limb through my own cruelty or treachery or carelessness? — Have I in my words and deeds not sometimes become offensive to the innocent and simple, and so in some respect wounded their soul? — Have I tried to correct an offense that I gave before, to satisfy the neighbor as much as possible for the injury which occurred, and to appease him? — Have I given my neighbor all possible help in his necessity, danger, and poverty, or assisted him with advice and consolation? — Have I had mercy and charity in my heart, kindness in my actions, and gracefulness in my words? Have I nurtured toward my offender a meek and reconcilable heart and tried to make peace between others? — Have I attended to my neighbor's good in spiritual and physical things?

Sixth Commandment

Have I earnestly pursued chastity and purity of body and soul, to be suitable for service both to God and neighbor? — Have I used the proper means of chastity, such as devout prayer, moderation, fasting, and the like? — Have I frequently harbored wicked and impure lusts in my heart, delighted in them, and even pursued them for any period of time? — Have my actions not sometimes been shameless and frivolous? — Have I not frequently lent my ears to unchaste speech and my eyes to unchaste persons, pictures or other offensive things? — And have I myself offended others by unfitting words with double meanings? — Have I earnestly avoided all impurity and adultery, by whatever name they may be called? Idleness, drunkenness, intoxication, bad company, and lewd fashion?

Seventh Commandment

Have I at all times treated my neighbor justly with respect to his property, given to each what is his, and left to each what is his, and by advice, action, and prevention of all harm helped him to preserve it? — Have I restored to its rightful owner whatever I have found, or property otherwise obtained in an unjust manner, or have I tried to keep it away from him? — Have I not often coveted my neighbor's property, tried to get it by deceitful words or to acquire it by scheming? Have I faithfully given to authorities what is theirs, honestly and diligently labored in my office and vocation, gratefully and properly used the benefits shown me or the righteous alms given me? — Have I taken advantage of my neighbor in business and commerce through false measures and weights or wicked, unreasonable prices and stinging taxes? — Have I been a wise steward, guarded myself against debts and sureties, or tried to pay what I owe in an honest manner? — Have I loved idleness, waste, and luxury, or tried to use impermissible means such as gambling, luxury, foolish jesting, and flattery? — Have I oppressed or sucked dry anyone who was subject to me, or delayed and withheld the wages of any workers and staff? — How have I treated the poor? Have I shown true and genuine mercy by my actions?

Eighth Commandment

How have I treated my neighbor's honor and good name? Have I grieved him by any sort of treachery, slander, or sarcastic and pointed remarks, or hindered his well-being? Or have I deceived him by false compliments, and in judging his life generally sought my own honor and contentment — Have I continually and earnestly guarded myself against wicked suspicions, falsehood, lies, flattery, and useless chatter?

Ninth and Tenth Commandments

Have I earnestly resisted my wicked desires for increase, such as envy, pride, covetousness, and the like, and conversely pursued contentment and humility? — Have I come to the aid of my neighbor at every opportunity with prayer, good will, advice, and help, and rejoiced when he prospered? — Have I practiced moderation in all things, especially in eating and drinking, joy and sorrow? — Have I continued the fight against evil desires as one who belongs to Christ, and used the proper means, such as prayer, vigilance, shunning the occasion, repeated renewal of good resolution, and other such things? — For what has my greatest desire aspired: heavenly or earthly things? — How far have I come in putting on the new man, and how have I increased in that renewal? O my God, search me Yourself! Try me and know my thoughts! See if I am on the just way, and lead me in the way everlasting. You alone can understand the heart, which is deceitful and desperately wicked, and uncover all the guile of narcissism. Oh, how much good I have omitted, and how much evil I have committed! What good I find is only external. Rarely is there a true, good intention and good basis of true virtue. Therefore, O mighty and jealous God, make me to hear the thunder of Your holy and immutable Law, to be terrified by the curse and wrath which I have earned, and to turn in penitence to Your grace in Christ!

281. Repentant prayer of a sinner awakened after examination

Holy and righteous, merciful and gracious Father, Son, and Holy Spirit, since by Your grace I have come to know the multitude, quantity, and heinousness of my sins and to discern the depths of my misery and corruption, I not only thank You for the grace and salutary operation granted me to that end, but also hereby present to You, O Father, an honest confession of my sins and iniquities. I confess that I, being deprived of Your image by original sin, and fearfully corrupted in soul, body, and all my powers, am therefore (alas!) unequipped and unmotivated toward all good things. Besides this, even though I am obliged to crucify this my flesh with its desires and passions and to put off and mortify the old man, I have until now often given room, power, and honor to the old man and thereby fallen into many, indeed innumerable, and great actual sins, added sin to sin, accumulated burden after burden, increased the misery of my condition, and sunk deeper into ruin, even to the kingdom of hell. I confess that I have transgressed in manifold ways both tables of Your holy Law, which was given amid thunder and lightning, and fallen short of the love which I owe both to You and to my neighbor—You, whom I confess from Your Word to be the only true God, whom I honor according to Your will, yea, whom I fear for Your majesty's sake above all things, whom I love for Your goodness' sake above all things, and whom I trust for Your truth's sake above all things—You, I say, I have despised, O Highest God, and have not feared You as my Lord, nor loved and trusted You as my Father, and in short, have turned Your glory and honor which I ought to give You into idleness with my carnal and earthly thinking and with the unholy seeking after earthly things.

This Your most holy name, which is feared by all angels and seraphim, Your high name, which is honored by my prayer and grateful praises I have also misused in manifold ways, by cursing and swearing and various superstitions and foolishness. I have often invoked it without reverent fear or devotion. How often have I profaned the day consecrated to Your service and used it for idle and sinful pastimes or entertainments, and arrogantly despised Your holy and precious, indeed, saving, Word by not hearing it attentively, not believing it in my heart, and not living according to it! With sorrow I am reminded of my sins against parents, authorities, and others whom You set over me, which I have committed through contempt, self-love, and insubordination instead of obeying and honoring them. And how can I deny that, although my neighbor has been commended to my charity and assistance, I have often become a murderer toward him through my uncharitableness, hatred, irreconcilability, jealousy, unkindness, bitter and irritable words, infliction of pain, and frequent withholding of some good? In my disorderly self-love I have also erred and sinned against myself through excess of physical labor, or of food and drink, or of wrath or other emotional tendencies. You know better than I, O knower of hearts, what impure and unchaste desires are often stirred up in my heart and perhaps even evince themselves in offensive words, looks, and deeds. You also know best how often I have not only coveted my neighbor's property but even obtained it unjustly and have been more of a hindrance than a help to him in the maintenance of his living and physical advancement.

Indeed, You have also recorded in the book of Your omniscience all other injustices and undeserving judgments, irritable slanders and blasphemies. And how many more sins have been committed by me which I cannot wholly number or tell? They are above the number of the sands of the sea. To how many sins have I not grown accustomed, and how many have been concealed from my eyes and heart? My life until now has been a continual sinning, my thoughts and imaginations and the desires of my heart vain and unholy, my words unprofitable and offensive, and my actions a continual departing from

You and Your Commandments. I am ashamed and blush to lift my eyes to You, my God in heaven, for my iniquities have increased over my head, and my trespass has grown up to the heavens. Alas, that I have sinned so often, so willfully, and so maliciously, and resisted the operations, stirrings, and movements of Your Word, O God, and of the governing of Your Holy Spirit, and wandered so long in the paths of my sin! For this my heart is faint; for these things my eyes are dim. I acknowledge my transgressions, and my sin is ever before me. Against You, You only, O God, have I sinned and done this evil in Your sight. If You would contend with me, I could not answer You once in a thousand times. If You enter into judgment with me, my judgment will be condemnation and my punishment death and eternal destruction, the destruction of the body and the soul in the depths of hell. For that is the just reward of my labor in sinning and the fruit of my diligence in doing evil. Therefore if You were to reject my prayer now, turn Your face away from me, and kill me in Your wrath, I would have to proclaim and confess: righteous are You, O Lord, and upright are Your judgments. If I were silent or denied it, yet my own conscience, which You chose as the courtroom for my soul, would be my constant witness and judge.

Oh, what wounds I feel in my conscience! Oh, what a burden lies upon it! I wail for the turmoil of my heart, and do not know how to escape. For I see before me the open jaws of hell, to which I ran in my sinning; around me both my brothers offended or afflicted by me and the hordes of hellish spirits seeking after my soul; and above me I see Your wrath burning like a fire and Your fatherly face turned away from me, and feel Your hand, which day and night weighs heavily upon me. I feel them when I remember the calamity that awaits me, the rod which I have felt, and the sorrows which I already feel for my sins. Deep calls to deep at the roar of Your waterfalls. All Your waves and billows are to go over me and all the bowls of Your wrath to be poured out over my body and soul, a factory and habitation of sin. Ah, Lord, the anguish of my heart is great, its fear of Your judgment is powerful, its hatred for my sins is honest, and its detesting of my wickedness is in earnest! I weep when I think of Your love. I am terrified when I consider Your benefits. I can hardly contain my grief when I think of Your faithfulness to me, which has been new and abundant to me every morning, such that I can ascribe my life and preservation only to You. I am deeply ashamed of my ingratitude, that You might well have repented of having created, preserved, and protected me, who am so great a sinner! The fruit of Your blood and death, Lord Jesus, was to redeem me from sins and to gain me for Yourself, and to these I devoted myself, and yet I tore myself from You! They were to save me forever, and how diligently I worked for damnation by sinning! How often, O precious Holy Spirit, I closed my eyes to Your enlightening and my ears to Your Word, and hardened my heart to the working of Your grace, and to my great detriment resisted Your leading and guiding me!

Now, Lord, I stand here, a poor man, deserving only wrath. O giver of mercy, show me the eyes of Your favor! I ask You because of Your mercy; I hope because of Jesus Christ. O Lord God, merciful and gracious, long suffering, and abounding in goodness and truth, who forgive iniquity, transgression, and sin, who to seek and save me, a lost and condemned person, sent Jesus Christ into the world and set Him forth as the Mercy Seat in His blood: look to what He has done for me, suffered for me, and procured for me, and let me savingly partake of Him and His all-availing merits both now and always. Where I have transgressed Your Law, look to Him, who has fulfilled it for me. Where I have earned the curse and death, see what He has suffered for me. Where I am unworthy of Your grace and salvation, let me obtain the favor which He won for me, the blessing which He earned for me, and the righteousness which He was made for me.

So let me be purified in His blood, reconciled to You by His death, justified before You by His resurrection, and mercifully heard because of His intercession. I cling, O Father, to Your goodness; I cling, O Jesus, to Your satisfaction; I cling, O Holy Spirit, to Your truth. Forgive me, O triune God, the sins which my Savior bore; pardon the debt which my bailsman has paid; cancel the punishment which my propitiation endured; give me the righteousness which He won for me. Since His obedience avails before You, since His suffering is so innocent, since His blood cries for atonement, since His death is so highly prized, and we have been raised up with Him and made to sit together with Him in the heavenly places, let me be righteous in Him, and in this Beloved accepted by You. This is the foundation of my hope in You, my God; this is what makes my praying heart so glad. Oh, then hear me and help me, God of my salvation, for the honor of Your name! Deliver me and forgive me all my sins, known to me or unknown, for the sake of Your name. Do this, O Father, because of Your love; do this, Lord, because You are Jesus; do this, Holy Spirit, because You have taught me to pray in this way and have promised to hear me. Amen! Amen.

282. A poor sinner's lament over the impenitence of his heart

I, a miserable and afflicted sinner, come to You, my heavenly Father, bringing nothing with me but utter sin, for which reason I may not lift my eyes to Your high and most holy majesty, but must be ashamed because I have so often angered You and not hearkened unto Your voice. Oh, there is nothing good in me! I was conceived and born in sin. I am by nature so perverted and corrupt that I feel and perceive in myself no delight or love for virtue and heavenly goods, but only for temporal honor and pleasure and the inclination to all manner of evil. I have lived in sin from my youth up. I still live in sin, as long as I carry this sinful flesh of Adam in me. But I take comfort, dear Lord, in Your immeasurable, unfathomable, boundless, and indescribable grace and mercy, which You have promised in Your Word to all penitent sinners and confirmed with a holy oath. I take comfort in the precious merits of Your only-begotten Son, who was delivered up for my sin and raised for my justification also. Hide Your face from my sins, O heavenly Father, and look to the face of Your Son, who did no sin Himself and knew no sin, but by His most holy obedience, blood, and death, made satisfaction for all my sins and for those of the whole world. For the sake of this Savior, O Father, receive me again into favor, and let His bitter suffering and dying and His perfect, precious redemption price which He paid for my sin not be wasted on me, a poor sinner, but efficacious for me; then shall I praise and glorify You forever, here in time and hereafter in eternity. Amen.

283. Prayer for knowledge of sin

Dear God, govern me, that with spiritual eyes I may recognize and confess my inborn sickness and frailty, and so be brought to the right knowledge of Christ, and governed, purified, and sanctified by Your Holy Spirit. Amen.

284. A poor sinner's prayer to humble himself before God

Lord God, I confess to You my frailty and say with the prophet, "Lord, You are our Father; we are Your clay. You are our potter, and we are all the work of Your hand." Since You say that I am a sinner, I will agree that You be right, and gladly confess this sinful and damnable condition which is concealed in my flesh and entire nature, that You may be justified in Your words and glorified, and I be ashamed; that You may be righteous and life, but I and all men only sin and death; that You may be the highest good, but I and all men the worst calamity and heartache. This I confess, having learned it not from my own reason but from Your Law and promise; for my reason would like to prevent its viciousness and ungodliness from being exposed, and rather to cover and conceal it, indeed, to dress it up; but it is more important for me that Your honor may abide and be increased. Amen.

285. *Prayer for true repentance and genuine conversion*

O Lord God, heavenly Father, You stretch forth Your hands to us disobedient children all the day and have commanded all men in every part of the earth to repent, and still cause us daily to hear from Your Holy Word, through the voice of Your servants and ambassadors, the cry, "Repent! Repent! Return! Return, you who have turned aside, each one from his wicked way, and from his wickedness!" and confirmed with a holy oath that You have no pleasure in the death of the dying, but that the ungodly should turn and live, yea, that it is Your gracious and earnest will that all men should be saved and come to the knowledge of the truth; for which reason You also provide for us that our sin may be amended. But since it does not lie in any man's willing or walking, but in Your mercy, and therefore true repentance and conversion do not arise from our own natural abilities, but You alone work them in us, both to will and to do according to Your good pleasure: therefore I heartily beseech You to enlighten and mightily move my soul and mind by Your Holy Spirit, that I may be converted to You with my whole heart both now and always. And since I cannot see or discern my vile sin, especially the inborn, inherited disease without the subtle mirror of Your holy Law, enlighten my dark heart, that I may rightly see myself in the mirror of the Ten Commandments, and from it humbly recognize not only my thoroughly corrupt, wicked, profitless nature, but also the actual internal and external sins arising from it. Show me, O Lord, my many and various hidden faults and deficiencies, indeed, my countless debts of sin; and set before my eyes the terrible misery into which I have fallen by sin, that I, by virtue thereof being a child of wrath and of infernal damnation, for Satan's wages are none other than temporal and eternal curse and death. Grant me also, gracious Father, true and earnest remorse over my great and heavy sins so that I am truly sorry for them in my heart and heartily fear and hold in awe Your unendurable wrath and hot displeasure, which I have invited on my body and soul by sin. Your Word is as a fire and a hammer which breaks the rock. O dear Lord, use Your Word in this time of grace here to break and crush my heart of stone and rock, that it may be perfectly soft and receptive, and earnestly opposed to sin. For the sacrifices which please You are a broken spirit; a broken and a contrite heart, O God, You will not despise. Grant me also, by the word of the Holy Gospel, to know rightly Your only-begotten Son as the only Mercy Seat, that I may not despair under my heavy weight of sin, but heartily take comfort in the precious merits and most perfect satisfaction of my beloved Savior, and so be raised up again by a true, living faith in Him. O Lord my God, who are willing to accept repentance for sin, teach me to know how much it cost to redeem my soul, that I may not let sin reign any more in my mortal body, to obey its passions, but that by Your grace I may produce true fruits of repentance. Amen.

286. Prayer when someone comes to the true knowledge of his sins

Dear God, I confess to You that I am a great sinner, and the Ten Commandments drive and thrust me down to hell, but the Gospel teaches me that this is to be regarded as the highest wisdom: to know and believe that it is Your will to be gracious and help poor, condemned sinners, and to this end You have founded a kingdom through Christ. Therefore I take these together in one word and confession: I am a sinner, yet God is merciful to me; I am Your enemy, but You are my friend only; I ought to be condemned, but I know that You do not wish to condemn me, but to save me and have me as an heir in heaven. Indeed, You wish it to be so. You have preached this to me and commanded me to believe it for the sake of Your dear Son, whom You gave up for me. Amen.

287. Humble lament of one who, having fallen, has been reawakened by God's grace

O holy, righteous, and merciful God, with a sorry, downcast, contrite heart and a broken spirit, I lament and confess to You my transgressions and iniquities! O Lord, my sins are above the number of the sands of the sea! They have gone over my head, and like a heavy burden they are too heavy for me. How great is my iniquity! It ascends to heaven and cries out. If You decide to judge me, I cannot answer one in a thousand. Oh, what an unclean clod I am! How pitifully I have been corrupted in body and soul through the deadly poison of original sin! Behold, I was begotten of sinful seed; in sin did my mother conceive me. From my head to the soles of my feet, there is nothing sound in me. O Lord, who can find a clean man where none is clean? Oh, I am a worthless branch on a poisonous tree! All my powers are corrupted, my understanding is darkened, and my will is contrary. I do not rightly know You; I do not love You with my heart; I do not trust You entirely; the thoughts and intentions of my heart are only evil from my youth. As a fountain pours out its water, my heart pours out sin, from which flow contempt, slander, pride, falsehood, vainglory and self-love, disobedience, enmity, wrath, curiosity, impatience, immorality, unrighteousness, covetousness, and all manner of wicked passions, upon which You, O righteous God, my Maker and Redeemer, have pronounced the judgment that those who do these things shall not inherit the kingdom of God. O my God, my Maker and Redeemer, I lament to You that although I was created according to Your image, yet I have lost it and have become the image of Satan. The whole kingdom of Satan is (alas!) within me with all wickedness and vice, and I have become an instrument of Satan. O Lord my God, my misery is greater than I can declare to You! I am an abomination in all my ways and deeds; all my righteousness is like a filthy garment. I wither in my sins like a leaf, and my iniquities carry me away like the wind. O Lord, I have misused all Your benefits, fought against You with all my members and powers of body and soul, and with body and soul served sin and the devil! Oh, I have fallen from Your grace into Your eternal wrath, from salvation into eternal damnation, from life into eternal death, from heaven to the depths of hell! O Lord, I am the prodigal son who squandered his inheritance so shamefully! I am not worthy to be called Your servant. I deserve to be cast out of Your house and never received by You again. I am the servant who owed You, my master, ten thousand talents and could never repay it. I am the man who fell among robbers, who stripped me and stole from me the beautiful image of God and wounded me severely in body and soul so that no man can heal me.

Therefore help me, my God and Lord! Give me assistance in this trouble, for the help of man is of no avail here. Turn me, O Lord, and I shall be turned; help me, and I shall be helped; for You are my glory. O Lord, who can change the wicked heart and create a new one? You only, Lord, the faithful maker in good works. Who can heal the deep and abhorrent wounds of sin? You, Lord, and Your Word, which heals all things. Take away the evil, stony heart, and create in me a new heart, O God, and renew a right spirit within me. Cast me not away from Your presence, and take not Your Holy Spirit from me. Restore unto me the joy of Your salvation, and uphold me with Your free Spirit. I am the lost sheep. If You do not seek me, I will stray forever and remain lost eternally. Take me up on Your back and bring me to Your heavenly sheepfold. Give me godly sorrow, which works a salutary repentance to salvation which no one regrets, that my heart may by faith be enabled to receive Your comfort and the most worthy forgiveness of sins. Give me a broken spirit and a contrite and repentant heart. Let my eyes be fountains of tears, that I may mourn my sins heartily with Peter and Mary Magdalene. O my Lord and God, if I wept day and night,

I could not mourn my misery enough, lament my sins enough, or sigh for my disobedience enough. Ah, my God! I have sorrow and regret not so much that I have earned death, hell, and condemnation as that I have so deeply, so often, so rudely, and so shamefully offended and angered You, my God, my Maker, my dear Father, my Protector, my Deliverer, my Redeemer, my faithful Shepherd, my only true Comforter, and have been so ungrateful for Your great love and faithfulness, goodness and mercy. Oh, how will I stand before Your face, before Your just judgment, before all the holy angels and elect? Oh, where shall I go from Your Spirit; where shall I flee from Your presence? In every place Your right hand will find me and hold me fast. I can do no more and know no more than this: Father, I have sinned in heaven and before You and am not worthy to be called Your child. Oh, I have forfeited my status as Your child! I have ceased to be Your child through my disobedience and have lost all my rights as a child. But I believe that You have not ceased to be my Father, for Your mercy is great and endures forever. Therefore have mercy on me, and look not at my sin but at Your boundless, eternal grace and mercy; through Jesus Christ, Your dear Son. Amen.

288. Prayer for true faith

I thank You, my dear God, that I have learned that I am not to attack my sin with my own repentance or begin faith with my works and blot out my sin. Before men I might well do so; before the world and the judge, it avails, but before You, God, there is eternal wrath for which I cannot make satisfaction; I would have to despair. Therefore I thank You that Another has attacked my sin, borne it, paid for it, and atoned for it. I would like to believe it, and it seems excellent, right, and comforting to me, but I cannot devote myself wholly to it. I find nothing in my powers that I could do. I cannot comprehend it, even though I am supposed to. Lord, draw me, help me, and give me the power and gift that I may believe as the prophet David, in Psalm 51, sighed, "Create in me a clean heart, O God, and give me a new and certain spirit." I have no ability to make a new heart; it is Your creation and creature. Just as I cannot make the sun and moon to rise and shine brightly in the sky, so little can I make the heart to be clean and myself to have a certain spirit, a strong, firm courage, which is inflexible and does not bend, doubt, or waver from Your Word. Amen.

289. *A repentant sinner's appeal from God's judgment seat to His Mercy Seat*

O dear Lord, we cannot argue our case before You nor stand before Your judgment, nor will we treat our righteousness or sin before You. For if You, Lord, should mark our iniquities and examine us to see whether we are righteous, we will perish. Therefore we will appeal from such judgment to the seat of His mercy and flee for refuge to Your loving kindness. If we have done any good, it has been by Your grace. Turn, therefore, the eyes of Your divine mercy to us and not the righteousness of Your strict judgment. For if You should mark or look at our iniquities, no one will be saved. Our Father who art in heaven, hallowed be Thy name, Thy kingdom come, Thy will be done on earth as it is in heaven. Give us this day our daily bread; and forgive us our trespasses as we forgive those who trespass against us; and lead us not into temptation, but deliver us from evil. For Thine is the kingdom and the power and the glory forever and ever. Amen.

290. *Refuge in the grace of God*

Lord, I receive all Your mercy, goodness, and grace as a sinner and hopeless man, whatever I do, deserving eternal wrath and hellfire if You should treat me according to justice and merits. But I do not look at my own sin, nor what I have earned, but Your Word and earnest command, by which You call, admonish, and threaten all of us to bring no work before You in order to earn something, but to receive the forgiveness of sins and every benefit from Your fatherly goodness, and stand and abide in the pure confidence of Your grace. Amen.

291. *The power of grace*

Lord, I am Your sin, You are my righteousness; therefore I am safe. My sin will not suppress Your righteousness and Your righteousness will not leave me a sinner. Blessed be God, my merciful Lord and Redeemer! I trust in You alone, and thus I will never be put to shame. Amen.

292. *Prayer for grace with God*

I am a poor sinner, O God; forgive me my sin! I will make no mention of merit, only make no mention of judgment! O God, with my works I will earn nothing in Your sight. They are only done so that by them I may serve my neighbor. Meanwhile, I will hold fast to Your naked mercy. Amen.

293. *Prayer for sincere mercy and forgiveness of sins*

O God, no man or creature can help or comfort me, so great is my misery; for my ailment is not physical or temporal. Therefore You, being God, and the One always able to help me, have mercy on me! For without Your mercy all things are terrifying and averse to me. But I beseech You of Your kindness to have mercy on me—not the lesser mercy which You show temporarily for physical distress, but Your greater mercy which You show for the distress of the soul. Have mercy on me, and forgive me my sin. Amen.

294. *A sigh for the forgiveness of sins*

I believe and confess that I am a poor sinner before God and deserve condemnation, and I am heartily afraid because I have disobeyed my God again and again and not rightly regarded or considered His Commandments, much less kept the greatest or least of them. Yet I entertain no doubts, but let myself be pointed to Christ that I may seek grace and help from Him and believe firmly that I will find them. For He is the Lamb of God provided from eternity to the end that He might take away the sin of the whole world and by His death make full atonement for it. Amen.

295. *Fervent prayer of faith*

My Lord Jesus Christ, You are the only Shepherd, and I, alas, am the lost sheep which went astray, and I am in anguish and fear and wish that I might be righteous and have a gracious God and peace in my conscience. Thus I hear that You are as worried about me as I am about You, and I am anxious and distressed until I come to You and am helped. Likewise, You are anxious and concerned and desire nothing other than that You may bring me back to You. Therefore come to me, seek and find me, that I may come to You and praise and honor You forever. Amen.

296. *Prayer for the forgiveness of sins*

Everlasting and merciful God, I, a poor, miserable, and afflicted sinner, come to Your divine majesty, bringing with me nothing other than utter sin, for which cause I may not lift up my eyes, but stand in shame before You, that You, my God, my maker and Father, have often been angered by all my great and manifold sins, so that if You were to treat me as I deserved, I would have to remain a child of wrath and eternal damnation. Yet, dear Lord God and Father, I take comfort in Your great mercy, Your immeasurable, unfathomable, infinite, and unspeakable grace, which You Yourself promised me and confirmed with a precious oath and pledge, saying, "As truly as I live, I do not desire the death of the sinner, but that he turn and live." I take comfort in Your only-begotten Son, my only Redeemer, Justifier, Mediator, and Savior, who by His whole obedience, suffering, and death regained Your favor for me and gave me, who believe in Him, the power to be and be called Your child and heir, and to remain so forever. Therefore I am not without hope, but confess to You my sins inward and outward, concealed and unconfessed, and admit my guilt before You as a great evildoer and criminal, and know nothing more to do than, at the promise of Your Word, to come to Your Mercy Seat with a humble heart and fearless spirit, in true faith and sure confidence on Your promised grace and on the bitter sufferings of Your beloved Son, and say from the depths of my heart, Abba, dear Father, Lord, have mercy! O God, be merciful to me, a poor sinner! Forgive me my inherited and actual sins and all that I have ever thought, said, or done against You knowingly or unknowingly. There is nothing good in me. I was conceived and born in sin, I have lived in sin, and I am still living in sin for as long as I still carry this sinful flesh and blood on me, and my sins are ever before You. You see a thousand times more in me—indeed, over a thousand times more and greater sins than I myself can see, know, and feel.

O Lord, enter not into judgment with Your servant, for before You none living is righteous. Be merciful to me for the sake of Jesus Christ, Your Son, my Lord and Savior, and blot out my sins according to Your great mercy, which is greater than the sins of all men. Wash me thoroughly in the pure blood and sprinkle me with the hyssop of Your Son, which He shed on the tree of the cross. Let me be and remain Your child and heir, a vessel of Your mercy, and a fountain and habitation of the Holy Spirit. O Lord, deliver, comfort, and quicken me! Help me up once more! Gladden my broken spirit and my broken and contrite heart with Your joyful and quickening Spirit. You will not break the bruised reed, O Lord, nor will You quench the smoldering wick. You will not cast me away from Your presence; of that I am certain. You will not let me despair, but will grace me with Your certain Spirit, who kindles and confirms in me true faith and consolation. O Lord, my God and Father, faithful God, hear my prayer, that I may be Your child and temple from henceforth and forevermore. Let me not fall into error and vice against my conscience. Deliver me from bloodguiltiness and from all evil. Let me always have a desire for Your Word, that I may hear, read, and study it gladly, and by it be of use to others, that I may speak of it day and night and declare Your righteousness and Your glory continually. Therefore with all angels and men will I eternally love, praise, thank, and serve You, my God and Lord, and Your Son, my Savior Jesus Christ, together with Your Holy Spirit from henceforth and forever. Amen.

297. Prayer for reconciliation with one's neighbor

Gracious Jesus, I have by Your grace prepared and equipped myself to receive the forgiveness of my sins in the confession chair. But I remember that You said and earnestly commanded, "If you offer your gift on the altar and there remember that your brother has something against you, leave your gift there before the altar and go; first be reconciled to your brother, and then come and offer your gift." Now I have unfortunately fallen into a misunderstanding and disagreement with my neighbor; wherefore grant me Your grace and govern me that my heart may be found willing for reconciliation. I acknowledge the hardness of my heart and confess that it is hard to control the flesh and blood and to avoid all wrath and vengeance. But I hope, indeed, I pray, that You, Lord, would take away the stony heart from my flesh and give me a fleshly, that is, loving and reconcilable, heart, and make me such a man as loves his enemy, blesses those who curse him, does good to those who hate him, and prays for those who injure and persecute him. Oh, let me remember the judgment and the heavy reckoning that I will have to give, that I may let go of the enmity which seeks death and destruction, and according to Your commandment be reconciled to my adversary while I am still on the way with him, and never let the sun go down on my anger. And as I pardon and forgive in Your name all those who have offended me, let me also find those amenable whom I have disturbed and angered, that for Your sake they, too, may forgive and pardon me that by which I have offended them. O Jesus, forgive all our sin and govern our hearts, to live Christian and peaceable lives together and to glorify Your name here in time until we praise You eternally hereafter. Amen.

298. Prayer before going to Confession and seeking Holy Absolution

Lord Jesus Christ, my Redeemer, You left the holy Office of the Keys to Your dear Church here on earth and to her faithful servants, with the attached promise that whatever they loose or bind in her behalf shall also be loosed and bound in heaven. For these gracious means I give You praise, honor, and glory and beseech You from the depths of my heart, that since I, as a poor, enslaved sinner, am in need of this comforting key of loosing, and that I may not be held under the rock of hell's prison-keeper, You would give me the consolation, through my Christian father confessor, of graciously unbinding me from all my sins for the sake of Your blood and death, and of granting me Your Holy Spirit, that I may receive the Holy Absolution in true repentance with undoubting confidence, good intent, brotherly love, and gratitude and finally obtain eternal salvation. Amen.

299. *Thanksgiving after the Absolution*

Dear God, who along with Your Holy Word have given me reliable signs to assure me that my Lord Christ's life, grace, and heaven, where He dwells, have canceled all my sins, death, and hell for my good: You will surely keep this promise to me; of this I am so certain that the words with which the church's minister has pronounced me free from sin are as firm and effective as if they had been heard from You Yourself, O God. Therefore, if it is God's Word, as indeed it is, it must certainly come to pass. On this I rest, and in this hope and confidence I will willingly die. Amen.

300. *Thanksgiving after receiving the Absolution*

Good, gracious, and merciful God and Father, I give You praise and thanks from my inmost heart that through Your servant You have once more forgiven me, a poor sinner, all my sins, renewed to me Your promise of eternal life, and received me back into favor. I heartily beseech You, give me Your Holy Spirit and create in me a clean heart, that I may firmly believe that all my sins are forgiven through Christ. As a certain pledge of this, I will eat and drink the true body and blood of Your Son, Jesus Christ, in the bread and wine for the salvation of my soul. Grant also, O faithful God, that from henceforth I may better guard myself against sin, hate it more, and amend my life; to which end may You graciously assist me for the honor of Your name. Amen.

301. *A communicant's morning prayer*

Lord Jesus, I rejoice this morning that I am to go with other good Christians into Your house for Your great goodness and to partake of Your body and blood with, in, and under the consecrated bread and wine. Oh, how my soul longs for the courts of the Lord and for Your holy altar! As the hart pants after fresh water, so my soul pants after You, my Redeemer. For You are my shepherd; I shall not want. O Lord Jesus, as You began the good work in me, a poor, sinful being, oh, therefore mercifully perfect it through the gracious assistance of Your Holy Spirit, to Your glory and the salvation and welfare of my soul! Dearest Redeemer, I am not worthy that You should come under my roof, yet let Your grace, which is capable of all things, make me worthy and perfectly equipped, that the blessed food and drink of Your true body and blood may refresh my soul in the heavenly feast of love and joy! Clothe me Yourself with the garments of salvation and with the robe of the righteousness of true faith, that I may not be found among the false guests and nominal Christians, but may be a worthy guest at Your table and a partaker of all the treasures of Your grace which You have won for me. Let Your grace, Lord Jesus, be and abide over me as I steadfastly hope in You. Let Your watching preserve my breath, my life, and my moving. By You shall all be given that I can need—true God indeed!—for this life and for heaven. Give sorrow true, my heart renew, my soul and flesh deliver; Lord, in Your care receive my prayer, keep me in peace forever—that I may please You here, and serve You in the heavenly sphere. Amen, in Jesus' name. Amen.

302. Meditation on Holy Communion

Jesus, my Lord and my God, my Redeemer and Savior, be praised and glorified forever and ever! You not only suffered the most contemptible death for me, a poor, lost sinner, to deliver me from the countless multitude of my sins, from the unbearable burden of God's wrath, and from the frightening condemnation of eternal death, but also instituted the Holy Supper, that by this I might be assured of the grace of Your heavenly Father, the forgiveness of my sins, and eternal salvation.

O most blessed Son of the Highest, You are the great Founder of this precious Sacrament. If a man on earth, whether a priest, king, or emperor, had founded and instituted this Supper, we would have to doubt whether He could keep and give what He promised therein. Only thus I am sufficiently assured that nothing will be lacking of that wherewith You have entrusted Your servant, for You are the true God, in whose mouth no deceit was ever found, the most wise Lord, in whom all the treasures of wisdom and of knowledge are to be found. Therefore I will not let my reason convince me otherwise, but will cling only to Your Word and promise.

For the institution of this Supper You chose the night in which You would be betrayed by Judas and delivered into the hands of Your cruel enemies, the night when You would begin Your bitter suffering for my sins, and on the Mount of

LUTHERAN PRAYER COMPANION

Olives would be pitted against the whole force of hell's darkness, even to the point of the bloody sweat of anguish, the night which won us eternal day and the light of the blessed joys of heaven. What else therefore can I recall in doing so than Your bloody Passion and precious merit? Dearest Savior, You took bread and wine for this purpose, and by them wished to indicate the powerful working of this Sacrament, that, just as bread strengthens the body of man, and wine gladdens our hearts, so in the Holy Supper my weary and troubled soul is to receive new strength and be gloriously refreshed. Therefore I will believe without wavering that it is a food of the sick, whose hearts are heavy with sin and very afflicted with anguish. At the same time, You prayed and gave thanks to remind me that I, with God-given devotion, should appear here at the holy altar and not forget the gratitude owed for Your benefits. Oh, then my heart and eye must now only be directed at You, and my mouth sigh with thankfulness:

Be welcome, noble Guest, who have not despised me. You come to me in my misery. How can I ever thank You? You broke the bread, and in this I see how my heart must be broken and crushed by true repentance if I would be a worthy guest at Your table of grace. Oh, then help by Your Holy Spirit, that I may come with a true, broken spirit and contrite heart! You give us, under the bread and wine, not a sign of Your absent body and blood, but Your true and essential body itself, which suffered so much for me, was so sorely flogged, so horribly tormented, and finally even killed on the cross, Your true and essential blood, which was shed so freely for my iniquities, that it might cleanse me from all sins, the blood which flowed from Your opened wounds and obtained for me an eternal redemption and reconciliation with God. No erring spirit will convince me of anything else; although I cannot with my own thoughts and senses fathom how it can be, I will nevertheless trust Your Word and not doubt it in the least. You command that I should use this Holy Supper in remembrance of You, and in so doing recall how You, O holy Lamb of God, were committed to the jaws of the fierce lion for my sins, atoned for my bloodguiltiness by Your blood, and won me life and salvation with Your death. Therefore, Lord, I remember Your fervent and unparalleled love, which compelled You to give up Your blood and life for me. I remember my dutiful debt that I ought to repay to You for this. Jesus, Your love and grace are greater than can be expressed. Yet I will not be silent, but as long as I live will declare Your praise, and even now will say with David, I give thanks to the Lord with my whole heart, in the assembly of the upright and in the congregation. The works of the Lord are great; he who studies them delights in them. What He ordains is honorable and glorious, and His righteousness endures forever. He has established a remembrance of His wondrous works: the gracious and merciful Lord. To Him be thanks and praise forever! Amen.

303. A repentant communicant's lament over the corruption of his nature

Oh, that my head were waters, and my eyes a fountain of tears, that I might weep day and night for the unholy destruction to which the fall of my first parents cast me! Where is the glorious image of God? Where is the wisdom, righteousness, and holiness imbued at creation? Where is the perfect purity, chastity, and immortality? Have they not all been lost, to my great detriment? For in the process I was not only robbed of likeness to God, but my nature was so corrupted that I must sigh with Paul, "Wretched man that I am!" What ignorance there is in my understanding and what perversity in my will! What disorder there is in my movements! How many sinful passions arise in my heart! How desirous is my flesh to carry them out! How are all my members eager for the works of unrighteousness! But why use many words? Nothing good dwells in my flesh! By Your grace I have the desire to do Your will perfectly, but how to perform what is good I find not. What imperfection is in my works! What mistrust and timidity I often feel in myself! Where is the constant serenity in the cross, persecution, and tribulation? How coldly disposed I am to pray! How scattered and thoughtless while praying! How slow my soul is to praise You! I ought to reprove all those who misuse Your most holy name, but how often it remains undone, and how frequently it is done without due zeal! How often the Sabbath day is profaned by me! How slow and unprepared my soul frequently is to hear Your Word! How easily I am moved to anger, and how often I sin by rash, untimely, and immoderate zeal! Oh, wretched man that I am! How careless and untended are my external senses! How willing toward evil and how reluctant toward good! Oh, how inconsiderate my tongue is in speaking, and how irresponsible in silence! How little I have gone beyond myself yet, for how much self-love, self-honor, self-desire, and self-profit there is, alas, in all that I do or do not! Oh, how many things I still have to die to before I can live entirely to You! How many inclinations and excitations to sin there are; for before one sin is mortified, another is already present! How soon a mere thought becomes a wicked desire, and this in turn a sinful indulgence! How violently passions attack me! Often, all that is left between me and spiritual death is to consent to sin and carry it out! The fact that this does not happen I can in truth ascribe not to myself (for who am I and what power do I have?) but to Your Spirit, O God, who comes to the aid of my weakness. Of duties toward God, toward myself, and toward my neighbor I cannot think; for if I consider how perfect Your Commandments are and how imperfect my obedience is, all my courage leaves me; for I find myself to be like the unclean, and all my righteousness like a filthy garment. Indeed, I am not worthy to be called Your child, let alone to sit at Your table which You have prepared for Your children.

But because it would not be well with my soul if I stayed away (for I would grow more and more miserable as time went on), much less if I were to go unworthily (for that would be to my judgment), therefore, my God, I come to the throne of Your grace, praying in deepest humility: Gracious God, merciful Father, Your wrath which You threaten upon all sinners is unbearable, but Your mercy which You promise to all the repentant is indescribable. Therefore I bend the knee of my heart before You. Let my supplication come before You, and forgive me; forgive me, O Lord, all my sins for Your name's sake; for You are gracious and long-suffering, and You abound in goodness and truth. Enter not into judgment with me, for before You no man living is righteous. Regard my weakness and deficiency. Oh, behold how I was corrupted by the fall of my first parents, and how evil possessed me to such an extent that by nature nothing good dwells in me. I acknowledge my inborn unholiness, from which, as from a polluted spring, so many idle thoughts, wicked lusts, useless words, and sinful works flow forth contrary to my will, horribly polluting my heart, eyes, ears, tongue, and other members of my body in turn. I also acknowledge by Your grace that this shameful evil makes me so disfigured and hideous that I am even displeasing to myself; how then shall I be pleasing to You, O Most High?

Yet, Lord, have mercy upon me, a miserable, weak, and mortal being. I would have nothing to complain about if You should punish me according to merit, but would rather have to say, "Righteous are You, O Lord, and upright are Your judgments." Yet let me find mercy, my Father, according to Your promise. You desire no more of a sinner than that He heartily repent of his sins and in true faith seek forgiveness. Therefore I come, my heavenly Father, beseeching You in the name of Your dear Son, to be merciful to me. Be merciful to me, according to Your loving kindness, and according to Your abundant mercy, blot out all my iniquities. Deal not with me according to my merits, but according to Your grace for Your goodness' sake. Create in me a clean heart, O God, and give me a new and certain spirit. Cast me not away from Your presence, and take not

Your Holy Spirit from me. Let me not die, but live; so will I praise Your name here in weakness and hereafter in perfection. Hear me, O Lover of life, for the sake of Jesus Christ, Your beloved Son, my only mediator and deliverer. Amen.

304. Prayer for a holy desire for the Holy Supper

My Lord Jesus Christ, see my unholiness, wretchedness, and neediness; I am poor and needy, and yet so reluctant for this medicine which You have ordained for the forgiveness of my sins and for my salvation that I do not even long for the riches of Your grace. Wherefore, O Lord, kindle in me a desire for Your grace and faith in Your promise, that I may not by my perverse unbelief and laziness offend You, my most faithful and gracious God, but may worthily eat and drink of the bread and wine of Your body and blood, and by this salutary food and drink be strengthened and sustained unto life everlasting. Amen.

305. Prayer for worthy reception of the Holy Supper

Lord Jesus Christ, eternal Son of God, I am not worthy to open my mouth and receive the most worthy Sacrament of Your body and blood, for I am a sinful man, but You are the Lord whom all the highest heaven cannot contain. How then shall man, who is dust and ashes, be worthy to partake of Your most holy body and precious blood? I know well and confess that my sins are many, and because of them I am an unworthy guest at this heavenly meal; but I also believe with my heart and confess with my lips that You can, with Your grace, make me worthy who am unworthy; for You are almighty and merciful, and You only can purify and sanctify that which comes from impure seed. From sinners You can make righteous, holy men, when in Your grace You forgive all our sin and renew us with Your Holy Spirit. Therefore I beseech You by Your power and love to grant grace that I may go ready to Your table and not make myself guilty of Your body and blood by unworthy participation, that I may not receive death for life. Grant grace that I may acknowledge myself to be a poor sinner; seek to have a heart that is sorry for my transgressions; rightly discern Your noble, tender body and precious, worthy blood; subject reason and sense to Your Word at all times; and by Your help earnestly think of amending my ways, that in this most worthy Sacrament, I may not only eat Your body and drink Your blood with my lips, but also receive You, my Savior and Redeemer, with true faith, enclose You in my heart, and so have life and salvation in You; for You are the living bread that comes down from heaven and gives life to men.

He who comes to You will never hunger, and he who believes in You will never thirst. He who eats Your flesh and drinks Your blood abides in You and You in him, and he shall never die. O sweet Lord, my spirit and my mind thirst for You. My soul thirsts for God, for the living God. When shall I come and behold the face of God? Fill me with Your grace. Amen.

306. Prayer for worthy participation of the Holy Supper

Behold, here I come, my Savior, at Your gracious invitation. Let me find favor in Your sight, O Lover of life. For who am I that You should call to me so tenderly? If I were holier than the angels, I would still not be worthy for this Supper. How then can I be worthy, seeing that I am a man of unclean lips, an abomination and detestable, unless You make me worthy? Therefore go before me with Your grace and prepare me. You said, "Whoever comes to Me, I will not cast him out." Therefore take up the cause of my soul according to Your great mercy. Remember, my Jesus, that of myself I have much evil, but nothing good, and help me for Your goodness' sake. Behold, how poor and needy I am. Remember Your faithfulness, O Savior of the world, and fill my heart with grace. How gladly I would appear with fervent devotion and fitting obeisance in full faith, but where is the performance if I do not receive it from You, the founder and perfecter of my faith? Therefore give me whatever is pleasing to You. Graciously remove from me what displeases You, or cover it at least, I most humbly beseech You, with the robe of Your righteousness. Blessed is the soul that You have found acceptable! Open my eyes, that I may see wonderful things in Your statutes. Awaken my heart and free me from all foreign thoughts, increase my hope, enlighten my desire, make my devotion fervent, purify me from all impurity, and sanctify me thoroughly, that I may come in joyful confidence, partake with pure lips and a holy heart, and with heartfelt desire eat and drink to the life, salvation, and blessing of my soul. Amen.

307. Prayer of a sick communicant before receiving the Holy Supper

Lord Jesus Christ, Son of God and Mary, my Redeemer and Savior, because You suffered death for me and redeemed me from sins and eternal damnation, saying, "Come to Me, all you who are weary and burdened; I will refresh you," I, who am burdened with many sorrows and great infirmity, come to You with a broken heart and the humble supplication that You would also quicken, refresh, comfort, and strengthen me on my bed. And inasmuch as You have instituted in Your Holy Supper an eternal memorial with all believers and established a new covenant, in which we receive Your true body and blood for the certain reassurance that You are and remain in us, and we in You, and no one shall separate us from You—neither life, nor death, nor devil, nor power, nor any created thing—therefore I beseech You from my inmost heart to cleanse me from my sins, refresh and restore, strengthen and comfort me in my infirmity with Your holy body and blood. Dearest Savior, enroll me in the number of those who worthily receive this high and precious gift to their salvation, that You may abide in me and I in You, and neither this infirmity nor even death itself may separate me from You, so that henceforth it is not I who live, but You live in me, and the life I live in the flesh I live in Your faith and remain Yours whether I live or die. Preserve me in this faith, my Lord Jesus, that through You I may overcome all tribulation, bear with patience this fatherly chastening, and persevere steadfast in the sure hope of the life everlasting. O Lord, remove from me whatever turns me from You, take me from myself, and make me wholly Your own. Let me be Yours forever until my final end, and hereafter in eternity; so will I without ceasing forever praise and glorify You with Your Father and the Holy Spirit. Amen.

308. Prayer before receiving the Holy Supper in church

To God the Father

O Lord, almighty, everlasting and merciful God and Father of our dear Lord and Savior, Jesus Christ! I, a poor, wretched, sinful man, ought not to lift my eyes up to You, nor to look for any grace or good from You, so full of sin am I, so disgracefully have I transgressed the covenant which You made with me in Holy Baptism, and ought justly to be shut up in the number of those of whom You said, in righteous anger, "Cast them away from Me and let them go forth. You have forsaken Me and fallen away from Me; therefore I stretched out My hand against you, because I will destroy you; I am weary with mercy." Yes, I have indeed forsaken You and fallen away from You, but, O good, faithful Father, You will not deal with us according to our sins, nor do You have any pleasure in our destruction, but rather desire that we should turn and live. For this reason, Your dear Son, Jesus Christ, according to Your fatherly counsel and will, instituted the Most Holy Sacrament, in which He gives us all grace, forgiveness of sins, life, and salvation. Therefore, being invited to this Your heavenly feast, I come now as a poor, hungry, and needy child; feed my soul and give it to drink, O faithful, heavenly Father, and receive me back into favor. Let not my sins separate me from You, for I am Your creature, for Your hands have made me and fashioned me for eternal life. Regard me with the eyes of Your boundless, fatherly goodness and mercy, and forgive me all that I have done against Your Commandments, even as You have truly already done and have pardoned and forgiven me all my sins in the confessional chair through Your ordained servant, in addition to which You will now give me a dear and precious pledge, the very body and blood of Your beloved Son, Jesus Christ. Therefore grant me Your Holy Spirit, and kindle in my heart a true and genuine faith, that I may worthily receive Your holy, most worthy Sacrament to the salvation of my soul, be assured of Your grace thereby, and be strengthened and preserved against all tribulation. Help me also, dear, faithful Father, that I may continue steadfast in this grace until my end and may not intentionally fall from it again by renewed sinfulness, but that I may continue to lead a Christian life well-pleasing to You, hold faith and a good conscience, and be a good and obedient child until what time I shall leave this frailty and come home to You and serve You in perfect holiness and righteousness. May You make it so, O faithful heavenly Father, for the sake of Your beloved Son, Jesus Christ, my only Redeemer and Savior. Amen.

To God the Son

O faithful Lord Jesus Christ, who can sufficiently extol Your boundless goodness and mercy? And with what words may express Your love and faithfulness toward me, a poor sinner? You not only redeemed me with Your blood and death, but You will also come to me now in the most worthy Sacrament, come into my heart, and make there Your temple and dwelling. O Lord, I am not worthy that You should come under my roof and surely deserve to be struck down to the pit of hell by Your thunder and lightning, yet since You, in Your grace, regard me as worthy of it and offer Yourself to me willingly with all the treasures of Your grace, come then; I will gladly embrace You heartily and come to receive You, my dear Lord and Savior, with a true, genuine hunger and thirst. Therefore have mercy on me, Your poor child, O good and faithful Lord Jesus Christ, and purify my heart for Yourself by Your holy crimson blood, that it may become Your holy temple. Dwell in me, and let me not perish in my sins. O Lord Jesus Christ, I confess and lament from my heart that, since from the outside I see and taste no more in this Holy and Most Worthy Sacrament than bread and wine, vile Satan never ceases to whisper through my blind reason that Your true body and blood are not present there, but I must ascend up to heaven with my faith and receive You there at the right hand of God. Therefore I beseech You from my heart to help me with grace that in this lofty and great Mystery, I may hold firmly to Your Holy Word and count it more than all the words and judgments of my reason. For Your Word is very truth; it will not deceive me, but because You have instituted this Sacrament as a testament which cannot be altered, strengthen my weak faith thereby, that I may take hearty comfort in all that You have obtained for me with Your blood and death, and let it also be for my good, and help me then to demonstrate this faith in deed with true godliness, to avoid sin from henceforth, to increase in piety and to amend my life, that I may not drive You out again, but may be Your permanent temple and residence until at last I leave this valley of sorrow and this frailty and attain to eternal perfection; for You live and reign with Your heavenly Father and the Holy Spirit, true God and man, our mediator, most blessed forever. Amen.

To God the Holy Spirit

O Holy Spirit, of the same essence, power, and glory with God the Father and His beloved Son, Jesus Christ, our governor, leader, and director: I beseech You from my inmost heart to grant me Your divine grace and to help me, that I may receive worthily the Holy Sacrament to the salvation of my soul, and then kindle in me, above all, a true and genuine faith, that I may learn to trust firmly the words of my dear Lord and Savior, Jesus Christ, and not doubt that I truly receive under bread and wine His essential body and blood, forcefully though my reason may strive against it, and especially that, in this precious pledge, I may sincerely remember and take comfort in the fact that my dear Lord Christ was given into death for me, and that all that He reaped by His bitter suffering and dying was also done for my good and is truly effective for me. Additionally, by the use of this high and heavenly feast, also work true love in my heart, that I may be true and faithful to my neighbor, serve him insofar as I may, and show him every good, even as my dear Lord and Savior has done for me. And help me, good and faithful God, from henceforth to amend my life, to guard myself against sin, to increase in piety, and never again to anger You, with my heavenly Father and His dear Son, Jesus Christ, O highest Counselor, Advocate, and Helper in every need, for the glory of Your holy name and the salvation and blessedness of my poor soul. Amen.

The Lord is my shepherd; I shall not want. He makes me lie down in green pastures. He leads me to the fresh waters. He restores my soul. He leads me in paths of righteousness for His name's sake. Even though I walk through the dark valley, I will fear no evil; for You are with me, Your rod and Your staff, they comfort me. You prepare a table before me in the presence of my enemies; You anoint my head with oil and fill my cup full. Goodness and mercy shall follow me all the days of my life, and I shall dwell in the house of the Lord forever.

309. *Prayer before the Holy Supper*
Father in heaven, who did not spare Your only Son but gave Him up for us poor sinners: have mercy on me, and prepare me as a worthy guest of the holy body and blood of Your beloved Son, my Lord, that my soul may be strengthened and my sins forgiven.

O Lord Jesus, my Redeemer and Savior, true God and Man, who suffered crucifixion and atoned for my disobedience: have mercy upon me, and help me by Your cross and death, in remembrance of which I receive this Holy Sacrament, to be reconciled to Your heavenly Father.

O God the Holy Spirit, who have enlightened our hearts by Your powerful Word: have mercy upon me, and strengthen me in the right and true faith, that in the same I may embrace and ever hold fast my Lord Jesus. Amen.

310. *Prayer before partaking of the Holy Supper*
My Lord Christ, I have fallen and would like to be strong. And for this reason You instituted this Sacrament, that by it we might kindle and strengthen our faith and so be helped. Therefore I am here and intend to receive it. Lord, behold, there is the Word; here is my deficiency and sickness. And You Yourself said, "Come to Me, all you who are weary and burdened; I will refresh you." Therefore I come and allow myself to be helped.

311. *Another*
I am a poor sinner; I am in need of help and comfort; I wish to go to the Lord's Supper and be fed with my dear Lord Jesus Christ's body and blood. For You, Lord Christ, have instituted this Sacrament so that all hungry and thirsty souls may be fed and refreshed. You will not scold me, much less kill me, if I only come in Your name wishing to be blessed and to have help and comfort. O Lord, I am a great sinner, for which reason I now come to Your Supper, desiring to eat with You, and doubting not that I will be to You a dear and worthy guest. Amen.

312. Lament over unworthiness

Lord, it is true that I am not worthy that You should come under my roof; yet I am needy and desirous of Your help and grace, that I may become godly. Therefore I come in no other confidence than that I have heard the sweet words with which You invite me to Your table and tell me, who am unworthy, that I am to have forgiveness of all sins through Your body and blood, if I eat and drink in this Sacrament. Amen. Dear Lord, Your Word is true; I do not doubt it. And on this basis I eat and drink with You. Let it be for me according to Your will and words. Amen.

313. Prayer when going forward

Lord Jesus Christ, You instituted and left us the Sacrament of Your body and blood, that forgiveness of sins might there be found. I feel that I have need of it; I have fallen into sin and stand in fear and trembling. I am not bold in confessing Your Word. I have so much and so many faults; wherefore I now come that You may heal, comfort, and strengthen me. Amen.

314. Brief sigh when about to receive Christ's body

Lord Jesus Christ, may Your holy body strengthen and preserve me in the true faith unto life everlasting. Amen.

315. Brief sigh when about to receive Christ's blood

Lord Jesus, may Your holy blood strengthen and preserve me in the true faith unto life everlasting. Amen.

316. Thanksgiving after partaking of the Holy Supper

Lord Jesus Christ, I heartily praise and thank You that You have again cleansed me, a poor, sinful being, from my trespasses, and for the true and certain cleansing and forgiveness of all my sins fed me with Your true body and blood, and, having washed me as a soiled child, received me again into the fatherly arms of Your grace and mercy, and now present me to Your Father blameless, pure, and without spot. I beseech You with my heart and with all that is in me that You would add to this an abundance of Your benefits and mercifully grant me Your grace, by the working of the Holy Spirit, that I may acknowledge Your great goodness and mercy, receive it with gratitude, and praise and glorify You all the days of my life. May You further work in me by Your Holy Spirit that I may also sincerely forgive my neighbor all that he has done against me, just as You, Lord, have completely pardoned and forgiven me all my great and manifold trespasses, and indeed, entirely extinguished them and will never remember them; that I also may love my neighbor and sincerely show him every good, just as You, Lord, have done for me, far more than I can ever thank You; that You, good and faithful God, may be forever praised and glorified with Your Father and the Holy Spirit. Amen.

317. Another

O almighty, everlasting God, merciful Father, I give You praise, honor, and thanks for Your boundless goodness and fatherly love, that You have so richly fed me with the true body and blood of Your beloved Son, my Savior and Redeemer, Jesus Christ. Now I can happily proclaim and say with David, The Lord is my shepherd; I shall not want. He makes me lie down in green pastures. He leads me to the fresh waters. He restores my soul. He leads me in paths of righteousness for His name's sake. I have partaken of my Savior, and my soul is preserved. Oh, how shall I repay the Lord for all His benefits to me? I give thanks to the Lord with my whole heart, in the assembly of the upright, and in the congregation. The works of the Lord are great; he who studies them delights in them. What He ordains is honorable and glorious, and His righteousness endures forever. He provides food for those who fear Him; He remembers His covenant forever. He has established a remembrance of His wondrous works: the gracious and merciful Lord. I beseech You, dear Lord, to work in me by Your Holy Spirit, that having by mouth received the Holy Sacrament, I may in this precious pledge and seal truly and firmly embrace and hold fast the gracious forgiveness of sins, union with Christ, and eternal life. Mercifully help me that my devotion and godly fear may endure long and not vanish like a rain shower or a cloud. Protect me, that I may not draw nigh to You with lips but with body and soul, remain devoted to You with all my powers and abilities, and be a living sacrifice, holy and pleasing to You. Lord God and Father, by Your goodness lead me in the way of righteousness. Lord God, protect me this day, that I may not go astray. Keep me firm in the faith in this evil day. Grant that I may be always ready for blessed eternity. Amen.

318. Yet another

Lord Jesus Christ, to You be praise, honor, and thanksgiving forever, both here and in eternity, that You have so graciously refreshed me, a poor, miserable sinner, with Your true body and blood. And I beseech You from my inmost heart to dwell mightily with and in me, Your poor worm, to regard and accept me with gracious eyes, and never to let me slip from Your hands of grace. So govern, lead, and direct me henceforth with Your Holy Spirit that I may not think, do, speak, or set to work anything contrary to You, but may always look to You, Your Word, or Your holy will, and in my cross laid upon me, may be patient and willing and not murmur against You, indeed, nor against my neighbor, but be content with everything according to Your good pleasure, and await the gracious deliverance and eternal joy which You will give to all believers who trust and rely on You. Help, Lord Jesus, that my faith may remain strong and firm in me. Preserve me in the true faith and confession, humility, patience, and hope until my last sigh, that I may praise You here and in eternity, and give thanks to You, who with the Father and the Holy Spirit are true, almighty, and everlasting God forever and ever. Amen. Lord Jesus! Amen.

319. Yet another

O my God, although I am a poor sinner, yet I am not a sinner. I am a sinner on my own account outside Christ; but on account of my Lord Christ and outside myself, I am not a sinner, for He has blotted out all my sin with His [precious] blood, as I firmly believe. In token of this, therefore, I have been baptized, absolved by God's Word, freed, released from my sins, and fed with the Sacrament of the true body and blood of my Lord Jesus Christ as by certain signs of grace; and I have received the forgiveness of sins, which my dear Lord Jesus Christ merited, purchased, and obtained for me by His dear blood; for which I will thank Him eternally. Amen.

320. A thanksgiving for the spiritual wedding

Dear God, how can I be so boastful as to claim that I am God's bride and God's Son is my bridegroom? How do I, a poor, stinking sack of worms, get a great honor that was not even given to the angels in heaven, that the eternal Majesty should thus [condescend to my poor flesh and blood, and] unite Himself with me and be one flesh with me? If I am so entirely full of filth, sores, scabs, leprosy, sin, and stench from head to foot, how can I be called the bride of the eternal, high, glorious Majesty and one body with Him? Yet since You will that it be so, thanks and praise be Yours forever! Amen.

321. *Comforting assurance concerning the Holy Supper*

Dear God, You pledged to me and gave me a sure sign of Your grace in the Sacraments, that Christ's life overcame my death in His death, His obedience blotted out my sin in His life, and His love destroyed my hell in His dereliction. This sign, this pledge of my salvation, will not deceive or disappoint me. For You said that You cannot lie, neither in words nor works. On this I remain, on this I die. Amen.

322. *Another*

Give me grace, O merciful God! I am a poor, sinful being and deserve nothing but wrath. Yet regardless how I have lived, I stand my ground, knowing and not doubting that I have been baptized and named a Christian for the forgiveness of sins and that my Lord Jesus Christ was born, suffered, died, and rose again for me and has given me His body and blood as food and strengthening for my faith. Lord Jesus Christ, I have been absolved and released from my sins in Your name; therefore I [my heart and faith] cannot fare ill or perish any more than God's Word can err or be false; for God Himself is my surety through His Word. Amen.

323. *Lament over lack of fruitfulness in good works*

Lord Christ, I go to the Sacrament and yet remain fruitless as before. I have received such a great treasure, and it simply lies there inactive in me. This is why I bring my complaint to You. Since You have given and granted me the treasure, grant also that it may bear fruit and new life in me and demonstrate and show itself to my neighbors, even as I ought to do. Amen.

324. *Comfort against unworthiness and the tribulation of the devil*

Lord God, through a brother You have absolved me, baptized me, and fed me with Your body and blood. Do with Your servant as You please; I will not be angry nor blaspheme You, but will bear all things patiently. For I do not want the covenant that You established with me in Holy Baptism and the Holy Supper to be destroyed. I know that I have been baptized, that I have eaten the body of Your Son and drunk His blood, that I have been absolved for God's sake, and released from my sins, indeed, that all my sins are forgiven and that victory over the devil, death, and hell has been promised me. What more can I want? Amen.

325. *Prayer for grace to accomplish God's will*

Merciful God, who through Jesus Christ, our Lord, have caused the light of Your grace to rise upon us once more: enlighten, admonish, and strengthen our hearts with the power of Your Holy Spirit, in firm faith and fervent love, to do in all things Your fatherly, gracious pleasure, to the glory and praise of Your Holy Gospel, to the comfort and benefit of all believers in Christ, Yours be the thanks, praise, and honor forever. Amen.

326. *Prayer that God would protect us from further sins, and where we sin, that He would not count it against us*

O gracious and merciful God, dear Father in heaven, in grace and divine love, You gave us Your dear Son and with Him all grace, salvation, and blessedness. We beseech You, dear Father, to preserve to us this salutary present and heavenly gift, the kindly countenance of Your dear Son, Jesus Christ, that we may not forfeit or lose it by ingratitude. We are truly poor, miserable, and faulty men, falling from one sin to another, as we sin now in thought, now in word, now in works, and it takes toil and effort to make us stand. There is never any rest or peace. The devil lurks about our thoughts, always fomenting and whispering. The world lurks about our words and works, our life and existence, giving us great offense and incitement to sin. Even our own flesh does not rest— quite apart from all the accidental sins, vices, and bad habits which daily attack us and oppress our consciences terribly, destroying the joy of our hearts and turning it into utter sadness and sorrow. Therefore, gracious and merciful God, although we may have become neglectful and ungrateful and may not conduct ourselves as we ought, nevertheless we beseech You still to remain our gracious God and to be kind, comforting, good, and merciful to us. Do not make us pay for our manifold sins, but purify our hearts and consciences by Your Word, that we may serve You in both sorrow and joy and praise, honor, and glorify You in time and in eternity. Amen.

327. *Prayer for new obedience after partaking of the Holy Supper*

Gracious God and Father, in mercy You forgave me all my sins and received me into favor for the sake of Christ, Your dear Son. I also promised You from my heart earnestly to improve my life and increase in piety by Your grace. O Lord and God, because the deeds of man are not in his own power, in the way he walks and directs his course, and the imaginations of the heart of man are only evil every day, but You can guide it and lead it in Your fear, as is pleasing to You, therefore I beseech You, give me a new heart, that I may oppose sin from my heart, let Your fear sanctify me, that I may begin a new and godlier life and live in holiness and righteousness which is pleasing to You. Let me never forget Your grace and promise, and help me earnestly to strive against my flesh and blood and against all wicked lusts and not fall again into sin and vice. Before me I have life and death; let me choose life and run undaunted so as to win the prize, that I may claim it and not disgrace myself. Teach me to do Your pleasure, that I may live an upright and godly life in this world and await the blessed hope and appearance of the glory of the great God and our Savior, Jesus Christ. Amen.

328. Meditation on the worth of Christ's suffering

O my God and my Lord, grant me to know and ponder the person who suffered for my sake. Is He not the only-begotten Son of God, the most dearly beloved Child of God? How then was He given up to such a shameful death? Is He not the One of whom the Father said from heaven, "This is My beloved Son, in whom I am well pleased"? How then is He now forced to endure the Father's wrath? Is He not the Lord of glory? How then does He now bear such contempt? Is He not the Most Mighty? How then has He become so weak as to be thus crucified? Is He not the eternal and all-powerful God? How then does He suffer such unspeakable distress? Is He not the spotless Lamb of God, and is He not led to the bloody slaughtering-bench? Oh, that tender body, that holy and spotless body—how it is wounded! Oh, those holy hands with which He blessed us! Oh, those holy feet, which walked the way of peace—how they have been pierced! Oh, that graceful mouth and those crimson lips—how they have grown pale! Oh, His holy, glorious head—how it is shredded with thorns! Oh, His loving heart—how He has shown it to us by His opened side! Oh, may the holy, tender, pure blood of His heart, which flowed from His side, cleanse me from all sins! Oh, those tender eyes, which are brighter than the sun—how they are darkened! How full of lamentation they seem! How they run with water as it were fountains of tears and springs of love! Lamentable and pitiful indeed is all His appearance. Oh, He is so beaten that there is nothing whole in His body; these are the chastisements and afflictions of my sins. My iniquities gave Him these wounds. O great mystery! O great love! That my sin should be paid for in the most holy body of Christ. Indeed, by this holy sacrifice I had to be reconciled—the Holy One bears my unholiness; the Righteous One my unrighteousness; the Upright One bears my wickedness; the Innocent One bears my guilt; the Master gives Himself up for His servants; the Son of God for the children of men; the King of glory lays upon Himself our scorn; God gives Himself up for His creature; the Deliverer for the imprisoned; the God of all the world for the lost; the Blessed One, yea, the Blessing Himself, gives Himself up for the accursed; the Beatific for the condemned; the Life for the dead. I have sinned; what has this innocent Lamb done? I was wicked; how did this Righteous One do wrong? O Lord, You were humbled for my pride, scourged for my disobedience, beaten with torment and wounds for my happiness. I earned the death and You must die; I was sold through sin, and You became my redemption price and put up the dearest payment for my sins. O my Lord Jesus, how could a sin be so great that it could not be paid for with this most valuable treasure? How could a trespass be so detestable that it could not be atoned for by such great shame, sorrow, and pain? How could there be so many sins that they could not be taken away by such great obedience, high patience, tremendous meekness, and deep humility? O my God! How can Your wrath be so great that it cannot be reconciled by this obedience, sorrow, trembling, terror, bloody sweat, and bitter death? Therefore, O God, be gracious to me and do not look at my sins, but take up my cause and let me eternally enjoy the precious blood that was shed by Your dear Son, Jesus Christ. Amen.

329. *Prayer on the sufferings of Christ*

O my Lord Jesus Christ, when I behold Your sorrow and how for Your great anguish Your sweat fell like great drops of blood in the garden, and You were taken captive and bound, and mocked and reviled all night in the hour of darkness, and in the morning lamented as the innocent Lamb, struck with rods, and finally condemned to death, hung on the cross, pierced with nails in hands and feet, and no part of Your holy body was left unwounded, I see nothing but my own sin, guilt, and iniquity which brought You to that end and for which You gave Yourself up to such anguish, distress, sorrow, suffering, and pain. Alas, Lord, I deserved all that You suffered! I am the cause of it all. How wonderfully God acted, ordaining that the Guiltless must pay what the guilty man owes, that the Godly must pay what the evil has earned! The debts which the servant has accrued, the Master must pay; what the sinful man has brought on himself, God must bear. O Son of the living God, how great is Your love and favor toward us men! What have You not done and endured to redeem me, a poor, lost sinner, and to deliver me from death and eternal damnation? I have done wickedly and You were chastised; I have sinned and You had to atone for it. I was disobedient, and You must have anguish and distress for my disobedience. O Lord of glory, how can I thank You for all the mercies and kindnesses which You have shown me? How can I, a poor, needy man, repay You? O Lord, it remains unpaid and will never be repaid with anything in heaven or on earth. It is Your grace and favor, Your love and faithfulness, and it will remain unpaid by me, a poor sinner. And because I cannot pay my debt, O Lord, I will give You heartfelt thanks for what You have done for me and will praise, extol, and glorify Your name from henceforth and forever. Amen.

330. Thanksgiving for the sufferings of Christ

O most holy and most gracious Lord Jesus Christ, we give thanks to You for Your heartfelt sorrow, when Your soul was grieved unto death for our sake, that You might turn away from us our eternal sorrow and win for us eternal glory; for Your humble step which You took toward Your heavenly Father when You fell down to the ground on Your holy face, that You might obtain grace for us, and that our faces might not be ashamed; for Your most holy prayer and holy obedience, when You sacrificed Your will entirely to Your heavenly Father, saying, "Not what I will, but what You will," that You might atone for and heal our wicked will and sanctify us in the will of God; for Your sharp and bitter struggle with death, by which You took away the power of death and overcame it; for Your most holy sweat of blood that was freely pressed from Your tender body and fell to the ground in abundance, that You might sanctify our cold sweat of death and change the anguish of death into gentle sleep. O innocent, spotless Lamb of God, we thank You that You were taken captive for our sake, that we might be redeemed; bound, that we might be freed from sin; falsely accused, that we might be acquitted of God's stern judgment; struck in Your holy face, that we might have peace. O most patient and meek heart, we thank You that You were mocked for our sake, that You might be made eternal wisdom for us; spit upon, that we might be delivered from our shame; blasphemed, that we might be honored; scourged, that our disobedience might be atoned for. O King of glory and Lord of glory, we thank You that for our sake You were mocked with robes of purple, that You might procure for us the wedding garment of glory; crowned with thorns, that You might set on us the crown of righteousness; given a reed in Your right hand, that You might not break the bruised reed; and were struck on Your holy head, that we might lift our heads with joy. O dearest and kindest Lord, we thank You from our heart for Your presentation to the people, when Pilate said, "Behold the Man!" O most Beloved, You were rejected and spurned by Your people, that You might become the cornerstone of Your believing Church. You were condemned to eternal death that You might free us from the judgment of eternal death. O most righteous and most humble Servant of God, most obedient Son of God Your Father, we thank You that You carried Your cross Yourself to Your holy death, that You might teach us willingly to take up our cross; that You were nailed to it hand and foot, that You might become a sacrifice for our sin; that You were crucified between two murderers, and reckoned among evildoers, even though You did wrong to no man and no deceit was found in Your mouth, that You might atone for us by Your innocence; and that You endured great, great blasphemy and scorn on the cross, that You might release us from eternal contempt. O Blessed of the Lord, we thank You that You became a curse on the tree, that in You all the peoples of the earth might be blessed; that You became as a worm, and were least among the children of men, that You might make us lovely in the sight of God; that You became the most despised among men, that You might make us glorious; that You hung wholly comfortless on the cross, that we might be comforted eternally; and that You were made to die naked and bloody, that You might clothe us with the garment of salvation and with the robe of righteousness. O eternal High Priest and our only Mediator, we thank You that You prayed for us on the cross and offered Yourself up with loud cries and tears to Your heavenly Father. We thank You for the comforting word, "Today you will be with Me in paradise," by which You opened paradise to poor sinners, which word is a very key of paradise. We thank You for Your anguish and distress, when You cried, "My God, My God, why have You forsaken Me?" that we might not be forsaken by God eternally. We thank You for Your holy thirst on the cross and the sharp draught of vinegar, with which You redeemed us from eternal thirst and from the bitterness of hell. We thank You for Your comforting word, "It is finished!" That is, sin is blotted out, God is reconciled, Scripture is fulfilled, and an eternal redemption is established! We thank You for Your holy death and for Your last word on the cross; for with it, all our sin is paid, life restored, and the souls of all believers in Christ delivered into the hands of the heavenly Father. May we therefore, O most loving and blessed King, with Joseph of Arimathaea crave Your holy body, wrap it in the pure linen of our faith, anoint it with the myrrh and aloes of sincere remorse and sorrow for our sins, preserve it in our devout remembrance, and lay it by faith in our new and purified heart, as in a new tomb, that He alone and no other may rest therein. Seal this tomb with Your Holy Spirit, that neither the world nor the devil may steal it from our hearts, that we may not lose You, but die, rise again, and live with You, and ascend to You in heaven, and be and abide with You forever. Amen.

331. Prayer of a troubled person worrying about unworthy reception of the Holy Supper

Heavenly Father, almighty and merciful God, my refuge and strength, my salvation and help in the great troubles which come upon me! I call to You from my inmost heart in the name of Jesus Christ, Your dearest Son, beseeching You graciously to hear my prayer, nor to hide Yourself from my supplication, but to look upon me who lament and wail with such anguish. For behold, Lord, my heart is afflicted in my body; fear and trembling have come upon me for the great sorrow of my heart, because I am worried that I may have come to the holy table of Your most worthy Supper unworthily and sinned against You. And it is true, my dear God, when I look at myself, I am unworthy in all things and cannot stand before Your holy righteousness. At the same time, it is also true that You have given us Your dearest Son, Jesus Christ, for our righteousness and sanctification, that in Him and His propitiation, we might obtain Your eternal favor and be accepted as righteous. Therefore, my Lord and God, by Your holy and good Spirit, drive out of me these and similar sad and false sentiments, lighten my heart and my eyes, and mercifully grant that I may turn away from myself and look with ardent devotion only upon Christ Jesus, Your dear Son, and take comfort in His most blessed holiness against my unholy impurity, and in His eternal righteousness against my damnable unrighteousness, and be firmly devoted to Him. I know from Your Holy Word that the righteousness of the same Your dear Son dwells in me, His Spirit bearing witness to my spirit that I am Your child and You my Father. Confirm it in my heart and increase my trust; keep me in Your grace and lead me in Your way, that I, as a limb engrafted in the body of Your dear Son, may never be separated from You, for the glory of Your most praiseworthy, divine name, most blessed forever. Amen, Amen.

IX. CATECHISM

332. Prayer for true knowledge of God

Eternal, true, righteous, living, holy God and Father: I lament and confess to You with a troubled and humble spirit the great inborn blindness and darkness of my heart. By nature I cannot know You rightly, and in my natural, carnal folly and ignorance, I have no love or delight for Your divine knowledge, in which eternal life nevertheless consists. Oh, forgive me this harmful folly, gracious Father, and do not reckon it against me. Take away the heavy punishment from me, with which, by the prophet Isaiah, You threaten all who refuse to know You, saying, "An ox knows its master, and an ass its owner's crib, but Israel does not know, and My people do not consider. O woe to the sinful nation, to the wicked seed!" But enlighten me with Your Word and Holy Spirit, that I may in true faith acknowledge that according to Your nature, You are to be adored as three persons and one true essential God, who from eternity begot Your only Son out of Your divine essence and sent Him to us as our Savior. Oh, grant me, dear Father, that I may acknowledge Your almighty power, glorify Your mercy, fear Your righteousness, believe Your truth, and extol Your wisdom! Oh, let Your power be my protection, Your mercy my consolation, Your righteousness my strength, Your truth my shield and buckler, Your wisdom my governing principle, Your love my gladness, Your grace my light and life, Your praise and worship my glory. Grant me to know Your dear Son, Jesus Christ, as the eternal, almighty God, of the same divine nature with You, and in His assumed human nature, the Second Person of the Holy Trinity, my Lord and God, the Brightness of Your glory and the exact image of Your nature, Light of Light, very God of very God, by whom You made all things, who is the life and light of men, whom You gave to us complete and entire with all that He is: God and man, with all His eternal riches and benefits, who by His incarnation became my Brother, by His Gospel my Prophet and Teacher, by His wondrous works my Physician, by His suffering and death my Redeemer, by His resurrection my victory and righteousness, by His ascension into heaven my hope, by His glory my praise and honor, by His Holy Spirit my anointing, by His return my salvation. O my Lord Jesus, You are the Way, the Truth, and the Life! Be for me the way which I should walk; be for me the truth which I believe; be for me the life which sustains me and saves me. Grant me also, O good and gracious Father, to know Your Holy Spirit to be the Third Person of the Holy Trinity, one eternal, true, essential God with You and Your dear Son, proceeding from You and Your dear Son, and sent into the hearts of the faithful to enlighten, sanctify, and lead into all truth. Oh, let Him be my light against all the darkness and error, my comfort in all sorrow, my sanctification against all impurity, my eternal truth against all falsehood of Satan and of all heretics. Let Your Spirit, the Spirit of rebirth, renew me, sanctify me as the temple of God, that the Holy Trinity may come to me and make His home with me, that by Your Spirit I may become a new creature, that my Lord Christ may live in me, and that my members may be Christ's members. Grant me, O God, to know Yourself according to Your gracious will, that I may taste in my heart Your love, O God the Father, find in myself the kindness and gentleness of my Lord Jesus Christ, that I may always have within the fruit of His incarnation, of His Word, of His suffering, resurrection, and ascension, and may sense the comfort, light, peace, and joy of Your Holy Spirit in my conscience, and so continually have with me and in me the foretaste and treasure of my salvation and my highest good. This knowledge of You, O God, is eternal life; to know You is perfect righteousness, and to know Your power is the root of eternal life. Through this knowledge, we are justified and saved; through this knowledge, You share with us Yourself and all Your goods, by which our hearts are filled with God. Through this knowledge, Satan, with his darkness, cunning, and lies, is driven away, his kingdom destroyed, his power overcome, his palace and armor taken away. Through this knowledge, a man is governed in his whole life to the glory of God and the good of his neighbor, and to his own salvation. Where this knowledge is absent, Satan fills the heart with all manner of darkness, error, blindness, and godlessness, and the man becomes the dishonor and disgrace of God, an impure vessel of God's wrath and eternal damnation. Preserve me from this, O God the Father, through Your holy knowledge forever; through Jesus Christ, Your beloved Son, our Lord. Amen.

333. Prayer for true fear of God
Holy, merciful, gracious, and beloved Father: I lament and confess to You with remorse and groaning in my heart that I am so corrupted by the poisonous disease of original sin that by nature there is no fear of God before my eyes,

and on account of my deeply corrupted nature, I do not fear, love, or honor You as a child, nor, alas, have I always permitted Your godly fear to govern me, but my thoughts have been mostly without any fear of God, and wholly vain, as have been my words and works. Oh, how often I have forgotten Your Word and Commandments, put them behind me, and not feared them! How often I have followed more the passions of the world and of my own flesh than Your Word and instruction. Oh, forgive me, dear Father, this self-security and despising of Your Commandments and threats, and turn away from me the heavy punishment with which You threaten all who do not fear You, that You will reject them because they have rejected Your Word. But because the fear of God is the most beautiful wisdom, by which a man is pleasing to God, I therefore beseech You from my heart, first, to extinguish and blot out in my heart the inborn security and presumption, as well as the despising of Your Commandments and divine warnings, and instead by Your Holy Spirit (inasmuch as He is the Spirit of the fear of the Lord) stir up in me Your divine and childlike fear, that at all times and in all places, in all my thoughts, words, and works, I may learn to fear Your wrath and disfavor, and that I may have in my heart a continual and true sorrow and contrition for each and every sin, and that I may be far more sorrowful and afflicted to have done You any injury than that I myself should be chastised. Wherefore grant me Your grace, that I may heartily oppose all sins as the works of the devil, and in all my faults and frailties, cross and tribulation, take comfort in Your fatherly grace and mercy, and not fear You as my enemy, but fear and love You as my Father. Preserve my soul and inner man also by Your divine fear, that I may not think, speak, or do anything contrary to Your holy will, but that I may think, speak, and do all things as before Your holy eyes and countenance, that my inner eye also may be directed and turned only upon You, so that in Your fear I may well consider all my words and works beforehand, and in all things begin by humbly calling upon Your divine wisdom, power, and assistance, and that I may let no temporal thing—honor, riches, worldly joy, passion, or fear of man—turn me from Your godly fear, but that I may always be mindful of the gracious promise which You made to the godly of deliverance, mercy, blessing, grace, help, wisdom, preservation, salvation, and consolation; and that in all my life Your godly fear, grace, and mercy may always govern, lead, and direct me; through Jesus Christ, Your beloved Son, our Lord. Amen.

334. *Prayer for heartfelt, fervent love*

O loving God, kind and gracious Father, source and fountain of all love, kindness, goodness, grace, and mercy! With great sorrow I lament and confess to You that in my heart, all Your divine love, with which I should love You above all things, has been so utterly snuffed out and extinguished by original sin that I am by nature more inclined to myself, to the love of myself, and to the love of created things than to You, my dear God and Father; and that, accordingly, I have never truly loved You, my dearest Father, and my Redeemer, Jesus Christ, and the Holy Spirit, my true Comforter, above all things, whereas You are the highest and eternal Good, and above all things to be adored. Oh, forgive me my grave sin and great folly, and turn away from me the heavy punishment in the words: "If any man love not Jesus Christ, let him be accursed"! Root out of me all inordinate love, the love of the world and created things, the honoring of myself, the lust of the eyes, the desire of the flesh, proud living, which wrests the hearts of men away from You. Kindle in me by Your Holy Spirit the pure, unblemished flame of Your love, that I may heartily love You for Your own sake as the highest good, the most gracious loveliness, the all-surpassing goodness, the quintessential holiness, the purest truth, righteousness, and wisdom, and in short, every good, and the eternal source of every good, and so love without consideration of any reward, personal gain, or requital, but only for Yourself; and that I may subject my heart, will, and understanding to You, and keep Your Commandments with joy, and gladly do Your will, for therein true love toward You consists. O Lord Jesus, let the pure love of Your pure heart kindle my cold heart, the tender love of Your unspotted soul lighten my soul, the love of Your noble character fill my mind and senses, the love of Your godly power strengthen my powers of body and soul in Your love! For the sake of Your love let me forgo all that displeases You, and do and suffer all that pleases You, and persevere therein until the end; for to love You thus is the most beautiful wisdom, and he who sees her loves her, for he sees what great wonders she does. Let Your love also draw me to You, unite me with You, and make me one spirit, one body, and one soul with You, my Lord; that I may always think of You, speak of You, hunger and thirst for You, be satisfied in Your love, and remain in You, and You in me; and that through such love I may love all men in You and because of You; and that in pitying love I may forgive my enemies, love them, pray for them, do good to them, and overcome them with kindness. May all these things be granted for the great love of my Father in heaven, my merciful Lord, and for the perfect love of God the Son, my Redeemer, and for the fervent, fiery love of God the Holy Spirit, my only and true Comforter. Amen.

335. *Prayer for true and steadfast hope*

O God, eternal Truth, who keep faith forever, in whom those who hope in You are not ashamed! I lament and confess to You that my corrupt flesh and blood is very worried about temporal things, always looking to the physical and temporal comfort and often forgetting Your promise, power, and mercy. Oh, forgive me this grave sin, and turn away from me the harsh punishment which You threaten, that those who put their hope in temporal things shall not see the consolation to come! Blot out in me all false, deceiving hope, which passes away like a smoke or a light frost. Take from me all futile and useless cares. Let me believe from my heart that You care for me and watch over me. Let the hope and confidence of my heart be always set on You, that the loving and sweet influence of Your grace and goodness may not be hindered in me, nor my heart's repose and rest in You may be disturbed. For all hope and desire which do not rest in You must remain forever unrest. Let my hope cleave in You alone as an anchor in the solid earth and await Your help without doubting. Let my heart sense that Your mercy is boundless, Your goodness infinite, and Your promise true, that thereby my hope may be firmly fixed and not waver; my prayer made sure and heard with certainty; my confidence sealed; and myself protected in Your shade and shelter, as safe as in a fortress. The foundation of my hope, O Father, is the gracious incarnation of Your dear Son and His holy, precious merit, His resurrection and ascension, by which You gave us new birth to a living hope which will certainly not make us ashamed. For in Christ I am already saved; with Him and in Him I have already risen and ascended into heaven and been set in the heavenly places. Therefore, in Christ Jesus, my Lord, I already have eternal life and am only awaiting the revelation of the glory to come. Wherefore, O God, in all things, in all that I do or do not, let me hope only in You, that You may be to me all that my heart desires. And in sorrow over the delaying of Your help, let me not be too greatly troubled. For the longer You delay, the more gloriously You help at last. Yet ease my cross for me, that I may not grow too weary, and strengthen me continually with Your comfort, that with those who hope in the Lord, I may gain new strength and not fall, but like Mount Zion abide forever; through Jesus Christ, our Lord. Amen.

336. *Prayer for true humility*

O Lord Jesus, most humble heart, I confess and lament to You that I am by nature much inclined to honoring myself, and that the evil one has poisoned my heart with pride, which is the beginning of all sins, so that I have often sinned against You by arrogating glory to myself and not considering that all honor is due to You alone and not to any creature. I have often despised my neighbor, trusted in my own powers too much, and frequently relied on myself. O Lord, who give grace to the humble and resist the proud, do not reckon this sin against me, but turn away from me the heavy punishment with which You have threatened the proud, that You would cast them down and scatter them. Let my desire for honor be blotted out and atoned for by Your holy humility. Teach me to know my own wretchedness and to fear the lofty majesty of God. For what am I but a handful of dust and ashes, a rotten corpse, a vessel filled with uncleanness, a wretched worm, a sinful birth, by nature a child of wrath. I was conceived and born in sin, I live in toil and vanity, and I die with pain and misery. Who knows how and where my end will be? Oh, I am a pit of misery, blind in Your knowledge, dumb in Your praise, deaf to Your Word, lame in Your ways. I have of my own self nothing but sin, death, and condemnation, and whatever good I have is Yours and not mine. For what does a man have that he has not received? Therefore the glory is Yours alone and not mine. Rather, I have often robbed You of Your glory, and through pride appropriated it to myself, and like an unfaithful servant and unrighteous steward boasted in and flaunted the goods of others. O dear Lord, do not call me to account. I cannot stand! But grant me to be humble in heart, simple in words, and lowly in works, that I may not regard myself highly, but be lowly in my own eyes. Plant true humility in my heart, that I may obey You in all things for which You wish to use me. Grant that I may do the work of my calling in simplicity of heart and not look to myself, but to Your power and help, and await them with patience. Help me faithfully to fulfill my part which You have assigned to me, and not to seek that to which I have not been called. Let me not fall into such blindness and folly that I think I can do things through my own means. Let me remember that I carry my treasure in earthly vessels. Let there not arise in my heart any contempt of my neighbor, nor of the least human being, for through the humble You perform Your business on earth and great things; You give them Your grace, that they may be Your salutary instruments. Through humility teach me peace, and preserve unity, O God of peace. Teach me, O humble Jesus, to follow

Your example, who humiliated and humbled Yourself under God, angels, men, and all creatures. Oh, let Your word bring forth fruit in my heart, when You say, "Learn of Me. I am meek, and humble of heart"—not outwardly as a show, but from the heart. O Lord of glory, You humbled Yourself, and the wretched worm of the human heart was puffed up. O humble Heart, You fled all the honor of this world, and those who wish to be Your children cannot be content with worldly glory! But when will I die to the glories of this world, that I may regard myself worthy of no honor, crave glory from no man, learn to regard myself as nothing, not be pleased with myself but be displeased with myself, reprove myself, and count all my deeds as filth and as a polluted cloth in Your sight? Grant me also not to let the praising lips of flatterers deceive me, but consider that I am a thousand times more deficient. Give me lowliness of heart as a treasure and foundation of all virtue, as an imitation of Your holy humility. Let me remember Your words, when You say, "He who humbles himself as this child is the greatest in the kingdom of heaven," and, "The Most High looks upon the lowly in heaven and on earth." Let me not become an abomination in Your sight through pride, a robber of God through covetousness, an imitator and partner of Lucifer through arrogance. Turn away from me all arrogant thoughts, haughty actions, and boastful words, and shut my heart up within Your humble heart, that in it my soul may find its rest and habitation forever. Amen.

337. Prayer for true patience

O Lord God, dear Father, merciful and gracious, long-suffering and abounding in goodness and truth; O Lord Jesus Christ, patient Lamb of God; O God the Holy Spirit, the Spirit of comfort and peace: I lament and confess to You the inborn impatience and disobedience of my heart, that I have often murmured against Your holy will and angered You. Oh, forgive me this grave sin and disobedience, and do not reckon it against me. Turn away from me the harsh punishment with which You threaten those who do not want to bear Your yoke, for they can never find rest for their souls. Grant me grace, that I may be always obedient to You and not murmur against You, nor be angry with You, but acknowledge that my sorrows have been laid upon me by Your divine counsel, since apart from Your will not one hair can fall from my head; and that I may accordingly receive all cross and suffering from the hand of Your fatherly providence with a good, patient, and grateful heart; indeed, that I may count myself worthy of even greater punishment, since my cross and suffering are far less than my sin; yea, that I may not only not grow weary of the cross, but rather may long to suffer whatever is Your will and whatever attains to Your glory and my good. Oh, let me know that You have sent me my cross in great love, that You might humble me, crucify my flesh, try my faith, love, and hope, sustain my prayer through patience and constancy, teach me, comfort me, prepare me for the kingdom of God, and through the cross make me great in heaven, and bring me into glory. Therefore give me a heart to love my cross, thank You for it, rejoice in it, that by it I may become like a reflection of my Lord Jesus Christ. O Lord Jesus, give me a heart and mind always to behold in all my sufferings the image of You bearing Your cross with great patience; of Your sacred head smitten, crowned with thorns, and lacerated; of Your face spit upon and disrespected; of Your holy body scourged, wounded, and killed. Oh, with what patience You sacrificed Your will to Your heavenly Father! Oh, let me also sacrifice my will completely to You and rejoice that Your will, which is always good and does all things well, may be fulfilled in me. Drive out from my heart all impatience, sadness, anguish, fear, and timidity, that through patience I may be strengthened in You to overcome all things, yea, that I may patiently bear and suffer such pain and sorrow according to Your will and through Your will in You, with You, and through You, as long as it pleases You, that I may regard it as the sorrows of my Lord Jesus Christ, love and praise Him for it now and in eternity. Lord Jesus Christ, give me patience to suffer all that You decide; meekness not to murmur against You; Your humility to regard myself as deserving of all punishment; Your grace to endure all, by true faith to lay all of my burdens before You, to trust Your faithful promises; the confidence that You love me even in the midst of my cross; the hope that You will help me to bear and lighten my cross. Comfort me also with Your Holy Spirit, with the foretaste and vision of eternal life, that I may seek more after the inward, heavenly things than after outward comfort. Grant that I may not fear those who can kill the body but not the soul. In the midst of sorrow and adversity, let me nevertheless retain a quiet and peaceful heart and meekness toward my enemies, that I may not take revenge either in word or deed, desire or action. Give me true steadfastness in faith, that I may persevere until the end and be saved; and because no Christian's life, age, and calling can be without the cross, and You, O my heavenly Father, know the frailty of Your poor child, therefore give me only what I can bear, and do not make it too heavy or long-lasting for me. Let me lift and bear Your grace with my cross, or with my burden. Give me grace to endure sorrow until it pleases You to release me, that I may be preserved, cleansed, and purified. Let my Lord Christ live in me with His meekness, humility, and patience, that not I but He who is my life may live in me. Grant me a meek spirit also toward all those who injure me and a compassionate love, that I may say to You, "Father, forgive them"; a tender, gracious mouth; a generous and helpful hand, that I may remain eternally bound together and united with You and Your love. Amen.

338. *Prayer that one may hallow God's name*

O Lord and God, I confess and lament to You from my inmost heart that I have not always hallowed and rightly used Your holy, high, and precious name, but have inwardly and outwardly, in thought, word, and deed, often profaned it, misused it, and taken it in vain! O dear heavenly Father, pardon me this grave sin, and turn away from me the punishment with which You have threatened those who take Your name in vain! And grant grace that I may henceforth guard myself with utmost diligence against all profaning of Your name. O Lord Jesus Christ, who taught me to pray daily, "Our Father who art in heaven, hallowed be Thy name": grant grace that such hallowing of God's name may also be found with and be done by me. O most holy Son of the Highest, You perfectly hallowed the name of Your heavenly Father and revealed it to us men. For the sake of Your perfect obedience, forgive me whatever I have done against the hallowing of God's name, and grant grace that I may truly hallow it henceforth with prayer, praise, and thanksgiving. O Holy Spirit, who are the Spirit of hallowing and sanctification, sanctify me wholly, that I may ever continue in the hallowing of God's name and may daily become more perfect therein, and preserve my spirit, soul, and body until the coming of my Lord Jesus Christ. Amen.

339. *Prayer for the grace to praise God*

O almighty God, merciful Father, I confess and lament to You from my inmost heart that I have not devoutly considered Your manifold benefits which You show me and others, nor given You sincere thanks for them, as were fitting, nor declared Your praise and glory daily with the devotion which You require of me. O dear Father, pardon me this sin, and turn away from me the punishment with which You threaten all the ungrateful! Give me Your grace that I may henceforth sing praises to You daily with lips and heart and thank You for all Your benefits. Grant that I may praise You continually for Your great mercy and continually offer up to You a sacrifice of worship and praise. You are praised,

O Lord, by the heavens, the earth, the sea, the fountains of water, and all that is in them, and all Your creatures; help me, as Your rational creature, to worship You daily. You are praised by the holy angels, mighty champions, Your soldiers and ministers; help me to lift my voice with them and give You thanks. O Lord Jesus Christ, who in the days of Your flesh so often gave heartfelt thanks to Your heavenly Father, by which holy example to move me to the praise and worship of God and to thanksgiving, give me Your grace and Spirit, that at all times I may be grateful for all Your benefits and declare the praise of God. You have made me a spiritual priest before Your heavenly Father; help me through Yourself to offer continually the sacrifice of praise to God. O Holy Spirit, who are the Spirit of rebirth and renewal, give me a new tongue with which to praise the Lord my God. O heavenly Oil of Gladness, gladden and quicken my heart with spiritual gladness, that at all times I may praise the Lord my God with joyful lips, sing and make melody to the Lord in my heart, and give thanks at all times for all things to God the Father in the name of our Lord Jesus Christ. Amen.

340. Prayer for love and appreciation for God's Word

Almighty, everlasting, and gracious God, who have given us Your beloved Son, Jesus Christ, who is Your eternal and essential Word and express image, who in Your Word has made known to us Your nature and will: give us, we beseech You, Your Holy Spirit, that we may always have a delight and love for Your Word, and in it seek and find all true doctrine, comfort, joy, and refreshment, and conform and constrain our life, office, and calling according to it, and teach others by it, and through the same Word overcome all adversity and the devil himself, sin, death, and all misfortune. O Lord, grant that we may count Your Word the greatest and most glorious treasure, higher and greater than the whole world with all that it is, has, or may be. Let Your Word be a burning lamp in our hearts, a guideline by which we believe, an even way on which we walk in our life and calling, a comfort in cross, a relief in all distress, a mighty fortress against all enemies, a bastion against the devil, a shade and shelter, and joy for our heart and conscience. Lord, keep us steadfast in Your Word, and repel all the enemies and persecutors of Your Word, that we may rightly know and praise and glorify You from henceforth and forever; for You are the only eternal, almighty, true God, the Father of our Lord Jesus Christ, with Your Son, our Lord Jesus Christ, and the Holy Spirit. Amen.

341. *Prayer for a delight and love for God's Word*

O merciful God and Father, You see how, on account of my corrupt nature, I have no desire for Your Word and how easily I am turned from it by the devil, my own flesh and blood, the children of the world, and false teachers and preachers, indeed, very despicable causes, and how careless, inattentive, and reluctant I am to hear and to keep Your Word. Therefore I beseech You now, eternal God, to pardon my inborn sloth and reluctance, and give me a willing and awake heart, to hear and consider Your Word; awaken in me a heartfelt desire, that as a newborn babe I may long for the reasonable, pure milk of God's Word. Let nothing in this world be dearer to me than Your Word, that I may love Your Word more than gold, yea, than much fine gold, and always count it my most excellent treasure. But because I have, alas, experienced the time of which Your dear Son Himself prophesied, that false christs would arise and perform wonders, that even the elect, if it were possible, would be led aside into error, therefore I beseech You mercifully to protect and preserve me from error and false doctrine. Keep me in Your truth, for Your Word is truth, that I may cling to it as to the heavenly truth and abide steadfast therein until my final end. Do this all for the glory of Your most holy and blessed name. Amen.

342. *Prayer when people are about to read the Bible*

Everlasting God and Father of our Lord Jesus Christ, grant us Your grace that we may make good and diligent study of Holy Scripture, seek and find Christ therein, and through Him have eternal life. Graciously grant it, dear God. Amen.

343. *Prayer before reading the Bible*

Sweetest Jesus, who spoke with friendly lips, "Search the Scriptures, for in them you think that you have eternal life, and it is they that testify of Me": be pleased with my heart's desire for Your Word and bless what I now begin. Without You I can do nothing; neither does the natural man perceive anything of the Spirit of God. It is foolishness to him, and he cannot discern it. Therefore, open my understanding, that I may understand the Scriptures and behold wondrous things out of Your Law. Give me the Spirit of wisdom and of revelation in the knowledge of You, and enlighten the eyes of my understanding, that I may know the hope of our calling, and what are the riches of Your glorious inheritance in the saints. Let me bring into captivity every thought to the obedience of Christ, believing that all that was spoken therein by the holy men of God was by the movement of the Holy Spirit, that I may increase in the knowledge of God and be strengthened with all power according to Your glorious might, till we all come in the unity of the faith, and of the knowledge of You, each of us a perfect man, unto the measure of the stature of Your fullness; for Your own sake. Amen.

344. *Prayer after reading the Bible*

I thank You, dearest Jesus, the founder and perfecter of my faith, that You have worked in me a constant desire for Your Word, and thus both the desire and performance, according to Your good pleasure. Now I see the truth of what the Spirit said through David: "When Your Word is manifested, it gives joy, and makes wise the simple." Seal in me therefore all the words of prophecy in this book, and take not the word of truth out of my mouth, for I hope in Your judgments. It is ever my treasure and sweeter than honey to my mouth. It is a lamp unto my feet and a light unto my path. Yea, preserve unto us Your Word, for it is the joy and comfort of our hearts. Amen.

345. *Prayer that one may honor the holy ministry*

O almighty, everlasting, dear heavenly Father, I thank You from my inmost heart that You have given us faithful teachers and preachers who present to us Your holy and divine Word in its purity and without distortion. But I also sincerely confess to You that I have not always esteemed this precious and worthy treasure of Yours so highly as I ought and have not at all times honored my appointed teacher as Your minister and messenger. Oh, dear heavenly Father, pardon me this sin and grant grace that I may henceforth show him all due honor, obedience, and well-doing! O Lord Jesus Christ, who, being the only High Priest of the New Testament and the Head of Your Church, ascended on high, sat down at the right hand of Your heavenly Father, and even today give to Your Church shepherds and teachers, that by them Your spiritual body may be built up: I beseech You heartily to clothe with power from on high those whom You have sent out and provided, and grace them with Your Holy Spirit, that they may preach Your Word with all boldness. Put Your Word in their mouths and cover them in the shadow of Your hands, that they may plant the heavens and lay the foundations of the earth. Adorn them with rich blessings, that they may gain victory after victory against the devil and his kingdom, that it may be apparent that the true God is in Zion. O Holy Spirit, who on Pentecost poured Yourself out upon the apostles in the form of tongues of fire: fill our teachers with Your holy light, that they too may speak with fiery tongues, that it may strike the hearts of their hearers. O heavenly Teacher of truth, grant increase to their planting and watering. Give us attentive ears and willing hearts, that in willing obedience we may follow what is presented to us from God's Word and be sanctified, guided, and preserved thereby unto eternal salvation. Amen.

346. Prayer that one may honor one's parents

O almighty, everlasting God, heavenly Father, who commanded with great earnest that parents should be honored, I thank You from my inmost heart that You have caused me to be born of Christian parents and that they have preserved me until now; but at the same time, I confess and lament to You that I have not always held my parents in such honor as I ought to have done, nor loved and feared them, nor shown them every good, as I ought to have done, but often resisted them with words and works. O dear God and Father, pardon me this sin of my youth and my transgression, and remember me according to Your great mercy, for Your goodness' sake. Give me henceforth an obedient, loving heart, that I may honor my parents from the heart with words and works. O Lord Jesus Christ, who in the days of Your flesh were subject to Your parents and left to me an example for imitation, that I also should follow in Your footsteps, give me a thankful, submissive, willing, and obedient heart toward my parents, that I may honor them with obedience, love and fear, patience and humility. Look also on my dear parents with the eyes of Your mercy. Let them reach old age in peace, bless their livelihood, lighten their cross, and grant them temporal and eternal blessing. O Holy Spirit, who are the Spirit of love and discipline, govern and lead me such that I love my parents heartily and receive their chastisement with patience. Enlighten my heart by Your heavenly grace and light, that I may with a grateful heart acknowledge what great benefits have been shown me by God through my dear parents, that I may not be found ungrateful and disobedient, but may show all due submission and obedience toward God and my parents. Amen.

347. Prayer for Christian kindness

O dearest Jesus, most desirable friend of the soul, how kind You were to everyone in the days of Your flesh! Thus You fulfilled indeed what had long been prophesied of You, that You would not be sullen and unkind. How loving Your heart was, how beautiful Your countenance! How gracious were Your lips, how kindly Your eyes, how amiable Your actions, how helpful Your hands! By this You left me a model, that I should behave the same way with my neighbors. Therefore give me the grace to learn such virtue from You and to follow Your footsteps. Let the pleasant light of Your eyes shine from my eyes, the gracious sound of Your lips echo in my lips, the kindness of Your face be reflected on my face. Most beautiful Savior, make me to resemble Your image, that I may meet everyone with charity, goodness, and gentleness and visit the miserable with counsel, the afflicted with comfort, and the needy with help; that I may grieve no one with my lips, injure no one with my words, and terrify no one with my actions. Let me not through wrath and fury come to resemble the horrible devil and hideous dragon from hell, but that my face may always appear gracious and kind like the face of an angel, and that I may daily increase in grace and favor with God and man. Amen, O kindest and most gracious Jesus! Amen.

348. Prayer for chastity of the heart

O noble, holy, pure, chaste, unblemished, and modest heart, Lord Jesus Christ, lover of purity, crown of all honor and virtue: I lament and confess to You the inborn impurity of my heart, by which I have often stained my body and soul through impure thoughts, words, and deeds. Oh, forgive me, pure, generous, gracious heart, my grave sin, and turn away from me the heavy punishment with which You threaten the impure; for those who are saved are the pure in heart, and they shall see God; so are they without doubt condemned who are impure in heart, and they shall not see God. Therefore create in me a clean heart, O God, and cast me not away from Your presence because of my impurity. And because I acknowledge that I cannot live a continent life unless You grant it to me, and this knowledge also is a great grace, I therefore humbly beseech You to sanctify and purify my heart by faith, by the Holy Spirit, by repentance, and by the new birth, and to strengthen me, that I may not permit the unclean spirit to rule over me, or to take control and possession of me like an unclean house, lest he stain my soul, poison my thoughts, and pollute my body. Extinguish in me the flame of incontinence, gird my loins and reins with the girdle of chastity, O chaste, continent, and noble Bridegroom of my soul! Embrace my heart with Your pure love, purify and espouse my soul with Your chaste heart, fill my heart with pure and holy thoughts, that I may be and always remain a pure and spotless member of Your body, that I may not become an unclean vessel and member of Satan, a vessel of dishonor and disgrace, but a vessel of grace and honor, and not squander and lose my gifts which You have placed in me, as it were in a vessel of mercy; that by continence and purity I may set myself apart from the unclean spirits, demons, and all impure heathen, that I may not be cast out from the new Jerusalem, but remain united with You and be of one spirit, one heart, and one body with You, just as You, to that end, have washed and consecrated me in Baptism and anointed and sanctified me with the Holy Spirit to be Your holy temple and habitation. Oh, teach me to remember that my body is the temple and habitation of the Holy Spirit, that I may not break it, and that You may not break me in turn, and that I may be a member of Christ, and not be made a dishonorable member by sinning against my own body. O noble, chaste, virtuous, heavenly Bridegroom, who feed among the roses of purity, feed my soul with Your knowledge and pure love, and drive from me all impure thoughts, that You may dwell in me with Your Holy Spirit, and the holy angels may remain with me continually. Amen.

349. *Prayer for righteousness in trade and commerce*

Almighty, everlasting, merciful, and righteous God, I lament to You from my inmost heart that I have often envied my neighbor and taken advantage of him in trade and commerce, by which I have invited upon me the heavy punishment with which You have threatened all the unrighteous. But I heartily beseech You for the sake of Christ, Your dear Son, the Righteous One, to pardon me my sin and unrighteousness, and grant me grace, that henceforth I may strive for righteousness in all my doings and affairs, may not steal my neighbor's property by scheming or force, with or without the appearance of righteousness, but rather help and be of service to him in keeping it. Graciously prevent me, dear heavenly Father, from stealing and so offending against Your holy name. O Lord Jesus Christ, who in the days of Your flesh referred us in all trade and commerce to the law of nature, "Do unto others as you would have them do unto you," enable me to live faithfully by this rule. You frequently repeated the eternal, unchangeable commandment of God that we should not steal; help me never to let this out of my heart, but constantly to remember it and to guard myself against all unrighteousness. O Holy Spirit, suppress and mortify in my heart the inordinate passion and desire to become rich, which leads to stealing and unrighteousness. Strengthen and increase in me the love of neighbor, that it being the director and governor of all my trade and commerce, I may so conduct my affairs as to wrong no man and may be preserved in the grace of God and love of neighbor unto life everlasting. Amen.

350. *Prayer against covetousness*

O almighty, everlasting God, heavenly Father, I confess and lament to You from my inmost heart that I am by nature inclined to covetousness and have often given it room and place in my heart. O dear, heavenly Father, pardon me this sin, and grant grace that henceforth I may heartily oppose the love of money, since it is a root of all evil that springs up into unrighteousness, ruthlessness toward one's neighbor, reliance on temporal things, and many evil and harmful fruits. Purify my heart, O heavenly Father, of this noxious poison, and plant in me the noble virtue of contentment, that I may be content with what is present, in certain hope that You will not forsake or neglect me. O Lord Jesus Christ, You faithfully and fraternally warned us, "Take heed that you keep yourselves from all covetousness, for no man's life consists in having many possessions." Oh, grant grace and blessing, that I may heed this warning! You taught, "Lay not up for yourselves treasures on earth, where moth and rust consume and thieves break through and steal." Oh, help me to take this teaching to heart and rule my life by it! Covetousness is a shameful idolatry; root and drive it out of my heart, O my faithful Savior. Let me cling to You with pure love, O dear, heavenly Bridegroom, that I may not let the lust of the flesh, the lust of the eyes, and the pride of life reign in me. O Holy Spirit, suppress and mortify covetousness in me, which is a harmful, damnable work of the flesh. Renew my heart, that I may put off the old man with his works, and renew my members, that I may put to death my wicked passions and love of money. Graciously defend me, that the deceiving riches and cares of life may not tear my heart like piercing thorns and choke out the seed of God's Word in me. Help me to feed my soul not with the poison of unrighteous goods but with heavenly manna of God's Word; for since my soul is eternal and immortal, it must possess an eternal and immortal food. Give me the true rest of the soul, that by being content I may rest in God and finally enter into eternal rest. Amen.

351. *Prayer that one may do good*

Almighty, everlasting God, heavenly Father, I confess and lament to You from my inmost heart that I have often been remiss and weary in giving alms. I am sorry to say that I have often closed my heart to my brother in need and not offered him a helping hand. O dear, heavenly Father, pardon me this grave sin, and grant grace that henceforth I may have compassion on those who are like poor Lazarus, and eagerly give and share with them. What am I, that I should give willingly of my own power? But give me a generous, willing heart by Your

Holy Spirit, and always maintain such an attitude in my heart, and fashion my heart for Yourself. O Lord Jesus Christ, You faithfully admonished us, "Sell what you have, and give alms!" "Give to him who asks you, and do not turn away from him who will borrow from you." Give me Your grace and Spirit, that I may take these faithful admonitions to heart and never forget them. O my faithful Savior, govern and lead me by Your good Spirit, that I may so walk in this life that I may finally be set at Your right hand on the Last Day and hear the cheering voice: "Come, you blessed of My Father, inherit the kingdom prepared for you from the beginning of the world. For I was hungry and you fed Me. I was thirsty and you gave Me drink." O Holy Spirit, whose fruit is goodness and well-doing, change and improve my hard, unmerciful heart, remove from me the stony heart and give me a heart of flesh, that I may take pity on my neighbor in his distress and need. Help us as members of one spiritual body to be compassionate and helpful, that by so doing we may show ourselves to be children of God, members of Christ, and heirs of the eternal kingdom of heaven. Amen.

352. Prayer for truthfulness

Almighty, everlasting God, heavenly Father, I confess and lament to You from my inmost heart that I have not always loved the truth and sincerely spoken it to my neighbor, but have often lied to and deceived him, backbitten and slandered him, maligned his good name and given him a bad reputation. O dear, heavenly Father, forgive me this sin and turn away from me the heavy punishment with which You have threatened all liars, slanderers, and backbiters. Give me Your grace, that henceforth I may walk in the truth and diligently guard myself against all lying and falsehood. Let idolatry and lying, O dear God and Father, be far from me. O Lord Jesus Christ, who have called Yourself the Truth, govern my heart that I may detest lying and cling constantly to the truth. Mercifully defend me against liars, slanderers, and backbiters, that they may not beguile me or make me fall. Let them be put to shame who would oppress me with lying. Save me from those who persecute me falsely. Leave me not to the counsels of slanderers, and let me not fall by them! O Holy Spirit, who are the Spirit of truth, give me strength and power to confess and defend the truth freely. Suppress and mortify in me my sinful flesh, which continually incites me to lying and falsehood, hypocrisy and deceit. Grant grace, that I may not heed its inciting, but may cultivate in myself a harmony of heart and mouth, and, always walking in the way of truth, at last attain to the kingdom of truth. Amen.

353. *Prayer for control of one's tongue*

Almighty, everlasting God, heavenly Father, I confess and lament to You that I have often and grossly sinned against You, my dear God, and against my neighbor, with my mouth. I have not tamed my tongue so diligently as I ought, have not always used it to the glory of Your name and improvement of my neighbor, and have frequently spoken vain things. O dear God, pardon me this sin, and turn away from me the heavy punishment with which You threaten all who misuse their tongue to Your dishonor and their neighbor's detriment. Give me Your grace that henceforth I may bridle my tongue. Teach me to set a lock on my mouth and to press a firm seal on my lips, that I may not fall. O Lord Jesus Christ, tender Lamb of God, in whose mouth no deceit was found, who when You were reviled, reviled not again, and when You suffered, threatened not, who as a lamb led to the slaughter, and as a sheep before its shearer is silent, opened not Your mouth. By so doing You not only atoned for our first parents and my vain, useless words, but also wished to teach me to be silent and hold my peace patiently. O dear Savior, give me a quiet, patient spirit and a silent mouth, that I may not err with my words. Grant me grace to bridle my thoughts and tongue, and to discipline my heart with God's Word, and not to spare myself where I do wrong, that I may not cause sin and establish error and commit much evil. O Holy Spirit, who poured Yourself out upon the apostles in tongues of fire and so governed their tongues that they declared the mighty acts of God: fill my tongue also with the heavenly fire of wisdom, that I may not misuse it for useless speech, but according to the exhortation which You have given me by Your precious instrument, the apostle Paul, to speak and put forth only that which is profitable for edification, when it is necessary. Open my lips that I may declare the glory of God and faithfully advance the temporal and eternal salvation of my neighbor. Grant this all in Your grace, O faithful God, for the sake of Christ. Amen.

354. *Lament over the inherited corruption*

Holy God, just Judge, I know that I was conceived and born in sin; I know that I was formed from impure seed in the womb of my mother. This poison of sin has corrupted and ruined my whole nature so utterly that no power of my soul has been left free from infection. The holy deposit of the divine image, which in the father of our race was entrusted also to me, has been lost in me. There is no longer any power to embark upon a beginning of Your knowledge, fear, love, and trust, no longer any means to obey Your Commandments. My will is turned away from the Law, and the law of sin is in my members, striving against the law in my mind, making my whole nature to be corrupted and perverted. I, a poor, miserable man, feel the incursions of sin, which dwells in my members and clings to me continually. I feel the yoke of wicked lust that presses me heavily. For although I have been born again and renewed in the washing of Baptism by the Spirit of grace, I am still not entirely free from the yoke and bondage of sin, since the bitter root which lies concealed in me is always seeking to spread further. The law of sin rages in my flesh and wishes to take me captive. I am full of doubts, full of suspicions, full of desire for my own glory; from the heart come wicked thoughts, which wholly defile me before You; from poisoned springs flow poisonous rivers. Wherefore, O Lord, enter not into judgment with Your servant, but be gracious to me according to Your abundant mercy. Let the deep of my misery call to the deep of Your mercy. For this abomination of my unclean nature I set before You the most holy conception of Your Son. He was born for me, and He was conceived for me; He was made for me sanctification and righteousness; He was also made for me purification and spotlessness. By this Your Son, and for His sake, have mercy upon me, O Most High, and do not bring into the light of Your presence the hidden evil of the corruption which clings to my nature, but look at Your dear Son, my mediator; let His most holy and spotless conception come to the aid of my misery. Amen.

355. Prayer for true repentance

Almighty God, merciful Father, Your call to repentance and Your words of grace daily resound in my ears and heart, urging me and all sinful souls to be converted: "Turn again, O you fallen, and I will not set My face against you, for I am merciful and will not show anger forever. Only acknowledge your iniquity, and that you have sinned against the Lord your God." But alas, I have no power on my own to turn to You. As little as the Ethiopian can change his skin, and the leopard remove his spots, so little can I by my own powers cease from sin and do good. For the imaginations and thoughts of my heart are only evil continually from my youth up. If Your grace should work in me so that I resolve to arise, be reconciled to You because of my sins, and offer to You a broken spirit, a crushed and contrite heart, oh, then accursed Satan will put a thousand hindrances in my way. My own sinful flesh and blood resist me so that I do not fulfill the good that I wish, but continue in sin, in which I shall finally perish. Therefore, Abba, dear Father, I bow and kneel down before You in deepest humility, beseeching You of Your boundless mercy to turn to me, O Lord, that I may be turned, and save me, that I may be saved. Let Your grace, my God, not be in vain for me, but as You have given the desire, so grant the means to perform it. Break the counsels of the hellish foe, turn away the inclinations of my perverse heart, that my holy intentions may not be hindered or turned backward. Open my eyes, that I may heartily acknowledge, sorely lament and bitterly bewail my sins. Give me godly sorrow for my transgressions, which produces repentance unto salvation, of which I shall never repent. O God, let me not perish under the weight of sin or despair like Cain and Judas, but turn Yourself to me and be gracious unto me. Look upon my misery and wretchedness, and forgive me all my sins. Show me the loving and merciful heart of a father, a heart that desires not the death of the sinner, but that he should turn and live. Pledge to my soul the comfort that You will let mercy come before justice and will remember my iniquities no more. With Your divine finger of grace direct me to the Crucified Jesus, His dying for my sins, and His rising again for my justification. Open to me for my safe refuge His bloody wounds, in which so many a poor sinner has found salvation and comfort. Create in me a clean heart, and give me a new and certain spirit. Cast me not away from Your presence, and take not Your Holy Spirit from me. Restore unto me the joy of Your salvation, and let the fearless Spirit uphold me in the steadfast resolve to correct my sinful life, and as long as I live, to serve You in holiness and righteousness pleasing to You. O Lord, hear! O Lord, forgive! O Lord, pay attention and act; for the sake of Jesus Christ! Amen.

356. *Prayer for a right faith*

Lord, almighty God, the Father of light, in whom is no change or shifting of light and darkness, from whom every good and perfect gift comes down to us: I beseech You, inasmuch as faith is not the thing of every man, that You would plant and sustain in my heart by Your Holy Spirit a right knowledge of Your Son, Jesus Christ, and increase the same daily, that I may be filled with knowledge of Your will in all spiritual wisdom and understanding and walk worthily, pleasing to You in every way, and that I may be fruitful in all good works and increase therein according to Your glorious power, in all patience and long-suffering with joy. Give me power according to the riches of Your glory to be strengthened in the inner man by Your Spirit, and give me Christ to dwell in my heart by faith. O dear God, inasmuch as no man knows Your Son but You, the Father, and no one knows You, the Father, except Your Son, and he to whom He will reveal Him, I therefore beseech You to draw me to Him, and that He would draw me to You. Give me knowledge of salvation which is in the forgiveness of sins. Come to the aid of my weak faith, which is as small as a mustard seed, that it may increase, and I may be rooted and built up in You and be firm and immovable. Faithful God, who kindled in us the spark of faith and began the good work in us, I call on You to bring it to completion, that we may daily increase and abound in all knowledge and understanding, that we may be pure and without offense unto the day of Christ, filled with the fruits of righteousness which are by Christ Jesus to the glory and praise of God. Sustain what You have worked in us, that we may wage the good warfare, holding faith and a good conscience, and not be knocked about in cross and tribulation nor suffer shipwreck of the faith. Therefore protect me, my God, that I may not be led away by all the errors, divisions, and heresies of this world, nor err or have doubts in any article of the faith. To that end, therefore, grant grace, that my faith may not be dead, workless, or without power, but busy and active, breaking forth through love, that I may receive the end of my faith, even the salvation of my soul. Amen.

357. Prayer for deliverance from the curse of the Law

Lord God, who can keep Your Commandments? The more You command, the less we do. We should trust in You and keep Your Commandments, but we do not. We find nothing more in the Law than that there is nothing good in us. For this reason Moses gave it: that it might make manifest the curse, even if we do not see and feel it, that we might begin and say, "Come then, Lord, and give us a blessing; deliver us from this curse!" The Law gives no help to our consciences. The blessing alone can do it. Here in the Law there is only death and God's wrath. Yet the Gospel is Your Word. Therefore keep what You have said, and give us the blessing through the blessed Seed, who has come. May He give it to us and save us from death through life, from sin through righteousness. Amen.

358. Thanksgiving for creation

O almighty God, heavenly Father, who are neither created nor begotten, but existed eternally before anything began: I adore You, I honor, praise, and glorify

You, and give thanks to You from my inmost heart for all Your benefits, and above all that You created heaven and earth, the sun and moon, and all creatures, and all that is in them, by Your almighty power and divine Word, and govern and sustain them by Your wisdom. I also thank You that You have by Your goodness and mercy put under the dominion of mankind the whole earth, together with all created things, and apportioned them to us for our good. But most especially I praise You, my maker and Lord, that You formed and fashioned me, Your creature, in Your image as a rational human being, that You gave me body and soul and all my members, my reason and understanding, and all my senses, and still preserve them. Great and marvelous is Your goodness to me, for when I was still enclosed in my mother's womb, You sustained and delivered me and took me out, nor did You cause me to be born blind, deaf, unable to speak or to walk, or otherwise deficient. Great and manifold is Your mercy to me, that You have not made and created me as cattle, which are without reason or understanding. Who can utter the mighty acts of the Lord or declare His laudable works? Who can tell all His praise? There is none who can number all His benefits. And even if I, as a poor sinner, cannot praise You as much and highly as You are worthy and I am indebted, yet I will not keep silent, but extol Your holy name without ceasing insofar as I can and is possible for me. I will extol and praise Your righteousness, grace, and abundant mercy for as long as I live; and while I have a living breath, I will not forget the good that You have shown me. My mouth will declare Your righteousness and Your salvation daily, which I cannot number. My tongue which You have given me shall daily speak the fullness of Your glory and Your praise forever. I give thanks to the Lord in His sanctuary; I praise Him in the firmament of His power; I glorify Him in His works; I extol Him in His great glory. Let everything that has breath thank the Lord. Alleluia.

359. *Thanksgiving for all the benefits received since the mother's womb*
Lord, before I was or lived or moved or could do anything, You were over me in my mother's womb, graciously defending me as Your own creation, tenderly caring for me, and in wonderful manner sustaining me. Much more do You do this to me, O faithful Keeper of men, now that I am a "man born into this world," living, going, staying, acting, and knowing You through Your Word, even if it seems far different in the eyes of men, and even though my old Adam, which hangs about my neck until the grave, feels the opposite. But however it

may seem or feel, I pay no heed to it, nor am I misled by it, but hold to Your declaration that You are my Lord from my mother's womb. This will not deceive or fail. I confide in this, and by it I stir up and strengthen my faith, which does not regard what is seen (which is contrary to it) but by hope and patience awaits what is unseen. May You be ever blessed, my Lord and my God. Amen.

360. *Thanksgiving for the redemption*

O Lord Jesus Christ, Son of the living God, who are the express image and brightness of Your eternal Father, and the express image of His being, not made, nor created, but begotten of Him from all eternity, in one divine, indivisible nature, coequal in majesty and glory: I adore You, I honor, praise, and glorify You, and give thanks to You for all Your benefits, and most especially that at the appointed time, according to the will and pleasure of God, You took on a true human nature from the pure and chaste Virgin Mary; redeemed me, a poor, lost, and condemned person; purchased and won me from all sins, from death, and from the power of the devil, not with gold or silver, but with Your holy, precious blood and with Your innocent suffering and death, and all this only out of pure grace and mercy without any works, merits, or worthiness on my part. O dear Lord God, how great is Your love toward mankind, seeing You, the Righteous One, died for the unrighteous and ungodly! How can there be any greater love than that One should thus lay down His life for His friends? But You show Your supreme and most excellent love toward us, in that while we were yet sinners and Your enemies, You died for us and reconciled us to Your Father and appeased His righteous wrath, blotting out the handwriting of ordinances that was against us, which was contrary to us, and took it out of the way, nailing it to the cross. And having spoiled the principalities and powers of darkness, You made a show of them openly, triumphing over them through Yourself. In addition, with Your salutary resurrection from the dead, You restored the innocence and eternal life, true righteousness, and salvation to me and to all who heartily believe it. O faithful Savior, let Your holy, bitter sufferings not be ill spent on me, a poor sinner. Help me henceforth to live not for myself but for You, who died for me and rose again that I might arise from sin and live in You and be Your own, and live under You in Your kingdom, and serve You in everlasting righteousness; for You ascended into heaven and sit at the right hand of Your Father for all eternity. Amen.

361. Prayer to Christ Jesus that He would come for the Last Day

Lord Jesus Christ, although no man knows the hour of Your coming, not even the angels in heaven, but only Your Father, who has reserved this to His own power, nevertheless this world shall have an end and pass away; You will come with flames of fire, avenging Yourself on those who do not acknowledge You as God and do not obey Your Gospel. And that we may not doubt, You have from Your faithful heart made known and declared to us Your coming again; which even now is in preparation, and so demonstrated with certainty that the end of all things is near. Great signs occur in the sun, moon, and stars, which fall from the heavens and do not give their light. We hear of wars and rumors of wars. Nation rises against nation, and kingdom against kingdom. There are earthquakes in various places. There is famine and starvation. Unrighteousness abounds more and more. Brotherly love in many has grown cold. These times are so terrible that there is a fear and anguish among the people; they faint and pass quickly away for the sorrow and grief which is in the world. In the church, many men have arisen and taught perverse doctrines and twisted Your Word, and Your Word is denounced as heresy by many. In the temporal government, justice often yields to power. Justice has been turned into gall, and the fruit of righteousness into wormwood. The wicked is called good, and the good wicked, and black white. In the home, disloyalty, disobedience, disunity, conflict, strife, and quarreling abound, and in general the people lead an ungodly life, and no one regards sin. All these things are signs that the Last Day is growing late. Now therefore, since all these things are before our eyes, O Lord, mercifully grant that we may take it to heart, and not be secure in our sin, and as it may be, surprised and disappointed like the foolish virgins, but that we may continually watch and pray, do good, and not grow weary, that we may escape Your strict judgment and be worthy to stand before Your holy face when You shall come in the cloud with great power and glory, and send Your angels to gather together Your elect from the four winds and from the ends of the earth to the ends of the heavens. Lord, we wait daily for Your salvation. Therefore come, O Lord Jesus, and bring to an end all our misery, and with the believing thief take us up into paradise. Come, Lord Jesus, come. Amen.

362. Prayer that Christ would hasten His return to judgment

Dear Lord Jesus Christ, strengthen and complete Your work which You have begun in us, and hasten the glorious day of our redemption, which by God's grace we heartily desire; wherefore we sigh and wait for it in true faith and a good conscience, with which we have served the ungrateful world. For we cannot expect it to improve, but it is an enemy both of its own salvation and of ours. Come, dear Lord Jesus! And let him who loves You say, "Come, dear Lord Jesus." Amen.

363. Longing sigh for the Last Day

Lord Jesus Christ, hasten and usher in the blessed Day, when the hope of our glorious redemption shall be fulfilled, even as You have commanded in the Our Father that we should pray, "Thy kingdom come!" Since You have commanded us to pray for this, grant us grace, and help us to do it, firmly believing that we will at last attain to that glory. Grant also that the same joyous and blessed day of our redemption and glory may come soon, and that we may experience all these things as we now hear and believe them in the Word. Amen.

364. Contemplation of the Last Judgment

Lord Jesus, who will endure the Day of Your coming again for judgment? For then You will no longer appear, as in Your first coming in the flesh, in the poor, despised form of a servant, but in the clouds of heaven with great power, in the glory of Your Father, with all the holy angels and archangels, and will sit in the seat of Your majesty at the right hand of power. O how terrible it will be on that Day! For You will send Your angels with loud trumpets to gather Your elect from the four winds, from one end of the heavens to the other, and to separate the wicked from them and cast them into the fiery furnace, where there shall be wailing and gnashing of teeth. O Lord, who will stand at Your appearing? For You will take Your zeal as Your whole armor and will arm creation against Your enemies. You will put on righteousness as a breastplate and wear earnest judgment as a helmet. You will take holiness as an invincible shield and sharpen stern wrath for a sword. You will judge the whole earth with righteousness and give to each as he has done in the life of the body, whether good or evil. Then shall all that every man has thought or done in the whole time of his life be exposed to hair's breadth. For You will bring everything to light that was concealed in darkness and will reveal the counsel of the heart, and we will have to give an account of every vain word that proceeded from our mouths. Oh, wretched man that I am, how shall I stand in such stern judgment? How will I answer for all my wicked thoughts, sinful actions, vain words, and worthless works, which are beyond counting? Oh, how many sins are there of which I do not know, indeed, which I do not regard as sins, but as good works, which before Your judgment appear as truly open and coal-black sins? Alas, how wickedly I have done! Where shall I flee where I may abide? I cannot conceal myself, for if I fly to heaven, You are there; if I take the wings of the dawn and abide in the uttermost sea, Your hand would lead me there, and Your right hand would uphold me. Indeed if I bury myself in hell, Your hand would seize me from thence. Much less can I excuse myself. Oh, where shall I seek Your help and counsel? In You only, Lord Jesus Christ, who are not only my judge but also my advocate and defender, for You are my Brother and Savior, and You let Yourself be judged for my sake, that I might stand with joy at the Last Judgment. Praise be to You, O my dearest Immanuel! Hosanna in the highest! Blessed is He who comes in the name of the Lord, my King and my Bridegroom! Come, Lord Jesus, come soon. Amen.

365. *Thanksgiving for sanctification*

O God the Holy Spirit, who proceed from the Father and are sent by the Son, of the same substance with them, coeternal with them, in one divine and indivisible nature: I adore You, I honor, praise, and glorify You, and give thanks to You from my inmost heart for all Your benefits, and most especially that by Your grace You have called and brought me to the holy Christian faith, poured Yourself out in my Baptism, and never cease to work in me Your own works. Because I cannot by my own reason or strength believe in Jesus Christ, my Lord, or come to Him, I beseech You to teach me, lead and bring me into all truth, increase and nourish true faith in me, grace me with a right understanding of Your Word, sanctify me in true invocation with proper trust, and give and bestow inner peace and constancy. Write Jesus Christ in my heart, for You are the living finger of God. Assure me with Your testimony; comfort me against all the fear and dullness of the flesh. Be my faithful assistant against the accusation of the wicked foe. Strengthen me against wavering, that I may be sealed in the faith by Your grace of the promise, for You are the pledge of my inheritance for my redemption. Grant me also right devotion and sighing for prayer, that I may cry out in true confidence and childlike trust, and say, "Abba, dear Father!" Give me true simplicity of heart without any gall and bitterness, even as You appeared in the form of a dove when our Lord Jesus Christ was baptized at the Jordan. Kindle in me the fire of fervent love, which You caused to be seen in fiery tongues upon the holy apostles, that I may receive Your anointing. Renew me in the inner man, that by You, who are active in the Word and Sacraments, might be born again. Keep me from idolatry and lying and from all error and heresy. Take away the impurity of my mind. Extinguish and suppress in me all carnal desires. Let the sinful passions have no power in my body, but make Your habitation in me, and rule all my members, and escort me to the true fatherland. Amen.

366. *Thanksgiving for the resurrection of the dead*

O Captain of our salvation, Christ Jesus, my Lord and my God, who Yourself spoke, "I am the Resurrection and the Life; he who believes in Me shall live, even if He die": strengthen my faith in this mystery from day to day, that in word and deed I may not be found among those who think that there is no resurrection, but may firmly believe that, as You rose from the dead and became the firstfruits of those who sleep, so I, too, may not remain in the grave, but that You, with the heavenly Father and the Holy Spirit, would one day transform my lowly body, that it may be made like Your glorified body according to the working by which You are able even to subject all things to Yourself. O my most trustworthy Lord Jesus, if we hoped in You only in this life and did not believe that after this life a better one were to be expected, we would be the most miserable of men! But now You by Your resurrection have brought life and immortality to light, in addition to which You said, "I live, and you also shall live"—in the body also as in the soul. Therefore my heart is glad, and my glory rejoices; for I know that my Redeemer lives, and He will hereafter raise me from the earth, and I will then be surrounded with this my skin, and in my flesh I shall see God; Him shall I see for myself, and my eyes shall behold Him, and not another. If in time my faith should sink and start to doubt this mystery, help me then Yourself, and intercede for me with God, that my faith may not cease. Let not the smoldering wick in me go utterly out, but strengthen my faith, that I may both trust in Your almighty power, for which nothing is impossible, and ever give thanks to You with a believing heart, and confess that we have in You a God who helps, and a Lord of lords who by virtue of His victorious resurrection delivers from death. To You be glory forever and ever! Amen.

367. *Prayer after the seven petitions of the Holy Our Father*

O dear heavenly Father, triune God, we Your children beseech You from our heart that You would keep us from false doctrine and a sinful life, give and preserve to us faithful teachers, that they may preach Your Word purely and without adulteration, and administer rightly Your Holy and Most Worthy Sacraments, and that we may accordingly live holy and godly lives in Your fear. Give us Your Holy Spirit, righteousness, and peace and joy in our hearts, and guard in us the deposit unto the day of Jesus Christ. Govern us, that we may do what You desire of us in Your Word, that we may believe in Christ, amend our lives, be long-suffering, and remain steadfast. Hinder and break every wicked counsel and will, such as that of the devil, the world, and our own flesh, that Your will may be done by us on earth as it is done without hindrance by the angels in heaven. Comfort and strengthen all those who are sick, afflicted, or suffering tribulation, and sustain them in Christian patience and true faith until the end. Grant also to our authorities the grace, Spirit, and wisdom to govern their subjects rightly according to Your pleasure. Keep us from sedition, war, and bloodshed, from distress by fire and water, hail, tempest, blight, pestilence, and famine. Faithfully receive into Your care also the domestic estate, and in it both husband and wife, parents and children, masters and servants, poor widows and orphans, young and old, and let us partake of our daily bread with prayer and thanksgiving. O merciful God and Father, do not look at our sins and trespasses! Forgive us these, and release us from the punishment which we well deserve. Renew our hearts and minds, that we may increasingly die to sins and grow in godliness, and that we may readily forgive, love, and live in peace with one another. Keep us also from the severe tribulations of the devil, the world, and our own flesh, and strengthen us by the power of Your Spirit, that we may resist these our spiritual enemies, do all things well, and obtain the victory. And because our misery here is, alas, various and great, we beseech You, O faithful God and Father, to take up our cause and not to abandon us to any distress, but to relieve and diminish our misery and wretchedness, and in them to comfort and help us, indeed, to deliver us at last from all evil, to grant us a blessed death, and then graciously to take us in true faith from this valley of sorrows to Yourself in eternal joy and blessedness. Amen, in Jesus' name, Amen.

368. Prayer for constancy in confessing the truth in time of temptation

Most beloved Jesus, my Lord and my God, You Yourself said in the days of Your flesh, "Whoever confesses Me before men, him will I confess before My heavenly Father. But whoever denies Me before men, him will I also deny before

My heavenly Father." You know all things. You know that I love You. You know also my sorrows and the blasphemy of those who say that they are Christians and are not, but are the school of Satan. I beseech You heartily to sanctify me in Your truth; Your Word is truth. And grant that I may not let myself be driven and tossed about by every wind of doctrine, but that I may stand in Your truth which I have known and abide in that which I have learned. Make me strong by Your grace, that I may bear Your name before nations, princes, and kings, and not be as a reed shaken by the wind. For I well know that none but he who perseveres to the end shall be saved; wherefore keep my heart in the one thing, and turn me from every false way, that my heart may not turn away from You nor let itself be secretly persuaded, lest a root bearing gall and wormwood spring up in me. For what would it profit me to gain the whole world and yet to suffer injury to my soul? Should my adversaries and persecutors attack me, to devour my flesh, and to bring me by force to a contrary religion, give me strength and courage that I may not fear those who kill the body and cannot kill the soul, but rather Him who can destroy both body and soul in hell, so that I may not love my life even unto death. And because the spirit is willing but the flesh is weak, perfect Yourself that good work which You have begun in me, and let me remain faithful to You unto death. Be mighty in me, who am weak, that I may not suffer life nor death nor any other power to separate me from the love which is in You. And bring me finally there, where I, being freed from all persecution, may with heart and mouth sing that the Lion of the tribe of Judah has overcome! To Him who sits on the throne, and unto the Lamb, be blessing and honor and glory and power forever and ever. Amen.

369. Earnest prayer for protection against stubbornness and apostasy
O Lord God, if we should sin, let us do any other sin than go our way and avoid the blessing as if it were a curse, and receive a stubborn, blinded, and hardened heart that neither sees nor hears, but refuses counsel and thinks it is under the blessing and not under the curse! Dear God, let us not fall into that sin which will not tolerate the plain truth, for then there is no fix or help or pardon, and at last wrath will strike. Defend us from that, dear, faithful God! Amen.

370. Prayer for a blessed end
O gracious God, You have appointed a limit to man's life that he cannot pass, for his time is determined; the number of his months is with You. You have

numbered all our days, and yet they pass quickly as a flood, and we fly away. All our years are as a smoke or shadow that passes suddenly away. Man is like grass which soon dries up, and like a flower on the field that withers. Therefore teach me, O gracious God, to acknowledge and bear in mind that I must have an end, and I must leave it. Behold, my days are as a hand's breadth before You, and my life is as nothing in Your sight. Truly every man is altogether vanity, however securely he may live. Lord, teach me to remember that I must die, and in this pilgrimage I have no continuing city. Make known to me how brief and passing my life is, that I may often remember my end, that I may not live and die for myself in this world, but for You, that, alert and cheerful in the faith, I may await the day of my homeward journey and the appearing of Your beloved Son, Jesus Christ, and hasten toward it with holy conduct and godliness. Grace me, my God, with a blessed departure when my last hour draws near, that I may die a blessed death, keeping my reason and full awareness until my end, that my understanding and senses may not become impaired, and I do not speak anything absurd or blasphemous against You, my Lord, or against my own salvation. Keep me from a sudden and evil death and from eternal damnation. Let me not be taken suddenly and unawares in my last hour, but let me prepare myself first with true repentance and right faith. And when the end comes, make me fearless and unwavering for temporal death, which only opens the door for me to eternal life. Then let me, Your servant, depart in peace, my eyes having seen Your Savior, whom You have prepared before all peoples, a light to lighten the Gentiles, and the glory of Your people Israel. Grant that my final word may be that which Your dear Son spoke on the cross: "Father, into Your hands I commit my spirit." And when I am no longer able to speak, yet hear my last sighing; through Jesus Christ. Amen.

371. *Prayer for protection against a sudden and evil death*

O dearest Jesus, my Lord and God! By all Your labors and sorrows, by Your priceless blood, by Your last words, O my sweetest Jesus, which You spoke on the cross: "My God, My God, why have You forsaken Me?" by Your loud cries, when You cried out to Your heavenly Father, "Father, into Your hands I commit My spirit!" by all these things I devoutly beseech You mercifully to keep me from a sudden, hasty, and evil death. Your hands, O my Redeemer, created and fashioned me together with all that is in me. O dear Lord, do not cast me down so hastily. Grant, I beseech You, abundant time for repentance. Give me a blessed hour of death, that I may depart in Your grace, that with my whole heart I may love, praise, and bless You forever. Yet all things are in Your hands, O gracious Lord Jesus, and there is no man who can resist Your will. My life depends upon Your will; it will end when You Yourself desire. Therefore I, too, desire nothing else, O my dear God, than what You desire, where You desire, when You desire, and how You desire—so may it be. All this I leave to Your discretion. I will exclude no place, no time, no death, however shameful or painful it may be. Only this I ask, O Christ, my God, that I may not die a precipitous and unforeseen death. Yet not my will, but Yours be done. Wherefore, if it is pleasing in Your sight that I should die precipitously, neither am I opposed to it. Your will, O my God, be done in all things. For I am entirely of the hope and confidence that by Your great mercy by which I ask all these things, I will die in Your grace and love, and when I die in these, no sudden death will be able to separate me from You. For the righteous man, although he dies a temporal death, is nevertheless at rest. His is no unforeseen death whose life was careful and circumspect. If I do not then have the space and time (which, O my God, only You know) so that I may commit myself to Your keeping, behold, I do so now, and with all possible humility and devout heart I call from the depths to You in heaven, "Have mercy upon me, O God, according to Your abundant mercy." Thy will be done, O Lord, on earth as it is in heaven. Into Your hands I commend my spirit. You have redeemed me, O Lord, faithful God. All creatures bless and worship You, O God. In You, O Lord, I put my trust; You will not leave me confounded for eternity. Amen.

372. Prayer concerning Holy Baptism

O Lord Jesus Christ, the beginning, middle, and end of our salvation, who have instituted the Holy Sacrament of Holy Baptism, and testified to it in the work of redemption when blood and water flowed forth from Your opened side, wherefore St. John says, "Three are they on earth which testify: The Spirit, the water, and the blood, and the three are together"; and further confirmed and sanctified it by Your own Baptism in the Jordan, as through Your own example: I heartily thank You that You have incorporated me by this Sacrament into Your holy Christian Church and thereby place me in the communion of all Your heavenly and eternal goods, which You obtained by Your bitter sufferings and death; thereby purified and washed me of the horrible poison and leprosy of original sin; in Your grace forgave all my sins, trespasses, and iniquity; and purified me by the washing of water in the Word, blotting out all my transgressions so that nothing is left to condemn me, even as there is now no condemnation for those who are in Christ Jesus. Having forgiven my sins, You redeemed me from eternal death and from the anguish, fear, and terror of temporal death, and from the power of the devil. At the same time, You have incorporated me into Yourself, made me a member of Your spiritual body, transferred me into Your kingdom of grace, and espoused and pledged me to Yourself in eternity. And since through Baptism I have put You on, I am clothed with all Your holy obedience, merit, righteousness, holiness, and innocence as with the garment of salvation and the robe of righteousness. By the washing of rebirth and renewal in the Holy Spirit You have given me new birth, and of a sinner made a righteous man. I have been baptized into Your death, become a partaker of the fruit of Your death, and incorporated into Your obedience and merit. Thus I, a child of wrath, have become a child of grace. I was a poor, miserable, lost child of man, and You made me a child of God. You gave me the Holy Spirit and the adoption of sons, by which we cry out, "Abba, dear Father!" Thus You received me into Your eternal covenant of grace, and by Your promise bound Yourself to me to be my Father forever, and gave me the right of sons, which is the eternal, heavenly inheritance and salvation. Briefly, in Baptism You have given me the highest good—Your dear Son with all His benefits. Christ is mine, along with all that He is and has; what can sin do to me? Christ is my righteousness; what can death do to me? Christ is my life; what can the devil do to me? Christ is my strength and victory; what can the world do to me? Christ has overcome it. Indeed, my Lord Christ has saved me and given me all blessedness in Holy Baptism. Therefore I await in patience the glory to come. What harm can poverty, misery, cross, persecution, and contempt do to me? I am saved. I have received all the goods of grace in and with Christ, and only await the goods of glory. But because I, O my Lord Jesus Christ, by Baptism have died and been buried with You, help me as long as I live in the flesh not to live according to the flesh. Let my Baptism bear fruit in me each day and work the mortification of the flesh, that I may daily die with You through heartfelt remorse and contrition; for he who dies to himself daily always has a new beginning of his life in You. And since I have been incorporated into You, my Lord and God, as a graft upon the tree of life, let me bring forth fruit as a branch on the living vine—not fruit of the old man, but of the new man, the new creature, the fruit of the Spirit. And let me remember daily that I am baptized into a new life, that I have put You on as a gift of eternal righteousness and blessedness, and as a new life by which

You may live and abide in me forever, and I in You. Indeed, let me never forget the covenant which You have made with me, nor break it, nor renounce it with heart or mouth or ungodly life; but rather let me rejoice and take comfort in it at all times, and depend on it safely against all tribulation, and abide in this covenant, which is eternal and certain, and have eternal salvation. Amen.

373. *Thanksgiving for the Office of the Keys, to be prayed before Confession*

O dearest Lord Jesus, Son of the living God, how dearly You love Your people, that You not only became a partaker of our flesh and blood for our salvation and eternal blessedness, and by Your bitter suffering and dying delivered us from sin, and by Your victorious rising again obtained for us the righteousness which avails before God, and then by Your glorious and majestic ascension opened again the heavenly gate to Your Father that formerly was barred through sin, but You also, before Your ascension, left the keys of the kingdom of heaven to Your dear apostles, in the name and stead of Your spouse, the whole Church. All this, so that to all those who after receiving Baptism should exclude themselves from the kingdom of heaven by false doctrine or a sinful life and fall from grace, but then repent truly, heaven—and thus access to God, Your heavenly Father—would in all joy and confidence, through faith, be opened again by the key of loosing, according to Your faithful promise: "Whatever you (My disciples, and your successors in the public ministry of preaching) shall loose on earth shall also be loosed in heaven." And again: "Whose sins you remit, they are remitted to them." At this Your word, therefore, I will go in Your name with a contrite and sorrowful heart, in childlike trust, to Your grace, to Your regular minister and steward of Your Mysteries, there to receive the particular Absolution or forgiveness of sins from his mouth in Your stead, for the strengthening of my faith. For I firmly believe what the minister ordained by You in Your stead speaks and does with me, particularly when at Your divine command and on the basis of Your precious merits he absolves me, as a repentant sinner, from my sins and pronounces me clear, loosed, and released, that his unbinding is as powerful and certain as if it had been done by You Yourself with Your own mouth in heaven, and thus the voice of the Absolution is truly Your own words. O faithful Savior, uphold this highest, most precious treasure until the end of the world, and govern my heart, that I may regard this work of grace high and dear, and seize, accept, and retain it by strong faith. Grant me grace also that I may sincerely forgive my neighbors, even my enemies, and eagerly do good to those who sin against me. Then I will enter into Your house on the basis of Your abundant mercy and will worship in Your fear. Lord, guide me in Your righteousness, and direct my ways before me. Lord, I call to You; come to me quickly, receive my voice when I call to You. Let my prayer avail before You as incense, the lifting up of my hands as the evening sacrifice. Grant me in the Holy Absolution to hear the words of life, by which I am saved. Indeed, grant me to hear joy and gladness, that the bones which You have broken may rejoice. Now I go; oh, let me return home justified like the repentant tax collector, and grant that I may embark upon a new life! Amen.

374. *Thanksgiving for the institution of the Holy Supper*

Dearest Lord Jesus Christ, what is this poor being, man, that You are so devoutly mindful of him, and the son of man, that You so eagerly visit him? Dearest Lord Jesus, in the night when You were betrayed, You cared more for our salvation than for Your own welfare. You instituted the most worthy Supper, that by it we might be incorporated into You, strengthened in the faith, and fed unto life everlasting. Thanks and praise be to You for this unspeakable benefit! Your works, O Lord, are great; he who studies them delights in them. What You ordain is honorable and glorious. You have established a remembrance of Your wondrous works, O gracious and merciful Lord. You provide food for those who fear You; You remember Your covenant forever. O Lord, for Your Holy Supper You took bread and wine. Oh, grant that as bread and wine nourish and sustain the body, so our souls may be mightily fed by these wondrous signs. You gave thanks and prayed over the bread and wine; stir up in us also true devotion at all times, that as in other matters, so above all in this holy rite, we may call fervently upon You and thank You sincerely. You broke bread; oh, let my heart also be broken and crushed by true repentance and contrition! You distributed it; oh, let me also willingly share the blessings which You give me. You said, "Take, eat"; at such works stir up in me a heartfelt desire, that I may come with great longing and fulfill Your command. You did not say "This signifies," but, "This is"; not, "a sign of My body," but, "My body"—even the body "which is given for you." These are Your words; You spoke them that we might see in them Your will and intention. Therefore I believe them as they read and will not let myself be torn from the clear letters. You are the wisest and well know how and what to speak. You are the mightiest and are certainly able to fulfill what You have spoken. You are the truest and will certainly do what You have said. O Lord, confirm in us this faith. Sanctify us and sustain us in Your truth. Your Word is truth. Restore all the erring and enlighten the eyes of those who by imperfect reasons and ill-founded quibbles have permitted themselves to be blinded. Lord Jesus, You also said, "This do in remembrance of Me." Therefore, O Lord, mercifully give me a fresh and strong memory of all Your benefits and especially of Your bonds and wounds, Your blows and stripes, Your suffering and dying. You graciously remembered me before time, when You chose me as a living member of Your Church and a fellow citizen of Your heavenly kingdom. You graciously remembered me in time, when You were made man, paid my debt, and prayed for me to Your heavenly Father in Your last sigh on the cross. You will graciously remember me after time, when You will bring me into the heavenly paradise. Do I then not owe it to You, indeed, should I not be willing in turn to remember You, and, especially when partaking of Your Holy Supper, to proclaim Your love and faithfulness, Your grace and favor, Your graciousness and mercy? You were not content to suffer and die for us; You also had to ordain and institute for us Your own body and Your own blood under the bread and wine to be received by mouth! When Mary, the mother of the Lord, came to her cousin Elizabeth, she said with amazement, "Whence is this to me, that the mother of my Lord should come to me?" Here it is not the mother of the Lord, but the Lord Himself. Should not I then say in amazement, "Whence is this to me, that my Lord should come to me?" When the Lord told the centurion in Capernaum that He would come to him, the good soldier acknowledged at once his unworthiness, and said, "Lord, I am not worthy that You should come under my roof." O Lord, how much more I ought to humble myself when You wish to enter into my sinful and unclean mouth and to give me Your body to eat and Your blood to drink! How much more I ought to kneel, and beat my breast, and lift up my voice and say, "Lord, I am not worthy that You should enter into my mouth!" But since it pleases You to ordain for me Your body as food and Your blood as drink, thanks and praise be to You, and may Your superabundant mercy be extolled and glorified forever and ever! Amen, Lord Jesus, Amen, Amen.

375. Prayer against the Sacramentarians

My dear Lord Jesus Christ, a dispute has arisen over Your words in the Supper. Some people try to interpret them otherwise than as they read. But since those people teach me nothing certain, but only cause confusion and uncertainty and neither can nor will prove their reading in any way, I have therefore kept to Your reading, as the words sounds. If there is something obscure in it, You wanted it to be obscure, for You have not given, nor commanded to be given, any other explanation of this. Neither do we find in any writing or language that "is" means "signifies," or "My body" means "a sign of My body." Now if there were some obscurity here, You would surely overlook it if I did not get it exactly right, as You overlooked it when Your apostles did not understand many things when You told them of Your suffering and resurrection. Yet they maintained the words as they sounded and did not turn them into other words. Likewise, Your dear mother did not understand when You said to her [Luke 2], "I must be in that which is My Father's," and yet in simplicity she kept the words in her heart and did not change them. So I, too, have stuck to these Your words, "This is My body," and have not tried to change them into others, nor have them changed, but commended it and left it to You whether there is something obscure here, and kept them as they read, especially since I do not find that they conflict with any article of the faith. Amen.

X. WEATHER

376. Prayer in time of drought

O faithful, true, and righteous God, who in Your faithful Word have indicated in the most comforting manner how a true, earnest, zealous, believing, and persistent prayer pierces mightily the clouds of heaven and not only comes with certainty before Your presence, but also is capable of much and accomplishes much: we poor children, in this unseasonable and exceedingly long-lasting period of heat and drought, come here at Your comforting indication, with our believing, sincere, and truly earnest prayers before the presence of Your high, divine majesty, humbly beseeching You that You would graciously hear us according to Your promise, kindly turn away from us Your great and relentless wrath, moisten again the sorely parched earth according to our need, and cause a nourishing rain from heaven to fall, drop drown, and rain upon it again, that it may bring forth and produce again the fruits committed to it for the necessary support of our temporal life, to which You appointed it with fatherly attention in the first creation. Now therefore, as at the earnest prayer of Your faithful servant and prophet Elijah opened again the heavens which You had shut, and caused rain to fall on the thirsty ground, so we look to You, that You might deal mercifully with us in this great dryness and heat, and with fatherly care answer our earnest prayer, to Your own praise and to our salvation; through Jesus Christ, Your beloved Son, our only Savior and Redeemer. Amen.

377. Thanksgiving after receiving fruitful rains

O faithful God, we poor sinners have awakened Your wrath and deserve nothing but punishment, which You have visited upon us for a time. For the sun rose with a burning heat and withered the grass, and its flower fell, and the beauty of its shape perished; then You commanded the clouds not to rain and afflicted us with a time of drought. But now You have covered the heavens with clouds and prepared rain for the earth. You make the grass to grow on the mountains; You give food for the cattle, and so restore to life the parched soil. We give thanks to You, Lord, for though You were angry with us, Your anger is turned away, and You have comforted us with Your help. Nevertheless You did not leave Yourself without witness, in that You have done much good to us by giving us rain from heaven, and fruitful seasons, filling our hearts with food and gladness. — Therefore shout unto God, all you lands, sing praises to the glory of His name, extol Him gloriously, and say to God, "How wonderful are Your works! All the earth worships You and sings praise to You and to Your holy name!" Yet help us, faithful God, that we may turn and forsake our sinful life, cease to do evil, and begin to do good, and continue steadfast in doing so, that we may not anger You again and by intentional sin invited upon ourselves, either the former punishment or one yet greater. Govern us with Your Holy Spirit, that we may serve You with joy and delight in our hearts, that all Your blessings may fall once more upon our city, country, field, and all that we have; indeed, that we may be blessed in our coming in and going out, until the day when we receive perfectly the rich spiritual blessing in heavenly riches through Christ; to whom with You, O heavenly Father, and the Holy Spirit, one true God, be praise, honor, and glory forever and ever. Amen.

378. Prayer for the relief of warm sunshine in a long period of wet weather

Lord, almighty God, who clothe the heavens with blackness, and sackcloth their covering: in Your wrath You punished the impenitent first world for their great wickedness and malice with the waters of the flood and destroyed all that on dry ground had had a living breath, spirit, and being. We also in our own time, because of our transgressions which we have committed against You, have, according to Your strict judgment, been visited by abnormal rain and a long and steady period of wet weather, by which the land and its produce have suffered great damage. Merciful Father, who in the flood stopped the fountains of the deep and the windows of heaven and prevented the rain from heaven: take from us all our sin and iniquity, and turn the punishment and damaging rains and great waters away from us. For the land is afflicted, and the heavens above us mourn. Behold the testimony of the bow in the clouds, and remember Your promise. Give us good weather, that the fruits of the field and in the garden may prosper and progress and not be devastated by the manifold and excessive wet weather, nor any famine ensue. Lord, very God, who cannot lie! You said, "There shall no flood destroy the earth any more." Therefore be gracious, Lord, and do not withhold mercy because of wrath. Take Your grace and mercy not away from us. Give us not idle teeth and lack of bread. Bless our bread, that we may eat, and glorify Your name. So shall we see that we are Your true children whom You care for faithfully, and honor and glorify You as our heavenly Father all our life long. Amen.

379. Prayer for the fruits of the field

Dear Lord God, mercifully preserve the fruits of the field, purify the air, grant blessed rain and good weather, that produce may ripen well, that it may not be rendered poisonous, nor we nor our livestock by consuming it be afflicted with pestilence, fever, or other disease; for such plagues derive from the evil spirits which poison the air, and so the fruit, wine, and grain in turn, so that by Your permission we are made to eat and drink death and disease by our own goods. Wherefore let them be blessed, dear God, that they may serve for our health and happiness, and we not misuse them to the harm of our soul or the multiplication of sin, gluttony, and idleness, which leads to unchastity, adultery, cursing, swearing, murder, war, and all calamity. But grant us grace to use Your gifts for the salvation of our soul and the amendment of our life, and that the fruit may be a cause of preserving the health of body and soul. Amen.

380. Prayer when the fruits of the field are damaged by mildew and various pests through God's delaying

True and great are all Your judgments; wonderful and unsearchable are all Your works, O mighty and all-powerful Lord of heaven and earth. For as in Your Holy Word You long ago threatened with terrible punishments and plagues all who willfully resist Your Commandments, and among other things intimated that You would equip and employ vermin in every place; likewise, we, as the unrepentant, experience and see in this day how with the greatest damage and detriment to ourselves and our livelihood, said punishments and plagues have come upon us also because of our sin, to frighten us from our ungodly way of life. For what we and our people expect to gather, harvest, reap, and afterwards enjoy and use each year, are eaten, consumed, and destroyed before our eyes by harmful wild animals, filthy grubs, abominable grasshoppers and beetles, indeed, troublesome mildew, and other troublesome insects and vermin. In this present misery and affliction, therefore, we beseech You, O God, through Your beloved Son, Jesus Christ, not to punish us in Your fiery indignation, as You nevertheless punished the shameless Egyptians, but mercifully take away from us the present trouble; protect and preserve all that we need and use daily for the necessary support of the body, for ourselves and our people. But especially, dear Father, keep us from the pest of hell and from the wicked, undying worm of a wicked, restless conscience which ever gnaws and stings us, that we may be graciously preserved by You here in time and hereafter in eternity; for You live and reign eternally with Your only-begotten Son and the Holy Spirit, true God, blessed forever. Amen.

381. *Prayer during stormy weather*

O Lord God of heaven, great and awesome God, who reign over all the kingdoms of the earth and are mighty, awesome, and doing wonders: Your voice is upon the great waters: You, the God of glory, thunder: Your voice is powerful; Your voice, Lord, is full of majesty, and its wrath is a consuming fire, and it is a fearful thing to fall into the hands of Your wrath! You touch a land and it melts, and all who dwell in it mourn. Our iniquities have earned Your punishment; yet help us in this distress, for the sake of Your name. Let not Your wrath wax greater than Your fervent and sincere mercy. You are our Father; Your name is from of old. You are our hope, and You have promised us that if we will turn to You, You will repent of the evil which You thought to do to us. Therefore blot out our iniquities like a cloud and our sins like a mist. O Lord, do not leave us, and do not withdraw Your hand from us, God of our salvation! Take the payment for our sins from the bloody merit of Your Son, Jesus, with which He procured us and established an eternal redemption and which cleanses us from all our sins. He is the propitiation for our sins, and through Him we have peace with You. Turn back now from the hotness of Your anger, and forgive the iniquities of Your people, according to Your great mercy. Do not destroy Your people and inheritance which You have redeemed by Your great power and have purchased by the very blood of Your beloved Son; keep our life and limb as the apple of Your eye. Preserve also in this great storm our house and home, goods and sustenance which Your blessing has granted us. Turn from us in Your fatherly care all our well-deserved calamity, and help us, God of our salvation, for the glory of Your great name, for all Your mercy and for the blood of Jesus, our Savior. Amen.

382. *Prayer when the stormy weather continues a long time*

Almighty, everlasting, powerful, and awesome God, we see from the present storm how angry You are with us, for You have commanded Your firmament to rise up against us and to punish us because of our sins, and terrible lightning and thunder follow one after another, so that we are in fear of life and limb if You do not give us Your fatherly protection. Therefore, O Lord, be not far from us, for anguish is near, and there is no other helper. O dear Lord and God, spare us, protect us and the fruits of the field, that we may have wherewith to sustain our bodies. Be gracious unto us and have mercy upon us. Continually grant us here in time Your grace and mercy, and after this life eternal and unceasing blessedness. Amen.

383. *Prayer in a severe storm*

O Lord, our Lord, great and awesome God, we, Your needy children, hear with terror and trembling what a fearsome tempest, roaring, and fury You have stirred up, by which You indicate to the ungodly and wicked world Your righteous wrath and the punishment justly deserved. O Lord, do not look at our great sins, but graciously release us from them. Set us free from all afflictions, and assist us in our misery. Rebuke the tempestuous wind to relent from its terrible blast and rage. Restrain Satan, that he may not have any power over our life and limb, house and home, possessions and property. Defend us from dangerous conflagration and from all harm to home and building, man and cattle, by land or sea. Dear Father, let us be enclosed in Your almighty hand and there remain; and neither this wind nor any other creature in heaven or on earth will be ever able to harm us or tear us from You. Save us, Lord God, and we shall be saved, that afterward we may be able to thank You heartily, obey Your Word, and glorify You continually, both here and hereafter, for the sake of Your dear Son, Jesus Christ, our Redeemer and Savior. Amen.

384. *Prayer during stormy weather*

O great and mighty God of heaven and earth, by whose present thundering and lightning we are reminded of Your great anger toward us sinful men: by this noise, at which all creatures tremble with terror, as by a repentance-bell, You call us to the knowledge of our sins and to true repentance, that we may not be condemned with the ungodly and wicked world. You are mighty and powerful, O Lord, and if You should deal with us according to Your strict righteousness, the whole world would perish instantly in a single thunderclap and bolt of lightning. But we fall to the knees of our hearts and humbly beseech You to relent from Your fierce anger, which burns against sin as a fire. Have mercy upon us, spare us, lift up upon us Your gracious countenance, and be merciful unto us. Preserve our life and limb, house and home, city and nation, our possessions and property, and all that we have, as also fruit of the field, from hail and sleet, and conflagration of the tempest, from great floods of water, and from all harm. Keep us also from a sudden, evil death, and mercifully grant that many sinners may be frightened from their ungodliness by Your Word and by Your thunder and lightning, and sincerely turn and be converted to You. Let us at every moment remember Your glorious coming for judgment, and be ready to receive You with gladness, and to go in with You to everlasting joy. Amen. O Lord, be gracious and merciful unto us poor sinners in body and soul, here in this life and hereafter in the life to come! Amen.

385. *Thanksgiving when the stormy weather is happily past*

Almighty God, heavenly Father, who said to us, "Call on Me in the time of need, and I will deliver you; then you shall glorify Me": we give You praise and thanks from our inmost hearts that You have graciously heard our prayer and caused the furious tempest to pass by without any harm to our bodies or property, by which You have manifested once again Your faithful fatherly heart, not desiring to deal with us according to our sins, and not repaying us according to our iniquities. Grant us, merciful Father, for the sake of Your only-begotten Son, Jesus Christ, that our lives may be constantly amended by Your earnest warnings, and that we may live in Your fear and prepare for the coming of Your beloved Son, that we may go out with gladness to meet Him, enter with shouts of joy into the new heaven, in which righteousness dwells, and forever possess it with You in Your blessed sight, through the same Your beloved Son, Jesus Christ, our Lord. Amen.

386. *Prayer when a comet or other wondrous sign is seen in the heavens*

Great God, You show wonders in the heavens above and signs on the earth below. You determine the number of the stars and call them all by their name and do great things which are beyond understanding. O hidden God, who made the eye: open our eyes, that we may marvel at this wondrous sign in the heavens now present and know that it is not by chance but by Your divine provision, to terrify the ungodly and to comfort the good. O Lord Jesus Christ, this reminds us of Your coming again and reassures us that the Last Day, and so our redemption, is at the door. O God, the Holy Spirit, since the signs in the heavens are our preachers of repentance, help us by them to be reminded of our sins, and according to such signs to amend our lives; through Jesus Christ. Amen.

XI. CROSS & TRIBULATION

387. *Prayer in dire weakness of faith*

O Lord, I see now in truth that "all men have not faith." I believe, dear Lord, yet help my unbelief! You will not break the bruised reed, nor quench the smoldering wick, O Jesus, for You sit at the right hand of God, representing and interceding for me, that my faith may not die. Be the founder and perfecter of faith, that I may extinguish the fiery darts of the evil one. Let me believe, even though I do not see, and so obtain salvation. Amen.

388. *Lament over a lack of devotion in prayer*

My God and Lord, I lament to You with groaning that, while I am eager with fervent devotion to call upon You and offer the sacrifice of zealous prayer, yet my heart is too heavy and cold. It will not be rightly and fervently lifted up from earthly things to heavenly things. I find myself disinclined and unworthy for prayer, and must often compel my flesh and blood to devotion with all my strength, which troubles me and causes me to imagine that You have become ungracious, because I feel no true moving of the Holy Spirit to speak to You. Dear Father, where I have earned this with my thoughtless conduct and negligence, where I have not listened diligently to You in Your Word when You called me to repentance, where I have not obediently hearkened to the urging of the Holy Spirit, where I set my thoughts too much on earthly things, forgive me for the sake of Your dear Son, Jesus Christ. Strip from before me all hindrances which keep me from blessed devotion, and in Your fatherly compassion bear with my weakness, for which I am sorry. Take all spiritual reluctance from my heart, and let me be willing and ready to serve You devoutly and with a mind turned away from the world. I long for Your heavenly grace. Come to the aid of my soul, and let me joyfully hold childlike conversation with You as my heavenly Father, as the Holy Spirit cries to You daily, "Abba, dear Father!" In this I will heartily rejoice and take comfort, that my poor prayer is acceptable and pleasing to You as a willing sacrifice, and I shall be and abide with You in grace forever. Amen.

389. *Prayer when one's heart is in anguish and afraid*

God of all comfort, who bountifully quicken all who in anguish and sorrow take childlike refuge in You: I, a poor and very afflicted being, know nowhere to flee except to Your mercy. Hear my cry and hearken to my prayer! From my trouble I call to You. I am anguished in my heart daily. The anguish of hell has gotten hold of me, and I am very anxious for consolation. Fear and trembling have come upon me. Lord, You make me to know many and sore afflictions; make me also to live again, and bring me back from the depths of the earth. You have made me fall into a hard school of anguish according to Your fatherly will, O Lord. Anguish is near, and here there is no helper except You only. Help me by Your grace to overcome this high mountain of anguish, and give me joy for anguish and gladness for fear, heart and courage for trembling, comfort and life for travail, that I may forget the past anguish and be glad in Your divine redemption, and my bones which are now very terrified may rejoice. Lord, I know that You do not afflict Your dear children from Your heart, but only hide Your friendly countenance a while for their salvation and their good. How often You have wonderfully delivered me and others of Your believers from anguish and distress! Demonstrate Your grace toward me also; I will hope in Your help at every hour. I know that You will not leave me without consolation, for I heartily desire it. Turn toward me and be gracious unto me, for I am lonely and afflicted. The anguish of my heart is great; bring me out of my troubles. Behold my sorrow and wretchedness, and forgive me all my sins for the sake of Your mercy. Amen.

390. *Prayer in great anguish over sins*

O Lord, gracious and merciful God, rebuke me not in Your wrath, and chasten me not in Your anger, for Your arrows pierce me and Your hand presses down on me; there is no health in my body because of Your indignation, neither is there any peace in my bones because of my sin. My heart trembles, my strength has failed me, and the light of my eyes is gone from me. Sorrows have surrounded me without number; my iniquities have taken hold upon me so that I cannot see. They are more than the hairs of my head, and my heart has forsaken me. O gracious Father, because I have angered You with my manifold sins, I am therefore suffering in my conscience the heavy and terrible tribulation, wherein I do not so much doubt Your grace as despair of it and feel that it is utterly exhausted, and there is no more for me. O God, how my heart is anguished and tormented! Oh, strengthen and sustain me by Your Holy Spirit in this my great anguish and anxiety! O Lord, deliver me, make haste to help me. Bring my soul out of the anguish of hell. Forgive me all my sins, out of which the devil makes great, high mountains, so as to hide Your grace from my sight. But cause me to see Your mercy, and withhold not Your divine help from me. Comfort me again, my God, that my heart may be quieted and rejoice. You are greater than our conscience, and although it accuses us, You can surely quiet it by Your Gospel. And although my sins are mighty and red as blood, yet Your grace is far mightier and can make them white as snow. Therefore be at peace again, my soul; why are you cast down, and so disquieted within me? Wait for God, who is the help of my countenance, and my God. He will pull you from anguish, for the Lord does good to you and delivers you from all your sins by the innocent death of Jesus Christ, who was made the spotless sacrifice for our iniquities. Therefore be not cast down, my soul, nor disquieted within me. Wait for God, for I will yet thank Him, for He is the help of my countenance, and my God. Write this all, my God, in my heart, and by it strengthen my faith, that I may fight valiantly in every tribulation and through Your powerful grace do well in all things and gain the victory. Amen.

391. Prayer after falling deep into sin

O my beloved heavenly Father, O just Judge of the world, how grossly I, a wretched man, have sinned! Alas, what I have done! How shamefully and despicably I have forgotten Your Holy Commandments, Your mercies toward me, Your severe threats against sin, indeed, Your manifest and fearsome judgment, to have committed this great sin which day and night afflicts me in my heart! O God, how anxious my soul is, how my heart quakes, how ashamed I am in my conscience before You! What a deep pit of sin and condemnation I see before my eyes! Wherefore, Lord my God, O dear Father, as a trusting child I flee from my anguish to the refuge of Your boundless mercy, imploring Your grace through Jesus Christ. Oh, how numerous are my sins! How great are my trespasses; I will never be able to count them! Yet have patience with me, a poor sinner, dear God, and blot out my iniquities according to Your surpassing mercy for the sake of Christ, who made atonement for me. I have done wickedly and sinned greatly. Yet I am heartily sorry and daily afflicted on account of it, even as You see in me, O Searcher of hearts. And I know, dear God, that You will not deny the broken and contrite heart. You are near to those who are of a contrite heart and save the humble of spirit. Oh, then, deny me not either! Heal, Lord, my broken heart, my wounded conscience. Help me, a poor sinner, for the sake of Christ, and bind up my wounds. You are my Father, my maker, and You know what kind of creature I am and perceive that I am dust. Your Son, Jesus Christ, also came into the world to save poor sinners, and His blood cleanses us from all sins. Oh, then, God, let the precious merit of Jesus Christ not be in vain on me, a poor, afflicted, penitent sinner! You swore that You did not desire the death of the sinner, but that he should turn and live. Therefore, dear God, I heartily desire to repent by Your grace. Only enter not into judgment with me, and let me not despair in my tribulations. O God, how often I have been cast down because of my sins and do not know where to go or what to do! O Lord, cast me not away from Your presence, and take not Your Holy Spirit from me! Pull my foot out of the net. Forgive me my iniquities, and by the power of the Holy Spirit, let me know joy and gladness, that the bones which You have broken may rejoice. Now I find that even as Satan brought me quickly to sin and made me fall into it, he also fills my conscience with horror and heaviness to bring me to despair. O my God, forsake me not in this difficult struggle, but let Your strength be powerful in my weakness. Arm me by the power of Your might, that I may be able to withstand the crafty assaults of the devil. Enlighten my eyes, that henceforth I may walk circumspectly, and guard myself against similar sins. O God, if You make my heart rejoice with Your grace, how heartily I will thank You, how diligently I will, by Your grace, amend my life, how eagerly I will teach other transgressors Your ways, that sinners may be turned unto You. Let it be a warning to me, dear God, and I will guard myself against such affliction of the conscience all my life long. I trust, O God, in Your mercy, and my heart rejoices in Your salvation and that You reject no one who comes to You. Therefore I come now and beseech You once more to be gracious to me, a poor sinner, and for the sake of Your beloved Son, my only Savior and Advocate, Jesus Christ, who promised that whatever we would ask You in His name, You would give it to us, and thereupon commanded us to pray: Our Father who art in heaven, hallowed be Thy name, Thy kingdom come, Thy will be done on earth as it is in heaven. Give us this day our daily bread; and forgive us our trespasses as we forgive those who trespass against us; and lead us not into temptation, but deliver us from evil. For Thine is the kingdom and the power and the glory forever and ever. Amen.

392. Prayer in tribulation of doubt

Merciful God, I have often and willfully transgressed Your Holy Commandments and despised, angered, and sorely offended You, my God and Lord, and thereby so oppressed and wounded my conscience that I am duly cast down and afraid because of it. Although Your Holy Word irrefutably promises me the forgiveness of my sins out of pure grace, yet my faith is weak, and the devil is strong and eagerly seeks to steal all comfort and pluck it from my heart. Therefore I call to You, O Holy Father, let me never despair of Your divine grace, that I may neither fall into nor consent to the supreme sin of unbelief and of doubt. Strengthen me that in the midst of death I may hope in You, my Life, and not despair of Your mercy and succor, nor like ungodly Cain regard my sins as greater than may be forgiven me. O Christ, the Son of God and living fountain of all grace, overflowing with wells of mercy, I cry to You with my whole heart, that You would increase my faith in Your holy suffering and death, for that is certainly and undeniably true that a single drop of Your most holy blood shed for me is far mightier and more efficacious than all my greatest and most powerful sins. Look on me with the eyes of Your mercy, as You looked on Peter after he denied You and cursed himself, that I may not doubt and sin against the Holy Spirit, like the traitor, Judas. O God the Holy Spirit, bountiful Treasure, assist me in my last distress, when the wicked foe accuses me and my conscience casts blame on me, when the thought of hell terrifies me, and I am surrounded by mortal dangers and dreadful tribulations. When the whole world forsakes me, and everything is set against me, then comfort me, that I may not lose hope. Confirm my heart with Your testimony and Your sealing, that I may believe firmly in the forgiveness of sins, which will come to me and to all who trust in the promise of God. Let me be mindful of the covenant of my Holy Baptism, and in so doing take hold of the promise, "He who believes and is baptized will be saved," and take comfort in it. Amen.

393. Refuge in Christ when one is distressed by sin

Dear Lord Jesus Christ, I feel my sins; they gnaw at me, pursue me, and terrify me. Where shall I go? I look to You, Lord Jesus Christ, and believe in You, albeit weakly; yet I cling to You, and am certain that You have said, "He who believes in Me will have eternal life." Although my conscience is burdened and sins terrify me and make my heart tremble, yet it is written, "Be of good cheer, My son, your sins are forgiven you, and you shall have eternal life, and I will raise you up at the Last Day." Amen.

394. Another prayer

I believe in Christ, who was born of the Virgin Mary, suffered, and died; and I trust in His promise that whoever comes to Him He will not cast out. I trust these words and on their basis come to You, dear Lord Christ, for this is Your will and heart, and Your mouth also. Your words are sufficient and certain to me. I am sure that You are not lying to me; the words will not fail me. You will not cast out those who come to You. Even though I am an evildoer and not holy and upright enough to be able to stand, You are true and desire that I should be raised up at the Last Day. Although I cannot stand, yet You, dear Lord Jesus Christ, will certainly stand and not cast me out. Amen.

395. In great melancholy and sorrow of the mind

Almighty, righteous, and merciful Father in heaven, You know that we poor men are so corrupted by original sin that we not only deserve Your just judgments with our many sins and sometimes painfully feel them in our hearts, but also are confronted by frequent sorrow and many adversities and often fall into severe melancholy of the spirit, and in our human frailty cannot get rid of it except by Your holy, divine comfort, which is able to set troubled hearts at ease, give them joy, and preserve them to eternal life. Therefore, O dear Father, look graciously upon me, for I am now troubled in heart and spend nearly all the day in sorrow. Lord, my soul is aggrieved unto death, and because of the great sadness and reluctance in my heart, I have become almost useless for all the work of my calling, and in the process I even forget to eat my bread. O faithful God, let me not remain in this melancholy and sadness of my soul, in which the vile devil delights and takes pleasure, but turn away from me the sorrow by which I am afflicted! O Lord, cast me not away from Your presence; hide not Your face from me. How long shall I be troubled in my soul and sorrowful in my heart? Keep me from temptation and impatience, that I, being delivered from my distress, may extol You with all joy. You will not quench the smoldering wick, and the bruised reed You will not break; I also know that whoever sincerely holds to You will never be cast out. And although in my misery not one hour or day can rid me of my sorrow, yet I will hold patiently to You, O dear Father, and draw comfort from the remembrance of Your help, which You have often showed me with such fatherly care, mercifully delivering me in many an hour of sadness. Therefore I wait every moment for Your divine restoration by the Holy Spirit and for the change of my disposition. Let this be my joy, that I may cling to God in my sorrow. I know that I have God for my consolation, and if I have You only, Lord, I ask for nothing in heaven and earth. As the hart pants after fresh waters, so my soul, God, pants for You; my soul thirsts for God, for the living God. I will rejoice and be glad in Your loving kindness because You see my affliction and know the troubles of my soul. I know that the light must always spring up again for the righteous, and that for the sake of Your beloved Son, Jesus Christ, I will certainly be and abide an heir of eternal life, even if I am still subjected to so much misery in this world, even if I am still afflicted with many more hours of sadness. Therefore I also trust that after this great heaviness in my sorrowful heart, You will refresh me by Your Holy Spirit, that I may heartily rejoice in Your grace. And for this will I sing to the Lord all my life long and praise my God while I am here. For You have shown me great and sore troubles and shall quicken me again. Your praise shall continually be in my mouth; my lips and my soul, which You have redeemed, shall rejoice and sing praise to You. Why are you cast down, my soul, and so disquieted within me? Wait for God, for I shall yet thank Him, for He is the help of my countenance, and my God. I trust, O God, in Your mercy, and my heart rejoices in Your salvation. I will sing unto the Lord, because He deals so bountifully with me. Amen.

396. Prayer when one is in tribulation because of eternal predestination

Everlasting, good, and gracious God, who in Your Son, Jesus Christ, elected us to eternal life before the foundation of the world and created us, and after the fall of our first parents sent the same Your dear Son as a Savior to all men without any distinction, to reveal to the world through Your Holy Word this Your gracious will and caused it to be confirmed by the Holy Sacraments as by certain and infallible foundations and signs: I, a poor, afflicted person, lament to You that the crafty and evil foe torments and afflicts me with the cunning and dangerous temptation and thought that I do not belong to the number of the elect but to the number of the damned and can never be saved, in order to tear me from Your revealed Word and cause me to blaspheme and revile You like other wicked men, not to recognize as my own Savior Your Son, whom You sent as Savior to the whole world, but to tread underfoot His holy, precious blood which He shed for me, and to cast myself into eternal despair. O gracious and merciful God, leave me not among these dangerous, fiery darts of the wicked foe, lest I die and perish in them eternally! But send me the Comforter, the Holy Spirit, that by His help I may cling to Your revealed Word in simple faith, recognize as my Savior Your Son, whom You sent to me as to the whole world, never forget Him, but always remember, take comfort in, and rejoice in all that He accomplished for the salvation of the whole world, including my own. Grant that I may hold up my Baptism, Absolution, and Supper of Your beloved Son as a trusty shield against all the poisonous darts of wretched Satan, and in great fearlessness boast and exult in them and wholly depend on them, that I, being delivered from the fiery darts of the devil, may with a glad heart and mouth praise and glorify You in the company of the elect, who suffer similar tribulations, in Christ Jesus, my Savior, by the power of the Holy Spirit, both here and hereafter. Amen, and again Amen in Christ Jesus, most blessed with the Father and the Holy Spirit. Amen.

397. *Prayer in satanic tribulations*

O Lord, how many are my spiritual foes that rise up against me! They say to my soul, "There is no help for you." Deliver me, and I will not fear many hundred thousand wicked spirits that seek to afflict my soul. In You, O Lord, I put my trust; let me not be put to shame, but deliver me, that the devil, my persecutor, may be turned back lest he snatch my soul like a lion, tearing it in pieces, while there is none to deliver. Lord Christ, lift Yourself up against the rage of my enemy, who has dug a pit for me, that I should perish therein. Look upon my misery, and lift me up out of the gates of death, that I may recount Your glories, that the ancient serpent in hell may be turned back. Lord, do not hide Yourself from me, for the evil one in his arrogance boasts over me; he lies in wait secretly as a lion in his den, devising wicked plots to catch me; he stretches his bow and shoots his fiery arrows secretly at my troubled heart. Lighten my eyes, that I may not be blinded by the spirit of hell nor die in my sins. Grant not that my enemy may claim to have prevailed against me, nor that my adversary may claim that I am defeated. He desires my soul as a lion his prey; he opposes me and afflicts me; therefore, O God, hide me under the shadow of Your wings. Let not the ancient, guileful serpent deceive me. Preserve my soul and deliver me. When wicked spirits come upon me to devour me, let them stumble and fall. Hide me in Your tents and conceal me from their fury. I call to You with great longing: Lord, do not be silent, lest I be like those who go down into hell. Know my soul in this great distress; fight with those who fight against me; say to my soul, "I am your help." Let Satan become as chaff before the wind. Let the angel of the Lord cast him away, because he thought to do me mischief. Let him be confounded and put to shame, for You are my God and strength. Though the whole world were filled with wicked spirits eager to devour me, yet because You are with me, they shall not overpower me. Lord, make peace for my soul, because the prince of this world is against me. God, be merciful unto me, for the evil one wishes to make me drown and daily fights against me. But gain glory for Yourself, and scatter my physical and spiritual enemies. Rebuke the devil, that he may flee from me. Good and faithful Shepherd, Christ, who redeemed me from the power of the devil with Your precious blood, deliver my soul from the jaws of the infernal wolf. Let Your loving kindness be for my comfort; bring me out from the anguish of my heart; let Your good Spirit give me joy, that I may glorify Your wondrous works and give thanks to You for Your help. Amen.

398. Short prayer against Satan's murderous darts

I give thanks to You, my dear Lord Jesus Christ, that You, as the stronger One, have attacked and overcome the strong, armored man, taken away his weapons and armor in which he trusted, spoiled his kingdom, cast out the prince of the world, and made a show of all my enemies, triumphing over them through Yourself. And I beseech You, O most beloved Lord Jesus Christ, mightily to curb and restrain the condemned, shameful filth, that he may not cast me down in presumption and doubt, nor wound me with his murderous arrows of predestination apart from God's revealed Word and make me fearful and desperate because of the weakness of my faith or some other reason. O dearest Savior, grant me power and strength hereby to overcome and beat back these and all his fiery arrows, and finally to obtain the crown of life and the imperishable wreath of glory in life everlasting. Amen.

399. Thanksgiving after overcoming tribulation

O eternal God, who permit no man to be tempted above his means, but make the temptation to have an end, that he may be able to bear it, and who have promised, "For a brief moment I have forsaken you; but with great mercies I will gather you. In the moment of My wrath I hid My face from you; but with everlasting kindness I will have mercy on you": I lift up my hands to You; I will bless Your name at all times; Your praise shall continually be in my mouth, for You know in what sorrow and distress, affliction of the soul and spiritual temptation I lay so long, how my spirit was afflicted within me, and my heart was almost consumed in my body because of turmoil and the assaults of the devil.

But when I cried to You with my mouth, You attended to my supplication, for You are a God who does not despise the sighs of the needy nor reject the desires of afflicted hearts. You regard the prayer of the destitute and do not despise their prayer; You loose those who are appointed to death. Praised therefore be Your divine power and omnipotence, blessed be Your infinite kindness and mercy, glorified be Your eternal truth! If You, O Lord, had not helped, my soul would soon have been in hell, but Your grace sustained me, O Lord; I had great anxiety in my need, but Your comforts gladdened my soul. You have made me see great and sore anguish and have comforted me again and restored me to life and taken me out of the depths. Therefore I give thanks to You for Your great faithfulness, my God! My lips and my soul, which You have redeemed, rejoice and sing praises to You. You are good, and Your mercy endures forever, and Your truth throughout all generations. O faithful God, protect me henceforth from such temptation by Your great goodness! And when wretched Satan (who wanders through dry places, seeking to make his dwelling in the house from which he was driven out before) would attack me again, assist me, O mighty God, Lord of Sabaoth; give me the weapon of the Spirit against the devil's cunning arrows, that I may overcome him valiantly; grant me Your good Spirit to destroy the works of the evil one, and suppress in me all that is contrary to Your divine glory and my salvation. To that end grant me grace, that I may heartily oppose all vice, and devote myself wholly and only to You, pass the whole time of my life in true fear of God and devout prayer and Christian virtues, wage a good warfare, and hold the true faith and a good conscience, that there might be laid up for me, and I obtain, the crown of righteousness which Jesus Christ shall give to all who love His appearing. Grant this to me, Holy Trinity, God the Father, Son, and Holy Spirit, most blessed forever. Amen.

400. Prayer in the peril of being led astray

Merciful God, who have warned us that we should beware of false prophets who come to us in sheep's clothing but inwardly are ravenous wolves: in the last days, in which we now live, dreadful times will come, when Satan will transform himself into an angel of light and will transform false teachers and deceiving workers into apostles of Christ, having the appearance of godliness but denying its power. In addition, people will fall away from the pure doctrine, and the man of lawlessness and the son of perdition, who is an abomination, shall be revealed. Therefore help us, eternal God, to have a love for the truth, to shun and flee from all lying spirits and errors and all false appearance, that we may not be moved from the true faith, nor let any man disqualify us, but continue steadfast in Your Word until the end, and in no way let any man mislead us by false powers, signs, and wonders, nor with any seduction to unrighteousness, so that we allow ourselves not to consider or weigh the various winds of doctrine, through the mischief of men and trickery, by which they deal with us and think to gain something from us by scheming. Defend Your elect, dear God, in this poor world, that they may not be misled into any error. Shorten the evil days in these dangerous times. Put an end to the Antichrist, that malignant son of perdition, with the breath of Your mouth. Bring about his death by the appearing of Your beloved Son. Preserve us also from all sectarian spirits and schisms, from the terrible wolves which do not spare the flock, from men who speak perverse doctrines and win disciples to themselves, from those who have a troubled mind and cause division or offense, from the tares which the enemy sows, from thieves and murderers of the soul. Let us listen only to Your voice and follow it heartily in true faith and simple obedience so that we have Your Word for our only norm and measure, judge all doctrine according to it, flee from what is foreign to it, and take no delight in unrighteousness. So shall we have boldness and not be put to shame on that day when Jesus Christ, our Savior, shall appear. Amen.

401. Prayer of those innocently persecuted (imprisoned)

Lord, I lift up my voice. Lord, I seek You. Lord, I call upon You! Cross and trouble have come upon me. I wait for You, O my God! Graciously incline Your ear unto me and hear my crying. Oh, how the ungodly persecute me and tread me underfoot! They have set their snare without a cause and prepared a pit for my soul, to destroy it. They give me evil for good and gnash their teeth over me, to bring me into distress of heart. They are glad at my harm and do not cease to hate and afflict me unjustly. How great is my cross, how my distress is increased, how my afflictions are multiplied! My God, my soul is disquieted within me, my heart is afflicted, my thoughts are afflicted, all that is in me is afflicted, and I do not know where to abide in this world, or where I may get help and comfort. Therefore I must turn and look up to You on high, my God, my fortress, my help, my deliverer in whom I trust! I knock at the door of Your grace, seeking Your fatherly help and mighty deliverance, for which I have long sighed and shed many tears. For You are a faithful God and will not burden or oppress me or any man with more affliction than we can bear. God Almighty, whose strong hand is not shortened, can deliver us from all distress. Abba, dear Father! I depend on Your fatherly heart, with which You are certainly devoted to me still; oh, look upon my great cross and misery! Hear how with great yearning I cry to You, and turn not Your mercy away from me. Let Your goodness and faithfulness always keep me, and deliver me from the horrible pit and from the hand of those who hate me and who seek to do me harm. Lord, fight against those who fight against me, and arise for my help, as You showed Your succor in former times and proved Yourself a mighty deliverer, the examples of which I, a poor and much afflicted man, view for my comfort, seeing that my cross also is not too great for You to help me. My Lord and my God! Let my enemies and persecutors not prevail against me nor put me to silence. Let them not rejoice over me or say, "Aha, aha, that is our desire! We have swallowed him up," but awake Yourself and arise for my justice, defend my cause, give me Christian patience, and say to my soul, "I am your help." Lord, do not charge their sins against them, but turn them and forgive them the evil which they have done me. Let them see with fear and trembling that You are with me, giving me justice, and make me rejoice and live happily forever because You have seen my misery and know the distress in my soul. Amen, Amen.

402. Prayer of exiles and the persecuted

O faithful God, only refuge of the forsaken, hear us according to Your wonderful righteousness! O God of our salvation, the confidence of all on the earth and afar off on the sea, You are our refuge throughout all generations; before the mountains came to be, and before the earth and the world were created, You are God from everlasting to everlasting. Have mercy upon our misery! Behold, the world will not tolerate us in any place. We are persecuted and have no continuing city anywhere and find fulfilled in ourselves the words of our Redeemer, Christ Jesus, which He spoke before: "Behold, I send you as sheep in the midst of the wolves; you shall be hated by everyone for My name's sake; but he who endures till the end shall be saved." O dear Father, let us endure in patience and steadfastness! And because You said, "When they persecute you in one city, flee to another," we have hope and comfort that with these words You have appointed for us the dwelling place, and will be with us in our flight as You were with the infant Jesus and with the patriarch Jacob when the army of God met him. O Lord Jesus Christ, let Your example be our comfort, when You say, "If the world hates you, know that it hated Me before you; the disciple is not above his master.

I have chosen you from the world, wherefore the world hates you!" Grant patience, therefore, since it cannot be otherwise, and because all those who wish to live godly lives in You, O Christ, must suffer persecution, grant grace that we may take up our cross patiently and remember the examples of the holy apostles, as St. Paul says of them, "I think that God has set us apostles forth as the littlest of all, like men sentenced to death; for we have been made a spectacle to the world and to angels and to men. To this present hour we suffer hunger and thirst, and are naked, and are buffeted, and have no certain dwelling place; being reviled, we bless, being persecuted, we suffer it, being slandered, we entreat; we are always as the curse of the world and expiatory sacrifice of all people." O Lord Christ, let us find our comfort in Your words, "Blessed are those who are persecuted for righteousness' sake, for theirs is the kingdom of heaven. Blessed are you when men revile and persecute you and say all kinds of evil against you falsely for My sake. Rejoice and be of good cheer, for great is your reward in heaven; for so they persecuted the prophets who were before you." O Lord God, let us also find comfort in the words of the holy apostle Paul, who says, "We are persecuted, but we are not forsaken"; and again, "through much affliction we enter into the kingdom of God!" Let us also remember the tender words of St. Peter, where he says, "Rejoice that you suffer with Christ, that in the time of the appearing of His glory you may have joy and gladness. Blessed are you if you are reviled for the name of Christ, because the Spirit of the glory of God rests upon you; on their part He is slandered, but on your part He is glorified." O God, what a great comfort it is to all who boldly confess You, when You say, "He who touches you touches the apple of My eye." Therefore we, Your pilgrims, who are driven into exile, all trust that You will keep us as the apple of Your eye and hide us under the shadow of Your wings, and in all places be with us, accompany us, and provide for us; for the earth is the Lord's and the fullness thereof, the world and those who dwell therein. Lord, Your grace reaches to the heavens, and Your truth to the clouds. Count up our flying, catch our tears in Your bottle; without doubt You number them. Blessed is he whose help is the God of Jacob, whose trust is in the Lord his God, who made heaven and earth, the sea, and all that is therein, who keeps faith forever, who gives justice to those who suffer violence, who feeds the hungry. The Lord releases the captives; the Lord makes the blind to see; the Lord raises up those who are bowed down; the Lord loves the righteous; the Lord watches over strangers and orphans, sustains widows, and perverts the way of the ungodly; the Lord is king forever, even your God, O Zion, throughout all generations. Alleluia!

403. Prayer of a Christian who must live among unbelievers

O God, You see how I must, alas, live among people with whom Your saving Word is not taught in its purity nor the Holy Sacraments administered without alteration. Since my flesh and blood are dull and may easily be seduced by either fear of bitter hatred or desire for worthless glory, I devoutly beseech You to strengthen me with Your Holy Spirit, that I may account the acknowledged evangelical truth higher than the riches of the whole world and let neither promise nor threat make me fall away. Grant me Christian circumspection also, that I may act and walk in such a way that no one may find in me cause to imprison or punish me, unless it be for my necessary and bold confession and answer for the hope that is in me. And help me in due time to return to my fellow believers and to the true worship of God, which rests alone on Your comforting Word revealed to us; for the sake of my dearest Lord Jesus Christ. Amen, Amen.

404. Prayer against the fear of strange apparitions

O Lord Jesus, faithful mediator between God and man, who did not desire that Your disciples should be afraid when You came in to them through the shut doors, but dispelled all their fear, saying, "Why are you so troubled, and why do such thoughts enter your hearts?"; who for my comfort were visited by Satan in the lonesome wilderness and by Your mighty Word dismissed him and were attended by angels: I heartily beseech You to let no sudden terror trouble me such that I can find no relief. You know that the human heart is a desperate thing and that many, surprised by fear, have fallen in distress and death; wherefore cover me with Your feathers, that I may not be afraid for the terror by night nor for the arrow that flies by day. If Satan tries to trouble and frighten me with his host, lift up Your divine voice upon me and say, "Depart, Satan"; and command Your heavenly spirits to protect and free me, poor man that I am, from this fear. Let me know that not one hair of my head may fall apart from Your will, and call to me in my heart: "Fear not, for I am with you; turn not aside, for I am your God. I will strengthen you, I will help you, yea, I will uphold you by the right hand of My righteousness." My sins may well terrify me, but Your blood cleanses me from all my sins. Therefore quicken me always in my anguish, and say to my soul, "I am your help." Arise, and let all Your enemies be scattered, and those who hate You flee before You, that I may dwell in quiet and safety and no one may do me harm. Amen.

405. Prayer against slanderers

My God and Father in heaven, I cry to You with an afflicted and sorrowful heart, lamenting the contempt which I now receive from hostile men through shameful suspicion and slanderous gossip. For You try hearts and reins and know best how unjustly they treat me; You are God Almighty and are best able to defend my cause for good and save me from the deceitful lips. Of course it is not without Your righteous permission that my enemies thus revile me and pour out the poison of their tongues against me, and although I may be innocent before men in this case, I have nevertheless earned this with countless sins which I have committed against You. But I rely with childlike confidence in Your great mercy, trusting that You will look mercifully upon my misery, hear my weeping and groaning, and for Christ's sake not remember my sins, but make my innocence manifest to the world at the proper time, that they may see it who seek my hurt and be ashamed. Jesus, my Savior! I remember now what slanders and contemptuous speech You had to hear from Your enemies even though You had done no sin, and in this I take comfort amid all the undeserved slanders which I am made to suffer. You were reviled for my sin, and spit upon, and were the most despised and esteemed not at all, a reproach of men and despised of the people. I will therefore bear this contempt gladly for Your sake and to Your glory. Yet, my bridegroom, have mercy upon me according to Your abundant mercy, and deliver my soul from the wicked men and mischievous people, who imagine evil in their hearts and whet their tongues like snakes. Yet do not blot them out according to their wicked works, nor reckon this sin against them for their damnation, but be merciful unto them because of Your merit and help them to turn and live. To You I commend and entrust my cause; You will finally bring forth my righteousness as the light and my justice as the noonday. Lord God, Holy Spirit, Comforter of all who grieve! You have assured me in Your Word that all things must work together for good to those who love God. Therefore I most humbly beseech You to let me see this in my present distress. Grant that all repugnant lies and mockery may turn my adversities to my advantage here in time, that I may walk more circumspectly, living always a chaste and upright life; and attain to my good hereafter in eternity, when, according to the promise of my Jesus, all who are innocently reviled by men may await a gracious reward. Meanwhile, however, grant me Christian patience, that I may bear this cross without murmuring and not repay evil for evil, nor curse for curse, but bless those who curse me, love those who hate me, do good to those who offend me. O Lord, triune God, do this all graciously, so will I honor and praise Your name in time and eternity. Amen.

406. *Prayer when children are sick*

Dear Father, Your whip stings, and yet You are still my Father; I know this in truth. And You, dear Lord and Savior, Jesus Christ, who were an example for all our suffering, comfort and compel Your way into our hearts, that I may fulfill the sacrifice of this afflicted spirit, and with a willing spirit deliver our Isaac up to You. Amen.

407. *A poor, imprisoned sinner's prayer for forgiveness of sins*

Lord, righteous and merciful God, Your judgments are righteousness and truth. In righteous judgment You have withdrawn Your grace, and because I have willfully and scornfully transgressed Your Holy Word and prayer according to the shameful will of the devil, wicked company, and my own corrupted flesh, and thus brought myself to sink and fall into gross and detestable sin, and so into peril of body and soul, so that I now suffer what I am worthy of and as I deserve—not only bound up in chains and bonds and awaiting the judgment unto death, indeed, a violent death, but also sorely troubled in my soul for the sins which I have committed, and afflicted with great anguish by the gnawing worm in my conscience, and by hell, the devil, Your anger, and my death. Yet in this distress and sorrow I recall how You said in Your Word that Your mercy and love are far greater and more powerful than the great burden of my sins, and how You have sworn an oath promising grace and mercy, yea, and forgiveness, to all poor, sorry sinners without distinction; that Your dear Son, my Redeemer, came into the world to save all poor sinners—and thus myself, the chief of sinners—by His suffering and death; that in Holy Baptism You adopted me as a child and heir of eternal life, sanctified me in the true faith by Your good Spirit, and promised, implanted, and gave me the fruit of Jesus Christ's suffering and death, indeed, Christ Himself together with all His merits. Wherefore with cheerful confidence I cry to You: God, be merciful unto me, a poor sinner, and do not deal with me according to my sins. Look upon Your boundless grace and mercy, and do not take account of me according to Your strict righteousness. Remember the wounds and death of Your beloved Son, Jesus Christ, my most precious Redeemer; Your gracious promise; and the covenant of my Baptism; and let me, Your dearly-bought creature and Your sanctified child, not fall eternally under the power of the devil and hell. Comfort me again with Your help, and strengthen my soul in true faith and genuine repentance against all tribulation, anguish, and hardship. Oh, have mercy upon me, Lord, triune God, and let my miserable state move Your heart, that hereafter I may forever live with You and praise You! Amen.

408. *Prayer of a criminal who has been condemned to death*

O Lord, righteous God, I, a poor sinner, lament and confess to You this day my grief which I have well deserved, and in the evil hour which is now approaching, how Satan has kept me from Your Word, torn from my sight every token of Your righteous wrath, and brought to the point of not believing that You, the enemy of sin, would punish me. I have despised the counsel of my instructors and cast their admonitions to the wind, not sought You in prayer to keep me from sin (I have loved bad company, lying, idleness, unchastity, and other profane living, and have done my own pleasure). For this reason You have withdrawn Your hand from me and left me to go my way, so that now, because You could no longer watch my wanton life, I have been assigned a speedy and contemptible death as a warning to others and must die in all disgrace. O Lord my God! I go this day with the prodigal son in my conscience and confess to You in true remorse all my evildoing! Pardon me for the sake of Jesus Christ. Righteous are You, O Lord, and all Your judgments are above reproach; wherefore I now receive the due desert of my actions. Merciful God, You have granted ample time for repentance, although You were not unaware that, in my inborn wickedness, I would not change my thinking and doing, but I have become worse rather than better. Hence my soul is now in great anxiety. The cords of death have surrounded me, and the anguish of hell has gotten hold of me. I have come into sorrow and distress. O dear God, let me not despair, but be merciful unto me, a great sinner. For a brief moment of wrath You have forsaken me and hidden Your face from me, but with great mercies You will have pity on me and gather me again to eternal life; for the sake of Jesus Christ. Amen.

409. *Three prayers of someone condemned to death, in his final hour*
To God the Father

O Lord my God, my dearest Father, the final hour of my departure from this valley of tears is now near at hand, when no one but You can help me. O Lord, who have never spurned anyone, cast me not off at this hour either, wretched though I am, but let the door of grace stand open to my poor soul and let it enter the heavenly paradise; mercifully grant me that, together with my final hour, all my other temporal and eternal distress, sin, and disgrace and vice which I have committed may be ended; yea, grant that this my final hour on earth may be the first with You in eternal blessedness; through Jesus Christ. Amen.

To God the Son

O Lord Jesus Christ, I beseech You, on account of the great bitterness which Your noble and innocent soul had when it departed from Your holy body, to have mercy, dear Lord and God, upon my poor soul this hour and in the moment when it departs from my sinful body! Lord, hear me! Christ, hear me! O Lamb of God, who took away the sin of the world, hear me! Amen.

To God the Holy Spirit

O Holy Spirit, who are sent forth by the almighty and everlasting God as a comforter and counselor for all the afflicted: oh, grant true assistance to my poor, weak heart and wavering, weary conscience in this hour, in my final, terrifying moments, that I may persevere steadfast in my Redeemer and Savior Christ until my end. And even if my mouth should never speak, oh, then speak for me and my poor soul, "Father, into Your hands I commend my spirit. You have redeemed me, O Lord God!" Amen.

410. Prayer of a poor, abandoned orphan

O beloved Lord Jesus Christ, who said, "I will not leave you as orphans": fulfill in me, a poor orphan, Your most gracious promise and true word! O Lord, take me up; You are merciful and gracious, patient and abundant in mercy and truth, for You show grace, forgiving iniquity, transgression, and sin. You see it, for You behold misery and sorrow. It is in Your hands; the poor commit it unto You. You are the helper of the fatherless. Lord, You hear the desire of the humble; their heart is sure that Your ear hearkens to it, that You will give justice to the poor and fatherless. Oh, forgive me my ignorance, sin, and folly, with which I have ever offended You and earned this and other punishments, sorrows, and griefs! Remember, O Lord, Your tender mercies and Your loving kindnesses, for they have been ever of old. You are truly the Father of the fatherless, and You are my Father. Protect me with Your mercy, preserve me with Your almighty power, and let Your Word be a strong wall round about me. O dearest Lord Jesus, give me food and clothing, grant me good friends, faithful guardians and benefactors, who assist me with counsel and deed. Govern me also and especially by Your Holy Spirit, that I may walk blameless and hold myself according to Your Word, upright and God-fearing, like the abandoned Joseph and godly Daniel, and like God-fearing Esther, for godliness is profitable for all things and has the promise of this life and of the one to come. Grant that I may have You before my eyes all my life long and guard myself against consenting to any sin and breaking Your Commandments. Help me to refrain from fleshly lusts which war against the soul, to shun all adultery, and to preserve my body and my soul in holiness and honor, and that I may gladly live among my elders, not despise what they say, but conform myself to their instructions. Let me be quiet and slow to speak and ashamed to repeat all that I hear or to reveal private words spoken in confidence. If You give me a friend and benefactor, help me to keep him like my own eye, to be faithful and discreet, and also to be modest, chaste, and honorable, and to speak only what is necessary; for many a poor child and miserable orphan, being furthered by modesty, chastity, faithfulness, and honesty, has attained to property and honor. Keep me also from wicked company and frivolous men, lest I learn their ways and get a snare to my soul, and lest I learn pride from them, and they burden me with evils, and I be made to perish for their folly. Lead me in Your righteousness; teach me to do Your will. Let Your good Spirit lead me in an even way, and preserve me unto life everlasting for the sake of Your mercy. Amen.

411. *Prayer in poverty*

Merciful, gracious God, dear Father, You have laid on me the cross of physical poverty, and I am sure it is for my good. Grant me patience to bear this cross rightly and to submit obediently to Your gracious will. Prosperity and adversity, life and death, poverty and riches all come from You. You make poor and make rich; You bring low and lift up. Yet, O faithful God, show me the means and way to sustain myself and my family honestly, and bless my occupation and labor. You have said that all the poor are to be fed by the work of their hands; let this blessing fall on me also; let me, too, eat from Your generous fatherly hand and be fed, together with my family, like the birds under the heavens, which neither sow nor reap, and yet You, their heavenly Father, feed them. You clothe and adorn the lily of the field each year with new robes; indeed, year by year You give a new robe to each according to his kind; You will certainly not forget me and my family, for You, heavenly Father, know that we need all these things.

Accordingly teach me to seek first Your kingdom and Your righteousness; so shall You, according to Your promise, add the temporal necessities as well. And because I have no comfort on earth–for no man is a friend to the poor—be my comfort Yourself, who are called the refuge and strength of the poor and lowly. Let my poverty not move me to evil and to forbidden means, but to stronger faith and trust in You and to all Christian virtues, to humility, meekness, patience, prayer, hope, and steadfastness. Grant that I may burden no one with my poverty, yet raise up for me willing benefactors whom You love, and grant that all manner of grace may dwell in them. O dear God, a poor man is like a stranger on the earth: no one will know him, and no one will take up his cause! Yet I find comfort in Your saying: "You shall love orphans and widows, and give them food and clothing, and fear the Lord your God." I am also comforted that it is written: "The Lord raises up the poor from the dust, and exalts the needy from the ash heap, to set them among princes, and to make them to inherit the seat of glory." Dear Father, You appointed that rich and poor should dwell together, yet, Lord, You made them all. Therefore, dear Father, take up my cause, and let me not suffer injustice or violence, lest I be oppressed. You say, "Better is a poor man that walks in his godliness than a rich man that walks in erring ways." Let me be mindful of what old Tobias says to his son: "Though we be poor, but we have much wealth if we fear God, depart from sin, and do what is good"; and what David says: "A little that a righteous man has is better than the riches of many wicked," and: "I have been young, and now am old; yet have I not seen the righteous forsaken, nor his seed begging bread." I take comfort in these promises and am content; for it is better to have a little with righteousness than much money with lawlessness; for we brought nothing into the world, and we shall take nothing out of it. Therefore I ask You for a heart that cares more for the eternal riches than for temporal wealth—You will certainly give me my portion. Let me follow the beautiful teaching of that wise domestic preacher, Sirach, when he says, "Trust God and remain in your calling; for it is quite easy for the Lord to make a man poor or rich." Let me look to the example of my Redeemer, Jesus Christ, when He says, "The birds under the heavens have their nests, and the foxes their holes, but the Son of Man has nowhere to lay His head." Lord, You are my wealth and my portion. You preserve my inheritance, and You put gladness in my heart, even though they abound in wine and grain. I am poor and needy, but the Lord provides for me. I trust also that I will see the goodness of the Lord in the land of the living. Be strong and let your heart take courage, all you who wait for the Lord.

412. Consolation in poverty and destitution

Even though I suffer poverty here, it does no harm, for in spite of that I know, dear God, that You will not let me suffer distress, since You have given me Christ, and in Him all blessedness. You will also add to this whatever my body needs for the brief period of its life. Amen.

413. Prayer that one may overcome in all distress

O Father and God of all comfort, grant us by Your Holy Word and Spirit a firm, cheerful, and grateful faith, that we may blessedly overcome this and every distress and finally taste and see that it is true when Christ, Your beloved Son, Himself says, "Be of good cheer, I have overcome the world." Amen.

414. Prayer of one who is suppressed because of the truth

I suffer many things and do poorly while my enemies prosper. They live; I die without ceasing. They are strong and mighty; I am continually oppressed. They are in honor, I in disdain. They are in peace, I in strife. They increase in number and abound in admirers who praise those who join them; I am alone, forsaken, and no one joins me, no one shows me any favor. I am lonely, forsaken and despised by all men. Therefore, dear Lord God, take me up and do not forsake me. Make haste to help me, for all others help me to destruction. I seek no salvation or blessedness, neither in myself nor in any other, but only in You. Amen.

415. Prayer of Christians participating in a trial

O Lord, You are a righteous God and love righteousness; but in the world justice is often perverted and the ungodly favored over the righteous. Unrighteousness, alas, has gained the advantage! There are many who hate the good and love the evil, who pervert justice into wormwood and gall and cast righteousness to the ground. How many are found who pervert the right of the needy for money, sell the needy for a pair of shoes, and make widows their prey and orphans their spoils! What the prince desires, the judge speaks aloud, that he may do him a service in turn, as Your Holy Word laments. The great men give counsel according to their mischievous desire, and turn it to their will. Justice yields to wicked gain, as many poor men now complain. Lord, You know their transgressions, how they afflict the just and take a bribe, and turn aside the poor in the gate from their right; for it is an evil time. Therefore, O righteous Judge, give ear in heaven, and give justice to the needy. But if I cannot obtain justice in this world, but the defiance of the mighty continues, grant me patience, that I may not be filled with rage, but rather suffer injustice and yield the advantage than try to fight with evil and undertake wickedness. Govern me also with You Holy Spirit, that I may not be quarrelsome in court, but hold the judge in honor, and be ashamed to confess justice for my soul; and, if I have done some wrong in this case, not to speak against the truth. But if I and my just cause are defeated, O Lord, then strengthen me, that I may possess my soul in patience, and in childlike obedience commit my cause and vengeance to You! Amen.

416. Prayer in loss of temporal possessions

Dear God, You see and know all my needs, burdens, losses, and damages in possessions, property, and honor. You see and behold my misery and sorrow. Receive these all into Your care and keeping alone. Save me, and I shall be saved! Grant patience and comfort in this great anguish and distress. Behold, here I am; do with me as You please. Once I have suffered the affliction of Job, let me, Your faithful servant, also find the comfort and joy of long-suffering Job, both here in time and hereafter in eternity. Amen.

417. Prayer in danger by fire

O Lord, our Lord, gracious and merciful, long-suffering and abounding in mercy and truth! We acknowledge with sincere regret and repentance that we have earned the fire blazing before our eyes, which may easily gain the upper hand and judge us like Admah and Zeboiim. But because You do not delight in our destruction, but rather desire that the sinner turn and live, we heartily beseech You mercifully to turn away even this deserved punishment for our sins, together with all worrisome, ravaging, and raging fury, and in the midst of Your wrath to remember grace and mercy and to command the terrible fire and say, "Enough!" for the sake of Your dear Son, Jesus Christ, who freed us from Your just anger and rebuke, bore all our sins, and fully atoned and paid for us. O Lord, hear us! O Lord, be merciful! O Lord, take note and do it, and do not delay, for Your own sake, Lord our God. Lord God, Father in heaven, have mercy upon us! Lord God, the Son, the Savior of the world, have mercy upon us! Lord God, the Holy Spirit, have mercy upon us! Be merciful unto us; spare us, dear Lord God. Be merciful unto us, help us, dear Lord God. In this great distress of fire, protect us, dear Lord God. Christ, the Lamb of God, who take away the sin of the world, have mercy upon us! O Jesus Christ, Son of God, have mercy upon us. So shall we, Your people and the sheep of Your pasture, with due obedience and earnest amendment of our sinful life, give thanks to You forever and declare Your praise throughout all generations. Amen.

418. *Prayer in great distress by water*

Lord God, You are our refuge from generation to generation, our help in the great troubles which have come upon us. The name of the Lord is a strong tower, and the righteous runs into it and has safety. Therefore to You shall all flesh come. Oh, behold from Your holy height, and look upon our affliction and trouble! For Your waves and billows pass over us. We pass through deep waters, and the rivers overwhelm us, and besides You, O Lord, there is no one who can save us. Therefore help us, O God of our salvation, for the glory of Your name! Our sins are not less than those of the first world, which You also drowned in great waters and visited with Your wrath. Nevertheless, remember Your mercies and Your loving kindnesses, for they have been ever of old! Fulfill in us the promise spoken through David, that when the floods of great waters come, they shall not come near those whose transgression is forgiven, whose sin is covered, and against whom the Lord counts no iniquity. The floods lift up, O Lord, the floods lift up their voice; the floods lift up their roaring. Yet, O Lord on high, be mightier than the noise of many waters! Break their course with Your dam, and set bars and doors for it. Say to the waters, "Thus far shall you come, but no further: and here shall your proud waves be stayed." Shut up the fountains of the deep and the windows of heaven, that the rivers may be turned away from the earth, and the ground may be dried up. Forget not what You promised to Your servant Israel, that when they passed through water, You would be with them, and the rivers would not overwhelm them. Therefore remember all those who are truly in such danger and for whom the waters have come up to their soul. Draw them forth from the waters as the daughter of Pharaoh did Moses, or preserve them like Noah and his family in the midst of such peril by water. But if according to Your just judgment these torrents of Your wrath should drown anyone, be merciful to Your people, do not retain their sins, but take up their spirits and let it not be to the harm of their souls. Indeed, if I, too, should meet with any adversity, Your will be done. Into Your hands I commend my body and soul and all things which pertain to me. For naked I came from my mother's womb, and naked shall I return. Wherefore, O God, be not far from me; my God, make haste for my help and assistance; for the sake of Christ. Amen.

419. Prayer when someone has been crippled

Dearest Lord Jesus, who in Your Word did not forget the lame, the crippled, and the maimed, and in the days of Your flesh came to their aid with all faithfulness: oh, have mercy upon me, a miserable and maimed man! Inspire Christian sympathy in honest people, that they may give me the help that I need. Above all, give me a healthy soul, keep me in a Christian life, and let me remember well that I might easily commit some grave sin with these limbs of mine if they were still whole and strong. But now that they have been maimed, You seek the good of my soul, and it is better for me to enter life as one crippled than as a whole man to be cast into the fires of hell. I also know that this my indisposed body will leave all its faults and frailties in the grave, and I will be raised up whole and vigorous in full strength to eternal life. Preserve this comfort in my heart, O faithful God, for the sake of the bitter sufferings and death of Jesus Christ, through the grace of Your Holy Spirit. And grant that when the wicked mock me, I may not become impatient nor despair in my misery, nor begrudge any man his health, but pray diligently, put my trust in You, and believe surely that You will nourish, clothe, feed, carry, and lift me up to life everlasting. Amen.

420. Prayer in great trouble and danger

O almighty and saving God and Father, You see and know that we live in great trouble and danger, knowing neither help nor counsel, and there is no strength or power in us to escape this great distress; wherefore our eyes look to You, our only comfort, refuge, and helper, who said, "Call on Me in the day of trouble, and I will deliver you, and you shall glorify Me." Our hearts remind You of Your word of promise, and in childlike humility and confidence seek Your face. O Lord, hide not Your face of mercy far from us; put not Your children away in anger! Forsake us not, and take not Your hand away from us, O God of our salvation, working all help in the midst of the earth. Let us therefore see Your help, and be merciful unto us also! Our souls trust in You, O Lord, and in the shadow of Your wings will we take refuge till these calamities pass by. Turn to us again, and satisfy us early with Your grace, and we will offer to You a sacrifice of rejoicing and give thanks to Your name because of its comforts. Make us glad according to the days in which You have afflicted us, and the years in which we have suffered evil. Give us assistance in trouble, and we will glory and rejoice in Your help all our life. Amen.

421. Another

I know for certain that the Lord our God heartily loves me, even though I am in this great distress and do not see how I might be helped. But I commend it to my dear God, who in this sorrow looks upon me as a mother upon her little child which she has carried under her heart. He will do it well, so I will ask Him and certainly believe that He will hear me and deliver me. For when the righteous cry, the Lord hears them and delivers them out of their troubles. Amen.

422. Another

O dear Father, You are my dear Father, for You gave up Your only dear Son for me; therefore You will not be angry with me or cast me away. You see my distress and weakness, so help me and deliver me! Amen.

423. Yet another

O Father of all mercies and God of all comfort, strengthen and confirm me by Your Spirit until the appearing and advent of that work for which You bid us wait in all afflictions, for You do not willingly afflict or grieve the children of men, nor do You permit any evil to happen which You cannot work to some good. Amen.

424. Prayer in great adversity

O God, rebuke me not in Your anger; let it be in grace, and not eternal. Be a father and not a judge. O God, rage here, cut here, strike here, and spare hereafter! Amen.

425. Another

Dear Father, do not hesitate to strike and beat me; I well deserve it, alas! But let it be a father's rod, for You correct all Your children whom You love, and those whom You do not discipline for their sins are not children but illegitimate. Therefore beat, whip, and thrash us at once, O righteous Judge and yet merciful Father, only without turning Your divine, fatherly heart away from us, that we may praise and glorify You both here and forever hereafter. Amen.

426. Prayer in time of famine

Gracious and merciful God, dear Father, we acknowledge and confess with contrite hearts that we have spent the time of our life very evilly and lived ungodly lives. But we beseech You by the most precious merits of Your beloved Son, Jesus Christ, our Savior, to be gracious to us poor sinners and pardon and blot out our transgressions, and grant us further to bear and endure this cross and chastisement with patience. Under the second cross, however, which You lay upon us, our flesh and blood has nothing more unbearable than the bitter distress of hunger and the most difficult and disdainful lack of daily physical sustenance. We have certainly earned such punishment by great excess, shameful luxury, and abuse of Your manifold gifts, for which we have, alas, given You little thanks. But as a gracious Father, You have promised in Your Word that You would give us Your generous hand and physical support. Your dear Son says in Matthew 6, "Do not be anxious and say, 'What shall we eat, what shall we drink?' Your Father knows that you need all these things." Omniscient God, You know best what is beneficial and good for us, Your poor children. Therefore we beseech You from the bottom of our hearts, inasmuch as severe hunger and the lack of various things oppress and afflict us on every side, be mindful of Your fatherly promise and with fatherly care apportion to us our daily bread. We trust surely in Your faithful promise, for what You promise, You surely keep. Those who in faith constantly seek and love You shall not want any good thing. You open Your bountiful hand and satisfy every living thing with good pleasure. The afflicted shall eat and be satisfied, and those who seek after the Lord shall praise Him. The Lord will give you bread in affliction and water in anguish. The Lord will send you rain for your seed which you sow in the field, and bread from the increase of the field, and full abundance thereof. You once sustained Elijah the prophet by an angel and a raven; You fed the prophet Elisha by a widow; You satisfied Daniel in the lions' den. By Your Son You readily satisfied five thousand men with a little and very poor supply, five loaves of bread and a few fish, and there were twelve baskets of fragments remaining. Therefore we have bold trust and confident hope in this time of famine, that You will have the knowledge and power to nourish us during this difficult time until we take leave of this miserable life by a natural death and finally, with You and all the elect, at Your table in Your kingdom, eat and drink the eternal and imperishable food and drink of everlasting joy and blessedness solemnly promised by You and dearly won through Christ. For You neither can nor will forsake Your children while we wander in this valley of misery; You have a father's and mother's heart. Since You feed us spiritually, neither will You deny us physical food and drink in time of need. You give to the cattle his food, and in wonderful manner feed the young ravens; much less will You forget us, whom You have washed and cleansed with the precious blood of Your dear Son. Do all these things, O everlasting Father, for the sake of Your beloved Son, Jesus Christ, our only Redeemer and Savior. Amen.

427. Prayer in contagious epidemics and plagues

Almighty, everlasting God and Father of our Lord Jesus Christ, Lord of heaven and earth: we poor, miserable sinners must confess that we have most dreadfully angered You, O God, with our sinful life and being, wherefore You justly pour out Your wrath upon us and attack us with various plagues, epidemics, and diseases. What then should we do? Should we despair? Far be it! We know that we deserve not only the epidemic which now rages as a punishment for our manifold sins, but even greater and more heinous plagues than this. Where then shall we flee, and where shall we turn, that we may be safe from this and other plagues and pandemics? To You alone, Lord Jesus Christ. We have no other comfort either in heaven or on earth except You, who have redeemed us. Surely You will not cast off Your creation; therefore we humbly call, sigh, and cry out to You with our whole heart, saying, "God be merciful unto us and blot out all our sins according to Your exceeding great grace, goodness, and mercy!" Cease from Your displeasure, wrath, and indignation toward us. Show us again Your grace, and spare us from the epidemic and abominable sickness which now rages. Listen to our pleas, O Lord; listen to our pleas and spare us. Kindly protect and shelter us, that this epidemic may not hurt or come near us, nor seize or take us away. But if it be Your divine will that we should end our life in this epidemic and depart this world, Your gracious will be done, for it is always the best. Hereupon we commend ourselves, our body and soul, wife and child, and all our household, into Your divine grace and fatherly hand, humbly beseeching from our heart that, if we should meet our final hour unexpectedly, and even now approach the time when our body and soul must be separate, You would mercifully preserve our faculty of reason, that we may be able with a clear mind to commend our soul to You. And grant us further a blessed end, that we, passing through temporal death, which is the end of all sorrow and misery and opens to us the door of eternal life, may the more speedily enter into that same eternal life and come to our Redeemer and Savior, and with all the elect of God in heaven eternally rejoice. Amen.

428. Prayer of one who because of his duties cannot flee in time of pestilence

Begone, devil, with your inspiring of terror! Since it annoys you, I will defy you and go the sooner to my sick neighbor and help him and will not regard you, but trust in the Lord my God. For I know in truth that this work pleases God and all angels, and if I do it, I walk in His will and in true worship and obedience. Yea, since it displeases you so much and you so violently attack it, it must indeed be especially pleasing to God! How gladly and cheerfully I would do it even if it pleased only one angel, who looked on and rejoiced at it! But since it pleases my Lord Jesus Christ and the whole heavenly host and is the will and command of God, my Father, how then can your terror tempt me to hinder such joy in heaven and my Lord's delight, and give you and your devils in hell cause to deride and mock me, all for your pleasure? No, you shall not end it. Christ has shed His blood for me and gave Himself into death for my sake. Why should I not also subject myself to a little danger for His sake? What need to regard a powerless pestilence? Where you can terrify, my Christ can strengthen; where you can kill, my Christ can give life; where you have poison on your lips, Christ has far more medicine. Should my dear Christ and His prayer and His benefits and all His consolations not avail more in my spirit than you, despicable devil, with your false terror in my feeble flesh? God forbid it! Begone, devil, get behind me. Here is Christ, and I His servant in this work. He will take care of it. Amen.

429. When a man is not bound to stay, but leaves and takes refuge in times of pestilence and mortality

Lord God, I am weak and afraid, and so I am fleeing from this evil and doing as much as I can to keep away from it. All the same, I am in Your hands in this and every evil which may befall me. Your will be done, for my fleeing will not do it. For the devil does not rest or sleep, and he is a murderer from the beginning and seeks to cause death and disaster on every side.

430. Prayer in distress of war

O Lord of Sabaoth, we confess before Your holy presence that we have kindled and caused this terrible fire of war and abhorrent destruction of the land by our manifold, grave, and serious sins. For while we were forgetful of Your manifold benefits and abused the blessing of peace for all manner of sin and unrighteousness, always ready to do evil, so according to Your righteousness You were ready with this calamity and caused it to come upon us. Yet help us and deliver us, Lord, according to Your great goodness. Let the plunder, slaughter, pillaging, and burning be brought to an end. Be moved to pity by the misery of so many thousands of souls, which You purchased for Your own possession by the blood of Your Son, and restore peace and tranquility to our borders. O Prince of Peace, Jesus Christ, true man and true God, who called us to peace, seal fast the bars of our gates. And because You have the hearts of all men in Your hands and lead them like streams of water, let all the mighty men on the earth have thoughts of peace, that the land may not, by war and bloodshed, be filled with wickedness and unrighteousness, but that henceforth we may lead a quiet and peaceable life and extol and glorify You for Your grace and wonderful goodness as long as we are here and our life continues. Amen.

431. Another

Heavenly Father, we have earned Your punishment, yet rebuke us Yourself according to Your grace and not in Your anger. It is better for us to leave discipline in Your hands than to put it in the hands of men or of the enemy, as David also requested (2 Sam. 2), for great is Your mercy. We have sinned against You and have not kept Your Commandments, but You know, almighty God and Father, that we have not sinned against the devil, pope, and Turk, neither do they have the right or power to punish us, but You can and should employ them as Your furious rod against us, who have sinned against You and earned all this misfortune. Yea, dear God, heavenly Father, we have committed no sin against them for which they might have the right to rebuke us, but rather they desired that we should join them in sinning against You in the most detestable manner. For they do not care if we disobey You, slander You, commit all manner of idolatry, as they do, and deal in false doctrines, beliefs, and lies, adultery, immorality, murder, theft, robbery, witchcraft, and do all evil against You; about such things they do not care. Rather our sin against them is that we preach, believe, and confess You, God the Father, the only true God, and Your beloved Son, our Lord Jesus Christ, and the Holy Spirit, the one, eternal God—yea, this is the sin which we commit against them. Yet if we would deny You, the devil, the world, pope, and Turk would be content. As Your dear Son says, "If you were of the world, the world would love you."

Here look down, O merciful Father to us and zealous Judge to our foes! For they are more Your enemies than our enemies, and if they persecute and strike us, they persecute and strike You Yourself, for the Word which we preach, believe, and confess is Yours, not ours—all the work of Your Holy Spirit in us. The devil will not stand for this but wishes to be our god in Your place and to establish lies in us instead of Your Word. The Turk wishes to set up his Mohammad in place of Your dear Son, Jesus Christ, blaspheming and saying He is no true God, and his Mohammad is higher and better than He. If therefore it is a sin for us to hold, confess, and claim You, the Father, and Your Son, and the Holy Spirit to be the only true God, then You Yourself are the sinner, working this in us and calling for and desiring this of us. Therefore they hate, strike, and rebuke themselves when they wish to hate, strike, and rebuke us for such things. Arise, then, dear Lord God, and sanctify Your name, which they disgrace; strengthen Your kingdom, which they destroy in us, and do not let Yourself be trampled underfoot because of our sin by those who do not rebuke our sin in us, but who wish to root out Your Holy Word, name, and work in us so that You are not a God and have no people to preach, believe, and confess You. Amen.

432. *Prayer for peace in times of war*
Lord of Sabaoth, let it stir Your pity that all other ungodly kings and lands dwell in peace, and Your own people alone are made to have discord, although it would be more fitting if the others had discord and Your people peace. Because You are righteous and true in Your words, regard Yourself and remember Your own righteousness and truth, if You will not regard us; and give us peace again. Amen.

433. *Prayer during general punishments and national afflictions*
O gracious God, merciful Lord, You have turned away from us in Your furious anger over our sins and threatened and exceedingly afflicted us all our life with anguish and sorrow, hell and eternal death. Now therefore, dear Father, relent, turn to us again, listen to our plea, and be gracious to Your servants! Satisfy us early with Your grace, that we may rejoice and be glad all our days. Amen.

434. *Another*
O gracious and merciful God, by Your anger and wrath You have caused us, like the grass that flowers early, to wither and fade, our life to be cut short, and Your disfavor to be poured out on us. We beseech You, dear, merciful God, to turn back to us and satisfy us early with Your grace—not with the plain, simple,

everyday grace by which the household, temporal government, preaching office, or bodily health are sustained. Rather, give us a rich, abundant, eternal grace, by which we are sustained eternally and delivered from the devil, death, sin, and hell. Amen.

435. *Prayer for patience and victory*

Lord God, grant us a peaceable heart and good courage in the struggle and strife with the devil, that we may not only endure and finally prevail, but also in the midst of the struggle and strife have peace, praise and thank You, and not murmur against Your divine will, so that peace may triumph in our heart, that we may not through impatience undertake anything against You, our God, nor against men, but both inwardly and outwardly, toward God and man, remain quiet and peaceable until the final and eternal peace. Amen.

436. *The Litany, or humble intercession for the general needs of the whole Church*

Who the author was and who composed it no one can say for sure. It was already common in the days of the ancient doctor, Basil, ca. AD 370, in Neo-Caesarea and several places in Greece, and in the days of Ambrose, bishop of Milan, in AD 380, in Italy and other regions. But since it was later corrupted in the papacy with the invocation of dead saints, blessed Luther was moved to correct, along with the other errors introduced by the papacy, the Litany also, and to conform it to the content of Divine Scripture, even as it is sung and used today in all the evangelical churches. This vernacular Litany was expounded with devout supplications by the famous Lutheran theologian and worthy professor at the University of Jena, Dr. Johann Gerhard, as follows:

Kyrie: eleison. O Lord, our Lord. *Lord of lords, †the true Father of all who are named children in heaven and on earth: have mercy upon us.

Ps. 8:1. *1 Tim. 6:15. †Eph. 3:15.

Christe: eleison. Anointed of the Lord, *our King and †High Priest forever, ‡our only Mediator, Savior, and Redeemer: have mercy upon us.

Ps. 2:2. *v. 6. †Heb. 5:6. ‡1 Tim. 2:5.

Kyrie: eleison. O Holy Spirit, who with the Father and Son are *one Lord and †one God, ‡our Comforter: have mercy upon us.

1 Tim. 2:5. *1 Cor. 12:5. †v. 6. ‡John 15:26.

O Christ: hear us. O Lord Jesus, our *only Advocate with the Father, †who are at the right hand of God, interceding for us: pray for us and hear us.

1 John 2:1. †Rom. 8:34.

Lord God, the Father in heaven: have mercy upon us. You who fashioned us and *so loved us that You gave us Your only-begotten Son: †O Lord, bless and keep us.

*Job 10:8. *John 3:16. †Num. 6:24.*

Lord God, Savior of the world: have mercy upon us. You who loved us and gave Yourself up for us to redeem us: *O Lord, make Your face shine upon us and be gracious to us.

*Gal. 2:20. *Num. 6:25.*

Lord God, the Holy Spirit: have mercy upon us. You who regenerate, renew, and *sanctify us, who †represent us with groanings too deep for words: ‡O Lord, lift up Your countenance upon us and give us Your peace.

*Titus 3:5. *1 Cor. 6:11. †Rom. 8:26. ‡Num. 6:26.*

Be gracious to us: spare us, dear Lord God. O Lord, *deal not with us according to our sins, nor repay us according to our iniquities, †rebuke us not in Your anger, nor discipline us in Your wrath.

Ps. 103:10. †Ps. 6:1.

Be gracious to us: help us, dear Lord God. Help us, O God, our Helper, for the glory of Your name; deliver us and forgive us our sins for Your name's sake.

Ps. 79:9.

From all sin: preserve us, dear Lord God. Keep us from sinning against You. *O Lord, teach us to do Your will. Let Your good Spirit lead us on level ground!

*Gen. 20:6. *Ps. 143:10.*

From all error: preserve us, dear Lord God. Turn our eyes away from looking at worthless doctrines. *Let Your Word be a lamp to our feet and a light to our path.

*Ps. 119:37. *v. 105.*

From all evil: preserve us, dear Lord God. O heavenly Father, as You have delivered us through Christ from the evils of sin, *so deliver us from all evils of punishment, †and help and bring us into Your heavenly kingdom.

2 Cor. 1:10. †2 Tim. 4:18.

From the craft and assaults of the devil: preserve us, dear Lord God. Arm us in the strength of Your might, *that we may be able to stand against the schemes of the devil.

*Eph. 6:10. *v. 11.*

From sudden and evil death: preserve us, dear Lord God. O Lord, *do not sweep us away with sinners, nor our life with bloodthirsty men. †Teach us to number our days, and help us not to meet our last hour unprepared and unawares.

*Ps. 26:9. †Ps. 90:12.

From pestilence and famine: preserve us, dear Lord God. Let us dwell in Your shelter and abide in Your shadow, *that we may be delivered from the deadly pestilence; †do not break our supply of bread, and ‡lay no famine upon us.

*Ps. 91:1. *v. 3. †Ezek. 14:13. ‡Ezek. 36:29.*

From war and bloodshed: preserve us, dear Lord God. Scatter the peoples who delight in war; *make wars cease to the end of the earth; †strengthen the bars of our gates and make peace in our borders.

*Ps. 68:30. *Ps. 46:9. †Ps. 147:13–14.*

From sedition and rebellion: preserve us, dear Lord God. O *Lord of peace, govern all subjects that they may †not instigate sedition in the land, but live together peaceably and ‡in unity.

*2 Thess. 3:16. †Ecclus. 7:7. ‡Ps. 133:1.

From hail and tempest: preserve us, dear Lord God. Turn back the destroying hail for rain, and the terrible tempests; *hide us in the time of thunder †under the shadow of Your wings.

*Ps. 105:32. *Jer. 30:23. †Ps. 17:8.*

From everlasting death: preserve us, dear Lord God. Ransom us from hell and redeem us from everlasting death. *Guard us by Your power through faith unto salvation.

*Hosea 13:14. *1 Peter 1:5.*

By Your holy nativity: save us, dear Lord God. Sanctify our sinful conception and unclean birth, O Lord Christ, by Your conception and birth which are pure in every respect.

Ps. 51:5.

By Your mortal agony and bloody sweat: save us, dear Lord God. You have *trodden alone the winepress of God's anger at our sins, and in so doing sweated blood; †because of which deliver us from the wrath to come.

Is. 63:3; Rev. 19:15. †1 Thess. 1:10.

By Your cross and death: save us, dear Lord God. You Yourself bore our sins in Your body on the tree. Let us never despair because of our sins. *You through Your death have destroyed the power of death. Oh, assist us in distress and death!

*1 Peter 2:24. *2 Tim. 1:10 [Heb. 2:14].*

By Your holy resurrection and ascension: save us, dear Lord God. Help us *daily to die to sin and to walk in a new life, †that we may seek the things that are above and not those that are on earth.

Rom. 6:2 [, 4]. †Col. 3:1.

In our last distress: save us, dear Lord God. Be our light and guide *when we walk through the valley of the shadow of death; †in the darkness of death let us see Your glory, and ‡take up our souls into Your hands.

Ps. 23:4. †Acts 7:55. ‡Ps. 31:6; Acts 7:59.

At the Last Judgment: save us, dear Lord God. Grant us, O Lord, *to find mercy from the Lord on that final Day of Judgment. Let us hear the joyful saying, †"Come, you blessed, inherit the kingdom which is prepared for you from the beginning of the world."

2 Tim. 1:18. †Matt. 25:34.

We poor sinners beseech You: to hear us, dear Lord God. *Do not in anger shut up Your compassion from us because of our sins. †Let our prayer come before You; incline Your ear to our cry.

Ps. 77:9. †Ps. 88:2.

To rule and govern Your holy Christian Church: hear us, dear Lord God. Save Your people, O Lord, and bless Your heritage! *Feed them and lift them up forever; govern and guide Your holy congregation, †which Your Son obtained with His own blood; ‡visit the stock that Your right hand planted.

*Ps. 28:9. *Ps. 48:14. †Acts 20:28. ‡Ps. 80:15.*

To preserve all bishops, pastors, and ministers of the Church in the wholesome Word and holy living: hear us, dear Lord God. O Lord, help teachers and preachers *to hold the mystery of the faith in a pure conscience, †that they may hold firm to the trustworthy Word, and ‡in everything adorn doctrine.

1 Tim. 3:9. †Titus 1:9. ‡Titus 2:10.

To put an end to all schisms and causes of offense: hear us, dear Lord God. Grant grace, *that we may be eager to maintain the unity of the Spirit in the bond of peace. Restrain all †erring spirits, which cause division and offense.

Eph. 4:3. †Micah 2:11.

To bring back those who err and are deceived: hear us, dear Lord God. O faithful *Shepherd of our souls, †seek the lost and bring back the strayed sheep, ‡and guide their feet into the way of peace.

Ps. 23:1. †Ezek. 34:16. ‡Luke 1:79.

To beat down Satan under our feet: hear us, dear Lord God. O Lord, make us partakers of the *victory which Your dear Son gained over Satan, that in His strength we may ††trample the infernal lion and dragon, and ‡soon crush Satan under our feet!

Matt. 4:10. †Ps. 91:13. ‡Rom. 16:20.

To send faithful laborers into Your harvest: hear us, dear Lord God. Give faithful *shepherds and teachers, †give Your Holy Word richly with a great host of evangelists. ‡Give us teachers according to Your heart, who feed us with doctrine and wisdom.

Eph. 4:11. †Ps. 68:12. ‡Jer. 3:15.

To accompany the Word with Your Spirit and power: hear us, dear Lord God. To the planting and watering of teachers give the increase. Water the *seed of Your Word †with the rain of Your divine blessing. ‡Give strength to Your thunder, that Your Word may **increase and ††have free course.

*1 Cor. 3:6. *Luke 8:11. †Is. 55:10. ‡Ps. 68:34. **Acts 12:24. ††2 Thess. 3:1.*

To help and comfort all the distressed and weakhearted: hear us, dear Lord God. O Father of mercies and God of all comfort, *refresh the weary soul, †give power to the faint, increase the strength of him who has no might, ‡revive the spirit of the lowly, and the heart of the contrite.

*2 Cor. 1:3. *[Jer. 31:25]. †Is. 40:29. ‡Is. 57:15.*

To give to all kings and princes peace and concord: hear us, dear Lord God. We beseech You in behalf of *all authorities, that among them we may live a quiet and peaceable life in all godliness and honesty; †draw the hearts of all high potentates to peace, that ‡there may be peace and truth in our days.

1 Tim. 2:2. †Ps. 33:15. ‡Is. 39:8.

To grant our emperor perpetual victory over his enemies: hear us, dear Lord God. O God, *the king's heart is in Your hand as the rivers of water. Grant our emperor a gracious heart toward Your Word and Church. †Restrain all those who put forth their hands against such as are at peace with You, seeking to break Your covenant. ‡Subdue the enemies of Your Church and turn Your hand against her foes.

Prov. 21:1. †Ps. 55:20. ‡Ps. 81:14.

(To direct and defend our gracious ruler with all his magistrates: hear us, dear Lord God.) (Grant grace that our gracious ruler may be a *foster father and nursing mother of Your Church; †Lord, be the strength of Your anointed, and ‡fulfill all his Christian petitions; **meet him with rich blessings, and through Your mercy let him not be moved.)

*Is. 49:23. †Ps. 28:8. ‡Ps. 20:5. **Ps. 21:3, 8.*

To bless and preserve our council and congregation: hear us, dear Lord God. Grant to all councilors *the Spirit of wisdom and understanding, †that they may decree justice according to Your Word; ‡bless our whole congregation, bless all those who fear You, both the small and the great; **bless us more and more, us and our children.

*Is. 11:2. †Prov. 8:15. ‡Ps. 115:13. **v. 14.*

To visit with succor all who are in distress and danger: hear us, dear Lord God. O Lord, *be a refuge for the poor, a refuge in time of need, †deliver the afflicted from their affliction. ‡Pull them from the wide mouth of distress, which has no foundation, and **save them out of all their troubles.

*Ps. 9:9. †Job 36:15. ‡v. 16. **Ps. 34:6.*

To grant all women with child, and all mothers with infant children, joyful fruition and success: hear us, dear Lord God. O Lord, the God of all living flesh, who *wonderfully form the children of men in their mother's wombs: strengthen all women with child, protect them from mishap, and †when their children come to the point of birth, give them strength to bring them forth.

*Num. 27:16. *Ps. 139:13–14. †Is. 37:3.*

To care for and attend to all children and sick persons: hear us, dear Lord God. Bless, Lord, all children, *that they may increase in wisdom, stature, and favor. Lord, †our healer, ‡heal all the sick according to Your gracious will, and grant grace **that in their disease they may seek You, the Lord.

*Ps. 147:13. *Luke 2:52. †Ex. 15:26. ‡Ps. 41:4. **2 Chron. 16:12.*

To defend all widows and orphans and provide for them: hear us, dear Lord God. You are *the Father of the fatherless and protector of widows; †protect all the fatherless and widows, ‡let the tears of the widow come before Your throne and **give justice to the fatherless.

*Ps. 68:6. †Ps. 146:9. ‡Ecclus. 35:17–19. **Ps. 10:18.

To have mercy on all men: hear us, dear Lord God. You, O Lord, are *the Savior of all men; †Your immortal Spirit is in all things, and Your dear Son ‡gave Himself as a redemption for all men; therefore have mercy on all.

*1 Tim. 4:10. †Wis. 12:1. ‡1 Tim. 2:6.

To forgive our enemies, persecutors, and slanderers, and to convert them: hear us, dear Lord God. Forgive, Lord, our enemies and persecutors, *for they know not what they do; †lay not this sin to their charge: that they ‡hate and persecute us without a cause.

*Luke 23:34. †Acts 7:60. ‡Ps. 119:161.

To give and preserve the fruits of the earth: hear us, dear Lord God. Visit our land, Lord, and water it, and greatly enrich it; let our grain ripen, *satisfy the earth with fruit of Your works; †give us the early and the latter rain in its season.

Ps. 65:9. *Ps. 104:13. †Jer. 5:24.

And graciously to hear us: hear us, dear Lord God. Incline, *Lord, Your ear to our prayer, †hear the desire of the afflicted; ‡O Lord, hear; O Lord, forgive; O Lord, pay attention and act. Delay not, for Your own sake!

*Ps. 17:6. †Ps. 10:17. ‡Dan. 9:19.

O Jesus Christ, Son of God: hear us, dear Lord God. O Lord Jesus, *our Savior, save us for Your name's sake, †O Anointed of the Lord; make us partakers of Your spiritual ‡anointing and of the **oil of gladness of the Holy Spirit. O only-begotten Son of God, ††make us children of Your heavenly Father.

*1 Chr. 16:35. †John 1:41. ‡1 John 2:27. **Ps. 45:7. ††John 1:12.

O Lamb of God, who take away the sin of the world: have mercy upon us. O innocent and spotless Lamb of God, by whose blood we are cleansed from our sins.

*1 Peter 1:19.

O Lamb of God, who take away the sin of the world: have mercy upon us. When You were afflicted for our sake, *You opened not Your mouth; like a lamb that is led to the slaughter, and like a sheep that before its shearers is silent and opens not its mouth.

*Is. 53:7.

O Lamb of God, who take away the sin of the world: grant us continual peace. You became a curse for us, *so that the blessing might come to us. †Upon You lay the chastisement of our sins that brought us peace.

Gal. 3:13–14. †Is. 53:5.

O Christ: hear us. O Lord Jesus, our *only Advocate with the Father, †who are at the right hand of God, interceding for us: pray for us and hear us.

1 John 2:1. †Rom. 8:34.

Kyrie: eleison. O Lord, our Lord. *Lord of lords, †the true Father of all who are named children in heaven and on earth: have mercy upon us.

*Ps. 8:1. *1 Tim. 6:15. †Eph. 3:15.*

Christe: eleison. Anointed of the Lord, *our King and †High Priest forever, ‡our only Mediator and only Savior: have mercy upon us.

Ps. 2:2. †v. 6. ‡Heb. 5:6.

Kyrie: eleison. O Holy Spirit, who with the Father and Son are *one Lord and †one God, ‡our Comforter: have mercy upon us.

*1 Tim. 2:5. *1 Cor. 12:5. †v. 6. ‡John 15:26.*

Kyrie: eleison. O Lord Jesus, our *only Advocate with the Father, †who are at the right hand of God, interceding for us: pray for us and hear us.

1 John 2:1. †Rom. 8:34.

XII. PRAISE & THANKSGIVING

437. Prayer for Christian gratitude

O gracious, good, and exceedingly generous God and Father, how great is Your grace! How good is Your generous, fatherly heart! How great are Your benefits, love, goodness, and mercy toward us! I lament and confess to You that my heart is by nature so dull of understanding, so beastlike and uncouth, that I have never acknowledged with my heart Your good works of creation and preservation, redemption and sanctification. I have never given You my heartfelt thanks nor Your due honor for them. Oh, I acknowledge and confess that I am of far too little account for all Your mercies which You have shown me from my mother's womb! I acknowledge that I am not worthy of Your least benefit, but rather deserving and worthy of Your wrath and disfavor. Yet out of pure grace and loving kindness You have shown me, who am unworthy, this great mercy. I never merited it nor could I ever earn it. For Your grace is ultimately what I am. You had the right on account of my ingratitude to reclaim all Your gifts, bodily and spiritual, for it is Your property! Oh, forgive me this gross ingratitude, and turn from me the threatened chastisement, "Evil shall not depart from the house of the ungrateful," and give me a discerning and grateful heart, that I may see that You are the fountain and source of every good gift, and without You I am nothing but a dead, lifeless shadow in all my doings. Oh, how heartily Your saints all thanked You, saying, "It is a good thing to give thanks to the Lord; and to give praise to Your name, O Most High," and, "With a joyful offering I will sacrifice to You; I will give thanks to Your name, O Lord, for it is good," and, "Bless the Lord, O my soul, and forget not all His benefits."

Grant that I may receive all from Your hand with a grateful heart and accept Your gifts from the treasures of Your grace and mercy, and that I may learn to see that it is only You who preserve Your mercies and gifts to me, and not I myself, that I may entreat, love, honor, and glorify You; and that I may use and dispose of all that You give me for the praise and honor of Your name, and in all things give honor not to myself but to You. For this is the gratitude and righteousness which I owe You, since all is Yours. And this is the truth: that I acknowledge and glorify this, and if You work any good through me, that

I ascribe to You and not to myself, but when I have done all things, that I say that I am an unprofitable servant, an unworthy instrument of Your grace. It is not I, but Your grace which is in me, that does all things through me. Let me also show my thanks to those through whom You do good to me, and love and honor them for Your sake, and by Your grace serve them in turn, and do good to them from the good things given by You, and pray for them! Yea, let me even love my enemies and do good to them for Your sake. Let not ingratitude, which is the most disgraceful vice, take root in me, lest the curse come to me, but let there always dwell in me the noble virtue and mother of many blessings: To join with all holy angels and eternally praise and glorify You with cheerful heart and conscience for all Your benefits; through Christ our Lord. Amen.

438. *Thanksgiving for the love of God*

O merciful, gracious, kind, and amiable God, lover of men, I give thanks to You from my inmost heart for Your great, unspeakable, fatherly, and heartfelt love with which You, O loving God and Father, have always loved me. You have carried me in Your love as in Your heart. You always remember me and never forget me. You care for me, hear my prayer, count my tears, number my groanings, know all my sorrows and my heart, and have given and revealed to me very dear and precious promises of Your grace, help, comfort, forgiveness of sins, and eternal life. You have given me Your beloved Son and by His incarnation assured me of Your grace and favor, by His Holy Gospel given me wisdom and comfort, by His example shown me the way and pattern of holy living, by His suffering and dying redeemed me from eternal death, by His resurrection delivered me from death, by His ascension opened paradise to me and prepared for me a place in heaven. By Your Holy Spirit You have enlightened, sanctified, comforted, strengthened instructed, and refreshed me, and given me assurance through Him that I am a child of God and eternal heir. You have not only shown me great benefits but also given me Your own self with Your beloved Son and Holy Spirit. How can I thank You for this great love? It is greater than heaven and earth; it is eternal and never ceases. It is infinite, higher than the heavens, wider than the earth, deeper than the abyss, farther than east and west. For as high as the heavens are above the earth, so great is His steadfast love toward all who fear Him; as far as the east is from the west, so far does He cause our transgressions to be from us, even as a father has mercy upon his children.

XII. PRAISE & THANKSGIVING

Oh, give me such a heart that I may never forget Your love! Let me walk and rest, sleep and wake, stop and go, live and die in it, and in Your love rise again and live in it forever. For Your love is eternal life and eternal rest. And eternal life is nothing other than eternal love. Oh, let it never be extinguished in my heart, but always increase, that nothing in my soul may surpass, outshine, outlive, or overwhelm Your love; that for Your love I may pour out my tears like Mary Magdalene and joyfully welcome You into the house of my heart like Zacchaeus! Oh, You have never despised anyone, Lover of man; do not despise me, either! True, I am not worthy to love You or to be loved by You; I am a wretched worm, stinking filth, a dead dog! But make me worthy through Your love. Turn my heart from all love of created things to Yourself, that You alone may be my love, my joy, my hope, my strength, my light, my salvation, my life, my physician, my food, my drink, my shepherd, my refuge, my power, treasure, and eternal riches. O happy am I if I abide in Your love with which You love me! O holy am I if I love You continually! O unhappy am I if I fall from Your love, for then I would lose my highest good, and go from light to darkness, from life to eternal death! O pure, divine love, kindle my heart, lighten my mind, sanctify my will, gladden my remembrance, and unite myself with You forever. Amen.

439. Thanksgiving for the eternal election of grace in Christ

O merciful, good, and gracious God, how generously, richly, and abundantly You have apportioned the riches of Your grace in Your beloved Son, Jesus Christ, to us poor, unworthy, lost, and condemned men, and preceded all our merit. You loved us in Your Beloved before the foundation of the world. Your mercy is upon all men. You desire that none should be lost, but that all should turn to repentance and live. You desire that all men should be saved and come to the knowledge of the truth. Therefore You gave and revealed Your beloved Son to the world, and in Your eternal election of grace foreordained Him to save all who believe on Him. Therefore You gave Him up for the sin of the world and laid on Him, as on the innocent Lamb of God and only atoning sacrifice, all our sins, to bear them, take them away, and make atonement for the world. Therefore He is the atonement for the sins of the whole world. He came to seek and save what was lost. And indeed, all men were lost; therefore He came to save all men. For this reason, O faithful God, You caused the Gospel to be proclaimed to all nations, and Your beloved Son called to Himself all those who are weary and burdened, that He might refresh them. You also promised through Your Word to stir up faith in us. For Your Word shall not return to You empty, but shall accomplish that for which You sent it; and You made it the power of God to justify and save those who believe in it. You also promised to sanctify believers in love, and to sustain them in the faith until the end, so that no one should pluck them out of Your hand, that the work which You had begun in us You would also bring to completion until the day of Jesus Christ. You also promised Your believers Your gracious protection against the devil and the world, attaching to Your Word the comforting seals of Your grace, Holy Baptism and the Supper, that we should never doubt Your grace. For this great love, the universal redemption and atonement of our sins, the general calling of all people, and the power of Your divine Word and the Holy Spirit, who awakens faith in us (since faith is Your work); and for preserving us in that faith; for the comforting promise of Your eternal grace, which shall not depart from us, though the mountains and hills fall down; and for the comforting seal of the Holy, Most Worthy Sacraments, I give You my heartfelt thanks. And I pray that You would keep me in this thankful state, defend me from severe tribulations, and let my heart be grounded on Your indescribable, universal love, on the all-encompassing merit of my Redeemer, on the general promises, calling, and comfort of the most worthy Sacraments, of which benefits You have graciously made me a partaker also, in which I acknowledge that I am Your elect child chosen in Christ before the world by pure grace, and appointed to the sonship through my Lord Jesus Christ, in whom You loved me and sealed me with Your Holy Spirit. Grant also that I may be holy and blameless in love to the praise of Your glorious grace; and assure my heart according to Your promise, that I may be certain that neither death nor life nor any created thing may separate me from Your love in Christ Jesus, my Lord. Amen.

440. Thanksgiving for the holy Christian Church

O good, gracious, and merciful Father, Love of man, I thank You that since the beginning of the world, You have gathered and called to Yourself from mankind one holy Christian Church, to which You have revealed Your Holy Word, which has rightly known You, the Father and the Son and the Holy Spirit, believed in You, called on You, honored, praised, and glorified You[. I thank You] that You have made with her a holy covenant of grace, to be her gracious God and forgive her sins for the precious merit of Christ, Your beloved Son, and promised to her Your Holy Spirit to enlighten, instruct, strengthen, comfort, and sanctify her, guide and preserve her in all truth, and renew her, that she may serve You in holy living, wisdom, and righteousness; whom You have also promised graciously to save and hallow; to whom You said through Your beloved Son, "Fear not, little flock, it is the Father's will to give you the kingdom"; to whom You gave many glorious, gracious promises of union with Yourself, "I will betroth you to Myself forever, yea, I will espouse you to Myself in faith, and you shall know the Lord"; likewise, "On this rock I will build My Church, and the gates of hell shall not prevail against her"; whom You have purified for Yourself by the washing of water in the Word, and fashioned for Yourself as a Church which is glorious, having no spot or wrinkle or anything, but being holy and blameless; which You have called and appointed that she should be conformed to the image of Your beloved Son; and which You have justified and shall glorify also. You also call her by a graceful name, the bride of Your beloved Son, Jesus Christ, her eternal Bridegroom. She is His spiritual body, and He her only, eternal head, from whom she receives all gifts and fullness, light, life, comfort, strength, power, and victory. She is His royal priesthood, a people of His possession, the chosen race, His beautiful inheritance, and His pleasant place in which the lot has fallen to Him, in whom He alone is King and High Priest; His fold of which He alone is Shepherd, a beautiful city of God and heavenly Jerusalem, the pillar and foundation of truth resting on the cornerstone, Jesus Christ; the vineyard in which Christ is the living Vine and we His branches, to whom You have pledged Your presence until the end of the world.

For this I heartily thank You that You have called me also to the fellowship of this Your holy Church, that I should be a member and citizen of heavenly Jerusalem in the fellowship of many thousand saints, in which I have in common with all saints all heavenly riches and treasures of grace in Christ, namely, one Redeemer and Savior, one Head, one Shepherd, one Baptism, one Supper, one faith, one God and Father of us all, who is in us all, through us all, and over us all; where all members of believers have true comfort, light, life, refreshment pasture, and protection, and even if the world give away, and the mountains are sunk in the midst of the sea, yet the city of God shall remain glad with her streams, where the holy dwellings of the Most High are. God is in the midst of her and shall help her early; therefore shall she not be moved. Help us, therefore, and strengthen us, dear God, that we may take comfort in Your presence during time of persecution, fearlessly confess Your name, valiantly contend for Your honor, bear witness to Your name and Word, with our blood if needs be, and finally be taken from this Church Militant to the Church Victorious, where one Church will be made of angels and men and shall praise and glorify You in eternity. O blessed are they who dwell in Your house, forever and ever. Amen.

441. *Thanksgiving for the protection of holy angels*

O faithful God, lover, protector, and preserver of mankind, Lord of hosts, before whom stand a thousand times a thousand, and ten times a hundred thousand which minister to You, through whom were made all things, visible and invisible, the thrones and dominions: how dearly You love mankind, that You should set over them from childhood Your holy angels—those steadfast, humble, friendly, God-praising angels; those obedient, chaste, lovely, true, good spirits; those beautiful, gleaming, heavenly flames of fire; those mighty champions, the host of God, the holy watchers who encamp round about those who fear Your name! These angels always behold the face of our Father in heaven as they stand before Your throne, some of whose names You have revealed to us, such as the archangel Gabriel, which means "the power of God"; Michael, which is "who is like God?"; and Raphael, "physician of God." With these holy angels You defend the three estates which You Yourself established on earth. For the archangel Gabriel, who stands before God, as the glorious angel of the Church brought greetings to the Virgin Mary, and announced the birth of John the Baptist to the holy priest Zachariah, and revealed to the holy prophet Daniel the time of the coming of the Messiah; the high prince Michael, as an angel of rulers and defense, protects both lord and land and fights for the people of God; and the angel Raphael, who is appointed as the angel of the home, binds the devil and the household demon in the wilderness. O dear, faithful God, what is man that You are mindful of him? I give You everlasting praise and thanks for this benefit, that You have sent out these ministering spirits to serve those who are heirs of salvation. And I beseech You to give Your angels charge over me, to keep me in all my ways; that they may bear me up by their hands, lest I dash my foot against a stone; that I may tread on the lion and adder, and trample the young lion and dragon underfoot. Drive far from me all wicked spirits, which are liars and murderers from the beginning. Defend me from their wrath and fury, from their lying and slander, from their crafts and assaults, that they may not sow their tares in among the wheat of my heart. Curb the lying spirits in the mouths of all false prophets, the spirit of murder in all tyrants, the devil of pride and covetousness in the domestic estate. Let Your holy angels always accompany me like Jacob, protect me with fiery chariots and horses like the prophet

Elisha, and bring me bread and water, that is, counsel and comfort, like Elijah. Let them be with me in my cross like the three young men in the fiery furnace and the prophet Daniel in the lions' den; let them deliver and bring me out of all my distresses like Lot from the burning of Sodom, Peter from prison, and Paul from shipwreck. Let my house and home, children, and all that I have, be watched over by Your holy angels like the house of Job, that the enemy may not gain entry. Let me live in Your fear and love Your Word and Gospel, into which things even angels long to look. Put true repentance in my heart, that the angels in heaven may rejoice over me. Kindle in me fervent prayer and praise of Your name, that I may fulfill the office of an angel, and with them sing, "Holy, Holy, Holy Lord God of Sabaoth," and that my soul may at last be carried by the angels to Abraham's bosom. Then on the day of resurrection, make me like Your holy angels, that in their fellowship I may dwell forever. Amen.

442. *Thanksgiving for gracious support and protection in various dangers*

Bless the Lord, O my soul, and all that is within me, bless His holy name. Bless the Lord, O my soul, and forget not all His benefits to you, who forgives all your iniquity and heals all your diseases, who redeems your life from the pit, who crowns you with grace and mercy. My God, I thank You that You have preserved my progress in Your way and not suffered my foot to slip. You have shown me Your wonderful goodness against those who have set themselves against Your right hand, O Savior of those who trust in You. You have protected me as the apple of Your eye. You have hidden me under the shadow of Your wings from the ungodly who destroy me, from my enemies, who seek after my soul continually. Therefore will I behold Your face in righteousness. I will be satisfied when I awake after Your likeness. Lord, You lighten my lamps; the Lord my God makes my darkness bright. O my God, You have often heard me in my distress! Your name has often protected me. You have often sent me help from the sanctuary and strengthened me out of Zion.

Therefore I extol Your salvation for me, and in Your name I lift up the banner. You have poured out Your blessing upon me and made me rejoice with the joy of Your countenance. You did not despise the misery of the poor, nor did You hide Your face from me. And when I cried to You, You delivered me. O faithful Shepherd, You have not let me, Your poor sheep, want anything. You have always fed me on green meadows of Your divine Word and led me to the fresh streams of consolation. You have always restored my soul and led me in the right way for Your name's sake. And though I have often walked through the dark valley of the cross and various dangers, yet have I feared no evil: for You have been continually with me. You have prepared a table for me in the presence of my enemies. You have anointed my head with the heavenly oil of gladness of Your Holy Spirit and filled my cup full with Your divine comfort and counsel. You have caused goodness and mercy to follow me all the days of my life, and I have hope that I shall dwell in Your house forever and ever. O Lord, You brought up my soul from hell; You have kept me alive when others go down to hell. You have instructed and taught me the way which I should go; You have guided me with Your eye. How excellent is Your loving kindness, O God! The children of men put their trust under the shadow of Your wings! They feast on the abundance of Your house, and You give them drink from pleasure as of a river. For with You is the fountain of life, and in Your light do we see light. My God, You have made me know many and sore afflictions, and have restored me to life, and from the depths of the earth will bring me up again. Therefore be content, my soul; the Lord does good to you. For You have delivered my soul from death, my eyes from tears, my feet from slipping. I will walk before the Lord in the land of the living. How shall I repay the Lord for all His benefits to me? I will take the wholesome cup and preach the name of the Lord. O my God, how often You have defended me from the prowling lion, the devil, that he might not devour my soul! How often Satan desired to sift me like wheat, but You, my Lord Jesus Christ, my advocate, interceded for me, that my faith might not cease! How often You have delivered me from lying lips and from quarrelsome tongues, which sharpen their tongues as an adder! How often You have delivered me from distress and danger, and hid me in Your shelter in the day of trouble, and concealed me under the cover of Your tent from the boasting of every man! How often You have guarded me from anger, vengefulness, and other fleshly passions so that I did not suffer a horrible fall! Indeed, how often I have fallen, and You have not cast me away, but held me by my hand and set me up again. O God, how can I thank You enough for Your gracious help, deliverance, strength, and comfort? How often You have given Your angels charge over me, to keep me in all my ways, to bear me up in their hands, lest I dash my foot against a stone! Blessed be You, O my Lord and God, who alone do wonderful things, and blessed be Your glorious name forever, and let all the earth be filled with Your glory. Amen, Amen.

443. Thanksgiving after working

Almighty, everlasting, gracious God, I give You sincere praise and thanksgiving for Your most holy help and assistance which You have shown me this day, for without You I would truly have been powerless to do anything. Therefore praise is due to You alone. I beseech You to let this work be pleasing to You and to serve for the good of myself and my neighbor in body and soul; through Jesus Christ, our Lord, who lives and reigns with You and the Holy Spirit, ever true God, world without end. Amen.

444. Thanksgiving after completion of a new dwelling

Gracious and merciful God, I am not worthy that You should come under my roof, but You have promised to come to Your own and bless them. Upon this Your counsel I undertook, according to my ability, to construct this building for the improvement of my domestic life, and by Your almighty help it has now been completed. For this I praise and thank You from my inmost heart. O Keeper of Israel, defend my building from fire, hail, and tempest by Your holy watchers. Let our children's children dwell therein, and help it to be inherited by our successors. O God the Father, Son, and Holy Spirit, Holy Trinity, come with Your holy angels to me and mine, dwell among us, that we and this house may be and abide in Your habitation and temple. Teach us to remember that we are strangers and guests before You. Let us love peace and unity, and always enter in with all the holy angels and blessed to the eternal tents and habitations by the merit of the blood of Jesus Christ, and rejoice forever and ever. Amen.

445. Prayer of thanks upon completion of a prosperous journey

Gracious God, heavenly Father, I thank You from my inmost heart that You have permitted me to complete my journey successfully, and by the protection of Your dear angels brought me home again with joy, and with such fatherly care defended me from all evil so that I was not killed by robbers and murderers, nor torn apart by wild beasts, nor maimed or injured by distress of water and other perils; but that I have been conducted on all my ways in health and good cheer, just as young Tobias was by the angel Raphael. For all this I have Your fatherly care and almighty power to thank. And I beseech You from my heart mercifully to keep me and my family further, to take us into Your powerful protection, and to preserve us mightily in body and soul unto life everlasting; through Jesus Christ. Amen.

446. Prayer of thanks after finishing a dangerous journey at sea (especially for immigrants)

O mighty Ruler of heaven and earth, let our mouths be full of Your glory and praise daily, for we will praise You at all times; Your praise shall continually be in our mouths. We give thanks to the Lord with our whole heart, in the assembly of the upright, and in the congregation. The works of the Lord are great; he who studies them delights in them. Yet how shall we repay the Lord for all His benefits unto us? We are not worthy of all the mercies and of all the truth which You have shown to Your manservants and maidservants. You have made us to see many and sore afflictions on this journey; You have made us to see and experience the peril of the sea, as the waves lifted up, roared and thundered fearsomely, making us in our ship mount up to heaven and go down again to the depths, and reel to and fro and stagger like a drunken man. You cast us into the deep, in the midst of the seas, and the floods surrounded us; all Your waves and billows passed over us, and it seemed as if the throat of the fearsome sea would swallow us. I said in the cutting off of my days, I shall go to the gates of the grave. I shall behold man no more. Often I thought, O that I might live till morning! How I groaned in the ship—like a crane or a swallow I chattered, and I mourned as a dove: For comfort I had great anxiety. But You, O Keeper of men and Lover of life, You came to the aid of my soul and of the souls of my loved ones, that they might not drown. For I cried to the Lord in my distress, and He answered me; I cried from the belly of the sea, and You heard my voice. You calmed the roaring of the sea, the roaring of its waves, and its proud waves were stayed. You delivered my life from destruction; You were with me in trouble; You delivered me and brought me back to life and took me from the earth. You have increased my greatness and comforted me again. Therefore praise is due to You, O God, in the place of peace, and to You shall vows be performed. Just as You have brought me again to land, according to my heart's desire, like Noah; so I now come and set up an altar of thanksgiving, to sacrifice the bullocks of my lips, heartily saying: Now give thanks, all you people, to God, who everywhere works great wonders, who preserves us alive from our mother's womb, and deals with us according to His mercy. Make a joyful noise to God, all you lands, sing to the honor of His name, make His praise glorious. Say to God, how wonderful are Your works! Bless our God, you peoples; make the sound of His glory to be heard afar off, who keeps our souls alive and does not suffer our feet to slip. For You, O God, have tested us and tried us as silver is tried. We came into fire and water, but You brought us out and revived us. Therefore I will go into Your house with burnt offerings, and pay to You my vows, which my lips have uttered and my mouth has spoken when I was in trouble. And this I will not only declare in the congregation, but also tell to our children, and to those who come after, that our successors may learn it, and the children which are yet to be born, when they appear, may announce it also to their children, that they may put their hope in God and not forget the works of God. I further beseech You, O gracious God, with sincerity and devotion, that You would not cease, but also multiply Your benefits to me and my loved ones in time to come. Keep us always in Your fatherly protection, preserve us from misfortune, graciously remove from us whatever is harmful, and give us what is beneficial to our bodies and souls. Let us always be safe under Your shelter. Give success, prosperity, and blessing to each person's undertaking in his office and estate; further the work of our hands; indeed, the work of our hands may You further. Direct all that we undertake, carry out, or forgo to the praise of Your name, the honor and glory of Your Church, and the edification of our neighbor.

O Lord, I (and my dear ones) have now entered a new land! Renew us and renew all things to us: create in us a clean heart, O God, and give us a new and certain Spirit. Save us, O Lord! O Lord, grant us success! The earth is Yours and You dwell everywhere. Yet be and abide our gracious God and Father, our provider and benefactor, in these new places. Grant that we may find all things before us as we would ourselves desire or as will be beneficial to us in body and soul. Grant also, O Prince of Peace, at all times the blessing of long-lasting peace in our land, protect and preserve the authority of every land, and sustain them in successful, peaceable governance, health, and long life. Receive also into Your care our dearly beloved friends whom we have left behind, from whom we parted with so many tears. Comfort, protect, and preserve them from all adversity and misfortune in body and soul. Bless them at home and at work, give them and us the joy of always receiving glad and awaited tidings from one another. Now then, may our God bless us, and grant the request of our mouths and the desire of our hearts. May He take pleasure in all our doings. The Lord bless us; the Lord keep us; the Lord make His face to shine upon us and be gracious unto us; the Lord lift up His countenance upon us and give us His peace! Amen.

447. *Thanksgiving for deliverance from affliction*
I give thanks to You, O Lord my God, with my whole heart, and glorify Your name forever. I thank You forever because You can do it well. Behold, for

comfort I had great anxiety, but You came eagerly to my help, that it might not be destroyed. I cried to You in my anguish, and You heard my voice, and my cry came before Your ears, and You comforted me. You stood by me faithfully, graciously upheld my soul, and finally in Your fatherly care delivered me from great sorrow. O my Lord and my God, how shall I repay all Your benefits which You show me daily? I will glorify Your name as long as I live, I will sing Your praise before all Your people, and Your praise shall ever be in my mouth. Help me, O faithful God, by Your Spirit, that I may pay these my vows and at no time forget what You have done for my soul. Let me not only spread Your praise abroad in this mortality, but also with the elect sound forth my eternal Alleluia to Your glory hereafter in eternity. Amen.

448. *Thanksgiving after obtaining peace*

We thank You, gracious God, that You have given us rest from our enemies round about us and have turned our sorrows into joy and our suffering into good days. We thank You that You have plucked us out as an ember from the fire so that we saved our life as the spoils of war. O merciful Father, how can we repay You enough for this great benefit which You have so mercifully shown us who are not worthy, when, in order to lift our eyes up to heaven, You heard and granted what we asked and desired of You? O Lord, You have clearly dealt with us according to all Your mercy, that our land (city), which before was filled with fear and terror, is now filled with delight and joy. We humbly beseech You that we, being delivered and preserved from the sword, may also find grace henceforth to let our horn increase again, that we may take root below and bear fruit above. Build us up, Lord, that we may dwell safely, and grant grace that the cities which have recently been destroyed, laid waste, and torn asunder, may be inhabited again and rebuilt, and the desolate land plowed once more, that all nations may see that You are the Lord who builds what is torn down and plants what has been devastated.

O God and Lover of peace, grant us henceforth continual peace, and let us occupy our borders and houses with peace and quietness, that the voice of those who announce war to us may no longer terrify us, nor the soldier harm us. Establish us in our land and plant us, that we may not be driven out of it and go astray, nor the children of wickedness disgrace and overpower us. O Lord, let us come into such misery no longer, but if we sin against You again, punish us in mercy! Give us peace in our times, for there is none other who can fight for us but You alone, O our God.

449. Praise of the power, mercy, and righteousness of God

I will extol You, my God and King, and bless Your name forever and ever. Great is the Lord and greatly to be praised, and His greatness is unsearchable. One generation shall commend Your works to another and shall declare Your mighty acts. I will speak of the glorious splendor of Your majesty and of Your wondrous works. They shall speak of the might of Your awesome deeds, and I will declare Your greatness, so that men shall tell of Your glory, so that men shall praise Your abundant goodness and sing aloud of Your righteousness. The Lord is gracious and merciful, slow to anger, and of great mercy. The Lord is good to all and has mercy on all His works. All Your works shall give thanks to You, O Lord, and all Your saints shall bless You! They shall speak of the glory of Your kingdom and tell of Your power, to make known to the sons of men His mighty acts and the glorious majesty of His kingdom. Your kingdom is an everlasting kingdom, and Your dominion endures throughout all generations. The Lord upholds all who are falling and raises up all who are bowed down. The eyes of all wait upon You, and You give them their food in due season; You open Your hand and satisfy every living thing with good pleasure. The Lord is righteous in all His ways and holy in all His works. The Lord is near to all who call on Him, to all who call on Him in earnest. He fulfills the desire of the God-fearing; He also hears their cry and saves them. The Lord preserves all who love Him, but all the wicked He will destroy. My mouth will speak the praise of the Lord, and let all flesh bless His holy name forever and ever. Blessed is he whose help is the God of Jacob, whose hope is in the Lord his God, who made heaven and earth, the sea, and all that is in them; who keeps faith forever; who works justice for those who suffer violence; who gives food to the hungry. The Lord sets the prisoners free. The Lord opens the eyes of the blind. The Lord lifts up those who are bowed down; the Lord loves the righteous. The Lord watches over the sojourners and the fatherless; He upholds the widows and turns back the way of the wicked. The Lord is King forever; Your God, O Zion, to all generations, Alleluia. Praise the Lord! For it is good to sing praises to our God; for it is pleasant, and a song of praise is fitting. He heals the brokenhearted and binds up their wounds. He determines the number of the stars; He gives to all of them their names. Great is our Lord and of great power; His governance is unfathomable. The Lord lifts up the humble; He casts the wicked to the ground. Sing back and forth to the Lord with thanksgiving; with the harp, praise our God, who covers the heavens with clouds and prepares rain for the earth. He makes grass grow on the hills; He gives to the beasts their food and to the young ravens that cry to Him. His delight is not in the strength of the horse, nor His pleasure in the legs of a man. The Lord takes pleasure in those who fear Him, in those who hope in His mercy. Praise the Lord, O Jerusalem! Praise your God, O Zion! For He strengthens the bars of your gates and blesses your children therein. He makes peace in your borders and fills you with the finest of the wheat. He sends out His saying upon the earth; His Word runs swiftly. He gives snow like wool; He scatters hoarfrost like ashes; He casts forth His ice like crumbs. Who can stand before His cold? He speaks, and it is melted. He makes His wind blow and it thaws. He shows His Word to Jacob and His judgments to Israel. The Lord takes pleasure in His people; He saves the humble gloriously. Let the saints be joyful and glory; let their mouths exalt God highly, and let them have sharp swords in their hands, to execute vengeance on the heathen and punishments on the peoples, to bind their kings with chains and their nobles with fetters of iron; to execute on them the judgment written! This honor shall all His saints possess. Alleluia!

450. *Praise of the glory, majesty, and goodness of God*

O eternal, true, living God, who have created me for Your praise, grant that I may praise You worthily. You are the most glorious, the most worthy, the most holy, the most righteous, the kindest, yea, You are the truest. You are righteous in all Your works and holy in all Your ways. You are the wisest; all Your works are known to You from eternity. You are the mightiest; no man can stand against You. Lord of Sabaoth is Your name, great in counsel and mighty in deed. Your eyes look upon all the children of men. You are infinite, seeing, hearing, and governing all things; You uphold and carry all things with Your powerful word. You are to be feared! When You utter judgment, the earth fears and is still. You will be exalted in the earth! You are exalted among the heathen! You cut off the spirit of princes and are to be feared by the kings of the earth. You are to be feared when You are angry! Who can stand before You when once Your anger is roused? The heathen rage and the kingdoms totter; at Your utterance the earth melts. You are also very gracious and merciful, slow to anger, and of great kindness, and You soon relent of punishment. You do not always chide, nor do You keep Your anger forever. As great as Your power is, so great also is Your mercy. Your power is infinite, and Your mercy has no ending. O eternal Light! O eternal Love! O eternal Sweetness! Let me see You, let me feel

You, let me taste You. O eternal Loveliness! O eternal Comfort! O eternal Gladness! Let me rest in You, for I find in You all that I lack in this misery. You are all abundance, and apart from You is nothing but poverty, sorrow, and misery. Life without You is bitter death. Your kindness is better than life. Oh, treasure beyond price, eternal good, sweet life, when shall I be perfectly united with You, that I may perfectly taste You and perfectly see You? Holy God, immortal God, righteous God, omniscient God, eternal King, to You be praise, honor, and glory forever and ever! Amen.

451. A soul glorifying Jesus Christ after being inspired to praise Him

O Jesus Christ, my Love, my Joy, my Light, my Salvation, my Glory, my King, my Shepherd, my Bridegroom, my eternal High Priest, my Life, my Wisdom, my Peace and Rest for my soul, my Righteousness, my Sanctification, my Redemption, my Sacrifice, my Advocate, my Mercy Seat, my only Mediator, my only Helper in need, my only Hope, my highest Treasure, my strong Defense and only Refuge! How shall I praise You worthily? O Radiance of the glory of God, most beautiful and essential image of the Father! Holy, righteous, and blessed am I in You, but without You, unrighteous, unholy, and condemned. Wherever I am, I am unhappy if You are not with me and in me. Come, my Joy, into my heart, and give me joy. Come, Consolation of the heathen, and console me. Come, my Love, and revive me. Come, my Life, and strengthen me. Come, my Light, and illumine me. Come, my Sweetness, that I may taste Your tender affection. Come, beautiful, noble Form, that I may see You. Come, my Delight, that I may hear You. Come, noble Flower, that I may smell You. Come, tender Stirring, that I may feel You. Let Your noble face stir me, Your gracious appearance cheer me, Your noble smell refresh me, Your holy remembrance kindle me, Your noble love satisfy me, Your indwelling delight me. O noble Humility, holy Meekness, unite my heart and mind with You! That will be the finest jewel of my soul! You are more precious to me than all diamonds, more priceless than all rubies, more worth than all pearls. O Rose ever-blooming, O Paradise of every spiritual, heavenly delight, O sweetest Fruit of God's garden! Let me taste You forever; kiss me with the kiss of Your mouth! O eternal Word of the Father, speak in me, that the whole world may be silent in me. O eternal Glory, shine in me. O eternal Truth, teach me. O wholesome Physician, heal me. O heavenly Treasure, come into my heart. O heavenly Noah, stretch forth Your hand and receive to Yourself the poor dove of my soul, for it can find no rest.

How amiable are Your tabernacles, Lord of Sabaoth! My soul longs and faints for the courts of the Lord. My body and soul rejoice in the living God. For the bird has found its home and the swallow its nest where it may lay its young, at Your altars, O Lord of Sabaoth, my King and my God! Blessed are those who dwell in Your house, ever singing Your praises. Blessed are those men who hold You as their strength and follow You with their hearts. O Lord Jesus, how amiable is Your incarnation! How wonderful is Your name! How mighty are Your works! How holy is Your Word! How comforting is Your Passion! How victorious is Your resurrection! How glorious is Your ascension! How great is Your glory! How high and lifted up is the throne of Your kingdom, where all the angels of God worship You! How unsearchable is Your power! Who would not fear You, O King of Glory! Make wide the gates and lift up the doors of the world, that the King of Glory may come in. Who is this King of Glory? It is the Lord, strong and mighty, the Lord, mighty in battle. Make wide the gates, and lift up the doors of the world, that the King of Glory may come in. Who is this King of Glory? *Selah.* Blessed is He who comes in the name of the Lord. The Lord is God, and He has given us light. Give thanks to the Lord, for He is good, and His mercy endures forever.

XIII. SICKNESS & DYING

452. An invalid's morning prayer

O faithful God and Father of our Lord Jesus Christ, I give You praise and thanks that You have graciously kept me, protected me, and strengthened me in my weakness this night. I heartily beseech You in the name of Jesus Christ that this day also, and for the remaining time of my life, You would give me Your mercy, pardon my sins, comfort me by Your grace, strengthen me by Your power, and lead me by Your Holy Spirit, that I may live, yea, and suffer, according to Your will. Into Your holy hands I also commend my sick body and my soul. Let Your holy angel be with me, that the evil foe may find and have no power or authority over me; through Jesus Christ, Your beloved Son, my only Comfort and Savior, in the power of the Holy Spirit. Amen.

453. An invalid's evening prayer

O God the Father, I thank You that You have graciously helped me through this day, and I heartily beseech You to help me, frail and sick as I am, through this night also with Your grace, with Your strength, with Your comfort, and with Your Spirit. Into Your hands I commend my body and soul. Let Your holy angel be with me, that the evil foe may find no power over me; through Jesus Christ, Your dear Son, our Lord. Amen.

454. An invalid's morning benediction

I commend myself this morning, and the whole time of my life, to You, God, the everlasting Father, who created me, to You, God the everlasting Son, who redeemed me, and to You God, the Holy Spirit, who sanctified me in my Baptism. O eternal Godhead, O true Humanity, O Holy Trinity, make me this day and always to be as You would have me in eternal blessedness. Amen.

Gracious, merciful God, dear Father, by Your grace I have once more passed another night and lived to see the light of day again. I thank You that You have been my Keeper and Watchman, Comforter and Helper, tenderly kept my weak body and the troubled soul that dwells in it, and have mightily preserved me from sudden death, severe tribulations, and other evils, and powerfully protected me by Your holy angels against the devil, the prince of darkness. It is by Your grace and mercy that I am still alive. I beseech You with my whole heart that You would turn Your divine face to me, a poor creature, this day also, and so govern and guide me, that I may not think, speak, or do any evil. Feed and conduct me, Your poor sheep, with and to Your Holy Word, which is my comfort in my affliction. Preserve me, O Lord, for I trust in You. You are my only strength, my God and highest good. Oh, direct my heart and mind that I may fear You and love You. Turn away from me all that is not purely Yours. Bury me in Yourself, that in my cross and misery, I may leave my will under You, and entrust it to You only, since my own help, and that of all created things, cannot save me. But You are the true physician of all the ailing, the comfort of all the afflicted, the helper of all the dying. Heal me, comfort me, help me, O dearest Father. Defend me especially this day from sin and all evil, from the crafts of the devil, the offenses of the world, and the wicked lusts of my sinful flesh. Grant patience, hope, and steadfastness. And when my time to live is done, grant me a gentle and blessed end; through Jesus Christ, Your dear Son, my Savior. Amen.

455. An invalid's evening benediction

God be gracious, kind, and merciful to me, and grant me His divine blessing. God make His face to shine upon me in the darkness, that I may not fall asleep in death. The Holy Spirit be with me and remain continually in my heart, whether I sleep or wake, live or die. Amen.

Almighty and merciful God, dearest Father, who said, "Call on Me in the time of trouble, and I will deliver you": I beseech You in this hour of night to have mercy upon me and to forgive me all my sins, by which I may have offended You this day. Take me into Your care this coming night, that I may have my rest in You—in soul if not always in body. And graciously keep me, that I may not be hastened away by a sudden death without acknowledging Your dear Son. If it be Your gracious will, let me sleep free from pain of body or sadness of soul and live to see another day. But if, according to Your unsearchable counsel, this night should be my last in this world, and You decide to summon me then, I humbly beseech You to let me attain to the eternal day of heaven and be the lowliest doorkeeper in Your kingdom. Now then, I go to sleep in Your name. Whether I awake to this mortal life or the eternal, I will heartily love and praise You, my faithful God. Amen. In Jesus' name. Amen.

456. Prayer in time of sickness

Merciful and righteous God, Lord of both health and sickness, I acknowledge before You with an honest heart that the grave misuse of many days of health and well-being which You granted me have certainly and justly deserved this present affliction. O Lord, in true humility I heartily wish to accept this punishment for my sins from Your hand and to bear the Lord's anger, since I have sinned against Him. I beseech You, O gracious and merciful Father, who discipline for our amendment and not for our destruction, that You would by Your grace also sanctify this discipline for me, that this sickness of my body may be an instrument for the health of my soul. Heal my soul, O Lord, which has sinned against You, and if it be Your holy will, heal my body also and help me in the future to dispose my life to Your praise and to bring forth true fruits of repentance. But if, according to Your wisdom, You have decided that this sickness must be unto death, I beseech You to prepare me and make me ready for it. Grant me a heartfelt and unfeigning repentance, to which You have pledged Your grace and forgiveness. Draw my heart away from the world and all its fleeting vanities and make me long and yearn for Your glorious and permanent riches, which are at Your right hand forevermore. Lord, lift up the light of Your countenance upon me, and in all my pains of body and afflictions of soul let Your comfort refresh my heart, that I may able to wait with patience till my change comes. Grant me, O Lord, that if my earthly house of this tabernacle is broken, I may have a building built by God, a house not made with hands, but eternal in heaven. Do this for the sake of Him who by His precious blood obtained it for me, even Jesus Christ. Amen.

457. Prayer of one terminally ill

Lord God, Father in heaven, have mercy upon me, who am sick and dying! You created me, body and soul, and for the sake of Jesus Christ adopted me as Your child in Holy Baptism, and mercifully promised that, as a father has compassion for his children, You would have compassion for me in the days of my life. Into Your faithful, fatherly hands, therefore, let my body and soul be now commended, and let Your compassionate, fatherly heart be moved for me, Your child. O heavenly Father, do not reckon my disobedience, indeed, all my sins committed from childhood, to my condemnation, but regard the all-availing atonement of Your Son, Jesus Christ, and for His sake spare me, a poor sinner, and do not repay me according to my sins. Remember the precious oath which

You swore: "As truly as I live, I do not desire the death of the sinner, but that he turn and live." Remember not the sins of my youth, nor my transgressions, but remember me according to Your great mercy. Look upon my sorrow and misery, and forgive me all my sins. — *Let me be Thine forever, Thou faithful God and Lord; let me forsake Thee never, nor wander from Thy Word. Lord, do not let me waver, but give me steadfastness, and for such grace forever Thy holy name I'll bless. — Lord, when my eyes are failing, my breath comes heavily, and words are unavailing, oh, hear my sighs to Thee! When mind and thought, O Savior, are flickering like a light that to and fro doth waver ere 'tis extinguished quite, in that last hour, oh, grant me to slumber soft and still, no doubts to vex or haunt me, safe anchored on Thy will.*

Lord God the Son, Jesus Christ, Savior of the world, have mercy upon me, who am sick and dying! You came down from heaven for my sake, and for my sake suffered and endured so many things; indeed, You shed Your blood for me so freely on the cross, and thereby redeemed me from sin, death, the devil, and hell: oh, then, dear Lord Jesus, let Your efforts and toil, Your agony and torment, Your cross and death, not be in vain for me, a poor sinner, but by virtue of Your merits intercede for me above in heaven, that I may receive grace and mercy in the time when I need grace and mercy. — *Oh, let me not in this distress meet death, nor hopeless languish; but come, O God of faithfulness, and help me bear my anguish; remember me, Thy very own, a sprig upon Thy body grown, and in Thy peace receive me.* — Cry even now, O my Comfort, into my heart and ears: "Fear not, dear child, I have redeemed you. I have called you by name. You are Mine. I am with you in trouble, I will deliver you and honor you; with long life I will satisfy you, and will show you My salvation." *Appear Thou in that fashion (to comfort me in need) when, Thou, Lord, in Thy Passion Thyself to death didst bleed! — Thy fearless Spirit strengthen me, Thy wounds, Lord, be my mending; Thy mortal sweat my cleansing be when life must here be ending, and when it please Thee, take me hence in faith and certain confidence to Thine elect in heaven.* Be, dearest Savior, my advocate on the Day of God's stern judgment; and *save me by Thy wounds that Day, that I may not be smitten, but in the Book of Blessing may find that my name is written. I doubt this not, it shall be so, for Thou hast judged the evil foe and paid my debts completely.*

Lord God, the Holy Spirit, have mercy upon me, who am sick and dying! Represent me above all, in my greatest weakness, before God with groanings too deep for words, and bear witness to my spirit that I am a child of God and heir of eternal salvation. Assist me with Your powerful comfort against all tribulations of the evil one. Drive away from me the fear of death by reminding me of the cheering resurrection and glorious reward of grace. Sustain me in heartfelt love to God the heavenly Father and in true faith in Christ Jesus, my Redeemer, shorten for me my torment and the agony of death, and help me to contend valiantly and to pass through death and life to God. — *O Holy Ghost, O Spirit pure, our Comforter, Thy comfort send when life must end; forsake me not when I am fought by devil's might, by death's grim sight! My Rock, my Lord, fulfill Thy word, Thy blessing give, fore'er to live. Amen.*

O holy and most blessed Trinity, have mercy upon me, who am sick and dying. Be above me and protect me, be beside me and accompany me prosperously through the dark valley of death, be below me and bless me, be before me and preserve me unto life eternal. Amen. — *O Thou mighty God, now hearken to the prayer Thy child hath made; Jesus, while the night-hours darken, be Thou still my hope, my aid; Holy Ghost, on Thee I call, Friend and Comforter of all, hear the earnest prayer I've spoken: Yea, Thy word shall not be broken!* — I live to You, Jesus; I die to You, Jesus; I belong to You, Jesus, whether dying or living. Amen.

458. Comforting verses to read to the sick and dying

Genesis 3:15. The seed of the woman shall crush the head of the serpent.

Genesis 32:26. Lord, I will not let You go until You bless me.

Exodus 34:6-7. LORD, LORD God, merciful and gracious, long-suffering, and abounding in grace and truth; keeping grace for thousands, and forgiving iniquity and transgression, and sin, and before whom no man is innocent.

1 Kings 19:4. Elijah said, "It is enough; now take away my soul, O LORD; I am no better than my fathers."

Job 5:17-18. Blessed is the man whom God reproves; therefore do not despise the discipline of the Almighty. For He hurts, and He binds up; He breaks, and His hand heals.

Job 5:19. He will deliver you from six afflictions, and in the seventh no evil shall touch you.

Job 14:1-2. Man that is born of woman is of few days and full of trouble. He comes up like a flower and falls; he flees like a shadow and continues not.

Job 19:25-27. I know that my Redeemer lives, and He will hereafter raise me from the earth, and I will then be surrounded with this my skin, and in my flesh I shall see God; Him shall I see for myself, and my eyes shall behold Him, and not another.

Psalm 4:8. I will both lay me down in peace and sleep, for You, Lord, only help me to dwell in safety.

Psalm 10:17. O Lord, You hear the desire of the afflicted; their heart is sure that Your ear is attentive to it.

Psalm 13:5–6. I trust in Your mercy; my heart rejoices in Your salvation. I will sing to the Lord because He is good to me.

Psalm 17:15. I will behold Your face in righteousness; I will be satisfied when I awake according to Your likeness.

Psalm 22:27. The needy shall eat and be satisfied; and those who seek the Lord shall praise Him: your heart shall live forever.

Psalm 23. The Lord is my shepherd; I shall not want. He makes me lie down in green pastures. He leads me to the fresh waters. He restores my soul. He leads me in paths of righteousness for His name's sake. Even though I walk through the dark valley, I will fear no evil; for You are with me, Your rod and Your staff, they comfort me. You prepare a table before me in the presence of my enemies; You anoint my head with oil and fill my cup full. Goodness and mercy shall follow me all the days of my life, and I shall dwell in the house of the Lord forever.

Psalm 25:6–7. Remember Your mercies and Your loving kindnesses, O Lord, for they have been ever of old. Remember not the sins of my youth nor my transgressions; but remember me according to Your mercy for Your goodness' sake.

Psalm 27:1. The Lord is my light and my salvation; whom shall I fear? The Lord is the strength of my life; of whom shall I be afraid?

Psalm 27:9. Hide not Your face from me, and turn Your servant not away in anger; for You are my help. Leave me not, and take not Your hand from me, O God, my salvation.

Psalm 31:5. Into Your hands I commend my Spirit; You have redeemed me, O Lord, faithful God.

Psalm 34:19. The righteous must suffer many things, but the Lord delivers him out of them all.

Psalm 37:4–5. Delight yourself in the Lord; He will give you what your heart desires. Commit your way to the Lord; trust also in Him; He shall bring it to pass.

Psalm 39:5. Behold, my days are as a hand's breadth before You, and my lifetime is as nothing in Your sight. Surely every man is altogether vanity, however securely he may live.

Psalm 42:1–2. As the hart pants after fresh waters, so my soul, God, pants for You; my soul thirsts for God, for the living God. When shall I come where I may see the face of God?

Psalm 43:5. Why are you cast down, and so disquieted within me? Wait for God, who is the help of my countenance, and my God.

Psalm 51:10–12. Create in me a clean heart, O God, and give me a new and certain spirit. Cast me not away from Your presence, and take not Your Holy Spirit from me. Restore unto me the joy of Your salvation, and let the fearless Spirit uphold me.

Psalm 55:22. Cast your burden on the LORD. He will sustain you, and will not leave you in disquietness forever.

Psalm 68:19–20. Blessed be the Lord daily; God puts a burden on us, but He helps us also. We have a God who saves, and the Lord of lords who delivers from death.

Psalm 73:23–26. Nevertheless, I am continually with You; for You hold me by my right hand. You guide me with Your counsel, and afterward You will receive me with glory. If I have You only, I ask for nothing in heaven and earth. Though my flesh and my heart may fail, yet You, O God are the comfort of my heart and my portion forever.

Psalm 91:14–16. Because he desires Me, I will deliver him; I will protect him, because he knows My name. When he calls to Me, I will answer him; I will be with him in trouble; I will rescue him and honor him. With long life I will satisfy him and show him My salvation.

Psalm 94:19. I had many cares in my heart, but Your consolations cheered my soul.

Psalm 103:1–3. Bless the LORD, O my soul, and all that is within me, bless His holy name! Bless the LORD, O my soul, and forget not all His benefits to you, who forgives all your iniquity, and heals all your diseases.

Psalm 103:8–14. The LORD is merciful and gracious, slow to anger, and plenteous in mercy. He will not always chide, nor will He keep His anger forever. He does not deal with us according to our sins, nor repay us according to our iniquities. For as high as the heavens are above the earth, so great is His steadfast love toward all who fear Him; as far as the east is from the west, so far does He cause our transgressions to be from us. As a father shows compassion to His children, so the LORD shows compassion to those who fear Him. For He knows what kind of creature we are; He remembers that we are dust.

Psalm 143:2. Enter not into judgment with Your servant; for no one living is righteous before You.

Psalm 145:18–19. The LORD is near to all who call on Him, to all who call on Him in earnest. He fulfills the desire of the God-fearing; He also hears their cry and saves them.

Proverbs 18:10. The name of the LORD is a strong tower; the righteous man runs into it and is safe.

Isaiah 1:18. Though your sins are red as blood, they shall be as white as snow; though they are red like crimson, they shall become like wool.

Isaiah 35:10. The ransomed of the LORD shall return and come to Zion with singing; everlasting joy shall be upon their heads; they shall obtain gladness and joy, and sorrow and sighing shall flee away.

Isaiah 38:17. Behold, it was for my welfare that I had great bitterness; but You have delivered in love my soul, that it might not meet destruction; for You have cast all my sins behind Your back.

Isaiah 41:10. Fear not, for I am with you; be not dismayed, for I am your God; I will strengthen you, I will help you, I will uphold you with the right hand of My righteousness.

Isaiah 42:3. A bruised reed He will not break, and a smoldering wick He will not quench.

Isaiah 43:24–25. You have burdened Me with your sins; you have wearied Me with your iniquities. I, I am He who blots out your transgressions for My own sake, and I will not remember your sins.

Isaiah 49:14–16. Zion said, "The LORD has forsaken me; my Lord has forgotten me." —"Can a woman forget her child, that she should have no compassion on the son of her womb? Even if these forget, I will not forget you. Behold, I have engraved you on My hands."

Isaiah 53:4–5. Surely He has borne our disease and carried our sorrows; yet we esteemed Him stricken, smitten by God, and afflicted. But He was wounded for our transgressions and crushed for our iniquities. Upon Him lay the chastisement that we might have peace, and with His wounds we are healed.

Isaiah 54:7–8. "For a brief moment I deserted you, but with great compassion I will gather you. In the moment of wrath I hid My face from you a little, but with everlasting grace I will have compassion on you," says the Lord, your Redeemer.

Isaiah 54:10. "The mountains may depart and the hills fall, but My grace shall not depart from you, and the covenant of My peace shall not fall," says the

Lord, who has compassion on you.

Isaiah 55:8–9. My thoughts are not your thoughts, neither are your ways My ways, declares the Lord: but as the heavens are higher than the earth, so are My ways higher than your ways and My thoughts than your thoughts.

Isaiah 57:15. Thus says the One who is high and lifted up, who dwells eternally, whose name is Holy: I dwell on high and in the holy place, and also with those who a re of a contrite and lowly spirit, to revive the spirit of the lowly, and the heart of the contrite.

Jeremiah 31:20. Is Ephraim My dear son and My darling child? For I remember still what I have spoken against him; therefore My heart yearns for him, and I shall have mercy on him, declares the Lord.

Lamentations 3:31–33. The Lord will not cast off forever, but He causes grief and has compassion again according to the multitude of His mercies; for He does not willingly afflict or grieve men.

Ezekiel 33:11. As truly as I live, declares the Lord God, I have no pleasure in the death of the wicked, but that the wicked turn from his way and live.

Hosea 13:14. I will ransom them from hell and redeem them from death. O Death, I will be to you a poison; O Hell, I will be to you a pestilence.

Micah 7:18. Who is a God like You, pardoning iniquity and passing over transgression for the remnant of His inheritance? He does not retain His anger forever; for He is merciful.

Wisdom 3:1. The souls of the righteous are in the hand of God, and no torment touches them.

Matthew 5:3–4, 6. Blessed are the poor in spirit, for theirs is the kingdom of heaven. Blessed are those who mourn, for they will be comforted. Blessed are those who hunger and thirst for righteousness, for they will be filled.

Matthew 11:28. Come to Me, all you who are weary and burdened; I will refresh you.

Mark 16:16. He who believes and is baptized will be saved; but he who does not believe will be condemned.

Luke 2:29–32. Lord, now You let Your servant depart in peace, according to Your Word; for mine eyes have seen Your Savior whom You have prepared before the face of all peoples; a Light to lighten the Gentiles and the Glory of Your people Israel.

Luke 5:31–32. Those who are well have no need of a physician, but those who are sick. I have come to call sinners to repentance, and not the righteous.

Luke 15:21. Father, I have sinned against heaven and before You; I am no longer worthy to be called Your son.

Luke 18:7–8. Will not God also deliver His chosen ones who cry to Him day and night? And will He delay long in doing so? I tell you, He will quickly deliver them.

Luke 19:10. The Son of Man came to seek out and to save what was lost.

Luke 23:43. And Jesus said to him, "Truly I tell you, today you will be with Me in paradise."

John 1:29. Behold, the Lamb of God who takes away the sin of the world.

John 3:16–17. God so loved the world that He gave His only-begotten Son, that all who believe in Him may not perish but have eternal life. For God did not send His Son into the world to condemn the world, but that the world might be saved through Him.

John 5:24. Truly, truly, I say to you, he who hears My word and believes Him who sent Me has eternal life, and does not come under judgment, but has passed from death to life.

John 5:25. Truly, truly, I say to you, the hour is coming, and is now here, when the dead will hear the voice of the Son of God, and those who hear will live.

John 6:37. He who comes to Me I will never cast out.

John 6:40. This is the will of Him who sent Me: that he who sees the Son and believes in Him may have eternal life; and I will raise him up on the Last Day.

John 6:54. He who eats My flesh and drinks My blood has eternal life, and I will raise him up on the Last Day.

John 6:68–69. Lord, to whom shall we go? You have the words of eternal life; and we have believed and known that You are that Christ, the Son of the living God.

John 8:51. Truly, truly, I say to you, if any man keeps My word, he will never see death.

John 10:27–28. My sheep hear My voice. I know them, and they follow Me. And I give them eternal life; and they will never perish, and no one will snatch them out of My hand.

John 11:25–26. Jesus said to her, "I am the resurrection and the life. He who believes in Me will live, even though he die. And he who lives and believes in Me will never die. Do you believe this?"

John 12:26. Where I am, there will My servant be also.

John 14:6. Jesus said, "I am the Way, and the Truth, and the Life; no man comes to the Father except through Me."

John 16:16. A little while, and you will not see Me, and again a little while, and you will see Me, because I go to the Father.

John 16:20. Truly, truly, I say to you, you will weep and mourn, but the world will rejoice; you will be sorrowful, but your sorrow will be turned into joy.

John 16:22. You have sorrow now; but I will see you again, and your hearts will rejoice, and your joy shall no man take from you.

John 16:23. Truly, truly, I say to you, if you ask anything of the Father in My name, He will give it to you.

John 16:33. In the world you have tribulation; but be of good cheer, I have overcome the world!

John 17:3. This is eternal life, that they may know You, the only true God, and Jesus Christ whom You have sent.

John 17:24. Father, I will that those also, whom You have given Me, may be with Me where I am, that they may behold My glory, which You have given Me because You loved Me before the foundation of the world.

Acts 4:12. There is salvation in no one else, nor is there any other name under heaven given among men by which we must be saved.

Acts 7:59. Lord Jesus, receive my spirit.

Acts 10:43. To this Jesus all the prophets bear witness, that through His name all who believe in Him shall receive forgiveness of sins.

Romans 3:22–25. There is no distinction: all have sinned and fall short of the glory that they should have in God, and without merit are justified by His grace, through the redemption that came through Christ Jesus; whom God put forward as a propitiation by faith in His blood.

Romans 3:28. Therefore we hold that a man is justified apart from works of the law, by faith alone.

Romans 4:5. To him who does not work but trusts Him who justifies the ungodly, his faith is counted as righteousness.

Romans 4:25. Christ was delivered up for our trespasses and raised for our justification.

Romans 5:1–2. Therefore, since we have been justified by faith, we have peace with God through our Lord Jesus Christ, through whom we have also obtained access in faith to this grace in which we stand, and we rejoice in hope of the glory to come, which God shall give.

Romans 5:20. Where sin abounded, grace abounded all the more.

Romans 8:1. There is therefore now nothing condemnable in those who are in Christ Jesus, who walk not after the flesh, but after the Spirit.

Romans 8:17–18. If we are children, then we are also heirs—heirs of God and fellow heirs with Christ, provided we suffer with Him in order that we may also be glorified with Him. For I consider that the sufferings of this age are not worthy of the glory that is to be revealed in us.

Romans 8:28–30. We know that for those who love God all things work together for good, for those who are called according to His purpose. For those whom He foreknew He also predestined to be conformed to the image of His Son, in order that He might be the firstborn among many brothers. And those whom He predestined He also called, and those whom He called He also justified, and those whom He justified He also glorified.

Romans 8:31–34. If God is for us, who can be against us? He who did not spare His own Son but gave Him up for us all, how will He not also with Him give us all things? Who shall bring any charge against God's elect? God is here, who justifies. Who is to condemn? Christ is here, who died—yea rather, who was raised—who is at the right hand of God and interceding for us.

Romans 8:37–39. In all these things we are more than conquerors through Him who loved us. For I am sure that neither death nor life, nor angel nor principality, nor power, nor things present nor things to come, nor height nor depth, nor any other created thing, will be able to separate us from the love of God which is in Christ Jesus our Lord.

Romans 9:16. So then it depends not on a man's willing or running, but on God's showing mercy.

Romans 10:4. Christ is the end of the law; whoever believes in Him is righteous.

Romans 10:12–13. There is here no distinction between Jew and Greek; there is one Lord of all, rich toward all who call on Him. For whoever calls on the name of the Lord will be saved.

Romans 11:32. God has consigned all to disobedience, that He may have mercy on all.

Romans 14:8–9. If we live, we live to the Lord; if we die, we die to the Lord. So then, whether we live or whether we die, we are the Lord's. For to this end Christ died and lived again, that He might be Lord both of the dead and of the living.

1 Corinthians 1:30. God made Christ our wisdom and our righteousness and sanctification and redemption.

1 Corinthians 2:9. No eye has seen, nor ear heard, nor the heart of man imagined, what God has prepared for those who love Him.

1 Corinthians 10:13. God is faithful, and He does not let you be tempted beyond your ability, but makes the temptation to have an end, that you may be able to endure it.

1 Corinthians 15:54–57. Death is swallowed up in victory. O death, where is your sting? O hell, where is your victory? The sting of death is sin, and the power of sin is the law. But thanks be to God, who gives us the victory through our Lord Jesus Christ.

2 Corinthians 4:17–18. Our slight momentary affliction is preparing for us an eternal weight of glory beyond all comparison, as we look not to the things that are seen but to the things that are unseen. For the things that are seen are transient, but the things that are unseen are eternal.

2 Corinthians 5:1. We know that if our earthly home of this tent is destroyed, we have a building built by God, a house not made with hands, eternal in the heavens.

2 Corinthians 12:9. Let My grace be sufficient for you; for My power is made mighty in weakness.

Galatians 2:16. Yet we know that a person is not justified by works of the law but through faith in Jesus Christ, so we also have believed in Christ Jesus, in order to be justified by faith in Christ and not by works of the law, because by works of the law no one will be justified.

Galatians 2:20. I have been crucified with Christ. It is no longer I who live, but Christ who lives in me. And the life I now live in the flesh I live by faith in the Son of God, who loved me and gave Himself for me.

Galatians 3:13. Christ redeemed us from the curse of the law by becoming a curse for us.

Galatians 3:26–27. You are all sons of God, through faith in Christ Jesus. For as many of you as were baptized have put on Christ.

Galatians 4:4–5. But when the fullness of time had come, God sent forth His Son, born of woman and made under the law, to redeem those who were under the law, so that we might receive adoption as sons.

Galatians 6:14. Far be it from me to boast save only in the cross of our Lord Jesus Christ, by which the world has been crucified to me, and I to the world.

Ephesians 2:8–9. By grace you have been saved through faith. And this is not of yourselves; it is the gift of God, not of works, so that no one may boast.

Ephesians 6:10–17. Finally, my brothers, be strong in the Lord and in the strength of His might. Put on the whole armor of God, that you may be able to stand against the schemes of the devil. For we do not wrestle against flesh and blood, but against the princes and authorities, even the masters of the world who rule in the darkness of this world, with the evil spirits under heaven. Therefore take up the whole armor of God, that you may be able to withstand in the evil day, and having done all, to keep the field. Stand therefore, having girded your loins with the belt of truth, and having put on the breastplate of righteousness, and having shod your legs as being ready to promote the gospel of peace, that you may be prepared. But above all, take up the shield of faith, with which you can extinguish all the flaming darts of the evil one. And take the helmet of salvation, and the sword of the Spirit, which is the Word of God.

Philippians 1:6. I am sure of this, that He who began a good work in you will carry it through until the Day of Jesus Christ.

Philippians 1:21. Christ is my life, and death is my gain.

Philippians 1:23. I have a desire to depart and be with Christ.

Philippians 3:20–21. But our walk is in heaven, and from it we await a Savior, the Lord Jesus Christ, who will transform our lowly body to be like His glorified body, according to the working by which He is able even to subject all things to Himself.

Philippians 4:7. The peace of God, which surpasses all understanding, guard your hearts and minds in Christ Jesus.

Colossians 1:12–14. Give thanks to the Father, who has qualified us for the inheritance of the saints in light, who has delivered us from the dominion of darkness and transferred us to the kingdom of His beloved Son, in whom we have redemption through His blood, even the forgiveness of sins.

Colossians 3:3–4. Your life is hidden with Christ in God. When Christ who is your life appears, then you also will appear with Him in glory.

1 Thessalonians 5:23–24. Now may the God of peace Himself sanctify you completely, and may your whole spirit and soul and body be kept blameless at the coming of our Lord Jesus Christ. He who calls you is faithful; He will surely do it.

1 Timothy 1:15–16. This is certainly true, and a precious, worthy saying, that Christ Jesus came into the world to save sinners, of whom I am the foremost. But I received mercy for this reason, that in me, as the foremost, Jesus Christ might display His perfect patience as an example to those who were to believe in Him for eternal life.

1 Timothy 2:4–6. God desires all men to be saved and to come to the knowledge of the truth. For there is one God, and there is one mediator between God and men, the man Christ Jesus, who gave Himself as a ransom for all, that this testimony might be given at the proper time.

1 Timothy 3:16. Great indeed is the mystery of godliness: He was manifested in the flesh, vindicated in the Spirit, seen by angels, proclaimed among the heathen, believed on in the world, taken up in glory.

2 Timothy 2:8. Remember Jesus Christ, risen from the dead.

2 Timothy 2:11–13. The saying is certainly true: If we die with Him, we will also live with Him; if we endure, we will also reign with Him; if we deny Him, He also will deny us; if we are faithless, He remains faithful; He cannot deny Himself.

2 Timothy 4:7–8. I have fought the good fight, I have finished the race, I have kept the faith. Henceforth there is laid up for me the crown of righteousness, which the Lord, the righteous judge, will award to me on that Day, and not only to me but also to all who love His appearing.

2 Timothy 4:18. The Lord will deliver me from every evil and bring me safely into His heavenly kingdom; to whom be the glory forever and ever. Amen.

Titus 3:5–7. Not because of works of righteousness which we did, but according to His own mercy, He saved us by the washing of rebirth and renewal of the Holy Spirit, whom He poured out on us richly through Jesus Christ our Savior, so that we, being righteous by His grace, might be heirs of eternal life according to the hope.

Hebrews 2:14–15. Since the children have flesh and blood, He Himself likewise partook of the same things, that through death He might take away the power of him who has dominion over death, that is, the devil, and deliver those who through fear of death were all their life compelled to be slaves.

Hebrews 4:9. There remains yet a rest for the people of God.

Hebrews 4:15–16. We do not have a High Priest who was unable to sympathize with our weaknesses, but who in every respect has been tempted as we are, yet without sin. Let us then with confidence draw near to the throne of grace, that we may receive mercy and find grace to help in time of need.

Hebrews 7:24–25. Christ has a permanent priesthood. Therefore He is able to save evermore those who draw near to God through Him and ever lives to make intercession for them.

Hebrews 12:6–8. Whom the Lord loves, He disciplines; and He chastises every son whom He receives. If you endure discipline, God is treating you as children; for what son is there whom his father does not discipline? But if you are without discipline, in which all have participated, then you are illegitimate children and not children.

Hebrews 12:11. For the moment all discipline seems to us not joy but sorrow; but later it will yield the peaceful fruit of righteousness to those who have been trained by it.

Hebrews 12:22–24. You have come to Mount Zion and to the city of the living God, to the heavenly Jerusalem, and to the multitude of many thousand angels, and to the assembly of the firstborn who are enrolled in heaven, and to God, the judge of all, and to the spirits of the righteous made perfect, and to Jesus, the mediator of a new covenant, and to the blood of sprinkling that speaks better than that of Abel.

Hebrews 13:5. He has said, "I will never leave you nor forsake you."

Hebrews 13:8. Jesus Christ, yesterday and today, and the same forever.

James 1:12. Blessed is the man who endures trial; for after he has been approved he will receive the crown of life, which God has promised to those who love Him.

1 Peter 1:3–9. Blessed be the God and Father of our Lord Jesus Christ, who, according to His great mercy, has caused us to be born again to a living hope through the resurrection of Jesus Christ from the dead, to an imperishable, undefiled, and unfading inheritance that is kept in heaven for you, who by God's power are being guarded through faith for a salvation which is ready to be revealed in the last time; in which you rejoice, though now for a little while, if necessary, you are grieved by various trials, so that your faith might be found genuine and far more precious than perishable gold, which is tested by fire, for praise and glory and honor at the revelation of Jesus Christ, whom you have not seen, and yet love, and now believe in Him. Although you do not see Him, you will rejoice with inexpressible and glorious joy, obtaining the outcome of your faith, the salvation of your souls.

1 Peter 1:18–19. You know that you were redeemed from your vain conduct according to the manner of your fathers, not with perishable silver or gold, but with the precious blood of Christ, as of an innocent and spotless lamb.

1 Peter 1:24–25. All flesh is like grass and all the glory of man like the flower of grass. The grass withers, and the flower falls, but the Word of the Lord remains forever.

1 Peter 2:24–25. Christ Himself bore our sins in His body on the tree, that we, being dead to sin, might live to righteousness; by whose wounds you have been healed. For you were like straying sheep; but now you have now returned to the Shepherd and Bishop of your souls.

2 Peter 1:19. We have a sure prophetic word, and you do well to pay attention to it as to a light shining in a dark place, until the day dawns and the morning star arises in your hearts.

2 Peter 3:9. God is patient with us, not wishing that any should perish, but that all should turn to repentance.

2 Peter 3:13. We are waiting for new heavens and a new earth (according to His promise), in which righteousness dwells.

1 John 1:7. The blood of Jesus cleanses us from all sin.

1 John 1:8–9. If we say we have no sin, we deceive ourselves, and the truth is not in us. But if we confess our sins, He is faithful and just to forgive us our sins and to cleanse us from all unrighteousness.

1 John 2:1–2. If anyone sins, we have an advocate with the Father, Jesus Christ, who is righteous. And He is the propitiation for our sins, and not for ours only but also for those of the whole world.

1 John 2:25. This is the promise that He promised us, even eternal life.

1 John 3:1–2. Behold what kind of love the Father has shown to us, that we should be called children of God. Therefore the world does not know you, for it does not know Him. Beloved, we are God's children now, and what we will be has not yet appeared; but we know that when He appears we shall be like Him, because we shall see Him as He is.

1 John 3:20. If our heart condemns us, God is greater than our heart, and knows all things.

1 John 4:9. In this the love of God was made manifest toward us, that God sent His only-begotten Son into the world, that we might live through Him.

Revelation 2:10. Be faithful unto death, and I will give you the crown of life.

Revelation 3:11–12. Behold, I am coming soon. Hold fast what you have, so that no one may take your crown. He who overcomes, I will make him a pillar in the temple of My God, and he shall never go out of it, and I will write on him the name of My God, and the name of the city of My God, the new Jerusalem, which comes down from My God out of heaven, and My own new name.

Revelation 3:20–21. Behold, I stand at the door and knock. If any man hears My voice and opens the door, I will come in to him and eat with him, and he with Me. He who conquers, I will grant him to sit with Me on My throne; as I also conquered and sat down with My Father on His throne.

Revelation 7:14. These are the ones who came out of the great tribulation, and washed their robes, and made their robes white in the blood of the Lamb.

Revelation 12:10–12. I heard a loud voice in heaven, saying, "Now the salvation and the power and the kingdom of our God and the authority of His Christ have come, for the accuser of our brothers has been thrown down, who accuses them day and night before our God. And they have overcome him by the blood of the Lamb and by the word of their testimony, for they loved not their lives even unto death. Therefore, rejoice, O heavens and you who dwell in them!"

Revelation 14:13. Blessed are the dead who die in the Lord from now on. "Indeed," says the Spirit, "because they rest from their labors; for their deeds follow them."

Revelation 19:9. Blessed are those who are invited to the marriage supper of the Lamb.

Revelation 21:7. He who overcomes will inherit all these things, and I will be his God and he will be My son.

Revelation 22:20–21. He who testifies to these things says, "Surely I am coming soon." Amen. Even so, come, Lord Jesus! The grace of our Lord Jesus Christ be with you all. Amen.

459. Hymns and hymn stanzas

1

1 My Savior, be Thou near me
   When death is at my door;
   Then let Thy presence cheer me,
   Forsake me nevermore!
   When soul and body languish,
   Oh, leave me not alone,
   But take away mine anguish
   By virtue of Thine own!

2 Be Thou my consolation,
   My shield when I must die;
   Remind me of Thy Passion
   When my last hour draws nigh
   Mine eyes shall then behold Thee,
   Upon Thy cross shall dwell,
   My heart by faith enfolds Thee.
   Who dieth thus dies well.

2

1 From depths of woe I cry to Thee,
   Lord, hear me, I implore Thee.
   Bend down Thy gracious ear to me,
   My prayer let come before Thee.
   If Thou rememb'rest each misdeed,
   If each should have its rightful meed,
   Who may abide Thy presence?

2 Thy love and grace alone avail
   To blot out my transgression;
   The best and holiest deeds must fail
   To break sin's dread oppression.
   Before Thee none can boasting stand,
   But all must fear Thy strict demand
   And live alone by mercy.

3 Therefore my hope is in the Lord
  And not in mine own merit;
  It rests upon His faithful Word
  To them of contrite spirit
  That He is merciful and just;
  This is my comfort and my trust.
  His help I wait with patience.

4 And though it tarry till the night
  And till the morning waken,
  My heart shall never doubt His might
  Nor count itself forsaken.
  Do thus, O ye of Israel's seed,
  Ye of the Spirit born indeed;
  Wait for your God's appearing.

5 Though great our sins and sore our woes,
  His grace much more aboundeth;
  His helping love no limit knows,
  Our utmost need it soundeth.
  Our shepherd good and true is He,
  Who will at last His Israel free
  From all their sin and sorrow.

3

1 Why should cross and trial grieve me?
  Christ is near / With His cheer;
  Never will He leave me.
  Who can rob me of the heaven
  That God's Son / For my own
  To my faith hath given?

2 Naked was I, nothing owning,
  When on earth / At my birth
  My breath came with groaning,
  Naked hence shall I betake me,
  When I go / From earth's woe
  And my breath forsake me.

3 Naught—not e'en the life I'm living,
  Is mine own, / God alone
  All to me is giving.
  Must I then His own restore Him?
  Though bereft / Of each gift
  Still shall I adore Him.

4 Death cannot destroy forever;
  From our fears, / Cares, and tears
  It will us deliver.
  It will close life's mournful story,
  Make a way / That we may
  Enter heavenly glory.

5 There I'll reap enduring pleasure,
  After woe / Here below
  Suffered in large measure.
  Lasting good we find here never,
  All the earth / Deemeth worth
  Vanisheth forever.

6 Lord, my Shepherd, take me to Thee.
  Thou art mine / I was Thine,
  Even ere I knew Thee.
  I am Thine, for Thou hast bought me;
  Lost I stood, / But Thy blood
  Free salvation brought me.

(cont.)

7 Thou art mine; I love and own Thee.
  Light of Joy, / Ne'er shall I
  From my heart dethrone Thee.
  Savior, let me soon behold Thee
  Face to face, / May Thy grace
  Evermore enfold me!

4

I fall asleep in Jesus' wounds,
There pardon for my sins abounds;
Yea, Jesus' blood and righteousness
My jewels are, my glorious dress.
In these before my God I'll stand
When I shall reach the heavenly land.

5

Who knows when death may overtake me!
Time passes on, my end draws near.
How swiftly can my breath forsake me!
How soon can life's last hour appear!
My God, for Jesus' sake I pray
Thy peace may bless my dying day.

6

1 When my last hour is close at hand,
  Lord Jesus Christ, attend me;
  Beside me then, O Savior, stand
  To comfort and defend me.
  Into Thy hands I will commend
  My soul at this my earthly end,
  And Thou wilt keep it safely.

2 My sins, dear Lord, disturb me sore,
  My conscience cannot slumber;
  But though as sands upon the shore
  My sins may be in number,
  I will not quail, but think of Thee;
  Thy death, Thy sorrow, borne for me,
  Thy sufferings, shall uphold me.

3 I am a branch in Thee, the Vine,
  And hence the comfort borrow
  That Thou wilt surely keep me Thine
  Through fear and pain and sorrow;
  And when I die, I die to Thee,
  Thy precious death hath won for me
  The life that never endeth.

4 Since Thou the power of death didst rend,
  In death Thou wilt not leave me;
  Since Thou didst into heaven ascend,
  No fear of death shall grieve me.
  For where Thou art, there shall I be
  That I may ever live with Thee;
  That is my hope when dying.

5 My spirit I commend to Thee
  And gladly hence betake me;
  Peaceful and calm my sleep shall be,
  No human voice can wake me.
  But Christ is with me through the strife,
  And He will bear me into life
  And open heaven before me.

7

1 Farewell I gladly bid thee,
  False, evil world, farewell.
  Thy life is vain and sinful,
  With Thee I would not dwell.
  I long to be in heaven,
  In that untroubled sphere
  Where they will be rewarded
  Who served their God while here.

2 By Thy good counsel lead me,
  O Son of God, my Stay;
  In each perplexing trial
  Help me, O Lord, I pray.
  Mine hour of sorrow shorten,
  Support my fainting heart,
  From every cross deliver,
  The crown of life impart.

3 When darkness round me gathers,
  Thy name and cross, still bright,
  Deep in my heart are sparkling
  Like stars in blackest night.
  O heart, this image cherish:
  The Christ on Calvary,
  How patiently He suffered
  And shed His blood for me!

4 Lord, hide my soul securely
  Deep in Thy wounded side;
  From every danger shield me
  And to Thy glory guide.
  He has been truly blessed
  Who reaches heaven above;
  He has found perfect healing
  Who rests upon Thy love.

5 Lord, write my name, I pray Thee,
  Now in the Book of Life
  And with all true believers
  Take me where joys are rife.
  There let me bloom and flourish,
  Thy perfect freedom prove,
  And tell, as I adore Thee,
  How faithful was Thy love.

8

O Christ, Thou Lamb of God,
That takest away the sin of the world,
Have mercy upon us.

O Christ, Thou Lamb of God,
That takest away the sin of the world,
Have mercy upon us.

O Christ, Thou Lamb of God,
That takest away the sin of the world,
Grant us Thy peace. Amen.

9

1 Lamb of God, pure and holy,
  Who on the cross didst suffer,
  Ever patient and lowly,
  Thyself to scorn didst offer.
  All sins Thou borest for us,
  Else had despair reigned o'er us:
  Have mercy on us, O Jesus! O, Jesus!

2 Lamb of God, pure and holy,
  Who on the cross didst suffer,
  Ever patient and lowly,
  Thyself to scorn didst offer.
  All sins Thou borest for us,
  Else had despair reigned o'er us:
  Have mercy on us, O Jesus! O, Jesus!

3 Lamb of God, pure and holy,
  Who on the cross didst suffer,
  Ever patient and lowly,
  Thyself to scorn didst offer.
  All sins Thou borest for us,
  Else had despair reigned o'er us:
  Thy peace be with us, O Jesus! O, Jesus!

10

Thy fearless Spirit strengthen me,
Thy wounds, Lord, be my mending;
Thy mortal sweat my cleansing be
When life must here be ending,
And when it please Thee, take me hence
In faith and certain confidence
To Thine elect in heaven.

11

1 Help, Helper, help in misery,
　Have mercy, faithful God, on me!
　Thy child I am, Thy dearest one:
　Let devil, world, and sin begone!

2 My God and Lord, I trust in Thee;
　And having Thee, what faileth me?
　Lord Jesus Christ, I have Thee now—
　My God and my Redeemer Thou.

3 In this my heart's delight I find,
　And wait on Thee with cheerful mind,
　And wholly on Thy name rely.
　Help, Helper, help! Amen! I cry.

12

1 Look up to thy God again,
　Soul, sunk in affliction!
　Shall He be reproached by men
　Through thy sore dejection?
　Satan's wiles dost thou not see
　Who by sore temptation,
　Gladly would keep far from thee
　Jesus' consolation?

2 Shake thy head, bid Satan, "Flee!
　Wouldst thou, O deceiver—
　With thy thrusts renewed at me
　Make me fear and shiver?
　Serpent! bruised thy head I see;
　Christ my Savior freed me
　From thee by His agony,
　And to joy will lead me.

3 "Dost thou charge my sin to me?
　When hath God in heaven
　Ordered that my judgment be
　From thee sought and given?
　Who did pow'r on thee bestow,
　Sentence to deliver,
　Who thyself art sunk so low
　In hell's flames forever?"

4 Though I've not done as I should,
　And it grieves me truly,
　I lay claim to Jesus' blood,
　Death, and Passion fully.
　These the ransom price repay
　Set for my transgression,
　These before God's throne I lay,—
　Choicest intercession!

5 Often God's own children here
　Sow in tears and sadness,
　But at length the longed-for year
　Comes to joy and gladness;
　For the reaping time appears,
　All their labors after,
　When are turned their grief and tears
　Into joy and laughter.

6 Come, then, Christian heart, today,
　Take thy desperation,
　Cast it joyfully away;
　Let God's consolation
　Burn within thee more and more,
　Praise and honor giving
　To thy God's great name and power,
　Source of thy relieving.

13

1 Seems it only in my anguish
  As though God would let us languish,
  Yet I hold this knowledge fast:
  God will surely help at last.

2 Though by some delay He try us,
  He will not His aid deny us,
  Though it come not oft with speed,
  It will surely come at need.

14

1 Lord Jesus Christ, true Man and God,
  Who borest anguish, scorn, the rod,
  And diedst at last upon the tree,
  To bring Thy Father's grace for me:

2 I pray Thee, through that bitter woe,
  Let me, a sinner, mercy know,
  When comes the hour of failing breath,
  And I must wrestle, Lord, with death.

3 When from my sight all fades away,
  And when my tongue no more can say,
  And when mine ears no more can hear,
  And when my heart is racked with fear.

4 When all my mind is darkened o'er,
  And human help can do no more;
  Then come, Lord Jesus, come with speed,
  And help me in my hour of need.

5 Lead me from this dark vale beneath,
  And shorten then the pangs of death;
  All evil spirits drive away,
  But let Thy Spirit with me stay,

6 Until my soul the body leave;
  Then in Thy hands my soul receive,
  And let the earth my body keep,
  Till the Last Day shall break its sleep.

7 Joyful my resurrection be,
  Thou in the Judgment plead for me,
  And hide my sins, Lord, from Thy face,
  And give me Life, of Thy dear grace!

8 Implicitly I trust Thee, Lord,
  For Thou hast promised in Thy Word:
  "In truth I tell you, who receives
  My word, and keeps it, and believes,

9 "Shall never fall God's wrath beneath,
  Shall never taste eternal death;
  Though here he must return to dust,
  He still is noways therefore lost;

10 "For I will with a mighty hand
  Deliver him from Death's strong band,
  And lift him hence that he shall be
  Forever in My realm with Me.

11 "Forever living there in bliss."
  O let us not that glory miss!
  Dear Lord, forgive us all our guilt,
  Help us to wait until Thou wilt

12 That we depart; and let our faith
  Be brave, and conquer e'en in death,
  Firm resting on Thy sacred Word,
  Until we sleep in Thee, our Lord.

15

1 In Thee alone, O Christ, my Lord,
My hope on earth remaineth;
I know Thou wilt Thine aid afford,
Naught else my soul sustaineth.
No strength of man, no earthly stay,
Can help me in the evil day;
Thou, only Thou, canst aid supply.
To Thee I cry;
On Thee I bid my heart rely.

2 My sins, O Lord, against me rise,
I mourn them with contrition;
Grant, through Thy death and sacrifice,
To me a full remission.
Lord, show before the Father's throne
That Thou didst for my sins atone;
So shall I from my load be freed.
Thy Word I plead;
Keep me, O Lord, each hour of need.

3 O Lord, in mercy stay my heart
On faith's most sure foundation
And to my inmost soul impart
Thy perfect consolation.
Fill all my life with love to Thee,
Toward all men grant me charity;
And at the last, when comes my end,
Thy succor send.
From Satan's wiles my soul defend.

4 All praise to God in highest heav'n,
The Father ever gracious;
And to the Son, for sinners giv'n,
Who guards His children precious;
And to the Holy Ghost on high;
Oh, may He keep His comfort nigh,
And teach us, free from sin and fear,
To please Him here,
And serve Him in the sinless sphere.

16

1 God the Father, be our Stay,
Oh, let us perish never.
Cleanse us from our sins, we pray,
And grant us life forever.
Keep us from the evil one;
Uphold our faith most holy,
Grant us to trust Thee solely
With humble hearts and lowly.
Let us put God's armor on:
With all true Christians running
Our heavenly race and shunning
The devil's wiles and cunning.
Amen, Amen, this be done,
So sing we, Alleluia!

2 Jesus Christ, be Thou our Stay,
Oh, let us perish never.
Cleanse us from our sins, we pray,
And grant us life forever.
Keep us from the evil one;
Uphold our faith most holy,
Grant us to trust Thee solely
With humble hearts and lowly.
Let us put God's armor on:
With all true Christians running
Our heavenly race and shunning
The devil's wiles and cunning.
Amen, Amen, this be done,
So sing we, Alleluia!

(cont.)

3 Holy Ghost, be Thou our Stay,
   Oh, let us perish never.
   Cleanse us from our sins, we pray,
   And grant us life forever.
   Keep us from the evil one;
   Uphold our faith most holy,
   Grant us to trust Thee solely
   With humble hearts and lowly.
   Let us put God's armor on:
   With all true Christians running
   Our heavenly race and shunning
   The devil's wiles and cunning.
   Amen, Amen, this be done,
   So sing we, Alleluia!

17

1 Oh, whither shall I flee,
   Depressed with misery?
   Who is it that can ease me,
   And from my sins release me?
   Though all the world should aid me,
   Of grief they could not rid me.

2 O Jesus, Source of Grace,
   I seek Thy loving face,
   Upon Thy invitation,
   With deep humiliation;
   Oh, let Thy blood me cover,
   And wash my soul all over.

18

O Jerusalem, how glorious
Dost thou shine, thou city fair!
Lo, I hear the tones victorious
Ever sweetly sounding there.
Oh, the bliss that there surprises!
Lo, the sun of morn now rises,
And the breaking day I see
That shall never end for me.

19

1 In God, my faithful God,
　I trust when dark my road;
　Though many woes o'ertake me,
　Yet He will not forsake me.
　His love it is doth send them
　And, when 'tis best, will end them.

2 My sins assail me sore,
　But I despair no more.
　I build on Christ who loves me;
　From this Rock nothing moves me.
　To Him I all surrender,
　To Him, my soul's Defender.

3 If death my portion be,
　Then death is gain to me
　And Christ my Life forever,
　From whom death cannot sever.
　Come when it may, He'll shield me,
　To Him I wholly yield me.

4 O Jesus Christ, my Lord,
　So meek in deed and word,
　Thou once didst die to save us
　Because Thy love would have us
　Be heirs of heavenly gladness
　When ends this life of sadness.

5 "So be it," then I say
　With all my heart each day.
　We, too, dear Lord, adore Thee;
　We sing for joy before Thee.
　Guide us while here we wander
　Until we praise Thee yonder.

20

Give, Lord, this consummation
To all our heart's distress;
Our hands, our feet, e'er strengthen,
In death our spirits bless.
Thy truth and Thy protection
Grant evermore, we pray,
And in celestial glory
Shall end our destined way.

21

1 For me to live is Jesus,
　To die is gain for me;
　Then, whensoe'er He pleases,
　I meet death willingly. *(x2)*

2 For Christ, my Lord and Brother,
　I leave this world so dim
　And gladly seek that other,
　Where I shall be with Him. *(x2)*

(cont.)

3 My woes are nearly over,
  Though long and dark the road;
  My sin His merits cover,
  And I have peace with God. *(x2)*

4 Lord, when my pow'rs are failing,
  My breath comes heavily,
  And words are unavailing.
  Oh, hear my sighs to Thee! *(x2)*

5 When mind and thought, O Savior,
  Are flick'ring like a light
  That to and fro doth waver
  Ere 'tis extinguished quite, *(x2)*

6 In that last hour, oh, grant me
  To slumber soft and still,
  No doubts to vex or haunt me,
  Safe anchored on Thy will; *(x2)*

7 And so to Thee still cleaving
  Through all death's agony,
  To fall asleep believing
  And wake in heav'n with Thee. *(x2)*

8 Amen! Thou, Christ, my Savior,
  Wilt grant this unto me.
  Thy Spirit lead me ever
  That I fare happily. *(x2)*

22

1 Jesus Christ, my sure Defense
  And my Savior, ever liveth;
  Knowing this, my confidence
  Rests upon the hope it giveth
  Though the night of death be fraught
  Still with many an anxious thought.

2 Jesus, my Redeemer, lives;
  I, too, unto life shall waken.
  Endless joy my Savior gives;
  Shall my courage, then, be shaken?
  Shall I fear, or could the Head
  Rise and leave His members dead?

3 Nay, too closely am I bound
  Unto Him by hope forever;
  Faith's strong hand the Rock hath found,
  Grasped it, and will leave it never;
  Even death now cannot part
  From its Lord the trusting heart.

4 I am flesh and must return
  Unto dust, whence I am taken;
  But by faith I now discern
  That from death I shall awaken
  With my Savior to abide
  In His glory, at His side.

5 Glorified, I shall anew
  With this flesh then be enshrouded;
  In this body I shall view
  God, my Lord, with eyes unclouded;
  In this flesh I then shall see
  Jesus Christ eternally.

6 Then these eyes my Lord shall know,
  My Redeemer and my Brother;
  In His love my soul shall glow—
  I myself, and not another!
  Then the weakness I feel here
  Shall forever disappear.

7 They who sorrow here and moan
  There in gladness shall be reigning;
  Earthly here the seed is sown,
  There immortal life attaining.
  Here our sinful bodies die,
  Glorified to dwell on high.

8 Then take comfort and rejoice,
  For His members Christ will cherish.
  Fear not, they will hear His voice;
  Dying, they shall never perish;
  For the very grave is stirred
  When the trumpet's blast is heard.

9 Laugh to scorn the gloomy grave
  And at death no longer tremble;
  He, the Lord, who came to save
  Will at last His own assemble.
  They will go their Lord to meet,
  Treading death beneath their feet.

10 Oh, then, draw away your hearts
  Now from pleasures base and hollow.
  There to share what He imparts,
  Here His footsteps ye must follow.
  Fix your hearts beyond the skies,
  Whither ye yourselves would rise.

23

1 Christ is arisen
  From the grave's dark prison
  We now rejoice with gladness;
  Christ will end all sadness.
  Lord, have mercy!

2 All our hopes were ended,
  Had Jesus not ascended
  From the grave triumphantly.
  For this, Lord Christ, we worship Thee.
  Lord, have mercy!

3 Alleluia! Alleluia! Alleluia!
  We now rejoice with gladness;
  Christ will end all sadness.
  Lord, have mercy!

24

1 We now implore God the Holy Ghost
  For the true faith, which we need the most,
  That in our last moments He may befriend us
  And, as homeward we journey, attend us.
  Lord, have mercy!

2 Shine in our hearts, O most precious Light,
  That we Jesus Christ may know aright,
  Clinging to our Savior, whose blood hath bought us,
  Who again to our homeland hath brought us.
  Lord, have mercy!

(cont.)

3 Thou highest Comfort in ev'ry need,
   Grant that neither shame nor death we heed,
   That e'en then our courage may never fail us
   When the foe shall accuse and assail us.
   Lord, have mercy!

25

1 By grace! This ground of faith is certain;
   So long as God is true, it stands.
   What saints have penned by inspiration,
   What in His Word our God commands,
   What our whole faith must rest upon,
   Is grace alone, grace in His Son.

2 By grace to timid hearts that tremble,
   In tribulation's furnace tried—
   By grace, despite all fear and trouble,
   The Father's heart is open wide.
   Where could I help and strength secure
   If grace were not my anchor sure?

3 By grace! May sin and Satan hearken!
   I bear the flag of faith in hand,
   And pass—for doubts my joy can't darken—
   The Red Sea to the Promised Land.
   I cling to what my Savior taught,
   And trust it, whether felt or not.

26

Though it may seem, He hears thee not,
Count not thyself forsaken;
Thy wants are ne'er by Him forgot,
Let this thy hope awaken;
His word is sure, here is thy stay.
And though thy flesh say only nay,
Let not thy faith be shaken.

27

1 Now I have found the firm foundation
   Which holds mine anchor ever sure;
   'Twas laid before the world's creation
   In Christ my Savior's wounds secure;
   Foundation which unmoved shall stay
   When heav'n and earth will pass away.

2 It is that mercy never ending
   Which human wisdom far transcends,
   Of Him who, loving arms extending,
   To wretched sinners condescends;
   Whose heart with pity still doth break
   Whether we seek Him or forsake.

3 Our ruin God hath not intended,
  For our salvation He hath yearned;
  For this His Son to earth descended
  And then to heav'n again returned;
  For this so patient evermore
  He knocketh at our heart's closed door.

4 O depth of love, to me revealing
  The sea where my sins disappear!
  In Christ my wounds find perfect healing,
  There is no condemnation here;
  For Jesus' blood through earth and skies
  Forever "Mercy! Mercy!" cries.

5 I never will forget this crying;
  In faith I'll trust it all my days,
  And when o'er all my sins I'm sighing,
  Into the Father's heart I'll gaze;
  For there is always to be found
  Free mercy without end and bound.

6 Though I be robbed of ev'ry pleasure
  That makes my soul and body glad
  And be deprived of earthly treasure
  And be forsaken, lone, and sad,
  Though my desire for help seem vain,
  His mercy shall with me remain.

7 Though earthly trials should oppress me
  And cares from day to day increase;
  Tho' earth's vain things should sore distress
  And rob me of my Savior's peace;
  Though I be brought down to the dust,
  Still in His mercy I will trust.

8 When all my deeds I am reviewing,
  The deeds that I admire the most,
  I find in all my thought and doing
  That there is naught whereof to boast.
  Yet this sweet comfort shall abide—
  In mercy I can still confide.

9 Let mercy cause me to be willing
  To bear my lot and not to fret.
  While He my restless heart is stilling,
  May I His mercy not forget!
  Come weal, come woe, my heart to test,
  His mercy is my only rest.

10 I'll stand upon this firm foundation
  As long as I on earth remain;
  This shall engage my meditation
  While I the breath of life retain;
  And then, when face to face with Thee,
  I'll sing of mercy, great and free.

28

1 My Savior sinners doth receive
  Who find no rest and no salvation,
  To whom no man can comfort give,
  So great their guilt and condemnation;
  For whom the world is all too small,
  Their sins both them and God appall;
  With whom the Law itself hath broken,
  On whom its judgment hath been spoken,
  To them the Gospel hope doth give:
  My Savior sinners doth receive. *(x2)*

(cont.)

2 Oh, couldst thou but His heart have seen,
  And how to lost ones e'er it bore Him,
  For those who long in sin had been,
  Whose eyes poured out their tears before Him!
  He cleansed the publican of blame,
  And to Zacchaeus quickly came;
  When Magdalene mourned her transgression,
  He dried her tears with sweet compassion;
  Despite their sins, He would not leave.
  My Savior sinners doth receive. *(x2)*

3 How love-filled as His tender look
  When Peter's deep-dyed sin He pondered!
  Ah, not alone this course He took
  When in the vale of tears He wandered!
  Eternal love is still the same,
  The Friend of sinners is His name.
  As on the cross His love was given,
  So from His glorious throne in heaven
  He gives to sinners kind reprieve.
  My Savior sinners doth receive. *(x2)*

4 O come, then, child of sinful men,
  Come, well thy griefs and sorrows knowing!
  Approach the One who knew no sin,
  And stoops to sinners, lowly bowing!
  What, wilt thou stand in judgment's light
  And perish without heart contrite?
  Wilt thou let sin and hell enslave thee
  When Christ is manifest to save thee?
  Oh, nay, the sinful byways leave!—
  My Savior sinners doth receive. *(x2)*

5 Say not: "My sins are far too great,
  His mercy I have scorned and slighted,
  Now my repentance is too late;
  I came not when His love invited."
  O trembling sinner, have no fear;
  In penitence to Christ draw near.
  Come now, though conscience still is chiding;
  Accept His mercy, e'er abiding.
  Come; blest are they who this believe:
  My Savior sinners doth receive. *(x2)*

6 Oh, draw us ever unto Thee,
  Thou friend of sinners, gracious Savior;
  Help us, that we may fervently
  Desire Thy pardon, peace, and favor.
  When guilty conscience doth reprove,
  Reveal to us Thy heart of love.
  May we, our wretchedness beholding,
  See then Thy pard'ning grace unfolding
  And say: "To God all glory be:
  My Savior, Christ, receiveth me." *(x2)*

29

All righteousness by works is vain,
The Law brings condemnation;
True righteousness by faith I gain,
Christ's work is my salvation.
His death, that perfect sacrifice,
Has paid the all-sufficient price;
In Him my hope is anchored.

30

1 If God Himself be for me,
  I may a host defy;
  For when I pray, before me
  My foes, confounded, fly.
  If Christ, my Head and Master,
  Befriend me from above,
  What foe or what disaster
  Can drive me from His love?

2 I build on this foundation,
  That Jesus and His blood
  Alone are my salvation,
  The true, eternal good.
  Without Him all that pleases
  Is valueless on earth;
  The gifts I owe to Jesus
  Alone my love are worth.

3 My heart for joy is springing
  And can no more be sad,
  'Tis full of mirth and singing,
  Sees naught but sunshine glad.
  The Sun that cheers my spirit
  Is Jesus Christ, my King;
  That which I shall inherit
  Makes me rejoice and sing.

31

1 In peace and joy I now depart
  At God's disposing;
  For full of comfort is my heart,
  Soft reposing.
  So the Lord hath promised me,
  And death is but a slumber.

2 'Tis Christ that wrought this work for me,
  My faithful Savior,
  Whom Thou hast made mine eyes to see
  By Thy favor.
  Now I know He is my Life,
  My Help in need and dying.

3 Him Thou hast unto all set forth
  Their great Salvation
  And to His kingdom called the earth,
  Ev'ry nation,
  By Thy dear and wholesome Word,
  In ev'ry place resounding.

4 He is the Hope and saving Light
  Of lands benighted;
  By Him are they who dwelt in night
  Fed and lighted.
  He is Israel's Praise and Bliss,
  Their Joy, Reward, and Glory.

32

Now let all the heav'ns adore Thee,
Let men and angels sing before Thee,
With harp and cymbal's clearest tone.
Of one pearl each shining portal,
Where, dwelling with the choir immortal,
We gather round Thy radiant throne.
No vision ever brought,
No ear hath ever caught,
Such great glory;
Therefore will we
Eternally
Sing hymns of praise and joy to Thee.

33

Ah, dearest Jesus, holy Child,
Make Thee a bed, soft, undefiled,
Within my heart, that it may be
A quiet chamber kept for Thee.

34

1 Now I will cling forever
To Christ, my Savior true;
My Lord will leave me never,
Whate'er He passes through.
He rends Death's iron chain,
He breaks through sin and pain,
He shatters hell's dark thrall,—
I follow through it all.

2 To halls of heavenly splendor
With Him I penetrate;
And trouble ne'er may hinder
Nor make me hesitate.
Let tempests rage at will,
My Savior shields me still;
He grants abiding peace
And bids all tumult cease.

3 He brings me to the portal
That leads to bliss untold
Whereon this rhyme immortal
Is found in script of gold:
"Who there My cross hath shared
Finds here a crown prepared;
Who there with Me has died
Shall here be glorified."

35

1 A mighty Fortress is our God,
A trusty Shield and Weapon;
He helps us free from ev'ry need
That hath us now o'ertaken.
The old evil Foe
Now means deadly woe;
Deep guile and great might
Are his dread arms in fight;
On Earth is not his equal.

2 With might of ours can naught be done,
Soon were our loss effected;
But for us fights the Valiant One,
Whom God Himself elected.
Ask ye, Who is this?
Jesus Christ it is.
Of Sabaoth Lord,
And there's none other God;
He holds the field forever.

3 Though devils all the world should fill,
All eager to devour us.
We tremble not, we fear no ill,
They shall not overpower us.
This world's prince may still
Scowl fierce as he will,
He can harm us none,
He's judged; the deed is done;
One little word can fell him.

36

From evil, Lord, deliver us;
The times and days are perilous.
Redeem us from eternal death,
And when we yield our dying breath,
Console us, grant us calm release,
And take our souls to Thee in peace.

37

1 Jesus, Thou my heart's delight,
  Sweetest Jesus!
Thou my soul's salvation quite,
  Sweetest Jesus!
Of my mind assuring sight,
  Sweetest Jesus,
  Jesus, sweetest Jesus!

2 Thousand times I think of Thee,
  My Redeemer!
Longing for Thee filleth me,
  My Redeemer!
How I yearn with Thee to be,
  My Redeemer!
  Jesus, my Redeemer!

3 Feed Thou me and satisfy,
  Heav'nly Manna!
Quench me, for my heart is dry,
  Help, Hosanna!
  Be the bed on which I lie,
  Soul's Reposing,
  Jesus, soul's Reposing!

4 Naught is lovelier than Thou,
  Love most precious!
Naught is friendlier than Thou,
  Love most gracious!
And naught sweeter is than Thou,
  Love most pleasing,
  Jesus, Love most pleasing!

5 I am sick, come, strengthen me,
  Strength in weakness!
Faint am I, refresh Thou me,
  Sweetest Jesus!
When I die, console Thou me,
  Thou Consoler!
  Jesus, my Consoler!

38

O worldly pride and leaven!
What good in you is found?
My spirit would to heaven
And thither shall be bound
To Jesus' light unfailing;
I long that place to see,
Where Jesus builds my dwelling,
There is it good to be!

39

1 A sinner, I my course must run,
  And then this world be leaving;
  So let me say: "Thy will be done,"
  By faith to Thee still cleaving,
  And at my end
  My soul commend,
  God, to Thy faithful keeping,
  O'er sin and hell,
  And death as well,
  Through Thee the vict'ry reaping.

2 Lord Jesus, this I ask of Thee,
  Deny me not this favor:
  When Satan sorely troubles me,
  Then do not let me waver.
  Keep watch and ward,
  O gracious Lord,
  Fulfill Thy faithful saying:
  Who doth believe
  He shall receive
  An answer to His praying.

40

1 Should this night prove the last for me
  In this sad vale of cares,
  Then lead me, Lord, to dwell with Thee
  And all Thy chosen heirs.

2 And thus I live and die to Thee,
  Strong Lord of hosts indeed.
  In life, in death, deliver me
  From ev'ry fear and need.

41

Spread out Thy wings to hide me,
Jesus, with joy provide me,
Thy own dear child receive!
Seeks Satan harm to bring me,
Then let the angels sing me:
"No harm shall here this child aggrieve."

42

1 O Jesus, when my time is come
  Receive me to Thy heav'nly home,
  That there in peace and joy I may
  Enjoy Thee in eternal day!

2 O Jesus, take my pray'r on high!
  O Jesus, here me as I sigh!
  O Jesus, Thou my hope shalt be!
  O Jesus, Jesus, help Thou me!

43

A rest remaineth for the weary;
Arise, sad heart, and grieve no more;
Though long the way and dark and dreary,
It endeth on the golden shore.
Before His throne the Lamb will lead thee,
On heav'nly pastures He will feed thee.
Cast off thy burden, come with haste;
Soon will the toil and strife be ended,
The weary way which thou hast wended.
Sweet is the rest which thou shalt taste.

44

The power of God the Father bless me:
The truth of the Son with goodness grace me,
The love of God the Holy Ghost preserve me
To life everlasting by His mercy. Amen.

460. A repentant invalid's prayer

O almighty God and Father, who because of sin visit men with all manner of plagues, and especially with physical infirmity, to discipline them, that they may not be condemned with the world: full of sins I come to You, confessing that I have thereby earned not only this infirmity but also eternal condemnation, since I am not only by nature a child of wrath and sold under sin, but also have transgressed all Your Commandments countless times in the span of my life. But I take refuge in Your boundless mercy, humbly beseeching You not to enter into judgment with me, for before You no man living is righteous. Remember not the sins of my youth, nor all my transgressions, but for the sake of Your name be gracious to my iniquities, which are great. Turn Your plague away from me, and give ear to my cry; be not silent at my tears. Spare me, that I may be refreshed, before I go hence and am here no more. Behold, dear Father, for comfort I have great bitterness, and cast all my sins behind You. Let the distress of my body move Your heart to pity, and either take it away or diminish it by Your consolation. Grant patience, help me to bear my cross, or simply bring me to blessedness. — *Let all in Your good will be placed; Dear God, do as may please Thee best* — I am Yours, and will remain Yours. Amen.

461. *Prayer for the blessing of medicine*

Lord Jesus, my most faithful helper and physician of body and soul; because You say, "The healthy need no physician, but the sick," and I, being now afflicted with sickness, desire to use the medicine which You cause to spring up from the ground for our good, therefore I humbly beseech You to add Your beneficial power to this medicine, which I will now use in Your name, and by Your blessing cause it to work in me the effect for which You created it, for without You all toil and effort is in vain. But according to Your Commandments and will, all created things must appear, help, and serve for our salvation, and there is no sickness too great for You, Lord, to heal it. Accordingly, Lord, show Your power to deliver from all distress, as You have promised, that my mouth may praise and glorify You eternally. Amen.

462. *Brief hourly prayers for the infirm*

One o'clock

O everlasting, true God, my Creator and Father, from whom health and sickness, prosperity and adversity proceed: because it is Your fatherly will that I should bear so long a cross and so heavy a physical infirmity, give me Christian patience and constant hope. I know that You are my dear Father, whether I suffer good or ill. It is required of all true church members that they bear the cross and misery. Amen.

Two o'clock

Dearest Lord Jesus, my faithful Mediator and Savior, I know well that with my sins I have earned this physical burden and every cross. But I take comfort in Your unfathomable grace and precious satisfaction, by which You have redeemed me in body and soul. Whatever happens to the body, I am assured that body and soul, freed from hell, shall at last attain to eternal life and be graced with heavenly glory and health. Grant it, Lord Jesus! Amen.

Three o'clock

O precious Holy Spirit, dearest Guest of my soul and true Witness to my heavenly adoption and salvation: I beseech You in my persistent physical burden to continue to dwell in my heart and quicken me with Your divine comfort, that I may abide steadfast in Your pure Word and most worthy Sacraments. Maintain faith, love, and hope in me as the three pillars of my Christianity, and grant me to know aright God's fatherly will for myself, that I may remain in it, and so live and die in it. Amen.

Four o'clock

O dear, faithful God, teach me to number my days, that I may not sin: a blessed death give me, at the Last Judgment absolve me, from hell preserve me, into heaven bring me. In death I will both lie down and sleep in peace. At the Last Day help me, that I may avoid hell and dwell safely in heaven. Let my heart take hold of Your divine Word and keep it and be refreshed by it until You come and take me to Yourself. Amen.

Five o'clock

My dearest Jesus, where else can I go for refuge in my cross and sorrow than to Your five holy wounds? If my senses and thoughts vanish, I will find the best protection. I abide in You; oh, abide also in me! Adorn the lamp of my heart with the true oil of faith, and make me ready by Christian repentance to go out to meet Your coming again with joy and to share in the gladness of the eternal wedding together with all the elect. Amen.

Six o'clock

I thank You, dear God and Father, that You have created me in Your image with a human body and a reasonable soul, and I pray that You would not forsake me, Your creature, in my need, but care for me with fatherly attention and mightily deliver me. Many are my afflictions, and every day has its plague, but I know that You will finally deliver me from every plague and affliction. I trust in You; let me not be put to shame. Amen.

Seven o'clock

O God, heavenly Father, who rested on the seventh day of creation, rest and keep Your Sabbath in my heart also, O only Rest and Refreshment of my soul! O Lord Jesus, let the seventh and last word that You spoke on the cross also be my last word when I am in the throes of death, that I may commit my spirit to God, Your heavenly Father. O God, Holy Spirit, heavenly prayer-master, Spirit of prayer, kindle in me constant devotion toward prayer, that in my holy Our Father, in the seven penitential psalms, and in other prayers and sighs, I may bring my concerns before God and be graciously heard by Him. Amen.

Eight o'clock

Dearest Lord Jesus, who on the eighth day of Your temporal life began to suffer pain and to shed Your blood for my sake: give me a willing spirit to bear my bodily pains patiently to Your glory, and the hope that You will preserve me and my poor soul in the water of great afflictions like the eight souls in the ark of Noah. Let me also be among the eight flocks which You declare to be blessed, that I may be poor in spirit, patient in cross, meek toward my enemies, hungry and thirsty for righteousness, merciful toward Christians in need, pure in heart, peaceable toward my neighbors, steadfast in persecution. Oh, let me advance through all the classes of the school of patience until I am promoted from the last through perseverance into the joyful high and exalted school of eternal life, where I will love and worship You with the Father and Holy Spirit forever. Amen.

Nine o'clock

O my dearest Lord Jesus, although Your suffering was unimaginable, it obtained a desirable end when You were delivered from it by a blessed death. Oh, let me also experience a blessed last hour and make my long-lasting cross to have an end! For this I will heartily thank, praise, worship, and glorify You. Now I know that You will not forget me, and my hope will not be lost forever. I am here Your member in the Church Militant. Oh, then let me also be and abide a member in the Church Triumphant hereafter. Amen.

Ten o'clock

O just and merciful God and Father, I confess with sincerity and sorrow not only that I was conceived and born in sin, but also that I have frequently transgressed Your holy Ten Commandments in thought, word, and deed, by which I have earned not only this my infirmity and other temporal crosses, but also eternal punishment in hell. But because Your dearest Son, my faithful Savior, Jesus Christ, with His precious merit and holy blood made satisfaction for all my original and actual sin, I beseech You to be gracious to me for His sake, let it remain a temporal punishment, and in Your mercy release me from the eternal. Govern me also with Your Holy Spirit, that I may separate myself from the great multitude of the ungodly and continually cultivate in myself the true faith and the Christian works which flow from it; and particularly that I may be patient in my cross, wage a good warfare, holding faith and a good conscience, and at last dwell forever in Your tents. Ease my bodily pain according to Your good will, and dispose my cross that I may be able to bear it; through Jesus Christ. Amen.

Eleven o'clock

O faithful Lord Jesus, who after Your resurrection mightily comforted Your sorrowful disciples many times and tenderly call to Yourself all the weary and burdened, promising to refresh them: visit me also in my infirmity; comfort and refresh me who find my refuge in You alone and from You seek my help and counsel. I long for that holy eve of a blessed death and desire the joyful resurrection of my flesh. Oh, let me meet with both as soon as possible; so shall I praise and glorify You forever with the Father and the Holy Spirit. Amen.

Twelve o'clock

Dearest Lord Jesus, I heartily thank You that You have granted me to know in the writings of the holy prophets and apostles that I am to believe in You and by faith have eternal life. I beseech You to keep me steadfast in the true faith and to let me have the end thereof, even eternal salvation. Make me also watchful and ready, my dearest Bridegroom, so that when You come, I may go out to meet You with joy. Bring me then with You into the heavenly wedding hall, where I will truly love and praise You. Amen.

463. Prayer of an invalid afflicted by sadness

O Lord Jesus, Comforter of all sorrowful and afflicted hearts, You were tempted in all things as we were, yet without sin, that You might have sympathy with us poor, afflicted hearts. I come to You for refuge in my grief and heavy tribulations, in which I cannot help myself nor find a way out, nor can I cast this burden on any man. Oh, help and advise me! Let me know mercy and find grace, indeed, when I most need help, comfort, and assistance! Have mercy upon me because of Your temptation and sorrow which You endured and overcame for my sake, that by Your power I, too, might overcome and endure my sorrow and sadness. Terror got hold upon my heart, the anguish of hell surrounded me, the fear of death fell upon me. Oh, let me not sink or despair! Oh, let not the smoldering wick of my faith be wholly extinguished, but stoke it by Your Holy Spirit. Speak to my afflicted soul: "I am Jesus, your help." Then I will repeat myself, and say to You, "Why are you downcast, O my soul, and disquieted within me? Wait for God, for I shall yet thank Him, because He is the help of my countenance, and my God." Amen. Help, O Jesus! Amen.

464. Prayer during a long and painful infirmity

Merciful God and Father, I, Your poor child, lie here with terrible pain, captive to the awful sickbed. As a master longs for the shade, and as a laborer for the end of his labor, so I have waited day by day (month by month, year by year) for Your help and deliverance, and the nights of my misery have multiplied. Oh, turn again to me, and be gracious to me, after hiding Your face for (so long) a season. The affliction of my heart is great, O Lord; bring me out of my distresses, look upon my sorrow and misery, and forgive me all my sins. Let my crying, groaning, and lamentation reach Your ear, and let Your heart be moved with pity for my distress. If I must continue in agony, and my affliction abide every morning, let Your grace also be renewed upon me every morning; ease my pains, and grant Christian patience, until the time appointed according to Your wisdom, when You shall take them all away. Speak but one word, O Lord, and Your poor servant (maidservant) shall be healed! You will certainly do it! — *Since Thou my God and Father art, I know Thy faithful, loving heart will ne'er forsake Thy child; I am a wretched thing of dust, on earth is none whom I can trust.*

Jesus, my precious Savior and Redeemer! I now think of Your bitter Passion, Your unspeakable sorrows. How great was Your torment and agony which You suffered for me, a poor sinner! But how great was Your patience when You obeyed Your Father even to the painful death of the cross! In the midst of Your suffering, dearest Savior, You did not open Your mouth, but were as patient as a lamb that is led to the slaughter. By this You gave me an example, that I should follow in Your footsteps. Oh, dearest Jesus, the spirit is willing in this, but the flesh within me is weak. Therefore I beseech You for Your great anguish and sorrow to plant and sustain in my heart by Your Holy Spirit a godly patience, willingly to bear all that is laid on me by the hand of my heavenly Father. Show me, O my Savior, Your holy wounds and opened side when I am distressed by my cross, and let the stings of Your Passion be the refreshment of my soul. Grant that I may be conformed to Your likeness in suffering here, that I may share Your glory in eternal joy hereafter.

O Holy Spirit, Comfort of the sorrowful and Strength of the weak! Forsake me not, and take not Your hand away from me. Have patience with my weakness, and depart not from me with Your heavenly power. Revive my poor, anxious soul with Your sweet consolations, that it may not despair under the heavy and persistent cross. When I cannot speak or pray as fitting because of my anguish and sorrow, represent me before the throne of God with groanings too deep for words. Sustain my heart always in the true faith and living hope, that even in the utmost need and extreme affliction I may nevertheless be a child of God and heir of heaven. Amen.

465. *Prayer for deliverance from the distress of infirmity*

O gracious God and Father, I know that You love me, because in this infirmity You discipline me with such fatherly care. For it is Your usual way to subject to the rod of discipline those whom You love. Yet I know that You hold my breath, my lifespan, and all my ways in Your hand. From You proceed both health and sickness; You have the power over life and death; You bring down to hell and back again. If therefore it is Your will that I should recover from this sickness, then heal me, O God, and answer my prayer! Let me see Your mercy, and deliver me from these bonds. Do good to me, and sustain me by Your Word, that I may live, and let me not be put to shame in my trust. Strengthen me, that I may recover, and let my soul live, that I may praise You. Quicken me upon the bed of my sickness, and save me from all my infirmity. Remove Your plague away from me, for I faint from the rebuke of Your hand. Hear my prayer, O Lord, and receive my cry, and be not silent at my tears. Make my flesh to spring up again as in my youth, and let me be rejuvenated as an eagle. Speak but one word, and I, Your servant (maidservant), shall be healed. But if it is better for me that I should now depart this valley of sorrows than to linger here a long season, preserve me in steadfast faith and strong hope until my blessed end, and help me to overcome all the sorrows of death, that I may pass through to life everlasting. O Lord, I am in Your hands! Whatever seems good to You, do it, even as You know shall tend to the good of my temporal and eternal prosperity; through Jesus Christ. Amen.

466. *Thanksgiving after recovery*

I thank You, Lord God Almighty, that You visited and disciplined me for my sins in such a fatherly way. Yes, Lord, it is dear to me that You have humbled me, that I might learn Your statutes. O my God, how often I thought like King Hezekiah, "Now is my age departed, and I am removed like a shepherd's tent; now like a weaver the Lord has cut off my life and ends my day before evening." Yet, my God, I see that my infirmity was not unto death, but it was for the glory of God, that You, my Lord Jesus Christ, might be glorified thereby. For You had mercy on me and tenderly came to the help of my soul. You cast behind You all my sin and delivered my life to me. How well You have used my infirmity and graciously helped me! I thank You, my God, yea, I thank You from my inmost heart, that You have restored and strengthened me, that I may behold Your holy temple once more, and go my way, and carry out my work. Were it not for Your mercy, I would have been finished long ago. Oh, how often I will remember Your chastening rod and all my life avoid and keep myself from Your wrath. Help therefore, Lord my God, that with my new health I may also begin a new life. Grant that I may bless Your name at all times, and Your praise may continually be in my mouth. Govern me by Your Holy Spirit, that I may live to Your glory and no longer devote my members to the service of sin as weapons of unrighteousness, but to the service of You, my God, as weapons of righteousness, that I may sing Your hymns as long as I live, and praise and glorify You in Your congregation. Amen.

467. A sick person's prayer for the forgiveness of sins before partaking of the Holy Supper

O gracious God and Father, I am sick in body and soul, and my misery is not hidden from You. My sincere desire is to be healed in soul, that I may be able more patiently to endure the infirmity of my body. I know and confess to You, O God, from my inmost heart, that I was not only conceived and born in sin, but also that I have passed my temporal life in many actual sins, so that there is no health in me, from the soles of my feet to the crown of my head. Therefore I well deserve my bodily infirmity in addition to other temporal punishments, indeed, eternal damnation. O good and gracious God, mercifully forgive me my sins for the sake of Your dear Son, Jesus Christ. Heal me, Lord, in my poor soul, and I shall be healed; save me, and I shall be saved. You are the Physician of Israel, but the strong have no need of a physician, but rather the weak. Therefore receive my ailing soul and make it whole. Reach Your almighty hand of grace to me, Your feeble child, and quicken me by the comforting word of Absolution, that all my sins may be forgiven me. Say to my soul, "I am your salvation." Speak but one word, and it shall be healed. When it has recovered, let the body be as You have determined in Your holy, divine will and counsel. Come then, dearest God and Father, unfathomable fountain of mercy. I do not doubt that You will also make a river of Your grace to pour and flow over my poor soul. With You there is grace and plenteous redemption. Hear the voice of my supplication, O Lord, and do not despise the wailing of my heart; through Jesus Christ. Amen.

468. Invalid's prayer after receiving the Holy Supper

Almighty God, heavenly Father, I, a poor sinner, give You my heartfelt praise and thanks that You have not only graciously pardoned all my sins for the sake of Jesus Christ, but also added as a pledge thereof Your body and blood in the Holy Supper. By what further and more trustworthy means could You assure me of Your grace and promise of eternal life? O Lord, grant me Your grace that I may never let this out of my heart, but may at all times remember that in Christ I have grace, forgiveness of sins, life, and salvation. Grant that it may strengthen my weak faith, comfort my weary conscience, quicken my mind, and produce strength in me for every good. Take into Your care my body and soul, and if it tends to Your praise and my soul's salvation, heal me not only in soul but also in body. Yet if not, give me steadfast faith, Christian patience, and firm hope until the end, that according to Your promise through Jesus Christ, whose body and blood I have received, I may obtain and possess the eternal and blessed joy of heaven. Amen.

469. An infirm communicant's prayer for a yearning for eternal life

O my dearest Lord Jesus Christ, my Life! Since You have by the partaking of Your Holy Supper and by the seal and pledge of Your body and blood assured me of eternal life, I humbly beseech You to suppress and extinguish in me all love of the world and every vain thing, to guide and turn my heart against it, that I may seek, long for, and desire only You and eternal life. Lord Jesus, You said, "In My Father's house are many mansions, and I go to prepare a place for you." Oh, what a beautiful house the house of the heavenly Father must be! Oh, when shall I be delivered from the dark house of this world and come to these heavenly mansions? You said, "I will come and take you to Myself, that you may be where I am." O my Lord Jesus, come soon, and take me to Yourself, for I have a desire to depart and be with You. I have had a foretaste in Your Holy Supper. Oh, let the joy, oh, let the longing daily grow and increase! As the hart pants for fresh waters, so my soul pants for You, O God; my soul thirsts for God, for the living God; when shall I go there, that I may see the face of God? To see You, my Redeemer, with Your Father and the Holy Spirit in eternal life, face to face, will be the highest joy, the most excellent life, the most perfect blessedness. Oh, let me go there soon, where I shall enjoy this joy, this life, and this blessedness with all the elect, there I shall eternally behold You, heartily love You, and tirelessly and unceasingly praise and glorify You. Grant and bestow this to me, dear Lord Jesus, for You are Yourself eternal Life. Amen, Amen.

470. *Comforting word of encouragement to the terminally ill, based on the three articles of the Apostles' Creed*

Dear Christian friend, according to God's will you are now in the final struggle with sin, death, the devil, and hell. Well then, wage a good warfare and hold faith, and there will be laid up for you the crown of righteousness, which the Lord, the righteous judge, will give to you on that Day (2 Tim. 4:7–9). Be strong in the Lord, and in the strength of His might. But above all, take up the shield of faith, with which you will be able to extinguish all the fiery darts of the evil one (Eph. 6:10, 16). Hold fast in your heart your Christian faith, which you learned and have confessed until this day.

You believe that God Almighty is the true Father of all who are named children in heaven and on earth (Eph. 3:5). Therefore He will also be your Father and reserve a heavenly inheritance for you.

You believe that He has made you and given you your body and soul. Neither, therefore, will He forget you, whom He created. For He hates nothing which He has made (Wis. 11:25).

You believe that the only Son of God, Jesus Christ, came into the world to destroy the works of the devil and to save sinners (1 John 3:8). Therefore you have no need to fear the devil or doubt your salvation.

You believe that Jesus Christ suffered, was crucified, and shed His innocent blood for all poor sinners. Therefore you have been cleansed by His blood from all your sins (1 John 1:7).

You believe that Jesus Christ descended into hell and destroyed it for all His believers (Hosea 13:14). Therefore the flames of hell can never touch you.

You believe that Jesus Christ rose again from the dead on the third day [Acts 10:40]. Therefore He overcame death, that you might never have to taste it and that temporal death might only be a slumber and a door to eternal life.

You believe that Jesus Christ ascended into heaven. Therefore you will also have an entrance into it. For He said to His Father, "Father, I will that where I am, they whom You have given Me may also be, that they may see My glory which You have given Me" (John 17:24).

You believe that Jesus Christ sat down at the right hand of God. Therefore you have an advocate with the Father, interceding for you in the best manner (Rom. 8:34; 1 John 2:1).

You believe that Jesus will come again to judge the unbelievers. And so long as you believe steadfastly, you will not come into judgment (John 5:24).

You believe in the Holy Spirit. Therefore He will help you in your weakness, and when you can no longer speak yourself, He will represent you before God with groanings too deep for words, crying, "Abba, dear Father!" (Rom. 8:15, 26).

You believe in the forgiveness of sins. Therefore it will be for you as you believe. God has had compassion on you. He has trodden your iniquities underfoot and cast all your sins into the depths of the sea (Micah 7:19).

You believe in the resurrection of the body. Therefore you are not burdened when imagining your death, since you will not remain in the grave but only rest in it until the happy day of your resurrection dawns [1 Thessalonians 4:14].

You believe in the life everlasting. Therefore you go out of this perishable and accursed life into an imperishable and blessed life [1 Corinthians 15:42], in which your Lord Jesus Christ has long since prepared a place for you, and will now graciously admit you to it [John 14:2–3].

Now then, go confidently and in peace in the name of your heavenly Father, in the name of your dear Redeemer Jesus Christ, and in the name of your highest Comforter, the Holy Spirit. Cling firmly to the Lamb of God who takes away the sin of the whole world (John 1:29) and say in your heart: "Lord, into Your hands I commit my spirit; You have redeemed me, Lord God of truth!" (Ps. 31:6).

The Lord, who has kept your going in to this life, also keep your going out and take you to Himself in eternal joy. Amen, in the name of Jesus Christ. Amen.

471. Sighs in the throes of death

I am a poor sinner, as You know, my dear Lord. Yet through Your dear Son, Jesus Christ, You have shown me that You will be gracious to me, forgive sin, and put away all wrath and condemnation, and You call me to believe this and not to doubt it. This is my trust, and with it I cheerfully depart. Lord, I know no one in heaven or earth to whom I can run for comfort and refuge but to You through Christ; I must depart naked of all other works and merits. Lord, I have no refuge but in Your divine embrace where the Son dwells; if I do not have that hope, it is all in vain.

472. Prayer for a blessed release through a gentle ending

O Christ, our dear Lord and Savior, be gracious to us, that we may not fall into temptation; but keep us pure, blameless, and innocent in the true faith, and deliver us from all evil by a blessed departure from this vale of misery, even from the wretched devil's kingdom and from his world. Yours be the praise and thanksgiving with the Father and the Holy Spirit forever. Amen.

473. Prayer in the fear and terror of death and hell

Dear Lord Christ, even if I do not fulfill the Law and even though sin is still present, and I am afraid of death and hell, yet I know from the Gospel that You have given and bestowed on me all Your works. I am sure that You do not lie, and You will keep Your promises in truth; and as a sign of this, I have received Baptism. [In this I confide, etc.] Since You are mine, dear God, I will readily die; for it pleases You, my Father, and death cannot hurt me; it has been swallowed up in victory. And thanks be to You, dear Lord God, who have given us the victory through Jesus Christ, our Lord. Amen.

474. A comforting prayer in our last hour

Almighty, everlasting, and merciful Lord and God, the Father of our dear Lord Jesus Christ! I am assured that You can and will keep all Your promises, for You cannot lie; Your Word is true. In the beginning You promised me Your dear and only Son, Jesus Christ, who came and redeemed me from the devil, death, hell, and sin, and then in Your gracious will and for my greater assurance bestowed on me the Sacraments of Baptism and of the Altar, in which I am invited to receive the forgiveness of sins, eternal life, and all heavenly riches. Being so invited, I have made use of them and, firmly trusting in His Word, have received them in faith. Therefore I do not doubt that I am well, safe, and at peace from the devil, death, hell, and sin. If this be my hour and Your divine will, I will happily depart this world in peace, rejoicing in Your Word. Amen.

475. Prayer in the throes of death

I am a poor sinner, as You know, my dear Lord. Yet through Your dear Son, Jesus Christ, You have shown me that You will be gracious to me, forgive sin, and put away all wrath and condemnation, and You call me to believe this and not to doubt it. This is my trust, and with it I cheerfully depart. Amen.

476. A dying husband's prayer for his family

Merciful God, faithful, heavenly Father, You are hurrying me to my end and wish to summon me to Your eternal kingdom, and I am glad to follow You there. But since I am leaving behind my dear family in great sorrow, I beseech

You for the sake of my Intercessor that You would comfort them richly in their grief, and not turn Your fatherly heart from them nor withdraw Your bountiful hand from them, but let them readily sense that You can provide for them without me no less than with me, and in due time let them blessedly follow after me to the true fatherland, where together we will praise and glorify You unceasingly in gladness. Now therefore, as You gave and entrusted them to me, I give and entrust them back to You. Dear loving Father, You will do better than this troubled flock believes; I cast all my and their cares upon You; You will provide well for them. Amen. In Jesus' name. Amen.

477. Prayer of those attending a dying man, to commend him to God

Almighty and gracious God, who sustain our life even in the midst of death and dying: turn the eyes of Your mercy, we beseech You, upon this invalid, revive him in body and soul, and mercifully forgive him all his sins. Accept for the atonement of his iniquities the offering of the innocent death of Jesus Christ, Your dear Son, in whose name he has been baptized, and washed and cleansed with His blood. Deliver him now from bodily pain and agony, shorten his sorrows, preserve him from the accusations of his conscience and all the temptations of the evil foe, that he may fight valiantly in faith and overcome. Grant him a blessed journey homeward to life everlasting and send Your holy angels to accompany him to the assembly of all the elect; in Christ Jesus, our Lord. Amen.

478. Another

O gracious God, merciful Father, our refuge, our strength, and helper in our distresses: let Your holy countenance shine upon this dying man, who is now to appear before You. Wash away all his sins, O Lord God, with the precious blood of Jesus Christ, that they may never be mentioned in the judgment! Increase his faith, deliver his soul from the dominion of the roaring lion and wicked angel. Comfort him by Your Holy Spirit, and give him to understand in this hour that You are his gracious and merciful Father, and that he is Your dear child by pure grace. Let him, whom You have so dearly purchased with Your holy blood, not perish. Take his soul up into the heavenly paradise, as You received the soul of the thief on the cross. Let his soul be carried by angels like the soul of poor Lazarus, and grant him a joyful resurrection on the Last Day. Hear us, O Father of all grace, in his stead. Hear Your dear Son, our only Redeemer and Mediator, who sits at Your right hand, interceding for him and for us all, and be gracious to us for the sake of the merits of His precious blood and bitter death. In this confidence we commend his soul into Your fatherly hand, calling upon You with the prayer which Jesus, our Savior, Himself taught and commanded us to pray: Our Father who art in heaven, hallowed be Thy name, Thy kingdom come, Thy will be done on earth as it is in heaven. Give us this day our daily bread; and forgive us our trespasses as we forgive those who trespass against us; and lead us not into temptation, but deliver us from evil. For Thine is the kingdom and the power and the glory forever and ever. Amen.

479. Brief litany with collects for the dying

O Lord: Have mercy.

O Christ: Have mercy.

O Lord: Have mercy upon this sick person.

God, the Father in heaven: Have mercy upon him.

God, the Son, Redeemer of the world: Have mercy upon him.

God, the Holy Spirit: Have mercy upon him.

Holy Trinity, everlasting God: Have mercy upon him.

O Lord: Be merciful and spare this dying person.

From the evil one: Preserve him, dear Lord God.

From the devil's cunning and deceit: Preserve him, dear Lord God.

From all evil: Preserve him, dear Lord God.

From the torment of hell: Preserve him, dear Lord God.

By Your holy incarnation and nativity: Help him, dear Lord God.

By Your mortal agony and bloody sweat: Help him, dear Lord God.

By Your cross and bitter death: Help him, dear Lord God.

By the grace of the Holy Spirit: Help him, dear Lord God.

In the hour of his death: Help him, dear Lord God.

On the Last Day: Help him, dear Lord God.

At the last judgment: Help him, dear Lord God.

We poor sinners do beseech You: To hear us, dear Lord God.

That this sick person may have consolation: Hear us, dear Lord God.

That all his sins may be pardoned: Hear us, dear Lord God.

And that after this misery he may be granted everlasting life: Hear us, dear Lord God.

O Christ: Hear us.

O Lamb of God, who take away the sin of the world: Have mercy upon this sick person, and grant him everlasting peace.

O Lord: Have mercy.

O Christ: Have mercy.

O Lord: Have mercy upon him.

Our Father who art in heaven, hallowed be Thy name, Thy kingdom come, Thy will be done on earth as it is in heaven. Give us this day our daily bread; and forgive us our trespasses as we forgive those who trespass against us; and lead us not into temptation, but deliver us from evil. For Thine is the kingdom and the power and the glory forever and ever. Amen.

Collect

Almighty, everlasting God, dear, faithful, heavenly Father: comfort and strengthen Your poor creature, and in Your loving kindness spare him; deliver him from all anguish and distress, release him in Your grace, and receive him to Yourself in Your kingdom; through Jesus Christ, Your dear Son, our only Lord, Redeemer, and Savior. Amen.

Another

Almighty, everlasting God: let the anxious sighs and lamentations of this dying person find mercy with You. Receive him into the heavenly kingdom which by grace You have prepared for him and for all believers from the foundation of the world. Graciously release him, O Lord, and when he has paid his mortal debt, comfort him forever together with Your elect; through Your dear Son, our Lord Jesus Christ. Amen.

480. Sigh when dying

I live to You, Jesus,

I die to You, Jesus,

I belong to You, Jesus;

Whether I live or die,

Save me and take me on high! Amen.

481. Prayer after a sick person has departed in the Lord

To Jesus Christ, the Lord of glory and Prince of Life, be praise and thanksgiving, for so graciously delivering this blessed man today and receiving his soul into His holy hands. May He reunite his soul and body in heavenly glory on the Last Day, and grant us together with him a blessed voyage at the time appointed by God, and quicken all afflicted hearts with sweet consolation, and keep us all in His eternal grace for the sake of His unceasing goodness and mercy. Amen, O most holy and glorious Trinity. Amen! Amen.

482. Final supplication to be read by one condemned to die

O my only Savior and Redeemer, Jesus Christ: I commend myself wholly into Your keeping! I devote my entire self to You! On You all my comfort and hope are founded. For You I long earnestly, that I may be with You. In You I will joyfully fall asleep and rise again unto life everlasting. Lord Jesus Christ, who on the cross commended Your soul and spirit into the hands of Your heavenly Father: now in my final hour I also commend my spirit into Your hands. You have redeemed me, Lord God of truth! — *With Thee, Lord, would I cast my lot; my God, my God, forsake me not! For, Lord, I am commending my soul to Thee; deliver me now and when life is ending.* — I live to You, Jesus! I die to You, Jesus! I belong to You, Jesus, whether I live or die! Amen.

INDEX

OF SELECT TOPICS

All references are to the prayer number.

a storm 385; thanks after Holy Communion 316, 317, 318, 319; thanks after overcoming temptation 399; thanks after receiving rain 377; thanks after recovery 466; thanks after successful birth 151; thanks after the Absolution 299; thanks after working 443; thanks for all benefits shown 359; thanks for Christ's Passion 330; thanks for creation 358; thanks for deliverance from affliction 447; thanks for preservation in danger 442; thanks for redemption 360; thanks for sanctification 365; thanks for the Christian Church 440; thanks for the election by grace 439; thanks for the institution of the Holy Supper 374; thanks for the love of God 438; thanks for the Office of the Keys 373; thanks for the protection of angels 441; thanks for the resurrection from the dead 366; thanks for the spiritual wedding 320; thanks for the Word of God being heard 55; thanks that God makes us worthy to pray 2; thanks when peace has been secured 448

Tongue. Restraint of the tongue 353

Travel. During travel 181; prayer for those traveling 242, 243, 245, 247; prayer of a housefather traveling 132; when about to travel 180

Trial (in court). 415

Tribulation. After overcoming tribulation 399; prayer in tribulation unto despair 392; tribulation of Satan 397

Truth. Prayer for truth 352

Unrepentance. Lament over unrepentance 282

Unworthiness. Comfort against unworthiness 4, 324, 331; lament over unworthiness 312

War. Prayer in time of war 430, 431

Watch. Prayer of a soldier while standing watch 223

Water. In distress of water 418

Weakness. Weakness of faith 387

Weather. Prayer in unseasonable weather 381, 382, 383

Widow(er). 160, 161

Wife. Prayer of a wife who has a bad husband 157, 158

Will. Doing God's will 325

Word of God. For love of the Word 340, 341; thanksgiving for the Word being heard 55

Work. Prayer before working 175; unfruitfulness in good works 323

Worry. Prayer against worry 178

Wounded. Prayer of one who is wounded 227

Young man. Prayer of a young man 164, 165

LUTHERAN
PRAYER
COMPANION

HAUSGESANGBÜCHLEIN

Hymns for Home Use

TRANSLATED FROM THE GERMAN
by Matthew Carver
and other translators as noted

CONTENTS

I. MORNING HYMNS

1. FOR EACH DAY OF THE WEEK

Beginning of the week

1

Tune: Wo Gott zum Haus nicht gibt sein Gunst.

1 Praise God! The week I now begin,
Praise God! Who good to me has been;
Praise God! His grace and faithfulness,
Each morning new, my day shall bless.

2 God grant me comfort, help, defense
From morn to eve instruct my sense,
Bless all my actions till day's end,
And keep my heart in faith unstained.

3 God thwart all causes of lament,
A sudden, evil death prevent;
And if this week my last will be,
Grant me to slumber blessedly.

4 To God the Father, God the Son,
And God the Spirit, ever one,
Most holy, blessed Trinity,
Be laud and praise eternally.

J. Olearius; tr. M. Carver.

Sunday

2

Tune: Wo Gott zum Haus nicht gibt sein Gunst.

1 Praise God! For Sunday now has come,
A new week gladdens Christendom;
This day God first created light,
This day Christ bro't true life to sight.

2 This is the day when for my sake
Christ Jesus did from death awake;
He gives me righteousness this day,
Salvation, joy, and life alway.

3 This is the day of jubilee,
Our joy for all eternity,
For we, with God now reconciled,
May each be called God's very child.

4 Lord, lead me by Your Word of life,
To heaven's gate, with glory rife:
Here let me live in holy love,
And ever give Thee thanks above.

J. Olearius; tr. M. Carver.

Monday

3

Tune: Wo Gott zum Haus nicht gibt sein Gunst.

1 Praise God! This morn has Monday bro't,
The day that God such blessings wro't!
My God the firmament did make,
And He will never me forsake.

2 What heav'nly is doth heaven seek,
To heav'n aspires the Christian meek
What changes oft must fade away,
But steadfastness remains for aye.

(cont.)

353

3 My God, preserve this mind in me
  So long as here on earth I be,
  That I may have a steadfast faith
  And persevere e'en unto death.

4 The moon is changing constantly;
  Oh, let me ever cling to Thee,
  That I, when all things pass away,
  In heaven's realm with Thee may stay!

5 To God the Father, God the Son,
  And God the Spirit, ever one,
  Most holy, blessed Trinity,
  Be laud and praise eternally.

J. Olearius; tr. M. Carver

Tuesday

4

Tune: Wo Gott zum Haus nicht gibt sein Gunst.

1 Praise God! For Tuesday sheds its ray,
  And I cannot be still this day;
  I must serve God with life and limb,
  And heart sincere, as pleaseth Him.

2 This day God parted land and seas,
  And made the plants and fruiting trees;
  Now since all this was for my good,
  Shall I not serve Him as I should?

3 God must be served by all He wrought,
  So may I seek, as well I ought,
  That all my deeds serve Him alone;
  Then is my Tuesday duty done.

4 May I a holy life possess,
  Not serving sin and wickedness:
  For he who truly here serves God
  Will ever gladly give Him laud.

5 My God, be Thou my only guide,
  Let me Thy servant true abide,
  With peace and joy take me at last
  To glory when this life is past.

6 To God the Father, God the Son,
  And God the Spirit, ever one,
  Most holy, blessed Trinity,
  Be laud and praise eternally.

J. Olearius; tr. M. Carver.

Wednesday

5

Tune: Wo Gott zum Haus nicht gibt sein Gunst.

1 Praise God! For now is Wednesday come,
  God's grace again shines on my home,
  This day God made the sun and moon
  To rule the night, the day, the noon.

2 The sun and moon their hour possess
  But Christ, the Sun of righteousness,
  Shines evermore, makes glad my heart,
  All blessedness His hands impart.

3 E'en though the sun may hide its ray,
  His gracious gleam fades not away;
  God, let me find Thy heav'nly height
  And enter in Thy joyful light.

4 There mid the angel company
  Thy glorious presence I will see;
  This grant thro' Jesus Christ Thy Son,
  My Mediator at Thy throne!

5 To God the Father, God the Son,
And God the Spirit, ever one,
Most holy, blessed Trinity,
Be laud and praise eternally.

J. Olearius; tr. M. Carver.

Thursday

6

Tune: Wo Gott zum Haus nicht gibt sein Gunst.

1 Praise God! For Thursday now is here
And fills the hearts of men with cheer,
For God, in whom each creature lives,
Fills us with joy, and blessings gives.

2 This day God filled the sky and sea
With birds and fish most wondrously;
He keeps them for us by His pow'r,
Which governs all things hour by hour.

3 This is the day when as our priest,
Christ made for us His sacred feast,
When He set forth, by His dear blood
To save us all from Satan's brood.

4 This is the day when Jesus went
To heav'n by wonderful ascent;
Who, seated at the Father's right,
Gives us a fatherland more bright.

5 His Word like thunder fills the air,
Inspiring penitence and pray'r,
And bids us from this world to call
And seek Him in His heav'nly hall.

6 This is the day of glory, when
A home is made for us in heav'n;
Oh, grant, my Savior, that I may
Behold and praise Thee there for aye!

7 To God the Father, God the Son,
And God the Spirit, ever one,
Most holy, blessed Trinity,
Be laud and praise eternally.

J. Olearius; tr. M. Carver.

Friday

7

Tune: Wo Gott zum Haus nicht gibt sein Gunst.

1 Praise God! Our Friday now begins,
The day that saw us freed from sins,
For on this day my Savior died,
And for my sins was crucified.

2 This day was Adam given breath,
Who into all the world brought death;
This day by death God's very Son,
Secured for us the heav'nly throne.

3 This day, Lord Jesus, my distress
Was in Thy death made nothingness;
Thou, Prince of Peace, my Keeper art!
Sin, devil, death, and hell depart!

4 Lord, let me know my freedom now,
And never to sin's yoke to bow;
Then, when life ends, for me there waits
A *free*-day in Thy heav'nly gates.

(cont.)

5 To God the Father, God the Son,
   And God the Spirit, ever one,
   Most holy, blessed Trinity,
   Be laud and praise eternally.

J. Olearius; tr. M. Carver.

8   Saturday

Tune: Wo Gott zum Haus nicht gibt sein Gunst.

1 Praise God! It is the day of rest,
   In all our deeds may He be blest,
   And may my heart in Him retire,
   That I may do His whole desire.

2 This day Christ rested for a time
   When He was buried for my crime,
   And thus prepared a resting-place
   In heaven's blessed realm of grace.

3 God, bring me to that rest at last
   When this my time of toil is past;
   Here comfort, concord, peace bestow,
   There glory that no end shall know.

4 To God the Father, God the Son,
   And God the Spirit, ever one,
   Most holy, blessed Trinity,
   Be laud and praise eternally.

J. Olearius; tr. M. Carver.

9   Close of the week

Tune: Wo Gott zum Haus nicht gibt sein Gunst.

1 Praise God! The week is ended now!
   To Thee in gratitude I bow,
   For granting life, this hour to see,
   And giving still Thy grace to me.

2 Praise God, whose grace and faithfulness
   Each morning new, my day shall bless!
   He strengthens me by His great pow'r,
   Gives comfort, wisdom, help each hour.

3 God, when I sin, oh, pardon me
   By Jesus' cross and misery;
   Grant blessing, peace, and gladness still,
   And rest at last from ev'ry ill.

4 To God the Father, God the Son,
   And God the Spirit, ever one,
   Most holy, blessed Trinity,
   Be laud and praise eternally.

J. Olearius; tr. M. Carver.

2. GENERAL MORNING HYMNS

10

Tune: Der lieben Sonnen Licht und Pracht.

1 To God, my soul, thank-off'rings pay,
With all thy heart's pure feeling!
The clear light drives the stars away,
This morning hour revealing.
To thee His sun displays
God's kindness, love, and grace,
Whose beauty God's own children view,
Reflected in the morning dew.

2 But vain the toil of heart or head,
Thy mercies, Lord, to number;
Which on my soul Thy love hath shed,
Through safe and balmy slumber.
Nor mind nor mem'ry knows
The good Thy hand bestows
On all whom living faith makes one
With me, and Thee, and Thy dear Son.

3 Thee, Lord, my help, my shield, I praise,
Thy faithful truth adoring;
Which shines in ev'ry morning's rays,
Anew Thy saints restoring:
All nightly perils o'er,
My heartfelt thanks I pour;
Since me and mine, the while we slept,
Thine angel-guards have watched and kept.

4 Blest God, in Christ's own lore today
May I be still proceeding;
In all I wish or do or say,
My ev'ry duty heeding!
E'en thus, in deed and will,
Thy name be honored still!
Thus may my soul find aid and health;
Thus may I help my brethren's wealth!

5 From all which flesh or soul may harm,
With guardian pow'r defend me!
And all that life or mind can charm,
With Thine own blessing send me!
Drive peril, grief afar,
Death, famine, fire, and war;
But if Thy cross is on me laid,
Give patience, comfort, peace, and aid!

6 I'll gladly take whate'er befall,
Of joy as well as sadness;
Since Thy good hand can change it all
And turn my grief to gladness;
Thou ne'er canst him forget,
Who in Thy heart is set:
O ever happy, ever blest,
He who in faith on Thee can rest!

7 Life, goods, rank, station, body, soul
I yield to Thy protection;
By Thy good pleasure guide the whole,
Resigned to Thy direction:
O guard both town and field,
Priest, warrior, lab'rer shield!
Thy Word, Thy Sacraments defend;
Give all a peaceful, happy end!

8 My God, I ne'er will let Thee go,
By earnest pray'r prevailing,
Till Thou Thy blessing wilt bestow,
The balm for ev'ry ailing;
Till meat and drink from heav'n—
Thy choicest boon—are giv'n;
Which Thy good Spirit from above
Show'rs down, thro' Jesus' dying love.

(cont.)

9 In weal or woe, whate'er betide,
I'll own Thy grace, adoring;
Me let Thy Spirit upward guide,
Through paths of gladness soaring,
In Paradise above
To praise and sing Thy love:
E'en thus, the day with God begun
From first to last in bliss shall run.

C. Scriver; tr. H. J. Buckoll.

11

Tune: Christe, wahres Seelenlicht. [Melody Appendix 2]

1 Christ, the soul's eternal Light,
Sun on Christians shining,
Face of glory, fair and bright,
Joy of spirits pining!
Lord, the sweetness of Thy grace
Springs anew each morrow;
Truly glad in Thine embrace,
I've no cause for sorrow.

2 Rouse me from the sleep of sin,
Thou, our Life from heaven,
Thy new life create within,
For, as Thou hast given
Sunlight to our earthly vale,
All with gladness filling,
Nor will my renewing fail;
Thou each day art willing.

3 Without light, we see no light;
Without God's enlight'ning,
Christ is hidden from our sight;
And our sense needs height'ning
From His shining heav'nly dew,
Jesus' sweet instruction;
Therefore, Jesus, look on me,
Turn me Thy direction.

4 Grace, O Lord, to me impart,
In Thy mercy view me,
Quicken Thou my inmost heart,
With new life endue me.
Let me taste that sweet desire
Filled with heaven's yearning;
Nothing else could joy inspire,
Or inflame its burning.

5 Let all lusts be far from me:
Pride and carnal passion,
Feasting eyes, hypocrisy—
Lord, my sense refashion,
Worldly passions to discard,
From their ruin flying;
For what they as best regard
Brings but death undying.

6 Be my light and constant stay,
Jesus, Thou my gladness,
Till shall dawn the joyful day,
When, beyond all sadness,
I, in robes of radiant white,
Soaring and rejoicing,
Sing how all God's deeds are right,
Endless praises voicing.

C. Prätorius; tr. M. Carver.

12

Tune: Wo Gott zum Haus nicht gibt sein Gunst.

1 O God Almighty, Father, Son,
And Holy Ghost on heaven's throne,
We thank Thee ere the sun arise,
At dawn we stand before Thine eyes!

2 This morn, right early, Lord, to Thee
With rev'rence due I bend the knee,
And cry to Thee with anxious care;
Thine ear incline, accept my pray'r!

3 Thy kindness, Lord, my heart shall bless,
Thy gracious guardian pow'r confess;
Since now I've passed, till morning light,
In rest and peace the darksome night.

4 I slept without a fear or doubt,
While Satan wandered round about,
Thy pow'r repelled him as I slept,
In safety was my slumber kept.

5 Through Jesus' precious blood, I pray,
Oh, keep me safe, my God, this day;
Me let Thy blessed angel-band
Attend and guard on either hand!

6 By Thee be soul and body swayed,
With all Thy Spirit's grace arrayed;
O guide me in Thy path and will,
Give pow'r for good, prevent from ill.

7 Grant grace that I may gladly do
My work and duty all day through,
In praise of Thee, and naught in vain,
And to my neighbor ev'ry gain.

8 Help me to know with sense discreet
How best to rule my hands and feet
Eyes, ears, and lips, and all my limbs,
Drive far from me all vicious whims.

9 Oh, keep from sin and shame mine heart,
That so, from evil drawn apart,
My soul to guilt I ne'er may bend,
My conscience ne'er in aught offend!

10 Keep me this day and evermore
From danger, shame, and heartache sore,
Set Thee betwixt me and my foe,
Both those unseen and those I know.

11 My ev'ry path protect today;
Let naught that's ill beset my way;
From sudden death preserve me free;
Where help I need, oh, help Thou me!

M. Behm; tr. sts. 1–3, 5–6, 11, H. J. Buckoll; sts. 4, 7–8, 10, M. Carver.

13

Tune: Lobet den Herren alle, die ihn fürchten.

1 Now let me praise Thee in this hour of morning,
O God, my Father, Thou the heav'ns adorning,
For all Thy grace to me, I come before Thee,
Here to adore Thee.

(cont.)

2 Thou to the daylight, Lord, hast kindly brought me,
  Thou through the font hast for Thy kingdom got me,
  Thou in Thy Son hast granted me remission
  Of all transgression.

3 Thou sendest down to me Thy Holy Spirit,
  To guide and teach me in a life of merit,
  That I may learn to build upon Thee solely,
  And trust Thee wholly.

4 Thou as a father ever hast sustained me,
  Ever my needs hast granted me and gained me.
  And when necessity and ills possessed me,
  Thou hast released me.

5 Thou by Thine angel hosts this night hast kept me,
  Suff'ring no ill to harm or intercept me,
  Nor any fright'ning sight from sleep to shake me,
  Stir me, or wake me.

6 Lord, with my lips and mind I'll sing and number
  Thy bounteous mercies in my hours of slumber,
  Which I have ever known, by Thy good favor,
  And shall know ever.

7 Ever defend me still, O Lord, I pray Thee,
  Through all the coming day let naught dismay me,
  Keep me from Satan's guile and arrows cunning,
  False byways shunning.

8 Help me, like all good Christians, to walk blameless,
  Safe from the passions of the world so shameless,
  Lest I pursue some evil wish or longing
  Within me thronging.

9 Lord, to Thy keeping be all things commended:
  Body and spirit be by Thee defended,
  Kinsmen and neighbor, and what things soever
  Come by Thy favor.

10 Guard and preserve all rulers in their station,
   Grant us Thy peace, success, health, and salvation;
   Graciously keep us, Lord, from shame and error,
   Danger and terror.

11 Strengthen me on this day of Thy creation
   For the important work of my vocation,
   That I may do my duty in full measure,
   All for Thy pleasure.

12 Finally grant me, when this life of sorrow
   I must depart, on this day or the morrow,
   That I may die in Jesus' death and merit,
   And heav'n inherit.

13 Thus will I prosper in my earthly station
   And soul and body see their true salvation;
   Here having conquered, there I'll find with pleasure
   Heav'n's highest treasure.

14 So grant me, Father, with the Son and Spirit
   Living and reigning, One in might and merit;
   Vouchsafe to grant Thy Yes and benediction
   To my petition.

J. Gesenius; tr. M. Carver.

14

Tune: Lobet den Herren alle, die ihn fürchten.

1 Our Lord be praising, / All His glory raising!
   Let us with joy His holy name be singing,
   Our laud and thanks unto His altar bringing;
   Praise ye Jehovah!

2 Life's primal blessing / From His hand possessing,
   Life through the night to Him we owe adoring;
   He now hath raised us, life and joy restoring:
   Praise ye Jehovah!

3 That we enjoy them / And can still employ them—
   Our mind and senses and our ev'ry member,
   Thanks do we owe for this, let us remember.
   Praise ye Jehovah!

4 By flames o'erpow'ring, / Us and ours devouring,
   From house and homestead that we've not been driven—
   We owe it to the care of God in heaven.
   Praise ye Jehovah!

(cont.)

5 That no thief, breaking / Through our doors and taking
   Our property, and us assaulting, hurt us,
   Is that He sent His angels to support us.
   Praise ye Jehovah!

6 Refuge from sadness! / Spring of all our gladness!
   Still through our life, by day, by night, direct us;
   Still may Thy love, Thy guardian wings protect us!
   Praise ye Jehovah!

7 Onward proceeding— / Thou our footsteps leading,—
   May we Thy paths still follow unimpeded!
   Still, Lord, Thy grace supply, where grace is needed!
   Praise ye Jehovah!

8 Lord, make us willing— / Thy pure Word fulfilling,—
   Good deeds and holy still to be pursuing;
   Where we are weak, help Thou, our strength renewing!
   Praise ye Jehovah!

9 Our hearts resigning, / Make us ne'er repining,
   Grow we in grace, Thy kind correction sharing,
   Through earthly trials still for heav'n preparing!
   Praise ye Jehovah!

10 Thou, Lord, descending, / Time wilt soon be ending,
   With Thee Thy saints to endless glory bringing,
   Where all Thy hosts are ever, ever singing,—
   Praise ye Jehovah!

P. Gerhardt; tr. sts. 1–2, 6–10, H. J. Buckoll; tr. sts. 3–5, J. Kelly.

15

Tune: Wer nur den lieben Gott läßt walten.

1 My God, again the morning breaketh,
   The night hath fled from earth away;
   Once more my sense of need awaketh
   When I arise to greet the day.
   My rest is o'er—sleep fled from me,
   And what I am again I see!

2 Within this lowly vale I'm dwelling,
   Where ev'ry soul must suffer need,
   Where years creep o'er, of weakness telling,
   And sin reigns over ev'ry deed.
   In Thee alone true light I see;
   Would I, my God, could perfect be!

3 Through Thee alone this morn I've risen;
   I pray Thee, Father, o'er me reign.
   Thou knowest what today must happen,
   May ev'ry work Thy praise proclaim:
   Constrain me—of Thy presence give,
   That I in all to Thee may live.

4 Remove, O Father, all my burden
   Of sin which from my bed I bring,
   And let me find Thy gracious pardon;
   Give ear to what I pray and sing,
   For if I seem but good to Thee,
   I care not how life else may be.

5 In all things help me and advise me,
   For I am simple and unwise.
   Keep me from sins that may surprise me,
   From wicked men's deceit and lies;
   Let me use well the coming day
   And do some good where'er I may.

6 Protect, O God, both soul and body,
   All those I know—all I possess,
   And when my hand to please Thee striveth,
   So let Thy grace my labors bless.
   Help, that I may in all succeed;
   I do not doubt Thy pow'r to lead.

C. Neumann; tr. sts. 1–3, 6, A. Manington; sts. 4–5, M. Carver.

16

Tune: Was willt du dich betrüben.

Thanksgiving

1 I meet the day glad-hearted
   With God, whose name be praised!
   For now the night's departed
   And day its face hath raised
   My heart, thy rest eschew!
   Acknowledge all God's graces,
   And in all times and places
   Resolve, good works to do.

Petition

2 O Lord, Thou seest clearly
   That we are sinners born,
   And cares are absent rarely
   On earth from eve to morn;
   Wherefore my heart keep pure,
   Curb what to ruin tendeth,
   And if today life endeth,
   A blessed death ensure!

Prayer

3 Whatever well may serve me,
   Send down from heaven's throne!
   O Father God, preserve me,
   And govern me, O Son!
   Grant strength, O Spirit, Lord!
   Defend and bless me ever,
   Shed Thou Thy rays of favor,
   And blessed peace afford!

Intercession

4 And Father, as Thou makest
   The sun on all to shine,
   And when Thou pleasure takest,
   Thou dost not soon resign:
   Have mercy, I implore,
   On all without exemption:
   Bring all to their redemption
   Both now and evemore!

C. Neumann; tr. M. Carver.

17

A sick person, upon waking

Tune: O Ewigkeit, du Donnerwort.

1 Now from my rest I rise again,
   To greet a day of toil and pain—
   My lot which God would give me.
   Unknowing what new grief may be
   With this new day in store for me,
   But it will not aggrieve me;
   I know full well my loving God
   Will send me not a hurtful load.

2 My burden ev'ry day is new,
   But ev'ry day my God is true,
   And bears my ev'ry sorrow;
   Ere eventide can no man know
   What day shall bring of joy or woe,
   And though it seem each morrow
   To some new path of suff'ring call,
   With God I can surmount it all.

3 How often did I scarce believe
   From each day's load to find reprieve
   And be from hence transported;
   Yet in the evening well I knew
   That Thou, Most High, didst bear me thro':
   By Thee I was escorted,
   And by Thy light was made to go
   And bear like Thee my cross of woe.

4 Since this I know, oh, wherefore sink,
   My faithless heart? And why thus shrink
   To take again thy burden?
   Bear what thou canst, God bears thy lot,
   The Lord of all, He stumbleth not;
   Pure blessing is thy guerdon,
   If thou with Him right onward go,
   Nor fear'st to tread the path of woe.

5 My heart grows strong, all terrors fly
   Whene'er I feel, O God Most High,
   Thy love doth safely hold me.
   But would I have Thee for my shield,
   No more to sin my soul must yield,
   But live as Thou hast told me;
   Thou, God, wilt never walk my way
   If from Thy paths my feet should stray.

6 But let me feel Thou guidest me,
   And, dearest God! I'll follow Thee
   In sorrow true, unfeigning;
   Then strong and dauntless in Thy might
   Against this wicked world I'll fight,
   With Thee the vict'ry gaining.
   Then bravely I can meet each day,
   And fear it not, come come what may.

7 My God and Lord, I cast on Thee
   The load that weighs too sore on me,
   The yoke 'neath which I waver;
   I lay my rank, my high command,
   In my almighty Father's hand,
   Well knowing, Lord, Thou never
   Wilt hence withdraw it, for Thy truth
   Hath let me onward from my youth.

8 To Thee my household I commend,
   For it is safe if Thou defend;
   Oh, ever watch and guard it!
   I bid my needy soul reside
   Within the cleft of Jesus' side—
   Thou never wilt discard it;
   When soul and body part at last,
   Then all myself on Thee I cast.

Anthony Ulrich; tr. sts 1–2, 4–8, C. Winkworth, alt.; st. 3, M. Carver.

18

Tune: O Christe Morgensterne. [Melody Appendix 6]

1 O Christ, Thou Star of Morning,
  Now shed Thy light abroad;
  From heav'n, the darkness scorning,
  Shine on us here, dear Lord,
  With Thy pure, glorious Word.

2 O Comfort of the lowly
  I lift my heart to Thee;
  O Christ, in grace console me,
  And pity have on me;
  I trust alone to Thee.

3 I cannot rest or slumber,
  No joy or peace I know,
  Deep wounds my soul encumber,
  And fears of pains below;
  O Christ, Thy pity show!

4 O Jesus, Lord, I love Thee,
  Son of the Father's heart,
  My hearfelt pray'r let move Thee
  Thy goodly help impart—
  The Mercy Seat Thou art.

5 Thou shed'st for me, my Maker,
  Thy blood of rosy hue;
  Make me thereof partaker,
  By grace my hope renew;
  Lord, for Thy help I sue.

6 (*Jesus*) Poor soul, if thou dost suffer
  By many a wound beset,
  Thyself to Me but offer;
  A Helper thou shalt get
  To loose thee of thy debt.

7 Forsaking sin, endeavor
  Thy Christian way to wend;
  I will refresh thee ever
  And will My Spirit lend
  To guide thee toward thine end.

8 With food I will supply thee—
  My body and My blood—
  Nor any love deny thee,
  But in true brotherhood
  Share with thee ev'ry good.

9 (*soul*) Then Jesus, I will praise Thee
  And ever sing to Thee;
  Increase my faith, and raise me
  Someday that I may see
  Eternal joys with Thee!

10 He who this hymn did sing us,
  Hath sung it passing well;
  God grant, it good may bring us
  Though living, yea, or dead,
  By Jesus' wounds so red.

B. Förtsch; tr. C. Winkworth, sts. 1–3, 9, alt.; sts. 4, 5–8, 10, M. Carver.

19

Tune: Freu dich sehr, o meine Seele.

1 Tender Jesus, thanks I give Thee
For Thy goodness through this night;
Thou hast suffered naught to grieve me,
Putting ev'ry foe to flight—
That my mortal enemy
Might no powèr have o'er me—
That I might, in health arising,
See the sun, with glad rejoicing.

2 As this night I lay in slumber,
Lord, were not Thy mercy near,
Oh, what sorrows without number
Oh, what griefs might then appear!
Satan and the wicked world
Would have then my soul assailed.
But because of Thy protection
None could cause me any affliction.

3 Jesus, Thou my Rock abiding,
Thou my Fortress, Hope, and Stay!
'Neath Thy wings of grace confiding,
May I rightly pass the day,
That, preserved from dangers all
I, without complaint or fall,
May bring all to good conclusion,
Nor be put to some confusion.

4 Take my body, soul, and senses,
Thoughts, and words, and things I do—
Any work my mind commences—
Govern them, my Refuge true!
Thou the Guide and Ruler be;
Do with me as pleases Thee;
All I am is in Thy keeping,
Living, dying, waking, sleeping.

5 Wash away my sins forever,
Jesus, by Thy precious blood;
Let me find Thy grace and favor
When afflictions round me flood;
Be my wealth, defense, and light
When all else is failing quite;
In the clefts where Thou wast riven
Let my soul her rest be given.

6 Let all those in need and anguish
Find Thy help when they implore;
In the hearts of those who languish
Comfortless, Thine essence pour.
Blessings give to each estate
Crown our land with mercy great,
Let Thine angel hosts attend us,
From all danger to defend us.

7 Oh, Lord Jesus, by Thy Spirit
Govern me and guide me here;
Let my life that form inherit
Taught me in Thy Scripture dear;
Let my conversation tend
Ever to the heav'nly end;
On the day for death appointed,
Bring me there, an heir anointed.

J. Lassenius; tr. M. Carver.

II. EVENING HYMNS

1. EVENING HYMNS FOR EACH DAY OF THE WEEK
Sunday

20

Tune: Nun ruhen alle Wälder.

1 The Sabbath now is over,
  What most I would discover
  Its Lord has given me:
  He by His truth has led me,
  With bread of life has fed me,
  And from its thirst my soul is free.

2 God by His Word indwells me;
  Now that no care compels me,
  My body, too, may sleep:
  Sins cannot now distress me,
  For Jesus' robe doth dress me,
  My eyes no anxious vigils keep.

3 Eternal Source of being,
  Now, Thy salvation seeing,
  My soul on Thee is cast:
  Thy face shines forth with favor,
  O Light of Light, my Savior,
  My gloomy doubts and fears are past.

4 Thou surely wilt be near me,
  And make a sun to cheer me,
  E'en in the midnight hour,
  Till come, with cherubs soaring,
  That brilliant Sunday morning,
  That shall all gloomy nights o'erpow'r.

5 But peaceful now my slumber,—
  Each breath will angels number
  With ever-watchful care;
  The world away is driven,
  I'll dream of God and heaven,
  And, when I wake, may find me there.

B. Schmolck; tr. sts. 1–3, 5, H. Mills, 1856, alt.; tr. st. 4, M. Carver.

Monday

21

Tune: O Jesu, treuster Heiland mein. [or Nun laßt uns den Leib]

1 O Jesus, faithful Savior mine,
  Now to my bed my steps incline;
  I go to take my rest once more:
  Do Thou Thyself secure the door.

2 In grace forgive my sins, I pray,
  Drive noxious visions far away,
  Spread over me Thy shelt'ring wing,
  And round my home Thine angels bring.

3 Now as I sleep, watch Thou and wake,
  And drive all ills and perils back,
  Let me arise, due thanks to show,
  And joyful to my labors go.

4 From fire and flood preserve my breath,
  And from a sudden, evil death;
  Keep me and ev'ry Christian soul
  From ev'ry danger safe and whole.

(cont.)

5 O Father, keep me in Thy care,
  O Son, Thy blood to cleanse me spare,
  O Holy Ghost, enlighten me,
  That I may come to heav'n with Thee.

6 And when this present life is past,
  And Thou shalt bid us cease at last—
  What rest awaits on heaven's shore
  That lasts forever, evermore!

Breslau Hymnal (ca. 1690), sts. 5–6 later; tr. M. Carver.

22   Tuesday

Tune: Wir danken dir, Herr Jesu Christ. [*LSB* 275; *TLH* 173]

1 Lord Jesus Christ, our thanks to Thee,
  That Thou hast died to set us free,
  And hast all dangers kept at bay
  By blessed angel hosts this day.

4 Thine angels ever with us be,
  To guard and keep us constantly,
  That Satan o'er us have no pow'r
  By day or night at any hour.

2 Now, Lord, we go to rest once more,
  Forgive our sins, which we deplore,
  Account them not against our soul,
  O Son of God, but make us whole!

5 From all distress of fire and flood,
  Of body and soul, save us, Lord God!
  Now in Thy name our heads we bow,
  Oh, help Thy needy children now.

3 Whate'er may happen, we are Thine,
  Bought by Thy five dear wounds divine;
  To Thee we live, to Thee we die,
  Thy sons we are eternally.

6 Amen! Amen! And so, good night;
  God's angel keep us by his might;
  To God be praise eternally,
  We take our rest from sorrow free.

N. Selnecker; tr. M. Carver

23   Wednesday

Tune: Christ, der du bist der helle Tag.

1 Day follows day, and morning eve,
  While yet to this brief life I cleave;
  Time passeth on; life too must flee,
  But Thou, O God, art still with me.

4 My hope on Thy dear grace is set,
  For it is greater than my debt;
  To Thee I'll cling and not let go
  Till Thou Thy blessing wilt bestow.

2 Thou grantest me to put to rest
  So many days, by prayers blest;
  And when some load weighs heavily,
  'Tis Thou who then dost quicken me.

5 Oh, Father, bless my hour of rest;
  Go with me, that my sleep be blest,
  As long ago dear Jacob slept
  While angel troops their vigil kept.

3 Yet is my conversation not
  Directed by Thy will and thought.
  I am not worthy that Thy grace
  Should shine so long upon my face.

6 O faithful Jesus, be my stay,
  Tread down the devil's head this day,
  That, where his cunning plots I meet,
  He soon is lying at my feet.

7 Good Spirit, never let Thy light
  E'en in the darkness fade from sight;
  My mind and senses watchful make,
  That though I sleep they still may wake

8 Thine, Holy Trinity, be praise,
  Whose own I am for endless days!
  Oh, if this night my last will be,
  I live and die alone to Thee!

B. Schmolck; tr. M. Carver

Thursday

24

Tune: Jesu, meine Freude.

1 God, Thy vigil keeping
  While Thy sheep are sleeping,
  Shepherd, Staff, and Stay:
  How Thy deep affection
  Served as our protection
  Through this passing day!
  Still this night / Be sharp Thy sight,
  Let Thy circling hosts attend me,
  Lest some ill offend me.

2 By Thy grace from heaven
  Let all foes be driven
  From my place of rest;
  Let my bed be pillowed
  By forgiveness billowed
  From Thy loving breast;
  For Thy Son / My soul hath won,
  From the prowling fiend concealed me,
  By His stripes hath healed me.

3 Let not those I cherish
  Suffer pain, nor perish,
  They are mine and Thine;
  In Thy mercy fold us,
  In Thy kindness hold us
  Without cause to pine;
  Thou with me / and I with Thee—
  Thus in peace I'll slumber ever,
  From Thee parted never.

4 Watch me till the morrow,
  Shut out ev'ry sorrow,
  Be the lock and bar!
  In Thy wings, Defender,
  Take Thy hatchlings tender,
  Chasing dangers far;
  By Thy shield / of peace concealed,
  We will fear not Satan's clutches;
  Here he cannot touch us.

5 Though my bed this even
  Be a tomb new-graven,
  And I yield my breath—
  Since Thou hast commanded
  When my time is ended,
  I must meet my death,
  I will not / oppose my lot:
  If in Jesus' wounds I'm lying,
  I am always dying.

6 Come, then, eyes, be closing,
  Lips, contently dozing,
  Naught shall you offend!
  Soul and body sleeping,
  Keeper, to Thy keeping
  Hereby I commend!
  Then good night! / Keep me in sight,
  And should life tomorrow leave me,
  Still Thou wilt receive me.

B. Schmolck; tr. M. Carver.

Friday

25

Tune: O Jesu Christ, wahr Gottes Sohn. [Br 79, p. 60f.]

1 When in the morning I awake
  And in the night my slumber take,
  I lift my eyes, O Lord, to Thee;
  Lord Jesus Christ, my Keeper be!

2 Thy hands, Thy feet, Thy piercèd side
  Be for the bed where I reside;
  My body, soul, my ev'ry good
  Are safe beneath Thy holy blood.

3 Thy blood defend me, as the blood
  That from the lamb in Goshen flowed;
  And whether I may wake or sleep,
  Thy station ever near me keep!

4 If in Thy holy blood I dwell,
  I fear not devil, death, or hell;
  Where'er I be, art Thou with me,
  My cross and fortune lie in Thee.

5 Alive or dead, Thine own am I!
  This be, when comes my hour to die,
  My final, firm confession still:
  My faithful God so grant and will!

Leipzig Hymnal, 1582; tr. M. Carver.

Saturday

26

Tune: Der Tag hat sich geneiget [Br 203, p. 160f.]

1 The day is at its ending,
  The night is under way.
  To God your blessing sending,
  Thank Him for grace this day
  Who kept us in His favor;
  Of body and of soul
  May He remain our Savior
  And keep them ever whole.

2 Naught long on earth resideth,
  Here is no constancy,
  God's love alone abideth
  And lasts eternally,
  By all 'tis freely taken;
  God ne'er forsakes His own;
  My hope a ground unshaken,
  Has found in Him alone.

3 He is my mighty tower,
  On earth my sole repose;
  Man's life is like a flower
  That in the meadow grows.
  The dew falls on the morrow,
  Its color blushes fair,
  But soon, cut down in sorrow,
  It withers and is bare.

4 Forgive, dear Lord, I pray Thee,
  My sins and vicious crimes,
  For which, when I betray Thee,
  I seek Thy grace oft-times.
  If Thou shouldst mark my errors,
  O Lord, how could I stand?
  Guilt, filling me with terrors,
  Would endless death demand.

5 Show pity and compassion
  Through Jesus Christ, I pray!
  Release me from transgression,
  Thy Spirit send alway,
  To teach me and prepare me,
  To lead me, yea, to prod,
  Lest I should stray or tarry,
  And lose the path of God

6 My body, soul, and living,
  Name, house, and property—
  All that is of Thy giving,
  Lord, I commit to Thee,
  And to Thy holy keeping!
  In mercy me defend,
  Let death be but a sleeping,
  Thy Kingdom be my end!

7 My inmost heart now raises
  In this fair evening hour
  A song of thankful praises
  To Thine almighty pow'r,
  And ever would adore Thee!
  O God, protect us here,
  That we may sing Thy glory
  Nor doubt that Thou art near.

P. Oderborn; tr. M. Carver.

2. GENERAL EVENING HYMNS

27

Tune: Der lieben Sonnen Licht und Pracht. [Br. 202, p. 160]

1 The lovely sun hath ushered west
  The day in pomp and splendor;
  The world is settled to its rest;
  Now, soul, thy duty render:
  To heaven's gate draw near,
  And with thy hymn appear;
  Thine eyes, and heart, and senses let
  On Jesus be devoutly set.

2 Ye brilliant stars in heaven shine
  And cast your beams so brightly,
  Ye fill the night with candles fine
  That none can number rightly;
  Yet in my heart more clear
  Shines heaven's Candle dear:
  My Jesus, glory of my soul,
  My prize, protector, light, and goal.

3 Now all in slumber's net is caught,
  Both man and beast are sleeping;
  Yet One there is who sleepeth not,
  Who still His watch is keeping,
  No rest will Jesus take,
  His eye for thee doth wake
  So now, my heart, thy Keeper own,
  Let not thy Jesus watch alone.

4 O Jesus, do not scorn my song,
  Though poorly I may sing it;
  My heart for peace must ever long,
  Until to Thee I bring it.
  I'll bring it as I may,
  Oh, gracious be, I pray!
  'Tis meant with love most genuine,
  O Jesus, dearest friend of mine.

(cont.)

5 With Thee I now to sleep will go,
  My soul to Thee commending,
  Thou shalt, my Keeper, watch also
  With constant, close attending;
  No trouble will I fear,
  No, nor death's exit drear!
  For he who down with Jesus lies
  With Jesus gladly will arise.

6 Ye haunts of hell, disperse, begone,
  This house no more molesting!
  For it is home to Jesus' throne,
  So leave it safely resting;
  The angels' Keeper strong
  Protects it from all wrong;
  And heaven's host is my defense,
  So fly, ye devils all, from hence!

7 Now let me in Thine arms be laid
  And sleep in Thine affection!
  Thy watchfulness shall be my bed,
  Thy mercy, my protection,
  My pillow be Thy breast,
  My dream, that bliss of rest
  That from Thy cloven side outflows
  Which in my heart Thy Spirit blows.

8 At night, as oft my blood may thrill,
  My spirit will embrace Thee;
  As long as my heart stirreth still,
  I long once more to praise Thee,
  Yea, I would fill the sky
  With such a thund'rous cry,
  "O Jesus, Jesus, Thou art mine,
  And I am now and ever Thine!"

9 Faint members, take thy sweet repose;
  May peace and stillness fill it!
  Ye drooping eyelids, softly close,
  For so thy God doth will it.
  And with these words resign:
  "Lord Jesus, I am Thine!"
  Then wilt thou close the day aright!
  O Jesus, Jesus, now, good night!

C. Scriver; tr. M. Carver.

28

Tune: Christe, der du bist Tag und Licht.

1 To God be praise! The day is done,
  Wherefore to Him my thanks I own
  That I have lived the night to see,
  And yet His grace abounds to me.

2 Be merciful and patient, Lord,
  Forgive the debts which I've incurred;
  Thy holy angel keep me e'er
  From danger, trouble, and despair.

3 Grant me, when comes the morning-hour,
  To rise in joy, renewed in pow'r,
  That I may spread Thy praise abroad
  And ever worship Thee, my God!

J. Olearius; tr. M. Carver.

A sick person's evening hymn

29

Tune: Wenn wir in höchsten Nöten sein.

1 Praise be to God, the day is o'er!
 Frail body, now Thy praise once more,
 With feeble hands and spirit faint,
 To God the Highest Good present.

2 Now, heart and lips, your prizes bring,
 Thank-off'rings to the Father sing,
 By whom ye have your burden borne
 While yet another day has worn.

3 For Satan tried within his sieve
 To sift these ailing limbs that grieve—
 My fleshly burden, borne within—
 By lack of patience, love of sin.

4 Yet, Father, did Thy grace the while
 Protect me from his craft and guile;
 Though he came nigh, my soul to charm,
 He had no chance to do me harm.

5 When, by this heavy weight oppressed,
 Which Thou hast laid upon my breast,
 The flesh its frailty often told,
 Thou didst my spirit still uphold.

6 Thou didst sustain my light of faith,
 Lest ever it should sink to death,
 Didst wake in me true sighs and pray'r,
 That I might speak more free from cares.

7 So poured I out my heart to Thee,
 E'en in my painful agony;
 Oft quiet hours assuaged my soul,
 Though yet my body is not whole.

8 Yea, though my body still is pained,
 Another day of life I've gained,
 Was furnished with my ev'ry need,
 And was not snatched away with speed.

9 With thanks, I freely must declare
 Myself unworthy of the share
 Of grace and faithfulness bestowed,
 Of all the gifts from Thee, O God!

10 A feeble child, this day I fell
 In sins more oft than I can tell,
 Yet, tender Father, I would cease:
 Have mercy on me! Grant release!

11 Forgiven be the sins I've done
 As here, so there before Thy throne!
 O Father, call me son again
 Thro' Thy Son's bloody sweat and pain.

12 My soul and body heartily
 I now commend, O Lord, to Thee.
 Repel by watchful guard this night
 All evil causes of affright.

13 Say to my sorrows, Be at rest;
 Or else, if not, grant patience blest;
 Thy night of grief my solace make
 When sickness would my slumber break.

14 Lord, if Thou wilt, 'tis in Thy pow'r,
 To let me see the morning-hour;
 But if Thou say it please not Thee,
 Then as Thou wilt, so let it be!

15 Then if this night must be my last,
 In pleasant sleep let it be passed!
 When I life's finished course must leave,
 My spirit, Jesus, Lord, receive!

16 Now in Thy wounds to bed I go;
 Thy purple mantle o'er me throw;
 My pillow be Thy thorny crown,
 Thy blood, O Son of God, my gown!

(cont.)

17 In Thee I fall asleep content,
   And pray that those 'neath crosses bent,
   Who like myself await the light,
   By Thee may have a blest good night!

Weimar Hymnal [J. Schwentner]; tr. M. Carver.

30

Tune: Geduld, die solln wir haben. [*TLH* 544]

1 Come, in this hour of evening,
   Let us with gladsome voice
   To God all praise be giving,
   And in His grace rejoice,
   Which safe till now hath brought us
   And kept us from all woe.
   Now may His grace allot us
   Forgiveness for our sins.

2 For any good effected,
   Lord, Thine be all the praise,
   To Thee all thanks directed.
   All honor Thine always.
   We praise Thy gifts so plenteous
   And further Thee we pray,
   Good rest this night to grant us,
   And safety where we stay.

3 Lord, with Thy hand, o'erveil us
   Whilst we in slumber lie,
   Lest e'er the foe assail us,
   Or seek to terrify
   With fire or tempest raging,
   Where'er his army rides;
   Our warfare for us waging,
   Defend us on all sides!

4 In sleep a type of dying,
   And picture clear we have:
   When we asleep are lying
   The bed is then our grave.
   While death its form displayeth,
   Now sight, now hearing dims,
   Not yet our flesh decayeth,
   But life soon fills our limbs.

5 Our pray'r is therefore ever,
   O God of truth and faith,
   Thy people to deliver,
   From sudden, evil death;
   Thy help always supplying,
   Let each, with trusting heart,
   Be well prepared for dying,
   Nor from Thy Son depart.

6 Those whom for fondness tender
   We fear to leave behind—
   Be Thou their good Defender,
   Their Father true and kind;
   Till all who trust the Savior
   In sainted company
   May praise Thy name forever;
   Oh, grant that it may be!

J. Mühlmann; tr. M. Carver

31

Tune: Werde munter, mein Gemüte.

1 Now our weary eyelids, drooping
'Neath the weight of labors, close,
And the body's members, stooping,
Greet their evening-tide repose.
For the dark and gloomy night
Hath o'ercast day's splendor bright
With her ocean, deep and tangled,
And the sky with starlight spangled.

2 Ah, consider, ere thou slumber,
O thou spirit in my breast,
What transgressions thee encumber,
'Gainst thy Maker's high behest!
Hast thou angered Him today?
Oh, repent, repent, and pray,
That He graciously would pardon
And relieve thy sin's due burden.

3 Say: From Thee, Lord, naught is hidden,
All those actions are not veiled,
Which defy what Thou hast bidden;
In my duties I have failed,
O my God, my labor's end
I did not with care attend
But Thy way I have forsaken
And in shame my own have taken.

4 Grant me, Lord, Thy grace and favor,
Give me not my just reward.
Hold me in Thy keeping ever,
Thy beloved Son regard,
Who did full atonement make;
Father, Him my Ransom take:
He endured with humble spirit
What my wicked actions merit.

5 Open wide Thy gate of graces,
Send Thy watch, my soul to guard,
Lest the devil's spirit-races,
Nor the grave, so cold and hard,
Nor the evil, which by night
Seeks to steal our life outright,
May by any net ensnare me,
Nor some wicked vision scare me.

6 Ever, Lord, on Thee relying,
Soft and gentle be my rest!
Holy thoughts be Thou supplying,
Soon as slumber fills my breast.
Bid Thou yet my spirit wake,
Still its course right heav'nward take,
Till the morn new light is pouring,
Man from sleep to life restoring.

7 Father, Thou, in heav'n abiding,
Honored be Thy name, Thy sway!
May Thy will our hearts be guiding;
Daily bread vouchsafe today!
Pardon all our load of sin;
Pour Thy grace and love within;
Break temptation's fatal powèr;
Shield us in the evil hoùr!

J. Franck; tr. sts. 1–5, M. Carver; sts. 6–7, H. J. Buckoll.

32

Tune: Herzlich tut mich verlangen.

1 Now in God's name I've ended
My work for one more day;
The sun, with glory splendid,
Conceals its final ray;
Its course is now completed,
It sinks to slumber blest;
So I, with thanks indebted,
Go to my evening rest.

2 My eyes, hands, heart, and spirit,
O Son of God I pray,
Accept by Thy good merit
As wages due this day;
At work Thou wast my neighbor
In all my tasks assigned,
Hast helped me in my labor,
And ruled my heart and mind.

3 My head Thou, Lord, hast strengthened,
My hand with pow'r endued;
Thine hours of blessing lengthened
The source of ev'ry good;
Thus all my toil succeedeth
My trade is forward brought
'Tis Thee all labor needeth,
Without Thee all's for naught.

4 For this I will adore Thee
And praise with all my heart,
And earnestly implore Thee
Thy mercy to impart,
And hear this hour of even
My Vespers pray'r to Thee,
And let Thy grace be given
To work all good in me.

5 In many a generation
Thou didst at evening-tide
Do good unto Thy nation,
When they on Thee relied
With hearts in Thee confiding;
So vouchsafe now to do,
To those in faith abiding
Thy benefits renew.

6 Once from the ark forth faring
A dove by Noah sent,
Returned, a message bearing,
When daylight far was spent;
An olive leaf it carried,
A blessed word of peace,
From which he was assurèd
God's wrath was now to cease.

7 Two angels, high and holy,
To Lot at eve came down,
Charged as his guardians duly
Against the wicked town;
The prophet they, sustaining,
Saved from their evil spell
Ere came God's judgment raining,
And fire and brimstone fell.

8 Likewise, we hear reported
How God Elijah kept,
And fowl his hunger thwarted
While famine round him swept.
For ravens, eve and morning
Upon the seer did wait,
With bread and flesh adorning
His humble supper plate.

9 So, Lord, do Thou renew us
  Each morn and eve with bread
  And all things needful to us
  By which life here is sped;
  Thine angel also send us
  To break the craft and snares
  Of Satan; so defend us
  From threats and noisome cares.

10 Receive our supplication
  O faithful God and Lord,
  From need and conflagration
  Be Thou our city's guard;
  While nations rage together,
  And stir up war and strife
  Send down like gentle weather
  Peace in our time of life.

11 Foes threaten with their terror
  And hide Thy Word of grace,
  And Satan works great error
  Its glory to efface;
  Stay, Lord, with splendor gracious,
  With grace and comfort pure;
  Preserve Thy Word so precious,
  And we will be secure.

12 Herewith, therefore, be ended
  The day with its affairs,
  Yet with this last petition:
  Lord, end at last these cares,
  And bring that Sabbath morning
  Which countless years shall know,
  Yea, which endures forever!
  Amen, may it be so!

M. Ziegenspeck; tr. M. Carver.

III. THE WORD OF GOD

33

Tune: Allein auf Gottes Wort will ich. [Br 195, p. 155]

1 God's Word alone can e'er afford
  Sure ground for faith's foundation;
  It is a treasure from the Lord,
  Brings trust for full salvation.
  No human wisdom can compare
  With that of God's own giving,
  What God's Word clearly doth declare
  Sufficeth for our living.

2 On God and His pure Word alone,
  My heart can rest confiding;
  From its bright pages light is thrown,
  Our pilgrim footsteps guiding.
  O God, let no false doctrine turn
  My heart from true devotion;
  O fire my soul, that it may burn
  For truth, with strong emotion.

3 In God alone I put my trust,
  On His rich care depending;
  He will ward off each deadly thrust,
  'Gainst Satan's craft defending.
  By Thy dear Word, uphold me, Lord,
  And let me keep it purely,
  Against the devil's wrath and sword
  And wiles, preserved securely.

4 In Christ alone, th' eternal Son
  True God from everlasting,
  One with the Father on the throne
  My hope and trust are resting:
  Him to this world the Father sent—
  To all men here residing,
  For all our sins a testament,
  A sacrifice providing.

(cont.)

5 In Christ alone my comfort stands
   Who died for me, to save me,
   From death by His own bloodied hands,
   Salvation thus He gave me.
   My sins He bore, redemption won,
   That so I might receive it;
   The Father sees what He hath done;
   God, help me to believe it!

6 'Tis Christ alone who did this thing
   And reconciled the Father.
   No human work can succor bring,
   Though fairer than all other;
   Christ only as my wealth I own,
   My life eternal bringing;
   Works serve my neighbor's good alone,
   As fruit from faith up springing.

7 And this pure doctrine comes alone
   From God the Holy Spirit
   Who to the Church doth make it known
   By virtue of Christ's merit.
   It is not gained by secret art,
   Nor mind nor learning clever,
   Free will does naught, the captive heart
   But ever hangs in error.

8 God through His Spirit makes alone
   This good in us to flourish
   By which the will in us is grown
   And which the deed doth nourish,
   The man, to good both dead and blind,
   Seeks not for God nor riseth;
   By sin corrupted in his mind,
   He nothing good deviseth.

9 God's Spirit and His Strength alone
   The heart to good compelleth.
   The second birth by God is done,
   The way to truth it telleth;
   O God my Lord, enlighten me,
   To Thee my heart be bending,
   In Thy Word keep me blessedly
   Until my life is ending.

10 May God the Father and the Son
   And Holy Spirit grant me
   That by my faith His praise be done,
   And in that faith so plant me
   That flesh to spirit yield in faith
   With fruit for demonstration.
   Lord Christ, save me in throes of death
   And bring me to salvation.

J. Walther; tr. sts. 1–3. C. A. Miller; sts. 4–10, M. Carver.

34

Tune: Gott des Himmels und der Erden.

1 Lord, I bless Thy gracious mercy,
   Goodness, faithfulness, and truth,
   Who hast brought me, poor, unworthy,
   To this world, and since my youth
   Raised me where Thy people lives,
   Where Thy Word salvation gives.

2 Oh, what pastures rich and pleasant
   Here within Thy Church I've known!
   Where the Gospel, good and pleasant,
   Life and peace and joy hath shown.
   Fair the light and sweet to eye
   Which the thousands never see.

3 Heathen men, no truth possessing,
   Of their speechless gods inquire,
   Jews, who lack the true Light's blessing,
   Stand in blindness as a mire—
   Christians, too, a man may find
   In their superstitions blind.

4 Blest am I to be a bearer
   Yea, and reader, of Thy Word!
   Thus I'm blinded by no error;
   For Thy books the truth record;
   Yea, they are Thy brilliant light
   On the blind bestowing sight.

5 Who would read it not nor hear it,
　Lives on earth as though a beast.
　Only those taught by the Spirit
　Come to Thee and share Thy feast;
　Knowledge is His gift alone
　Who salvation maketh known.

6 In the dark, oh, do not leave me
　Like the blinded flock that strays!
　But Thy Word forever give me,
　Light thereby my heart always!
　Let it be my quick'ning meat
　Like as milk and honey sweet.

7 Then may I in light forever
　As a child of Christ proceed,
　More like Thee in each endeavor,
　Glad in faith and chaste in deed;
　O Lord Jesus, by Thy blood
　Mine is now and ever good!

E. G. Woltersdorf; tr. M. Carver.

35

Tune: Lobt Gott, ihr Christen allzugleich.

1 Praise God the Lord, ye sons of men,
　Before His highest throne;
　His Word doth show us heav'n again
　Through Jesus Christ, His Son.

2 What God at sundry times of old
　Spake through the prophets blest
　And was in divers manners told
　Is now made manifest.

3 His Son Himself to us doth show
　The way to blessedness,
　That we, thro' Him, our God may know
　And heav'nly joy possess.

4 Here is the truth and here the light
　And dayspring which He gave,
　For all God's words are true are right,
　And He delights to save.

5 And when the world shall pass away
　This still shall be my lot:
　The Word of God endures for aye
　And He forsakes me not.

6 To God the Father and the Son
　And Holy Ghost be praise—
　One God supreme on heaven's throne
　Forever and always.

Unknown; tr. M. Carver.

36

Tune: Erhalt uns, Herr, bei deinem Wort.

1 O God, Thou highest Hiding-place,
　Grant that Thy Holy Word by grace
　May pierce us deep from ear to heart
　And so its pow'r and form impart.

2 Its pow'r is but the faith alone
　Which Jesus Christ as Lord doth own;
　Its form is but the works of love
　By which we Christ's disciples prove.

(cont.)

3 Work in us all, dear Lord, that we
May in Thy knowledge constantly
Grow stronger, by Thy Spirit blest,
And find at last in Thee our rest.

K. Huber; tr. M. Carver

37

Tune: Herzlich tut mich verlangen.

1 How blest are they who cherish
Christ and His heav'nly Word!
They shall not yield, nor perish
By Satan's bloody sword;
For where the Lord is dwelling
His own shall hold their ground,
And theirs is life excelling
Who on this Rock are found.

2 Have wayward trails amused thee
And lured thee from Life's road?
Have worldly lies confused thee?
Come, here's the Word of God,
Wherein the course is given,
Life's highway true and tried;
This, if thou wilt to heaven,
Must be thy faithful guide.

3 Hast thou endured great crosses,
Yea, art thou sorely fed
On troubles, needs, and losses?
Leave not God's Word unread!
This Word shall so renew thee
That, should both earth and hell
Endeavor to subdue thee
They never shall prevail.

4 Art thou in blindness tumbling,
And wearied by the blows,
'Gainst ev'ry block of stumbling?
God's Word can give repose;
The blind it can enable
To find their way again
To highways straight and stable,
From erring paths of sin.

5 Yea, though thy walk be tending
Through valleys dark and drear,
To realms of death descending,
Come, see God's Word is here—
A rod for thy salvation,
A staff to comfort thee;
When Satan sends temptation,
'Twill keep thee mightily.

6 Within me, Jesus, nourish
Love for Thy saving Word,
And let my study flourish;
Oh, grant me, gracious Lord,
That it may aid me ever
And in my heart take root,
And mid the cross's fever,
With patience bear its fruit.

Anna Sophia, Landgravine of Hessia; tr. M. Carver.

IV. HOLY BAPTISM

38

Tune: Wer nur den lieben Gott läßt walten.

1 Baptized into Thy name most holy,
　O Father, Son, and Holy Ghost,
　I claim a place, though weak and lowly,
　Among Thy seed, Thy chosen host.
　Buried with Christ and dead to sin,
　Thy Spirit now shall live within.

2 My loving Father, Thou dost take me
　To be henceforth Thy child and heir;
　My faithful Savior, Thou dost make me
　The fruit of all Thy sorrows share;
　Thou, Holy Ghost, wilt comfort me
　When darkest clouds around I see.

3 And I have vowed to love and fear Thee
　And to obey Thee, Lord, alone;
　Because the Holy Ghost did move me,
　I dared to pledge myself Thine own,
　Renouncing sin to keep the faith
　And war with evil unto death.

4 My faithful God, Thou failest never,
　Thy cov'nant surely will abide;
　Oh, cast me not away forever
　Should I transgress it on my side!
　Though I have oft my soul defiled,
　Do Thou forgive, restore, Thy child.

5 Yea, all I am and love most dearly
　I offer now, O Lord, to Thee.
　Oh, let me make my vows sincerely
　And help me Thine own child to be!
　Let naught within me, naught I own,
　Serve any will but Thine alone.

6 Depart, depart! Thou Prince of darkness!
　No more by thee I'll be enticed.
　My conscience, tho' it may be tarnished,
　Is sprinkled with the blood of Christ.
　Away, vain world! O sin, away!
　Lo! I renounce you all this day.

7 And never let my purpose falter,
　O Father, Son, and Holy Ghost,
　But keep me faithful to Thine altar
　Till Thou shalt call me from my post.
　So unto Thee I live and die
　And praise Thee evermore on high.

J. J. Rambach; tr. sts. 1–5, 7, C. Winkworth, st. 6, ELHB, alt.

39

Tune: Es wollt uns Gott genädig sein.

1 O what a prize beyond compare
  Thou, Lord, Thy children givest!
By blood and water, treasures rare,
  Thou sinful men receivest!
Three things in earth do testify:
  The water, blood, and Spirit,
Which three agree, and lift us high
  By Jesus' perfect merit
    To life of heav'nly gladness.

2 By Thee this very Sacrament
  Was hallowed and empowered,
That, as Thou wast to Jordan sent
  And with its waters showered
At John's own hand, so by Thy blood
  In Baptism we are given
A cleansing and a promise good
  That such great things of heaven
    Can work in us weak beings.

3 We by this Sacrament are brought
  And in Thy Church implanted,
And after Thee, by whom 'tis wrought,
  The name of Christian granted,
Which in Thy Book Thou dost record;
  This bath and washing truly
Hath cleansed our sins in Thy true Word;
  Henceforth Thy Spirit duly
    Will plant Thy love within us.

4 Lord, to Thy kingdom we are come
  By this Thy cov'nant gracious,
Where soul and body find a home
  And yet a feast more precious.
Thou hast by this pure, cleansing bath
  Adorned us with such wonder,
That henceforth neither spite nor death
  From us can ever sunder
    Thy goodly grace and favor.

5 The Lord makes heirs of hell to drown
  And heirs of mercy raises;
This is the Christian's highest crown,
  Deserving of all praises;
Yea, Christ Himself with all that's His,
  His blood, and death victorious,
By grace our property now is—
  His gift to us most glorious,
    To live with Him forever.

6 He also gave us graciously
  The sonship of salvation
And cast into the deepest sea
  Our sin and our transgression.
What pow'r have devil, death, and hell,
  Which always strove against us?
Christ hath o'ercome all these well,
  And from all sins hath cleansed us,
    And here we find salvation!

7 As branches, Lord, in Thee, the Vine,
  May we good fruit be bearing,
And, zealous be for realms divine,
  All worldly things forswearing;
Let us by honest penitence
  With Thee be daily dying
As the old Adam must go hence
  By thorough mortifying,
    If we would heav'n inherit.

8 Grant that we nevermore neglect
  This cov'nant, nor defile it,
Nor brazen heart this gift reject
  Nor brazen mouth revile it.
May Baptism in affliction be
  Our joy and consolation—
E'en in our final agony,
  That, leaving worldly sadness
    We may instead gain heaven.

J. Rist; tr. M. Carver.

V. HOLY COMMUNION

40

Tune: Ich hab mein Sach Gott heimgestellt

1 I know a fair and handsome flow'r,
In which I take great pleasure.
My heart is its adoring bow'r—
My precious flow'r!—
Its beauty none can measure.

2 This flow'r, it is the Word divine,
Whom God to us hath given.
Upon the narrow way doth shine
That light divine,
To endless life in heaven.

3 It is the way, the light, the door,
The truth and life forever.
Here sorry hearts which sin abhor,
And grace implore
Are pardoned by God's favor.

4 He says to all, "Come unto Me
Ye weary!" beck'ning sweetly:
"All that your heart desires, I see,
Believe ye Me,
And I will heal completely."

5 "Take, eat, this is My Body true
Which for your sake is given
And with it all My bounties, too;
Believe and do,
Rememb'ring Me, the riven."

6 "Take, drink; this is My very Blood
Poured out for you, to save you—
For sin a satisfying flood
That pleases God:
Do oft what here I gave you."

7 We pray Thee, O Lord Jesus Christ,
By all Thy suff'ring, hear us!
Since Thou for us wast sacrificed,
O Jesus Christ!
Abide Thou always near us.

8 Embrace us as Thy children dear
That we may praise Thee ever,
Thy Word confessing without fear
Both far and near
Through Jesus Christ our Savior.

B. Förtsch; tr. M. Carver.

41

Tune: Herr Jesu Christ, meins Lebens Licht.

1 Now in God's name I go my way
Unto the Lord I serve each day
That He may show me ev'ry good,
And feed me with His flesh and blood.

2 As countless angels circle me
Filled with great longing, Him to see;
Shall I not come with godly fear,
Worthy before Him to appear?

3 My carnal eye, Lord, cannot see
Nor can my reason let it be;
Yet faith can here salvation view
In flesh and blood, which life imbue.

4 Sin's poisons all my frame pervade:
Therefore this antidote was made
To be my soul's great help and good:
Such pow'r is in Thy flesh and blood.

(cont.)

5 I am a patient, helpless, poor,
　My fev'rish heart is burning sore,
　Wounds fill my body and my soul—
　Thy flesh and blood let make them whole.

6 Because I'm weak, I come to Thee
　Afflicted with great misery,
　I thirst and hunger, and implore:
　Thy flesh and blood may me restore!

7 All poor and needy am I here,
　The wealth I prize and hold most dear
　Is heaven's treasure, giv'n for me—
　Thy flesh and blood my riches be!

8 My spirit without Thee is blind;
　The good I cannot seek or find,
　But evil do, and Thee neglect;
　Thy flesh and blood my heart direct!

9 I yearn not for God's discipline,
　But wayward go by wanton sin;
　Far from the blessed way I live;
　Thy flesh and blood new blessing give!

10 I have been cast away in wrath,
　And bound to suffer endless death
　For all my dreadful sins and debt;
　Thy flesh and blood shall save me yet.

11 To heaven take me, Lord, on high
　My soul and body glorify!
　This is my longing and my care:
　Thy flesh and blood let bring me there!

Torgau Handbook (1676); tr. M. Carver.

42

Tune: Ach Gott und Herr, wie groß und schwer.

1 My soul, rejoice, / With gladsome voice!
　Adorned with faith unfeignèd,
　Where Christ is host / This day thou go'st,
　By Him to be sustainèd.

2 Behold with care / The sumptuous fare:
　His Body for thee given;
　The bev'rage good, / His precious Blood,
　Doth strengthen thee to heaven.

3 Art thou by sin / Oppressed within,
　And plunging to damnation?
　This table grand / Will help thee stand
　And work thy restoration.

4 Tho' great your sum / Of sin, yet come!
　Relieve your heart's sad burden;
　In Christ, your kind / Physician find
　All remedy and pardon.

5 All feasters here / By rights appear
　In robes of Christian beauty;
　Then dress thy heart / With proper art,
　As is thy sacred duty.

6 With heav'nly bread / Thou here art fed
　By God before His table;
　The Rock gives thee / Life's vintage free.
　Praise Him as thou art able.

7 Now heartily / I'll joyful be
　By Christ my Lord invited;
　He is both mine / and also thine
　My soul is well delighted.

8 I sadly weep / That few will keep
　This joy, and many scorn it,
　Nor will commence / in confidence
　To take this cup and drink it.

The believer asks Christ for grace.

9 This day I will / come gladly still
And with Thee, Christ, be seated,
And at Thy side / Be satisfied,
In body, soul repleted.

10 And wash me clean / From all my sin,
O Most High, by Thy favor;
Then shall I know / The evil foe
Can harm or hurt me never.

11 A contrite heart / Let not depart
Despised for its transgression;
I fondly pray / Grant me this day
Forgiveness and remission.

12 No sacrifice / Or worthy price
Have I to win Thy favor;
Lord, let these bones / so filled with groans
Leap with delight forever.

13 This feast, O Lord, / Like heav'nly cord
Binds us, that none may sever;
Abide in me, / And I in Thee:
So shall I praise Thee ever.

14 I know by grace / This holy place
By angels is attended
When we in faith / Go as He saith,
Before His table splendid.

15 When in this rite / There comes in sight
The cup of Thy bestowing,
My mind sees there / Thy blood, as 'twere
A stream from Thy wounds flowing.

Reason cannot fathom this lofty Sacrament.

16 How it may be / I cannot see,
Nor will have it disputed;
The Sacrament / By th' Element
And Word is constituted.

17 This wonder's high, / Too weak am I;
'Tis by some wondrous story
That faith alone / My heart leads on
To this Thy feast of glory.

18 When from the priest / I take the feast,
I find a pledge supernal
That gives me strength / And shall at length
Bring me to life eternal.

The believer receives a foretaste of eternal joy.

19 O God, how strong / The joys that throng
And through my limbs are driven!
In Christ I yearn / And gladly burn
For higher things of heaven.

20 With Stephen's eye / I now descry
The heavens open standing;
Thy love and grace / My soul embrace
And answer its demanding.

21 O harp and string, / For gladness ring,
Resound, violas splendid,
And fairly let / True faith's motet
With tuneful song be blended!

22 Let pipes now play / Their wonted way,
God's house with music filling,
Let horns rejoice / And dress the voice
With tones now sweet, now thrilling.

(cont.)

23 Each banquet guest / Within his breast
　　May then feel jubilation,
　　And chase away / The mind's dismay
　　And ev'ry sad sensation.

24 Oh, that I might / In such delight
　　Be brought by hosts of heaven
　　To that fair land, / Where by God's hand
　　I shall a crown be given!

25 Lord, from my heart / Let ne'er depart
　　This joy of joys excelling;
　　Thy Spirit be / My guarantee
　　And pledge within me dwelling!

26 Oh, how I yearn / Now to discern
　　Thy face with eyes unhindered!
　　Yet till life cease / I'll wait in peace
　　My will to Thine surrendered.

27 Meanwhile I'll be / Devout to Thee,
　　Beneath my crosses bending;
　　Someday I shall / In heaven's hall
　　Enjoy Thy feast unending.

28 By God's true Word / I am assured,
　　Christ gained me that bright morrow,
　　Upon the cross / Repaired my loss
　　And died in bitter sorrow.

S. Schererz; tr. M. Carver.

VI. REPENTANCE

43

Tune: Zion klagt mit Angst und Schmerzen.

1 Ah! What then shall be the ending?
　　Ah! What profit shall I gain,
　　Eyes to earth-ward ever bending,
　　Heart so seldom seeking heav'n,
　　Onward speeding, numb in sense,
　　Callous with impenitence?
　　Jesus, stir my heart and sting me!
　　To a true repentance bring me!

2 Ah! I feel no true contrition,
　　And my heart of sin is cold;
　　Without guile I make admission
　　That my guilt is manifold,
　　Yet I live from sorrow free,
　　In my false security.
　　Jesus, grant me to be proving
　　True repentance by Thy moving!

3 Ah! I fail to think of heaven
　　And my God sufficiently!
　　Thither is my spirit driven
　　Whence it rightly ought to flee,
　　Holds too tightly to the thing
　　Which the pit of hell may bring.
　　Jesus, grant Thy gracious pardon,
　　Loose me from my heavy burden.

4 Ah! Since o'er my fainted spirit,
　　Flesh doth reign, I scarcely sense
　　All the ills which I inherit
　　From my vile impenitence—
　　Scarcely the corruption see,
　　For to flesh I've yielded me,
　　Jesus, grant me by Thy favor
　　To discern my danger ever.

5 Ah! Therefore from sin awake thee,
 Spirit in thy fetters bound!
 Seek thy God, to Him betake thee,
 Seek Him while He may be found.
 Go while yet the door of grace
 Still is open to thy face!—
 Jesus, set this work in motion,
 Strengthen me with true devotion.

6 Ah! My heart, thy trespass measure,
 See how far from God thou art!
 How thou hast His grace and pleasure
 Mocked and banished from thy heart,
 And how thou thyself dost speed
 From His peace to hell indeed.
 Jesus, guide my heart to ponder
 This distress with earnest wonder.

7 Ah! While there is time for turning,
 Let me now my ways amend;
 Jesus, this my pray'r discerning,
 To my soul Thy hand extend
 I am weak; oh, help Thou me!
 Curb my vile iniquity.
 Lord, for all Thy bitter Passion
 Thou wilt answer my petition.

8 Ah! What soothing consolation
 Jesus, in Thy blood I find:
 Cleansing for all my transgression,
 Strengthening my heart and mind,
 In my soul restoring me,
 Though a sinner still I be.
 Jesus, henceforth lead and guide me,
 With a godly life provide me.

J. Scheffler; tr. M. Carver.

44

Tune: Nun sich der Tag geendet hat.

1 My God! I bring my heart to Thee
 A gift and offering;
 Thou hast demanded this of me,
 And, mindful, this I bring.

2 "Give Me thy heart, My son," Thou say'st,
 "To Me it has great worth.
 Thou findest else no peace or rest
 In heaven or on earth."

3 O Father, then my heart receive,
 Despise it not, I pray;
 I give with all my pow'r to give,
 Turn not Thy face away!

4 It may be full of vice and crude,
 Corrupt with vanity,
 And conscience of no virtue good
 Nor of true piety.

5 But now it looks in bare disgust
 Upon its evil state,
 Repents of all its former lust
 And all its sins doth hate.

6 It falls here at Thy feet and cries:
 Oh, smite me, break me now,
 That I may all false pride despise
 And in true penance bow!

7 Oh, crush my heart as hard as stone,
 And melt my sense like snow,
 That I with sorrow sigh and groan,
 And tears may overflow.

8 Then take me, Jesus Christ, to Thee,
 Deep sink me in Thy blood;
 I own Thy cross and agony
 Borne for all mankind's good.

(cont.)

9 Brace Thou my limping hand of faith,
Thy blood to keep e'ermore,
The pledge of pardon, life from death,
That all things doth restore.

10 In favor grant salvation free,
And righteousness bestow,
And take my sinful debt on Thee,
The portion that I owe.

11 In Thee vouchsafe my soul to dress
My body so to clad,
That, purified from sinfulness,
I may behold my God.

12 God, Holy Spirit, make me part
Of Thy communion blest;
For Jesus' sake indwell my heart
And stir my waiting breast.

13 Pour into me Thy godly light
And love's unspotted fire,
Snuff out all darkness, falsehood, spite,
Drive Thou my whole desire.

14 Help me to be steadfast in faith,
To trust in God, my Rock,
To do the good, not fearing death,
Though world may strive or mock.

15 Help me! In hope and patience make
My soul unmoved to be,
That, while Thou dost not me forsake,
Thy love may comfort me.

16 Help me to love with purest glow,
And clearest proof afford
That what I do is not for show
But for Thy glory, Lord.

17 Help me to be upright and true
Free from deceit and guile,
That none may fault the works I do,
Nor lies my lips defile.

18 Help me a lowly heart to prove
In meek and humble wise,
That, blemished not by worldly love,
Though falling, I may rise.

19 Help me to have true godliness
Without hypocrisy,
That all my life Thy name may bless
And pleasing be to Thee.

20 O God, adopt my heart by grace,
Thy temple here in time;
Yea, let it be Thy dwelling-place
E'en in th' eternal clime.

21 To Thee I give it for Thine own,
Employ it to Thine end
I know that I am Thine alone;
I call the world no friend.

22 And so it ceases not, nor will,
To get its hold on me;
It tempts and threatens with all skill,
That I its slave should be.

23 But nevermore to thee I'll fall,
Thou false, demonic bride!
Praise God! I do not care for all
Thy gleaming serpent-hide.

24 Away, thou world! O sin, away!
My heart is not for thee;
But Jesus, 'tis Thy gift, I say
To keep eternally.

J. C. Schade; tr. M. Carver.

VII. FAITH & JUSTIFICATION

45

Tune: Ich ruf zu dir, Herr Jesu Christ.

1 God loved the world so heartily
   That He did Christ deliver,
   His own dear Son, to agony,
   That we might live forever.
   O God, Thy love so great must be,
   No man its breadth can measure;
   Grant Thy pleasure
   O Lord, and grace that we
   May ne'er forget this treasure!

2 Christ brought us unto heaven's throne
   Without man's strength or vigor,
   And we are saved by faith alone;
   No works in this can figure.
   He who believes in Christ has bliss
    As his assured possession,
   And confession,
   For where faith absent is,
   No man can have salvation.

3 He who believeth not is damned;
   He hath no word of blessing,
   Christ will not pity those who stand
   On works, no faith possessing.
   In soul and body wracked with fear,
   They see all comforts flying,
   Captives lying,
   Denied all grace both here
   And in death's bonds undying.

4 He that is steadfast till his death
   Will surely have salvation;
   And he that boldly owns his faith
   In Christ before creation,
   Christ, too, will at the throne on high,
   Before the Father own him,
   And will crown him,
   His fellow-heir with joy
   And greater joys be shown him.

Old hymn, from Crüger's Praxis; *tr. M. Carver.*

46

Tune: Gott Lob, es geht nunmehr zu Ende.

1 Though devil hordes be multiplying
   As grains of sand upon the shore,
   As specks of dust in sunbeam flying,
   As drops upon the ocean floor,
   With Jesus I will take no fright:
   He's my salvation and my light.

2 Tho' hells may number ten times over
   The fissures which the mountains crack,
   The holes that ev'ry hillside cover,
   And all the forest caverns black,
   With Jesus I will take no fright:
   He's my salvation and my light.

3 Tho' e'en so many foes may meet me
   As fish in ocean, lake, and stream,
   As fowl in heaven winging fleetly
   As insects ev'rywhere that teem,
   With Jesus I will take no fright:
   He's my salvation and my light.

4 Yea, if more tongues of slander shouted
   Than ears of grain upon the field,
   Than blades of grass that ever sprouted,
   Than thorns that ever hedge did wield,
   With Jesus I will take no fright:
   He's my salvation and my light.

(cont.)

5 O bellow then, ye dragons cursèd!
Ye hell-bound kindling, boast on high!
Ye fiends, be all your taunts rehearsèd!
Ye liars, freely vilify!
With Jesus I will take no fright:
He's my salvation and my light.

6 Wherefore, ye devils, thus abuse me
For all my sins with furious cries?
Of what great debt can ye accuse me?
The payment stands before your eyes:
Christ—my salvation and my light:
Now at your cries I take no fright.

7 Ye lash in vain, ye flames infernal!
Ye frighten not my heart and sense!
Ye shall not be my doom eternal,
I'm dressed in Jesus' innocence.
He's my salvation and my light:
Now at your pit I take no fright.

8 What, foes, shall come of your aggressions?
Come, persecute with torments grim!
Come, burn and plunder my possessions!
Yea, slay me, tear me limb from limb!
Still at this all I take no fright:
Christ's my salvation and my light.

9 Ye lying lips with sland'rous story,
What tales have ye to bring my fall?
Here is the pillar of my glory,
Unstained to keep me from you all:
Christ's my salvation and my light,
Now at your lies I take no fright.

10 Therefore I boldly bid defiance
To wicked spirits, foes, and hell!
Come, ye who make of lies a science!
My Jesus will protect me well.
He's my salvation and my light:
Naught in the least can give me fright.

11 Oh, Jesus! never this deny me,
Nor let my trusting be in vain,
Then shall no danger terrify me;
Have mercy, Jesus, and remain
Still my salvation and my light,
Then e'en at death I'll take no fright.

J. Mentzer; tr. M. Carver.

VIII. JESUS HYMNS

47

Tune: Wer nur den lieben Gott läßt walten.

1 Alone, yet not alone completely—
Alone, this is my comfort dear;
My lonely hours are spent most sweetly
With Jesus, who is always near!
I am with Him and He with me:
Therefore what hour can lonely be?

2 What of all worldly conversation?
It only knows of vanity;
There, words of heav'nly consolation
Are met with smiles or mockery.
Therefore I'd rather be alone
Than without God by all be known.

3 A man is soon by bad perverted;
  Who, touching pitch, is not defiled?
  To go where God is soon deserted—
  Should I to this be reconciled?
  Oft suspect fellowships amuse
  Until the tragic fall ensues.

4 Can ever man be comprehended?
  Who may search out his heart and mind?
  How many a fellow was befriended
  Whom we at last did fickle find,
  And he who had been kind and sweet
  Soon proved a serpent in deceit?

5 Therefore let no one here reprove me
  If I this lonely manner keep,
  And only ask that none should move me
  From joying in God's comforts deep.
  Great craft and guile on earth are found:
  Blest, he who to his God is bound!

6 Let worldly men be people-seekers!
  I love my God in still repose;
  And if I'm curst by envious speakers,
  I'll shut me in my chamber close
  And take God with me secretly,
  That envy may confounded be.

7 I speak with God, His Scripture reading,
  And thro' His Word He speaks to me:
  He hears me in the silence, pleading,
  And He is there immediately.
  If in my cross I counsel need,
  'Tis He consoled me then indeed.

8 My plans in silence while I'm making,
  He keeps His hand there at my side;
  Then whether I'm asleep or waking,
  He doth His likeness, too, provide;
  Nor in my dreams doth He forsake,
  But tarries there as when I wake.

9 Who then would dare this truth deny me,
  That I am never quite alone?
  Though world for lonely ways decry me,
  I let them mock me on and on;
  Enough that God is with me there,
  And many thousand angels fair!

B. Schmolck; tr. M. Carver.

48

Tune: Ich laß dich nicht! [Melody Appendix 5]

1 I leave Thee not! Thou art my Jesus ever,
  Though earth rebel, / And death and hell
  Would from its steadfast hold my faith dissever.
  Ah, no! I ever will / Cling to my Helper still.
  Hear what my love is taught:
  Thou art my Jesus ever,
  I leave Thee not, I leave Thee not!

(cont.)

2 I leave Thee not, O Love! of love the highest,
  Though doubt display / Its battle-day;
  I own the pow'r which Thou, my Lord, appliest.
  Thou didst bear guilt and woe; / Shall I to torment go,
  When into judgment brought?
  O Love! of love the highest, I leave Thee not!

3 I leave Thee not, O Thou who sweetly cheerest!
  Whose fresh supplies / Cause strength to rise,
  Just in the hour when faith's decay is nearest.
  If sickness chill the soul, / And nights of languor roll,
  My heart one hope hath caught;
  O Thou who sweetly cheerest, I leave Thee not!

4 I leave Thee not, Thou Help in tribulation!
  Heap ill on ill, / I trust Thee still,
  I hope when all seems near to desolation,
  Do what Thou wilt with me, / I yet will cling to Thee;
  Thy grace I have besought;
  Thou Help in tribulation, I leave Thee not!

5 I leave Thee not: shall I forsake salvation?
  No, Jesus, no! / Thou shalt not go;
  Mine still Thou art, to free from condemnation.
  After this fleeting night, / Thy presence brings me light,
  Whose ray my soul hath sought;
  Shall I forsake salvation? I leave Thee not!

6 I leave Thee not; Thy Word my way shall brighten:
  With Thee I go / Through weal and woe,
  Thy precept wise shall ev'ry burden lighten.
  My Lord, on Thee I hang, / Nor heed the journey's pang,
  Though thorny be my lot;
  Let but Thy Word enlighten, I leave Thee not!

7 I leave Thee not, e'en in the lap of pleasure;
  For when I stray / Without Thy ray,
  My richest joy must cease to be a treasure.
  I shudder at the glee, / When no delight from Thee
  Has heartfelt peace begot;
  E'en in the lap of pleasure, I leave Thee not!

8 I leave Thee not! I fear no condemnation,
  For how could share / Thy child and heir
  The lot of those who spurn their soul's salvation?
  Thy blood, Lord, cleanseth me, / And therefore I am free
  From hell, the sinner's lot.
  I fear no condemnation; I leave Thee not!

9 I leave Thee not, my God, my Lord, my Heaven!
  Nor death shall rend / From Thee, my Friend,
  Who for my sake Thyself to death hast given.
  Thou diedst for love to me, / And love goes back to Thee;
  My heart has but one thought:
  My God, my Lord, my Heaven, I leave Thee not!

M. C. Deßler; tr. J. W. Alexander / ELHB.

49

Tune: Jesu, der du meine Seele. [Br 93, p. 71]

1 Jesus, Shepherd good and gracious
  Of the flocks of saints elect:
  Let me be a lamb most precious,
  Which Thy rod and staff direct.
  Ah! In love Thy life Thou gavest
  For Thy sheep—the fold Thou savest—
  Yea for me as well, I know:
  I in turn my love will show!

2 Sheep hold dear their shepherds ever,
  And the shepherds love their sheep:
  Show in heav'n Thy love and favor,
  I on earth love's law will keep;
  Let Thy love below be sounding,
  And my love on high rebounding.
  "Thee I love!" Thou call'st to me;
  Let my heart cry, "I love Thee."

3 Sheep their shepherd know most truly,
  And he knows them certainly:
  Let me hasten to Thee duly,
  As Thou cam'st in haste to me.
  When the wolf infernal sought me,
  In his clutches would have caught me;
  "Thee I know," Thou toldest me,
  I, too answer, "I know Thee."

4 Sheep unto their shepherd hearken
  Following his voice alone.
  Shepherds, too, when heavens darken
  Hear their sheep that cry or groan:
  Let me hear when Thou art calling;
  At Thy threat'ning not forestalling.
  Let me e'er submit to Thee,
  Jesus, also hear Thou me.

5 Hearken, Jesus, to my crying,
  Hear Thy sheep that longs for Thee;
  Teach me, too, the art of sighing
  When the wolf should come for me.
  Let my praying give Thee pleasure,
  Send me solace in good measure;
  When I pray Thee, hear Thou me!
  Jesus, answer: "I hear Thee."

6 Hearken, Jesus, I beseech Thee,
  When I call, and knock, and cry;
  Jesus, let my prayèr reach Thee,
  Graciously Thy help supply.
  In Thy name all our petitions
  Are "Amen" and "Surely" granted.
  Thus I do believe, and feel,
  Son of God, Thy comfort real.

S. von Birken; tr. M. Carver.

50

Tune: Den die Hirten lobten sehre. [Quem pastores]

1 Come, and Christ the Lord be praising,
Heart and mind to Him be raising,
Celebrate His love amazing,
Worthy folk of Christendom.

2 Sin, death, hell may all be grieving,
Satan shame feel to him cleaving;
We, salvation free receiving,
Cast our ev'ry care away.

3 See what God for us provideth,
Life that in His Son abideth,
And our weary steps He guideth
From earth's woe to heavenly joy.

4 His soul deeply for us feeleth,
He His love to us revealeth,
He who in the heavens dwelleth
Came to save us from the foe.

5 Jacob's Star his advent maketh,
Soothes the longing heart that acheth,
And the serpent's head He breaketh,
Loathing all the powers of hell.

6 Opened hath He, freedom gained us,
Now the prison that contained us;
Where much grief and sorrow pained us,
And our hearts were bowed with woe.

7 O blest hour when we receivèd
From the foe who us deceivèd
Liberty, when we believèd,
And Thee, gracious Spirit, praised.

8 Beauteous Infant in the manger,
O befriend us! beyond danger,
Bring us where is turned God's anger,
Where with angel hosts we'll praise.

P. Gerhardt; tr. J. Kelly.

51

Tune: Schmücke dich, o liebe Seele.

1 King, to whom no king compareth,
Whose renown to tell none dareth:
God, o'er heaven's kingdom reigning,
Man, all scepters here sustaining;
Son eternal of the Father,
Thine the throne o'er ev'ry other,
Perfect beauty for His dressing,
Ev'ry perfect trait possessing.

2 Earth and heaven, tribe and nation,
Bird and beast and all creation,
In the forest, field, or ocean
All that lives and showeth motion
Unto Thee have all been given
Lord of life and death in heaven,
All things trembling fall before Thee,
Son of Man and King of Glory.

3 In Thy kingdom where Thou dwellest,
  Thou in beauty all excellest,
  Ever loyal oaths receiving
  From unnumbered souls believing,
  Who, with Thine own Word complying
  Priv'leges of grace enjoying,
  Yield themselves to Thy directing,
  With Thee ev'ry wrong rejecting.

4 Ever in Thy realm of glory
  Heav'nly souls rehearse Thy story,
  Multitudes with love increasing
  Sing Thy praises without ceasing,
  Without fear the saints victorious
  There behold Thine aspect glorious,
  And unwearying adore Thee,
  Honor, worship bring before Thee.

5 Ruler, whose three kingdoms fear Thee,
  No kings else can e'er come near Thee
  In the bounty of Thy treasure,
  In Thy statutes, will, and pleasure,
  In the gifts which Thou hast given
  Fitting to the heirs of heaven
  With Thy shield Thy friends surrounding,
  And Thine enemies confounding.

6 Reign Thou in my heart, and vanquish
  Anger, fear, and lust, and anguish,
  In Thy shelter safely place me,
  And with faith in Thee, Lord, grace me;
  Let me kiss Thee, honor, fear Thee,
  Love Thee, and obedient hear Thee,
  Striving, suff'ring, till in heaven,
  I a throne from Thee am given!

J. J. Rambach; tr. M. Carver.

52

Tune: Wer Jesum bei sich hat. [Melody Appendix 8]

1 He that hath Jesus near
    can stand securely,
  Upon misfortune's sea
    he saileth surely.
  He that hath Jesus near—
    what can alarm him?
  His heart, with comfort filled,
    knows naught can harm him.

2 He that hath Jesus near
    hath also heaven;
  Peace from all worldly noise
    he would be given.
  He that hath Jesus near
    contently liveth
  With all that he may have
    from God, who giveth.

3 He that hath Jesus near
    finds little pleasure
  In earthly vanity
    and ev'ry treasure.
  He that hath Jesus near
    hath all he wishes,
  And in eternity
    far greater riches.

4 He that hath Jesus near
    in safety goeth;
  The road to heaven true
    his Savior showeth;
  He that hath Jesus near,
    though great the danger,
  Need fear no devil, death,
    nor murd'rous stranger.

(cont.)

5 He that hath Jesus near
  hath shelter wondrous
Against the lightning dread
  and weather thundrous;
He that hath Jesus near
  need not be shaken,
When his transgressions would
  his fears awaken.

6 He that hath Jesus near
  need not be doubting,
He can the evil foe
  be quickly routing.
He that hath Jesus near
  can perish never,
But cheerfully can die,
  and live forever.

7 He that hath Jesus near
  can perish never,
He that hath Jesus near
  dies in God's favor;
He that hath Jesus near
  hath ev'ry blessing;
He that hath Jesus near,
  hath peace unceasing.

C. F. Connow; tr. M. Carver.

53

Tune: Seelenbräutigam.

1 Who, O Jesus blest,
  Is like Thee, sweet Rest!
  From the multitude elected,
  Life of those who were dejected,
  Light that gladdens best,
  Jesus, dearest Rest!

2 Life, that with my load
  Down to death hast trod,
  From distress hast me delivered,
  All my debts hast freely covered
  And from highways broad
  Brought back to God!

3 Brightness of His Face!
  To redeem our race,
  Ere time was, Thou wast appointed,
  Thou didst veil Thee, God's Anointed,
  In our human race:
  Brightness of His Face!

4 Conqu'ror of renown,
  Thou hast smitten down
  Death and sin, the world astounded,
  And the dragon's might confounded
  Gained by blood Thy crown,
  Conqu'ror of renown!

5 Majesty most dear,
  Mightiest King and Seer,
  I will kiss Thy scepter holy,
  At Thy feet will sit me lowly,
  And like Mary hear;
  Majesty most dear!

6 By Thy Spirit's rays
  Let me know Thy praise;
  Thine by faith, may I ne'er perish;
  Warm love may I always cherish,
  Thine through all my days,
  Thou, my beauteous Praise!

7 Into Thee draw me,
  That for love of Thee,
  I may melt and, daily bolder,
  Cast all mis'ry on Thy shoulder,
  Which I feel in me;
  Draw me into Thee.

8 Thy humility
  And Thy kindness be
  As Thine image in me dwelling,
  Pride and anger thence dispelling,
  Naught avails in me
  Lest Thyself Thou see.

9 Curb my foolish mind,
  To the world inclined,
  That from Thee it may not waver,
  In Thy fold abiding ever,
  Wealth in Thee to find;
  Grant me, Lord, Thy mind.

10 Wake me up apace
  That the Christian race
  I pursue, unwearied, running;
  And, preserved from Satan's cunning
  Yield my foe no place,
  Quicken me apace.

11 Thy Good Spirit, Lord,
  To my soul afford,
  That I watch and pray with fervor,
  Trusting Thee, my soul's Preserver.
  Love unfeigned, O Lord,
  Unto me afford.

12 When the billows' might
  In the gloomy night
  O'er my heart's frail bark is sweeping
  Let Thy hand my soul be keeping;
  Lose me not from sight,
  Watcher in the night.

13 Give me courage good,
  That my wealth and blood
  I for Thee could lose, my Savior,
  Hating world and sin forever.
  Grant me this, my God,
  Through Thy precious blood.

14 And when death's at hand,
  Lord, then with me stand:
  Through death's shadows gently bear me,
  And for light of bliss prepare me,
  That I there may stand,
  Lord, at Thy right hand.

J. A. Freylinghausen; tr. Composite.

54

Tune: Wo ist Jesus, mein Verlangen. [Melody Appendix 11]

1 Where is Jesus, my Desirèd,
  My Beloved, and my Friend?
  Whither hath He now retirèd?
  Where to find Him shall I send?
  Soon my soul for sin would perish,
  Wearied and afflicted quite!
  Where is Jesus, whom I cherish?
  Whom I long for day and night?

2 Ah! I cry for pain and anguish
  Where hath He, my Jesus, gone?
  Restlessly my heart doth languish,
  Till with Him I shall be one.
  Ah! If I had wings for flying,
  I would seek the night around,
  Over hill and mountain sighing,
  Where my Jesus might be found.

(cont.)

3 Pain and anguish He dispelleth,
Sin and death He bids begone;
When our heart for sorrow faileth,
He delivers ev'ry one!
Therefore I will tarry never,
But will seek Him here and there,
In the fields and highways ever
Seek Him still, and seek Him e'er.

4 Dearest Jesus! Hide no longer,
For Thee now my soul doth cry.
Show Thine eyes, and make me stronger;
Grant my soul to find Thee nigh!
Grant my soul Thy grace and favor,
Jesus, dearest one to me!
Take my soul Thy captive ever,
Let it ever dwell with Thee.

5 Ah! I've found the best of treasures!
Jesus, Joy and Fount of grace!
I will cast off worldly pleasures
And will find with Him a place!
No more is that grief distressing
That distressed me heretofore;
Now my soul, its prize possessing,
Naught but Jesus will adore.

6 Dearest Jesus! Joy most thrilling,
Fairest Jewèl of my soul;
Pasture of my heart most filling,
Thou my long-desirèd Goal;
Heart and thoughts and senses ever—
All I now commend to Thee
Let me wander from Thee never,
Mine abide eternally!

Unknown; tr. M. Carver.

IX. THE CHRISTIAN LIFE

55

Tune: Machs mit mir, Gott, nach deiner Güt.

1 Arise, O Christian, join the strife,
A conqu'ror's glory testing;
This busy world, this little life
Affords no time for resting.
Who will not fight bears not away
The crown of everlasting day.

2 The devil comes with guileful heart,
The world with pomp to please thee;
The flesh, with lusts, to where thou art,
To snare thy heart and seize thee;
And fight'st thou not as hero brave,
Thou'rt lost—no human pow'r can save.

3 Recall thy pledge of loyalty
Sworn to the Captain's banner!
And that for strife He's chosen thee
To fight in manful manner;
Yes, think, without the strife of war,
No man can e'er to triumph soar.

4 How shameful when a warrior turns
His back on those assailing;
How shameful when his post he spurns,
In battle-duties failing.
How childlike when he lays him low,
And yields the glory to the foe.

5 Gird on! The devil soon will fall,
The worldly pomp soon flieth
The fleshly lust will cease withal
Though hard it thee defieth.
Oh, shame, if champion e'er should be
Compelled to yield to this vile three!

6 Who overcomes and wins the field
O'er foes in league infernal
Will eat the fruits of paradise
The tree of life eternal
Who conquers, him no agony
Nor death shall touch eternally.

7 Who overcomes and doth complete
His course in honor bidden,
The Lord will give him then to eat
Of that fair manna hidden;
A white stone He will give him, too,
And in the stone a name that's new.

8 Who overcomes, the pow'r is giv'n
With Jesus to be reigning—
With might the nations under heav'n
In holy union chaining;
And he receives the morning star
From God, as banner in the war.

9 Who here o'ercomes, will there receive
White robes by heav'nly favor;
And in the Book of those who live
His name shall shine forever;
Yes, Christ will own the victor's song
Before the angels' mighty throng.

10 Who overcomes shall never quit
God's holy habitation,
But like the golden vessels sit
In high angelic station;
And there the name of God the Lord
To all his ways will light afford.

11 Who overcomes will on a throne
With Jesus Christ be seated
And shine in splendor like the sun,
And as God's child be treated.
Yes, heav'n will be his heritage,
And he will rule from age to age.

12 So fight then well, be bold and brave—
The victory obtaining;
Gird on thy strength, that thou at last
May be to this attaining.
The man who strives to win no crown
Eternal shame he calleth down.

J. Scheffler; tr. sts. 1–5, 8–9, 12, A. Manington, alt.;
sts. 6–7, 10–11, M. Carver.

56

Tune: Meine Hoffnung stehet feste. [Br 226, p. 177]

1 Rise, ye children of salvation,
All who cleave to Christ, the Head.
Wake, awake, O mighty nation,
Ere the Foe on Zion tread.
He draws nigh, / and would defy
All the hosts of God Most High.

2 Follow Christ and fear no evil,
Trust His arm and all is well;
Face to face with ev'ry devil,
With the mighty hosts of hell:
More than they / the bright array
Guarding us by night and day.

3 Conqu'rors by the blood of Jesus,
Fearless in our faith and pray'r;
He from ev'ry terror frees us,
Makes us strong to do and dare:
By His blood / shed for our good
We fear not the devil's brood.

4 Lo, the banners cross-emblazoned
Of the army of the Lord:
White and crimson, they are stationed
Mid the field, and strength afford;
In His cause / there is no loss
Victory is in His cross.

(cont.)

5 Saints and martyrs long before us
  Firmly on this ground have stood;
  See their banner waving o'er us,
  Conqu'rors through the Savior's blood.
  Ground we hold / whereon of old
  Fought the faithful and the bold.

6 He who loveth slav'ry better,
  Slav'ry now and evermore:
  He who loves sin's galling fetter,
  Follows not the shout of war:
  Lost in night / dread Satan's might
  Holds him slumb'ring lest he fight.

7 But the man to whom is given
  Light to know his freedom's worth,
  All whose treasure is in heaven—
  God his all in heav'n and earth—
  Joys to be / Christ's servant free;
  Serving Christ is liberty!

8 He whose fetters are not riven,
  Lives a life that is not life;
  Hearts but half to Jesus given,
  Know of naught but care and strife:
  He alone / goes bravely on
  Whose desire and aim are one.

9 Fighting, we shall be victorious
  By the blood of Christ our Lord;
  On our foreheads, bright and glorious,
  Shines the witness of His Word;
  Spear and shield / on battlefield,
  His great name we cannot yield.

10 Deathless, we are all unfearing,
  Life laid up with Christ in God
  In the morn of His appearing
  Floweth forth a glory-flood;
  Tears we sow, / but joys shall grow
  Where those living waters flow.

11 When His servants stand before Him,
  Each receiving his reward;
  When His saints in light adore Him,
  Giving glory to the Lord,
  "Victory!" / our song shall be
  Like the thunder of the sea.

J. Falckner; tr. E. F. Bevan, alt.

57

Tune: Fahre fort, fahre fort.

1 Zion, rise, Zion, rise,
  Zion, wake, arise, and shine!
  Let thy lamp be brightly burning,
  Never let thy love decline.
  Forward still with hopeful yearning.
  Zion, yonder waits the heav'nly prize;
  Zion, rise! Zion, rise!

2 Bear the cross, bear the cross.
  Zion, till thy latest breath
  Bear the cross of scorn and jeering
  And be faithful unto death;
  See the crown of life appearing.
  Zion, count all other things as loss.
  Bear the cross, bear the cross!

3 Watch and pray, watch and pray!
　Zion, ever watch and pray
　Lest the wicked world misguide thee
　From the narrow path to stray
　And thy God reprove and chide thee.
　Zion, work with zeal while it is day.
　Watch and pray, watch and pray!

4 Prove the good, prove the good,
　Zion, now thy choice declare!
　Two would have thee, try the spirits,
　Guide thy steps by Jacob's Star;
　Try which Lord thy fealty merits!
　Zion, by two masters warmly sued,
　Prove the good, prove the good!

5 Force thy way, force thy way!
　Zion, upward! Be not thou
　Like to branches dry and withered;
　From thy green and fruitful bough
　May good grapes by Christ be gathered!
　Zion, upward to the light of day
　Force thy way, force thy way!

6 Pass along, pass along,
　Zion, with the victor's song!
　Fervently let love be burning;
　God can make the weakest strong!
　Heav'nward let thy thoughts be turning,
　Zion! None may do God's chosen wrong!
　Pass along, pass along!

7 Run thy race, run thy race,
　Zion, swiftly run thy race!
　Let no languor ever find thee
　Idle in the marketplace.
　Look not to the things behind thee.
　Zion, daily strengthened by His grace,
　Run thy race, run thy race!

J. E. Schmidt; tr. 1–3, 7, TLH (1941);
sts. 4–5, E. Massie; st. 6, H. Burlingham, alt.

58

Tune: Zion klagt mit Angst und Schmerzen.

1 Hold that fast which thou wast given,
　O my Christian, dearly bought!
　Wicked spirits, foes of heaven,
　Now with wicked cunning plot
　Shamefully to draw thee far
　From the bright and Morning Star,
　Or obscure Him, faith thus shaking:
　Ah! 'Tis time for pray'r and waking!

2 Yea, 'tis time for pray'r and waking,
　Now salvation nearer draws,
　And the serpent, coiling, snaking,
　Spews the venom from his jaws.
　Therefore be thou not so blind
　Do not thrust it out of mind,
　As if it thou needst never ponder
　Whether from thy God to wander.

(cont.)

3 Whether from thy God to wander,
　Or to take the highway straight—
　'Tis a matter well to ponder
　And consider, ere too late.
　If in life thou careful art
　Ere with temp'ral things thou part,
　Why should so few thoughts be given
　To hold fast the way to heaven?

4 To hold fast the way to heaven
　Takes a keen and careful sense,
　For God's little Church is riven
　By great lies and dissidence.
　Some say here's the house of God,
　Other, yonder, or abroad.
　Ah, with such disputes all over,
　Who may here the way discover?

5 "Who may here the way discover
　By which we to heaven go?"
　Sighs the tender conscience ever.
　Lo, the Word our way doth show!
　Thou art not so simple yet;
　Gold thou knowest by its weight.
　Precious ware from false provision
　Eyes distinguish with precision.

6 Eyes distinguish with precision
　Finest wheat from worthless chaff,
　Well thou tellest with thy vision
　Good or bad, and bull or calf,
　Yea, the tongue can soon divine
　If some dregs are in the wine:
　All these things thou knowest quickly
　Since these skills thou usest weekly.

7 Since these skills thou usest weekly,
　Which, however, are but vain,
　Therefore thou thy conscience strictly
　In this matter shouldest train.
　With great care and vigilance
　Take thy heav'nly journey hence
　Mark the evil flocks nearby thee—
　Those who chaff for grain supply thee.

8 Those who chaff for grain supply thee
　Scattered are the world around.
　God by them would test and try thee,
　That thou may'st be faithful found:
　What's thy faith, thy love, thy truth?
　Is it thy intent forsooth
　In His Word to stand forever
　When such babblers round thee hover?

9 When such babblers round thee hover,
　God directs thee to His Word;
　As by grinding, iron ever
　May a useful tool afford,
　As the sieve that sifts the wheat
　Makes it pure and fit to eat,
　So God brings by lore deceiving
　Greater light and more believing.

10 Greater light and more believing
　Oft God's children here may gain
　By the wind of wolves deceiving,
　Who the Scriptures twist in vain.
　As the wolf that plunders much
　Puts the shepherd to his watch;
　As by foes who ramble careless,
　Swords are called to strike more fearless.

11 Swords are called to strike more fearless
　When the heretics, in swarm,
　Spreading doctrines false and cheerless,
　Sound unwitting the alarm.
　But a seasoned mind and sense
　Casts it all as stubble hence,
　Soundly from the Word defying
　All that with that Word is vying.

12 All that with that Word is vying,
　All that will not death survive—
　All from which a Christian, dying,
　No true comfort can derive—
　All that doth its luster quit
　When the touchstone touches it
　When by Scripture 'tis traversèd—
　All such teaching be accursèd!

13 All such teaching be accursèd,
   Though it were by angels taught!
   Him who hath such lies dispersèd,
   Jesus, bring at once to naught!
   Faithful Shepherd, to the way
   Bring all souls that go astray!
   Church and doctrine pure, unstainèd,
   Plant, increase, and keep maintainèd!

F. Vogt; tr. M. Carver.

59

Tune: Freu dich sehr, o meine Seele.

1 Lord, I'll trust in Thee unfailing;
  Grant me also good to do:
  In Thy land let me be dwelling;
  I will give Thee worship true.
  Give me holy love and trust,
  Let me know no worldly lust.
  Grant my heart its whole desiring
  As on Thee it hangs untiring.

2 All my ways to Thee commending,
  I will trust in Thee, my God.
  Bring me on the path unbending,
  Leave me not in danger's road.
  Thou wilt bring all things to right,
  Brace my heart and give me light,
  That I may be Thine completely,
  And in Thee live ever meetly.

3 Lord, according to Thy pleasure
  Teach me evermore to go;
  Thou'rt my God, my highest treasure,
  Grant Thy Spirit mine to know;
  Lead me on the even way,
  And to heaven me convey.
  Never let me stray, nor lose me,
  Nor let Satan's crafts confuse me.

4 Teach me, Lord, my days to number,
  And that here my life must end;
  I must go at last, and slumber,
  And my foot must thither tend
  Past this present age to see
  Yonder pure eternity:
  Ah! Lord, let me dwell beside Thee
  And forever there enjoy Thee!

M. Geier; tr. M. Carver.

60

Tune: Höchster Priester, der du dich. [Melody Appendix 4]

1 Great High Priest, who deign'dst to be
  Once the sacrifice for me,
  Kindly hear my supplication:
  Let my heart be Thine oblation!

2 Love, I know, accepteth naught,
  Save what Thou, O Love, hast wrought;
  What without Thy hand is offered
  Is not to God's presence proffered.

3 Slay in me the wayward will,
  Earthly sense and passion kill,
  Wrest my heart from self-affection
  Though it cost me sore affliction.

4 To the Altar bear the wood,
  Quick consume old Adam's brood:
  Love most dear of heav'nly graces,
  I would die in Thine embraces!

(cont.)

5 So shall God, the Righteous, brook
On my sacrifice to look,
Then e'en in my earthly station
I will be God's dear oblation.

J. Scheffler; tr. Composite.

61

Tune: O daß ich tausend Zungen hätte.

1 Thee will I love, my Strength, my Towèr;
Thee will I love, my Hope, my Joy;
Thee will I love with all my powèr,
With ardor time shall ne'er destroy.
Thee will I love, O Light Divine,
So long as life is mine.

2 Thee will I love, my Life, my Savior,
Who art my best and truest Friend.
Thee will I love and praise forever,
For never shall Thy kindness end;
Thee will I love with all my heart,
For Thou my Bridegroom art.

3 Alas! that I so late have known Thee,
Who art the Fairest and the Best;
Nor sooner for my Lord could own Thee,
Our highest Good, our only Rest!
Now bitter shame and grief I prove
O'er this my tardy love.

4 I wandered long in willing blindness,
I sought Thee, but I found Thee not,
For still I shunned Thy beams of kindness,
The creature-light filled all my thought;
And if at last I see Thee now
'Twas Thou to me didst bow!

5 I thank Thee, Jesus, Sun from heaven,
Whose radiance hath bro't light to me;
I thank Thee, who hast richly given
All that could make me glad and free;
I thank Thee that my soul is healed
By what Thy lips revealed.

6 Oh, keep me watchful, then, and humble;
And suffer me no more to stray;
Uphold me when my feet would stumble,
Nor let me loiter by the way.
Fill all my nature with Thy light,
O Radiance strong and bright!

7 Oh, teach me, Lord, to love Thee truly
With soul and body, head and heart,
And grant me grace that I may duly
Practice fore'er love's sacred art.
Grant that my ev'ry thought may be
Directed e'er to Thee.

8 Thee will I love, my Crown of gladness,
Thee will I love, my God and Lord,
Amid the darkest depths of sadness,
Not for the hope of high reward—
For Thine own sake, O Light divine,
So long as life is mine.

J. Scheffler; tr. C. Winkworth.

62

Tune: Liebe, die du mich zum Bilde [Br 222, p. 174]

1 Love, who didst the image lend me
  Of Thy Godhead from above;
  Love, who, when I fell, didst send me
  Restoration in Thy love:
  Love, I give myself to Thee,
  Thine for all eternity!

2 Love, by whom I was ordainèd
  To Thy bliss ere I was made;
  Love, who hast true Manhood gainèd
  And art in our flesh arrayed:
  Love, I give myself to Thee,
  Thine for all eternity!

3 Love, who hast for me endurèd
  All the pains of death and hell;
  Love, whose contest hath procurèd
  Endless joys and life as well:
  Love, I give myself to Thee,
  Thine for all eternity!

4 Love, my Life, Pow'r, and Salvation,
  Light and Spirit, Truth and Word!
  Love, who borest condemnation,
  My soul's comfort to afford:
  Love, I give myself to Thee,
  Thine for all eternity!

5 Love, who to Thy yoke hast bound me
  And my mind and senses taught;
  Love, who in Thyself hast drowned me
  Till my eyes for heaven sought:
  Love, I give myself to Thee,
  Thine for all eternity!

6 Love, who nevermore forsakest,
  But dost intercede for me;
  Love, who full atonement makest,
  And defendest mightily:
  Love, I give myself to Thee,
  Thine for all eternity!

7 Love, who at the end wilt raise me
  From the grave and dust of death:
  Love, who on that day wilt grace me
  With a glorious golden wreath:
  Love, I give myself to Thee,
  Thine for all eternity!

J. Scheffler; tr. M. Carver, after J. C. Jacobi.

63

Tune: O Gott, du frommer Gott.

1 What earnest care and fear
  Ought Christians to be waking,
  Their hearts and eyes alert
  And minds e'er cautious making.
  "With fear and trembling, work
  The saving of your soul."
  If just men scarcely stand,
  What is the sinners' toll?

2 The devil walks about
  And seeketh to devour us,
  Conceals a thousand snares
  And means to overpow'r us.
  The foolish world, deceived,
  Prepares its own sharp rod;
  And yet our greatest foe
  Is our own flesh and blood.

(cont.)

3 How many sins we do
  Of which we have no knowing!
  Yea, in the eyes of God
  E'en thinking counts as doing!
  One sheep amid the flock
  By sickness sickens all;
  Let him who thinks he stands
  Take heed lest he should fall.

4 "Ye shall be as I am,"
  Saith God, "uprightly living;
  And unto Me your souls
  Not half but wholly giving;
  Nor have I many called
  Of high or princely line;
  Though many say, 'Lord, Lord,'
  To hell their ways decline."

5 And should a man, once just,
  To evil be converted,
  He shall not benefit
  From faith erstwhile exerted.
  The servant who doth know
  His master's will, but shirks,
  Earns all the greater stripes
  For his malicious works.

6 One apple bite alone
  Could work such evil for us,
  That Christ Himself must drown
  In God's great anger o'er us;
  Thy Baptism thus to breach
  Shall prove thy perjury;
  Mayhap thy mortal end
  Will come this hour for thee.

7 They have enough to do
  Who would one soul deliver;
  He that has many more
  How can he manage ever?
  The loftier the charge,
  The more the talent's price,
  The more severe and harsh
  A reck'ning must suffice.

8 The world in its first age
  Was by the deep surmounted;
  Eight souls alone by God
  As righteous then are counted;
  Ten righteous are not found
  In all of Sodom's plains;
  Of seeds but one in four
  Fruit for the sower gains.

9 Of those who Egypt left,
  Few crossed the Jordan's water;
  And Judas of the Twelve
  Himself did put to slaughter;
  One leper of the ten
  Praised God for His great skill;
  Ah! Would that five were wise
  Though five be foolish still!

10 The advent of the Judge
  Will be like lightning glowing;
  Naught common or unclean
  To heaven may be going.
  The final plague will strike,
  And scarce a house be left
  That knows no son condemned,
  That has no heart bereft.

11 Lord God! On all these things
  The longer that I ponder,
  My ev'ry vessel stirs,
  Aroused by fear and wonder.
  My skin is chilled with sweat,
  My ear rings deaf'ningly,
  My trembling lips and heart
  Are lifted up to Thee.

12 Yet confident by faith
  And love and hope I'm living.
  I know Thy grace stands free
  To all men for receiving;
  I know Thy love and truth
  My staff and stay will be;
  Yet will I pray the more
  For all the world and me.

13 Implant in all men's hearts
   Thy godly fear and rev'rence;
   Let none make light of faith
   Nor of a true repentance.
   Take from us lust and sloth
   Presumption, stubbornness,
   Hypocrisy, deceit
   Ill-will, unholiness.

14 Help us the vict'ry gain
   By Thee before obtainèd;
   Let Satan be destroyed
   And visibly restrainèd,
   That we with earnest care
   May him renounce and fight,
   And praying steadfastly,
   Flee and escape his might.

15 Grant patience in the strife
   And comfort in contending,
   Our careful vigilance
   With wisdom ever blending;
   Grant us in readiness
   And holy fear and love
   To stand, till boldly we
   May come to Thee above.

J. R. Hedinger; tr. M. Carver.

X. PRAYER, PRAISE & THANKSGIVING

64

Tune: Es war einmal ein reicher Mann.

1 Of all the joys upon this earth
   None can be found of greater worth
   Than what I with my song propound,
   And with so many a pleasant sound.

2 No evil humor can be here
   Where goodly fellows sing with cheer,
   No hatred, wrath, and strife abide,
   Nor spite—all heartache must subside;

3 Greed, care, and lonely heaviness
   No more do they the heart oppress.
   Each man can in his mirth be free
   Since such a joy no sin can be.

4 In music God more pleasure finds
   Than in all joys of earthly minds.
   The devil's works her art destroys,
   Thwarts oft his evil, murd'rous ploys.

5 To this King David's deeds attest,
   Who often put King Saul to rest
   By sweetly playing on the lyre
   And thus escaped his murd'rous ire.

6 To hear God's Word and truth divine
   She hushes hearts and doth incline;
   Such did Elisha once propound
   When harping he the Spirit found.

7 Mine is the fairest time of year
   When all the birds in song appear:
   The heavens and the earth they fill
   By much good singing sung with skill.

8 And o'er them all, the nightingale,
   That gladdens ev'ry hill and dale
   With her sweet-sounding melody—
   Thanks be to her eternally!

(cont.)

9 But thanks be first to God, our Lord,
  Who made her by His mighty Word
  To be the songstress of His heart
  And mistress of His tuneful art.

10 For our dear Lord she sings her song
  In praise of Him the whole day long;
  To Him I give my melody
  And thanks in all eternity.

Luther; tr. Composite.

65   Thanks for recovery from sickness

Tune: Herr, du Kraft und Arzt der Schwachen. [Br 211, p. 166]

1 Great Physician of the ailing,
  Lord, who bringest down to hell
  And deliv'rest thence as well;
  Thou who givest him all healing
  Who trusts in Thy grace
  And upon Thy love relies.

2 Ah! I have not words sufficient,
  All Thy glory to express,
  And show forth Thy worthiness!
  All things laud Thee, Lord omniscient,
  All creation sounds Thy praise,
  Lord of life and death always.

3 Ah! For tongues of angels glorious,
  That by such adornment fair
  Worthier songs might fill the air
  Of Thy help and pow'r victorious,
  When Thou with a father's grace
  Showedst me a tender face.

4 Thou art moved by our petition
  When from heart sincere 'tis made
  And in faith before Thee laid:
  Thou wilt leave Thine indignation
  And for Thy rebuke wilt send
  Blessing that shall never end.

5 Though a father's wrath be burning,
  When his child before him kneels
  And displays the grief he feels,
  Weeping, sighing, trembling, turning,
  Then the father's heart must bend,
  And his hand in help extend.

6 Therefore may my simple singing,
  Father, to Thy praise attain,
  Who hast brought me back again
  From the night of sickness stinging;
  Maker, whatso be Thy will,
  Do Thou e'er in me fulfill!

J. Franck; tr. M. Carver.

66   Thanks for peace being secured

Tune: Nun danket Alle Gott.

1 Lord God, our thanks to Thee!
  In loud and happy chorus,
  We praise Thy Love and power,
  Whose goodness reigneth o'er us.
  To heaven our song shall soar,
  Forever shall it be
  Resounding o'er and o'er,
  Lord God, our thanks to Thee!

2 Lord God, our thanks to Thee!
  We praise Thy loving merit,
  We glorify Thy strength
  With all our heart and spirit.
  Our hymn shall now arise
  To heaven's portal free
  With loud and joyful cries:
  Lord God, our thanks to Thee!

3 Lord God, our thanks to Thee!
  For Thou our land defendest;
  Thou pourest down Thy grace,
  And strife and war Thou endest.
  Since golden peace, O Lord,
  Thou grantest us to see,
  Our land, with one accord,
  Lord God, gives thanks to Thee!

4 Lord God, our thanks to Thee,
  Who for long years of fighting
  Have borne war's heavy yoke
  And conflict unremitting.
  Now we our mourning cease
  And cry most heartily,
  To God be praise for peace!
  Lord God, our thanks to Thee!

5 Lord God, our thanks to Thee!
  Who horse and man o'erturnest,
  Who breakest shield and sword,
  Who bow and arrow spurnest;
  The snare is broken now
  And so our songs rise free
  From heart and tongue and mouth:
  Lord God, we worship Thee!

6 Lord God, our thanks to Thee!
  Thou didst indeed chastise us,
  Yet still Thy anger spares,
  And still Thy mercy tries us;
  Once more our Father's hand
  Doth bid our sorrows flee,
  And Peace rejoice our land;
  Lord God, we worship Thee.

7 Lord God, our thanks to Thee!
  Who hast our land sustainèd,
  Defended church and home,
  The fam'ly tree maintainèd
  With branches flourishing;
  Yet grant those yet to be
  May in the future sing
  Lord God, our thanks to Thee!

8 Lord God, our thanks to Thee!
  We pray Thee, who hast blessed us,
  That we may live in peace,
  And none henceforth molest us;
  O crown us with Thy love
  And heed our cry to Thee;
  O Father, grant our prayer;
  Lord God, our thanks to Thee!

9 Lord God, our thanks to Thee!
  With trump and organ voicing;
  With harp and lute and horn,
  With strings and flute rejoicing;
  Let all that breathes intone
  Its praise forevermore
  Lord God, we worship Thee!

J. Franck; tr. sts. 1, 3, 6, 8, C. Winkworth, alt.;
sts. 2, 4–5, 7, 9, M. Carver.

67

Tune: Freu dich sehr, o meine Seele.

1 Help us, Lord, in each endeavor
   To begin our work aright,
   Likewise well to finish ever;
   Give us wisdom, pow'r, and might.
   If Thy help and love be gone,
   All our work in vain is done!
   Help us, Lord, in each endeavor
   And let all things prosper ever!

2 Help us, Lord, where'er we travel,
   Anywhere we need Thine aid;
   Hell's dominion here unravel,
   Give the flock which Thou hast made
   Love and peace and unity;
   Guard Thy Church continually:
   Help us, Lord, in each endeavor
   And let all things prosper ever!

3 Help us, Lord, when griefs alarm us,
   Help in sorrow and distress;
   Let no danger slay or harm us
   Keep us in Thy faithfulness
   Cross, annoyance, misery—
   Let them work all good for me!
   Help us, Lord, in each endeavor
   And let all things prosper ever!

4 Help us, Lord, from all affliction
   Ere we yield our final breath;
   Let us go with glad conviction,
   Bring us by Thy bitter death
   To Thy paradise divine
   And to bliss—the praise be Thine!
   Help us, Lord, in each endeavor
   And let all things prosper ever!

5 Help us, Lord, to finish glorious,
   As we put our trust in Thee;
   Let us stand at last victorious,
   Let us not confounded be
   O Lord Jesus, be our stay,
   Help us ever on our way,
   That when we are done contending
   We may sing Thy praise unending!

M. Rinckart; tr. M. Carver.

68

Tune: Nun preiset alle. [*TLH* 28]

1 Now let all loudly
   Sing praise to God the Lord;
   Christendom, proudly
   Laud Him with one accord.
   Gently He bids thee come before Him;
   Haste, then, O Israel, now adore Him. *(x2)*

2 For the Lord reigneth
  Over the universe,
  All He sustaineth,
  All things His praise rehearse,
  The angel host His glory telling,
  Psalter and harp are the anthem swelling. *(x2)*

3 Come, heathen races,
  Cast off all grief and cares,
  For pleasant places
  Your Savior doth prepare,
  Where His blest Word abroad is sounded,
  Pardon for sinners and grace unbounded. *(x2)*

4 Richly He feeds us
  Always and ev'rywhere;
  Gently He leads us
  With a true father's care;
  The late and early rains He sends us;
  Daily His blessing, His love, attends us. *(x2)*

5 Sing we His praises
  Who is thus merciful;
  Christendom raises
  Songs to His glorious rule.
  Rejoice! No foe shall now alarm us;
  He will protect us, and who can harm us? *(x2)*

M. A. von Löwenstern; tr. C. Winkworth.

Thanks for good weather

69

Tune: Wo Gott zum Haus nicht gibt sein Gunst.

1 O God, who mak'st the sun to rise
  Upon both good and wicked eyes,
  Dost all the world with light imbue
  And moisten with the rain and dew.

2 Thou wat'rest hills from chambers high,
  Dost earth with foliage satisfy,
  Thou fillest rock with precious vein,
  Peace, life, and law Thou dost maintain.

3 Thou freely givest bread and wine
  That make our hearts with joy to shine;
  Thou cov'rest sin, and by Thy Word
  Peace, rest, and comfort are conferred.

4 We now implore Thee of Thy grace,
  Grant us Thy Word and peace always,
  Preserve the produce of the field,
  And grant a year of plenteous yield.

5 Send fertile weather for increase,
  From hail and tempest grant us peace,
  By snow and rain and wind and sun
  Let Thy good will be ever done.

6 The pests that swarm and creep, O God,
  Are all Thy devastating rod;
  O Lord, the vermin horde repel,
  And keep Thy gifts intact as well.

411

(cont.)

7 Remember, we poor indigents,
　Thy creatures and inheritance,
　All wait upon Thy hand alone,
　And by Thy Word and works are known.

For sunshine

8 Cause Thou the blessed sun to shine,
　Bless ore and grass and bread and wine;
　That man and beast may nourished be,
　And by Thy gifts may know of Thee.

For rain

9 Thro' Christ, Thy Son, our pray'r attend,
　A clement rain upon us send,
　And crown the year, Lord, by Thy hand,
　And by Thy steps enrich the land.

10 The Lord of Zion is Thy name
　Thy mercies all the world acclaim;
　Receive our plea, and help afford,
　And grant us grace to thank Thee, Lord.

N. Herman; tr. M. Carver.

70　Thanks for a good harvest

Tune: Nun lob mein Seel den Herren.

1 Our thanks to God forever
　For all the mercies He hath shown;
　What benefits and favor
　He hath bestowed on what was sown!
　The fields with produce dressing,
　He fruitful made the land
　And by His gracious blessing
　Enriched our weary hand.
　Thus all that first was planted
　Became a bounty vast,
　And homeward we were granted
　To bear the sheaves at last.

2 Should we these goods not reckon
　To God's great pow'r and counsel wise?
　Nor should we be mistaken:
　Here stands God's grace before our eyes.
　For naught is he that soweth
　Or he that reaps the grain,
　Or he to field that goeth,
　Or brings it home again,
　Unless God all attendeth
　And grant His blessing there;
　On Him it all dependeth
　That it may prosper e'er.

3 No sooner hath God given
　A fruitful yield to field and town
　By blessings sent from heaven,
　Than we, His bounties so to crown,
　Should rightly praise and bless Him
　For all His kindnesses
　And glorious e'er confess Him,
　For such abundant grace,
　Our thanks and worship giving
　With heart and mind and pow'r,
　Nor waver in our living
　From Him at any hour.

4 O faithful God, assist us
　That we may do as we have said:
　Upon Thy way direct us,
　And bless to us our daily bread;
　So let us use it ever
　At home as Christians true,
　That it may be a river
　To help the poor, as due,
　And we may profit greatly
　Both here in fruits of love
　And then in manner stately
　As heaven's heirs above.

J. Weber; tr. M. Carver.

Closing hymn

71

Tune: Nun laßt uns Gott dem Herren.

1 Amen! All praise be given
   To Father, Son in heaven,
   The Spirit's confirmation
   Grant faith and true salvation.

2 Amen! 'Tis certain, truly!
   We shall see Jesus newly
   Upon the clouds descending,
   To give us life unending.

3 Amen! God, by Thy good favor
   Ours be the joy forever
   And Thine, eternal glory
   When all are brought before Thee!

4 Amen! Death cannot shake us,
   For Jesus will awake us:
   Once in a tomb though lying,
   He lives for time undying.

5 Amen! To God be praises!
   The Spirit, who conveys us
   To Jesus, also bring us
   Where death no more shall sting us!

L. Helmbold; tr. M. Carver.

XI. THE CHURCH

72

Tune: Auf, ihr Heiden, lobet Gott. [Melody Appendix 1]

1 Rise, ye nations, praise your God
   Who from shades of death released you,
   And, when in your former days
   Gloomy darkness had oppressed you,
   Did not scorn your wretched plight,
   But conveyed you to the Light!
   Praise His goodness all-abounding,
   Heartfelt thanks forever sounding.

2 All ye peoples, bless your God
   Who in grace that none could merit
   Hath by Jesus' death undone,
   Adam's curse which we inherit,
   Cleansing your unrighteousness,
   He saves you from all distress;
   Bless His goodness all-abounding,
   Heartfelt thanks forever sounding.

3 May all grace and truth—which came
   By this Christ, our Lord and Savior,
   And which we by faith receive
   From His full abundance ever—
   Always unto us be great,
   And no more from us abate!
   Shout His goodness all-abounding,
   Heartfelt thanks forever sounding.

Raumer's Sammlung; tr. M. Carver.

73

O Ewigkeit, du Donnerwort. [Br 143, p. 114f.]

1 The pow'r of Truth breaks to the fore
And knocks for entry at the door
Of many a heart benighted.
The knowledge of the kingdom grows,
And on its speedy course it goes
Till ev'ry street be lighted:
Yea, knowledge now and kingdom lie
Before all men beneath the sky.

2 Behold what wonders God performs!
With courage He His herald arms,
He makes His witness stronger;
He sends them forth by day and night,
To bring His teachings to the light—
It can be hid no longer!
They for His glory spread abroad
Th' eternal Gospel of their God.

3 The Alpha and Omega saith,
"I now will cause the word of faith
To sound with acclamation.
My peace and joy they shall declare,
And all the realms of earth prepare
For reconciliation."
My angel, who the errand cries,
All in the midst of heaven flies.

4 His form in ev'ry place is seen,
Clear sounds his cry of peace to men:
"Far shall My grace and favor
To nation, tribe, and tongue progress,
The riches of My graciousness
Be sung, nor silenced ever."
Now here, now there, the cry goes out—
"The year of jubilee!" they shout.

5 The myst'ries of the Holy Word
By worthy and unworthy are heard—
By all in this world living.
With gladness hearts these tidings hear,
This testimony great and dear,
Themselves entirely giving
To Him who o'er the world doth reign;
Love, grace, and cov'nant they maintain.

6 Oft in the past I've turned my glance
And not perceived my ignorance;
But now the light is risen:
I will not turn mine eyes away
As in so many a bygone day;
The truth will burst its prison,
And as is fitting, in plain sight,
Be hailed with thanks and true delight.

7 I, even I, make all things new,
And work a liberation true
For all My dear creation.
And blest is he who this doth see,
And in My Son takes hold of Me
Amid life's brief duration,
And blest is he who here can say,
This is in truth salvation's day!

Raumer's Sammlung; *tr. M. Carver.*

74

Tune: Freu dich sehr, o meine Seele.

1 Sons of God, with jubilation
  Join me now to praise God's might;
  Sinners poor, with exultation
  Leave the world its splendors bright:
  Sing how God the Gentiles called
  And has brought them to His fold,
  Calling lowly heathen ever
   Sons of God by His good favor.

2 Ever His dominion stretches
  Over ev'rything that lives;
  All that life and breath possesses
  Shelter from His hand receives.
  When He speaks, His Word goes forth
  Swift like lightning o'er the earth,
  Thunder-like, the spirit cleaving,
  Life and consolation giving.

3 Sinners, would ye have the blessing
  When this earthly life must end,
  And the sonship be possessing?
  Let your heart and mind amend!
  Glorify God's love and might;
  He will strengthen you aright
  To approach Him and be given
  To rejoice with heirs of heaven.

4 Christ, our light and consolation,
  Has gone forth to all earth's ends:
  Keeper of the faithful nation,
  Our protection and defense;
  Praise Him who is kind and true
  As He proves each morn anew,
  He will grant you then with wonder
  To be His both here and yonder.

J. Olearius; tr. M. Carver.

75

Tune: Erhalt uns, Herr, bei deinem Wort.

1 Like as the sparrow hath her rest,
  And as the swallow builds her nest;
  So, Christ my Lord, I long for Thee
  And for Thine altars.

2 Lord, help me this sad vale to trace!
  Send lab'rors forth to ev'ry place.
  Thy gracious waters well to tend,
  That we may hold the faith unstained.

3 Far better in Thy Church with Thee
  The littlest and the least to be,
  Than lacking Thee, to rule the earth
  With wealth, esteem, and all things worth.

4 Light, Sun, and Shield art Thou, O Lord,
  Grace, honor, mercy dost afford;
  Confirm our faith increasingly,
  And ever turn our heart to Thee.

N. Selnecker; tr. M. Carver.

76

Tune: Von Gott will ich nicht lassen.

1 Great is Thy kingdom, spreading,
   Lord, to earth's farthest ends
   Wherever foot is treading
   Thy glorious reign extends;
   This kingdom knows no bound:
   Unshaken its foundations,
   And men of countless nations
   Within its walls are found.

2 No kingdom e'er existed
   That could endure for aye.
   We read how none persisted,
   But all at last decay,
   And finally must cease;
   'Tis Christ's alone abideth,
   Naught in which man confideth
   Can ever break its peace.

3 The Lord raised up the Savior
   Foretold when Adam fell,
   Who graciously did cover
   The sins of Israel.
   This is His name alone:
   The Lord all men must name Him.
   The righteous know and claim Him,
   And He shall have the throne.

4 Forth out of Zion goeth
   His glorious rule and reign;
   A people that Him knoweth
   His scepter shall sustain—
   That scepter is His Word,
   Which heav'n to us supplieth,
   Through all the world it flieth,
   Victorious for the Lord.

5 From Zion too He sendeth
   Into the world His rod,
   Which to His pleasure bendeth
   A people called by God,
   Who live in purity,
   With love for Christ their Savior,
   And cling to truth forever
   With faith and constancy.

6 King born, and King anointed,
   Eternal God art Thou,
   The Governor appointed
   Of all Thy Church e'en now!
   O Brightness, Strength, and Pow'r!
   On Thy Amen we reckon
   When Thy true servants beckon:
   "Repent ye all this hour!"

7 O blest are we, whom kindly
   Christ doth His people name—
   Who, no more wand'ring blindly,
   Him o'er all others claim:
   Henceforth in Him, our Lord,
   We shall not yield nor waver,
   And nothing can us sever
   From God and from His Word.

8 O what high grace and blessing
   His kingdom brings us here!
   Our way to Him addressing
   We're safe from night's dark fear;
   In light we walk alway,
   As God's own Word hath taught us,
   Who hath repentance brought us;
   Our step shall hardly stray.

9 No groom's assistant ever,
   Nor man, nor wife pertain,
   But Christ, the faithful Savior,
   Doth all things for us gain:
   To His true friends imparts
   The right of heirs of heaven,
   And none is from Him driven
   Who gives to Him his heart.

10 Up, ev'ry fellow Christian!
   Come as one holy race;
   Let us the King petition,
   And seek His gates of grace,
   And do as He doth teach:
   Come, let us trust Him solely,
   Come, let us see right boldly
   How spreads His kingdom's reach!

11 That man to Him is pleasing
   Who walks a holy road
   With faith unfeigned, unceasing,
   Which moves the heart of God.
   That tribe is His delight
   Which heavenward is striving,
   And on this earth is living,
   Chaste, holy, and upright.

12 Lift up therefore your spirits
   Ye saints, in unison!
   Receive the goods and merits
   The mighty King hath won:
   Which loose from sin and hell,
   And take away the terror
   Of devil, death, and error:
   He's blest who heeds this well.

Dresden Kirchen- und Hausbuch (1694) [J. Rist]; tr. M. Carver.

77

Tune: Es woll uns Gott genädig sein.

1 Lord Jesus, grant us grace in mind
   And strength for all well-doing,
   Renouncing deeds of heathen blind,
   Their works and ways eschewing.
   Enlighten those in error's way,
   All to Thy gath'ring bringing,
   And cause them in Thy fold to stay,
   That ev'ry tongue be singing
   And Jesus Christ confessing.

2 As once by holy saints of yore
   Thy Word was scattered broadly
   From eastern sea to western shore,
   So raise anew men godly,
   Let faithful shepherds labor here
   To build Thy congregation,
   With righteous doctrine year by year
   To multiply Thy nation,
   All men to Thee conducting.

3 Grant that they ever well reprove,
   Exhort, encourage, punish,
   Go first in godliness and love,
   And in right faith admonish;
   May we be doers of Thy Word,
   And not be hearers merely,
   That sheep and shepherds of the Lord
   May walk in love sincerely,
   The end of faith obtaining.

Raumer's Sammlung; tr. M. Carver.

78

Tune: O Herre Gott, dein göttlich Wort.

1 O God my Lord, / we love Thy Word
And fearlessly believe it;
How is it then / that other men
Should hate us who receive it?
We patiently / bear misery
And shun all sin whatever,
While pope and Jew / and pagan, too,
Enjoy success and favor.

2 O Christ, this woe / comes from the foe
Who in this latter season
With craft and guile / doth all defile
And murder without reason,
His horde with lies / he doth disguise,
His will by them performing;
But lets God's Word / nowhere be heard
Amid the worldly swarming.

3 God's ark must e'er / such beatings bear
While Noah she containeth,
She yet doth sail / through wind and hail
And e'er intact remaineth;
Storm, wave, and fire / may fear inspire,
And viciously assail her.
Yet Satan may / not bar her way:
God's pow'r must e'er avail her.

4 For Christ is there, / our berth to share,
And though it seems He sleepeth,
Great care He gives / and never leaves,
His faithful vigil keepeth.
In season due / His succor true
Is clearly manifested;
And in that hour / the devil's pow'r
Will vanish still untested.

5 Then furious be, / thou raging sea,
O'erwhelm this little vessel!
Come, dragon old / breathe fire so bold,
With Christ's assembly wrestle
Wield, Antichrist, / thy weapons prized:
Pow'r, sword, and conflagration,
Hypocrisy / and treachery—
God yet doth know His nation.

6 This ship, though tried, / must safe abide
And know no harm forever;
And yet, must she / Thy martyr be?
Thou wilt prevent it never.
Here is the Lord / who by His word
Makes wind and sea to falter;
All things fulfill / His wish and will;
Who can His counsel alter?

7 Nor is the Star / of Morning far
Which shall bring night to ending.
We soon shall near / That heav'nly pier
Whereto this ship is tending.
O God, with speed / help us in need,
That we may enter safely
That port on high / for which we sigh
Here in Thy Church so greatly!

N. Chyträus; tr. M. Carver.

79

Tune: Ihr Gestirn, ihr hohlen Lüste. [Br 217, p. 170f.]

1 Shout, O Tyre! Laugh, Sheba stately!
   O rejoice, ye Gentiles all!
   Rise, ye peoples troubled greatly,
   See, new strength on you doth fall:
   For the glory of the Savior
   Now is ris'n on you with favor.

2 On the race in darkness dwelling,
   Worshiping their gods of stone,
   There hath shined a light revealing:
   Now to us (praise God!) 'tis known
   That we face no condemnation:
   Shem shares Japheth's habitation.

3 For today in Jacob rises
   On us Gentiles poor, a star.
   Therefore we with sacrifices
   Come to Him from lands afar.
   With the Magi much intending
   To give Jesus praise unending.

4 Take, O Jesus, what I give Thee,
   Take it, though it is not more;
   Yet I bring it, and believe Thee,
   And, though I am small and poor,
   I in Japheth's tents so lowly
   Heave it to Thy bosom holy.

5 Though as now I cannot give Thee
   Frankincense or gold or myrrh,
   Oh, let not my poorness grieve Thee!
   Look upon my faith sincere:
   This is an unfading treasure.
   In this golden gift take pleasure!

6 Incense too I'll burn before Thee
   When in pray'r to Thee I cry,
   And myrrh's bitter tears will pour Thee
   With a penitential eye:
   This, then, is the off'ring kingly
   Which it is my hope to bring Thee.

7 Jesus, kindly take this off'ring,
   Look with mercy and make do
   With what I would Thee be proff'ring!
   Give me heart and spirit new,
   That I may in each endeavor
   Bring a spotless off'ring ever.

J. Franck; tr. M. Carver.

80

Tune: Ein feste Burg ist unser Gott. [rhythmic]

1 Lord Jesus, Thou the Church's Head,
   Thou art her one Foundation;
   In Thee she hath her faith well laid,
   And waits for Thy salvation.
   Built on this Rock secure,
   Thy Church shall endure
   E'en though the world decay
   And all things pass away.
   Oh, hear, oh, hear us, Jesus!

2 O Lord, let us Thy flock so small,
   Thy name alone confessing,
   Continue in Thy care withal,
   True unity possessing.
   Thy Sacraments, O Lord,
   And Thy saving Word
   To us e'er pure retain.
   Grant that they may remain
   Our only strength and comfort.

(cont.)

3 Help us to serve Thee evermore
   With hearts both pure and lowly;
   And may that Light of saving pow'r
   Shine on in splendor holy,
   That we repentance show,
   In faith ever grow;
   The pow'r of sin destroy
   And all that doth annoy,
   And make us faithful Christians.

4 And for Thy Gospel let us dare
   To sacrifice all treasure;
   Teach us Thy blessed cross to bear,
   To find in Thee all pleasure.
   Oh, grant us steadfastness
   In joy and distress,
   That we Thee ne'er forsake.
   Let us by grace partake
   O endless joy and glory!

5 Have mercy on Thy Christians, Lord,
   Enlarge Thy congregation;
   Thy guidance to Thy flock afford,
   Fight for her preservation!
   Dispel offense and scorn,
   Thy despisers turn,
   Break all that will not bend,
   And save them in the end
   With Thy deliv'rance blessed.

6 Oh, Jesus, hear our pray'r to Thee,
   For on Thy name we plant it.
   Receive our cry and graciously
   Say, Yea, Amen, and grant it!
   Our Jesus if Thou be,
   Jesus, Thine are we!
   Then keep Thy promise dear
   And grant us even here
   And yonder to extol it!

J. Mentzer; tr. sts. 1–4, W. J. Schaefer, alt.; sts. 5–6, M. Carver.

81

Tune: O Herre Gott, dein göttlich Wort.

1 Dear is to me the holy maid,—
   I never can forget her;
   For glorious things of her are said;
   Than life I love her better:
   So dear and good, / That if I should
   Afflicted be, / It moves not me;
   For she my soul will ravish
   With constancy and love's pure fire,
   And with her bounty lavish,
   Fulfill my heart's desire.

2 She wears a crown of purest gold,
   Twelve shining stars attend her;
   Her raiment, glorious to behold,
   Surpasses far in splendor
   The sun at noon; / Upon the moon
   She stands, the Bride / Of Him who died:
   Sore travail is upon her;
   She bringeth forth a noble Son
   Whom all the world doth honor;
   She bows before His throne.

3 Thereat the Dragon raged, and stood
   With open mouth before her;
   But vain was his attempt, for God
   His buckler broad threw o'er her.
   Up to His throne / He caught His Son,
   But left the foe / To rage below.
   The mother, sore afflicted,
   Alone into the desert fled,
   There by her God protected,
   By her true Father fed.

Luther; tr. R. Massie.

XII. VOCATION & VARIOUS OCCASIONS

82

Tune: Erschienen ist der herrlich Tag.

1 I now invoke the name of God
Whose arm can help me bear my load;
With God work prospers all the way,
This therefore from the first I say:
God grant it me!

2 All that I undertake to do
By God's own pow'r is carried through.
My heart toward God is set always,
Wherefore my mouth with gladness says:
God grant it me!

3 If God helps not, I have no pow'r.
Where God gives not, alas that hour!
God gives and does all good to me,
Therefore my mouth says cheerfully:
God grant it me!

4 If God some good will grant me here,
I will repay Him thanks sincere;
All at His word I'll cast my net,
And as I work, this is my debt:
God grant it me!

5 From start to finish, all that stands
I leave to God and in His hands;
My ev'ry good be in His pow'r
Therefore I say at ev'ry hour:
God grant it me!

6 If God shall choose my work to bless,
According to His faithfulness,
I am content by night or day
And with my heart will gladly say:
God grant it me!

7 If woe befall me, never fear!
I do the work and let God steer.
He will assist me graciously,
This then my watchword e'er shall be:
God grant it me!

8 His hand can bless me morn and eve,
Until my deeds their end receive;
He gives and takes, does as He will,
Wherefore I say with spirit still:
God grant it me!

9 God is my helper in distress,
With daily bread He doth me bless
According to His tender way,
He does me good, wherefore I say:
God grant it me!

10 Apart from Him I work in vain,
Mind, skill, and reason nothing gain;
With God I prosper and succeed
And I can say in faith indeed:
God grant it me!

11 If God in mercy grant me aught,
I fear the spite of rivals not;
Let him despise me, whoso will,
With joy I will sing louder still:
God grant it me!

12 If I do as God counsels me,
Who is my help continually,
All then must well and rightly fare,
Wherefore I finally declare:
God grant it me!

Treuenbrietzen Hymnal, 1722 [J. Betichius]; tr. M. Carver.

83

Lullaby

Tune: Lobt Gott, ihr Christen, allzugleich.

1 Thou little child, how small thou art,
Of nothing art aware,
To good and evil blind in heart,
In body poor and bare.

2 Yet thou by Baptism hast been made
In God a perfect limb;
He sends an angel to thine aid
To keep thee safe with Him.

3 Although thy parents thee begot
In true iniquity,
God in His grace and favor sought
And came in love to thee.

4 He is thy Father, thou His child,
He loves thee heartily;
He takes the sin which thee defiled
And casts it in the sea.

5 The crimson blood of Christ the Lord
Has made thee white as snow;
In holy Baptism life is poured
And given thee also.

6 For God's true Son became for thee
An infant small and frail,
That thereby He might set thee free
From sin and flames of hell

7 And therefore Satan can obtain
O'er thee no right nor pow'r,
Thou art restored to life again
And saved forevermore.

8 And thus assured, thou mayest sleep
In safety, calm at heart;
For God will thee both save and keep
And ev'ry good impart.

9 The Church will hedge thee round about
With all her pray'rs in need;
That God will hear them, do not doubt,
For they from faith proceed.

10 Depart, thou Satan, leave us be,
This child has been baptized,
And long since purchased by the blood
Of our Lord Jesus Christ.

11 Then sleep, thou precious infant, sleep!
Around thee angels fly,
All pain and anguish far to keep
All dangers to deny.

12 O faithful God, we trust Thy might;
Forsake us not, we pray;
Be our salvation and our light
Upon our pilgrim-way.

13 Give to this child Thy grace while here
To honor Thee, O Lord,
And walk in faith and godly fear,
Obedient to Thy Word.

14 Then call at last its soul to Thee
And gentle death bestow,
And bid it from earth's misery
To heav'nly gladness go.

15 To Thee, dear Jesus, thanks be said,
Who for our sake didst dare
To be a feeble infant made:
Oh, keep us in Thy care!

A. H. Buchholtz; tr. M. Carver.

Summer song

Tune: Heut singt die liebe Christenheit. [Br 212, p. 167]

84

1 Go forth, my heart, and seek delight,
   While summer reigns so fair and bright,
   View God's abundance daily;
   The beauty of these gardens see,
   Behold how they for me and thee
   Have decked themselves so gaily.

2 The trees with spreading leaves are blest,
   The earth her dusty rind has dressed
   In green so young and tender.
   Narcissus and the tulip fair
   Are clothed in raiment far more rare
   Than Solomon in splendor.

3 The lark soars upward to the skies,
   And from her cote the pigeon flies,
   Her way to woodlands winging.
   The silver-throated nightingale
   Fills mountain, meadow, hill and dale
   With her delightful singing.

4 The clucking hen leads forth her brood,
   The sparrow gives her children food,
   The stork protects her dwelling;
   The stag and doe, with footsteps light,
   Come bounding from the neighb'ring height,
   Joy in their movements telling.

5 The brooklets murmur in the sand
   Surrounded there on either hand
   By myrtle deep in shadow;
   The shepherds and the sheep rejoice,
   In joyful mirth they send their voice
   Across the bounding meadow.

6 Th' unwearied bees, on busy wing,
   From flow'r to flow'r flit murmuring,
   And seek their honied treasure;
   While on the vine, from day to day,
   New strength the tender shoots display,
   Each day increase in measure.

7 Fast grows the wheat, like waving gold,
   And gives delight to young and old;
   All nature with thanksgiving
   Lauds Him whose mercy measureless
   Vouchsafed the soul of man to bless
   With goods that grace his living.

8 Nor can I rest when all around
   Such great and wondrous works abound,
   Their Maker's goodness showing;
   When heav'n and earth their praises swell,
   And field and wood God's glory tell,
   I join in praise o'erflowing.

9 Thy splendor, Lord, doth brightly shine
   And fills my heart with joy divine
   While here on earth abiding;
   What, then, may be in store for me
   And all who heaven's glory see,
   In golden halls residing?

10 What matchless rays, what light divine
   In Christ's own paradise will shine,
   What sounds be ever ringing,
   Where thousand seraph hosts rejoice,
   With ceaseless and unwearied voice
   Their Hallelujahs singing!

11 Oh, that with God's exulting band
   I even now might take my stand,
   With them might now adore Him,
   And, bearing high victorious palms,
   Sing praise in thousand joyful psalms,
   As angels do, before Him!

12 Nor will I, while I here remain
   And bear this yoke of flesh, refrain
   From praises and thanksgiving:
   My heart, in this and ev'ry place,
   Shall never cease to praise Thy grace
   As long as I am living.

(cont.)

13 Bless me with blessings from above,
And cause the fruits of faith and love
To grow in me and flourish;
Oh, may the summer of Thy grace
Make fruitful each unfruitful place
And ev'ry virtue nourish!

14 Make for Thy Spirit ample room,
That thus I may forever bloom,
Like plants which root have taken;
Oh, let me in Thy garden be
A flourishing and righteous tree,
Which never shall be shaken!

15 O choose me for Thy paradise,
Let soul and body, till I rise,
Still flourish, tiring never.
With Thee alone will I abide,
Thine honor serve, and none beside,
Both here and there forever.

P. Gerhardt; tr. Composite.

85   Travel song

Tune: Dies sind die heilgen zehn Gebot.

1 In God's name let us on our way,
His holy angel lead, we pray,
Like Israël in Egypt-land,
When they fled Pharaoh's hand.
Kyrieleis!

2 O Lord, be Thou our goodly Guide,
Through all our wand'rings at our side,
Our journey step by step to show
And dispel ev'ry woe.
Kyrieleis!

3 No hill so high nor dale so deep
Nor water can our errand keep,
With gladness we our goal shall see,
If Thou but help us graciously.
Kyrieleis!

4 Lord Christ, Thou art the Way alone
And the true Path to heaven's throne;
Bring home our pilgrim brotherhood,
Therefore Thou shedd'st Thy blood.
Kyrieleis!

N. Herman; tr. M. Carver.

86   Lullaby

Tune: Nun schlaf, mein liebes Kindelein. [Br 232, p. 182]

1 Now sleep my little infant dear
And let thine eyes fall close;
For God thy Father tarries near,
So sleep in sweet repose.

2 Thy Father is thy God indeed,
And ever will remain,
Who gave thee life and doth thee feed
Through thy dear parents twain.

3 And when like all the sons of men
Thou too in sin wast born,
And wast in wrath because of sin,
And Adam's fall forlorn:

4 God gave thee then His dearest Son,
Who died in bitterness;
He came to earth from heaven's throne,
Saved thee from all distress:

5 Was born a Man, and walked His path
  To shed His blood one day,
  And thereby stilled the Father's wrath
  And put thy sin away.

6 Behold what Christ for thee obtained
  By all His agony;
  The blessed bath of Baptism drained
  Out from His side for thee.

7 In Baptism thou art born again
  By Christ's own fountains red;
  God's wrath is swallowed in the stain,
  Thy debt repaid and dead.

8 He crowns thee with His Spirit high;
  His love for thee is true,
  His Spirit in thy heart doth sigh,
  And makes thee wholly new.

9 He sends to thee His angels strong
  To stand thy cradle by;
  They guard all day and all night long,
  And watch with sleepless eye:

10 Lest e'er the wicked foe succeed,
  Pow'r o'er thy soul to have,
  Christ works this for thy good indeed.
  And so His child doth save.

11 Thy father and thy mother dear
  He gives to rear and raise,
  That they may be thy keepers here,
  And train thee for His praise.

12 His Jesus dear He gives as well,
  Who is thy Friend sincere,
  Thy God with thee, Emmanuel,
  And thine own Brother dear.

13 So sleep, my dearest little one,
  Give God thy Father praise,
  Like Zacharias's son, Saint John,
  And blest art thou always.

14 The holy Christ His blessing share,
  And keep thee evermore.
  His holy name from harm thee spare,
  And guard thee from all woe.

15 Amen, Amen, this true remains,
  The Holy Spirit says.
  God grant that thou may'st from hence
  A bles'ed child always be.

J. Mathesius; tr. M. Carver.

87

Tune: Nicht so traurig, nicht so sehr. [Br 230, p. 180]

1 Full of wonder, full of art,
  Full of wisdom, full of pow'r,
  Full of kindness, grace, and heart,
  Full of comfort flowing o'er,
  Full of wonder, still I say,
  Is love's chaste and gentle sway.

2 Those who've never met before,
  Ne'er each other known nor seen,
  Never in the idlest hour
  Thus employed their thoughts have been,
  Yet whose hearts and hands in love
  Tieth God who lives above!

(cont.)

3 His child doth this father guide,
  That one traineth his each day,
  Each their special wind and tide
  Speed upon their sep'rate way,
  When the time appointed's there,
  Lo! they're a well-mated pair!

4 Here grows up a prudent son,
  And a noble daughter there;
  One will be the other's crown,
  One the other's rest from care
  Each will be the other's light,
  But from both 'tis hidden quite,

5 Till it's pleasing in His sight
  Who the world holds in His pow'r,
  To all giveth what is right
  Freely in th' appointed hour;
  Then appears in word and deed
  What hath been by Him decreed.

6 Then Ahasuerus's eye
  First doth quiet Esther see;
  To where Sara peacefully
  Dwells, Tobias leadeth He;
  David then, with pliant will,
  Fetcheth prudent Abigail.

7 Jacob flees from Esau's face,
  And he meeteth Rachel fair;
  Joseph in a foreign place
  Serves, and winneth Asnath there;
  Moses did with Jethro stay,
  And bore Zipporah away.

8 Each one taketh, each doth find
  What the Lord for him provides;
  What in heaven is designed,
  Ever shall the earth betide;
  And whatever happens thus
  Ordered wisely is for us.

9 "This or that might better be"—
  Oft this foolish thought is ours;
  But as midnight utterly
  Fails to be like noonday's hours,
  So the feeble mind of man
  God's great wisdom cannot scan.

10 What God joins, together leave,
   What the best is knoweth He,
   Our thoughts only can deceive,
   His from all defects are free;
   God's work standeth firm for aye,
   When all other must decay.

11 Look at pious children who
   Entered have the holy state,
   How well for them God doth do,
   See what joys upon them wait;
   To their doings God doth send
   Evermore a happy end.

12 Of their virtues the renown
   Blossometh forevermore,
   As a shadow when is gone
   Of all other love the flow'r;
   When truth faileth ev'rywhere,
   Theirs still bloometh fresh and fair,

13 Fresh their love is evermore,
   Ever doth its youth renew,
   Love their table covers o'er,
   Sweetens all they say and do.
   Love their hearts aye giveth rest,
   When they're burdened and opprest.

14 Though things oft go crookedly,
   Even then this love is still,
   Bearing crosses patiently,
   Knowing 'tis the Father's will.
   From this thought doth comfort taste,
   Better days will come at last.

15 Meanwhile God with bounty gives
    Streams of blessing rich and free,
    Mind and body He relieves,
    And the house too foundeth He;
    What is small and men despise,
    Makes He great and multiplies.

16 And when all is over here
    That the Lord designs in love,
    For His faithful children dear,
    Taketh them to courts above,
    And with great delight in grace
    Folds them in His warm embrace.

17 Now 'tis ever full of heart,
    Full of comfort flowing o'er,
    Full of wonder, full of art,
    Full of wisdom, full of pow'r,
    Full of wonder, still I say,
    Is love's chaste and gentle sway.

Paul Gerhardt; tr. J. Kelly, alt.

88

Tune: Wie schön leuchtet der Morgenstern.

1 Oh, Jesus Christ! how bright and fair
    The state of holy marriage where
    Thy blessing rich is given;
    What gracious gifts Thou dost bestow,
    What streams of blessing ever flow
    Down from Thy holy heaven,
    When they / True stay
    To Thee ever, / Leave Thee never,
    Whose troth plighted,
    In one life have been united.

2 When man and wife are mated well,
    In harmony together dwell,
    Are faithful to each other,
    The streams of bliss flow constantly
    What bliss of angels is on high
    From hence may we discover;
    No storm, / No worm
    Can destroy it, / Can e'er gnaw it,
    What God giveth
    To the pair that in Him liveth.

3 He giveth of His grace the boon,
    And in its bosom late and soon
    His own beloved He keepeth,
    His arms He daily spreadeth o'er,
    Guards as a Father by His pow'r
    Us and our house, nor sleepeth.
    Still we / Must be
    Here and thither / Roaming ever,
    Till He gives us
    Pious homes, and thus relieves us.

4 The husband's like a goodly tree
    Whose branches spread so fair and free;
    The wife a vine that giveth
    Much fruit, and nurtures what it bears,
    Whose fruit increaseth with the years,
    Fruit that remains and liveth.
    Jewèl, / All hail!
    Husband's treasure! / House's pleasure!
    Crown of honor!
    On His throne God thinketh on her.

(cont.)

5 O wife! the Lord hath chosen thee
  That from thy womb bro't forth should be
  The folk His Church that buildeth;
  His wondrous work goes on for aye,
  The mighty word His mouth doth say,
  What thou beholdest, yieldeth,
  Sons fair / Stand there,
  Daughters sitting / Working, knitting,
  Finely spinning,
  And with art time wisely winning.

6 Be of good cheer, it was not we
  Who first this order did decree,
  It was a higher Father,
  Who loved and loveth us for aye,
  And from whose lips when grieved each day
  We friendly counsel gather;
  Good end / He'll send,
  What we're doing / And pursuing,
  Or conceiving
  Wise and happy issue giving.

7 A time will come, it cannot fail,
  When we 'neath trials sore shall quail,
  And tears be freely flowing;
  To him who bears it patiently,
  By God's grace shall his sorrow be
  Turned into joy o'erflowing.
  Toil now, / Wait thou,
  He arriveth / Who rest giveth,
  Who can ever
  Banish care and soon deliver.

8 Come hither then, my King so blest!
  In trials guide, in pain give rest,
  In anxious times relieving!
  To Thee we shall ascribe the praise,
  Our hearts and voices we shall raise
  In one loud song, thanks giving,
  Till we / With Thee
  Ever dwelling, / And fulfilling
  Thy will ever,
  Thy name cease to praise shall never.

Paul Gerhardt; tr. J. Kelly.

XIII. CROSS & COMFORT

FOR PEACE

89

Tune: Du Friedefürst, Herr Jesu Christ. [Br 204, p. 161]

1 Lord Jesus Christ, the Prince of Peace,
  True God and Man art Thou!
  Mighty to help in life and death,
  O hear and help us now!
  'Tis through Thy name / alone we claim
  The mercy of Thy Father!

2 The times are sore and perilous
  With heavy woes and wars,
  Whence no man can deliver us
  But Thou! Oh plead our cause,
  That God may lay / His wrath away,
  Nor deal with us in anger!

3 Remember, Lord, Thy work and pow'r,
  The Prince of Peace Thou art,
  And graciously this present hour
  To all Thy help impart,
  Grant that Thy Word / may long be heard,
  In peace's shelter ringing.

4 We have deserved, and patiently
  Would bear, whate'er Thou wilt,
  But grace is mightier far with Thee
  Than all our sin and guilt;
  Forgive us then, / dear Lord, again,
  Thy love is ever faithful.

5 Danger and grief around us stand,
   When plagues are in the air;
   But far more wretched is the land
   When cruel war is there;
   Men scorn the good / in reckless mode
   All holy things despising.

6 There law and judgment yield to force,
   None asketh what is right;
   Thy Word is hindered in its course,
   And quenched its blessed light;
   Then drive afar / this harmful war,
   Help, save us from its terrors.

7 And let Thy grace, O Lord, control
   Our minds and hearts, that none
   Should make a sport, that kills the soul,
   Of evils war hath done.
   'Tis Thou alone / who from Thy throne
   Canst rule us thus, and save us!

8 Take heart, then, friends, and fear you not,
   What cause for such great sorrow?
   Ye by the blood of Christ are bought:
   From this your courage borrow;
   The shield and boast / of heaven's host
   In life and death will keep you.

9 And Thou wilt keep Thy Word for sure,
   And wilt forsake us never;
   Our confidence in Thee is sure,
   O Thou our Refuge ever!
   Alone in Thee / our hope shall be.
   Oh, save us, Thou our Savior!

J. Ebert (sts. 8–9 later); tr. sts. 1–2, 4–7, C. Winkworth; tr. sts. 3, 8–9, M. Carver.

90

Tune: Auf meinen lieben Gott.

1 Come, soul, in thy distress,
   Trust in thy God to bless,
   Tell Him all ills that pain thee,
   He surely will sustain thee,
   When many griefs attend thee,
   He can deliv'rance send thee.

2 Art thou exceeding poor
   Or pained with sickness sore
   Or suff'ring persecution,
   Oppressed or in confusion?
   To God in pray'r commend thee,
   He shall deliv'rance send thee.

3 Do men thy heart dismay
   Amid this wicked day?
   Art thou affliction bearing?
   Be not therefore despairing;
   If thou to God commend thee,
   He shall deliv'rance send thee.

4 Do all laugh thee to scorn?
   Art thou distressed, forlorn,
   And by all men forsaken?
   Let not thy heart be shaken.
   If thou to God commend thee,
   He shall deliv'rance send thee.

5 Let him who Christ's will be
   Prepare such things to see,
   The cross in patience bearing,
   Of his own pow'rs despairing;
   When many ills offend him,
   God can deliv'rance send him.

6 Such is this day and hour,
   It passes human pow'r:
   As soon as one cross ceases
   Another cross increases;
   Thou must to God commend thee,
   When many griefs offend thee.

(cont.)

7 The more our cause to sigh,
  The more God draweth nigh,
  Oft in His mercy nears us
  Ere sin to error steers us.
  Deliv'rance He will send us
  When we to God commend us.

8 When trouble from us flies,
  All pray'r neglected lies,
  So God must send affliction,
  To turn us with conviction,
  And e'er to Him commend us
  That He deliv'rance send us.

9 Howe'er a Christian fare,
  Much suff'ring he must bear
  And falsely be accusèd,
  Unjustly be opposèd;
  He must to God commend him,
  That He deliv'rance send him.

10 For he who patiently
  Lets God his cause o'ersee,
  Can trust Him to deliver
  Nor must he wait forever,
  If he, when griefs attend him,
  To God in pray'r commend him.

11 Since trouble, need, and pain
  Our daily bread remain,
  And sorrows sting and burn us
  Wherever we may turn us
  We must to God commend us
  That He deliv'rance send us.

12 If ever was distress
  That should to pray'r men press,
  Distress e'en now assaileth,
  All earth in mis'ry aileth.
  Let us to God commend us,
  That He deliv'rance send us.

13 For such a Christian's pray'r
  Returneth empty ne'er.
  God hears with recognition
  And grants them their petition;
  If they to God commend them,
  He will deliv'rance send them.

14 Though naught at once be done
  We must not cease to groan,
  But constantly pursue it,
  And so leave God to do it.
  He can deliv'rance send us
  When many griefs attend us.

15 Through many afflictions here,
  We pass with many a tear,
  While yet in life contending
  For heaven neverending,
  Till God deliv'rance send us
  From ills that still attend us.

16 Not worthy is this day
  To be compared for aye
  With glories that will bless us
  Beyond the griefs that press us;
  If we in pray'r commend us,
  To God, who help can send us.

17 O godly Christian soul,
  Whose faith in God is whole,
  Fear not the cross before thee,
  Build on the Lord of glory,
  From ills that still attend thee
  He will deliv'rance send thee.

18 Walk in God's pathway true,
  Neglect not good to do,
  In patience still enduring,
  Thy innocence assuring,
  To God in truth commend thee,
  Who will deliv'rance send thee.

19 Though here it not be done,
   Do not despairing groan!
   Thou wilt thy wish be given
   And have all good in heaven;
   God will deliv'rance send us
   From ills that still attend us.

20 For griefs which here we've earned
   Will there to joy be turned,
   And we will join forever
   To praise our Lord and Savior,
   No ills will then attend us,
   Before God we will bend us.

J. Stegmann; tr. M. Carver.

91

Tune: Gib dich zufrieden und sei stille. [Melody Appendix 3]

1 Be thou contented, e'er relying
   On thy God, who life is giving;
   For He hath joys all-satisfying;
   Wanting Him—in vain thy striving;
   Thy Spring is He,
   Thy Sun that ever
   Rejoiceth thee,
   And setteth never.
   Be thou contented!

2 He lightens, comforts, and supports thee,
   True in heart, by guile unstainèd;
   When He is near naught ever hurts thee,
   E'en when smitten sore and painèd.
   Cross, need, and woe
   He soon averteth,
   O'er the last foe
   His pow'r asserteth.
   Be thou contented!

3 How it fareth with thee and others,
   Truly none from Him concealeth,
   He ever from on high discovers
   Burdened hearts, and for them feeleth.
   Of weeping eyes
   The tears He counteth,
   The pile of sighs
   Before Him mounteth.
   Be thou contented!

4 When not another on earth liveth,
   To whom safe thou may'st confide thee,
   He'll faithful prove, who ne'er deceiveth,
   And to happiest end will guide thee.
   The secret grief
   Thy soul that boweth,
   And when relief
   To give, He knoweth.
   Be thou contented!

5 The sighing of thy soul He ever,
   And thy heart's deep plaint, is hearing;
   What to another thou wouldst never
   Tell, reveal to God, ne'er fearing.
   He is not far,
   But standeth near thee,
   Who poor men's pray'r
   Marks, soon will hear thee.
   Be thou contented!

6 To God cleave, He'll salvation show thee,
   Let not anguish then depress thee;
   Altho' devouring floods o'erflow thee,
   Rise above it, He will bless thee.
   When 'neath the load
   Thy back low bendeth,
   Thy Prince and God
   Soon succor sendeth.
   Be thou contented!

(cont.)

7 Why do the cares of life so grieve thee,
   How to nourish and sustain it?
   Thy God, who ever life doth give thee,
   Will provide for and maintain it.
   He hath a hand
   With gifts o'erflowing,
   On sea and land
   For aye bestowing.
   Be thou contented!

8 Who for the forest songsters careth,
   To their daily portion leads them,
   For sheep and ox enough prepareth,
   Slakes their thirst, with plenty feeds them;
   He'll care for thee—
   Thee, lone one—filling,
   So bounteously
   Thy hunger stilling.
   Be thou contented!

9 Say not, the means nowhere appeareth,
   Where I seek, my effort faileth;
   God this high name of honor beareth:
   Helper when no help availeth!
   When thou and I
   Fail to discover
   Him, speedily
   He'll us recover.
   Be thou contented!

10 Although away thy help is staying,
   He will not forever leave thee;
   Tho' anxious makes thee His delaying,
   'Tis for thy greater good, believe me.
   What on the way
   To come ne'er hasteth,
   Doth longer stay,
   And sweeter tasteth.
   Be thou contented!

11 Tho' 'gainst thee hosts of foes are scheming,
   Let not all their lies affright thee;
   Still let them rage against thee, deeming
   God will hear it and will right thee.
   Doth God support
   Thee and thine ever?
   The foe can hurt
   Or ruin never.
   Be thou contented!

12 To each his share of ill is given,
   Would he only see and know it;
   No course on earth so fair and even,
   That no trouble lurks below it.
   Who can declare,
   "My house was ever
   All free from care,
   And troubled never?"
   Be thou contented!

13 So must it be, in vain our grieving,
   All men here must suffer ever,
   Whate'er upon the earth is living,
   Evil days avoideth never.
   Affliction's blow
   Doth oft depress us,
   And lays us low,
   And death then frees us.
   Be thou contented!

14 A day will dawn of rest and blessing,
   When our God will come and save us
   From the vile body's bands depressing,
   And the evils that enslave us.
   Death soon will come,
   From woe deliver,
   And take us home
   Then all together.
   Be thou contented!

15 He'll bring us to the hosts in glory,
    To the chosen and true-hearted,
    Who when they closed this life's sad story,
    Hence in peace to joy departed,
    And on the shore,
    The ever-vernal,
    Hear evermore
    The voice eternal.
    Be thou contented!

P. Gerhardt; tr. J. Kelly, alt.

Evening hymn in an epidemic

92

Tune: Mein Wallfahrt ich vollendet hab. [Br 229, p. 179]

1 To God, who watched us thro' this day
  Be praise and honor given,
  Who by His mighty pow'r and sway
  Assisted us from heaven,
  Lest we an evil end possess
  And die without a warning;
  In all our great and sore distress
  He heard our cry and mourning.

2 Before Thee, mighty God, we own
  Our measure of transgression,
  And yet in faith we pray and groan
  For Thy divine compassion.
  Take pity on our grievous fall,
  Lord Christ, from us be taken
  The deadly plague that weighs on all
  The needy and forsaken.

3 Turn from us, Lord, the pestilence
  That round us walks discreetly;
  Lest it come nigh us, drive it hence
  From house and land completely!
  O Christ, in grace defend our cause,
  Strength to the feeble giving,
  Deliver us from plague's grim jaws,
  And let us all be living!

4 O mighty God, whom wind and sea
  And earth obey, as fitting!
  We bow to Thee repentantly,
  Ourselves to good committing.
  Oh, with Thy mouth but say a word,
  And heal what now is stricken,
  And further health to them afford
  Who yet escape affliction.

5 While we are wrapped in shadows grim,
  May we all safely slumber!
  Who trusts in God and loveth Him—
  Such plagues cannot encumber,
  Nor even hurt a single hair
  Except at God's disposing.
  Pray therefore, ready and aware,
  Still in thy Lord reposing.

6 In sorrow yet do not despair,
  God shall be life supplying;
  Thou art the Lord's both here and there,
  In living and in dying.
  If then thou art to die, die on,
  Thy soul to God commending!
  For Christ shall be our life alone
  And death our gain unending.

(cont.)

7 No man in peace can breathe a breath
  While he on earth resideth,
  Until he shut his eyes in death,
  Where better life abideth.
  Then from this battle he is freed,
  No more by foes offended,
  Released from trial, cross, and need,
  With which he oft contended.

8 My hope in God I now set fast,
  On Him my spirit staying,
  For death must come to all at last:
  What use in long delaying?
  And he who falls alseep today
  Already shines in heaven
  Far from this tumult and decay,
  Crowned by his God in heaven.

9 O Jesus, I commit to Thee
  My living and my dying!
  As pleaseth Thee, so deal with me,
  Thy heav'nly grace supplying!
  Then, Jesus, I will be content,
  To be a porter lowly
  Above when life is spent;
  Oh, grant me this thing solely!

10 And if I die, I die in Thee,
   And Thou death too hast suffered,
   And life eternal won for me,
   When Thou wast freely offered.
   This is my comfort constantly
   And gives me sweetest slumber.
   He who repents and hopes in Thee,
   No ills his heart encumber.

Marburg Hymnal [1677, asc. "J.G.S"]; tr. M. Carver.

93

Tune: Dies sind die heilgen zehn Gebot.

1 The more the cross, the nearer heaven;
  Who hath no cross, he hath God not;
  By sin and world His face is hidden,
  Hell, curse, and death make Him forgot.
  Oh! Blessed is the child of God
  On whom He lays the cross, the rod.

2 The more the cross, the better Christian;
  God lays the touchstone to each soul;
  How many a garden must lie wasting
  Did not a tear-storm o'er it roll!
  As gold is by the furnace tried.
  So Christians by affliction's tide.

3 The more the cross, the more believing;
  The burdened palm will lofty soar;
  So too, the press, the grape receiving,
  Will make its sweetness flow the more
  In grief our virtues grow and shine,
  Like pearls beneath the ocean brine.

4 The more the cross, the more affection;
  When tempests blow, the flames arise;
  When darkness mars the day's complexion,
  What joy, when sunlight clears the skies!
  The cross increases love's pure glow,
  Like oil that men on embers throw.

5 The more the cross, the more the praying;
  The bruisèd plant yields sweetest balms;
  Man looks not for the star unswaying
  In quiet seas and steady calms;
  Had David spent no darksome hours,
  His sweetest songs had ne'er been ours.

6 The more the cross, the more the yearning;
  Out of the vale man upward goes;
  Who often treads the desert burning,
  For Canaan longs, where Jordan flows.
  The dove, discerning here no rest,
  Flies to the ark and builds her nest.

7 The more the cross—the dearer dying!
    For man rejoices then to die
    Whenas his body down is lying
    Much pain and sorrow are laid by;
    The cross that stands men's graves upon
    Is witness to their triumph won.

8 The more the cross, the brighter o'er us
    The crown that God makes for our own:
    Rich prize by many a victor glorious
    Who wears it now before the throne;
    Oh, think upon that jewel fair,
    And heaviest griefs are light as air!

9 O Crucified, Thy cross make dearer
    The more time passes constantly,
    Lest I lose patience and grow wearier;
    So plant Thou such a heart in me
    As tends to faith and hope and love
    Until my cross is crowned above.

B. Schmolck; tr. Composite.

Morning hymn in an epidemic

Tune: Ach Herr, mich armen Sünder. [Befiehl du deine Wege]

94

1 Now in these days distressing,
    Whose life is ever sure?
    For one, all health possessing,
    May leave his house secure,
    And yet upon returning
    Be taken unaware,
    And he in hell be burning—
    Since he did not prepare.

2 He who would die in blessing,
    Not in the devil's pow'r,
    Nor pains of hell possessing—
    Let him prepare each hour
    By honest, true repentance,
    For death at God's behest,
    And fearless meet his sentence,
    Nor be by death distressed.

3 For, sinner, thy transgression
    Doth part thee from thy God,
    And 'twas thine own secession
    That wrought this deadly rod,
    By which both field and city
    Are plagued most ev'rywhere,
    That it is much to pity—
    This for our sins we bear.

4 Now or upon the morrow
    I am prepared to die
    And leave this world of sorrow—
    When Thou art pleased, Most High.
    Oh, oft I've Thee offended,
    And earned such pestilence!
    Must my life soon be ended,
    Grant me a patient sense!

5 Here cut, here burn, here smite me,
    Here spare no pain or sting!
    With all Thy whips requite me,
    Yet let Thy suffering
    Be wasted not upon me!
    But after torment's o'er,
    O Prince of Peace, enthrone me
    In heaven evermore!

Marburg Hymnal; tr. M. Carver.

95

Tune: Nun danket alle Gott.

1 Stern, Lord, Thou mak'st Thy face,
Yet will I not cease crying;
Till for my great distress
I see Thee, grace supplying.
I have Thy pledge to me,
And Thou wilt hold it fast;
My pleasure I will see
When Thy help comes at last.

2 Lord, by my pray'r be moved,
My ev'ry ill redressing,
My heart and house be proved,
And bring to me the blessing!
No toil or pain of heart
Without Thee e'er avails;
But where in grace Thou art,
Thy blessing never fails.

3 Five thousand men with bread
Thou gavest satisfaction
Who with Thy Word were fed—
So great Thy love's attraction!
What need for agony
When hopeless seems my lot?
Who puts His trust in Thee,
Oh, he misplaces naught!

4 O Lord, see how I sink
And how my heart doth waver,
When on my sins I think,
And on Thy death, O Savior!
Yet Thou assurest me,
"Thou art My child so dear;
In grace I set thee free
From sin and scorn severe."

5 O Lord, Thine hours are slow,
Or seem so in appearing!
Often it seems as though
Thou never wilt be nearing.
Yet Thou dost come one day
And ev'ry wrong redress,
And make up the delay
With peace and blessedness.

Chemnitz Hymnal [J. Heermann]; tr. M. Carver.

96

Prayer in time of war

Tune: Da Christus geboren war. [Br 199, p. 158]

1 Thou who keepest Israel,
In whom I delight so well—
Ah! Thou dost all sorrows search
Of Thy needy Christian Church.
Therefore, Keeper, slumb'ring not,
Neither sleeping, help allot,
Show Thy face, which we have sought!

2 See what great distress and pain
Over all Thy flock remain:
Sorrow waxes without end;
Help, Thy doctrine pure defend.
See, we die and pass away;
Nothing else our eyes survey,
Save if Thou beside us stay.

3 Jesus Christ, Thou great High Priest,
  Who hast founded Thee a feast,
  Entered in the Holy Place
  By Thy bitter death and cross,
  Reconciled us with Thy blood,
  Snuffed hell's flame and fiery brood,
  And restored the highest good:

4 Seated at the Father's right
  One with Him in glory and might,
  Mediator, Advocate,
  Crown and Joy of high estate,
  Carried in the Father's breast—
  As He loves Himself the best,
  Never spurning Thy request.

5 In our grief we seek Thy face,
  Knocking at the door of grace;
  We by Thee were dearly bought,
  Thy possession dearly sought.
  O Thy Father's anger turn,
  Which as utter fire doth burn
  Running wild from eve to morn!

6 Show to Him Thy wounds so red,
  Show Thy cross, how Thou wast dead,
  And all else which Thou hast done
  For our sake let Him be shown!
  Tell how Thou hast paid our debt,
  On the altar-cross wast set,
  And salvation there didst get.

7 Jesus! as a Savior aid;
  On Thy name our hope is stayed:
  Help of man we seek in vain;
  With Thy hand our souls sustain.
  Be to us a wall around,
  So shall fear our foe confound,
  Brought with trembling to the ground.

8 Rock most high, Immanuel,
  Who around, within dost dwell,
  God with us in all distress,
  Who dost soul and body bless,
  God our aid till time shall end,
  Those who now our hurt intend,
  Let Thy heav'nly chast'nings mend.

9 Let Thy Father's mighty arm
  Send us mercy, save from harm.
  Let Thy mighty pow'r be seen,
  Which our constant hope hath been.
  Break the bonds of ev'ry foe,
  That of Thee the world may know:
  There the Lord of lords doth go!

10 Others in their strength confide,
  In their luck or skill or pride.
  But Thy Christians trust in Thee—
  Yea, in Thee unswervingly!
  Let them not be put to shame,
  Help and guard those who Thee claim,
  For Thou know'st them all by name.

11 On Thy thigh, oh, gird Thy sword,
  Fight for them, Most Mighty Lord!
  Scatter all Thine enemy,
  Where on earth they e'er may be.
  Crush them, all their hosts appal,
  As Thy footstool make them all,
  Break their pride and let them fall.

12 Mighty Champion, Lord, art Thou,
  Making wars to cease e'en now,
  Breaking bow and cutting spear
  Shatt'ring sword, inspiring fear
  Burning chariots in the fire,
  Changing e'en the man's desire
  That the end of war transpire.

(cont.)

13 Death the might of Thy great name
Did, O Prince of Peace, proclaim:
By Thy death the serpent fell,
Peace returned on earth to dwell.
Jesu, graciously give peace;
So Thy people's joys increase,
And our praise shall never cease.

J. Heermann; tr. sts. 1–6, 9–12, M. Carver; sts. 7–8, 13, A. T. Russel.

97

Tune: Wenn wir in höchsten Nöten sein.

1 When all men's help seems to depart,
The help of God doth often start;
When no one aids, His aid He gives,
And all my sufferings relieves.

2 Why seek the favor of the proud,
Which passes like a mist or cloud?
The worldly wise can yield no friend
Who faithful stands until the end.

3 To God alone for refuge fly,
Who in distress doth help supply;
Seek friendship with the One alone
By whom thy utmost need is known.

4 With God beside thee as thy friend,
Thy rival's pow'r is at an end.
Yea, though there many thousand be,
Not one could do thee injury.

5 As God doth please, so must it go,
Though all creation be thy foe;
Let God do only as He will,
And in His willing be thou still.

Anthony Ulrich; tr. M. Carver.

98

In excessive rain

Tune: Wenn wir in höchsten Nöten sein.

1 O Lord, whose tents in heaven stand,
What is it that now makes our land
And all the fruits that it may bear
So sad and spoilt an aspect wear?

2 Naught else, in truth, but that the flock
Of men have turned from Thee, their Rock,
And fallen utterly away,
Their guilt increasing ev'ry day.

3 They who as God's own property
His name should praise continually
And in His Word's great pow'r delight,
Are like the heathen without sight.

4 The heav'ns are all with darkness clad,
The firmament's clear light doth fade;
We wait to see the light again
At dawn of day, but wait in vain.

5 The strife of man proceeds apace,
And war abides in ev'ry place;
In ev'ry corner hate and spite,
In all estates they spar and fight.

6 The elements o'er all the land
Against us stretch their heavy hand,
And troubles from the sea arise,
And troubles meet us from the skies.

7 It is a time of great dismay
   For to the grave before their day
   All men are hunted, plagued, oppressed,
   And granted no reprieve or rest.

8 The sun, the source of joy, is sad,
   And seems to hide his radiance glad,
   And all at once the clouds descend,
   Shed tears that never seem to end.

9 Ah, child of man! go weep alone,
   Thy many grievous sins bemoan,
   Henceforward from thy crimes refrain,
   Repent, and be thou clean again.

10 Fall on thy knees, thyself now throw
    On God, that He may mercy show,
    That His deservèd wrath may be
    By Him to grace turn'd speedily.

11 He's faithful, and aye true will be,
    Naught else desireth but that we
    With reverence and godly fear
    To seek His mercy should draw near.

12 Ah! Father, Father, hear our cry,
    Redeem us, 'neath sin's yoke we lie,
    From out the world drawn may we be,
    And Thou Thyself turn us to Thee.

13 Subdue Thou our rebellious mood,
    And make us, sinners, pure and good;
    Whom Thou dost turn, soon turned is he,
    Who heareth Thee, is heard by Thee!

14 And let Thine eye now friendly be,
    The anguished cry that reacheth Thee
    From earth, from our sad hearts, O Lord,
    With gracious ear do Thou regard.

15 Remove Thine anger's gloomy pall,
    Refresh us and our land withal,
    And may the genial sun shine forth
    And ripen the fair fruits of earth.

16 And, Lord, as long as we may live
    Our daily bread in bounty give,
    And when the end of time we see
    The bread give of eternity!

P. Gerhardt; tr. J. Kelly, alt.

XIV. DEATH & ETERNITY

SONGS FOR DYING CHILDREN

99

Tune: Herr Jesu Christ, meins Lebens Licht.

1 Ah, Jesus, dearest to my heart,
   For Thee I fain would soon depart!
   This vale of tears doth naught possess
   But anguish, sorrow, and distress.

2 Grant me a blessed hour of death,
   And gently take my final breath,
   And let me with the angels see
   Thy glorious face eternally.

3 When this my flesh and heart shall fail,
   And this my mind no more avail,
   Yet Thou my strength and portion be,
   Since, Lord, Thou hast delivered me.

4 I shall not die, but I shall live
   And to the Lord all glory give.
   Lord Jesus, I hereby commend
   My soul to Thee when life must end!

(cont.)

5 My strength of life Thou wilt remain;
  In God, I know, death is my gain.
  I'll sleep in peace, and be restored,
  And ever be with Christ the Lord.

6 Farewell, false evil world, farewell!
  I'm destined for the heav'nly vale;
  Away, thou wretched den of grief,
  I count our parting pure relief.

J. H. Schein; tr. M. Carver.

100

Tune: Christus, der ist mein Leben.

1 Ah, were I there in heaven!
  My Savior, were I there!
  Where praise to Thee is given
  With Hallelujahs fair!

2 Where saints above adore Thee
  Where I shall see Thy face—
  'Tis good Lord, there in glory
  To build our dwelling place.

3 There all shall be revealèd—
  Creation's mysteries,
  All that Thy blood hath sealèd,
  And all Thy Spirit's deeds.

4 There saints are e'er rejoicing,
  A countless company
  With all Thy servants voicing
  The year of jubilee!

5 There strains divine and pleasant
  My lips in praise will sing,
  Where sin is never present,
  To Thee, my Life and King!

6 There tears shall all be thronging
  As joyful streams outpoured.
  Oh, quench my heart's deep longing
  And take me to my Lord!

E. G. Woltersdorf; tr. M. Carver.

101

Tune: Wie wohl ist mir, o Freund der Seelen.

1 A rest remaineth for the weary;
  Arise, sad heart, and grieve no more;
  Tho' long the way and dark and dreary,
  It endeth on the golden shore.
  Before His throne the Lamb will lead thee,
  On heav'nly pastures He will feed thee,
  Cast off thy burden, come with haste;
  Soon will the toil and strife be ended,
  The weary way which thou hast wended.
  Sweet is the rest which thou shalt taste.

2 The Father's house has many a dwelling,
  And there will be a place for thee.
  With perfect love His heart is welling
  Who loved thee from eternity.
  His precious blood the Lamb hath given
  That thou might'st share the joys of heaven,
  And now He calleth far and near:
  "Ye weary souls, cease your repining,
  Come while for you My light is shining;
  Come, sweetest rest awaits you here!"

3 O come, come all, ye weak and weary,
  Ye souls bowed down with many a care;
  Arise and leave your dungeons dreary
  And listen to His promise fair:
  "Ye bore your burdens meek and lowly;
  I will fulfill My pledge most holy,
  I'll be your Solace and your Rest.
  Ye are Mine own, I will requite you;
  Though sin and Satan seek to smite you,
  Rejoice! Your home is with the blest."

4 Oh, what contentment hath the ailing
  Who wand'ring through the desert goes
  When he obtains a bed availing,
  Where he may have his sweet repose!
  Beneath a tree the weary stranger
  In cooling shadow, safe from danger,
  May rest his weary limbs and sore;
  But brief the solace both are given;
  Ah! There remains a rest in heaven
  Where we have peace forevermore!

5 Come in, the sheaves of glory bringing,
  The seed-time of our tears is past,
  More sweet than dreams of joy the singing
  That fills our Father's house at last.
  And grief and fear, and death and pain,
  Are fled, and are forgotten things;
  We see the Lamb that once was slain,
  He leads us to the living springs;
  Himself He wipes our tears away—
  Such blessedness words cannot say.

6 The day of deep refreshing dawneth;
  No sun lights on us, and no heat;
  No longer is there one who mourneth,
  And there the hearts long severed meet—
  And God Himself shall be with them;
  They who the weary desert trod,
  Shall be a royal Diadem
  Forever in the Hand of God;
  All hail! thou glorious Sabbath day
  When toil and strife are past away!

7 There rest and peace in endless measure
  Shall be ours through eternity;
  No grief, no care, shall mar our pleasure,
  And untold bliss our lot shall be.
  Oh, had we wings to hasten yonder—
  No more o'er earthly ills to ponder—
  To join the glad, triumphant band!
  Make haste, my soul, forget all sadness;
  For peace awaits thee, joy and gladness—
  The perfect rest is nigh at hand.

J. S. Kunth; tr. sts. 1–3, 7, TLH; st. 4, J. Borthwick, alt.; sts. 5–6, E. F. Bevan.

102

Tune: Freut euch, ihr Gotteskinder all. [Br 218, p. 171]

1 Rejoice, rejoice ye Christians dear,
  The Son of God will soon appear,
  Our Brother He hath come to be—
  Christ Jesus, our dear Lord is He.

2 The Final Day is drawing nigh.
  Come, dear Lord Jesus, from on high!
  Each day we wait expectantly
  And sorely long to be with Thee.

(cont.)

3 The Antichrist hath been exposed,
   His blasphemy and lies disclosed,
   And set beneath the shadeless light
   Wherefore he daily rues his plight.

4 O Jesus Christ, our Savior true,
   The time of fullness now we view
   Of which we have heard Daniel tell,
   So come, O dear Immanuel!

5 Saint Simeon awaited Thee
   And joyed at last Thyself to see.
   His pray'r its answer then acquired—
   He saw the Lord his heart desired.

6 He said, "With joy I now can die,
   For here Salvation greets mine eye,
   I need not have a grieving heart:
   In peace, not pain, I now depart."

7 So also we await the hour
   And pray to Thee with all our pow'r,
   No longer Thy return forestall,
   But shut for good the serpent's maul.

8 The murderer of all mankind
   His fill of lies can never find,
   So take him and his sland'rous school
   And cast them in the fiery pool.

9 Thy children all await the day
   When all the world must pass away,
   And Satan's reign is crushed at last
   And in eternal shame is cast.

10 The devil on Thy name hath hurled,
   Such foul abuse, and blinds the world
   He builds a crown of deaf and dumb,
   And wills not that Thy kingdom come.

11 What Thou commandest, he reviles,
   And fiercely plots with all his wiles,
   And all Thy gen'rous hand bestows
   He seeks to steal from 'neath our nose.

12 So hard a war doth Satan wage
   That few repent, and many rage
   Against Thy Word; he doth incite
   Great envy, murder, wrath, and spite.

13 The devil seeks to make us fall,
   Deceive, devour, and strip us all
   Of body, soul, good name, and gold,
   Lord Christ, restrain that dragon old!

14 The world is in its last travail,
   'Tis old and weak, and soon must fail,
   It groans and sighs beneath its load
   And makes as if 'twill soon implode.

15 Creation can no longer be
   Subjected to such vanity,
   It longs for freedom from the Turk,
   His blasphemy and bloody work.

16 The pope has crushed it with such guilt,
   And wrecked the order that was built,
   The world, with us, would fain be free,
   And thus we wait Thy help to see!

17 The fathers longed to see at last
   Thy coming at the trumpet blast
   With all Thy heav'nly company—
   They waited many a century.

18 Lord, come, Thy judgment bring apace,
   And show the glory of Thy face,
   The presence of the Trinity!
   God grant us this eternally!

E. Alber; tr. M. Carver.

103

Tune: O Jesu Christ, wahr Gottes Sohn. [Br 79, p. 60f.]

1 My sins and wretchedness I own.
God's Son remains my gain alone,
My hope—that He true Man was made,
My ransom—'twas His blood that paid.

2 O God the Father, govern me
With Thy good Spirit constantly;
Allow Thy Son, my Life and Stay,
To dwell within my heart alway.

3 Oh, when the final hour I see,
Take me, Lord Jesus Christ, to Thee!
For Thine I am, and mine Thou art—
To meet Thee soon how longs my heart!

4 Lord Jesus Christ, assist Thou me
Like as a branch to dwell in Thee,
And afterwards with Thee to rise
To see Thy glory o'er the skies.

5 Then with Thine angel hosts above
I'll praise Thee ever for Thy love;
This grant, Lord Christ, I pray Thee now;
My only Help in need art Thou!

J. Gigas, after Melanchthon; tr. M. Carver.

104

Tune: Machs mit mir, Gott, nach deiner Güt.

1 God, deal with me in mercy now,
Thy help in sorrow showing!
Thine ear to me in pity bow;
When hence my soul is going,
Receive it, as its God and Friend,
For all is right if right it end.

2 Now, dearest Lord, I follow Thee,
Safe where Thy steps I'm tracing;
Ah, now Thou art not far from me,
Though death I now am facing,
And I must leave the friends most dear
Who loved me well and truly here.

3 In earth the body calmly lies,
To Thee the spirit flying,
And in Thy hands unharmed doth rise
By death to life undying.
Here was a land of tears and woe,
Where toil and care are all we know.

4 Now death and Satan, hell and sin,
And world cannot offend me.
To Thee, in whom my life doth dwell,
For comfort I commend me;
For on the Son my debts were laid,
And He my ransom freely paid.

5 Why mourn, then, that I now go hence,
When I such good inherit,
Dressed as a bride in th' innocence
Of Christ, and in His merit?
Farewell, thou evil world, farewell!
With God I rather choose to dwell.

6 Dear friends, I bid you now good night,
God evermore defend you!
Ye who have loved me with delight,
May there no ill attend you!
Good night, good night! Your griefs dismiss!
I go to God in boundless bliss.

J. H. Schein; tr. sts. 1–5, C. Winkworth, alt.; st. 6, M. Carver.

105

Tune: O Jesu Christ, wahr Gottes Sohn. [Br 79, p. 60f.]

1 O Jesus, very Lamb divine,
  In life and death I yet am Thine.
  Let me be with Thee, I implore,
  Heir of Thy kingdom evermore.

2 What good were all Thy death to me,
  Thy stripes and wounds and agony,
  If I might not be ever brought
  The good which Thy redemption wro't?

3 And why wouldst Thou consent to have
  Thy body shut within the grave,
  Should my death not, O faithful God,
  Be crushed by feet that Calv'ry trod?

4 Therefore, O Jesus, be my aid,
  Let me be helped and comforted;
  Forsake not him, O Christ my Lord,
  On whom Thy cleansing blood is poured.

5 In peace grant me to fall asleep,
  And perfect rest in Thee to keep.
  Thy face, O Lord, let me behold;
  A happy end to me unfold.

6 I pray Thee by Thy Passion blest,
  Receive this as my last request;
  So will I ever give Thee praise
  O Lord my God, for endless days!

M. Moller; tr. M. Carver.

106

Tune: Wird das nicht Freude sein. [Melody Appendix 10]

1 What gladness there shall be
  When faith shall end in knowing,
  Hope to fruition growing,
  The Savior's face to see!
  To learn from Him the story,
  What vict'ries won our glory—
  What gladness there shall be!

2 What gladness there shall be
  When God again shall lead us
  To friends who did precede us,
  From pain and sickness free!
  Where sorrows show no traces,
  To meet their fond embraces;
  What gladness there shall be!

3 What gladness there shall be
  When foes that would destroy us
  Shall never more annoy us?
  Where dwells full harmony,
  Always to live a stranger
  To trouble, fear, and danger—
  What gladness there shall be!

4 What gladness there shall be
  Where angel chorus raises
  To God Most High their praises,
  With seraphs to agree?
  And, when the skies are ringing,
  To join "thrice Holy!" singing—
  What gladness there shall be!

5 O yes!—there's gladness there!
  Away, earth's glitt'ring bubbles!
  Your joys are full of troubles,
  Your bliss not worth the care.
  Then do not, friends, bewail me,
  When heart and flesh shall fail me—
  But think!—There's gladness there.

H. C. von Schweinitz; tr. H. Mills, alt.

INDEX OF FIRST LINES (GERMAN)

INDEX OF AUTHORS

INDEX OF TRANSLATORS

APPENDIX OF SELECT HYMN MELODIES

Here only those melodies are included
which are not found in the St. Louis Melodien-Büchlein

1. Auf, ihr Heiden, lobet Gott

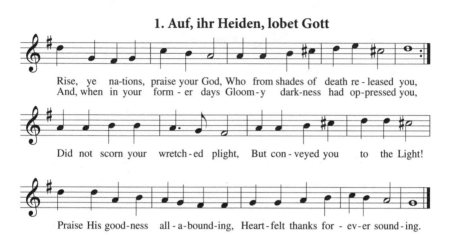

Rise, ye na-tions, praise your God, Who from shades of death re-leased you,
And, when in your form-er days Gloom-y dark-ness had op-pressed you,

Did not scorn your wretch-ed plight, But con-veyed you to the Light!

Praise His good-ness all-a-bound-ing, Heart-felt thanks for-ev-er sound-ing.

2. Christe, wahres Seelenlicht

Christ, the soul's e-ter-nal Light, Sun on Christ-ians shin-ing,
Face of glo-ry, fair and bright, Joy of spir-its pin-ing!

Lord, the sweet-ness of Thy grace Springs a-new each mor-row;

Tru-ly glad in Thine em-brace, I've no cause for sor-row.

3. Gib dich zufrieden und sei stille

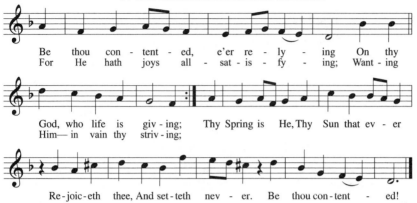

Be thou con - tent - ed, e'er re - ly - ing On thy
For He hath joys all - sat - is - fy - ing; Want - ing

God, who life is giv - ing; Thy Spring is He, Thy Sun that ev - er
Him— in vain thy striv - ing;

Re - joic - eth thee, And set - teth nev - er. Be thou con - tent - ed!

4. Höcshster Priester, der du dich

Great High Priest, who deign'dst to be Once the sac - ri - fice for me,

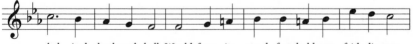

Kind - ly hear my sup - pli - ca - tion: Let my heart be Thine ob - la - tion!

5. Ich laß dich nicht

I leave Thee not! Thou art my Je - sus ev - er, Though earth re -

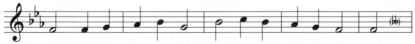

bel, And death and hell Would from its stead - fast hold my faith dis - sev -

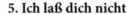

er. Ah, no! I ev - er will Cling to my Help - er still.

Hear what my love is taught: Thou art my Je - sus ev - er,

6. O Christe, Morgensterne

O Christ, Thou Star of Morn - ing, Now shed Thy light a -
broad; From heav'n the dark - ness scorn - ing, Shine on us here, dear
Lord, With Thy pure, glo - rious Word.

7. Sie ist mir lieb, die werthe Magd

Dear is to me the ho - ly maid,— I nev - er can for - get her;
For glo - rious things of her are said; Than life I love her bet - ter:

So dear and good, That if I should Af - flict - ed be, It

moves not me; For she my soul will rav - ish With con - stanc-y and

love's pure fire, And with her bount-y lav - ish, Ful-fill my heart's de - sire.

8. Wer Jesum bei sich hat

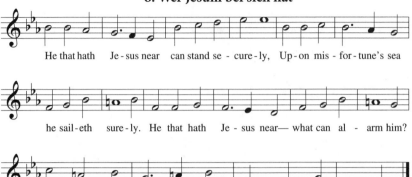

He that hath Je-sus near can stand se-cure-ly, Up-on mis-for-tune's sea he sail-eth sure-ly. He that hath Je-sus near— what can al-arm him? His heart, with com-fort filled knows naught can harm him.

9. Treuer Wächter Israel

Thou who keep-est Is-ra-el, In whom I de-light so well— Ah! Thou dost all sor-rows search Of Thy need-y Christ-ian Church. There-fore Keep-er, slumb'-ring not, Neith-er sleep-ing, help al-lot, Show Thy Face, which we have sought!

10. Wird das nicht Freude sein

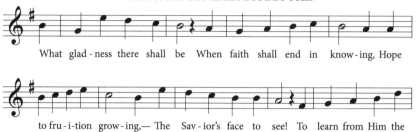

What glad-ness there shall be When faith shall end in know-ing, Hope

to fru-i-tion grow-ing,— The Sav-ior's face to see! To learn from Him the

stor-y, What vict'-tries won our glo-ry— What glad-ness there shall be!

11. Wo ist Jesus, mein Verlangen

(O mein Jesu, ich muß sterben.)

Where is Je-sus, my De-sir-èd, My Be-lov-èd, and my Friend?
Whith-er hath He now re-tir-èd? Where to find Him shall I send?

Soon my soul for sin would per-ish, Wear-ied and af-flict-ed quite!

Where is Je-sus, whom I cher-ish? Whom I long for day and night?

Concordia
Publishing House
CPH.ORG

ISBN   978-0-7586-5933-0

9 780758 659330

RELIGION /
Christian Life / Prayer
124533